Multicultural Issues in Social Work

Multicultural Issues in Social Work

Practice and Research

Edited by

Patricia L. Ewalt

Edith M. Freeman

Anne E. Fortune

Dennis L. Poole

Stanley L. Witkin

with a foreword by

Paula Allen-Meares

NASW PRESS
National Association of Social Workers
Washington, DC

Josephine A.V. Allen, PhD, ACSW, *President*
Josephine Nieves, MSW, PhD, *Executive Director*

Jane Browning, *Director of Member Services and Publications*

Paula Delo, *Executive Editor*

Christina A. Davis, *Senior Editor/Production Manager*

K. Hyde Loomis, *Senior Editor*

Marcia Roman, *Senior Editor*

Stephen D. Pazdan, *Staff Editor*

Sarah Lowman, *Staff Editor*

Nancy Winchester, *Proofreader*

Kargearies Indexing Services, *Indexer*

Chanté Lampton, *Acquisitions Associate*

Heather Peters, *Editorial Secretary*

Library of Congress Cataloging-in-Publication Data

Multicultural issues in social work / edited by Patricia L. Ewalt . . .
   [et al.] ; with a foreword by Paula Allen-Meares
      p.   cm.
   Includes bibliographical references and index.
   ISBN 0-87101-302-9
     1. Social service—United States. 2. Multiculturalism—United
States. I. Ewalt, Patricia L.
   HV41.M84   1999
   362.84'00973—dc20   99-3663
                                          CIP

Printed in the United States of America

Contents

PART V: HEALTH

PART VI: LONG-TERM CARE

Contents

Foreword

> Society in its full sense . . . is never an entity separable from the individuals who compose it. No individual can arrive even at the threshold of his potentialities without a culture in which he participates. Conversely, no civilization has in it any element which in the last analysis is not the contribution of an individual.
>
> –Ruth Benedict (from *Patterns of Culture*, p. 253)

Anyone who questions the relevance of multiculturalism need only look at how the face of America has changed in the past century. From 1880 to 1920 America experienced one of its largest periods of growth when hundreds of immigrants, primarily from southern, central, and eastern Europe, arrived daily on its shores (LeMay, 1987). During these times little thought was given to issues such as acculturation or assimilation, and little was done to help new immigrants navigate the choppy waters of conflict when their values, beliefs, and behavioral norms clashed with their new environment.

Now we are on the threshold of a new millennium, and we face similar cultural challenges. According to the U.S. Immigration and Naturalization Service (INS) (1998) immigration now occurs at a rate of about 700,000 to 900,000 individuals per year—about 200,000 more people per year than the boom years of the 1880s through 1920s when 23.5 million immigrants came to America. It is no surprise, then, that cultural issues remain extremely important and extremely complicated. Interestingly, according to the INS, Mexico, the Philippines, India, Vietnam, China, and the Dominican Republic are the top six countries of emigrés to the United States. These recent immigrants are, in a sense, like the Germans, Italians, Slavs, Poles, Russians, and Greeks of a century ago, coming to this country with a multitude of gifts, cultures, and needs, and interacting with a society that is largely unprepared to understand many of their norms, behaviors, or beliefs.

Cultural issues are important not only because of the arrival of today's immigrants—who happen to be from North America and Asia primarily—but also because there continue to be complexities surrounding the many existing cultures of people who have lived decades—and even centuries—in this country. Cultural issues result from the effects not only of immigration but also from what I like to call intraculturation, that is, the exchange among cultures within a society.

Why is culture so important? Quite simply, because culture is an integral part of the individual's very being. Any diminishment of culture diminishes the individual. Culture, here, takes on the additional rubrics of nationality, ethnicity, and religious belief. Conflict seems to arise when there is miscommunication about something so central to a people's lives as their culture. Huge conflicts arise when culture is misunderstood by people who hold authority or power over the lives of people of color.

With our history and our worldview, these are the issues that are foremost in our minds as a community and as a society:

- What are the historical traditions, values, beliefs, behavioral norms, and concerns of people from differing cultures?
- How can we facilitate communication among cultures in ways that are fruitful, meaningful, and beneficial to all of our lives and to our country's progress?
- How do we deliver culturally appropriate services?
- How do we as a profession cope with relatively new health issues such as HIV/AIDS, especially in culturally different environments?

These are the kinds of questions that social workers contend with daily, as they navigate the waters among cultures and even bring their own biases to the picture. We do know that instead of adapting existing social work practices to serve people of color, for example, we need to acknowledge that not all models work for all people.

This new edition, *Multicultural Issues in Social Work: Practice and Research*, brings such issues to light in ways that not only describe the concerns but also provide crucial insight, understanding, and even solutions. For social workers and other individuals in the helping professions, this book offers a variety of extremely useful perspectives for learning to navigate among different cultures, for mediating more effectively between differing cultures, and for empowering them.

This is a welcome edition to the continuing discourse on multiculturalism in social work practice. Whereas the edition published in 1996 identified a number of critical issues, addressed substantive gaps in our knowledge, and attempted to define multicultural practice across a variety of groups, this edition is organized into sections on multicultural practice, child welfare, education, youth, communities, health, long-term care, mental health, substance abuse, HIV/AIDS, and immigration. Cross-cutting each chapter are implications for practice, practical tools, and relevant theories and research findings. This timely work covers natural support systems; health-seeking behaviors and health care needs of various ethnic and racial groups; the concept of privilege; value-based practice; marital conflict; adoption; violence; environmental and behavioral risk factors; social indicators of community strengths; spirituality; alternative health practices in diverse rural communities; neighborhood-based health promotion; and the unique circumstances for refugees and immigrants.

Discussions of research methods and approaches show a greater sensitivity and awareness of the need to collaborate and to actively involve the stakeholders (the individual, the community, or the group). The outcome of this participatory research model is that stakeholders gain a voice and thus become empowered by the process, rather than merely its "subject matter." The profession has paid too little attention to this issue in the preparation of students for research roles to advance knowledge development. Theories and perspectives such as identity formulation, constructivism, empowerment, Afrocentrism, standpoint, communication, cognitive, ecological, stress, and role undergird various discussions.

What is fascinating about this edition is that it moves the discourse from a superficial "politically correct posture" to one of social conviction—what is just and rightful in a humane society. Underneath, hidden below the veneer of the "politically correct posture," one finds all of the "isms" that directly conflict with the espoused values of the social work profession. Perhaps this edition will facilitate the congruency that is sorely needed for the advancement of knowledge—that what we espouse becomes engrained in our belief systems and behaviors.

The contributors to this volume are recognized for their thoughtful and scholarly writings. They represent the diversity and breadth of the profession—in terms of points-of-view, gender, race, ethnicity, and contexts.

Given the texture that is America, the subject of multiculturalism is one of the most important factors shaping our society in the coming decades and generations. Examinations of multiculturalism help us glimpse the impact on future generations and the ways in which we view one another and appreciate and adapt each others' cultures to our own. In our ever-changing world—and the way in which greater communication and education has helped it to shrink—multiculturalism and books such as this one are immeasurably important. As social workers, striving for the greater good and for the betterment of our entire society, we embrace issues of culture in a positive manner, acknowledging that cultural differences are our country's strength and our country's challenge.

Paula Allen-Meares, PhD
Dean and Professor
School of Social Work
University of Michigan

REFERENCES

Benedict, R. (1934). Peter's quotations: Ideas for our time. In *Patterns of culture* (p. 253). Boston: Houghton Mifflin.

LeMay, M. C. (1987). *From open door to dutch door: An analysis of U.S. immigration policy since 1820.* New York: Praeger.

United States Immigration and Naturalization Service. (1998). *Immigrants admitted by region and selected country of birth: Fiscal years 1994–96* [Date on U.S. immigration] [Online]. Available: http://www.ins.usdoj.gov/stats/annual/fy96/

Introduction

Multicultural Issues in Social Work: Practice and Research extends the collective vision of multiculturalism in social work practice that was presented in Volume I. Volume II reflects some of the major social and political changes that have influenced multicultural practice since 1995, the end of the period addressed in Volume I. The following changes have shaped both the content and the organizational framework of this book:

- **The Status of Multicultural Practice Research.** Emerging research has documented how large systems, as well as culturally biased research paradigms and methods, can disregard the marginalized voices and realities of oppressed groups. Conversely, culturally sensitive research has identified collaborative political action strategies and stakeholder research methods that lead to systems change and help diverse groups and communities gain their voices and enhance their capacities. Such research has implications for shifting the roles of professionals to make them more complementary to new active roles for consumers.
- **Professional Social Work Standards Related to Multicultural Practice.** NASW revised its *Code of Ethics* in 1996. Among other changes, the revised *Code* clarifies, strengthens, and expands ethical principles and standards required for social work practice in terms of social justice; sexual harassment; cultural competence; and social diversity, discrimination, and social and political action. Changes in these ethical principles and standards require practitioners to be more knowledgeable about the ethics involved and to improve their multicultural practice skills. Organizational resources are needed to support these professional and individual changes.
- **The Cultural Patterns and Political Circumstances among Diverse Populations Currently Immigrating to this Country.** The cultural patterns of groups coming to this country from similar parts of the world cover a tremendous range of values, traditions, and beliefs that service providers may not recognize as important within-group differences (for example, among Asian and Pacific Islanders, groups from different Caribbean islands, and latinos from various South American countries). Groups from countries with totalitarian political systems may have difficulties understanding this country's democratic traditions, the political culture, and how to influence the system to address social justice issues. Practitioners in various settings will need to

recognize and develop skills for responding to these subtleties in cultural patterns.

- **Implementation of Public Policy Related to Multicultural Issues.** Many policies passed by Congress before 1995 and other more recent policies that are being implemented are affecting multicultural practice and the quantity and quality of services available to a range of diverse groups. Those policies include welfare-to-work; managed care in health, child welfare, mental health; and affirmative action reforms in education, employment, and other civil rights areas. Such policies reflect a shift away from cultural tolerance and an appreciation of diversity in this country toward victim-blaming and cost-containment in social and educational programs. Hate crimes may have increased as part of this atmosphere of intolerance. Practitioners and administrators will need to improve their resource development, advocacy, action research, dissemination, and policy impact skills based on these social, political, and cultural changes.

The focus in Volume I, from a developmental perspective, was on clarifying the importance of multiculturalism, identifying multicultural issues, and defining and conceptualizing the nature of multicultural practice across various groups. This volume builds on that foundation by addressing a broader range of multicultural practice in more diverse settings and practice arenas. The book is organized into sections on multicultural practice, child welfare, education and youths, communities, health, long-term care, mental health and substance abuse, HIV/AIDS, and immigration. The chapters in each section provide an in-depth analysis of multicultural practice and related professional issues, as well as practical tools and cogent research findings for improving such practice.

Some chapters include implications for enhancing multicultural practice through innovative curriculum developments in social work education. The focus on diversity and multiculturalism in Volume II has been extended to include issues of gender and location in terms of the special needs and cultural strengths of rural populations. The also is a larger number of chapters on age-appropriate services for elderly people.

The breadth and scope of this book should challenge social workers and other helping professionals, as well as policymakers, to move beyond concerns about political correctness in their perspectives and actions. This book clarifies the dynamic balance required between supportive policy, research, and practice in the multicultural area and the related shift in language and thought that is necessary for real commitment to honoring diversity. Concepts such as culturally informed, values-based, culturally relevant, social construction, alternative health practices, cultural values and health care decision making, cultural care practices, and culturally appropriate services reflect an emphasis on consumers' interpretations and meanings and on their role as experts. Consumers' perspectives about their cultural strengths, the quality of service networks, the effects of oppression and cultural privilege, culturally appropriate help-seeking behaviors, and their needs are highlighted in the book as well. In a complementary fashion, some chapters identify culturally sensitive roles for professionals, including those of partners, coaches, advocates, and nonexperts.

Multicultural Issues in Social Work: Practice and Research is designed to assist social work students and practitioners in a broad range of practice settings and fields to improve the quality of and resources available for effective multicultural practice. Its contents are relevant to social work administrators in social agencies and other organizations, educators, researchers, community advocates, and policy analysts and reformers. The book should be useful also to students and professionals from other helping fields and related areas.

Many gifted authors have contributed to the expanded perspective about multicultural issues and practice presented in this volume. The breadth and depth of their work parallel an increase in the overall number of articles on this topic in the literature. This trend reflects an increased concern and commitment to understanding and disseminating multiculturalism within the range of social work practice. Furthermore, it provides fertile ground for the future development of practice literature in this extremely important area.

Patricia L. Ewalt
Edith M. Freeman
Anne E. Fortune
Dennis L. Poole
Stanley L. Witkin

Part I

MULTICULTURAL PRACTICE

1 A Constructivist Perspective on Clinical Social Work Practice with Ethnically Diverse Clients

Gilbert J. Greene, Carla Jensen, and
Dorothy Harper Jones

R esearch has found that virtually all therapeutic approaches are equally effective (Smith, Glass, & Miller, 1980). The one thing essential to therapeutic success, regardless of theoretical orientation, is a good working relationship between the clinician and the client (Frank, 1982; Marziali & Alexander, 1991). Integral to establishing and maintaining such a relationship is the clinician's use of self in the application of a specific approach or technique (Lambert, Bergin, & Collins, 1977; McConnaughy, 1987).

Awareness of use of self is especially important for clinicians working with clients ethnically different from themselves. Much has been written on ethnicity issues in clinical practice (Ho, 1987; Pinderhughes, 1989), with some emphasis given to the clinician's use of self in cross-cultural practice (Boyd-Franklin, 1989; Pinderhughes, 1989). Although the use of self by the clinician in client empowerment has been discussed (Baldwin & Satir, 1987; Pinderhughes, 1989), it has not been sufficiently operationalized in the broader context of cross-cultural clinical social work practice.

In cross-cultural clinical practice, the importance of considering the client's worldview (conception of reality) vis-à-vis the clinician's has been noted (Ibrahim, 1985). One's conception of reality is constructed through social interaction with significant others, and ethnicity is a critical factor in this process (Berger & Luckman, 1966; Hoffman, 1988). The fact that reality is socially constructed is the basis of the constructivist perspective in family therapy and social work (Hoffman, 1988; Jones, Greene, & Ruhala, 1993; Witkin, 1991).

CONSTRUCTIVISM

Constructivism holds that people do not discover reality but rather use language to construct a conception of reality through social interaction (Goolishian & Winderman, 1988). A person's conception of reality consists of the meanings he or she has given to his or her interpretation

This chapter was originally published in the March 1996 issue of *Social Work*, Vol. 41, pp. 172–180.

of the world (Goolishian & Winderman, 1988). Meanings are coconstructed in the dialogue between two people (or more) in which ideas are exchanged (Goolishian & Winderman, 1988).

Through conversations with numerous people over a lifetime, one's reality continually evolves. One major aspect of this socially constructed reality is one's sense of self—self-concept (Gergen, 1985). Integral to the social construction of the self are experiences in the family of origin (Reiss, 1981; Wamboldt & Wolin, 1989). According to Minuchin (1979), the family of origin is the matrix (context) for the development of the definition of self.

Also important in the socially constructed reality of the self is one's ethnic and cultural heritage (Pinderhughes, 1989). Different ethnic groups have different values, beliefs, rituals, and traditions that form the context of the family of origin. Just as the family is the context for one's construction of self, one's ethnic and cultural heritage provides the larger context for the family's construction of its reality. Having a sense of and connection with one's ethnic and cultural heritage is important to positive self-esteem and mental health (Pinderhughes, 1989).

Society is assumed to provide the larger context for the construction of ethnic identity. Experience shows, however, that the unique attributes of groups in the minority tend to be devalued by those in the majority as a way of coping with perceived threats from the minority. Consequently, a person from an ethnic group in the minority may construct a sense of self that is influenced by this devaluation, lack of power, and discrimination in the societal context.

CONSTRUCTIVISM AND CLINICAL PRACTICE

Consistent with the constructivist orientation is the narrative approach to clinical practice (Borden, 1992; Howard, 1991; Laird, 1989). Several authors have mentioned the connection between constructivism and narrative theory in their writings (Dean & Fleck-Henderson, 1992; Gallant, 1993; Hoffman, 1991). People's construction of reality is reflected in the stories (narratives) they tell (Howard, 1991), which allow them to organize and make meaning out of their lives (Borden, 1992). These stories–meanings are contained in the narratives–conversations that transpire between people where meaning is coconstructed (Dean, 1992; Hoffman, 1991).

Family of Origin

In clinical social work the self of the client encounters the self of the clinician, and the clinician's family-of-origin issues encounter the client's family-of-origin issues. Consequently, there is a risk that the clinician will unconsciously undermine client growth (Baldwin & Satir, 1987) or contribute to client deterioration (Lambert et al., 1977).

To help ensure treatment success, clinicians must become aware of their unresolved family-of-origin issues and consciously monitor their reactions so that they do not reinforce the clients' problematic behaviors (Kramer, 1985; Meyer, 1987). In effective treatment, clinicians are diligent in keeping their own family-of-origin issues from interfering with the clinical work as much as possible (Papero, 1990). Using systems theory and systemic questioning helps the clinician avoid getting his or her family-of-origin issues caught up with those of the client (Bowen, 1978; Papero, 1990).

Ethnicity

In clinical social work the ethnicity of the clinician encounters the ethnicity of the client. Just as clinicians are affected by the client's family-of-origin issues, they also are uncomfortable to some extent with ethnic and cultural differences. A challenge for clinicians is how to therapeutically use self with ethnically diverse clients while recognizing the effects of cultural differences.

In discussing ethnic-sensitive clinical practice, Pinderhughes (1989) consistently emphasized the importance of clinician comfort in working with clients' ethnic and cultural differences. To feel as comfortable as possible in cross-cultural work, clinicians need to be aware of and feel positive about their own ethnic and cultural identity (Pinderhughes, 1989). Pinderhughes stated that clinicians must monitor and manage their "feelings, perceptions, and attitudes mobilized as a result of one's clinical and cultural group status role" (p. 133) to practice effectively with ethnically diverse clients.

Desired outcomes of clinical social work include increases in self-esteem and empowerment for clients. Such outcomes can occur when the therapeutic discourse causes the client to have an empowered sense of self. Essential to this empowerment process is the client's feeling more connected to his or her ethnic identity. In taking a constructivist or narrative approach to clinical work with clients of color, clinicians must include ethnicity and issues of discrimination and powerlessness in the therapeutic discourse for such clients to successfully restory their lives. Howard (1991) stated that some examples of clinical work could be viewed as cross-cultural experiences in story repair. Clients develop new stories as models for future action (Laird, 1989).

Use of Self

A constructivist approach to therapy lends itself well to client empowerment and, thus, is well suited to cross-cultural clinical social work. A constructivist approach to therapy de-emphasizes therapeutic hierarchical power and control and emphasizes therapy as collaborative and empowering (Hoffman, 1988). Thus, from a constructivist perspective, the clinician does therapy with clients rather than to them.

Clinicians using a constructivist approach do not attempt to impose "reality" but rather facilitate through the therapeutic conversation the clients' construction of a more workable reality for themselves. This perspective can allow clinicians to transcend their discomfort arising from cross-cultural differences with clients. According to Anderson and Goolishian (1988), a therapeutic conversation involves "a mutual search and exploration through dialogue, a two-way exchange, a criss-crossing of ideas in which new meanings are continually evolving toward the 'dissolving' of problems" (p. 372).

Coconstruction. Because reality is socially constructed, a constructivist therapist believes that there is no one truth but many possible explanations—multiple realities—for the phenomena under discussion (Cecchin, 1987). This belief allows the clinician to take a position of curiosity about which explanation fits the client rather than insisting on discovering the "truth" (Cecchin, 1987).

Lax (1992) stated that it is the clinician's job to join with clients "in the development of a new story about their lives that offers them a view that is different enough from their situation, yet not too different, to further the conversation" (p. 74). In this coconstructing process, clinicians and clients both contribute words and ideas. Clinicians continually translate the clients' words into their own and share these words with them to see if there is a match with the clients' language and interpretations (Lax, 1992).

During the therapeutic conversation the clinician may offer suggestions and ideas that build on what the client has said; the clinician presents them in a tentative way, leaving plenty of room for the client to come up with his or her own answers (Lax, 1992). The successful coconstruction of the client's story no longer includes the presenting problem.

Novelty. The clinical situation is more than an ordinary conversation between the social worker and client. The therapist must be skilled at facilitating the conversation in a therapeutic manner (Anderson & Goolishian, 1988). As a participant in the process of change, the therapist must interact with clients in a manner that results in the interruption of the problematic, repetitive patterns in which clients find themselves (Dowd & Pace, 1989; Fruggeri, 1992; Watzlawick, Weakland, & Fisch, 1974). Consequently, the clinician hears and feeds back to the client a slightly different perspective than the client's description of his or her situation; in this manner, the clinician introduces novelty to the client system (Lax, 1992).

The experience of "novelty" by the client as a result of the therapeutic conversation is integral to a constructivist approach (Anderson & Goolishian, 1992; Fruggeri, 1992). The clinician should have some guidelines for asking questions during the therapeutic conversation so that the client experiences such novelty in the coconstruction of a new reality (or a new story) that does not include the problem and the vicious cycles that maintain it.

Real (1990) pointed out "that the only behavior directly accessible to the therapist's control is the therapist's own behavior. How the therapist moves, the selections he makes, where he places his weight, so to speak, in other words his use of self, is the only tool available to him" (p. 260). Given constructivism's emphasis on language and conversation in reality construction, the use of self in contributing to the process of empowering ethnically diverse clients involves bringing the issue of ethnicity into the therapeutic discourse in a way that allows the clinician to transcend any discomfort with cultural differences. The literature on operationalizing the use of self in general and with ethnically diverse clients in particular is limited. In response to a lack of literature on the operationalization of constructivist–systemic family therapy, Real (1990) developed five stances for guiding therapeutic use of self: eliciting, probing, contextualizing, matching, and amplifying. The following adaptation of Real's stances for the therapeutic use of self from a constructivist–systemic perspective provides a map for operationalizing such an endeavor with ethnically diverse clients.

CONSTRUCTIVIST USE OF SELF WITH ETHNICALLY DIVERSE CLIENTS

Eliciting Stance

The initial stories clients tell clinicians contain problems that they have not been able to solve themselves (Laird, 1989; Penn & Sheinberg, 1991). From the eliciting stance the therapist asks clients about their ideas and explanations about the presenting problem and respectfully accepts each one (Real, 1990). Conflicting explanations are not countered, but instead each is explored through open-ended questions. When using the eliciting stance, the clinician does not present himself or herself as an "expert" but rather takes a "one-down" position and thus reinforces the client as the expert on his or her situation; this can be experienced by clients as empowering.

By using the eliciting stance, the clinician, according to Real (1990), "invites greater variety in system members' thinking, not by countering their ideas or by suggesting alternatives, but by simply asking individuals to focus their attention on constructs that may have received only scant attention before" (p. 261). The eliciting stance allows the clinician to bring the issue of ethnicity into the therapeutic discourse in a way that reflects curiosity and acceptance.

Case Example. Initially the Smiths were referred because T, a 13-year-old African American boy, assaulted a student at school; as a result, charges were filed against him in juvenile court. At the time, T, his 11-year-old brother D, and nine-year-old sister S had been in the legal custody of their great-grandparents, Mr. and Mrs. Smith, for almost nine years. The great grandparents received legal custody after the children's mother, C, was charged with child neglect. C requested that the children be placed in her grandparents' custody, and the court agreed. C lived separately from her children and grandparents during the nine years but did visit them periodically.

T was placed on probation by the court, and after several months of working with T, the family, and the school system, the clinician closed the case with the family's consent, because the agreed-on goals had been met. Six months later, Mr. Smith called the clinician to resume family treatment after the mother moved into the household where her children, grandparents, and an uncle's family resided. Mr. Smith thought that resuming family sessions would be an opportunity for the children and their mother to re-establish their relationship.

The first session was with the children, C, and the elder Smiths. C was seen alone by design for the second session so she and the clinician could get better acquainted. Several times during the first session and the first part of the second session, C said she just wanted T to communicate with her more openly.

> **C:** I just want T to open up to me about his feelings.
>
> **Therapist:** What was it like for you when you were growing up? Who could you open up to about your feelings?
>
> **C:** I could talk easiest to Grandma.
>
> **Therapist:** And how about your brother? Who could he talk with the easiest?
>
> **C:** Oh there's no doubt it was Daddy [referring to great-grandfather].
>
> **Therapist:** Who do you think has been the easiest for T to talk to?
>
> **C:** Again, I have to say Daddy.
>
> **Therapist:** From what I know about teenage boys, especially African American teenage males, they do find it easiest to open up to other males. To what extent do you think this has been true for T?

In Real's (1990) discussion of the eliciting stance, questions are used in a straightforward manner to elicit more specificity and concreteness. The clinician hopes that the result is a "chink" in the armor of the client's "airtight" reality, which then might be increased by further questioning (Real, 1990). The previous series of questions could gently and indirectly get C to rethink her position about T having to open up to her, thereby putting a chink in C's position. This rethinking would then help her avoid a power struggle with T that could lead to estrangement and feelings of inadequacy in her parental role. C could rethink "openness" and come to a different perception about T's behavior; she could then possibly experience it as her idea rather than the social worker's. Also, paradoxically, T might become more open with her if he were not feeling pressured.

Circular Questioning. Real (1990) did not include the use of circular questioning (see Fleuridas, Nelson, & Rosenthal, 1986; Penn, 1982) in the eliciting stance. However, we believe that circular questioning should be considered part of the eliciting stance. *Circular questioning* involves asking different family members their views about the beliefs, behaviors, and patterns of behavior of other family members and their relationships (Penn, 1982). Because problems do not occur in a vacuum, such questioning highlights the interpersonal context (Fleuridas et al., 1986). As a result, clients view and experience their situations systemically rather than focus on individual symptomatology. This shift in perspective results in significant positive change for clients. Straightforward questions can elicit "each person's construction of the situation" (Real, 1990, p. 262). Circular questioning enlarges the contextual definition of the problem.

Reframing Stance

In Real's (1990) framework the second stance is called the "probing" stance. However, the terms "eliciting" and "probing" are similar in meaning and, thus, could cause the two stances to be confused. Because the clinician's primary activity in the second stance is reframing, we have decided to refer to this stance as the "reframing" stance to avoid confusion.

Reframing the Situation. In the eliciting stance, the clinician draws out distinctions and explanations from the system members; in the reframing stance the opposite is true. The clinician now contributes potentially new, plausible ideas to be considered in the therapeutic dialogue. These ideas consist of ways clients can redefine or reframe important aspects of their situations. One important aspect of a client's reality in which positive reframing may be useful is the area of ethnicity, especially when clients of color seem to have bought into society's devaluation. Client empowerment is reinforced when heretofore negatively defined ethnic attributes are positively reframed.

Case Example. C put herself down several times during the first two interviews:

> **C:** I tell these kids, "Don't drop out of school, don't be like me."
>
> **Therapist:** You want a lot for these kids.
>
> **C:** Yes, I do.
>
> **Therapist:** Sounds like you're also pretty down on yourself.
>
> **C:** I just don't want them to carry a shadow like I'm carrying.
>
> **Therapist:** You have a shadow? What's the shadow?
>
> **C:** That I had my kids taken from me.
>
> **Therapist:** It's pretty painful.
>
> **C:** Yeah, but I deal with it. I talk to my sister, my mother, sometimes with Grandma. My brother is there for me, too.
>
> **Therapist:** You've had a really tough time. I'm also wondering, in terms of you being down on yourself and feeling that you are carrying a shadow, how much has the way the system does things and the way it treats African Americans been a factor in your developing these feelings?
>
> **C:** I haven't thought of it that way, but as an African American, I have been jerked around by the system a lot.
>
> **Therapist:** So it's been a real struggle for you. You've been a young, single, African American mother of three children trying to make it in a system that doesn't, in many instances, consider what the African American experience is like.

Later in the interview the therapist took the reframing stance:

Therapist: You must be real proud of your kids.

C: Yeah, but I definitely don't want my kids to follow in my footsteps.

Therapist: You are real down on yourself, aren't you?

C: I can't picture my kids doing the same thing I did.

Therapist: Look what you did for them. That was a real act of love. You signed custody over to your grandparents because you knew they would be safe and taken care of, and that showed a lot of courage to do something like that. This is something that really impresses me about African American families—the ability to rely on extended family.

C: Even though I had my sister and brother, the first person I thought of was grandma.

Therapist: They have really been there for the kids, but I also think that your kids have really been missing you. Mothers are always important.

The clinician used the reframing stance to help C reframe giving her grandparents custody of her children as "an act of love." The reframing was extended to include ethnicity by situating this act of love within the strengths of the African American extended family.

Contextualizing Stance

Using the contextualizing stance, the clinician helps clients connect the presenting problem situation to their interpersonal or family-of-origin realities (Real, 1990). The contextualizing stance is typically in use whenever the clinician convenes two or more generations for a family session. Having such sessions implicitly conveys to the family the message that the problem situation has meaning and relevance to all family members. Another implicit contextualizing message in sessions involving multiple generations is that everyone is needed to resolve the problem situation. The use of the contextualizing stance is especially relevant to working with African American families because of the importance of the extended family in African American culture (Hines & Boyd-Franklin, 1982).

Frequently clients see a problem in dichotomous terms in which they hold themselves or other people responsible; either view of the problem can be disempowering. Frequently clients are not aware of the complex interactive and ecological nature of their problem situation. The contextualizing stance allows the client to see the problem with a wide-angle lens. The clinician uses circular questioning in the contextualizing stance to help clients view problems interpersonally, generationally (up or down at least one generation), or societally. Contextualizing is illustrated in the previous dialogue when the social worker asked C who in the family it was easiest for certain family members to open up to. The ease of opening up depends on the interpersonal context, which includes issues of gender and ethnicity.

Matching Stance

Using the matching stance, the clinician mirrors (feeds back) to clients key aspects of their reality (Real, 1990). The clinician shares with clients his or her hypotheses about their reality. Real stated that an example of this at the individual level is the clinician's use of empathic responding. In applying this stance to working with ethnically diverse clients, the relevance of their ethnic reality becomes a key point. The use of the matching stance in an empathic manner is illustrated in the previous dialogue when the clinician stated, "So it's been a real struggle for you. You've been a young, single, African American mother of three children trying to make it in a system that doesn't, in many instances, consider what the African American experience is like."

Bicultural Awareness. The matching stance is especially relevant when the client has conflicts or dilemmas that are integral to his or her problem situation, especially if these conflicts are outside conscious awareness. In everyday life clients of color are presented with conflicts and dilemmas arising from their bicultural lives (Chestang, 1979). Such experiences can be very uncomfortable, and in coping the client of color may be inclined to deny or minimize their existence. Real (1990) referred to this use of the matching stance as "reflecting."

> **Therapist:** C, to what extent do you think having to live in two worlds—the white world and the African American world—might have contributed to your depression?
>
> **C:** I don't think that's been a problem for me at all. I just go about my business and don't give that any thought at all.
>
> **Therapist:** Yes, it is important to take care of business. I wonder though if a part of you finds it difficult to live in these two worlds but you just don't have the time or energy to worry about it. And I wonder if there's another part of you that feels it won't do any good anyway to think about the problems of living in two worlds. This is just food for thought for you at this time and at some point it might be helpful for us to take some time and talk about this.

Reflection. After becoming increasingly aware of forgotten strengths and competencies, the client may then have the energy to reflect on the possibility of being in a "bicultural dilemma" and later bring this up in the therapeutic conversation for further exploration. However, if the client does not initiate discussion of this dilemma at a later time, the clinician can revisit and explore its effect on the client by using Socratic, circular, and reflexive questioning. These types of questions, according to Tomm (1987), aid clients in self-healing by getting them to reflect on their current interpretations of reality and generating new patterns of interpreting and behaving. When clients of color are reflective, they become objects of their own observations (Lax, 1992) and, consequently, are able to define the reality of their bicultural dilemma and its resolution themselves.

Amplifying Stance

Taking the amplifying stance, the clinician focuses on a particular idea, affect, theme, or behavior that is a client resource; he or she hopes to evoke more client attention to it as a result of this focus (Real, 1990). According to Real, this stance is based on the constructivist axiom that "Often, all one needs to do to evoke more of any given quality within a system is to attend to it" (p. 267). Real saw the amplifying stance as similar to the emphasis on identifying "exceptions" in solution-focused therapy (Walter & Peller, 1992) or "unique outcomes" in narrative therapy (White & Epston, 1990), in which the clinician and clients identify what has worked previously in problem resolution so that the client will do more of it.

Extended Family. Many clients of color who have been devalued and disempowered by society may deny or downgrade the strengths and resources they have. The amplifying stance is a way to facilitate clients' awareness and use of their strengths and resources. In extended African American families like the Smiths, it is common to have an older male member in the family in the role of "Daddy" or "Big Daddy" and an older female family member in the role of "Big Mama." These roles represent strengths in an extended African American family that need to be maintained in treatment.

Amplifying Family Changes. In the case example there is a change that also needs to be supported and amplified—the re-entry of C into the family. C's successful re-entry and ongoing involvement can be an asset to both her grandparents and her children. The great-grandparents were reluctant to turn responsibility over to C after nine years. C's re-entry into the family was still in its early stages and had not been solidified. Her re-entry and the importance of the great-grandparents to the family system needed to be supported; these facts are not mutually exclusive.

The amplifying stance is used by the clinician in the reintegration process, as the following excerpts from the first session illustrate:

> **Therapist:** T, what was it like to have your mom come to the session today?
>
> **T:** Happy.
>
> **Therapist:** Great! [to C] So you're back with the kids now. What's that like for you?
>
> **C:** Okay.
>
> **Therapist:** When I saw T last week, the first thing he said was "My mom is back." This is a pretty exciting time for him. D, what was that like for you to have your mom back in?
>
> **D:** Great!

> **Therapist:** S, what was it like for you when your mom moved back in?
>
> **S:** Fun.
>
> **Therapist:** What's fun about it?
>
> **S:** We get an allowance.
>
> **Therapist:** So everyone is pretty excited about having her back, including you [talking to the great-grandparents].
>
> **Mrs. S:** Yes, quite a bit.

Later in the session C pointed to the great-grandfather and said, "He's been Daddy to everyone."

> **Therapist:** [speaking to the great-grandfather] How about you, what do you want to see happen in our work here?
>
> **Mr. S:** To express our feelings. To pull no punches.
>
> **Therapist:** That's something T and I have been working on. And you've [great-grandfather] been so helpful. T's done some amazing things, and he couldn't have done what he did without you. It's like you've been there as "Daddy," as C said, to help him.

A few minutes later in the session:

> **Therapist:** This is a powerful thing to have four generations in one house. I think I'm going to learn a lot. You're going to have to teach me what it's like to have this kind of support system. This is a wonderful thing about extended African American families—that there's room for everyone and everyone has a part to play.
>
> **Mr. S:** It isn't every day you see this many generations.
>
> **Therapist:** It's very unusual in my work with white families.

In the dialogue above, the clinician, very early in the first session, began amplifying the importance of the mother to her children and her re-entry into the family. The process continued with the emphasis on how important Mr. Smith had been to T's progress and his prominent position in the extended family. The clinician's last comments amplified the African American extended family as a source of strength and support and further enhanced C's re-entry.

DISCUSSION

Cross-cultural clinical social work is most effective when clinicians are comfortable working with clients ethnically different from themselves. The clinician's comfort is increased in such situations when he or she is knowledgeable about the client's culture. However, it is impossible to be knowledgeable about every culture. The clinician's position of curiosity—knowing that there are many possible realities— and use of the five stances discussed in this chapter can facilitate the therapeutic conversation and help prevent discomfort from interfering with cross-cultural clinical work.

The constructivist theoretical framework can be used to operationalize the therapeutic use of self with ethnically diverse clients. Clinicians using the five stances can engage in appropriate use of self regardless of the client's ethnicity. In a constructivist approach, the clinician's job is to keep the conversation going until the presenting problem "dis-solves" (Anderson & Goolishian, 1988). Continuing the conversation with clients of color involves skillfully bringing ethnicity and the issues of discrimination and disempowerment into the therapeutic conversation. Clients of color will find it difficult to successfully dis-solve problems and restory their lives without bringing these topics into the story. The clinician's awareness of the different ways to use self ultimately allows the clients, rather than the clinician, to construct reality or repair the stories and thus increases their sense of empowerment in a valued ethnic context.

REFERENCES

Anderson, H., & Goolishian, H. A. (1988). Human systems as linguistic systems: Preliminary and evolving ideas about the implications for clinical theory. *Family Process, 27,* 371–393.

Anderson, H., & Goolishian, H. A. (1992). The client is the expert: A not-knowing approach to therapy. In S. McNamee & K. J. Gergen (Eds.), *Therapy as social construction* (pp. 25–39). Newbury Park, CA: Sage Publications.

Baldwin, M., & Satir, V. (1987). *The use of self in therapy.* New York: Haworth Press.

Berger, P., & Luckman, T. (1966). *The social construction of reality.* New York: Doubleday.

Borden, W. (1992). Narrative perspectives in psychosocial intervention following adverse life events. *Social Work, 37,* 135–143.

Bowen, M. (1978). *Family therapy in clinical practice.* New York: Jason Aronson.

Boyd-Franklin, N. (1989). *Black families in therapy: A multisystems approach.* New York: Guilford Press.

Cecchin, G. (1987). Hypothesizing, circularity, and neutrality revisited: An invitation to curiosity. *Family Process, 26,* 405–414.

Chestang, L. W. (1979). Competencies and knowledge in clinical social work: A dual perspective. In P. Ewalt (Ed.), *Toward a definition of clinical social work* (pp. 1–12). Washington, DC: National Association of Social Workers.

Dean, R. G. (1992). Constructivism: An approach to clinical practice. *Smith College Studies in Social Work, 63,* 127–146.

Dean, R. G., & Fleck-Henderson, A. (1992). Teaching clinical theory and practice through a constructivist lens. *Journal of Teaching in Social Work, 6,* 3–20.

Dowd, E. T., & Pace, T. M. (1989). The relativity of reality: Second-order change in psychotherapy. In A. Freeman, K. H. Simon, L. E. Beutler, & H. Arkowitz (Eds.), *Comprehensive handbook of cognitive therapy* (pp. 213–226). New York: Plenum Press.

Fleuridas, C., Nelson, T. S., & Rosenthal, D. (1986). The evolution of circular questions: Training family therapists. *Journal of Marital and Family Therapy, 12,* 113–127.

Frank, J. D. (1982). Therapeutic components shared by all psychotherapies. In J. H. Harvey & M. M. Parks (Eds.), *Psychotherapy research and behavior change* (pp. 9–37). Washington, DC: American Psychological Association.

Fruggeri, L. (1992). Therapeutic process as the social construction of change. In S. McNamee & K. J. Gergen (Eds.), *Therapy as social construction* (pp. 40–53). Newbury Park, CA: Sage Publications.

Gallant, J. P. (1993). New ideas for the school social worker in the counseling of children and families. *Social Work in Education, 15,* 119–128.

Gergen, K. J. (1985). Social constructionist inquiry: Context and implications. In K. J. Gergen & K. E. Davis (Eds.), *The social construction of the person* (pp. 3–18). New York: Springer-Verlag.

Goolishian, H. A., & Winderman, L. (1988). Constructivism, autopoiesis and problem determined systems. *Irish Journal of Psychology, 9,* 130–143.

Hines, P. M., & Boyd-Franklin, N. (1982). Black families. In M. McGoldrick, J. K. Pearce, & J. Giordano (Eds.), *Ethnicity and family therapy* (pp. 84–107). New York: Guilford Press.

Ho, M. K. (1987). *Family therapy with ethnic minorities.* Beverly Hills, CA: Sage Publications.

Hoffman, L. (1988). A constructivist position for family therapy. *Irish Journal of Psychology, 9,* 110–129.

Hoffman, L. (1991). A reflexive stance for family therapy. *Journal of Strategic and Systemic Therapies, 10,* 4–17.

Howard, G. S. (1991). Culture tales: A narrative approach to thinking, cross-cultural psychology, and psychotherapy. *American Psychologist, 46,* 187–197.

Ibrahim, F. A. (1985). Effectiveness in cross-cultural counseling and psychotherapy: A framework. *Psychotherapy, 22,* 321–323.

Jones, D. H., Greene, G. J., & Ruhala, T. R. (1993). On campus practicum: A model for accelerating the social construction of professional social work identity. *Journal of Teaching in Social Work, 7,* 3–16.

Kramer, J. (1985). *Family interfaces: Transgenerational patterns.* New York: Brunner/Mazel.

Laird, J. (1989). Women and stories: Restorying women's self-constructions. In M. McGoldrick, C. M. Anderson, & F. Walsh (Eds.), *Women in families: A framework for family therapy* (pp. 427–450). New York: W. W. Norton.

Lambert, M. J., Bergin, A. E., & Collins, J. L. (1977). Therapist-induced deterioration in psychotherapy. In A. S. Gurman & A. M. Razin (Eds.), *Effective psychotherapy: A handbook of research* (pp. 452–481). New York: John Wiley & Sons.

Lax, W. D. (1992). Postmodern thinking in a clinical practice. In S. McNamee & K. J. Gergen (Eds.), *Therapy as social construction* (pp. 69–85). Newbury Park, CA: Sage Publications.

Marziali, E., & Alexander, L. (1991). The power of the therapeutic relationship. *American Journal of Orthopsychiatry, 61,* 383–391.

McConnaughy, E. A. (1987). The person of the therapist in psychotherapy practice. *Psychotherapy, 24,* 303–314.

Meyer, P. H. (1987). Patterns and processes in a therapist's own family work: Knowledge required for excellence. In P. Titelman (Ed.), *The therapist's own family: Toward the differentiation of self* (pp. 43–69). Northvale, NJ: Jason Aronson.

Minuchin, S. (1979). Constructing a therapeutic reality. In E. Kaufman & P. Kaufman (Eds.), *Family therapy of drug and alcohol abuse* (pp. 5–18). Boston: Allyn & Bacon.

Papero, D. V. (1990). *Bowen family systems theory.* Boston: Allyn & Bacon.

Penn, P. (1982). Circular questioning. *Family Process, 21,* 267–280.

Penn, P., & Sheinberg, M. (1991). Stories and conversations. *Journal of Strategic and Systemic Therapies, 10,* 30–37.

Pinderhughes, E. (1989). *Understanding race, ethnicity, and power: The key to efficacy in clinical practice.* New York: Free Press.

Real, T. (1990). The therapeutic use of self in constructivist/systemic therapy. *Family Process, 29,* 255–272.

Reiss, D. (1981). *The family's construction of reality.* Cambridge, MA: Harvard University Press.

Smith, M. L., Glass, G. V., & Miller, T. I. (1980). *The benefits of psychotherapy.* Baltimore: Johns Hopkins University Press.

Tomm, K. (1987). Interventive interviewing: Part II. Reflexive questioning as a means to enable self-healing. *Family Process, 26,* 167–183.

Walter, J. L., & Peller, J. E. (1992). *Becoming solution-focused in brief therapy.* New York: Brunner/Mazel.

Wamboldt, F., & Wolin, S. (1989). Reality and myth in family life: Changes across generations. *Journal of Psychotherapy and the Family, 4*, 141–165.

Watzlawick, P., Weakland, J., & Fisch, R. (1974). *Change: Principles of problem formation and problem resolution.* New York: W. W. Norton.

White, M., & Epston, D. (1990). *Narrative means to therapeutic ends.* New York: W. W. Norton.

Witkin, S. L. (1991). The implications of social constructionism for social work education. *Journal of Teaching in Social Work, 4*, 37–48.

An earlier version of this chapter was presented at the 39th Annual Program Meeting of the Council on Social Work Education, New York, February 1993.

2 Differential Effects of Racial Composition on Male and Female Groups: Implications for Group Work Practice

Larry E. Davis, Li Chin Cheng, and
Michael J. Strube

Race continues to be among the most affect-laden and problematic issues in U.S. society. Interactions between black people and white people are often tense and conflictual (Fairchild & Gurin, 1978; Hacker, 1992). Fortunately, over the past 20 years, social workers have increasingly acknowledged race as a salient consideration in helping relationships (Davis & Proctor, 1988; Devore & Schlesinger, 1988; Jacobs & Bowles, 1988; Mindel, Habenstein, & Wright, 1988). Although race per se has not always been discussed, group practitioners have long argued that the attributes or characteristics that individuals bring to small groups have the potential to influence the effectiveness of those groups (Bertcher & Maple, 1985; Garvin, 1987; Northen, 1969; Vinter, 1985; Yalom, 1995). Moreover, with the increasing racial diversification of this society, race dynamics are likely to remain a major concern for group workers.

Unique to group workers has been the concern of small-group interracial dynamics. Given that working with a racially homogeneous group is not always feasible or desirable, the question often faced by group workers is, What racial composition is optimal? Despite its clear importance, this question has only in the past decade or so begun to receive major attention from group workers (Brower, Garvin, Hobson, Reed, & Reed, 1987; Brown & Mistry, 1994; Chau, 1990; Davis, 1979; Mistry & Brown, 1991; Muston & Weinstein, 1988). However, guidance in this area is frequently derived from anecdotes, theory, and practice experience (Brayboy, 1971; Davis, 1980; Muston & Weinstein, 1988). Scant empirical data are available to corroborate or enhance existing practice wisdom.

Even less is known about how gender and race together affect small groups. Historically, race-related group research has involved male participants (Davis & Burnstein, 1981; Katz, 1955; Katz & Benjamin, 1960), requiring practitioners to generalize observed "male dynamics" to women. Yet it seems reasonable that men and women differ in small-group racial dynamics as they do in other respects (for

This chapter was originally published in the September 1996 issue of *Social Work Research*, Vol. 20, pp. 157–166.

example, task versus social–emotional levels of communication) (Aries, 1976; Bales, 1970; Bartol & Butterfield, 1976; Herschel, Cooper, Smith, & Arrington, 1994; Kimble, Yoshikawa, & Zehr, 1981; Stein & Heller, 1983; Strodtbeck & Mann, 1956). Power dynamics in women's groups differ from those in men's groups. For example, evidence suggests that struggles for dominance and efforts to establish hierarchical relationships are less pronounced in groups of women than in groups of men (Aries, 1976; Eagly & Karau, 1991; Stogdill, 1974; Wood, 1987). At the same time, there is less than complete consensus regarding gender dynamics; some efforts have failed to find gender differences in the group dynamics of homogenous groups of men and women (Chapman, 1975; Kerr & Sullaway, 1983; Verdi & Wheelan, 1992).

RELATED LITERATURE

Three primary conceptualizations are used to explain the compositional dynamics of black–white interactions. First, there is a linear explanation, which contends that the quality of interactions between black people and white people will increasingly worsen as the percentage of one racial group increases relative to the other (Giles, 1977; Pettigrew & Cramer, 1959; Wright, 1977). There is some evidence that clients are reluctant to join groups in which they will be in the racial minority (Brayboy, 1971). Indeed, a wealth of research evidence suggests that individuals are inclined to become increasingly comfortable with individuals like themselves (Byrne, 1971).

However, what is perhaps most interesting about the dynamics of black–white racial compositions is that they are commonly found to be nonlinear (Crain, Mahard, & Narot, 1982; Farley, Schuman, Bianchi, Colasanto, & Hatchett, 1978; Longshore, 1982; Matthews & Prothro, 1963; Pettigrew, 1967). Both the second and third major conceptualizations about racial group dynamics are nonlinear—that is, that racial difficulties occur with specific racial groupings. Such racial compositions have sometimes been referred to as "tipping points" (Farley et al., 1978; Giles, Cataldo, & Gatlin, 1975; Myerson & Banfield, 1955; Stinchcombe, McDill, & Walker, 1969). These nonlinear critical racial balances have tended to resemble either a J or a U (or inverted U) pattern. The J model contends that the behaviors and attitudes of white people are not negatively affected by the percentage of black people in a given setting until the percentage of black people increases beyond a certain point, usually around 30 percent (Farley et al., 1978; Matthews & Prothro, 1963; Pettigrew, 1967). Such findings are consistent with the idea that the presence of one or two black people in an otherwise all-white group may arouse little attention from other group members, and the sole racial outgroup member may even be treated as a mascot (Criswell, 1937; Davis, 1980; Moreno, 1934). Yet the presence of additional racially dissimilar people may result in the rejection of all members of that group. Others (Tajfel, 1982; Tajfel & Turner, 1979) have argued that imbalanced racial groupings, like similarly imbalanced gender groupings (Kanter, 1977), and those containing a "solo status" member may accentuate ingroup–outgroup distinctions and thereby promote negative stereotyping and lessen group harmony (Brewer & Kramer, 1985). They offered experimental evidence indicating that groups that contain people of color and solo status members promote stereotyping and biased behavior (Mullen, 1983; Pettigrew & Martin, 1989; Sachdev & Bourhis, 1984).

A third conceptualization of racial group dynamics is the U model. Most evidence in support of this notion of racial conflict has been derived from macro research rather than small-group research. The U model contends that interracial groupings that contain equal numbers of black people and white people will be the least harmonious. Proponents of this model contend that harmony will be lowest in racially balanced groups because neither group is dominant and both groups are struggling for control (Longshore, 1984; Longshore & Prager, 1985). There is in fact considerable support for the U model of racial conflict accompanying racial shifts in school populations (Coleman et al., 1966), neighborhood racial composition (Farley et al., 1978), and voting trends (Matthews & Prothro, 1963).

The preponderance of research evidence for each of these conceptualizations (the linear, J, and U models) has usually suggested the existence of negative racial sentiments of both black people and white people based on the behaviors of the white people (Crain et al., 1982; Matthews & Prothro, 1963). Less frequently have both white and black individuals been queried about how they felt regarding their membership in specific racial group compositions (Farley et al., 1978; Longshore, 1984). Even less frequently have the sentiments of women, either black or white, been queried (Fenelon & Megaree, 1971). Hence, it was of major concern in this study to include gender as a consideration.

The study described in this article sought first to assess which racial group composition affected most favorably or disfavorably the perceptions of group atmosphere, satisfaction, success, and enjoyment of group members. Specifically, we wanted to assess which racial grouping—that is, a white majority, a white minority, or an equal black–white racial composition—was most satisfactory to black and white members and to male and female members. Second, we sought to determine if men and women responded differentially to these variations in racial group compositions.

METHOD

Participants

A total of 120 undergraduate students participated: 30 white men, 30 black men, 30 white women, and 30 black women. These students responded to a posted notice asking for volunteers to participate in a small-group experiment, for which they would be paid $10 each.

Group Monitors

Two graduate students monitored the groups. One white male social work graduate student monitored all of the male groups, and one white female social work graduate student monitored all of the female groups. Group monitors welcomed each of the students as they arrived at the meeting room, explained the group task to each member, and thereafter had only minimal contact with the group. It would have also been interesting to have assessed the effects of both black and white and male and female monitors across all group conditions. This, however, would have increased the size of the study beyond the resources available for this effort. Instead, we held the race and gender of the monitors constant across group conditions. We elected to use white facilitators because of the more common appearance of white students on our predominantly white college campus. That is, because of the more frequent appearance of white people on campus, we felt that a white monitor would arouse less suspicion about the racial nature of our study. However, the use of group monitors from a single race does limit the external validity of our findings.

Procedure

Group members were randomly assigned by race and gender to 30 four-person groups, 15 all male and 15 all female. Three group conditions were established: 25 percent–75 percent (one black and three white members), 50 percent–50 percent (two black and two white members), and 75 percent–25 percent (three black members and one white member). These four-person groups provide the minimum condition for inspection of the linear, J, and U models of racial conflict.

Group members were asked to participate in a decision-making task. Each group was provided with very brief descriptions of 10 individuals. This information did not specify their race. The group was given the hypothetical scenario that war had been declared and that an existing fallout shelter could support only six individuals. Thus, four individuals must be excluded from the shelter so that six could live to rebuild a new society. Participants were required to reach a group consensus as to which four must be excluded. Each group was given 30 minutes to reach a decision. All groups were able to reach a consensus within the time allotted.

At the end of 30 minutes, the group monitor asked each group for its decisions and thanked the members for completing the task assigned them. They then asked each group member to complete a questionnaire packet. Following completion of the questionnaire, group members were told the nature of the study, received $10, and were asked not to discuss the study with others for at least one month.

Measures

Several measures were included in the questionnaire that participants completed. The first, the Desirability of Control Scale (Burger

& Cooper, 1979), is a 20-item scale designed to measure individual differences in the general desire for control over events in one's life—for example, "I enjoy being able to influence the actions of others" and "I enjoy making my own decisions." Group members responded to each of the 20 statements on a scale ranging from 1 = this statement doesn't apply to me at all to 7 = this statement always applies to me; possible scores ranged from 20 to 140. We used this measure to check for pre-existing racial, gender, or group differences in the desire for power. This measure had a total sample coefficient alpha of .73 (.73 for black men, .77 for white men, .62 for black women, and .81 for white women).

A second measure we used was the Group Atmosphere Scale (Fiedler, Chemers, & Mahar, 1976), a 12-item measure of how participants perceived the group on general evaluative dimensions (for example, warm–cold, effective–ineffective, open–closed, formal–informal, pleasant–unpleasant). Each dimension was rated on an eight-point bipolar scale, with possible scores ranging from 12 to 96. The total sample coefficient alpha for this measure was .89 (.91 for black men, .90 for white men, .91 for black women, and .87 for white women).

A third measure, which we constructed for this study, consisted of 18 questions intended to assess a variety of members' perceptions of the group experience. Four of the questions attempted to assess members' feeling of comfort with the group: (1) How much did you enjoy working with the other group members? (2) How willing would you be to participate in a group with these same members again? (3) Overall, how comfortable were you during the group's deliberations? (4) To what extent did the group make members feel or look foolish because of their ideas? Three questions measured satisfaction with the group process: (1) How successful was the group at arriving at a decision? (2) How satisfied were you with the decision your group reached? (3) How well would you expect your group to perform on a similar task in the future? Eight questions measured the amount of control or authority exhibited during group deliberations: (1) How much authority did you feel you had? (2) How much authority did you feel others had? (3) How much did you control the group discussion? (4) How much did others control the group discussion? (5) Approximately how much of the time did you participate in the group discussion? (6) Approximately how much of the time did you want to participate in the discussion? (7) How much were your ideas taken into consideration during the group decision-making process? (8) How much were the ideas of others taken into consideration during the group decision-making process? Three questions measured the clarity of the task and the participants' seriousness in trying to solve it: (1) How clear an understanding did you have of your task in the group? (2) To what extent were the steps necessary to accomplish the task clearly defined? (3) How seriously did you take the task? Group members were asked to respond to the questions on scales ranging from 1 = not at all to 5 = a great deal.

RESULTS

Overview

We analyzed the data using hierarchical analysis of variance. Group composition and gender were treated as between-subject variables; race of participants was treated as a within-group variable. Racial groups of participants were nested within levels of group composition and gender. The group composition effect was partitioned into linear and quadratic components so that linear and nonlinear models of racial composition could be distinguished. (Analysis of data from the men's groups has been reported previously [Davis, Strube, & Cheng, 1995]. The current analyses include the women's group data and provide an explicit test of sex differences.)

Preliminary Analysis

The overall means and standard deviations for all measures are reported in Table 2-1. These means suggest that, overall, the groups exhibited substantial harmony, high perceived success, high satisfaction, and high enjoyment. Indeed, some of the variables exhibit means so extreme that little variability remained for detection of racial composition differences. This overall character of the data must be kept in mind when evaluating the racial composition effects.

An analysis of the Desirability of Control Scale indicated no racial or gender differences in basic motives for control (all $Fs < 3.47, p > .05$). Thus, both black and white participants and both women and men appeared equally motivated to control the situation in which they perceived themselves. We had not anticipated finding racial or gender differences but believed that an examination was warranted given the central position of control in discussion of the J and U models.

Analyses

We analyzed each of the 18 items from the questionnaire constructed for this study (Table 2-1). Although forming compositions from items measuring similar constructs might ordinarily provide a simpler picture of the data, such a strategy is eliminated in the present case by two features of our data. First, the items from the questionnaire were only moderately correlated, suggesting that unique perceptions were being assessed by many of the items. Second, some of the items exhibited high mean scores and low variances; hence, their utility in composites is of questionable value. Exploratory analyses using these approaches, as well as transformations of the data, were not fruitful. However, several single items from the questionnaire did produce significant findings.

The analysis of the major outcome variable, group atmosphere, yielded a single significant result for the quadratic component of the group composition variable [$F(1, 24) = 5.83, p < .05$] (Figure 2-1). Groups with a clear majority of black members ($M = 82.69$) or of white members ($M = 78.39$) reported more positive group atmosphere

Table 2-1

Means and Standard Deviations for Study Measures

Measure	M	SD
Group atmosphere	78.57	0.88
Desire for control	94.04	8.60
Questionnaire items		
1. How successful was the group at arriving at a decision?	4.14	0.59
2. How clear an understanding did you have of your task in the group?	4.62	0.57
3. To what extent were the steps necessary to accomplish the task clearly defined?	3.83	1.03
4. How much authority did you feel you had?	3.32	0.61
5. How much authority did you feel others had?	3.35	0.56
6. How much did you control the group discussion?	3.18	0.67
7. How much did others control the group discussion?	3.26	0.53
8. How much did you enjoy working with the other group members?	3.70	0.78
9. How satisfied were you with the decisions your group reached?	3.99	0.81
10. How well would you expect your group to perform on a similar task in the future?	4.18	0.71
11. How willing would you be to participate in a group with these same members again?	3.94	0.78
12. Approximately how much of the time did you participate in the group discussion?	3.88	0.80
13. Approximately how much of the time did you want to participate in the group discussion?	3.97	0.78
14. How much were your ideas taken into consideration during the group decision-making process?	3.95	0.78
15. How much were the ideas of others taken into consideration during the group decision-making process?	4.01	0.67
16. To what extent did the group make members feel or look foolish because of their ideas?	1.38	0.69
17. How seriously did you take the task?	3.95	0.75
18. Overall, how comfortable were you during the group's deliberations?	4.12	0.79

NOTE: Questions appear in their order of presentation on the questionnaire.

than groups with an equal number of black and white members ($M = 74.54$). Importantly, this quadratic effect was not moderated by race or gender (both $Fs \leq 1.52$, $p > .05$), nor were any linear main effects or interactions evident in the analysis ($Fs \leq 1.91$). Thus, the U model is supported by these data and is equally true of men and women and of black and white participants.

Three additional findings also involved the quadratic component of the group composition variable. First, a main effect for the quadratic component emerged from the analysis of the questions that asked participants to indicate how much of the time they wanted to participate

Figure 2-1

Group Atmosphere Scores, by Group Composition

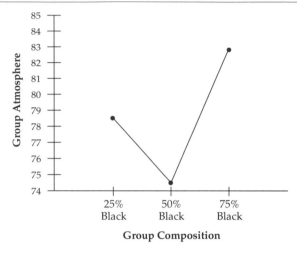

Group Composition

NOTE: Twelve items were rated on an eight-point bipolar scale. Possible scores ranged from 12 to 96.

in the group discussion [$F(1, 24) = 4.87$, $p < .05$] (Figure 2-2). The highest desire to participate was voiced by participants in the 50 percent black condition ($M = 4.20$). Lower ratings were given by the participants in the 25 percent and 75 percent black conditions ($M = 3.73$ and $M = 3.97$, respectively). The second finding was a significant gender ×

Figure 2-2

Amount of Time Participants Wanted to Participate, by Group Composition

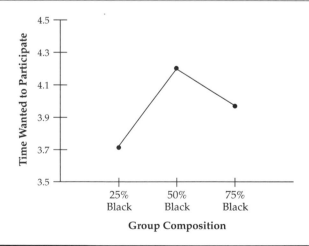

Group Composition

NOTE: Participants responded to the question "Approximately how much of the time did you want to participate in the group discussion?" on a scale ranging from 1 = not at all to 5 = a great deal.

group composition (quadratic) interaction for the question that asked participants to rate how satisfied they were with the decision reached by their group [$F(1, 24) = 7.55, p < .05$]. As Figure 2-3 indicates, the U model received clear support for the men but not for the women. The third finding involving the quadratic component of the group composition variable was a race × group composition (quadratic) interaction for the question involving expected success on a future task [$F(1, 24) = 4.93, p < .05$]. As Figure 2-4 indicates, the black and white participants appeared to have different critical compositions for high expectations.

Four effects are directly relevant to the issue of racial composition models. First, the analysis of the question that asked participants to rate how much they enjoyed working with the other group members revealed a significant linear effect for the group composition variable [$F(1, 24) = 8.90, p < .05$] (Figure 2-5). Participants in the 25 percent black condition rated their enjoyment lower ($M = 3.38$) than participants in the 50 percent black condition ($M = 3.55$), who in turn rated their enjoyment lower than participants in the 75 percent black condition ($M = 4.02$). A similar linear pattern emerged for the question that asked participants to rate how well they would expect their group to perform on a similar task in the future [$F(1, 24) = 10.47, p < .05$] (Figure 2-6). The lowest expectations were indicated by the participants in the 25 percent black condition ($M = 3.87$), the next highest expectations were given by the participants in the 50 percent black condition ($M = 4.15$), and the highest expectations were given by the participants in the 75 percent black condition ($M = 4.47$).

One final effect emerged from the analysis of the question that asked how clearly defined the steps necessary to accomplish the task

Figure 2-3

Satisfaction with Decision Scores, by Group Composition and Gender

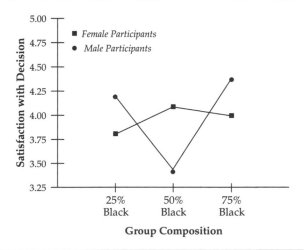

NOTE: Participants responded to the question "How satisfied were you with the decision your group reached?" on a scale ranging from 1 = not at all to 5 = a great deal.

Figure 2-4

Expected Future Performance Scores, by Group Composition and Gender

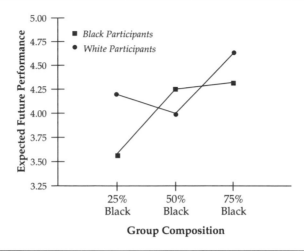

NOTE: Participants responded to the question "How well would you expect your group to perform on a similar task in the future?" on a scale ranging from 1 = not at all to 5 = a great deal.

were: The men ($M = 3.70$) rated the steps as less clearly defined than the women ($M = 4.12$) [$F(1, 24) = 5.97, p < .05$].

Last, to our surprise we noted no significant racial composition effects on our eight items intended to assess member perceptions of control or authority. Again, adherents to the U model of racial confrontation contend that numerically equal groups of black and white

Figure 2-5

Enjoyment of Working with Others Scores, by Group Composition

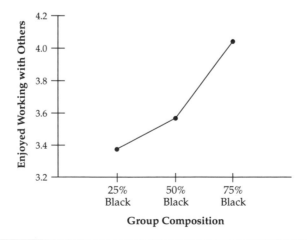

NOTE: Participants responded to the question "How much did you enjoy working with the other group members?" on a scale ranging from 1 = not at all to 5 = a great deal.

Figure 2-6

Expected Future Performance Scores, by Group Composition

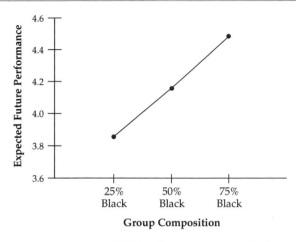

NOTE: Participants responded to the question "How well would you expect your group to perform on a similar task in the future?" on a scale ranging from 1 = not at all to 5 = a great deal.

members result in competition for power and dominance of the situation (Longshore, 1984, 1988). Despite the plausibility that control was the underlying dynamic in our noted support for the U model, analyses of our eight items measuring control failed to confirm this hypothesis. Perhaps the measures were insufficiently sensitive. It may also have been the case that the temporary nature of the task required of the groups did not bring the issue of control to the conscious attention of the group members. That is, perhaps the participants perceived that it just was not worth getting into a power contest with the other group members. There is evidence that intergroup relations that are noncompetitive should reduce racial conflict (Longshore & Prager, 1985). However, others have contended that black and white group members will inevitably engage in social competition even in the absence of clear conflicting interests (Hogg & Abrams, 1988; Tajfel & Turner, 1979). Hence, it is possible that had the group task been more "task" oriented or, for that matter, more social–emotional in nature, our observations may have been different. Clearly, additional research designs that use alternative group manipulations are needed to answer these questions.

DISCUSSION

This study was an effort to provide some empirical data to assist group practitioners in their attempts to construct and lead effective groups of black and white and male and female members. Of course, it would be a mistake to consider only the attributes of race and gender in group composition. Many other factors, such as group purpose, client problem, and personality or behavioral concerns, must always be considered. In short, race and gender are rarely the sole criteria used for group member inclusion or exclusion. Still, we felt that rudimentary insights into how group members perceived various racial configurations would be useful to those confronted with the decision of how best to compose groups containing black and white participants.

By varying the racial compositions of our four-person groups, the perceptions of black and white members and men and women were affected significantly. General support, albeit inconsistent, was obtained for the U model of racial conflict. Member perceptions of group atmosphere, the major outcome variable for this study, supported the U model. Specifically, members of groups with equal numbers of black and white members perceived a less favorable group atmosphere, regardless of gender. This was an important finding, as it is open to question whether black people and white people experience the same reactions in groups with the same racial compositions. Given that some research evidence suggests that black and white individuals might prefer different racial compositions (Davis, 1979; Massey & Denton, 1993), it is conceivable that white people might find one racial balance to have the most favorable group atmosphere and black people another.

It is also curious that evidence in support of the U model was observed in group member aspirations to participate. That is, they reported wanting to participate most when the racial balance of their groups was 50–50. It is possible that this desire was fostered by the struggle for control as posited by the U model. This would seem to be the case at least for the men, who reported least satisfaction with their groups when the racial balance was equal. However, no similar racial composition effects were observed for women. This observation warrants us to raise a major question for race-related group dynamics: Is most of what we know about black–white racial conflict in general more applicable to men than women? In other words, is intergroup racial conflict more a male phenomenon? There is some evidence to support this assertion (Ekehammar, 1985; Sidanius, Cling, & Pratto, 1991; Sidanius, Pratto, & Mitchell, 1994). Women have been noted to be less concerned with dominance behavior in small groups than men (Aries, 1976; Eagly & Karau, 1991; Ridgeway, Johnson, & Diekema, 1994; Stogdill, 1974; Wood, 1987). Yet it must be kept in mind that there were no gender differences in perceptions of the favorableness of the group atmosphere or in desire for group participation.

Some of our expectations were supported, but we had a number of surprises. First, we were surprised by the differences reported by black and white participants with respect to expectations for future group success. The expectations of the white members were consistent with the U model, but the expectations of the black participants were the reverse of those predicted by this model: In evenly divided groups, the white group members expected less future success, but the black members did not. Second, we found some evidence in support of linear racial effects. However, these effects were asymmetrical: As the percentage of black people in their groups increased, both black and white participants reported enjoying working with others most and expecting that their group would perform well in the future. These racially asymmetric linear findings may be an artifact of social desirability effects on the part of the white students. That is, the white participants may have been responding to societal pressure to include and accept people of color in groups. By contrast, the black participants may have felt no such pressure to include greater numbers of white individuals and hence experienced feeling no benefit. Finally, we were unsure why the men reported having a less clear understanding of the group task than did the women. We can only conjecture that perhaps this task was not concrete enough in that there were no real right or wrong decisions, so the women may have been more comfortable with the assignment.

The finding that groups containing equal numbers of black and white participants, and men in particular, may be problematic poses potential dilemmas for group practitioners. The possibility that constructing racially balanced groups (that is, groups with equal numbers of white and black members) may exacerbate racial confrontation is disconcerting. Intuitively, groups that are racially balanced are most fair and therefore most desirable, a belief that probably comes from general notions of fairness and equity (Adams, 1963). Yet the reactions of our groups suggest that practitioners may want to pay special attention to the possibility that evenly divided group compositions may pit subgroups of different-race members against each other.

Finally, the groups constructed in this study can best be classified as discussion groups, in that members were required to come to a group consensus. Groups of a more intimate or task nature may affect white and black members and male and female members differently.

Furthermore, the findings and interpretations of this study are limited. Our sample size is small and consists of college-educated men and women, who may behave differently than more diverse groups of black people and white people interacting in the world beyond the civility of the university. Hence, caution must be used in generalizing the observations of this study. However, these data do suggest that small group dynamics are apt to be significantly affected by the racial composition of the groups, and groups that include equal numbers of black and white men may be most at risk for conflict.

REFERENCES

Adams, J. (1963). Toward an understanding of inequity. *Journal of Abnormal and Social Psychology, 67,* 422–436.

Aries, E. (1976). Interaction patterns and themes of male, female and mixed groups. *Small Group Behavior, 7,* 7–18.

Bales, R. (1970). *Personality and interpersonal behavior.* New York: Holt, Rinehart & Winston.

Bartol, K., & Butterfield, D. (1976). Sex effects in evaluating leaders. *Journal of Applied Psychology, 61,* 446–454.

Bertcher, H., & Maple, F. (1985). Elements and issues in group composition. In M. Sundel, P. Glasser, R. Sarri, & R. Vinter (Eds.), *Individual change through small groups* (pp. 180–202). New York: Free Press.

Brayboy, T. (1971). The black patient in group therapy. *International Journal of Group Psychotherapy, 21,* 288–293.

Brewer, M. B., & Kramer, R. (1985). The psychology of intergroup attitudes and behavior. *Annual Review of Psychology, 36,* 219–243.

Brower, A., Garvin, C., Hobson, J., Reed, B., & Reed, H. (1987). Exploring the effects of leader gender and race on group behavior. In J. Lassner, K. Powell, & E. Finnegan (Eds.), *Social group work: Competence and values in practice* (pp. 129–148). Binghamton, NY: Haworth Press.

Brown, A., & Mistry, T. (1994). Group work with mixed membership groups: Issues of race and gender. *Social Work with Groups, 17,* 3, 5–21.

Burger, J., & Cooper, H. (1979). The desirability of control. *Motivation and Emotion, 3,* 381–393.

Byrne, D. (1971). *The attraction paradigm.* New York: Academic Press.

Chapman, J. (1975). Comparison of male and female leadership styles. *Academy of Management Journal, 18,* 645–650.

Chau, L. (1990). Social work with groups in multicultural contexts. *Groupwork, 3,* 8–21.

Coleman, J. S., Campbell, E. Q., Hobson, C. J., McPartland, J., Mood, A. M., Weinfield, F. D., & York, R. L. (1966). *Equality of educational opportunity.* Washington, DC: U.S. Government Printing Office.

Crain, R. L., Mahard, R., & Narot, R. (1982). *Making desegregation work: How schools create social climates.* Cambridge, MA: Ballinger Press.

Criswell, H. H. (1937). Racial cleavage in Negro–White groups. *Sociometry, 1,* 81–89.

Davis, L. (1979). Racial composition of groups. *Social Work, 24,* 208–213.

Davis, L. (1980). When the majority is the psychological minority. *Group Psychotherapy and Psychodrama, 33,* 179–184.

Davis, L., & Burnstein, E. (1981). Preference for racial composition of groups. *Journal of Psychology, 109,* 293–301.

Davis, L., & Proctor, E. (1988). *Race, gender and class: Guidelines for practice with individuals, families and groups.* Englewood Cliffs, NJ: Prentice Hall.

Davis, L., Strube, M., & Cheng, L. (1995). Too many blacks, too many whites: Seek a racial balance. *Basic and Applied Social Psychology, 17*(1/2), 119–135.

Devore, W., & Schlesinger, E. (1988). *Ethnic-sensitive social work practice.* St. Louis: C. V. Mosby.

Eagly, H., & Karau, S. (1991). Gender and emergence of leaders: A meta-analysis. *Journal of Personality & Social Psychology, 60,* 685–710.

Ekehammar, B. (1985). Sex differences in socio-political attitudes revisited. *Educational Studies, 11,* 3–9.

Fairchild, H., & Gurin, P. (1978). Traditions in the social psychological analysis of race relations. *American Behavioral Scientist, 21,* 757–778.

Farley, R., Schuman, H., Bianchi, S., Colasanto, D., & Hatchett, S. (1978). Chocolate city, vanilla suburbs. *Social Science Research, 7,* 319–344.

Fenelon, J. R., & Megaree, E. I. (1971). Influence of race on the manifestation of leadership. *Journal of Applied Psychology, 55,* 353–358.

Fiedler, F., Chemers, M., & Mahar, L. (1976). *Improving leadership effectiveness: The leader match concept.* New York: John Wiley & Sons.

Garvin, C. (1987). *Contemporary group work.* Englewood Cliffs, NJ: Prentice Hall.

Giles, M. W. (1977). Percent black and racial hostility. *Social Science Quarterly, 58,* 412–417.

Giles, M., Cataldo, E., & Gatlin, D. (1975). White flight and percent black: The tipping point reexamined. *Social Science Quarterly, 56,* 85–92.

Hacker, A. (1992). *Two nations: Black and white, separate, hostile, unequal.* New York: Charles Scribner's Sons.

Herschel, R., Cooper, T., Smith, L., & Arrington, L. (1994). Exploring numerical proportions in unique context: The group support systems meeting environment. *Sex Roles, 31,* 99–123.

Hogg, M. A., & Abrams, D. (1988). *Social identifications.* London: Routledge.

Jacobs, C., & Bowles, D. (Eds.). (1988). *Ethnicity and race: Critical concepts in social work.* Silver Spring, MD: National Association of Social Workers.

Kanter, R. M. (1977). *Men and women of the corporation.* New York: Simon & Schuster.

Katz, I. (1955). *Conflict and harmony in an adolescent interracial group.* New York: New York University Press.

Katz, I., & Benjamin, L. (1960). Effects of white authoritarianism in biracial work groups. *Journal of Abnormal and Social Psychology, 61,* 448–454.

Kerr, N., & Sullaway, M. (1983). Group sex composition and member motivation. *Sex Roles, 9,* 403–417.

Kimble, C., Yoshikawa, J., & Zehr, H. (1981). Vocal and verbal assertiveness in same-sex and mixed-sex groups. *Journal of Personality and Social Psychology, 40,* 1047–1054.

Longshore, D. (1982). Race composition and white hostility. *Social Forces, 61,* 73–78.

Longshore, D. (1984). School control and intergroup relations. *Social Science Quarterly, 63,* 674–687.

Longshore, D. (1988). Racial control and intergroup hostility: A comparative analysis. *Research in Race and Ethnic Relations, 5,* 47–73.

Longshore, D., & Prager, J. (1985). The impact of school desegregation: A situational analysis. *Annual Review of Sociology, 11,* 75–91.

Massey, D. S., & Denton, N. A. (1993). *American apartheid: Segregation and the making of the underclass.* Cambridge, MA: Harvard University Press.

Matthews, D., & Prothro, J. (1963). Social and economic factors in Negro voter registration in the south. *American Political Science Review, 57,* 24–44.

Mindel, C., Habenstein, R., & Wright, R. (Eds.). (1988). *Ethnic families in America.* New York: Elsevier Science.

Mistry, T., & Brown, A. (1991). Black/white co-working in groups. *Groupwork, 4,* 2.

Moreno, J. L. (1934). *Who shall survive? A new approach to the problem of human interrelations.* Washington, DC: Nervous and Mental Disease Publishing House.

Mullen, B. (1983). Operationalizing the effect of the group on the individual: A self-attention perspective. *Journal of Experimental Social Psychology, 19,* 295–322.

Muston, R., & Weinstein, H. J. (1988). Race and groupwork: Some experiences in practice and training. *Groupwork, 1,* 30–40.

Myerson, M., & Banfield, E. (1955). *Politics, planning, and public interest.* Glencoe, IL: Free Press.

Northen, H. (1969). *Social work with groups.* New York: Columbia University Press.

Pettigrew, T. (1967). Social evaluation theory: Convergences and applications. *Nebraska Symposium on Motivation, 15,* 241–304.

Pettigrew, T., & Cramer, R. (1959). The demography of desegregation. *Journal of Social Issues, 15,* 61–71.

Pettigrew, T., & Martin, J. (1989). Organizational inclusion of minority groups: A social psychological analysis. In J. P. Van Oudehoven & T. M. Willemsen (Eds.), *Ethnic minorities: Social psychological perspectives* (pp. 169–200). Amsterdam: Swets & Zeitlinger.

Ridgeway, C. L., Johnson, C., & Diekema, D. (1994). External status, legitimacy, and compliance in male and female groups. *Social Forces, 72,* 1051–1077.

Sachdev, H., & Bourhis, R. Y. (1984). Minimal majorities and minorities. *European Journal of Social Psychology, 14,* 35–52.

Sidanius, J., Cling, B. J., & Pratto, F. (1991). Ranking and linking as a function of sex and gender role attitudes. *Journal of Social Issues, 47,* 131–149.

Sidanius, J., Pratto, F., & Mitchell, M. (1994). In-group identification, social dominance orientation, and differential intergroup social allocation. *Journal of Social Psychology, 134,* 151–167.

Stein, T., & Heller, T. (1983). The relationship of participation rates to leadership status: A meta-analysis. In H. Blumberg, A. P. Hare, V. Kent, & M. Davies (Eds.), *Small groups and social interaction* (Vol. 1, pp. 401–406). New York: John Wiley & Sons.

Stinchcombe, A. L., McDill, M., & Walker, D. (1969). Is there a racial tipping point in changing schools? *Journal of Social Issues, 25,* 127–130.

Stogdill, R. (1974). *Handbook of leadership.* New York: Free Press.

Strodtbeck, F., & Mann, D. (1956). Sex role differentiation in jury deliberation. *Sociometry, 19*, 3–11.

Tajfel, H. (1982). Social psychology of intergroup attitudes. *Annual Review of Psychology, 33*, 1–39.

Tajfel, H., & Turner, J. (1979). The social identity theory of intergroup behavior. In S. Worchel & W. G. Austin (Eds.), *Psychology of intergroup relations* (pp. 7–24). Chicago: Nelson-Hall.

Verdi, R., & Wheelan, S. (1992). Developmental patterns in same-sex and mixed-sex groups. *Small Group Research, 23*, 356–378.

Vinter, R. (1985). The essential components of group work practice. In M. Sundel, P. Glasser, R. Sarri, & R. Vinter (Eds.), *Individual change through small groups* (pp. 11–34). New York: Free Press.

Wood, W. (1987). Meta-analytic review of sex differences in group performance. *Psychological Bulletin, 102*, 53–71.

Wright, G. C. (1977). Contextual models of electoral behavior: The southern Wallace vote. *American Political Science Review, 71*, 497–508.

Yalom, I. (1995). *The theory and practice of group psychotherapy* (4th ed.). New York: Basic Books.

The research reported in this chapter was supported by grant MRI-8918199 from the National Science Foundation. An earlier version of this chapter was presented at the Annual Program Meeting of the Council on Social Work Education, February 1996, Washington, DC.

3

Marital Conflict Management:
Gender and Ethnic Differences

Richard A. Mackey and Bernard A. O'Brien

This chapter discusses how spouses in marital relationships that had lasted for more than 20 years managed conflict (Mackey & O'Brien, 1995). The focus of the discussion is on gender and ethnicity influences on modes of coping with conflict within these marriages. The couples participating were selected purposefully to represent ethnic, religious, and educational diversity.

Three trends influenced the design of the research on which this chapter is based:

1. The United States has the highest divorce rate in the world; it reached nearly 50 percent of all marriages by the late 1980s (Billingsley, 1990; Chadwick & Heaton, 1992; Lewis, 1988).
2. Marital difficulties are one of the leading reasons people seek psychological help from social workers and other human services professionals (Cowing et al., 1985; Lewis, 1988). Given increased life expectancies of the U.S. population (Ade-Ridder, 1985), it is important to understand the relational dynamics of lasting marriages, because research suggests that couples who are both dissatisfied and satisfied with their marriages remain together (Kelly & Conley, 1987; Lewis & Spanier, 1979; Swensen & Moore, 1984). With these couples living together for longer periods of time, there may be increasing numbers of older couples seeking the services of social work practitioners.
3. Relatively little research has been reported on lasting relationships and even less on ethnically diverse marriages. Research on marriage has tended to focus on white, college-educated, middle-class couples (Lauer, Lauer, & Kerr, 1990; Levenson, Carstensen, & Gottman, 1993; Wallerstein & Blakeslee, 1995). Although findings from these studies may be helpful in treating couples with marital difficulties, the results have limitations for practice with clients from different social and ethnic groups (Billingsley, 1990; Vega, 1990; Wamboldt & Reiss, 1989).

Although working-class and middle-class couples may face similar issues in their relationships, there are differences in how diverse groups resolve conflicts (Rubin, 1976). Factors important to marital

This chapter was originally published in the March 1998 issue of *Social Work*, Vol. 43, pp. 128–141.

stability among white, middle-class Americans may be different from factors important to other cultural groups (Frisbie, Bean, & Eberstein, 1980).

Our research is in response to a challenge that social workers encounter in their daily practice: helping couples to manage conflicts in their relationships and to manage interpersonal differences in ways that enrich marital satisfaction. Given demographic trends, social workers increasingly will be working with ethnically diverse and older couples who may need help with these problems. The findings from our study have implications for prevention of debilitating conflicts through psychoeducational interventions informed by sensitivity to gender and ethnic differences in an older population.

FRAMING THE DIMENSIONS OF THE STUDY

As part of our research on lasting relationships, we adopted a developmental, life span perspective (Dilworth-Anderson & Burton, 1996) in exploring how spouses coped with conflict over the years. On the basis of that perspective, we organized the study to explore several dimensions of marital relationships over time. This chapter focuses on one of these dimensions: conflict and its management. Other dimensions included decision making, sexual relations, psychological intimacy, parenting, communication, and satisfaction with relationships (Mackey & O'Brien, 1995).

Levinson's (1986, 1996) hypothesis of adult life structures and transitions was useful in understanding how spouses adapted to marriage. Levinson conceptualized structures as dynamic plateaus in which modifications in various dimensions of relationships were integrated and consolidated, albeit tenuously and temporally. Transitions involved changes as people negotiated modifications in the structure of existing dimensions. In terms of marriage, the engagement period was conceptualized as a transition into the structure of early marriage. Planning for children involved another transition into a new marital life structure, parenthood. In middle age, when children were leaving home, couples were on the road to another marital configuration, the postparenting or "empty nest" structure. This hypothesis of structural and transitional cycles was useful when placed within a cultural context that often has been overlooked in marital research. Differences grounded on gender and ethnicity, which have been internalized as parts of the self, shape the ways in which spouses interact and adapt to each other as dimensions of their relationships evolve.

In framing marriage as a developmental process, we assumed that individual and marital changes were interrelated so that modification in one sphere may have triggered changes in another; that is, marriage may be a stimulus for developmental changes in individuals, and individual change in a spouse may also lead to change in the marital relationship. Earlier research provides enough evidence to support the interdependent nature of marriage as a development opportunity or threat (Belsky, Spanier, & Rovine, 1983; Bumagin & Hirn, 1982; Lewis, 1988; Miller & Sollie, 1980; Spanier, Lewis, & Cole, 1975).

The long-term relationships of couples in this study occurred during a period of significant sociocultural change. In the era after World War II, when most of the couples married, roles of men and women were changing as were personal and social expectations of marriage. Despite trends toward integration of and equity in marital role behaviors, research suggests that gender differences continued to play a central role in marital stability. Lewis (1988) found that wives were more interpersonally oriented than husbands and more likely to take the initiative in problem solving. Other studies have found that women valued interdependence and connection, whereas men valued independence and achievement (Gilligan, 1982; Levinson, 1986; Miller, 1986).

Longitudinal studies have found that couples who are inclined to avoid conflict are less satisfied with their marriages than couples who confront conflicts (Gottman & Krokoff, 1989). Vaillant and Vaillant (1993) reported that wives were less satisfied than husbands in evaluating the success of couples in resolving disagreements. Chronic inability to resolve disagreements erodes marital stability and satisfaction, leading to more psychological and physical impairments among wives than husbands (Levenson et al., 1993).

METHODS

We used semistructured interviews to study the marital histories of 120 spouses in 60 marriages. An interview guide was developed after a review of the marriage literature (Gottman & Krokoff, 1989; Kelly & Conley, 1987; Lewis & Spanier, 1979; Rubin, 1983; Spanier & Fleer, 1980). The four-page interview guide included items about the effects of individual and interpersonal characteristics and family and cultural influences on marital relationships. Questions focused on perceptions of initial attraction, role expectations, communication patterns, problem-solving styles, marital roles, management of marital conflict, and sexual and psychological intimacy. Additional questions centered on the influence of culture, economic status, ethnicity, religious background, and experiences in the family of origin on marital relationships. Respondents were asked to consider how these factors influenced their marriages during the early years of marriage before their children were born, during the child-rearing years, and during the empty nest years. The object was to acquire in-depth information from the perspectives of individuals to develop an understanding of how spouses adapted to marriage over the life of their relationships.

An open-ended style of interviewing was followed to allow for freedom of expression (Kvale, 1983). Focal questions elicited information from the perspectives of each respondent and asked them to describe their marital interactions within their own frames of reference (Moon, Dillon, & Sprenkle, 1990; Strauss & Corbin, 1990). Interviews were held in the homes of the respondents, providing additional information about their lifestyles and environments. Before each interview, respondents were told about the purpose of the study, were given an overview of the interview schedule, and were assured that their identities would remain anonymous. Interviewers obtained informed consent for audiotaping and the research use of interviews. Each spouse was interviewed separately; the length of each interview was approximately two hours.

Respondents

The sample was chosen purposively to fit with the goal of developing an understanding of adaptation among a diverse group of couples in lasting relationships. Couples were selected who met the following criteria:

- married at least 20 years
- youngest child at least age 18 or out of high school
- no current psychotherapy or history of extensive marriage counseling
- racial, ethnic, educational, and religious diversity.

Couples were recruited through business, professional, and trade union organizations, as well as churches, synagogues, and a variety of other community organizations. Most couples resided in the northeast part of the country with the exception of Mexican Americans, who lived in the Southwest. Although there were a variety of relational difficulties reported, most frequently during the child-rearing years, the couples had been able to maintain intact relationships without receiving any significant social services, such as marital counseling.

Of 120 respondents (60 wives and 60 husbands), 57 percent were white; 23 percent were African American, and 20 percent were Mexican American. Forty-two percent were Roman Catholic; 33 percent were Protestant, and 25 percent were Jewish. Thirty-five percent were college graduates, and 65 percent were noncollege graduates.

By age, 16 percent of respondents were in their forties, 64 percent in their fifties and sixties, and 20 percent in their seventies. Twenty-seven percent of couples had been married more than 40 years, 42 percent between 30 and 40 years, and 31 percent fewer than 30 years. Thirty-five percent of couples had one or two children; 47 percent had three or four, and 18 percent had five or more. By total family income, approximately 12 percent of couples earned less than $25,000 a year, 32 percent between $25,000 and $49,999, 25 percent between $50,000 and $74,999, 12 percent between $75,000 and $99,999, and 19 percent more than $100,000.

Data Analysis

All interviews were transcribed, and categories based on key themes from a subsample of cases were developed using the constant comparative method of qualitative analysis (Strauss & Corbin, 1990). The categories that served as a guide for data analysis were generated by a research team of two women and two men. Once the categories were identified by the four-member research team, the 120 interviews were coded independently by two raters (one woman and one man). One of the authors coded all interviews to ensure continuity in the operational definitions of variables and consistency of judgments from case to case. Using opposite-sex researchers helped control for possible gender differences in identifying themes and coding them. The two raters coded each interview separately, marking the passages on the transcripts that identified themes. The raters then met to review their codes. When discrepancies occurred, they discussed their differences referring to the relevant interview passages until an agreement was reached. The interrater reliability across all cases was .87.

After the interviews were coded, the data were analyzed using SPSS (Norusis, 1990) software. We used chi-square analyses to examine the relationship between the independent variables of educational level, religion, gender, and ethnicity and the dependent variables of major conflict and styles of managing conflict. The alpha criteria were set at .05.

The use of chi-square with a nonrandom sample is appropriate when certain conditions are met. First, it is very difficult to ensure randomness of samples, especially in research that focuses on new territory (Edgington, 1980). This nonprobability sample was selected deliberately to include couples who had not been studied in earlier research, namely, ethnically diverse couples who had been married more than 20 years. Second, compared to other tests of statistical significance, chi-square has fewer requirements about population characteristics. Third, chi-square assumes independence of observations, a condition the data met. Fourth, the expected frequency of five observations in most cells was met. Finally, the intention in using this test of significance was to develop hypotheses that might be helpful in understanding diverse marriages that last and not to generalize to the general population (Nachmias & Nachmias, 1981). This last point is very important in understanding the substantive rather than statistical importance of the study. Through the process of logical yet parsimonious generalization, the data may be useful to practitioners in understanding clients as well as to researchers who wish to design future studies.

Chi-square analysis offered direction to the qualitative analysis. The latter included the use of HyperRESEARCH software (Hesse-Biber, Dupuis, & Kinder, 1992), which enabled the researchers to identify, catalogue, and organize specific interview passages on which codes had been based. HyperRESEARCH allowed us to do a thorough content analysis of the 120 interviews, which totaled over 4,000 double-spaced pages.

RESULTS

The data suggest that patterns in the severity of marital conflict over time varied among white, African American, and Mexican American respondents. Significant differences were found in how husbands and wives managed conflict. Ethnicity also had an effect on how husbands and wives perceived themselves and their spouses in the management of conflict. There were no statistically significant differences between the educational level of respondents and management of conflict or between religion and conflict management.

Conflict and Ethnicity

Respondents were asked about examples of conflict during the pre-child-rearing, the child-rearing, and the empty nest years. All respondents reported at least minimal conflict in their relationships, so that the challenge for the researchers was to assess and code the severity of conflict. We focused on understanding disagreements from the perspectives of individual spouses. The points of view of respondents were respected, and judgments were made on the basis of how disruptive disagreements were to marital relationships. If conflicts were assessed to have minimal effect on marital relationships, they were coded as minor. If respondents described disagreements as highly distressing to them personally and as having significantly disruptive effects on their marital relationships, they were coded as major. Major conflicts occurred most often during the child-rearing years. A father of four children related the following example of a major conflict: "I think the worst was after we started having the children, because in my opinion I kind of took her for granted. We've had our rough times. We've been on the verge of trying to get a divorce, but it didn't go through because I told her I was going to shape up my life."

The frequency of reported major conflict remained relatively stable for African American respondents from the beginning of marriage (18 percent) through the child-rearing years (21 percent) (Figure 3-1). In contrast, major conflict among white respondents more than tripled during the same time period (10 percent to 32 percent) and more than doubled among Mexican American (13 percent to 29 percent). Major conflict for the three groups declined after children had grown to maturity. The differences among the three groups in reporting major conflict were not statistically significant.

The reason for the differences between African Americans and the other two groups may have been related to the following characteristics about their relationships. Recollections of expectations about marital roles before marriage were different for African American than they were for white and Mexican American respondents. Twenty-five percent of African Americans said that they had expected nontraditional roles for themselves and their spouses compared with fewer than 3 percent of white people and 8 percent of Mexican Americans $[\chi^2(2, 120) = 11.62, p = < .01]$. A 51-year-old African American woman

Figure 3-1

Percentage of Respondents Reporting Major Conflict over the Years, by Ethnic Group

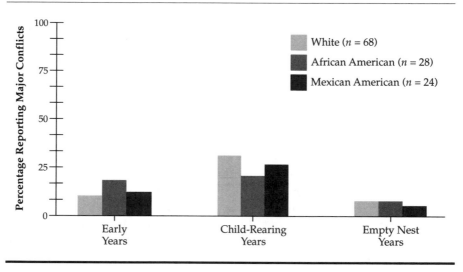

told of her nontraditional role expectations: "Equal, because I had seen too many of my friends and my own mother in the circumstances that I was not going to put up with in any way, form, shape or fashion; decision-making and every aspect of married life, I felt, should entail the husband and wife together."

In traditional marriages, women expected to take care of the home, support their husbands in their careers, and nurture children; men expected to work to support and take care of their families. One manifestation of nontraditional roles was in child rearing. When children were in infancy and latency, African Americans reported higher rates of mutuality in child rearing than the other two groups: 50 percent of African Americans reported mutual responsibilities for child rearing during the children's infancy compared with 25 percent of white couples and 17 percent of Mexican Americans [$\chi^2(2, 120) = 8.27, p = .02$]. Comparable rates for mutual child rearing during the children's latency years were 61 percent for African American, 46 percent for white, and 29 percent for Mexican American couples. By the adolescent years, mutuality in parenting was reported by half of white and Mexican American couples compared with 75 percent of African Americans.

Nontraditional roles in African American marriages, which needed to be negotiated as spouses moved through the early years of marriage, apparently led to conflicts, which may have been quite different from those in white and Mexican American marriages, in which roles were ascribed and accepted by spouses without great ambiguity. When roles were allocated according to accepted cultural mores, as most gender roles were in the era when these couples were married, there may have been less need to negotiate one's place in the relationship, at least in the early years of marriage. African Americans may have worked out the ambiguities in marital roles earlier than white and Mexican American couples. As white and Mexican American husbands became involved in child rearing during the children's latency years, new roles and responsibilities needed to be negotiated leading to an increase in major conflict.

Conflict and Gender

After exploring the nature and severity of relational conflict, respondents were asked to describe their styles of handling conflict with spouses. A confrontational style included any efforts to express one's thoughts and feelings to the spouse in a face-to-face manner. Other conflict management styles that included any stratagem to deny or escape face-to-face encounters about conflict were coded avoidant. Wives and husbands differed significantly in their predominant styles of managing conflict. The following example of a confrontational style was taken from an interview with a woman who had been married for 30 years: "We have very different styles. Yes, I'm quick to anger, but then I forget and say, 'OK, I'm done.' He's the opposite." Her husband commented, "I think she preferred to discuss and talk it out but that's just not my shtick and I know that and it's not a particularly admirable trait, but it's a trait I have . . . she would rather face it head on."

Although patterns of managing conflict by wives and husbands were similar from early marriage to the empty nest years, there were

Figure 3-2

Percentage of Respondents Reporting Confrontational Styles of Managing Conflict over the Years

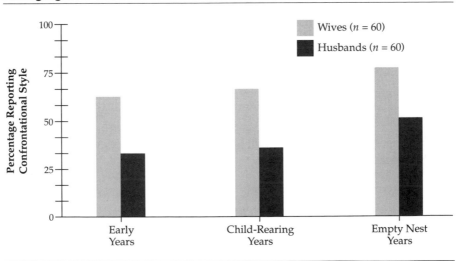

Figure 3-3

Percentage of Respondents Reporting Spouse's Confrontational Style of Managing Conflict over the Years

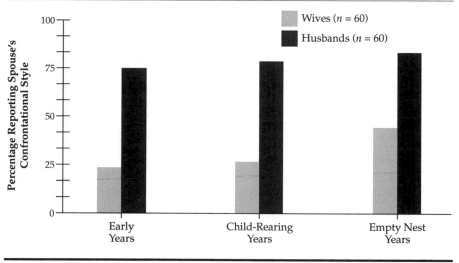

shifts in how respondents viewed their styles of managing conflict. In the early and child-rearing years, a majority of husbands avoided face-to-face discussion of conflict, whereas a majority of wives used confrontational styles (Figure 3-2). Before the birth of their children, 32 percent of husbands and 62 percent of wives described themselves as confrontational [$\chi^2(1, 120) = 10.85, p < .01$]. During the child-rearing years, there were slight shifts in those patterns; 35 percent of husbands and 67 percent of wives were confrontational [$\chi^2(1, 120) = 12.04, p = .01$]. Styles of managing conflict among husbands and wives shifted further in the empty nest years, when 48 percent of husbands and 77 percent of wives reported themselves as confrontational, a difference that was not statistically significant.

Respondents were also asked to describe how they viewed their spouses' styles of managing conflict. The results are shown in Figure 3-3. An important aspect of the data in Figure 3-3 is the correspondence in the observations of respondents about spousal behavior compared with observations of their own behavior as shown in Figure 3-2. That is, 75 percent of husbands described their wives as confrontational during the early years of marriage; in the same phase, 23 percent of wives described husbands as confrontational [$\chi^2(1, 120) = 32.04, p \leq .01$]. Slight shifts were found during the child-rearing years, when 27 percent of wives reported husbands as confrontational and 80 percent of husbands reported wives as confrontational [$\chi^2(1, 120) = 34.29, p \leq .01$] (Figure 3-3). By empty nest phase, the shift toward face-to-face modes of managing conflict continued: 42 percent of wives and 83 percent of husbands described their spouses as confrontational [$\chi^2(1, 120) = 22.22, p \leq .01$].

Figure 3-4

Percentage of Husbands Reporting Confrontational Styles of Managing Conflict over the Years, by Ethnic Group

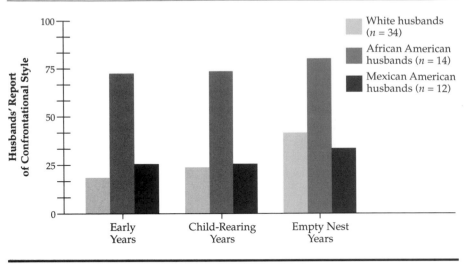

CONFLICT, GENDER, AND ETHNICITY

The findings about styles of managing conflict by gender raised the question of whether gender differences varied by ethnicity. African American husbands reported higher confrontational styles than white and Mexican American husbands (Figure 3-4). Seventy-two percent of African American husbands compared with 25 percent of Mexican American and 18 percent of white husbands reported that they used confrontational styles of dealing with marital conflict early in marriage [$\chi^2(2, 120) = 13.56, p \leq .01$]. An African American husband, married for 45 years, reported, "We have done a lot of screaming at each other, and pouting, if you will, and storming off and screaming . . . definitely we're confrontational. We don't keep anything down. If something is there you let it out. Get it out in the open. And then it'll be over with. You can be mad but then that's not going to last that long. And then it'll be over with. And you start over again. Each day's a new day."

Styles of managing conflict among husbands changed only slightly during the child-rearing years [$\chi^2(2, 120) = 10.66, p = .01$]. During the empty nest years, 41 percent of white, 79 percent of African American, and 33 percent of Mexican American husbands reported face-to-face styles of managing conflict with their wives [$\chi^2(2, 120) = 6.90, p \leq .05$].

We also examined how wives in the three ethnic groups viewed their husbands' styles of managing conflict. Wives in the three groups did not differ significantly among each other in reporting their observations of spousal styles of managing conflict. Somewhat higher numbers of African American wives (36 percent) viewed their

Figure 3-5

Percentage of Wives Reporting Spouse's Confrontational Style of Managing Conflict over the Years, by Ethnic Group

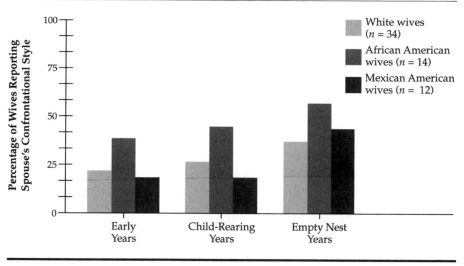

spouses as confrontational in the early years of marriage than did white wives (21 percent) or Mexican American wives (17 percent) (Figure 3-5). Slight changes were found during the child-rearing years in the observations of African American and white wives. By the empty nest phase, 35 percent of white, 57 percent of African American, and 42 percent of Mexican American wives reported that their husbands dealt with conflict through face-to-face discussions.

Limitations of the Study

Although this research has potential for enhancing an empathic understanding of relational dynamics in marriages, there are limitations in the method. Concern about the validity and reliability of self-reported data is an issue in retrospective studies. Memories may become distorted with the passage of time; respondents may not be candid or present themselves in ways that are not congruent with how they think or feel (Norton, 1983). Distortion of the data may lead to inaccuracies and incorrect findings (Belsky et al., 1983; Gray-Little & Burks, 1983). A focus on the subjective experiences of respondents may compromise the objective aspects of the findings and requires careful monitoring of the reactions of researchers to the data. Open and honest dialogue among team members was a critical resource in addressing these issues.

Sampling that fit the goals of this research is another limitation. Participant recruitment was selective and targeted to specific populations with the goal of understanding marital couples who have received little attention in marital studies. The researchers were interested in substantive rather than statistical significance of the findings (Nach-mias & Nachmias, 1981) in generating understanding of these select groups that might be useful to practitioners who need empirical infor-mation about the importance of ethnic and gender differences and to researchers in offering direction for future studies. Use of logical gen-eralization in which data are assessed against known parameters for a particular group was a valuable tool in that process.

The validity of the data was enhanced by interviewing spouses separately. That procedure allowed us to compare individual re-sponses of spouses about common social realities in their lives. Most respondents were remarkably similar in reporting on their own be-haviors, as well as the behaviors of their spouses. For example, hus-bands remembered themselves as avoidant and their spouses as con-frontational early in marriage; wives remembered themselves as confrontational and their spouses as avoidant. The overall congru-ence in these reports supports the internal validity of the data.

Regardless of gender or ethnicity, spouses talked with surprising honesty about personal and seemingly difficult issues, such as sexual dysfunction and avoidant behaviors. Given the centrality of inter-viewing skills in social work practice, we think that social workers are well equipped to conduct this type of research.

DISCUSSION

This study was designed to generate an understanding of a popula-tion that social workers will be serving with increasing frequency. Semistructured interviews elicited patterns in the nature of major conflict and conflict management styles in the relationships of cou-ples from early years, through child rearing, and into the empty nest years. The findings may help practitioners in planning interventions and researchers in designing future studies.

Styles of managing conflict by husbands and wives in this study resonated with the findings of research on gender differences that hypothesize that socialization experiences create differences in how men and women behave in relationships. Women have been hypoth-esized to define their sense of self within the context of relationships in which attachments and interpersonal connections are central (Chodorow, 1978; Gilligan, 1982; Surrey, 1984). Men may experience more anxiety than women in dealing with conflict matters in a face-to-face manner (Levant, 1996). The overall patterns of managing con-flict between spouses in this study supported the general themes re-ported in earlier research.

Despite their usefulness, hypotheses based on research focused only on group differences do not account for the variations within groups. Although there was movement toward face-to-face modes of conflict management over the years, almost one of two husbands con-tinued to avoid face-to-face discussion of conflict during recent years compared with fewer than one of four wives. To appreciate these variations within groups, we must look beyond general themes about gender-based behaviors. The mellowing of men as they negotiate the late middle years of the life span may lead to the construction of a different sense of self. With the pressures of a career receding, husbands may attend to relationships in ways that did not fit with their sense of self or their priorities in the past. The data support a post-modern perspective of how human beings construct a sense of self on the basis of differing contexts and developmental experiences (Sands & Nuccio, 1992). Such a perspective is faithful to social work values of respecting individual differences within and between genders (Hoffmann, 1997).

Differences by gender in the patterns of managing conflict need to be understood within a wider relational context that includes ethnicity. The frequency of major conflict among African American couples, which was higher during the early years of marriage compared to Mexican American and white couples, was shaped, in part, by the nontraditional roles of the African American couples. Equity and sharing of role responsibilities, including the rearing of children, needed to be negotiated and may have fueled conflict among African American couples. Working out roles through negotiation was different for other respondents in which marital roles were ascribed along traditional gender lines. Differentiation of marital roles by gender, which fit with the predominant mores of the times, was apparently accepted by white and Mexican American spouses without major conflict.

The conflict management styles of African American couples were also different from those of white and Mexican American couples. Compared with the latter groups, African Americans had higher rates of face-to-face styles of dealing with interpersonal differences. Approximately eight of 10 African American husbands compared with four of 10 white and Mexican American husbands adopted confrontational modes of managing conflict in the later years of the marriage.

The observations of African American men about their conflict management styles needs to be understood within a social context that was even more oppressive to African American men than it is today. It was dangerous for most of these black men to assert themselves in conflict situations with white people. As a consequence, the home may have been one of the few safe places for African American men to deal openly with interpersonal conflict. These findings may reflect the legacy of racism, as that legacy shaped the observations of African American men about their conflict management styles with their spouses.

Earlier research suggests that confrontation is more adaptive than avoidance in managing conflict (Cahn, 1990; Hendrick, 1995). Habitual avoidance of differences leads to unresolved tensions, which may result in conflict that is distressing to individual partners and disruptive to relationships (Baucom, Notarius, Burnett, & Haefner, 1990; Gottman, 1994; Gottman & Krokoff, 1989; Levenson et al., 1993; Levinger, 1979). Given our findings that avoidance persisted into the most recent years in about one-half of these marriages, we must look beyond this dimension to understand why the marriages were stable and satisfying. The data suggest that conflict management needs to be understood within the context of marital relationships as a whole. Two elements are important in understanding how these marriages lasted even when one spouse, primarily the husband, was unable to engage regularly in face-to-face discussion of conflict. First, conflict that resulted from relational differences between spouses, especially during the child-rearing years, was contained by mutual values of trust, respect, and commitment to relationships. Differences in personal styles of managing conflict were contained by a symmetry in values that enabled spouses to develop an understanding and acceptance of differences in managing conflict as they grew older together.

Second, balance was another important element. As values supported the viability of relationships, especially through stormy times, personal qualities compensated for differences in conflict management styles. For example, a husband may have had considerable difficulty in expressing his feelings about interpersonal differences directly to his wife; at the same time, he may have been seen by her as having other strengths that made up for that limitation. It usually took considerable time for balances to become a reality in relationships; it never occurred unless other qualities, such as kindness and thoughtfulness, were valued as much as face-to-face skills in managing conflict.

CONCLUSION

Many couples today face challenges as they negotiate marital roles based on sharing of responsibilities and on equity between spouses. Social workers may become increasingly active in helping couples to negotiate marital roles for which there are relatively few models. The types of conflict couples experience today in negotiating marital roles for which there are relatively few models may be quite similar to those reported by African American spouses in this study. Negotiating conflict associated with the integration rather than differentiation of tasks and responsibilities within marriage may become a focal point for intervention with couples who are in the process of adapting to new ways of being together.

Differences in managing conflict shaped by gender are important for clinicians to consider in selecting modes of intervention. For many couples, an approach involving face-to-face discussion of one's thoughts and feelings may be appropriate and constructive. In other marriages, in which individual spouses may have significant difficulty with face-to-face discussion of their thoughts and feelings about conflict, interventions need to focus initially on strategies that strengthen positive elements in relationships. Within this strengths approach, which emphasizes respect for differences, both spouses need to be supported in examining their personal needs in the relationship, the roles that they see themselves playing in the relationship, and their expectations of their spouses. On the basis of the findings in this research, we have found such a structured approach to be effective in reducing destructive exchanges and enhancing trust, respect, and commitment to relationships. As a result, spouses become empowered to use mutually confrontational modes of talking about conflicts rather than avoiding them.

The people in this study had had no professional treatment for marital conflicts. As they discussed their marital histories, they did not sound that different from many couples whom we have treated for major conflicts, especially during the child-rearing years. Yet they were able to call on internal resources to achieve satisfying adaptations in recent years. Regardless of the theoretical orientation of the social worker, the principle of having respect for the innate resources of couples to help themselves emerged as an eloquent message from this research. A developmental perspective focuses on the adaptive resources within individuals and supports couples in finding and using their strengths. The couples whom we studied accomplished that gain without the help of professional intervention. They have much to teach us about effective practice, especially in reaffirming the central principle of helping people to help themselves.

REFERENCES

Ade-Ridder, L. (1985). Quality of marriage: A comparison between golden wedding couples and couples married less than fifty years. *Lifestyles: A Journal of Changing Patterns, 7*, 224–237.

Baucom, D. H., Notarius, C. I., Burnett, C. K., & Haefner, P. (1990). Gender differences and sex role identity in marriage. In F. D. Fincham & T. N. Bradbury (Eds.), *The psychology of marriage: Basic issues and applications* (pp. 150–171). New York: Guilford.

Belsky, J., Spanier, G., & Rovine, M. (1983). Stability and change in marriage across the transition to parenthood. *Journal of Marriage and the Family, 45*, 567–577.

Billingsley, A. (1990). Understanding African American family diversity. In J. Dewart (Ed.), *The state of black America 1990* (pp. 85–108). New York: National Urban League.

Bumagin, J., & Hirn, K. (1982). Observations on changing relationships for older married women. *American Journal of Psychoanalysis, 42*(2), 133–142.

Cahn, D. (1990). Confrontation behaviors, perceived understanding, and relationship growth. In D. Cahn (Ed.), *Intimates in conflict* (pp. 153–165). Hillsdale, NJ: Lawrence Erlbaum.

Chadwick, B. A., & Heaton, T. B. (Eds.). (1992). *Statistical handbook on the American family.* Phoenix: Oryx Press.

Chodorow, N. (1978). *The reproduction of mothering: Psychoanalysis and the sociology of gender.* Berkeley: University of California Press.

Cowing, C., Cowan, P., Heming, G., Garrett, E., Coysh, W., Curtis-Boles, H., & Bales, A. (1985). Transitions to parenthood: His, hers and theirs. *Journal of Family Issues, 6*, 451–481.

Dilworth-Anderson, P., & Burton, L. (1996). Rethinking family development: Critical conceptual issues in the study of diverse groups. *Journal of Social and Personal Relationships, 13*, 325–354.

Edgington, E. (1980). *Randomization tests.* New York: Marcel Dekker.

Frisbie, W. P., Bean, F. D., & Eberstein, I. (1980). Recent changes in marital instability among Mexican Americans: Convergence with black and Anglo trends? *Social Forces, 58*, 1205–1219.

Gilligan, C. (1982). *In a different voice: Psychological theory and women's development.* Cambridge, MA: Harvard University Press.

Gottman, J. M. (1994). *Why marriages succeed or fail.* New York: Simon & Schuster.

Gottman, J. M., & Krokoff, L. J. (1989). Marital interaction and satisfaction: A longitudinal view. *Journal of Consulting and Clinical Psychology, 57,* 47–52.

Gray-Little, B., & Burks, N. (1983). Power and satisfaction in marriage: A review and critique. *Psychological Bulletin, 93,* 513–538.

Hendrick, S. S. (1995). *Close relationships: What couple therapists can learn.* Pacific Grove, CA: Brooks/Cole.

Hesse-Biber, S., Dupuis, P., & Kinder, T. S. (1992). *HyperRESEARCH: A tool for the analysis of qualitative data.* Randolph, MA: Researchware.

Hoffmann, N. (1997). *A feminist comparison of self-in-relation theory as self-psychology.* Unpublished manuscript.

Kelly, E. L., & Conley, J. J. (1987). Personality and compatibility: A prospective analysis of marital stability and marital satisfaction. *Journal of Personality and Social Psychology, 52,* 27–40.

Kvale, S. (1983). The qualitative research interview: A phenomenological and hermeneutical mode of understanding. *Journal of Phenomenological Psychology, 14,* 171–196.

Lauer, R. H., Lauer, J. C., & Kerr, S. T. (1990). The long-term marriage: Perceptions of stability and satisfaction. *International Journal of Aging and Human Development, 31,* 189–195.

Levant, R. (1996). The new psychology of men. *Professional Psychology: Research and Practice, 27,* 259–265.

Levenson, R., Carstensen, L., & Gottman, J. (1993). Long-term marriage: Age, gender and satisfaction. *Psychology and Aging, 8,* 301–313.

Levinger, G. (1979). Marital cohesiveness at the brink: The fate of applications for divorce. In G. Levinger & O. C. Moles (Ed.), *Divorce and separation.* Westport, CT: Praeger.

Levinson, D. (1986). A concept of adult development. *American Psychologist, 41,* 3–13.

Levinson, D. (1996). *The seasons of a woman's life.* New York: Alfred A. Knopf.

Lewis, J. M. (1988). The transition to parenthood: II. Stability and change in marital structure. *Family Process, 27,* 273–283.

Lewis, R. A., & Spanier, G. B. (1979). Theorizing about the quality and stability of marriage. In W. R. Burr, R. Hill, F. I. Nye, & I. L. Reiss (Eds.), *Contemporary theories about the family* (pp. 268–294). Glencoe, IL: Free Press.

Mackey, R., & O'Brien, B. (1995). *Lasting marriages: Men and women growing together.* Westport, CT: Praeger.

Miller, B., & Sollie, D. (1980). Normal stresses during the transition to parenthood. *Family Relations, 29,* 459–465.

Miller, J. B. (1986). *Toward a new psychology of women.* Boston: Beacon Press.

Moon, S., Dillon, D., & Sprenkle, D. (1990). Family therapy and qualitative research. *Journal of Marital and Family Therapy, 16,* 357–373.

Nachmias, D., & Nachmias, C. (1981). *Research methods in the social sciences* (2nd ed.). New York: St. Martin's Press.

Norton, R. (1983). Measuring marital quality: A critical look at the dependent variable. *Journal of Marriage and the Family, 45,* 141–151.

Norusis, M. J. (1990). *SPSS: Introductory statistics student guide.* Chicago: SPSS, Inc.

Rubin, L. B. (1976). *Worlds of pain.* New York: Basic Books.

Rubin, L. B. (1983). *Intimate strangers.* New York: Harper & Row.

Sands, R., & Nuccio, K. (1992). Postmodern feminist theory and social work. *Social Work, 37,* 489–494.

Spanier, G., & Fleer, B. (1980). Factors sustaining marriage: Factors in adjusting to divorce. In *Families today* (U.S. Department of Health, Education, and Welfare Science Monographs, pp. 205–231). Washington, DC: U.S. Department of Health, Education, and Welfare.

Spanier, G. B., Lewis, R. A., & Cole, C. L. (1975). Marital adjustment over the family life cycle: The issue of curvilinearity. *Journal of Marriage and the Family, 37,* 263–275.

Strauss, A., & Corbin, J. (1990). *Basics of qualitative research: Grounded theory procedures and techniques.* Newbury Park, CA: Sage Publications.

Surrey, J. L. (1984). *The "self-in-relation": A theory of women's development* (Work in Progress No. 13, Stone Center Working Paper Series). Wellesley, MA: Stone Center.

Swensen, C. H., & Moore, C. D. (1984). Marriages that endure. In C. C. Nadelson & D. C. Polonsky (Eds.), *Marriage and divorce* (pp. 249–286). New York: Guilford Press.

Vaillant, C. O., & Vaillant, G. E. (1993). Is the U-curve of marital satisfaction an illusion? A 40-year study of marriage. *Journal of Marriage and the Family, 55,* 230–239.

Vega, W. A. (1990). Hispanic families in the 1980's: A decade of research. *Journal of Marriage and the Family, 52,* 1015–1024.

Wallerstein, J., & Blakeslee, S. (1995). *The good marriage: How and why love lasts.* Boston: Houghton Mifflin.

Wamboldt, F. S., & Reiss, D. (1989). Defining a family heritage and a new relationship identity: Two central tasks in the making of a marriage. *Family Process, 28,* 317–335.

4 Challenging Privilege through Africentric Social Work Practice

Mary E. Swigonski

Privilege permeates the social structure of the United States and the daily lives of its inhabitants. Access to unearned privilege sustains continued inequality in the distribution of power and resources (Brand, 1977; hooks, 1990; Hurst, 1976). Privilege accrues to those who (consciously or not) oppress others and it is generally invisible to those who enjoy it. Privilege is quite visible to those to whom it is denied. Access to unearned privilege also influences the process and outcomes of social work practice, particularly when it occurs in a context of ethnic or cultural diversity (McMahon & Allen-Meares, 1992; Pinderhughes, 1989). Too often, when privilege is invisible, the effects of the lack of privilege are misconstrued as pathology within the oppressed individual.

This chapter examines the pervasiveness of privilege throughout the daily lives of people in the United States and discusses Africentric theory to exemplify how knowledge developed from the standpoint of another culture can challenge the pervasiveness of privilege and can transform the practice of social work.

PRIVILEGE

Definition

Privilege has been defined as the right to reap private benefit from the use of the means of production (Brand, 1977). That is a fairly narrow conception of privilege, the privilege of the capitalist. A more encompassing understanding of privilege frames it as unearned advantages enjoyed by a group simply because of membership in that group. A comprehensive list of the kinds of privileges enjoyed by particular groups would be enormous, but some illustrative examples include capitalist privilege, racial (white) privilege, gender (male) privilege, socioeconomic (high income) privilege, sexual orientation (heterosexual) privilege, married privilege, religious privilege, and age (youth) privilege.

This chapter was originally published in the March 1996 issue of *Social Work*, Vol. 41, pp. 153–161.

McIntosh (1988) defined *privilege* as those conditions of daily experience that are taken for granted as normal, neutral, and universally available to everybody. McIntosh observed that

> Some privileges allow one to feel at home in the world. Other privileges allow some groups to escape penalties or dangers which others suffer. Through privilege, we escape fear, anxiety, and the sense of not being welcome or not being real. Some keep us from having to hide, or be in disguise, or to feel sick or crazy . . . most keep us from having to be angry. (p. 11)

Privileges are those daily interactions with individuals and society that help individuals experience themselves in the center of their world. The center is where power, resources, and money (and a concomitant sense of social efficacy) are located. Exclusion from this center of the social structure marginalizes individuals, who then have less access to social, economic, political, and other resources.

Basis of Privilege

Through social structural arrangements, marginalized groups are not only constrained in their access to money, education, and opportunity but also denied the right to define themselves in their own terms. Marginalized groups are denied the right to have their own terms or to define their experiences within their own contexts and meanings. To survive, they must understand themselves and the world in the terms of those at the center of power. Marginalized groups must fit their construction of reality into the knowledge base of those with the privilege of education.

The dominant culture in the United States has its roots in Judeo-Christian, European traditions. All other ethnic groups must adapt to that culture or constantly explain their deviation. The values embedded in the English language affirm white Judeo-Christian superiority—on our way to heaven, we will be bathed in a white light or on our way to hell, it will be a black day. Most publicly recognized holidays celebrate European customs and culture. The heroes and role models presented by the educational system and the media are primarily of European ancestry. The most desirable education and the highest-paying jobs are more readily accessible to healthy European American men. Socioeconomic status and race are even privileged in terms of life span: More affluent European Americans have longer life expectancies.

In response to these kinds of considerations, it is common for European Americans to say "But I don't think of myself as privileged or white. I don't feel very privileged. I just see myself as an average person who works hard for what I have." That self-conception is privileged: White people have the privilege of forgetting that they are white and middle-class. But it is impossible to be a person of color in the United States and not be deeply aware of that color and of white people.

It is important to recognize that most individuals have access to some kinds of privilege. Most individuals are members of a privileged group in some aspect of their lives, and many are members of marginalized groups in other aspects. Rave (1990) observed that this is one of the dynamics that both helps and inhibits individuals in understanding privilege. By being in the minority, individuals experience the limitations and negative consequences of the majority's privilege. That experience as an outsider, as a marginalized person, may then be a barrier to recognizing areas of one's own life that are privileged.

Conditions of Privilege

To make privilege visible, it is helpful to view privileged lives in contrast to the lives of those denied particular privileges. What are some of the advantages of being white, male, middle-class (or more affluent), heterosexual, married, and so forth? In *White Privilege and Male Privilege*, McIntosh (1988) listed 54 conditions of privilege, conditions that invisibly permeate the mundane activities of daily life yet significantly influence the texture of one's existence. I have identified six general types of privilege that McIntosh's conditions illustrate. Table 4-1 lists the general types of privilege and illustrates them with quotations from McIntosh.

European Americans usually are free to travel anywhere in the United States without being stopped and questioned. In contrast, it is a common experience for people of color, especially young men, to be stopped by police officers and asked why they are in a particular place, where they are going, and how they acquired the car they are driving. European Americans are able to blend in and avoid notice; people of color are constantly visible and subject to notice simply because of their skin color.

People of color learn their ethnic culture at home and learn the crazy-making double standards of social acceptance outside the home (Boyd, 1990). Boyd illustrated this point with a quotation from Lorde: "Those of us for whom oppression is as American as apple pie have always had to be watchers, to become familiar with the language and manners of the oppressor, even sometimes adopting them for some illusion of protection" (p. 159).

Awareness of Privilege

For members of marginalized groups, awareness of difference and awareness of privilege are needed for survival. All members of ethnic minority groups must be bicultural. People of color must know the patterns and habits of the culture of the dominant society; low-income people must learn middle-class values; gay men and lesbians must know how to act straight. Members of all marginalized groups must be able to function in the culture of their identity group and that of the dominant culture. European Americans, as members of the dominant culture, need only know that culture. European Americans

Table 4-1

Types of Privilege Reflected in Statements from *White Privilege and Male Privilege*

Type of Privilege	Sample Statement
The freedom to associate exclusively or primarily with members of your own group	I can, if I wish, arrange to be in the company of people of my race most of the time. (p. 5)
The level of social acceptance one can presume across varying contexts	If I should need to move, I can be pretty sure of renting or purchasing housing in an area in which I want to live. (p. 5)
	Whether I use checks, credit cards, or cash, I can count on my skin color not to work against the appearance of financial reliability. (p. 6)
	I do not have to educate my children to be aware of systemic racism for their own daily protection. (p. 6)
The ability to see members of your groups in a positive light, in the records of history, in texts, in media, and as role models	When I am told about our national heritage or civilization, I am shown that people of my color made it what it is. (p. 6)
	I can be pretty sure that if I ask to speak to the person in charge, I will be facing a person of my own race. (p. 7)
The freedom from stereotyping	I can swear, or dress in second-hand clothes, or not answer letters, without having people attribute these choices to the bad morale, poverty, or illiteracy of my race. (p. 7)
	I can do well in a challenging situation without being called a credit to my race. (p. 7)
	I can be late to a meeting without having the lateness reflect on my race. (p. 8)
The ability to be oblivious of other groups	I can remain oblivious of the language and customs of people of color who constitute the world's majority without feeling in my culture any penalty for such oblivion. (p. 7)
	My culture gives me little fear about ignoring the perspective and powers of people of other races. (p. 8)
The ability to feel at home in the world	I will feel welcome and normal in the usual walks of public life, institutional and social. (p. 17)

SOURCE OF SAMPLE STATEMENTS: McIntosh, P. (1988). *White privilege and male privilege: A personal account of coming to see correspondences through work in women's studies* (Working Paper 189). Wellesley, MA: Wellesley College Center for Research on Women.

can ignore the values and worldviews of other groups without endangering their existence.

Readers who are European American and believe that they are exceptions to these generalizations should ask themselves the following questions: How would your life be different if you were an African American man or woman? if you were a person with low income? if you were an Asian American man or woman? if you were an American Indian man or woman? if you were Latina or Latino? if you were a gay man or a lesbian of any culture? The freedom to not know the answers to these kinds of questions reflects privileged status. Members of all of the groups reflected in these questions clearly and explicitly know how their lives would be different if they were middle-class, heterosexual, white European Americans.

Privilege and Social Workers

Recognizing the pervasive effects of privilege may be difficult for many social workers. Social workers enjoy privileges as educated people. Professional language and knowledge are privileges not available to many of their clients. Many social workers enjoy the privilege that accrues to them as white European Americans.

To make privilege and its effects visible, social workers need to understand how they perpetuate and reinforce privilege in their lives and practice. Rave (1990) suggested that to understand one's part in the process, it is essential to understand and identify with the oppressors. That is not an easy task for social workers with strong commitments to social justice and empathy. But it is an essential one. White social workers are both members of the oppressor group and advocates for oppressed groups.

To further this task, it is necessary to begin a discourse on race that interrogates whiteness (hooks, 1990). It is important to analyze privilege in the lives of the privileged from the standpoint of those denied privilege. The profession knows what oppression looks like, and it is not a pretty picture. Yet it persists as a social phenomenon. To more effectively confront oppression, it is necessary to study the contexts of privilege that sustain oppression and to understand the unearned advantages that accrue from it.

Privilege is a dynamic that can help advance social workers' understanding of the interlocking nature of oppressions. All forms of oppression result in privileges for the oppressors. Privileges are not conditions of life that are normal, neutral, and universally available to everybody. It is not possible to give up privilege. But it is possible to learn to think and act not out of the spontaneous consciousness (Harding, 1991) of the social locations of one's birth, but out of the transformatory consciousness developed through the application of critical theories and through work in emancipatory movements.

AFRICENTRIC THEORY

Theories are powerful tools for the creation of shared realities. Africentric theory shows how developing knowledge of another culture from the perspective of that culture can transform social work practice. Knowledge developed in this way enables the professions to work more profoundly for the empowerment of clients. Nobles and Goddard (1985), leading Africentric scholar–researchers, said that the person who controls the information is in control:

> The most efficient way to keep black people oppressed and pow-
> erless is to provide them with ideas that justify and certify our sta-
> tus and condition. A powerful approach to the empowerment of
> all marginalized groups is to work together to develop critical
> consciousness, to develop together the tools to critique frames of
> reference, ideas, information, and patterns of privilege. (p. 27)

Definition

Africentric theory begins with the questions "Does this place Africans
in the center? Is it in the best interest of African peoples?" (Asante,
1988, p. 45). Africentric theory describes the ethos and values of
Africans and African Americans (Everett, Chipungu, & Leashore,
1991). Africentric work reorganizes the frame of reference so that
African history, culture, and worldview become the context for understanding Africans and African Americans (Asante, 1988). Africentric theory counteracts the application of deficit models that focus
exclusively on defects and problems in the behaviors of people of
color. This theory provides a standpoint from which to develop a
proactive stance emphasizing strengths. The construction of models
of human behavior from an Africentric perspective portrays African
Americans in ways that are free of European ethnocentrism and an-
drocentrism (Turner, 1991). This foundation is essential to more
clearly understand the effects of racism and privilege on the reality
of African Americans.

The Africentric perspective is holistic and includes recognition of
the interconnectedness of all things and the oneness of mind, body,
and spirit; development of collective rather than individual identity;
consanguine family structure; consequential morality; analog thinking rather than dualistic thinking (recognizing all points along the
continuum, in contrast to only either–or, right–wrong); phenomenological time (present oriented, tied to events); and a pervasive, experiential, and participatory spirituality (Turner, 1991). The European
American worldview is individualistic and mastery oriented, whereas the African worldview is cooperative and harmony oriented (Harvey, 1985).

Africentric theory is not ethnocentric because it does not claim or
aspire to hegemony. Eurocentrism is ethnocentric because of the cultural, economic, and epistemological hegemony that have historically become associated with it. Of course, there are significant variations in the degree to which individual African Americans
participate in every aspect of this worldview. It is as important to
recognize and respect differences within groups as it is to acknowledge differences between groups. It is equally important not to ro-
manticize cultural strengths by neglecting the profound effects of
racism and other forms of oppression.

However, understanding African American clients within their
context at least begins to challenge the privileged status of the European worldview and places them in the center of their conception of

reality. This stance is a profound operationalization of the social work practice imperative of beginning where the client is.

Knowledge Building

hooks (1990) observed that racism is perpetuated when blackness is associated solely with the concept that concrete experience either opposes or has no connection to abstract thinking and the production of critical theory. That kind of assumption perpetuates the privileged status of white Eurocentric systems of knowing. In contrast, the Africentric approach to knowledge building asserts that it is the prerogative of all peoples to understand their lived reality in their own terms—to define their own cultures and worldviews and to develop their own unique economic forms. By establishing the legitimacy of an alternative system of knowing, the Africentric cultural worldview provides a powerful challenge to that privilege. It poses a significant challenge to the understanding of human behavior and approaches to practice held by most social workers.

Loss of Terms

The Africentric analysis of the cultural and economic questions builds on the concept "loss of terms." Asante (1990) described loss of terms as a fundamental metaphor for both economic and social relationships of Africans to the Western world. Asante noted that to be moved off of one's terms is to be a victim of aggression, whether physical or mental. European slave traders moved Africans off of their physical terms. Missionaries and settlers moved Africans off of their religious terms. Capitalists moved Africans off of their economic terms. Educator Carter G. Woodson (1933) highlighted the power of the loss of terms:

> If you control a man's thinking, you do not have to worry about his action. When you determine what a man shall think, you do not have to concern yourself about what he will do. If you make a man feel that he is inferior, you do not have to compel him to accept inferior status, for he will seek it himself. (p. 84)

The right to define the categories or terms through which one sees the world, and is seen by it, is a fundamental political right of all peoples (Harding, 1991). Regaining the use of one's own terms to understand and define one's life affirms personal power. A challenge for social work practitioners committed to empowerment is to help clients define the terms through which they view the world and are seen by it. In regaining the use of their own terms, clients can create pathways to return from the margins to the center, laying claim to their own empowerment.

AFRICENTRIC CRITIQUE OF MONOCULTURAL RESEARCH

The Africentric critique of monocultural research demonstrates that research of the dominant culture advances in three directions: (1) by conferring negative or positive qualities on others and the manner in which others are evaluated by criteria and measures promoted by one's in-group (projection of values), (2) by interpreting one's own posture as reasonable (rationalization), and (3) by refusing to recognize the existence of the other's position (denigration) (Asante, 1990).

Projection of Values

European Americans act from common conceptions of time, work, productivity, the importance of material goods, relations with nature, family structure, the role of young and old in society, and the relative importance of cities and countryside. Many European Americans presume the universality of these concepts. This kind of projection conceals diversity and imposes a worldview that blankets and obscures the unique perspective of other cultures.

Language consolidates these projections, for example, in the attachment of negative or inferior connotations to the word "black" and their application to African Americans and in the attachment of positive or superior connotations to the word "white" and their application to European Americans. These attachments result in the implication that African American culture is inferior and white culture is superior (Solomon, 1976).

Rationalization

Rationalization denies or minimizes the value of intuitive, spiritual, and other forms of knowledge. Rationalization is apparent in European American scholars' assumption that their conception of knowledge and knowledge production is the only reasonable one (Asante, 1990). Asante noted that such a posture fractures communication and imposes a particularism as universal. This posture privileges the approaches to knowledge and limits what passes for legitimate information.

European American scholars and leaders foster Judeo-Christian faiths, the way of life of representative democracy, particular forms of art and music, the Industrial Revolution, the scientific revolution, and technology (Tucker, 1968). Other forms of religion are merely cults, other ways of life are backward or repressive, other forms of art and music are crafts or primitive.

Denigration

Denigration is the symbolic and consequent intellectual refusal to recognize the "other." The other remains invisible, unimportant, concealed, and irrelevant (Asante, 1990). For example, U.S. public policy on the family is based on the assumption of a single homogeneous family type, the nuclear family, assumed to be the only reasonable form. Nobles and Goddard (1985) noted that this assumption results in the underdevelopment and oppression of families belonging to ethnic groups who do not conform to the presumed norm.

Further illustration of the effects of denigration can be seen in the early research on the internal dynamics of African American family life, much of which focused on socialization practices and concluded that those practices were inadequate and dysfunctional (Collins, 1990; Nobles & Goddard, 1985; Wilson, 1991). That denigration and refusal to recognize the realities of African American family life cause the considerable strengths of African American families to remain invisible. Subsequent research by African American scholars found contrary conclusions: A clear purpose of African American family socialization is to prepare children to cope with the concrete realities of both the African American and wider communities (Nobles & Goddard, 1985).

In a review of the literature produced by the strengths school of African American family studies, English (1991) extracted the following attributes of traditional African American family life:

> Strong kinship ties and obligations, care of the elderly and absorption of children into households by other relatives and fictive kin, strong religious consciousness, strong community ties, socialization of the young with emphasis on group welfare over individual welfare, strong helping and mutual-aid tradition, and a strong achievement orientation. (p. 23)

There are variations across and within families in terms of their adherence to these values. Nonetheless, they provide a striking contrast to earlier descriptions of African American family life.

IMPLICATIONS FOR SOCIAL WORK

In a rather stinging critique of white feminist efforts toward social change, equally applicable to social work practice, Gordon (1987) observed,

> The primary difference in the message which emanates from black women in contrast to those of white women would be that white women send a message that states "I have worked hard. I have been oppressed. It is past the time when I should take my rightful place in the structure beside you." The message that emerges from the black woman is "The structure is wrong. It works against us as black people, and it needs to be changed." (p. 42)

Striving for an adaptive balance between the person and the environment is not always desirable for people of color and members of marginalized groups (Gould, 1989). Instead, transformation of social institutions must be the basic goal.

Traditional multicultural social work practice acknowledges the unique culture of the client. As representatives of the dominant culture, practitioners often work to help clients adapt their lifestyles to fit with the dominant culture (Everett et al., 1991; McMahon & Allen-Meares, 1992; Montiel & Wong, 1983). The outcome of that kind of work is acculturation and assimilation. It serves to support existing social patterns and structures. That kind of work ensures the perpetuation of the privilege of the existing power structure and falls short of larger goals of social justice.

To more effectively honor the profession's commitment to social change and social justice, social workers need to consciously and intentionally take up the work of unlearning, undoing, transforming, and revolutionizing the patterns of social privilege. This work begins with self-awareness and extends to the critical analysis of the professional knowledge and skill bases.

In her book *Cultural Etiquette: A Guide for the Well Intentioned*, Three Rivers (1990) provided some basic strategies for beginning to confront privilege and to develop self-awareness while becoming more empowering within a context that respects diversity:

- Be an active ally to all oppressed people. Take the initiative in intercepting oppression.
- Don't let anyone be racist, sexist, heterosexist, classist, or anti-Semitic in your face.
- Have the courage and commitment to lovingly confront even your friends and your employers when they are offensive.
- Write letters to the editor and support boycotts.
- Seek out or start anti-oppression groups in your community.
- Read books by and about people of color, Jewish people, lesbians and gay men.
- Don't expect the work to be easy.
- Don't be afraid of pain and discomfort.
- Don't be afraid to grow. (pp. 26–27)

Developing self-awareness is a first step. The profession also needs to develop its knowledge in the terms of each particular oppressed or marginalized group. Practitioners must do more than read a book, although they must do at least that. Social workers need to find ways to confront the reality of the lives of all clients through reading, research, scholarly literature, popular writings, art (music, painting, and dance), food, and personal contacts that are more than tokenism. Beyond self-awareness and knowledge, this new information calls for translation into skills for action. Social workers need to work more effectively to transform the social structures that perpetrate racism, ethnocentrism, classism, sexism, heterosexism, and all other forms of oppression.

All of the interlocking oppressions need direct confrontation and transformation through social work practice that spans the micro–macro practice continuum. Africentric awareness and knowledge call for personal and political interventions to be woven into the fabric of all social work practice efforts by helping clients recognize the effects of institutionalized discrimination and oppression in their lives, sorting out more carefully the difference between the effects of oppression and pathology, strengthening advocacy skills, and working with clients to help them empower themselves.

From research building on the Africentric perspective, the considerable strengths of African American families have become visible. The African American valuing of extended families makes visible the privileges accorded to the nuclear family by law, social policy, and practice theory. The Africentric perspective redirects practice and policy to address family problems by developing supports and resources that include collective efforts, self-help, and mutual aid (Leashore, McMurray, & Bailey, 1991). Developing resources for family preservation through social, civic, fraternal, and religious groups explicitly emerges from the African value of collective work and responsibility (Leashore et al., 1991).

Social work practice from an Africentric perspective challenges the social work profession to work with clients to develop alternative social structures that are empowering and that confront the hegemony of existing systems and structures of oppression and domination. Too often social work has been content to look at culturally diverse groups as representing problems, anomalies, or victims for study and remediation. Social workers must learn to center the culture and lives of African Americans, Latinos, Asian Americans, and American Indians as unique groups. They need to explicitly incorporate those insights when working with individuals from that culture or group. But that is not enough. It is necessary, but not sufficient. Social workers must recognize the ways that the privileges of certain groups oppress members of other groups.

CONCLUSION

Through the process of learning to see reality from the standpoints of other groups, in their terms, one acquires the vantage point necessary to see privilege and its effects. Africentric theory provides a standpoint from which to begin to recognize the ways in which knowledge, culture, power, economics, spirituality, and even the family are sites of privilege. The theory also provides a standpoint from which to begin to recognize the ways in which knowledge, culture, power, economics, spirituality, and family can be forces of empowerment as the profession works to understand them in the terms of particular groups.

Learning to develop theories and methods of practice within the terms and standpoint of clients can profoundly transform the practice of social work. It challenges social work to develop ways of knowing and being that flexibly shift whose interpretation of reality is placed in the center. It provides a theoretical framework to ensure that practice efforts advance client empowerment and social justice as primary goals. It significantly transforms the social order by challenging the current hegemony of privilege. Privilege no longer needs to be understood as either yours or mine. The Africentric perspective invites all of the profession's participation in the collective work and responsibility of initiatives for freedom and justice within our global village.

REFERENCES

Asante, K. A. (1988). *Afrocentricity*. Trenton, NJ: Africa World Press.

Asante, M. K. (1990). *Kemet: Afrocentricity and knowledge*. Trenton, NJ: Africa World Press.

Boyd, J. A. (1990). Ethnic and cultural diversity: Keys to power. *Women and Therapy, 9*(1/2), 151–167.

Brand, H. (1977). Limits to social growth or limits to privilege? *Dissent, 24*, 425–430.

Collins, P. H. (1990). *Black feminist thought: Knowledge, consciousness, and the politics of empowerment*. London: HarperCollins Academic.

English, R. A. (1991). Diversity of world views among African American families. In J. E. Everett, S. S. Chipungu, & B. R. Leashore (Eds.), *Child welfare: An Africentric perspective* (pp. 19–35). New Brunswick, NJ: Rutgers University Press.

Everett, J. E., Chipungu, S. S., & Leashore, B. R. (Eds.). (1991). *Child welfare: An Africentric perspective*. New Brunswick, NJ: Rutgers University Press.

Gordon, V. (1987). *Black women: Feminism and black liberation*. Chicago: Third World Press.

Gould, K. (1989). Asian and Pacific Islanders: Myth and reality. *Social Work, 34*, 142–147.

Harding, S. (1991). *Whose science? Whose knowledge? Thinking from women's lives*. Ithaca, NY: Cornell University Press.

Harvey, A. R. (1985). Traditional African culture as the basis for the Afro-American church in America: The foundation of the black church in America. In A. R. Harvey (Ed.), *The black family: An Afrocentric perspective* (pp. 3–19). New York: United Church of Christ Commission for Racial Justice.

hooks, b. (1990). *Yearning: Race, gender, and cultural politics*. Boston: South End Press.

Hurst, W. (1976). Consensus and conflict in twentieth-century public policy. *Daedalus, 105*(4), 89–101.

Leashore, B. R., McMurray, H. L., & Bailey, B. C. (1991). Reuniting and preserving African American families. In J. E. Everett, S. S. Chipungu, & B. R. Leashore (Eds.), *Child welfare: An Africentric perspective* (pp. 247–265). New Brunswick, NJ: Rutgers University Press.

McIntosh, P. (1988). *White privilege and male privilege: A personal account of coming to see correspondences through work in women's studies* (Working Paper 189). Wellesley, MA: Wellesley College Center for Research on Women.

McMahon, A., & Allen-Meares, P. (1992). Is social work racist? A content analysis of recent literature. *Social Work, 37*, 533–539.

Montiel, M., & Wong, P. (1983). A theoretical critique of the minority perspective. *Social Casework, 64*, 112–117.

Nobles, W., & Goddard, L. (1985). Black family life: A theoretical and policy implication literature review. In A. R. Harvey (Ed.), *The black family: An Afrocentric perspective* (pp. 21–89). New York: United Church of Christ Commission for Racial Justice.

Pinderhughes, E. (1989). *Understanding race, ethnicity, and power*. New York: Free Press.

Rave, E. J. (1990). White feminist therapists and anti-racism. *Women and Therapy, 9*(1/2), 313–326.

Solomon, B. B. (1976). *Black empowerment: Social work in oppressed communities*. New York: Columbia University Press.

Three Rivers, A. (1990). *Cultural etiquette: A guide for the well intentioned*. Indian Valley, VA: Market Wimmin. (Available from Market Wimmin, Box 28, Indian Valley, VA 24105)

Tucker, F. (1968). *The white conscience*. New York: Frederick Unger.

Turner, R. J. (1991). Affirming consciousness: The Africentric perspective. In J. E. Everett, S. S. Chipungu, & B. R. Leashore (Eds.), *Child welfare: An Africentric perspective* (pp. 36–57). New Brunswick, NJ: Rutgers University Press.

Wilson, M. (1991). The context of the African American family. In J. E. Everett, S. S. Chipungu, & B. R. Leashore (Eds.), *Child welfare: An Africentric perspective* (pp. 85–118). New Brunswick, NJ: Rutgers University Press.

Woodson, C. G. (1933). *The miseducation of the Negro*. Washington, DC: Associated Press.

5 Afrocentricity: An Emerging Paradigm in Social Work Practice

Jerome H. Schiele

Although considerable attention in social work practice has been aimed at addressing the concerns of people of color, the general thrust in what is called ethnic-sensitive (or "minority") (Devore & Schlesinger, 1981; Lum, 1992) or cross-cultural (Greene & Ephross, 1991) social work practice is to adapt existing practice models to serve people of color, with special attention given to racism (Pinderhughes, 1989). Although this strategy is a step in the right direction toward cultural sensitivity and political consciousness, it de-emphasizes the legitimacy of using the cultural values of people of color as a theoretical base to develop new practice models. Moreover, the failure to use the cultural values of people of color in developing new models can be viewed as an implicit expression of Western ethnocentrism, or the belief that Eurocentric values are the only values that can explain behavior and should be the basis for solving people's problems. Consequently, the theoretical foundations of many established social work practice models do not mirror the diversity of cultural values and worldviews found in the broader U.S. society, which includes people of color. In addition, because people of color, especially African Americans and Hispanics, experience greater poverty and have fewer material resources than the general population (U.S. Bureau of the Census, 1994), it is important that practice models reflect the cultural values and worldviews of these most likely social work clients.

Social workers and social scientists from oppressed groups, especially African Americans, have begun to affirm and integrate their cultural values and worldviews into their scholarship and professional practice (see, for example, Abramovitz, 1988; Chau, 1992; Hill-Collins, 1989; Manoleas & Carrillo, 1991). As a consequence of slavery, African Americans have been particularly victimized by cultural denigration, which has been manifested in all areas of life, including the social sciences. African American social scientists and practitioners have responded by developing theoretical and practice models that reflect and affirm the values and worldviews of African Americans (see, for example, Akbar, 1984; Asante, 1988; Brisbane & Womble, 1991;

This chapter was originally published in the May 1996 issue of *Social Work*, Vol. 41, pp. 284–294.

Burgest, 1982; Daly, Jennings, Beckett, & Leashore, 1995; Everett, Chipungu, & Leashore, 1991; Jackson, 1976; Kambon, 1992; Phillips, 1990; Schiele, 1994).

This chapter describes and explains the Afrocentric paradigm that has been used in social work practice. It describes the reasons for and the theoretical assumptions of Afrocentricity; it describes the way Afrocentricity conceives social work practice and social problems. Although some people prefer the term "Africentric" (see Akbar, 1984; Daly et al., 1995; Everett et al., 1991), I prefer the term "Afrocentric," primarily because of its prevalence. There appears to be no political difference between Afrocentric and Africentric, and they are often used interchangeably. Some members of the African American community (Ani, 1994; Kambon, 1992) have begun to use what they refer to as a more politically and culturally correct label, which is Africancentric or African centered. I use Afrocentric to mean African centered.

AFROCENTRIC PARADIGM

Origins and Reasons

The Afrocentric paradigm is a social science paradigm predicated on the philosophical concepts of contemporary African America and traditional Africa. The origins of this worldview, however, are found in traditional Africa before the advent of European and Arab influences (Carruthers, 1981; Williams, 1987). Although the colonization of Africa by Europeans and Arabs modified traditional Africa somewhat (Serequeberhan, 1991), several writers maintain that the philosophical integrity of traditional Africa has survived among continental Africans (Mazrui, 1986; Mbiti, 1970; Zahan, 1979) and among people of the African Diaspora (Akbar, 1979; Asante, 1988; Dixon, 1976; Kambon, 1992). These writers imply that slavery and the denial of African culture did not destroy all of the cultural vestiges of Africa in African Americans.

Several writers believe that the social isolation of African Americans created by slavery and racial segregation, in addition to sustaining the desire to maintain tradition, helped preserve traditional African philosophical assumptions among African Americans (Franklin, 1980; Herskovitz, 1941; Martin & Martin, 1985; Nobles, 1980; Sudarkasa, 1988). The social scientists who have advanced the Afrocentric paradigm in the United States accept the veracity of these assumptions.

Although they acknowledge that African Americans vary in their internalization of traditional African values, Afrocentrists contend that traditional Africa has survived enough to render African Americans a distinct cultural and ethnic group. Furthermore, these writers maintain that the application of Eurocentric theories of human behavior to explain the behavior and ethos of African Americans is inappropriate (to varying degrees) (Akbar, 1979, 1984; Baldwin & Hopkins, 1990; Bell, Bouie, & Baldwin, 1990; Kambon, 1992).

Eurocentric theories of human behavior reflect concepts of human behavior developed in European and Anglo-American culture. The practice of using Eurocentric theories to explain the behavior and ethos of African Americans can be inappropriate because a major assumption of the Afrocentric paradigm is that social science theories are derived from the specific experiences and cultural perspectives of the theorist. Unlike the predominant Eurocentric ideal, the theorist, from an Afrocentric standpoint, is not viewed as an objective, detached observer but as an observer shaped by a particular cultural, autobiographical, and political standpoint. Therefore, Afrocentrists do not believe in social science universalism—that one theory or paradigm can be used to explain social phenomena among all people and in all cultures. Afrocentrists, who desire cultural pluralism without political hierarchy, recognize that there are similarities between and among people of various cultural and ethnic groups. However, they view differences, especially cultural differences, as important and feel that these differences should not be minimized. Afrocentrists believe that these differences speak to a cultural and ethnic group's ethos, which is and should be revealed in social work and social sciences. Moreover, Afrocentrists believe that an emphasis on difference does not necessarily lead to an emphasis on negativity or hostility. The Afrocentric perspective fosters the belief that there can be social unity among people sharing a particular time and space but that cultural uniformity is not essential (Asante, 1992).

Eurocentric Knowledge Hegemony. Afrocentrists also contend that the application and imposition of Eurocentric theories of human behavior, especially to explain the behavior and ethos of African Americans, are implicitly oppressive. Most of the theories of human behavior to which social workers and social scientists in the United States are exposed have sprung from a Eurocentric perspective because of the political and economic hegemony that European Americans exercise over U.S. social institutions.

European political and economic hegemony, Afrocentrists say, has led to a hegemony of knowledge production and knowledge validation (especially apparent in academia) that omits or marginalizes the indigenous worldviews of people of color (Akbar, 1984; Ani, 1994; Asante, 1990). It is interesting to note that several feminists make a similar observation, although from a gender hegemonic perspective (Abramovitz, 1988; Gilligan, 1989; Harding & Hintikka, 1983).

Eurocentric Basis for Racism. Eurocentric theories of human behavior and society have historically vilified people of African descent and other people of color (Akbar, 1984; Ani, 1994; Asante, 1990). This vilification can be discerned in Hegel's (1837/1956) *The Philosophy of History,* Terman's (1916) *The Measurement of Intelligence,* and the works of other writers who explicitly or implicitly have claimed that people of African descent were inferior or pathological in their personality, social, or moral development. The origins of this denigration can be found in the European slave trade; slave investors, traders, and owners were pressed to justify the enslavement of Africans (Ani,

1994; McIntyre, 1993). The first justification came from theology and was especially noticeable in the "Hamitic myth," which contends that Africans are the descendants of Ham, who in Genesis were cursed by Noah into servitude (see McIntyre, 1993).

After the European Enlightenment of the 17th and 18th centuries, the slave investors, traders, and owners turned to the emerging social sciences in Europe and America for justification of slavery. This justification was conspicuously noticeable in scientific theories of intelligence, family organization, and crime. The fallout of this historic scientific racism is the portrayal of the culture of people of African descent as "uncivilized" and the projection of the belief that people of African ancestry have contributed nothing to world development and human history, thus creating the perception that it was impossible for them to have developed a credible philosophy on which to base a social science (Ani, 1994; Asante, 1990).

Although explicit scientific racism is difficult—but possible—to find in social science theories today, what increasingly is found is subtle or symbolic scientific racism (Rothenberg, 1990), which involves the use of superficially race-neutral codes that carry racist connotations (that is, dysfunctional family values, affirmative action, urban crime and violence, youth violence, welfare cheats or frauds, and drug addicts).

Objectives of the Paradigm

Because of these historical factors and other factors discussed later in this chapter, Afrocentricity has three objectives: (1) It seeks to promote an alternative social science paradigm more reflective of the cultural and political reality of African Americans; (2) it seeks to dispel the negative distortions about people of African ancestry by legitimizing and disseminating a worldview that goes back thousands of years and that exists in the hearts and minds of many people of African descent today (Carruthers, 1981; Diop, 1978); and (3) it seeks to promote a worldview that will facilitate human and societal transformation toward spiritual, moral, and humanistic ends and that will persuade people of different cultural and ethnic groups that they share a mutual interest in this regard. As Karenga (1993) stated, Afrocentricity is both particularistic and universalistic; it speaks to the specific liberation needs of people of African descent and to the spiritual and moral development of the world.

Afrocentric Assumptions about Human Beings

The Afrocentric paradigm asserts three major assumptions about human beings: (1) Human identity is a collective identity; (2) the spiritual or nonmaterial component of human beings is just as important and valid as the material component; and (3) the affective approach to knowledge is epistemologically valid (Akbar, 1984; Asante, 1988; Bell et al., 1990; Boykin & Toms, 1985; Dixon, 1976; Everett et al., 1991; Harris, 1992; Kambon, 1992; Myers, 1988; Nobles, 1980; Schiele, 1990).

Individual Identity as Collective Identity. Considerable emphasis in the Afrocentric paradigm is placed on a collective conceptualization of human beings and on collective survival; individual identity is conceived as a collective identity (Akbar, 1984; Harris, 1992; Kambon, 1992; Myers, 1988; Nobles, 1980). The paradigm does not reject individual uniqueness (Akbar, 1984; Boykin & Toms, 1985), but it does reject the idea that the individual can be understood separately from others in his or her social group (Akbar, 1984; Nobles, 1980). Afrocentricity's disavowal of an isolated, detached identity is based on the belief that there is no perceptual separation between the individual and other people (Dixon, 1976). Mbiti (1970) used the African adage "I am because we are, and because we are, therefore, I am" (p. 141) to capture the essence of this value. Thus, the Afrocentric paradigm conceives of individual identity as a fluid and interconnected way of uniquely expressing a collective or group ethos. In addition, the focus on collectivity in the Afrocentric paradigm also encourages an emphasis on sharing, cooperation, and social responsibility (Daly et al., 1995; Kambon, 1992; Martin & Martin, 1985).

Spiritual Nature of Human Beings. The Afrocentric paradigm also acknowledges and underscores the importance of spirituality or nonmaterial aspects of human beings. *Spirituality,* from an Afrocentric perspective, can be defined as that invisible universal substance that connects all human beings to each other and to a Creator or a Supreme Being (Schiele, 1994). In traditional African philosophy, God, or the generative spirit, is thought to be reflected in all elements of the universe and is thus seen as the connective link between humanity and the universe (see Mbiti, 1970; Zahan, 1979). In the Afrocentric paradigm, the soul, which is the amorphous part of the human being that transcends time and space, is considered just as much a legitimate source of study as the mind and the body. In addition, soul, mind, and body are considered interdependent and interrelated phenomena (Mbiti, 1970; Nobles, 1980; Schiele, 1994). Furthermore, unlike many Eurocentric social science theories (with the exception of the existentialist, humanistic, and transpersonal schools of thought), the Afrocentric paradigm considers the soul a vital part of social science inquiry. The Afrocentric paradigm does not limit its concept of science to directly observable or quantifiable phenomena and does not impose distinct boundaries among science, philosophy, and theology.

Affective Knowledge. In the Afrocentric paradigm, affect (feelings or emotions) is viewed as a valid source of knowing. The scientist's or practitioner's life experiences, as expressed through emotion, are considered essential for furthering knowledge. A major tenet of Afrocentricity is that emotions are the most direct experience of self (Akbar, 1984). The focus on affect in the Afrocentric paradigm does not preclude recognition of the rational. Rather, rationality and emotionality are two transparent and penetrable sides of the same coin, that coin being the ways people experience life. In this paradigm, reasoning or thoughts do not occur in a vacuum but are filtered through the maze of people's emotions and values. Thus, thoughts do not occur independently of feelings, and feelings do not occur independently of thoughts. Thoughts are no more superior to emotions than emotions are to thoughts. Unlike the dichotomous logic characteristic of European American culture, the Afrocentric paradigm relies more on a holistic or diunital (that is, union of opposites) way of making sense of the world (Bell, 1994; Dixon, 1976; Nichols, 1987).

The emphasis on feelings as a source of knowledge is akin to social work's tradition of emphasizing feelings in practice. Many social work practitioners believe that for transformation to occur in practice, feelings must be shared between the helper and the client. The concept of practice wisdom, which recognizes the importance of the practitioner's feelings and life experiences, is another demonstration of how the profession places emphasis on emotions or feelings as a means of knowing. Furthermore, many concerns that social workers have about inequality and injustice arise not only from rationality but also from the emotional experience of the pain of injustice, either directly or vicariously. Despite this emphasis, however, the extent to which traditional social work has fully integrated concepts and assumptions of the Afrocentric paradigm is questionable.

Afrocentric Sources of Human Problems

From an Afrocentric perspective, the major sources of human problems in the United States are oppression and alienation. *Oppression* is defined as a systematic and deliberate strategy to suppress the power and potentiality of people by legitimizing and institutionalizing inhumanistic and person-delimiting values such as materialism, fragmentation, individualism, and inordinate competition. These values together undergird a society that teaches people to see themselves primarily as material, physical beings seeking immediate pleasure for their material, physical, or sexual desires. In this social context, values such as spirituality, collectivity, mutual aid, and co-operation are de-emphasized and underdeveloped (Myers, 1988). This situation leads to a kind of alienation from the spiritual and the moral. In this alienation, an individual's worth and sense of self become fragile and diminished, because the emphasis on materialism fosters a belief that human worth is equivalent to physical appearance, wealth, possessions, education, and so forth (Myers, 1988). This orientation leads to a lack of spiritual and moral development that prevents people from tapping into the spirit of the Creator and from viewing themselves as intimately connected to all people and world elements.

European Worldview. The Afrocentric paradigm posits that there is a reciprocal relationship between the values of materialism and individualism and the political and economic systems and social institutions that oppress people. For many Afrocentrists, these values are a result of a worldview that they argue has its origins in the geohistorical, political, economic, and philosophical traditions of Europe (especially Anglo-Germanic culture) (Ani, 1994; Asante, 1990; Diop, 1978; Kambon, 1992; Myers, 1988). Afrocentrists contend that this worldview emanated from Europe and sprang from several factors unique to Europe. They maintain that because of 500 years of political and economic domination, European nations were able to successfully disseminate and impose their worldviews onto the non-European nations that they colonized or conquered and to suppress and devalue the worldviews of these countries (Ani, 1994; Diop, 1978; Kambon, 1992). Thus, from an Afrocentric perspective, a major problem of the current era is the increased and pervasive Europeanization of human consciousness and culture (Karenga, 1993).

Spiritual Alienation. The Afrocentric paradigm maintains that although the Eurocentric worldview has been especially devastating to people of color throughout the world, it also has been detrimental to people of European descent. This worldview encourages individual alienation from spiritual and moral development for all. It also has led to global enslavement and imperialism, inordinate conflict between nations and ethnic groups, and unequal consumption of global resources (Akbar, 1984; Kambon, 1992; Karenga, 1993). It has fostered a nation like the United States that spends over 50 percent of its budget on a worldwide military–industrial complex but only 4 percent on social welfare programs (U.S. House of Representatives, Committee on Ways and Means, 1993). The Eurocentric worldview supports ludicrous debates by U.S. politicians that question the rights of people to equal opportunities for education and training, affordable housing and health care, and higher wages. Moreover, it supports the practice of denigrating groups and people based solely on their gender, skin color, weight, age, and other exterior characteristics and then uses this denigration as justification for excluding people from meaningful participation in major sectors of society (Myers, 1988; Schiele, 1994).

THE AFROCENTRIC PARADIGM AND SOCIAL PROBLEMS

How does the Afrocentric paradigm in social work explain specific problems that social workers deal with daily, and what recommendations for social work practice would it have? Street violence by youths and substance abuse are two social problems that have received considerable attention recently, not only in the social work literature but also in popular literature. These problems have had grave consequences for society and are in need of Afrocentric analysis if social work is to diversify and strengthen its arsenal against them. It is important to underscore that in explaining these problems, the Afrocentric paradigm does not claim universality; its explanations may not be appropriate for all youths who commit violence or all substance abusers.

Violent Crimes by Youths

Although violent crimes overall have decreased in the United States since 1991, violent crimes committed by youths have increased (U.S. Bureau of the Census, 1994). For youths who commit violent crimes, the Afrocentric paradigm maintains that oppression and spiritual alienation are the fundamental causes of the commission of these violent acts. It is my perception that youths commit violent acts because they live in a society that institutionalizes impediments to their economic mobility and livelihood and legitimizes the disconnection of people from nonmaterial and morally affirming values about human self-worth and social relationships.

Because much of youth street violence is related to participation in activities that are illegal (Myers & Drescher, 1994), the Afrocentric paradigm underscores the need to examine the effects of the U.S. political economy. From an Afrocentric standpoint, youths turn to violence because of the limited options and choices they have to advance themselves economically. The U.S. system of capitalism and labor exploitation causes many people, especially those at lower income levels, to develop a sense of hopelessness about succeeding in the legitimate labor market (Myers & Drescher, 1994).

Faced with minimum wages, layoffs, lack of opportunities for training or education, and more competition for existing jobs, many at the lower or moderate income levels consciously decide to participate in lifestyles that place them at risk of committing violent street crimes, even though these decisions may seem to lack grounding in reason by not considering adverse consequences of a life of street crime, such as being murdered or incarcerated (Cloward & Ohlin, 1960). An Afrocentric analysis contends that these decisions reflect the youths' political maturity and understanding that the United States clearly does not support the positive potentiality of all its citizens. These youths see a life of street crime as a logical means to cope with, and protest against, a society that practices pervasive employment discrimination (Lemelle, 1991). Moreover, these youths mentally calculate that they can make just as much, if not more, money from a life of street crime than from going through the prolonged experience of attending college and graduate school or from attempting the long shot of starting a legitimate business with very little start-up capital (Lemelle, 1991).

Victims in a Hostile Situation. Afrocentricity's focus on the role of political and economic oppression supports the view that in spite of their destructive behaviors, violent youth offenders are victims of U.S. exploitation and hypocrisy (Oliver, 1989). Social workers, therefore, are urged to adopt a "victim-in-hostile-situation" perspective: at-risk youths in the United States facing hostile practices of exploitation and hypocrisy. From this viewpoint, interventions should encourage and bring into existence socially caring policies and patterns of social behavior that economically and politically advance all people and enhance their positive potential. Instead of focusing intervention strategies more on individual adaptation or ego deficits, the Afrocentric paradigm advocates that more attention be placed on systems-accommodation and systems-replacement models of intervention. To this extent, the worker should take on the roles of policy practitioner (Jansson, 1994) and community organizer.

Violence and Spiritual Alienation. Spiritual alienation also can provide some explanation of youth street violence in the United States. Spiritual alienation is the disconnection of nonmaterial and morally affirming values from concepts of human self-worth and from the character of social relationships. The key concept here is disconnection, the disconnection that allows people to take on an insular, detached identity of self—individualism—and to view themselves primarily, if not exclusively, as material beings. I believe that the detached and materialistic identities of self cause youths to lack a spiritual connection to others, the sort of connection that allows them to see themselves and others as part of an interdependent web held together by the acknowledgment of the sacredness of, and the Creator's presence in, all human life.

The lack of awareness of this sacredness and spiritual interconnectedness provides a justification for exploiting and intentionally harming people, because people are seen as mere things or objects. In this objectification of human beings, people suspend—if only momentarily—caring or loving emotions toward others.

In my view, youth violence is a process of reciprocal objectification of human beings wherein physical aggression becomes the primary mode of expression that can be overcome only through an Afrocentric perspective. The reciprocal objectification of human beings that leads to violence is reinforced by ideas of human beings as inherently evil, aggressive, and selfish. Supported by the Judeo-Christian ethic and prominent Eurocentric theories of human behavior, these ideas, when internalized by young people, may lead to the false belief that humans lack the inherent capacity to be peaceful, caring, and morally affirming. Youths who commit violent acts often say, "I had to get him before he got me." Such statements reveal the internalization of the pessimistic vision of human behavior that is too often perpetuated by the values, philosophy, and social sciences of Western, Eurocentric societies (Akbar, 1984; Schiele, 1994).

Promoting Holistic Thinking. An Afrocentric analysis contends that this pessimistic, aggressive viewpoint is nurtured by the cruel effects of oppression, which too frequently engenders communities in which violence becomes a way of life (Oliver, 1989). The goal of the Afrocentric social worker is to try to eliminate spiritual alienation in young people and to begin to replace it with values that affirm a more holistic, spiritual, and optimistic viewpoint of human beings. This can be achieved by promoting and teaching holistic reasoning among youths as opposed to fragmented or analytic reasoning, which some say lays the foundation for the objectification and ultimately the exploitation of human beings (Ani, 1994; Burgest, 1981; Schiele, 1994).

Holistic reasoning or logic is thinking predicated on at least two concepts: union of feeling and thought (Ani, 1994; Bell, 1994) and the spiritual oneness of human beings. Acknowledging the interconnectedness of feelings and thought allows young people to make decisions that more completely tap the multidimensional makeup of their being. This acknowledgment allows them to get in touch with latent aspects of themselves that can serve as new avenues through which to achieve a greater capacity for positive potentiality and change.

The Afrocentric perception of human beings is based on the belief that at the core of the human being there is a spiritual essence that releases vast capabilities for interconnectedness or what Nobles (1980) called "spiritual oneness." Bringing young people into spiritual oneness helps them to understand that they are spiritually and socially connected to others, to acknowledge the sacredness of all human life, and to appreciate the many shades and variations of human beings and human experiences.

This transformation from materialistic–individualistic thinking to spiritual–holistic thinking among those who seek professional help can be brought about by a therapeutic process known as belief systems analysis (Myers, 1988). Although this helping process can be conducted through direct, one-on-one practice, the Afrocentric paradigm in social work practice invariably views the Eurocentric worldview as the primary target for change.

Substance Abuse

Most societies in history have sanctioned the use of some form of mood-altering substance, if for nothing more than ceremonial occasions (Goodman, Lovejoy, & Sherratt, 1995). Thus, the Afrocentric view is that the use of mood-altering substances is not deemed inherently deleterious (Christmon, 1995). What is damaging is the abuse or overuse of these substances and the reasons people use them in the first place. For this reason, the Afrocentric paradigm of social work acknowledges that substance abuse, like most other problems, must be viewed within the sociocultural and political–economic context in which it occurs (Oliver, 1989).

Sociocultural and Political–Economic Context. It is my perception that the Afrocentric paradigm in social work asserts that the political–economic and sociocultural attributes of the United States are the bases for the existence of substance abuse in this country. Specifically, substance abuse is a function of two phenomena: (1) Addictive substances are part of a broader arsenal used to dominate people more efficiently by rendering them politically passive and indifferent, and (2) substance abuse is a response to spiritual alienation. I believe that Afrocentric social work perceives the dominant group in the United States as having a vested interest in keeping the majority of citizens politically passive and indifferent. The idea is to contain people by any means necessary or appropriate so that power can remain in the domain of a few. Because insurgency and dissipation of their power base is always of concern to the dominant group, the Afrocentric paradigm contends that this group will stop at nothing to ensure and maximize its power. The broad availability of drugs in the United States, which contributes to the existence and increase in substance abuse, possibly helps the dominant group maintain its control and privilege over others as well as the material universe (Lusane, 1991).

Substance abusers are predictably politically passive; in the case of those in the worst socioeconomic conditions, such as African Americans, they too often participate in violent acts that destroy members of their own oppressed or exploited communities, thereby unconsciously capitulating to the political interests of the "white power elite" (Wilson, 1990).

Social workers working within the Afrocentric paradigm endeavor to expose the social contradictions, inequalities, and consequences of policies about drug trafficking, distribution, and control. For example, social workers could fight against the disproportionate location of liquor stores in urban communities of color. Social workers could also serve as educators to raise the political consciousness of those who abuse substances—especially those from lower socioeconomic groups and communities of people of color—by pointing out the relationship between substance abuse and the political oppression of affected communities. Finally, social workers could help organize boycotts of activities and organizations that are sponsored by the alcohol industry or that are known to be heavily financed by the illicit drug trade.

Substance Abuse and Spiritual Alienation. Substance abuse in the United States can also be viewed as a response to spiritual alienation. The effects of spiritual alienation have deep psychological consequences that the abuse of substances may help ease. The Afrocentric paradigm posits that humans at peace with themselves have the best chance of drawing on their vast potential when they acknowledge that the core of their being is spiritual. When people fail to admit this or when a society dissuades them from this belief, a limited view of life content and happiness emerges. Within this starved notion of human existence, happiness and human self-worth get translated into how much and what one owns, how one looks, and how fast or much one's career advances (Myers, 1988).

Furthermore, time, especially the future, is thought to be an enemy to compete against, because, in this worldview, all phenomena are regarded as things or objects the individual must compete against or overcome. This perspective places undue stress on the individual to succeed or to win, and the stress related to "winning" these material battles becomes even more pronounced for the oppressed. Thus, the Afrocentric paradigm should view substance abuse as a mode through which individuals attempt to compensate for their perceived failure to overcome life's material obstacles.

The role of the Afrocentric social worker whose specialty is substance abuse is to help bring into existence a new society in which relations between and among people and between people and the physical world are not based on conflict or antagonism. In doing this, the Afrocentric substance abuse worker explores and helps reinterpret experiences that abusers perceive occurred because of their failure to successfully overcome obstacles. Thus, eliminating spiritual alienation in abusers' lives becomes a primary goal of intervention. The Afrocentric substance abuse worker augments the examination of the detrimental corollaries of spiritual alienation on abusers and their families and integrates this knowledge in training seminars, schools of social work, and organizations that serve substance abusers. Social workers from an Afrocentric framework view spiritual alienation as a major public health problem. I believe such a view allows Afrocentric social workers to advocate a more complete definition of health that incorporates unobservable and too often untapped dimensions of human functioning and potential.

AFROCENTRIC ESSENTIALS IN THE HELPING PROCESS

The Afrocentric paradigm maintains that the personalization of the professional relationship and reciprocity within professional relationships are essential components of the helping or healing process (Brisbane & Womble, 1991; Jackson, 1976; Myers, 1988; Phillips, 1990).

Personalization of the Helping Relationship

Personalizing the professional relationship involves downplaying aloofness and emotional distance between the helper and the client. Professionalism is not associated with objectivity because objectivity, within the Afrocentric paradigm, is viewed as a false attribute of human beings.

For Afrocentric social work, emotional distance is seen as unproductive because it prevents the complete development of a trusting, authentic helping relationship. The demonstration of positive feelings by the helper cues the person being helped that the helper does indeed care about his or her life. This perception of caring provides the foundation for the relationship to be viewed and practiced as a sacred and special one—a unique point where people meet to advance human transformation. It leads to the formation of a shared consciousness between the helper and helped, and the helping relationship becomes an avenue through which both the helped and helper tune into an aspect of life that has implications for both their lives (Phillips, 1990).

Although the problem of the client is the focal point of the relationship, the helper understands that the problem is a human one that can and does have direct or indirect implications for his or her own life. Afrocentricity realizes that the worldview to which all are exposed can have detrimental consequences for all. Thus, "feeling" the client's problem (that is, personalizing the problem and understanding that it directly or indirectly affects the helper's life too) is an essential skill in Afrocentric social work.

Reciprocity in the Helping Relationship

The Afrocentric paradigm also emphasizes reciprocity in the helping relationship. Reciprocity not only implies the identification of problems mutually important to the client and helper but also means that the helper can learn and be assisted by the helped. Both the helper and helped can be the sources and recipients of information and assistance (Brisbane & Womble, 1991).

From an Afrocentric viewpoint, all human beings have the potential to help others; all human beings have experiences and knowledge that can be used to enlighten the thinking and enhance the lives of others. To this extent, the Afrocentric paradigm is not elitist; it does not view the worker as the only expert in the helping relationship. To do so is to de-emphasize and devalue the experiences and knowledge of the client in a way that is dehumanizing and oppressive. As Pinderhughes (1989) and Saleebey (1992) noted, practitioners must be willing to give up power to empower the client and be able to identify strengths of the client that can and should be integrated in the helping process. Afrocentricity agrees strongly with this observation and encourages a social work practice predicated on equality.

CONCLUSION

Afrocentricity is an emerging social work paradigm with particularistic and universalistic characteristics that can be used to uplift oppressed groups and advance spiritual and moral development in the world. Its call for spiritual and moral growth and the liberation of historically oppressed groups is in keeping with social work's mission of equality and justice for all. With its focus on the interaction between macro and micro problems, Afrocentricity fits well within social work's person-in-environment perspective. Probably Afrocentricity's most significant contribution to social work is its application of traditional African philosophical concepts as a foundation for a new social work practice model. By codifying the cultural values of people of African descent into a paradigm for explaining human behavior and solving societal problems, social work's knowledge base can be expanded and become more inclusive of the plurality of values found in a multiethnic and multicultural society and world.

REFERENCES

Abramovitz, M. (1988). *Regulating the lives of women: Social welfare policy from colonial times to the present.* Boston: South End Press.

Akbar, N. (1979). African roots of black personality. In W. D. Smith, H. Kathleen, M. H. Burlew, & W. M. Whitney (Eds.), *Reflections on black psychology* (pp. 79–87). Washington, DC: University Press of America.

Akbar, N. (1984). Africentric social sciences for human liberation. *Journal of Black Studies, 14,* 395–414.

Ani, M. (1994). *Yurugu: An African-centered critique of European cultural thought and behavior.* Trenton, NJ: Africa World Press.

Asante, M. K. (1988). *Afrocentricity.* Trenton, NJ: Africa World Press.

Asante, M. K. (1990). *Kemet, Afrocentricity, and knowledge.* Trenton, NJ: Africa World Press.

Asante, M. K. (1992, April). The painful demise of Eurocentrism. *World & I,* pp. 305–317.

Baldwin, J., & Hopkins, R. (1990). African-American and European-American cultural differences as assessed by the worldviews paradigm: An empirical analysis. *Western Journal of Black Studies, 14,* 38–52.

Bell, Y. R. (1994). A culturally sensitive analysis of black learning style. *Journal of Black Psychology, 20*(1), 47–61.

Bell, Y. R., Bouie, C. L., & Baldwin, J. A. (1990). Afrocentric cultural consciousness and African-American male–female relationships. *Journal of Black Studies, 21,* 162–189.

Boykin, W., & Toms, F. (1985). Black child socialization: A conceptual framework. In H. P. McAdoo (Ed.), *Black children* (pp. 35–51). Beverly Hills, CA: Sage Publications.

Brisbane, F. L., & Womble, M. (1991). *Working with African Americans: The professional's handbook.* Chicago: HRDI International Press.

Burgest, D. R. (1981). Theory on white supremacy and black oppression. *Black Books Bulletin, 7*(2), 26–30.

Burgest, D. R. (1982). Worldviews: Implications for social theory and third world people. In D. R. Burgest (Ed.), *Social work practice with minorities* (pp. 45–56). Metuchen, NJ: Scarecrow Press.

Carruthers, J. H. (1981). Reflections on the history of the Afrocentric worldview. *Black Books Bulletin, 7*(1), 4–7.

Chau, K. L. (1992). Educating for effective group work practice in multicultural environments of the 1990s. *Journal of Multicultural Social Work, 1*(4), 1–15.

Christmon, K. (1995). Historical overview of alcoholism in the African American community. *Journal of Black Studies, 25,* 318–330.

Cloward, R. A., & Ohlin, L. E. (1960). *Delinquency and opportunity.* New York: Free Press.

Daly, A., Jennings, J., Beckett, J., & Leashore, B. (1995). Effective coping strategies of African Americans. *Social Work, 40,* 240–248.

Devore, W., & Schlesinger, E. (1981). *Ethnic-sensitive social work practice.* St. Louis: C. V. Mosby.

Diop, C. A. (1978). *The cultural unity of black Africa.* Chicago: Third World Press.

Dixon, V. (1976). World views and research methodology. In L. King, V. Dixon, & W. Nobles (Eds.), *African philosophy: Assumptions and paradigms for research on black persons* (pp. 51–93). Los Angeles: Fanon Center Publications.

Everett, J. E., Chipungu, S. S., & Leashore, B. R. (Eds.). (1991). *Child welfare: An Africentric perspective.* New Brunswick, NJ: Rutgers University Press.

Franklin, J. H. (1980). *From slavery to freedom: A history of Negro Americans* (5th ed.). New York: Alfred A. Knopf.

Gilligan, C. (1989). Woman's place in man's life cycle. In L. Richardson & V. Taylor (Eds.), *Feminist frontiers II: Rethinking sex, gender, and society* (pp. 31–42). New York: McGraw-Hill.

Goodman, J., Lovejoy, P. E., & Sherratt, A. (Eds.). (1995). *Consuming habits: Drugs in history and anthropology.* New York: Routledge & Kegan Paul.

Greene, R. R., & Ephross, P. H. (1991). *Human behavior theory and social work practice.* New York: Aldine de Gruyter.

Harding, S., & Hintikka, M. (1983). Introduction. In S. Harding & M. Hintikka (Eds.), *Discovering reality: Feminist perspectives on epistemology, metaphysics, methodology, and philosophy of science* (pp. ix–xix). Boston: D. Reidel.

Harris, N. (1992). A philosophical basis for an Afrocentric orientation. *Western Journal of Black Studies, 16,* 154–159.

Hegel, G.W.F. (1956). *The philosophy of history.* New York: Dover Publications. (Original work published 1837)

Herskovitz, M. J. (1941). *The myth of the Negro past.* New York: Harper & Row.

Hill-Collins, P. (1989). The social construction of black feminist thought. *Signs, 14,* 745–773.

Jackson, G. G. (1976). The African genesis of the black perspective in helping. *Professional Psychology, 7*, 292–308.

Jansson, B. S. (1994). *Social policy: From theory to policy practice* (2nd ed.). Pacific Grove, CA: Brooks/Cole.

Kambon, K. (1992). *The African personality in America: An African-centered framework.* Tallahassee, FL: Nubian Nation Publications.

Karenga, M. (1993). *Introduction to black studies* (2nd ed.). Los Angeles: University of Sankore Press.

Lemelle, A. J. (1991). "Betcha cain't reason with 'em": Bad black boys in America. In B. P. Bowser (Ed.), *Black male adolescents: Parenting and education in community context* (pp. 91–128). Lanham, MD: University Press of America.

Lum, D. (1992). *Social work practice and people of color: A process-stage approach* (2nd ed.). Pacific Grove, CA: Brooks/Cole.

Lusane, C. (1991). *Pipe dream blues: Racism and the war on drugs.* Boston: South End Press.

Manoleas, P., & Carillo, E. (1991). A culturally syntonic approach to the field education of Latino students. *Journal of Social Work Education, 27*, 135–144.

Martin, J. M., & Martin, E. P. (1985). *The helping tradition in the black family and community.* Silver Spring, MD: National Association of Social Workers.

Mazrui, A. (1986). *The Africans: A reader.* New York: Greenwood Press.

Mbiti, J. (1970). *African religions and philosophy.* Garden City, NY: Anchor Books.

McIntyre, C. (1993). *Criminalizing a race: Free blacks during slavery.* New York: Kayode Publications.

Myers, L. J. (1988). *Understanding an Afrocentric world view: Introduction to an optimal psychology.* Dubuque, IA: Kendall/Hunt.

Myers, S. L., & Drescher, P. J. (1994, March). *The economics of violent crime.* Paper presented at the annual Black Family Conference, Hampton University, Hampton, VA.

Nichols, E. (1987, September). *Counseling perspectives for a multiethnic and pluralistic workforce.* Paper presented at the annual meeting of the National Association of Social Workers, New Orleans.

Nobles, W. W. (1980). African philosophy: Foundations for black psychology. In R. Jones (Ed.), *Black psychology* (3rd ed., pp. 23–35). New York: Harper & Row.

Oliver, W. (1989). Black males and social problems: Prevention through Africentric socialization. *Journal of Black Studies, 20*, 15–39.

Phillips, F. B. (1990). NTU psychotherapy: An Afrocentric approach. *Journal of Black Psychology, 17*(1), 55–74.

Pinderhughes, E. (1989). *Understanding race, ethnicity and power.* New York: Free Press.

Rothenberg, P. (1990). The construction, deconstruction, and reconstruction of difference. *Hypatia, 5*(1), 42–57.

Saleebey, D. (Ed.). (1992). *The strengths perspective in social work practice.* New York: Longman.

Schiele, J. H. (1990). Organizational theory from an Afrocentric perspective. *Journal of Black Studies, 21*, 145–161.

Schiele, J. H. (1994). Afrocentricity as an alternative world view for equality. *Journal of Progressive Human Services, 5*(1), 5–25.

Serequeberhan, T. (Ed.). (1991). *African philosophy: The essential readings.* New York: Paragon House.

Sudarkasa, N. (1988). Interpreting the African heritage in Afro-American family organization. In H. P. McAdoo (Ed.), *Black families* (2nd ed., pp. 27–43). Beverly Hills, CA: Sage Publications.

Terman, L. M. (1916). *The measurement of intelligence.* Boston: Houghton Mifflin.

U.S. Bureau of the Census. (1994). *Statistical abstract of the United States.* Washington, DC: U.S. Government Printing Office.

U.S. House of Representatives, Committee on Ways and Means. (1993). *Annual budget report, fiscal year 1992.* Washington, DC: U.S. Government Printing Office.

Williams, C. (1987). *The destruction of black civilization: Great issues of a race from 4500 B.C. to 2000 A.D.* Chicago: Third World Press.

Wilson, A. (1990). *Black-on-black violence: The psychodynamics of black self-annihilation in the service of white domination.* New York: Afrikan World Infosystems.

Zahan, D. (1979). *The religion, spirituality, and thought of traditional Africa.* Chicago: University of Chicago Press.

An earlier version of this chapter was presented at the Sixth Annual Chiekh Anta Diop Conference, October 1994, Philadelphia.

6   Culturally Informed Social Work Practice with American Indian Clients: Guidelines for Non-Indian Social Workers

Edith Ellison Williams and Florence Ellison

S ocial agencies mandated to provide services to American Indian populations are staffed predominantly by non-Indian social workers whose professional education may not have provided the tools to deliver culturally appropriate services. In a study of American Indian cultural factors in the interaction between Indian clients and non-Indian professionals (Miller, 1982), 65 percent of the professionals indicated that during client interviews there was no discussion related to Indian culture. Fifteen percent indicated that they did not need to ask for more cultural information to effectively provide services. Those who indicated the need for more cultural information stated that they did not know how much weight to place on cultural characteristics and were uncomfortable with gathering the information.

Alcoholism, child neglect, diabetes, incest, spiritual loss, suicide, and unemployment are but a few of the problems facing American Indians at disproportionate rates. Social workers must be prepared to address these issues while designing interventions for clients who may distrust the very agency they have come to for help. Fundamental to this process is the ability to design culturally sound interventions (Coggins, 1991; Locust, 1988; Yukl, 1986). This article provides guidelines that can assist social workers in this task.

AMERICAN INDIAN CULTURE

American Indian educators and health care practitioners maintain that interventions are effective only when American Indian clients are encouraged to become responsible in ways that are culturally relevant (Coggins, 1990, 1991; French & Hornbuckle, 1980; Yukl, 1986). In undertaking such a task, social workers need to educate themselves about the historical traditions, beliefs, and behavioral norms of the community being served; determine an Indian client's degree of assimilation into the dominant culture; and understand what any loss of culture may represent.

This chapter was originally published in the March 1996 issue of *Social Work*, Vol. 41, pp. 147–151.

Government Policies and the Protestant Work Ethic

Historical Western attitudes have caused cultural disruption and contributed to the alienation of American Indians from the mainstream of U.S. society. Early federal government policies, such as the removal policy of 1835, which displaced Indian populations to Indian territory, and the Dawes Act (Indian General Allotment Act), which made that same land available to white settlers two years later, separated Indians from their traditional lands and roles (French & Hornbuckle, 1980). Beginning in the 1870s and continuing for the next 100 years, the removal of American Indian children from their homes, attempts to eliminate native ways, and the urban relocation program of the 1950s contributed to the image of the Indian family as impoverished and unstable (Herring, 1989). Such a depiction renders functioning kinship networks invisible and leaves unacknowledged the problems of poverty and urban displacement.

The first immigrants to North America were Protestant separatists who brought with them the values of hard work, piety, and frugality. The Protestant work ethic promoted the notion that poor people are usually indolent and in need of moral guidance (Adrian, 1990). This ethic was at odds with the American Indian tradition of sharing to strengthen social bonds (Coggins, 1991). In the Indian tradition, receiving was not stigmatized, and needy people were seldom divided into the categories of deserving and nondeserving. Left unrecognized, the rich spiritual life of the American Indian deteriorated as Western influences dominated.

Religious and Health Beliefs

Values can exert powerful influences on behavior and beliefs about what constitutes appropriate, positive, prosocial behavior in others (Coggins, 1991; Tropman, 1989). Most American Indian cultures have a high degree of integration of religious and health beliefs (Coggins, 1990); healing cannot be separated from culture or religion (Locust, 1988).

Basic to the concept of the treatment of disease among many American Indian tribes is the idea that humans are made up of body, mind, and spirit (Coggins, 1991; Locust, 1988). What may be deemed a cure by Western health care professionals (for example, the treatment of a wound) may be seen as treatment only of the symptoms by American Indians. For Indians the underlying cause of the wound may be a spiritual matter. Treating the spirit involves determining why the wound occurred; understanding the events in a spiritual rather than physical sense; and changing whatever in the body, mind, or spirit was out of harmony enough to cause the wound. Becoming well emphasizes the patient's power to overcome the illness (Locust, 1988). In contrast, Western health care professionals treat illness by removing obstacles that prevent the body from being well, and the professionals are honored for removing the obstacle.

RECOMMENDATIONS FOR SOCIAL WORK PRACTICE

Only in the past two decades have health and mental health fields witnessed a shift toward other culturally based perspectives (Beiser, 1985; French & Hornbuckle, 1980; Rogoff, 1990). There is a growing literature that places American Indians on a cultural continuum emphasizing four styles of living: traditional, marginal, middle class, and pan-Indian. Each style contributes to a sense of family (French & Hornbuckle, 1980; Miller, 1982; Red Horse, Lewis, Feit, & Decker, 1978).

Traditional American Indians

Traditionalists live in accordance with culturally prescribed customs (French & Hornbuckle, 1980; Locust, 1988; Red Horse et al., 1978). A spirit of cooperation with each other and the environment is central to their thinking. Health care for traditional American Indians must operate from an Indian value orientation. For the traditional Indian, becoming ill may be more than simply experiencing a cluster of symptoms that fit into a diagnostic category; it may also be a function of the individual's perception of being unable to adequately fulfill traditional role obligations (Locust, 1988). An intervention will need to restore physical well-being to the body and harmony to the damaged social and spiritual relationships.

American Indian clients will involve themselves in interventions they perceive to be appropriate. Involving a traditional healer may increase the desirability of an intervention. Social workers should use ceremony and ritual—two important aspects of healing—in an intervention. Giving gifts, serving food, and involving family and friends emphasize the importance of an intervention. The inclusion of family members underscores that the family is a supportive and protective unit whose help is valued.

Case Examples. Roy, age 43, visited the Indian Health Services Clinic on the reservation because he had been suffering from headaches and blurred vision. The clinic's physician diagnosed hypertension and prescribed medication. In time, as Roy experienced relief from his symptoms, he began arriving late for his appointments and then stopped coming to the clinic and taking his medication.

When the symptoms returned, Roy returned to the clinic. This time Roy was treated by the physician and a traditional healer who was on the clinic's consulting staff. Members of Roy's family were encouraged to accompany him on clinic visits and were included in ceremonies that celebrated Roy's improvement. Appointment scheduling was changed to a more flexible format that allowed Roy to walk in on Thursdays anytime during the day. This accommodated Roy's sense of time and reduced the number of missed appointments.

Andy, a 70-year-old fisherman who had lived his entire life on a reservation, was hospitalized for a work-related back injury. Andy spoke very little to the hospital staff and was an unwilling participant in his physical therapy program. He appeared disinterested and depressed and had a poor appetite. Andy received one visit from his wife, who also was generally uncommunicative.

On one occasion Andy was visited by his youngest son, who lived in Chicago. The social worker learned from the son that Andy had been a member of a highly respected drum group. By showing interest in this activity, the social worker was able to engage both father and son in conversation and discovered that Andy had not been eating because he was unfamiliar with the food served by the hospital. Andy's wife had brought him some of the traditional foods, but lack of transportation prevented her from visiting often. The social worker arranged for transportation so that she could visit twice a week. The social worker also arranged for storage of extra food in a small kitchen used by the nursing staff. Andy's doctor agreed that the food could be served along with Andy's regular meals. In time Andy became less depressed and participated in his physical therapy program.

Marginal and Middle-Class American Indians

The marginal class (French & Hornbuckle, 1980) of American Indians, caught between traditional roots and white society, is at risk for sociocultural stress because they are not fully accepted in either culture. Middle-class Indians are more likely to subscribe to Western society's way of life. As a result, they are most likely to be comfortable with Western medicine.

Social workers working with marginal and middle-class American Indians must identify those who are most likely to adhere to traditional standards of health behavior and therefore be uncomfortable with Western health care. Harwood (1981) proposed several factors that can help identify clients who are more acculturated to general Western health norms: a relatively high level of formal education, greater generational removal from the reservation, a low degree of encapsulation within a family social network, limited traveling to and from the reservation, and previous experience with Western health care in the immediate family.

In planning interventions, social workers need to remember that marginal Indians, especially those in urban settings, must be able to cope effectively with the value constraints of the majority culture as well as with those of their own. Care needs to be taken to elicit the Indian client's concept of his or her problem in a way that is not judgmental and that communicates genuine interest in the response. Social workers who are aware of how much of a role traditional culture plays in an Indian client's life will be better able to design a program or treatment modality that fits that individual's lifestyle.

Case Example. Maggie, age 36, was brought by her husband to the psychiatric emergency room of an urban hospital because of suicidal ideation. She was being treated for major depression by the hospital's depression clinic with antidepressants and individual psychotherapy. Maggie was seen by the emergency room psychiatric social worker, who determined that Maggie and her parents had always lived in the city and that Maggie was currently enrolled in graduate school. This information indicated to the social worker that Maggie was probably accustomed to Western norms.

At first Maggie had great difficulty speaking to the social worker. Therefore, with Maggie's permission, her husband was also included. He reported that two days ago Maggie learned that as a youngster her grandfather had been forcibly removed from his parents' home and sent to a boarding school in another state, where he stayed until age 18. Her grandfather was not allowed to speak his native language and had no contact with his parents. He was severely punished for any display of his Indian heritage and became ashamed of being an American Indian. As an adult he refused to teach Maggie's father about tribal ways because he wished to spare his own child shame. As a result, his cultural heritage was lost.

The conversation had a profound effect on Maggie. It became clear to the social worker that Maggie was now uncomfortable in both mainstream and native cultures. By encouraging Maggie to search for her cultural roots, the social worker was able to support feelings of pride in her newfound heritage. This lessened Maggie's suicidal feelings and allowed her to plan with her husband for her safety until she was able to see her outpatient therapist.

Pan-Indians

Pan-Indians struggle to re-establish lost traditions in a way that encompasses tribal variation (Hall, 1986; Red Horse et al., 1978). For both reservation and marginal Indians, pan-Indianism represents a reformation of tradition. Belief systems are enlarged to include the mixing of several traditional forms while avoiding activities of the dominant society (French & Hornbuckle, 1980; Hall, 1986). Pan-Indianism is characteristic of multitribe groups who are more likely to accept traditional rituals that have been practiced by members of other tribes (Hall, 1986). Pan-Indian families are the least likely to use Western health and mental health agencies (Red Horse et al., 1978).

The ability of social workers to integrate Western medicine and psychological skills with traditional arts and beliefs is of primary importance. Such an ability requires trust in another mode of healing and different cultural beliefs and an understanding that use of tradition may in fact facilitate an accommodation to contemporary society (Hall, 1986). Accordingly, interventions should incorporate only those treatment approaches that are useful and acceptable to the client.

Case Example. John, age 12, had been referred to the school social worker by his teacher because he was not doing well in school and had become disruptive in the classroom. The social worker, who had made several unsuccessful attempts to engage John and his family in therapy, learned that the boy's father regularly attended the sweat lodge, a small, circular, ceremonial structure with heated rocks at the center. Participants sit along the outer edge facing the center. The ceremony is divided into several rounds, each of which consists of sprinkling water on the heated rocks and reciting prayers. The sweat physically cleanses the participants and induces a state of serenity. The central purpose of this ceremony is to bring each participant closer to the Creator and to reaffirm human kinship with all living beings (Hall, 1986). The social worker encouraged John's father to take him to the ceremony. The result was an enhancement of the father–son relationship and a reduction in disruptive classroom behavior.

CONCLUSION

Social work health and mental health interventions directed toward American Indians must be harmonious with the client's environment and degree of acculturation. The following guidelines will help social workers in their endeavors:

1. Listen for opportunities to show desire to learn about American Indian traditions.
2. Determine what importance Indian culture may assume in ongoing care.
3. Design interventions that are sensitive to the value constraints of both traditional and Western cultures.
4. Aim interventions at restoring a balance between physical well-being and spiritual harmony.
5. Emphasize the present and problem-solving skills.
6. Involve the Indian community in the planning and implementation of programs.
7. Understand the Indian client's definition of illness, and fit the intervention with that definition.
8. Include ceremony and ritual in interventions when appropriate.
9. Consult with traditional healers.
10. Include peers, family members, and community representatives in interventions when appropriate.

Historically, American Indians have felt that the loss of their freedom to express themselves in traditional ways is an undeserved oppression. Ethnocentrism, seen through the eyes of American Indians, is based on the premise that Western ways are superior to Indian ways. Interventions that involve Indian planning and implementation have the best chance for succeeding because they are likely to be more culturally appropriate.

REFERENCES

Adrian, F. (1990). *The Protestant work ethic.* New York: Routledge.
Beiser, M. (1985). The grieving witch: A framework for applying principles of cultural psychiatry to clinical practice. *Canadian Journal of Psychiatry, 30,* 130–141.
Coggins, K. (1990). *Alternative pathways to healing: The recovery medicine wheel.* Deerfield Beach, FL: Health Communications.
Coggins, K. (1991). *Cultural considerations in social program planning among American Indians.* Unpublished manuscript, School of Social Work, University of Michigan, Ann Arbor.

French, L., & Hornbuckle, J. (1980). Alcoholism among Native Americans: An analysis. *Social Work, 25,* 275–280.

Hall, R. L. (1986). Alcohol treatment in American Indian populations: An indigenous treatment modality compared with traditional approaches. *Annals of the New York Academy of Sciences, 472,* 168–178.

Harwood, A. (1981). *Ethnicity and medical care.* Cambridge, MA: Harvard University Press.

Herring, R. (1989). The American Native family: Dissolution by coercion. *Journal of Multicultural Counseling and Development, 17*(1), 4–13.

Locust, C. (1988). Wounding the spirit: Discrimination and traditional American Indian belief systems. *Harvard Educational Review, 58,* 315–330.

Miller, N. B. (1982). Social work services to urban Indians. In J. W. Green (Ed.), *Cultural awareness in the human services* (pp. 157–183). Englewood Cliffs, NJ: Prentice Hall.

Red Horse, J. G., Lewis, R., Feit, M., & Decker, J. (1978). Family behavior of urban American Indians. *Social Casework, 59,* 67–72.

Rogoff, B. (1990). *Apprenticeship in thinking.* New York: Oxford University Press.

Tropman, J. E. (1989). *American values and social welfare: Cultural contradictions in the welfare state.* Englewood Cliffs, NJ: Prentice Hall.

Yukl, T. (1986). Cultural responsiveness and social work practice: An Indian clinic's success. *Health & Social Work, 11,* 223–229.

7

Indigenous People in a Multicultural Society: Unique Issues for Human Services

Hilary N. Weaver

Discussions of a multicultural America abound in professional literature and popular media. Projections for increasing the diversity and the "browning" of America are plentiful as we approach 2000. There are many discussions about the changing waves of immigrants and their social services needs, but less commentary is devoted to the original inhabitants of North America, the Native Americans.

Human services providers who work with Native Americans must understand the unique issues of indigenous people in a multicultural society. Many people are not aware that the federal government and some state governments have specific moral and legal rights and responsibilities toward Native Americans, unlike other groups in the United States (Deloria & Lytle, 1984; Spicer, 1992). This chapter examines the unique status of indigenous peoples in the United States and explores the practice implications of that status. The chapter begins with an overview of the components of culturally competent social work with Native Americans, then examines specific issues with which social workers and other human services workers should be familiar to serve Native American clients effectively.

CULTURALLY COMPETENT SOCIAL WORK PRACTICE

For human services providers to be effective in their work with Native Americans, they must become culturally competent. Cultural competence can be summarized with three major principles: (1) The human services provider must be knowledgeable about the group in question, (2) the human services provider must be able to be self-reflective and to recognize biases within himself or herself and within the profession, and (3) the human services provider must be able to integrate this knowledge and reflection with practice skills (Browne, Broderick, & Fong, 1993; Sue, Arredondo, & McDavis, 1992; Weaver, 1997; Weaver & Wodarski, 1995).

The knowledge component of cultural competence must include a sense of the history of Indian people, their values, and their norms. Given the diversity of American Indians, it is important that human services providers be knowledgeable about the specific tribe or nation

This chapter was originally published in the May 1998 issue of *Social Work*, Vol. 43, pp. 203–211.

of the client. Accurate information on specific Native American groups can best be obtained from the groups themselves. The practitioner should begin by asking the client about his or her cultural background and the role that cultural identity plays in his or her life. In addition, most reservations and urban areas have social services and cultural agencies that are willing to provide information to practitioners working with Native Americans. Such organizations also may sponsor relevant workshops and conferences.

In addition to possessing and applying technical knowledge, many professions such as social work require that practitioners demonstrate a type of artistry to be truly competent (Schon, 1987). This artistry is developed through self-reflection. Many authors who discuss cultural competence emphasize the importance of social workers' ability to reflect on their own cultural backgrounds, to examine their biases and behaviors, and to analyze the implications of these factors for interactions with others (Chau, 1992; Hardy & Laszloffy, 1992; McRae & Johnson, 1991; Ridley, Mendoza, & Kanitz, 1994; Seliger, 1989; Van Soest, 1994). Recognition of biases begins with self-reflection. Human services providers must look critically at their own belief systems, values, and worldview and the ways in which they affect practice.

Similarly, it is important for social workers to reflect on the belief systems, values, and worldview inherent in the models and theories used within human services. A practitioner's discipline shapes the way that a situation is viewed and interpreted (Schon, 1987). Issues such as what is labeled as a problem, the origin of problems, the target of interventions, appropriate interventions, and desired outcomes are all grounded in a particular belief system that may be incongruent with the belief system of the client. For example, terms such as "enmeshment" and "codependency" have taken on negative connotations in the human services vocabulary (Anderson, 1994; Barker, 1991; Collins, 1993; Dell & Appelbaum, 1977; Miller, 1994; Murata, 1989; Prest & Protinsky, 1993; Troise, 1993). The negative connotations of these terms are based on assumptions about the desirability of independence, a trait that is highly valued in the dominant society. Within Native American cultures, interdependence is valued. Connections and close relationships between people are highly prized. The group is more important than the individual. Assessments and interventions must take into account the cultural norms of the client rather than assuming that models and theories fit all clients equally.

Knowledge and self-reflection must be integrated with practice skills to achieve cultural competence. For example, a human services provider can use knowledge about the value that many Native Americans place on interdependence, combine this with reflection on his or her own feelings about dependence and independence, and use practice skills to develop a culturally congruent intervention plan. An in-depth discussion of the self-reflection and skill components of cultural competence is beyond the scope of this chapter. (For fuller discussions of these topics, see Burstow, 1991; Chau, 1992; Hardy &

Laszloffy, 1992; Lammert, 1986; McRae & Johnson, 1991; Ridley, Mendoza, & Kanitz, 1994; Schon, 1987; Seliger, 1989; Swenson, 1988; Van Soest, 1994; and Wesselkamper, 1983.)

KNOWLEDGE BASE FOR CULTURAL COMPETENCE

The material discussed in this chapter adds to the knowledge base necessary for culturally competent practice with Indian people. The following is a discussion of four major areas of which practitioners should be aware to work effectively with Native Americans: (1) history, (2) citizenship, (3) cultural identity, and (4) sovereignty. Practice implications follow from these areas.

History

Estimates of the population of North America at the time of initial contact vary from around 1 million to 18 million (Stiffarm & Lane, 1992). Slavery, disease, introduction of alcohol, warfare, and the federal policy of forced removal from traditional lands all contributed to the devastation of American Indian populations. Most population estimates indicate that between 95 percent and 99 percent of the indigenous population was wiped out between 1500 and 1900. Even by the most conservative estimates, the population decreased by two-thirds during this time (Stiffarm & Lane, 1992).

Historical trauma and unresolved grief are a legacy with which many Indian people struggle today. Although discussed less frequently than the Holocaust in Europe, the genocide that took place in the Americas was no less devastating. American Indian nations experienced decimation of their numbers and sometimes complete extermination. Initial decimation was caused by diseases that had been previously unknown in the Americas. Although some epidemics may have been started accidentally, Stiffarm and Lane (1992) cited evidence that both Britons and Americans deliberately used biological warfare against American Indian nations as a strategy of war.

Forced relocation of Native American people led to further decimation. The Trail of Tears is the most famous of many relocations. In 1838, the U.S. military forced the "Five Civilized Tribes" of the Southeast to march to Oklahoma to clear the way for white settlement. Many died of disease, exposure, and malnutrition along the way. Eight thousand, or nearly 50 percent of the Cherokees that had survived earlier epidemics, failed to survive the Trail. Six thousand, or 15 percent, of the Choctaws died. Approximately 50 percent of the Creeks and Seminoles died. The Chickasaws suffered severe losses as well. The Navajos suffered a similar relocation known as the Long Walk. After 9,000 Navajos surrendered to Kit Carson in 1868, 3,500 died in captivity (Stiffarm & Lane, 1992).

Genocide continued through warfare and massacres. "By the mid-19th century, U.S. policymakers and military commanders were stating—openly, frequently, and in plain English—that their objective was no less than the 'complete extermination' of any native people who resisted being dispossessed of their lands, subordinated to federal authority, and assimilated into the colonizing culture" (Stiffarm & Lane, 1992, p. 34).

After the Civil War, U.S. policies began to shift from physical genocide to cultural genocide. Because adults were often viewed as recalcitrant and beyond help, policy efforts focused on redeeming American Indian children by taking them from their families, often by force, and assimilating them into the American way of life through boarding schools based on a military model. Most Native Americans have been affected, either directly or indirectly, by a legacy of boarding schools that broke apart families and forbade the speaking of American Indian languages, practicing of traditions, and expression of spirituality (Weaver & Yellow Horse Brave Heart, in press). Individuals who were taken to boarding schools had minimal contact with their families, leaving generations of Indian people with no role models for parenting. The physical, sexual, and emotional abuse that was common in the schools initiated a vicious cycle of poor parenting practices and child abuse (Morrisette, 1994). Even individuals who did not experience the boarding schools or other traumas themselves have been affected because of the pervasive influence of these events on native populations. The last of the government-run boarding schools closed in the 1970s. Some religious denominations continue to run voluntary boarding schools on various reservations.

Boarding schools have left a devastating legacy of sexual abuse in Canada and the United States. As they matured, some victims became perpetrators and preyed on people in their own communities. In some Indian communities in Canada, 80 percent to 90 percent of the population has reported being sexually abused (Canadian Broadcasting Corporation, 1990). In Alkali Lake, British Columbia, helping professionals were brought in to conduct survivors groups to help deal with the extreme pain and dysfunction in the Indian community. Mutual support was mobilized, and survivors who had begun to heal were able to help others who had not yet begun their journey.

Suspicion and mistrust are natural outcomes and important survival skills for people who have experienced attempts at genocide. Many interactions with the dominant society have had dire consequences for Native Americans. Practitioners and program planners who seek to work with Indian people must realize that their helping interventions may be viewed within this context. Patience, perseverance, and working with clients around concrete issues are ways in which social workers can begin to establish a trusting relationship with American Indian clients (Good Tracks, 1973).

Trauma experienced by generations of Native Americans has led to unresolved grief in many cases (Brave Heart-Jordan & DeBruyn, 1995). Social workers and community activists are beginning to address this grief directly through community and group-based interventions that recognize the trauma and review its implications for contemporary issues such as family violence, substance abuse, and suicide. The Bigfoot Memorial Ride in December 1990 memorialized the events leading to the massacre at Wounded Knee, South Dakota. People on horseback retraced the steps that the leader Bigfoot and his people had taken before being slaughtered by the U.S. 7th Calvary in 1890. The ride was viewed as bringing acknowledgment and closure to a 100-year period of mourning. It was also an acknowledgment and celebration of survival.

Because much of the trauma experienced by Native Americans has been perpetrated on them as a group, many of the interventions used to address these issues have been done on a group or community level. Also, American Indian identity is grounded in a sense of group membership, which makes this type of intervention appropriate. Ideally, issues of trauma should be addressed by the people within a native context. Community healing projects such as those described in British Columbia and South Dakota are becoming more common.

It is possible, however, for social workers who are working with individual Native American clients to begin to address issues of trauma. This important work can be started even when the social worker is non-native, although Native American–sponsored community-based interventions may be desirable as referrals or as the intervention of choice where available. First the social worker must be aware of the extent of the Native Americans' trauma so that he or she can include historical grief as one of many factors in the assessment process. The social worker can then explore the relationship between historical grief and the current presenting problem. Validation of grief can be an important healing tool.

Citizenship

No single criterion exists for determining who is an American Indian. Each Indian nation sets its own criteria for membership. Some nations require that a person document a certain percentage of Native American heritage to be considered a member. This criterion is referred to as "blood quantum." Some nations require that ancestry be traced to someone who was on a tribal census in a particular year. Other nations trace descent only through the mother or only through the father. Criteria for citizenship in Indian nations may or may not be directly linked to biological heritage or cultural identification. Only the nations themselves are capable of setting standards for citizenship, and these standards are subject to change just like any other policy. The federal government has no right to determine who is a member of an American Indian nation, but it does set criteria to identify who is Indian for the purposes of federal programs. These standards typically include measures of blood quantum and vary from program to program (Jaimes, 1992).

Citizens of American Indian nations are "enrolled" or listed on the tribal roles. Enrollment provides access to a variety of social and health benefits through the nations and through the federal government and some state governments as fulfillment of treaty obligations. Many American Indians are not enrolled for one reason or another.

They may have Native American heritage yet not meet the enrollment criteria of a particular nation. In addition, some individuals who qualify for enrollment may not have completed the necessary paperwork. This is particularly common for American Indians who have been adopted by non-Indian people or who were raised away from an American Indian land base.

In the 1950s the federal government adopted a policy of terminating Indian nations through legal proceedings that ended any recognition by the federal government that certain nations exist. In addition, more than 100 identifiable American Indian groups never have been recognized (Porter, 1983). Lack of recognition frequently means lack of access to benefits and services designed for native people.

Many nonrecognized nations are fighting to have their rights recognized or reinstated. The Menominee were successful in having their termination overturned in part because of the efforts of Ada Deer, a Menominee social worker who was later appointed by President Clinton to head the Bureau of Indian Affairs. A strong tradition of advocacy exists in the social work profession. In addition to recognizing and addressing issues on a clinical level, social workers can assist Native Americans on a macro level.

The varying standards of who is considered an American Indian are relevant in determining eligibility for services through various nations and through federal and state governments. Someone who is enrolled may be eligible for a variety of health and social services that are not available to nonenrolled people or non-native people. For example, services may be available through the Indian Health Service. Also, enrolled individuals are covered by the Indian Child Welfare Act of 1978. Under this act, Indian nations and organizations often have jurisdiction over any child welfare case involving a native child. (For a full discussion of the act and its implications, consult Johnson, 1981; Mannes, 1995; and Weaver & White, 1997.)

An individual who does not have citizenship in an Indian nation may struggle with his or her sense of identity and self-esteem. Lack of citizenship not only means inability to participate in political processes and lack of access to social and health benefits, but may also imply that an individual's place in the community is unclear, if that individual is accepted as a community member at all. The struggles are likely to be most severe if the individual is recognized neither by his or her nation as a member nor by the United States as an American Indian. Individuals recognized within their own nations may have a strong enough grounding and support network that lack of outside recognition is less problematic. Practitioners must be aware of these stresses around identity issues as potential areas for work.

Cultural Identity

American Indians usually identify themselves according to their particular nation rather than as members of a broad category such as Native American or American Indian. For some people, membership in a band or a clan may be equally or more important than membership in a nation as a primary source of identity. Bands or clans are groups of extended family networks, often labeled with the name of an animal such as eel or hawk. In some cases a sense of commonality and pan-Indian identification has developed among Native Americans. This form of identification may be particularly common in urban areas where people from various nations have come into contact with each other.

Although there is no agreement about appropriate labels, when speaking generally of American Indians rather than of a specific nation, it is best to remember that we are talking about people rather than objects or commodities, and therefore, terms that use the word "people" (Indian people, native people, indigenous people, first nations people) may be the most appropriate. When speaking of a specific nation such as Lakota, Onondaga, or Nez Perce, use of these specific labels generally is preferable to a broader term. When working with a specific client, asking about that client's preference of terms communicates respect.

A sense of connection to the land is a primary factor in the psychological makeup of Indian people. As the land is alienated, social cohesion erodes (Deloria & Lytle, 1984). Connection to the land is intimately intertwined with native religion, values, culture, and lifestyle. Loss of land presents enormous challenges for maintenance of culture.

Not all Indian people are equally connected to their heritage. Some, often through force and sometimes through choice, have taken on the values and norms of the dominant society to some degree. Others have maintained traditional values and ways of life. Many who have maintained traditional spiritual and healing practices will not openly discuss these practices because of their private nature, because of fear of exploitation and prejudice, and because of a long history of persecution for their beliefs.

Some American Indian groups have maintained their cultural identity while appearing to blend into the dominant society. Small family groups of Indian people remained in the eastern United States after forced removal by the U.S. military. To survive, these people took on the outward appearance of white people, yet were able to maintain their cultures (Porter, 1983). Theories of assimilation and acculturation initially developed by anthropologists but also generally accepted by members of the dominant society stated that mixing (both socially and biologically) between Indian peoples and other ethnic groups would eventually result in the loss of Indian culture. Those who are not seen as having easily identifiable native characteristics or phenotypical features often have been assumed not to be Indian, yet this is not necessarily an accurate reflection of cultural identity (Porter, 1983). In addition, it is possible for people to identify with more than one culture (Oetting & Beauvais, 1991; Weaver, 1996). This may happen because of mixed ethnic heritage or through extensive exposure to other cultures.

Practitioners must do a thorough assessment that includes cultural dimensions. Some American Indians are connected to their culture, others are not. Some identify with a blend of Indian cultures (pan-Indianness) or with an Indian culture and a non-Indian culture. An appropriate cultural assessment is important in planning and implementing a culturally appropriate intervention.

Whereas a variety of tools have been developed to assess cultural identity, the majority have not been normed with Native American clients. Many such assessment tools rely heavily on language usage as a primary indicator of attachment to culture. Although such measures may be appropriate for members of immigrant groups who made choices about language retention or adoption of English, these tools do not fit as well for Indian peoples, who often lost language abilities, not through a choice to assimilate but through assimilation policies that they were subjected to against their will.

A few notable exceptions of cultural assessment tools designed for Indian people exist. The Tri-Ethnic Center for Prevention Research at Colorado State University has developed a cultural assessment scale normed for American Indian children. Their concept of cultural identity is based on an orthogonal model. A strong identification with one culture does not necessarily limit identification with another culture. Generally, identification with a cultural group has been found to have positive implications for well-being. Using this model, social workers have applied groupwork interventions based in life-skills training to enhance the cultural identification of Indian children. Fuller discussions of this model and implications of cultural identity for substance abuse and health issues can be found in Oetting and Beauvais (1991) and Weaver (1996).

Another notable example of a cultural assessment scale normed for American Indians is the work of Cross at Portland State University. A full critique of this work, including an exploration of its validity, reliability, and how social workers can apply this cultural assessment scale with native people, can be found in Long and Nelson (in press).

Sovereignty

Sovereignty is the most basic principle of American Indian law, yet the U.S. courts have a mixed record of upholding it (Wilkinson, 1987). The inherent sovereignty of Indian nations, equal to that of foreign nations, is recognized in the commerce clause of the Constitution of the United States. The Supreme Court reaffirmed this sovereignty in *Cherokee Nation v. Georgia* (1831) (Deloria & Lytle, 1984; Porter, 1983; Wald, 1992). The 1924 Indian Citizenship Act bestowed U.S. citizenship on Indian peoples without infringing on the rights that they enjoy as citizens of Indian nations, essentially amounting to dual citizenship (Deloria & Lytle, 1984). It should be noted that not all Indian people desire or accept U.S. citizenship.

Historically, most American Indians expressed a strong desire to remain apart from the dominant society as a way of protecting the people. Many moved westward in an attempt to escape Western civilization (Deloria & Lytle, 1984). One aim of most treaties was to keep land for Indian people separate and apart from the rest of the United States. The dominant society has seen reservations as epitomizing poverty, but for many Indian people, reservations constitute homelands that provide an opportunity for self-preservation (Wilkinson, 1987). Emerging nationalism in the 1960s led to an emphasis on preserving culture, language, religious freedom, norms, self-determination, and ways of healing (Deloria & Lytle, 1984; Morris, 1992).

The issue of sovereignty places American Indians in a unique position relative to other groups of color in the United States. Indigenous people are not just ethnic or cultural minorities within a larger society (Morris, 1992). The unique historical relationship between Indian people and the United States has led to distinct social policies, programs, and obligations unlike those that apply to any other group. Examples of such policies and programs include the Indian Child Welfare Act of 1978 and the Indian Health Service.

Tremendous variation exists in how Indian people identify themselves (Green, 1995; Red Horse, 1978; Weaver, 1996). Some identify themselves only as members of Indian nations and reject membership in a multicultural society. Others consider themselves to be citizens of the United States and take pride in their role in a multicultural society. Some identify many issues that they hold in common with other people of color, but others reject all commonalities. The place of Indian people within the United States is varied and complex.

Within Indian nations there are divisions over the meaning of sovereignty. For some people, sovereignty is a concept related primarily to identity and self-determination. It represents the ability to be free from the reach of colonizing powers. For others, sovereignty is a key to economic freedom because it can include the right to sell items such as gasoline and tobacco without state taxation, and it can include operation of gambling casinos without state regulation.

The sovereignty of Indian nations has specific implications for human services. Practitioners, particularly those working for states, should be aware that their agencies may not have jurisdiction over local American Indian children. Tribal social services or urban Indian social welfare agencies usually bear the responsibility for these children unless they have specifically delegated this responsibility to the state or another agency. This principle of sovereignty is reinforced by the Indian Child Welfare Act of 1978. When a case involves an Indian child, a practitioner should check with the child's nation or an urban Indian social services agency to clarify who should provide services. Native nations have the power to make and enforce their own laws through tribal police and court systems. If a client is involved in a domestic violence situation, probation or parole, or other legal matter, consultation with an Indian organization about applicable laws and policies is recommended. The provision of services through Indian nations may also mean that a client is eligible for additional services not available to non-natives.

CONCLUSION

Indian people have a unique place within a multicultural society. The history of indigenous people in the United States differs from those who came as immigrants. For many, a primary goal has been self-preservation through separation and isolation rather than seeking a place within a multicultural society. Issues such as historical trauma, citizenship, sovereignty, and cultural identity have implications for the provision of culturally competent human services to native people. The primary goal of this chapter has been to raise practitioners' awareness of the unique status of Native Americans within a multicultural society so that they can provide informed, quality services to native clients.

REFERENCES

Anderson, S. C. (1994). A critical analysis of the concept of codependency. *Social Work, 39,* 677–685.

Barker, R. (1991). *The social work dictionary* (2nd ed.). Silver Spring, MD: National Association of Social Workers.

Brave Heart-Jordan, M., & DeBruyn, L. (1995). So she may walk in balance: Integrating the impact of historical trauma in the treatment of American Indian women. In J. Adelman & G. Enguidanos (Eds.), *Racism in the lives of women: Testimony, theory, and guides to antiracist practice* (pp. 345–368). Binghamton, NY: Haworth Press.

Browne, C., Broderick, A., & Fong, R. (1993). Lessons from the field: Social work practice with multicultural elders. *Educational Gerontology, 19,* 511–523.

Burstow, B. (1991). Freirian codifications and social work education. *Journal of Social Work Education, 27*(2), 196–207.

Canadian Broadcasting Corporation. (1990). *Circle of healing: Breaking the silence.* Man Alive Series.

Chau, K. L. (1992). Educating for effective group work practice in multicultural environments of the 1990s. *Journal of Multicultural Social Work, 1*(4), 1–15.

Collins, B. G. (1993). Reconstructing codependency using self-in-relation theory: A feminist perspective. *Social Work, 38,* 470–476.

Dell, P. F., & Appelbaum, A. S. (1977). Trigenerational enmeshment: Unresolved ties of single parents to family of origin. *American Journal of Orthopsychiatry, 47,* 52–59.

Deloria, V., Jr., & Lytle, C. (1984). *The nations within: The past and future of American Indian sovereignty.* New York: Pantheon Books.

Good Tracks, J. G. (1973). Native American non-interference. *Social Work, 18*(6), 30–35.

Green, J. W. (1995). *Cultural awareness in the human services.* Englewood Cliffs, NJ: Prentice Hall.

Hardy, K. V., & Laszloffy, T. A. (1992). Training racially sensitive family therapists: Context, content, and contact. *Families in Society, 73,* 364–370.

Indian Child Welfare Act of 1978, P.L. 95-608, 92 Stat. 3069.

Jaimes, M. A. (1992). Federal Indian identification policy: A usurpation of indigenous sovereignty in North America. In M. A. Jaimes (Ed.), *The state of Native America: Genocide, colonization, and resistance* (pp. 123–138). Boston: South End Press.

Johnson, B. B. (1981). The Indian Child Welfare Act. *Child Welfare, 60,* 435–445.

Lammert, M. (1986). Experience as knowing: Utilizing therapist self-awareness. *Social Casework, 67,* 369–376.

Long, C., & Nelson, K. (in press). Native American culture and the validity and reliability of a resiliency scale. *Journal of Human Behavior in the Social Environment.*

Mannes, M. (1995). Factors and events leading to the passage of the Indian Child Welfare Act. *Child Welfare, 74,* 264–282.

McRae, M. B., & Johnson, S. D., Jr. (1991). Toward training for competence in multicultural counselor education. *Journal of Counseling and Development, 70*(1), 131–135.

Miller, K. J. (1994). The co-dependency concept: Does it offer a solution for the spouses of alcoholics? *Journal of Substance Abuse Treatment, 11,* 339–345.

Morris, G. T. (1992). International law and politics: Toward a right to self-determination for indigenous peoples. In M. A. Jaimes (Ed.), *The state of Native America: Genocide, colonization, and resistance* (pp. 55–86). Boston: South End Press.

Morrisette, P. J. (1994). The holocaust of first nation people: Residual effects on parenting and treatment implications. *Contemporary Family Therapy, 16,* 381–392.

Murata, J. M. (1989). *Family values, delinquency and the Mexican American family in the U.S.* [American Sociological Association document delivery service.]

Oetting, E. R., & Beauvais, F. (1991). Orthogonal cultural identification theory: The cultural identification of minority adolescents. *International Journal of the Addictions, 25*(5A & 6A), 655–685.

Porter, F. W., III. (1983). *Nonrecognized American Indian tribes: An historical and legal perspective* (Occasional Papers Series 7). Chicago: Newbury Library.

Prest, L. A., & Protinsky, H. (1993). Family systems theory: A unifying framework for codependence. *American Journal of Family Therapy, 21,* 352–360.

Red Horse, J. (1978). Family behavior of urban American Indians. *Social Casework, 59,* 67–72.

Ridley, C. R., Mendoza, D. W., & Kanitz, B. E. (1994). Multicultural training: Reexamination, operationalization, and integration. *Counseling Psychologist, 22,* 227–289.

Schon, D. A. (1987). *Educating the reflective practitioner: Toward a new design for teaching and learning in the professions.* San Francisco: Jossey-Bass.

Seliger, J. (1989). A model curriculum for mental health paraprofessionals. In P. S. Denise & I. M. Harris (Eds.), *Experiential education for community development* (pp. 143–154). New York: Greenwood Press.

Spicer, E. H. (1992). The nations of a state. *Boundary 2, 19*(3), 26–48.

Stiffarm, L. A., & Lane, P., Jr. (1992). The demography of native North America: A question of American Indian survival. In M. A. Jaimes (Ed.), *The state of Native America: Genocide, colonization, and resistance* (pp. 23–53). Boston: South End Press.

Sue, D. W., Arredondo, P., & McDavis, R. J. (1992). Multicultural counseling competencies and standards: A call to the profession. *Journal of Counseling & Development, 70,* 477–486.

Swenson, C. R. (1988). The professional log: Techniques for self-directed learning. *Social Casework, 69,* 307–311.

Troise, F. (1993). An overview of the historical and empirical antecedents in the development of the codependency concept. *Journal of Couples Therapy, 4*(1–2), 89–104.

Van Soest, D. (1994). Social work education for multicultural practice and social justice advocacy: A field study of how students experience the learning process. *Journal of Multicultural Social Work, 3*(1), 17–28.

Wald, P. (1992). Terms of assimilation: Legislating subjectivity in the emerging nation. *Boundary 2, 19*(3), 77–104.

Weaver, H. N. (1996). Social work with American Indian youth using the Orthogonal Model of Cultural Identification. *Families in Society, 77,* 98–107.

Weaver, H. N. (1997). The challenges of research in Native American communities: Incorporating principles of cultural competence. *Journal of Social Service Research, 23*(2), 1–15.

Weaver, H. N., & White, B. J. (1997). The Native American family circle: Roots of resiliency. *Journal of Family Social Work, 2*(1), 67–79.

Weaver, H. N., & Wodarski, J. S. (1995). Cultural issues in crisis intervention: Guidelines for culturally competent practice. *Family Therapy, 22,* 213–223.

Weaver, H. N., & Yellow Horse Brave Heart, M. (in press). Facets of American Indian identity: Implications for social work practice. *Journal of Human Behavior in the Social Environment.*

Wesselkamper, M. C. (1983). *Developing cultural awareness and sensitivity: An experiential approach.* Unpublished dissertation, City University of New York.

Wilkinson, C. F. (1987). *American Indians, time and the law.* New Haven, CT: Yale University Press.

8 Toward a Values-Based Approach to Multicultural Social Work Research

Edwina S. Uehara, Sung Sil Lee Sohng,
Raymond L. Bending, Sherri Seyfried,
Cheryl A. Richey, Paula T. Tanemura Morelli,
Michael S. Spencer, Debora M. Ortega,
Lynn Keenan, and Valli Kanuha

An approach to multicultural social work research that is values based and process oriented is being developed by the authors and other faculty and doctoral students affiliated with the Multicultural Research Group at the University of Washington School of Social Work. Members of the group share an interest in the collective creation of models of social work practice, education, and research that reflect a multicultural worldview and a commitment to collaborative work with members of disenfranchised communities—that is, groups in the United States that experience economic, social, and political disadvantage or discrimination.

In particular, the authors share a commitment to working with communities of color, women, gay men and lesbians, and socioeconomically disadvantaged groups. We believe that too many models of social science research replay and reinforce the theme of disenfranchisement, providing little opportunity for community members to shape research questions, claim ownership of data, develop findings and implications for action, and hone their own critical inquiry skills.

The approach discussed in this chapter reflects the research group's ongoing dialogue on multicultural social work research, practice, and education. It represents a work in progress. An invitation to join a panel on research and diversity at the Council on Social Work Education's 1995 Annual Planning Meeting was the impetus for clarifying and consolidating our current thoughts on multicultural research. We accepted the invitation as an opportunity to struggle with the following questions: What is multicultural social work research? And what are the benefits and challenges associated with teaching, learning, and doing it? This chapter represents a response to these questions and an invitation to other social welfare researchers to ponder these and related questions individually and collectively.

This chapter was originally published in the November 1996 issue of *Social Work*, Vol. 41, pp. 613–621.

DEFINITION OF MULTICULTURAL SOCIAL WORK RESEARCH

Multicultural social work research should meet three general criteria: (1) It should involve the researcher in a constant process of both private and public reflection on a range of issues critically affecting collaboration—from how her or his own biases and motives affect the research process to the impact of the larger political economy on the sociocultural history of disadvantaged groups; (2) it should democratize the research process, supporting a continuous process of community collaboration rather than token representation of community members in limited advisory roles; and (3) its objectives should be linked to community empowerment, social justice, and social transformation goals. The centrality of empowerment with respect to both the process and aims of research differentiates the group's approach from other applied social work research models that also emphasize cooperation with and direct benefits to communities (for example, the Design and Development Model; Rothman & Thomas, 1994). Although redressing the power imbalance between researcher and community participant is an optional feature under other applied models, it is a defining characteristic or parameter of the approach we describe in this chapter.

Our approach is "values based" because it draws on fundamental values undergirding the profession and practice of social work: social justice, equality, self-determination, and empowerment. It is "process oriented" for two reasons: First, we assume that no single act or set of finite acts performed on research makes it "multicultural"; instead, reflection and collaboration must become organic to every part of the research process (Rogler, 1989). Second, we place trust in the assumption that a process of critically reflective and collaborative inquiry can lead to social transformation.

THE ULTIMATE GOAL: SOCIAL TRANSFORMATION

The social work values of justice, equality, and empowerment are currently given strong voice in the concept of multiculturalism. Multiculturalism offers to social work both a vision of society in the 21st century and a critical perspective on culture and power. As Sohng (1994) suggested,

> A social worker operating out of a multicultural perspective does not take for granted the surface manifestations of culture. She or he questions the [societal] power relations that have historically subordinated certain groups and rationalized their marginalized status as being the result of their "cultural" deficiencies. . . . Multicultural social work entails not just the pleasure of diversity but the realities of exclusion that minority groups face. Its mission is to build bridges of understanding [that span] peoples stratified by race, class, gender, sexual orientation, language, and other social group memberships. (p. 12)

Embracing multiculturalism as we define it places social workers on the side of groups whose members experience racism, xenophobia, sexism, homophobia, classism, or other forms of oppression and exploitation and on the side of those who, by virtue of extant social structural patterns, have relatively less control than dominant groups over critical aspects of their own lives (such as the nature and product of their labor). Ours is an explicit value stance. Our conception of multiculturalism does not support a radical relativist, "anything goes" orientation toward cultural diversity. It does not support the position of groups that advocate the subjugation or oppression of others.

From our perspective, the ultimate goal of multicultural social work research, like the goal of multicultural social work practice and education, is social justice and the transformation of contemporary sociocultural structures and processes that support injustice and inequality. We do not presume that any single research project can transform contemporary society, but believe in the emancipatory potential of social action based on critical reflection, collaboration, and research and in the cumulative effect of such action. Therefore, a primary criterion for "good" multicultural social work research is that its aims should be linked to transformational goals. Multicultural research projects thus facilitate the empowerment of marginalized groups and lead to group resistance to domination and exploitation. A good example of such a linkage is provided by a recent collaborative study conducted by students, a teacher, and a social work counselor of the experiences of students of color in an elite private school (Herr, 1995). In one component of the study, students developed a systemic view of the causes and implications of racist incidents within the school that departed both from the administration's perspective and from their initial "person-blaming" framework. Students moved from personalistic, physical responses to incidents (for example, beating up white perpetrators) to creating institutional change (including courses representing a diversity of histories and establishing a formal committee to educate the school on diversity issues) (Herr, 1995).

THE PROCESS: CONTINUOUS REFLECTION AND COLLABORATION

As critical theorists point out, creating social transformation requires democratic processes of inquiry that help us understand "what is, in order to ultimately liberate us from the destiny of what has been" (Morrow, 1994, p. 320). How do we get there from here? We believe that the most promising strategy involves the researcher in a continuous process of reflection and collaboration.

Reflection

Effective collaboration with disenfranchised communities requires that the researcher personally acknowledge current discrepancies in power, status, and influence between "the researcher" and "the researched" and recognize that such discrepancies can enter into interactions between the two in numerous overt and subtle ways. To avoid importing discrepancies into the collaborative process, the researcher must be constantly aware of how her or his own values, beliefs, behaviors, and customs may distort communication and promote domination. Therefore, constant introspection or self-reflection on the part of the researcher is critical. As Pinderhughes's (1989) work on race, ethnicity, and power implied, researchers must carefully examine the personal and professional gratification they receive as a result of their status vis-à-vis disenfranchised clients and community members.

At the same time, researchers must give constant attention to how the culture of the target group or community articulates with every part of the research, from the conceptualization of research goals through the processes and products of the inquiry itself. To paraphrase Rogler (1989), the researcher must possess "an incessant, basic and active preoccupation" with the culture of the target group "throughout the process of research" (p. 296). There is an obvious parallel here with the emphasis in cross-cultural research on taking an "emic," or insider's, stance as a safeguard against drawing false parallels between one cultural group and another. However, multicultural social work research must go beyond reflection on group culture and intergroup cultural differences to critical analysis of the social, political, and cultural forces that maintain patterns of intergroup domination and inequality.

Collaboration

Democratic collaboration with disenfranchised groups is fundamental to multicultural social work research for two reasons: First, as Hartsock (1983) suggested, those who experience disenfranchisement have the most potential for analyzing and understanding what that experience is and how that experience must be transformed; experiential expertise is therefore critical to social transformation. Second, the social work values of self-determination and empowerment suggest that people have the right to exert maximum control over their own destinies.

Meaningful collaboration requires that decision making about critical aspects of the project be open and responsive to disenfranchised community members. These decisions include what questions should be asked and how findings should be used. Meaningful collaboration also requires that all participants be committed to a joint process of inquiry, which may require collaborators to engage in such nontraditional research activities as mutual consciousness-raising, empowerment, and historical analysis of problems and issues (Flick, Reese, Rogers, Fletcher, & Sonn, 1994; Rappaport et al., 1985). At the same time, traditional research tools can be applied to collaborative work. For example, focus groups have been used to define research questions and delineate criteria for evaluating study outcomes. Collaborative projects have encompassed survey research, ethnography, secondary data analysis, and even experiments.

The term "democratic collaboration" is not used here to suggest that every person on the research team need be identical in knowledge, skills, or power. Rather, the term describes a condition in which everyone on the team claims equal responsibility for and ownership of the goals and processes of the project (hooks, 1994). Multicultural social work research teams should create a working environment in which academic researchers and community members participate as equally committed members in a joint process of inquiry and feel equal responsibility to the research endeavor because of its potential benefits to the community.

Envisioning new, egalitarian partnerships requires both the academic researcher and the community member to break with old hierarchical patterns of interaction between "researcher" and "research subject." Given the subtle and ingrained nature of these patterns, their re-enactment in the research process can be very nearly autonomic, even among the best-intentioned collaborators. Thus, academics committed to community empowerment and collaboration can find themselves articulating the research question "for the community," reasoning that this makes good use of their "advanced" training. By the same token, community members who initiate a study in collaboration with academics can find themselves deferring to the latter's conception of community issues, reasoning that academics have "better skills" for such tasks.

Old patterns may be most successfully broken and new roles created when all collaborators make a clear commitment to continually scrutinize their interactions. At appropriate times, community members must be willing to call academics on their unexamined assumptions of authority and expertise. In turn, academics must be willing to be confronted on such assumptions and to take a back seat to community experts. Researcher–community partnerships are more likely to succeed if all participants share responsibility for acknowledging and discussing patterns of interpersonal conduct. In this way, the collaborative researcher strives for an equivalent voice rather than a dominant voice in the research process (Gould, 1995).

Developing collaborative partnerships with community members may be the most daunting and anxiety-producing aspect of multicultural social work research; because it requires the researcher to share control, true collaboration requires profound trust in the democratic process. Typically, very little in the researcher's training prepares her or him for this step. Indeed, most formal research training rests on the premise of maximum researcher control over all aspects of scientific inquiry. However, we do not propose that "trusting in the process" means that anything goes. To the contrary, effective collaboration requires enormous self-discipline on the part of all participants lest the promise of democratic process devolve into the tyranny of structurelessness.

No single, specific act or set of finite acts performed on research can make it democratic. Research is made more collaborative and thus more multicultural through a "continuing and open-ended series of substantive and methodological insertions and adaptations" (Rogler, 1989, p. 296). Considerations pertinent to critical reflection and collaboration become an organic part of the research process, every bit as important to the success of the enterprise as the more technical research procedures codified in traditional research texts. These considerations span the entire research process, from conceptualization of goals, planning, and analysis and interpretation of data to dissemination and action.

CHALLENGES TO AND BENEFITS OF MULTICULTURAL SOCIAL WORK RESEARCH

Challenges

Even friendly critics can point to a number of daunting challenges facing a social work researcher who attempts to follow our general model of multicultural research. Four challenges come to mind:

1. Community collaboration is time and energy consuming for community members and researchers alike. Academics who engage in this type of research will surely be "punished" for low productivity when they are being considered for tenure or promotion.
2. Collaboration and cultural reflection require many new skills such as introspection, cultural analysis, critical and historical reflection, and cross-cultural communication, which few researchers can claim to have and for which few have been trained.
3. Social work researchers and educators have few models to follow on how to teach and do good multicultural social work research and no easy answers to key questions such as, What is the target group or community? And which community members should we collaborate with? Moreover, whether collaboration and reflection can be integrated with all or only some analytic techniques, research methods, and metatheories remains to be explored.
4. The requirements for collective ownership and trust in the collaborative process are generally at odds with current research funding priorities and accepted research protocols. Reviewers of grant applications that feature continuous collaboration throughout the research process often evaluate the process as insufficiently "scientific" and more like community development than "real" research.

The assertion that community-based models of research are not adequately scientific or scholarly appears to reflect an absence of metatheoretical and methodological pluralism on the part of many funding bodies and research review panels. Instead, such negative appraisals of collaborative research models exemplify an adherence to a monolithic view of scientific inquiry that is fast becoming obsolete in the social sciences and social work (Coulton, 1995; Gambrill, 1994; Klein & Bloom, 1994). Unfortunately, even as criticisms of "traditional" research grow apace within communities of color and some sectors of academia, federal agencies appear to be much slower to reflect these trends in their research funding criteria.

The criticism that few guidelines or models exist for conducting multicultural research appears to overlook the many useful suggestions, standards, and exemplars offered by researchers in other disciplines. An important example is the guidelines and models for research put forth by participatory action and feminist researchers (Brown, 1985; Fonow & Cook, 1991; Gergen, 1988; Maguire, 1987). Another example is the standards for conducting research in cross-cultural or international contexts developed in the 1970s by Tapp, Kelman, Triandis, Wrightsman, and Coelho (1974, cited in Ponterotto, Casas, Suzuki, & Alexander, 1995).

Similarly, the argument that few social work researchers have the requisite skills needed for successful collaborative efforts appears to ignore the potential resources available in cross-cultural practice in social work and other fields. The literature delineates a range of interpersonal and group skills relevant to multicultural research, including active listening, ethnographic interviewing, consciousness raising, managing and resolving conflict, mobilizing effective small-group processes, team building, and community organizing (Brunner, 1991; Gutierrez, 1990; Leigh & Green, 1989; Merta, 1995). Thus, although these competencies may be relatively new to social work research, they are not as new to social work practice. Many of these skills can be adapted to fit the emerging demands of different kinds of collaborative researcher–community partnerships.

Benefits

We do not wish to downplay the seriousness of these and other challenges to doing and teaching multicultural research. At the same time, however, these challenges represent relatively short-term, manageable costs, which are outweighed by longer-term and more important benefits: reinforcement of principles from multicultural practice models, integration of research and action, promotion of effective community-based services, reinforcement of requirements for "good" research with diverse groups, and facilitation of meaningful community relationships.

Reinforcement of Principles from Multicultural Practice Models. A research approach that places as much emphasis on reflection, community collaboration, and transformation as on the more technical aspects of inquiry is highly consistent with models of empowerment and culturally competent social work practice. For example, "empowerment" refers to both the phenomenological development of a certain state of mind (for example, feeling competent or worthy of esteem) and to the modification of societal conditions or opportunity structures that promote the reallocation of power (Gutierrez, 1990; Simon, 1994). Contemporary models of cultural competence in social work practice embrace a value base of "cultural pluralism" that promotes mutual respect for cultural value differences among racial and ethnic groups and recognizes these differences as sources of cultural strength and vitality (Chau, 1990). Attempts to identify practitioner skills for culturally competent practice have pinpointed the importance of self-reflection on one's own ethnic and socioeconomic background and ongoing vigilance against ethnocentric practice (Ho, 1991; Pinderhughes, 1989). Thus, an important benefit of teaching and conducting multicultural research is that it models for students the kind of social work practice they should embrace and promote in the field.

Integration of Research and Action. The failure of traditional research models to engage the field-based practitioner in addressing practice concerns has long been noted in the social work literature. Like other applied or action research frameworks, our approach to multicultural social work research uses reflection, analysis, theorizing, and action, thus providing a reparative mechanism for integrating social work research, education, and practice. Moreover, as the collaborative study in a private school described earlier suggests, social work practitioners can be important partners and catalysts in projects that integrate research and community action.

Promotion of Effective Community-Based Services. The theories and practice models that evolve from multicultural research may be more relevant to practice in the future than many past theories and models that build largely on an implicit assumption of monoculturalism. The usefulness and appropriateness of practice models evolving from collaborative multicultural research are likely to be much greater, given greater community ownership and participation in the development process and the empowering influence of multicultural research on people's perceptions that their community system is capable of influence and direction.

Reinforcement of Requirements for "Good" Research with Diverse Groups. There is an excellent fit between multiculturalism and requirements for "good" research in general, given the increasingly diverse populations to which researchers must generalize. For example, increased attention to such issues as extreme response sets among cultural groups or cross-cultural construct validity can yield concrete payoffs for the researcher in terms of measurement validity and reliability and statistical power (Hui & Triandis, 1989). Indeed, multiculturalism and good applied social science research may enjoy an even closer and more complementary fit within emerging models of construct validity that stress evaluation of the process by which construct meaning has been negotiated and the consequences of meaning construction to the community at large (Messick, 1995; Sheppard, 1993).

A recent study in King County, Washington, is instructive; the study assessed the reliability, concurrent validity, and cultural appropriateness of a consumer assessment instrument under consideration for countywide implementation. The assessment was undertaken by a coalition of community agencies serving special needs consumers (consumers of color, elderly people, deaf and hard-of-hearing consumers, and gay men and lesbians) and a social work faculty member.

The study's findings and recommendations resulted in substantial changes in the instrument (Uehara, Smukler, & Bates, 1993). The revised tool showed improved reliability and validity for the county's culturally diverse consumer population. Moreover, changes appear to have improved the appropriateness of the instrument for all consumers, both special needs and mainstream (Uehara et al., 1993).

Facilitation of Meaningful Community Relationships. Finally, a multicultural research model may fit most appropriately with the growing demand among clients and communities for the democratization of research. In fact, academic researchers are already seeing an increasing demand among communities of color for collaborative, community-based research approaches. In a recent neighborhood forum held by a health coalition representing several communities of color in Seattle, for example, residents talked to researchers about the problems they had with the way research was typically conducted in their communities. They complained that too often, researchers viewed all communities as basically the same; as a result, the researchers assumed that a single program or strategy could work equally well in all locales and that the best way to develop a program was to work from general theories of behavior, design an intervention, and test it in a number of communities. The community's role in this model was that of "laboratory." They argued for a new vision of applied research in which the balance of power is shifted so that "community members have more control over the way research is done in minority communities, including which questions are asked, how programs are developed and implemented, how data [are] gathered, and how the results are interpreted and presented" (Spigner & Cheadle, 1994, p. 2).

In fact, there appears to be a growing trend among communities of color to resist involvement in research projects that are not in accord with the community's perceived needs and goals; are more beneficial to academic researchers than to community members; or are naive, heavy-handed, or exploitative (Starr, Harris, & Edwards, 1994). In the future, community willingness to participate in social work research of any kind may very well depend on how seriously researchers take such community concerns and demands for partnership.

CONCLUSION AND RECOMMENDATIONS

Meeting the challenges to multicultural social work research will require a multilevel strategy of change in which the profession closely scrutinizes current patterns of "knowledge production"—who decides how social problems are constructed, what problems are worthy of research attention, how problems are researched, and how social science resources are allocated. Key actors in knowledge production, particularly funders, schools of social work, and educational oversight and accrediting bodies, must be asked to increase their accountability to disenfranchised communities and groups.

Some critics have already called for foundations and public funding bodies to incorporate criteria related to collaboration into their funding formula. For example, Starr et al. (1994) argued that research in American Indian communities should answer questions community members want to address, be rooted in American Indian epistemology, and protect Indian people from exploitation. At least one private funding body, the Kellogg Foundation, requires that research applicants demonstrate how the proposed study will promote change in ways that will benefit the community, enhance creation of community partnerships, and strengthen collaboration among community agencies (W. K. Kellogg Foundation, 1995). Public funding bodies, including federal health and mental health institutes, should be encouraged to follow suit.

Attempts to prepare multicultural social work researchers for the 21st century must confront the deficits in existing curricula and curricular policy at all levels of training, from bachelor-level degree programs through doctoral programs. As Van Soest (1995) suggested, the "moral vision" on which multicultural research and practice rest is largely provided at the MSW level. Unfortunately, most MSW programs have had only limited success in incorporating content on diverse populations, and the diversity content that does exist is too often "naive and superficial" (McMahon & Allen-Meares, 1992).

Infusion of diversity content and multicultural perspectives into social work doctoral-level curricula and training may be even more problematic at this time. For example, although the Council on Social Work Education's curriculum and accreditation standards appear to support multiculturalism as we have defined it, the *Guidelines for Quality in Social Work Doctoral Programs* (Task Force on Quality Doctoral Education, 1992) does not spell out the need for multicultural research training. Thus, an important next step for social work educators is the development of clear and consistent policies in support of multicultural research training at the doctoral level and support for infusion of diversity content into curricula at all degree levels.

Schools of social work should also consider modifying current incentives and supports for collaboration between faculty and community representatives. For example, hiring, promotion, and merit considerations for faculty should acknowledge the additional time investment required for developing and maintaining academic–community ties and give credit to the variety of products that emerge from these collaborative ventures in addition to peer-reviewed articles (for example, community training curricula, public service videos and other media, letters to the editor, service innovations, and changes in service policy). Small grant programs within universities could give greater priority to such collaborative projects. Finally, in those institutions where merit and promotion are tied to community service as well as scholarship, collaborative researchers could receive credit in both categories.

Perhaps most important, the challenges to multicultural social work research require progressive social workers to explicitly acknowledge the political and ideological debate surrounding the value of multiculturalism in the United States. The future development, or decline, of multicultural social work research will occur in a politically and intellectually contentious environment. As Van Soest (1995) implied, this contention is not primarily about research methods and technical skills, although overt clashes often arise around such topics. More fundamentally, the conflict concerns differing moral visions "over the meaning of America, who we have been in the past, who we are now, and perhaps most important who we, as a nation, will aspire to become in the new millennium" (Hunter, cited in Van Soest, 1995, p. 56).

In contrast to the ideological position the Multicultural Research Group supports, neoconservatives within academia have launched a sophisticated assault on multiculturalism in education (Bloom, 1987; D'Souza, 1992). As Rosaldo (1989) suggested, this "academic warfare" should not be trivialized: "At stake . . . are competing political and intellectual visions. What should count as knowledge and critical thought in the education of our country's future generations? How can we prepare students to enter the changing multicultural world of the coming century?" (pp. 218–219).

In such an environment, with many critical issues at stake, we agree with others who call on advocates of a progressive view of multiculturalism to actively encourage a broader, deeper debate on multiculturalism (Van Soest, 1995). This debate might also include a closer inspection of the usefulness of current conceptualizations of multiculturalism vis-à-vis the value of somewhat less ambiguous constructs of race, socioeconomic status, ethnicity, gender, and sexual orientation (Helms, 1994). Such a debate should move beyond "attention to mechanics and technical distinctions" to focus on important ideological differences (Van Soest, 1995) and conceptual vagueness.

As Rosaldo (1989) suggested, people who differ over essentially contested concepts such as multiculturalism "should sharpen debate on issues that divide them rather than pretend to be bedfellows" (p. 223). We are aware that an open and serious examination of such differences will be an emotionally laden undertaking. Participants in the debate must remain extremely respectful of one another while working to clarify rather than homogenize important differences among themselves. At stake is the future relevance or obsolescence of social work practice, research, and knowledge in an increasingly diverse society.

REFERENCES

Bloom, A. (1987). *The closing of the American mind.* New York: Simon & Schuster.

Brown, L. (1985). People-centered development and participatory research. *Harvard Educational Review, 55,* 69–75.

Brunner, C. (1991). *Thinking collaboratively: Ten questions and answers to help policy makers improve children's services.* Washington, DC: Education and Human Services Consortium.

Chau, K. L. (1990). Cross-cultural practice in social work. *Journal of Social Work Education, 26*(2), 124–133.

Coulton, C. J. (1995). Riding the pendulum of the 1990s: Building a community context for social work research. *Social Work, 40,* 437–439.

D'Souza, D. (1992). *Illiberal education: The politics of race and sex on campus.* New York: Vintage Books.

Flick, L., Reese, C., Rogers, G., Fletcher, P., & Sonn, J. (1994). Building community for health: Lessons from a seven-year-old neighborhood/university partnership. *Health Education Quarterly, 2,* 369–380.

Fonow, M., & Cook, J. (1991). *Beyond methodology.* Bloomington: Indiana University Press.

Gambrill, E. (1994). Social work research: Priorities and obstacles. *Research on Social Work Practice, 4,* 359–388.

Gergen, M. (1988). Toward a feminist metatheory and methodology in the social sciences. In M. Gergen (Ed.), *Feminist thought and the structure of knowledge* (pp. 87–104). New York: New York University Press.

Gould, K. H. (1995). The misconstruing of multiculturalism: The Stanford debate and social work. *Social Work, 40,* 198–205.

Gutierrez, L. (1990). Working with women of color: An empowerment perspective. *Social Work, 35,* 149–153.

Hartsock, N.C.M. (1983). The feminist standpoint: Developing the ground for a specifically feminist historical materialism. In S. Harding & M. B. Hintikka (Eds.), *Discovering reality: Feminist perspectives on epistemology, metaphysics, methodology, and philosophy of science* (pp. 283–310). Boston: D. Reidel.

Helms, J. E. (1994). How multiculturalism obscures racial factors in the psychotherapy process. *Journal of Counseling Psychology, 41,* 162–165.

Herr, K. (1995). Action research as an empowering practice. *Journal of Progressive Human Services, 6,* 45–58.

Ho, M. K. (1991). Use of ethnic-sensitive inventory (ESI) to enhance practitioners' skills with minorities. *Journal of Multicultural Social Work, 1*(1), 57–65.

hooks, b. (1994). *Teaching to transgress: Education as the practice of freedom.* New York: Routledge & Kegan Paul.

Hui, C. H., & Triandis, H. C. (1989). Effects of culture and response format on extreme response styles. *Journal of Cross-Cultural Psychology, 20,* 269–309.

Klein, W. C., & Bloom, M. (1994). Social work as applied social science: A historical analysis. *Social Work, 39,* 421–431.

Leigh, J., & Green, J. (1989). Teaching ethnographic methods to social service workers. *Practicing Anthropology, 11*(3), 8–10.

Maguire, P. (1987). *Doing participatory research: A feminist approach.* Amherst, MA: Center for International Education.

McMahon, A., & Allen-Meares, P. (1992). Is social work racist? A content analysis of recent literature. *Social Work, 37,* 533–539.

Merta, R. J. (1995). Group work: Multicultural perspectives. In J. G. Ponterotto, J. M. Casas, L. A. Suzuki, & C. M. Alexander (Eds.), *Handbook of multicultural counseling* (pp. 567–585). Thousand Oaks, CA: Sage Publications.

Messick, S. (1995). Validity of psychological assessment: Validation of inferences from persons' responses and performances as scientific inquiry into score meaning. *American Psychologist, 50,* 741–749.

Morrow, R. A. (1994). *Critical theory and methodology* (Vol. 3). Thousand Oaks, CA: Sage Publications.

Pinderhughes, E. (1989). *Understanding race, ethnicity, and power: The key to efficacy in clinical practice.* New York: Free Press.

Ponterotto, J. G., Casas, J. M., Suzuki, L. A., & Alexander, C. M. (1995). *Handbook of multicultural counseling.* Thousand Oaks, CA: Sage Publications.

Rappaport, J., Seidman, E., Toro, P., McFadden, L., Reischl, M., Roberts, L., Salem, D., Stein, C., & Zimmerman, M. A. (1985). Collaborative research with a mutual help organization. *Social Policy, 15,* 12–24.

Rogler, L. (1989). The meaning of culturally sensitive research in mental health. *American Journal of Psychiatry, 146*, 296–303.

Rosaldo, R. (1989). *Culture and truth: The remaking of social analysis.* Boston: Beacon Press.

Rothman, J., & Thomas, E. (1994). *Intervention research: Design and development for the human services.* New York: Haworth Press.

Sheppard, L. (1993). Evaluating test validity. *Review of Research in Education, 19*, 405–450.

Simon, B. L. (1994). *Empowerment traditions: History of empowerment and social work.* New York: Columbia University Press.

Sohng, S. (1994, June). *Critical feminist research in a multicultural context.* Paper presented at the Global Society of International Social Work Third Annual Conference, Chicago.

Spigner, C., & Cheadle, A. (1994, December). *Research in minority communities.* Workshop presented at Caring Community Partnerships: A Community Forum, sponsored by the Minority Health Coalition, Seattle.

Starr, E., Harris, C., & Edwards, T. (1994). Voice of the community: Culturally sensitive research targeting the needs of Native Americans will benefit everyone. *HIV Newsletter, 4*, 4.

Task Force on Quality Doctoral Education, Group for the Advancement of Doctoral Education. (1992). *Guidelines for quality in social work doctoral programs.* Washington, DC: U.S. Department of Health and Human Services, National Institutes of Health, National Institute of Mental Health.

Uehara, E. S., Smukler, M., & Bates, R. (1993). *Assessment of the reliability, validity and appropriateness of the Community Psychiatric Clinic's problem severity scales for special needs populations.* Unpublished manuscript.

Van Soest, D. (1995). Multiculturalism and social work education: The non-debate about competing perspectives. *Journal of Social Work Education, 31*, 55–66.

W. K. Kellogg Foundation. (1995). *The language of hope: Communities in action* (1995 program information and guidelines). Battle Creek, MI: Author.

An earlier version of this chapter was presented at the Symposium on Research and Diversity at the Annual Program Meeting of the Council on Social Work Education, February 1995, San Diego. The authors thank H. Anthony Ishisaka, Lewayne Gilchrist, Richard Catalano, and Lorraine Gutierrez for their helpful comments.

9 Navigating Two Cultures:
Deaf Children, Self-Esteem, and Parents' Communication Patterns

Debra D. Desselle and Lynn Pearlmutter

Social workers who work with families of deaf children should know which communication methods to encourage the family to learn: sign language, lipreading, finger spelling, or a combination of methods. Despite the growing body of literature and increasing media attention to the culture of deafness (Dolnick, 1993; Solomon, 1994), one practitioner (Desselle, 1992) found that in most cases, deaf children in a public school setting lived with parents who did not know sign language, and little communication involving sign language and finger spelling occurred between the deaf child and other family members. Tanksley (1993) found that the significant variable in maternal–child interaction for deaf preschoolers was not the extent of the child's hearing impairment, but rather the child's language development. Caissie and Cole (1993) found that communication was facilitated when deaf children's mothers' conversational behaviors were direct. Moreover, practice wisdom indicates that family communication patterns significantly influence self-esteem in deaf children.

Although dated studies were found that compared methods of communication (Stevenson, 1964; Stuckless & Birch, 1966; Vernon & Koh, 1970), neither dated nor recent studies have documented the relationship among communication, parents, and the self-esteem of the deaf child (Marschark, 1993). The study described in this chapter sought to address the dearth of valid data that support the clinical wisdom. This chapter explores primarily the mother's role in the development of the deaf child's self-esteem; only two of the respondents were fathers.

LITERATURE REVIEW

If the whole family participates in communicating with the child, Schlesinger and Meadow (1972) observed, the child will feel like an accepted member of the family. Furth (1973) indicated that deaf children are vulnerable to the reactions of significant others concerning their impairment. The family atmosphere into which a deaf child is

This chapter was originally published in the January 1997 issue of *Social Work in Education*, Vol. 19, pp. 23–30.

born has a lot to do with the child's self-esteem (Marschark, 1993; Meadow, 1969).

If a deaf child has grown up in a family where the child's deafness is considered a stigma (Goffman, 1974), the child is likely to have poor self-esteem. However, a deaf child born to deaf parents may feel much more accepted, because the impairment is not foreign to the parents and the child may experience a sense of inclusion (Schlesinger, 1978). Hearing parents can influence the deaf child's self-esteem by communicating acceptance to the child, done by treating the deafness as a family issue rather than as a deficiency in the child (Schlesinger, 1978).

Unfortunately, in hearing families, "the early development of the mother–child bond necessary for positive feelings of self is often impeded by the hearing-impaired child's ability to communicate" (Loeb & Sarigiani, 1986, p. 89). This impediment sets up a cycle where the parents are frustrated because they cannot communicate with the child and the child internalizes this frustration (Schlesinger & Meadow, 1972). Marschark (1993) noted that hearing impairment leads to psychological impairment, which leads to problem behavior. The deafness or hearing impairment itself does not directly cause poor self-esteem, but the ability to communicate may be a contributing factor to self-esteem (Schlesinger & Meadow, 1972). The mother–child dyad's ability to communicate effectively becomes more important as the child grows older because corresponding age-appropriate activities become increasingly dependent on language (Lederberg & Mobley, 1990).

Moores (1987) wrote that if the parents try to force the child to learn to function as a hearing person and forbid the use of sign language, the child's self-image could be negatively affected. If, however, the parents make every effort to communicate with their child through all available means (such as sign language, finger spelling, and getting auditory amplification for the child), then the child's self-esteem could be positively influenced.

A heated debate, not only among professionals working with the deaf population, but also among deaf people themselves, exists between using "oral-only" and "total" communication. With the oral-only method, the hearing-impaired person uses his or her residual hearing and lip-reads with the assistance of a hearing aid. Total communication involves the oral-only methods plus sign language and finger spelling (Moores, 1987). Many deaf people believe that having to learn to lip-read and wear hearing aids forces them to participate in life as defective hearing people. They are hearing impaired, they feel, so why should they pretend to be otherwise? American Sign Language (ASL) is a symbol for many deaf people of their identification with their deaf community and culture (Dolnick, 1993; Moores, 1987; Solomon, 1994).

Kelliher (1976) compared the family's mode of communication with the level of self-esteem in deaf adolescents and found that although hearing students had higher self-esteem than deaf students, no statistically significant differences existed between deaf students whose families used total communication and deaf students whose families used oral communication. Warren (1983) tested the impact of parental attitude and mode of communication on self-esteem in elementary school–age deaf children's families and found that parental attitude had a statistically significant effect on the deaf child's self-esteem. Nothing in the recent anecdotal or empirical literature has connected parents' communication patterns and the self-esteem of their deaf adolescents.

More data are needed to help professionals make informed decisions in counseling families of deaf children. This study examined the effects of parents' communication patterns on the self-esteem of a deaf adolescent.

METHOD

Instruments

Most of the previous research surveying deaf people was performed by hearing individuals. The instruments used to measure self-esteem were written by hearing people and were normed using the hearing population (Garrison & Tesch, 1978). These methods are slowly changing, but when interpreting the results of studies on deaf people, this issue must be considered. Beaudoin (1984) underscored this point: "The researcher must take seriously the subjective experience of deaf people rather than first establishing criteria for normality and deficiency" (p. 1).

Many instruments for measuring self-esteem exist (Coopersmith, 1959; Fitts, 1964; Hudson, 1982; Nunnally & Flaugher, 1963; Piers, 1969; Rosenberg, 1979). Several of these measurements of self-esteem have been used with the hearing-impaired population. Only tests that were used successfully with hearing-impaired people who are fluent in ASL were considered for this study.

The Coopersmith Self-Esteem Inventory is used with good reliability and validity across populations and was specifically designed to be used with 10- to 16-year-olds. In addition, Kelliher (1976) specifically modified it for deaf children and then retested it for reliability and validity. As revised, this test is known as the Modified Self-Esteem Inventory (MSEI). In this study, self-esteem was measured using the MSEI.

The Subject Communication Questionnaire (SCQ), in which students describe their communication methods, is a multiple-choice tool also taken from Kelliher's (1976) research. Kelliher administered the questionnaire to deaf students 12 to 14 years old to determine whether they would understand the questionnaire. Some of the vocabulary in the questionnaire was then revised by Kelliher to be better understood by the students. Kelliher's revised questionnaire was then expanded in the present study with eight additional questions to seek greater detail about the student's perceptions of family communication patterns.

Sample

The sample consisted of 53 deaf adolescent students who used ASL. This group attended a southern residential school for deaf students. At the time of the study, 90 high school students attended and stayed on campus during the week and returned home on the weekends. Of the 90 students, the 53 adolescents chosen for the study

- had severe to profound deafness
- had no other major disabilities
- were prelingually deafened
- used total communication
- were ages 13 to 19
- had IQs in the average range
- had hearing parents.

These criteria eliminated those youths, for example, who had autism, mental retardation, blindness, or deaf parents. Written consent to participate was obtained from both parents and students.

Data Collection

A separate questionnaire based on Kelliher's (1976) research was sent to the parents to determine the type of communication used in the home. The students whose parents participated in the survey were administered the MSEI and the SCQ. The questionnaires given to the students were administered in groups by one of the authors, who used ASL in explaining the instructions for completing the questionnaires. The researcher also answered the students' questions while administering the questionnaires.

When the data were collected, the SCQ was descriptively analyzed. Each parent was then contacted by phone to get clarification of their questionnaire answers. Many parents who had only a minimal knowledge of sign language had overstated their actual skill level. After telephone clarification, the parents' description of communication methods was changed by the researcher to reflect their skill level more accurately. The parents' communication skill level also was compared and confirmed with the students' SCQ.

Data Analysis

When parents relied on speech, finger spelling, and only a few signs, they were placed in the "low level of skill" group. When parents stated (and adolescents agreed on the SCQ) that the parent was fluent in ASL, they were placed in the "high level of skill" group. Self-esteem and parents' communication methods were tested using one-way analysis of variance (ANOVA), because multiple variables (such as reading levels and parental attitudes) reported elsewhere (Desselle, 1992) also were compared. The research hypothesis was tested at the .05 level of significance. The dependent variable was the self-esteem of the deaf child, and the independent variable was communication method (oral-only or total communication) used by the parents.

Table 9-1

Deaf Students' MSEI Scores, by Level of Parents' ASL Skill (*N* = 53)

Level of Skill	*M*	*SD*	*n*	%
Low	27.97	4.58	37	70
High	31.63	4.77	16	30

NOTES: MSEI = Modified Self-Esteem Inventory (Kelliher, 1976); ASL = American Sign Language.

RESULTS

The students' self-esteem scores ranged from 19 (low) to 40 (high) of a possible 50. Table 9-1 presents the descriptive statistics on parents in the ASL-proficient group and in the non-ASL-proficient group.

The ANOVA showed that a relationship existed between the parents' communication method and the deaf adolescents' self-esteem (Table 9-2). Parents who used total communication had adolescents whose self-esteem scores were higher than parents who used oral-only communication.

One of the study's limitations was that mostly mothers (89 percent, *n* = 51) answered the questionnaire. Fathers' and siblings' knowledge of sign language is underrepresented in the literature (Watson, Henggeler, & Whelan, 1990). Also, the original questionnaire to the parents was found to be invalid, and groupings were reconsidered after telephone clarification and confirmation through the students' SCQ. Only then did the researcher believe face validity was achieved.

DISCUSSION

The findings of the study support the practice wisdom that a deaf adolescent's self-esteem may be influenced by the parents' communication method. Hearing parents of deaf children, especially those with a high level of skill in ASL, may have an important role in influencing their deaf children's self-esteem. In this study, the deaf students whose parents knew only a few signs or communicated by letting their child

Table 9-2

Analysis of Variance for Students' MSEI Scores, by Parents' ASL Skill (*N* = 53)

Source of Variation	Sum of Squares	*df*	Mean Square	*F*	*p*
Levels of parents' ASL skills[a]	153.42	1	153.42	7.14	.01
Within levels of parents' ASL skills	1,096.51	51	21.50		
Total	1,249.92	52			

NOTES: MSEI = Modified Self-Esteem Inventory (Kelliher, 1976); ASL = American Sign Language.
[a]Levels are high and low.

lip-read had lower self-esteem. Parents who had learned ASL and used total communication may have made the deaf adolescent feel more accepted in the family and experience less sense of exclusion. This finding supports a study by MacKay-Soroka, Trehub, and Thorpe (1988) that found that a deaf child's communication success was "compromised by deficits in maternal signing skill" (p. 284).

Parents of deaf children may underestimate the impact they have on their deaf children. This influence of parents on a deaf child starts early (Altshuler, 1974; Meadow, 1969). If the deaf child feels accepted by the family, especially the parents, this feeling will positively affect self-esteem. Parents may need early guidance from social workers and other professionals when deciding how to communicate with their children. As they grow older, many deaf children go to residential schools during the week and see their parents only on weekends. Parents may mistakenly believe that being in school with deaf peers is more influential for deaf children than the parental role.

Although this contention is beyond the scope of this study, future researchers may wish to investigate the implications for self-esteem when parents start using ASL early in the child's life. The deaf child's grasp of language and communication may significantly increase if early efforts are made to introduce the child to ASL. Deaf children of deaf parents are exposed to ASL from the beginning, and consequently, the delay in language development is absent. In hearing families, deafness is too often not detected early, and when it is detected, the parents may go through a period of denial about their child's deafness, adding to the delay in language development (Altshuler, 1974; Vernon & Koh, 1970).

Sign language is of great importance in the deaf culture. Parents have a responsibility not only to help their deaf child use ASL but also to model the ability to travel between two cultures by learning and using ASL with the deaf child. For the deaf child to feel accepted in the deaf culture, he or she must be able to use ASL. It is documented that sign language helps create bonds among members of the deaf community (Dolnick, 1993; Moores, 1987; Schein & Delk, 1974; Solomon, 1994).

School social workers working with hearing parents of deaf children must address several issues. Intrinsic to a sound ecological approach (Germain & Gitterman, 1986) are the paradigmatic thinking that the child is a vital member of the dynamic environment and the provision of practical information and support to families (Meadow-Orlans & Steinberg, 1993). Parents' interaction strategies are best assessed through direct observation (Tanksley, 1993). The social worker can help hearing parents navigate through their feelings and reactions by acknowledging the parents' feelings of disbelief, grief, guilt, and anger. Even if the hearing loss was diagnosed years ago, it may not be until the child enters school that the parents confront the previously denied feelings of loss and their fears about their child's education and psychosocial development. The social worker needs to gently explain the importance of recognizing the significance of the child's hearing loss and the importance of early and ongoing intervention. Then the social worker can educate the parents about the various aspects of their child's deafness and how their acceptance of their child affects his or her self-esteem. The social worker should impress on the parents to accept their child not as defective but as different.

From that point, the school social worker can assist the parents in choosing the best method of communicating their acceptance to the child. The social worker can discuss recent studies with the parents (for example, Meadow-Orlans & Steinberg, 1993) that show the benefits of early intervention with children whose deafness is acknowledged and accepted. Soon after the diagnosis is made, the parents and child can begin learning sign language; it is not only the deaf child who needs to navigate between two cultures, but also the parents. Children receiving early intervention grasp learning skills more easily, and a developmental learning gap is prevented. In the long run, better reading skills will result in higher self-esteem for the deaf child (Meadow-Orlans & Steinberg, 1993). The social worker is in a unique position to address these issues with the parents.

REFERENCES

Altshuler, K. Z. (1974). The social and psychological development of the deaf child: Problems, their treatment and prevention. *American Annals of the Deaf, 119,* 365–376.

Beaudoin, J. P. (1984). The projected phantasies of the deaf: A psychoanalytic and cross-cultural perspective (Doctoral dissertation, Wright Institute, University of California, Berkeley, 1990). *Dissertation Abstracts International, 44,* 3922B. (University Microfilms No. 84–07040)

Caissie, R., & Cole, E. B. (1993). Mothers and hearing-impaired children: Directiveness reconsidered. *Volta Review, 95,* 49–59.

Coopersmith, S. (1959). A method for determining type of self-esteem. *Journal of Abnormal and Social Psychology, 59,* 87–94.

Desselle, D. (1992). Self-esteem, family climate, and communication patterns in relation to deafness (Doctoral dissertation, University of New Orleans, 1992). *Dissertation Abstracts International, 53,* 2763A. (University Microfilms No. 92-30595)

Dolnick, E. (1993). Deafness as culture. *Atlantic Monthly, 272,* 37–53.

Fitts, W. H. (1964). *Tennessee self-concept scale.* Nashville, TN: Counselor Recordings and Tests.

Furth, H. G. (1973). *Deafness and learning: A psychological approach.* Belmont, CA: Wadsworth.

Garrison, W. M., & Tesch, S. (1978). Self-concept and deafness: A review of the literature. *Volta Review, 80,* 457–466.

Germain, C. B., & Gitterman, A. (1986). The life model approach to social work practice revisited. In F. Turner (Ed.), *Social work treatment* (3rd ed., pp. 618–644). New York: Free Press.

Goffman, E. (1974). *Stigma.* New York: Jason Aronson.

Hudson, W. W. (1982). *The clinical measurement package: A field manual.* Homewood, IL: Dorsey Press.

Kelliher, M. H. (1976). The relationship between mode of communication and the development of self-esteem in the deaf child of hearing parents (Doctoral dissertation, Loyola University of Chicago, 1976). *Dissertation Abstracts International, 37,* 196A. (University Microfilms No. 76-15459)

Lederberg, A. R., & Mobley, C. E. (1990). The effect of hearing impairment on the quality of attachment and mother–toddler interaction. *Child Development, 61,* 1596–1604.

Loeb, R., & Sarigiani, P. (1986). The impact of hearing impairment on self-perceptions of children. *Volta Review, 88,* 89–100.

MacKay-Soroka, S., Trehub, S. E., & Thorpe, L. A. (1988). Reception of mothers' referential messages by deaf and hearing children. *Developmental Psychology, 24,* 277–285.

Marschark, M. (1993). *Psychological development of deaf children.* New York: Oxford University Press.

Meadow, K. P. (1969). Self-image, family climate, and deafness. *Social Forces, 47,* 428–438.

Meadow-Orlans, K. P., & Steinberg, A. G. (1993). Effects of infant hearing loss and maternal support on mother–infant interaction. *Journal of Applied Developmental Psychology, 14,* 407–426.

Moores, D. F. (1987). *Educating the deaf.* Boston: Houghton Mifflin.

Nunnally, J. C., & Flaugher, R. L. (1963). Correlates of semantic habits. *Journal of Personality, 31,* 192–202.

Piers, E. V. (1969). *Manual for the Piers-Harris children's self-concept scale.* Nashville, TN: Counselor Recordings and Tests.

Rosenberg, M. (1979). *Conceiving the self.* New York: Basic Books.

Schein, D., & Delk, M. T., Jr. (1974). *The deaf population of the United States.* Silver Spring, MD: National Association of the Deaf.

Schlesinger, H. S. (1978). The effects of deafness on childhood development: An Eriksonian perspective. In L. S. Liben (Ed.), *Deaf children: Developmental perspectives* (pp. 157–169). New York: Academic Press.

Schlesinger, H. S., & Meadow, K. P. (1972). *Sound and sign.* Berkeley: University of California Press.

Solomon, A. (1994, August 28). Defiantly deaf. *New York Times Magazine,* pp. 38–45, 62, 65–68.

Stevenson, E. A. (1964). A study of the educational achievement of deaf children of deaf parents. *California News, 80,* 1–3.

Stuckless, E. R., & Birch, J. W. (1966). The influence of early manual communication on the linguistic development of deaf children. *American Annals of the Deaf, 111,* 452–460.

Tanksley, C. K. (1993). Interactions between mothers and normal-hearing or hearing-impaired children. *Volta Review, 95,* 33–47.

Vernon, M., & Koh, S. D. (1970). Early manual communication and deaf children's achievement. *American Annals of the Deaf, 115,* 527–536.

Warren, C. J. (1983). The relationship between self-concept of deaf children and selected other variables (Doctoral dissertation, University of Virginia, 1983). *Dissertation Abstracts International, 45,* 2461A. (University Microfilms No. 84-15431)

Watson, S. M., Henggeler, S. W., & Whelan, J. P. (1990). Family functioning and the social adaptation of hearing-impaired youths. *Journal of Abnormal Child Psychology, 18,* 143–163.

Part II

CHILD WELFARE

Promoting Same-Race Adoption for Children of Color

Leslie Doty Hollingsworth

Opponents of policies to protect same-race adoption for children of color assert that it is necessary to lift all restrictions on transracial adoption (alternately referred to as "interracial," "interethnic," or "transethnic" adoption) of the many children of color believed to be "languishing" in foster homes, residential programs, and institutional settings. This chapter briefly presents the history of the transracial adoption controversy and discusses its current status; counters assertions typically used to oppose same-race adoption policies for children of color; summarizes the positions of several social work organizations regarding adoption and race; and makes recommendations for education, policy, research, and practice.

HISTORY OF TRANSRACIAL ADOPTION

The adoption of orphaned children from other countries by U.S. families began in the 1940s with the end of World War II (Simon & Alstein, 1977). A rise in the number of such adoptions accompanied later wars, including the Korean and Vietnam Wars (Silverman, 1993). In the 1960s, widespread use of artificial birth control, the legalization of abortion, and decreased social stigma associated with bearing a child outside of marriage were accompanied by a substantial decrease in healthy white infants available for adoption. There was, however, no corresponding decrease among African American and other children of color (although foreign countries began to establish rules that limited some adoptions in those countries).

It has been suggested that adoption agencies, feeling the pressure of reduced fee income, found in the availability of children of color an opportunity to increase adoption fees (McRoy, 1989). One writer (Bartholet, 1991) suggested that as the United States became accustomed to children of color from other countries in its communities, it became easier to accept the transracial adoption of African American children. By 1971 transracial adoptions had reached an annual high of 2,574 (Simon & Alstein, 1987). Responding to this increase, a 1972 meeting of the National Association of Black Social Workers (NABSW) ended with a resolution opposing transracial adoption:

This chapter was originally published in the March 1998 issue of *Social Work*, Vol. 43, pp. 104–116.

> Black children belong physically and psychologically and cultur-
> ally in black families where they can receive the total sense of
> themselves and develop a sound projection of their future. Only a
> black family can transmit the emotional and sensitive subtleties of
> perceptions and reactions essential for a black child's survival in a
> racist society. Human beings are products of their environment
> and develop their sense of values, attitudes, and self-concept
> within their own family structures. Black children in white homes
> are cut off from the healthy development of themselves as black
> people. (quoted in McRoy, 1989, p. 150)

In response to that resolution, and to the Indian Child Welfare Act
of 1978 giving tribal courts exclusive jurisdiction over American Indian child custody proceedings, some states established policies and
procedures limiting transracial adoption and requiring that serious
efforts be made to place children of color with adoptive parents of
their own racial or ethnic group. Agencies specializing in same-race
placements were established, and many traditional agencies modified their programs in the same direction.

Some parents who had adopted transracially were offended, however, by the NABSW resolution, perceiving it as not based in truth
and disagreeing with the assertion that they were not capable of adequately parenting their adoptive children of color (Hermann, 1993).
White foster parents began to file legal suits to prevent children of
color who were in their care from being placed with same-race adoptive parents and to be allowed to adopt the children themselves
(Elias, 1991). Advocates of transracial adoption, some of them transracial adoptive parents themselves (Bartholet, 1991; Mahoney, 1991),
began to speak and write publicly in its support and in opposition to
same-race protective policies. Criticism of protective policies for
same-race adoption has included the following assertions:

- that same-race placement policies result in retention of children
  in foster care for longer than necessary, which may result in delay or denial of placement for children of color and therefore in
  long-term harm
- that there is no systematic recruitment of white parents to correspond to that of families of color, and therefore families of color
  are being given unfair advantage
- that same-race policies give families of color an edge in receipt
  of adoption subsidies, because children of color (whom same-
  race parents adopt) are eligible for such subsidies by nature of
  their "special-needs" status
- that agencies apply differential screening criteria to prospective black parents than to prospective white families (such as
  socioeconomic status, age, and marital status requirements),
  even though these have not been ruled out as viable criteria for
  selection
- that empirical studies have been biased toward studying the
  negative aspects of transracial adoption

- that in spite of such biases, studies have failed to document a negative effect of transracial adoption in areas such as general adjustment and self-esteem and, in some instances, have indicated a possible benefit with regard to the transracial adoptee's ability to get along with and in a white world
- that there is no empirical support for the contention that parents of color do a better job at socializing their children ethnically
- that racial matching policies are in conflict with antidiscrimination legislation, such as the U.S. Constitution and Title IV of the Civil Rights Act of 1964 (Bartholet, 1991; Mahoney, 1991; National Coalition to End Racism in America's Child Care System, cited in McRoy, 1994).

A result of the opposition to same-race policies was that states began "to reassess their policies which include race as a viable consideration in placement decision making" (National Coalition to End Racism in America's Child Care System, cited in McRoy, 1994). Subsequently, transracial adoptions began to increase in the early 1980s (McRoy, 1989). Bill Pierce, president of the National Council for Adoption, estimated that 12,000 children were transracially adopted in 1992 (Richman, 1993). Accurate national data on the numbers of transracial and same-race adoptions are not available because after 1971 the federal government no longer required states to maintain and report such data.

On December 22, 1995, the U.S. Department of Health and Human Services published final rules implementing the Adoption and Foster Care Analysis and Reporting System, a mandatory system of data collection on all children covered by Title IV-B of the Social Security Act, Section 427 ("Foster Care," 1997). Included are rules requiring states to collect data on all adopted children who were placed by the state child welfare agency or by private agencies under contract with the public child welfare agency. However, national adoption data are not yet available.

The recent increase in transracial adoptions has been influenced by a trend among child welfare agencies toward greater flexibility in eligibility to adopt. Such changes have included less rigidity regarding age, income, housing, family composition, and infertility examination requirements; attempts to make application procedures and agency locations and hours more convenient for prospective adopters; less emphasis on the need for matching the characteristics of child and parent (which may have facilitated same-race placements); a willingness to select single parents or those who already have birth or adopted children; openness to adoption by foster parents, caretakers, and relatives of the child; use of adoption resource exchanges; use of active and ongoing recruitment methods, often using the mass media and featuring specific children; and expansion of adoption subsidy programs (Child Welfare League of America, 1988). Although some of these changes may facilitate same-race adoptions, they have also opened the way for increases in transracial adoptions. People interested in adopting transracially typically either originally desired a white infant or preschool child and became willing to adopt a child of a different race or were the child's foster parents (Child Welfare League of America, 1988).

The Multiethnic Placement Act of 1994 prohibited agencies or entities engaged in adoption or foster care placements that receive federal assistance from "categorically deny[ing] to any person the opportunity to become an adoptive or foster parent, solely on the basis of the race, color, or national origin of the adoptive or foster parent or the child" and "from delay[ing] or deny[ing] the placement of a child solely on the basis of race, color, or national origin of the adoptive or foster parent or parents involved" (p. 4056). However, this law allowed "an agency or entity to which [the preceding applied to] consider the cultural, ethnic, or racial background of the child and the capacity of the prospective foster or adoptive parents to meet the needs of a child of this background as one of a number of factors used to determine the best interests of a child" (p. 4056).

Opponents of same-race protective policies criticized the qualification in the Multiethnic Placement Act that allowed race, culture, and ethnicity to be considered at all and the absence of penalties for failure to conform to the requirements of the act. Advocacy efforts with regard to federal and state adoption policy continued, and in August 1996 legislation was signed that modified the Multiethnic Placement Act of 1994. This legislation, which was enacted as a part of the Small Business Job Protection Act of 1996, had two sections: (1) Section 1807 (Adoption Assistance), which allowed a tax credit to adoptive families with incomes not exceeding $75,000 of up to $5,000 ($6,000 in the case of children with "special needs") annually for qualified adoption expenses, and (2) Section 1808 (Removal of Barriers to Interethnic Adoption), which removed the qualification provided by the earlier act and simply prevented any entity that receives federal funds from denying any person the opportunity to adopt or provide foster care and from delaying or denying the placement of a child on the basis of the race, color, or national origin of the adoptive or foster parent or the child involved.

ALTERNATIVE CONSIDERATIONS

Given the history of transracial adoption, social workers need to be aware of alternative considerations to those that resulted in the current legislation. Delays in moving children of color out of the out-of-home care system are caused by factors other than restrictions on transracial adoption and can be resolved by actions other than lifting such restrictions. Improvements in the following six areas would alleviate such delays and lessen the need for transracial adoptions. First, because there are insufficient nonkin foster families of color, policies favoring adoption by foster parents are increasing the numbers of transracial adoptions. Second, there are indications that sufficient numbers of families of color are available to adopt healthy infants of color if such families are sought out and if traditional barriers to adoption are eliminated. Third, many children of color in the child welfare system are not available for adoption or have special needs. Fourth, overrepresentation of children of color in the child welfare system has been linked to disparities in services related to ethnic group. Fifth, children of color may be counted as being in foster placements when they are actually in permanent kinship care. Finally, poverty, which disproportionately affects families of color, has been associated with the abuse and neglect that often result in the out-of-home placement of children.

Policies Favoring Adoption by Foster Parents

Many children of color are placed with non-kin foster families (as many as 52 percent in California, according to Meyer & Link, cited in Barth, Courtney, Berrick, Albert, & Needell, 1994). Barth, Courtney, Berrick, Albert, and Needell noted that among the California children they studied, only two-thirds of African American children were placed in African American foster homes, and only 31 percent of Hispanic children were placed with Hispanic caregivers. (Because the figures for children of color include kinship placements, the actual proportion of placements of children of color with same-race, nonkin foster families is much lower than they found.) In contrast, 92 percent of selected white children in foster homes were placed with white foster families. The researchers noted that "when children were not placed with ethnically similar foster parents, they were almost always placed with Caucasians [and that] nearly one-half of Caucasian foster parents were caring for children of color" (Barth, Courtney, Berrick, Albert, & Needell, 1994, p. 245).

What has come to be known as the "fost adoption" program (Barth, Courtney, Berrick, & Albert, 1994) emerged in the mid-1970s (Meezan & Shireman, 1985) to promote the placement of children in foster homes with the explicit expectation that the foster parents would adopt the child if reunification with the birth parents failed. Before this program was implemented, foster placements were established in such a way that they would interfere neither with the reunification of the child with her or his birth parents nor with the permanent placement of the child in an adoptive home. Foster parents were considered temporary substitutes, and they were urged not to become attached to the child. If they did become attached, the child was often removed to another placement. With the advent of the fost adoption program, white foster families began to seek adoption of children of color placed in their homes, sometimes from birth, even when the children were not placed with the intention of their future adoption by those foster parents.

Thus, insufficient numbers of foster families of color reduce the likelihood that children of color will be adopted by a family of their same racial or ethnic group and gives an advantage to transracial placements. There is evidence that even children of mixed racial parentage tend to be confronted with racism or problems of racial identity while they are in placement, and researchers have recommended that these factors be considered in the selection and preparation of potential foster parents (Folaron & Hess, 1993). Increasing the numbers of available foster families of color has the potential, therefore, for increasing same-race adoptive placements (Rezendes, 1994).

Barth, Courtney, Berrick, and Albert (1994) compared children who were adopted within two years of entering foster care with children who remained in foster care for longer than two years before being adopted. Although they found that ethnicity had no effect on "the odds of a timely adoption," an item that was consistently related to length of time until adoption was whether the child welfare worker and the foster family with whom the child was placed planned, at the time of the placement, that the child would be adopted by the family. The authors added, "the fact that an adoption is planned at the time of foster placement or that a child is under one month of age both decrease the odds that a child will stay in foster care more than two years" (p. 167). Because ethnicity had no effect, it can be concluded that age and planned placement affected the adoption of children of color as well as of other children. If the pool of foster parents is less likely to contain foster parents of color, and if adoption plans continue to be made at the point of initial foster placement, especially within the context of the increased restrictions on same-race adoption protective policies, the likelihood that a child of color will be adopted by someone of her or his own race or ethnic group is diminished and the odds of a transracial adoption are increased.

Availability of Adoptive Families of Color

Evidence indicates that the number of families of color who are willing to adopt healthy infants may be sufficient if agency recruitment and eligibility policies are responsive to the cultures and lifestyles of such families. Early studies documented the failure of adoption agencies to implement culturally sensitive recruitment strategies and eligibility standards for potential adoptees of color (Day, 1979; Herzog, Sudia, Harwood, & Newcomb, 1971). Although many states and agencies took action to correct these circumstances, a recent survey by the North American Council on Adoptable Children (Gilles & Kroll, 1991) found that 83 percent of agencies in the 25 states studied acknowledged that organizational barriers continued to exist that prevented or discouraged families of color from adopting. The most frequently cited barriers were "institutional/systemic racism; lack of people of color in managerial positions; fees; 'adoption as business' mentality; communities' of color historical tendencies toward 'informal' adoption; negative perceptions of agencies and their practices; lack of minority staff; inflexible standards; general lack of recruitment activity and poor recruitment techniques; and 'word not out'" (pp. 7–8). With regard to the "adoption as business" mentality, one agency head was quoted as saying, "If your agency relied on fees, where would you place a minority kid . . . with a white family that can afford to pay, or a black family that can't?" (p. 14).

When adoption services and programs have become more responsive to families of color, such families have come forward to adopt. Haring reported in 1975 (cited in McRoy, 1989) that following changes in public and private adoption practices to encourage same-race adoptions, 70 families of color were approved for every 100 available children of color, reflecting an increase from 1971 (Herzog et al., 1971), when 39 families of color were approved for every 100 children of color (and 116 white families were approved for every 100 white children). More recently, a study by the North American Council on Adoptable Children (Gilles & Kroll, 1991) of 17 agencies specializing in finding same-race adoptive placements for children of color found that these agencies located same-race placements for 94 percent of their 341 African American children and 66 percent of their 38 Hispanic children; nonspecializing agencies obtained an average of 51 percent of same-race placements of 806 African American children and 30 percent of 168 Hispanic children.

A number of sources have identified agencies that are exemplars in successfully engaging same-race adoptive families ("Adoption," 1992; Gant, 1984; Hairston & Williams, 1989; "Homes," 1993; Jackson-White, Dozier, Oliver, & Gardner, 1997; McRoy, Oglesby, & Grape, 1997). Hairston and Williams (1989) found that more than half of the 58 African American adoptive families they surveyed viewed the services they had received from exemplary national African American adoption agencies or programs as having led to their decision to adopt. Others (Gant, 1984; Gilles & Kroll, 1991) have similarly identified agency characteristics associated with successful recruitment of same-race families.

Availability for Adoption and Special Needs

Many children in out-of-home placements either are not available for adoption or have characteristics that make them difficult to place. Thus, they should not be included in numbers of children "languishing" in the system who are considered easily adoptable. Regarding availability for adoption, the Voluntary Cooperative Information System (VCIS) (cited in Flango & Flango, 1994), estimated that nationally 71,000 children had a permanency plan for adoption at the end of fiscal year 1992, meaning that their child welfare workers expected that parental rights would be voluntarily or involuntarily terminated and that the children would then become eligible for adoption. Of that number, it was estimated that 17,000 adoptions had been finalized and that another 17,000 adoptions were in the process of finalization. VCIS estimated that 21,000 children were in substitute care and still awaiting a decision regarding a final disposition. (The plight of the remaining 16,000 children was not clear, but because they were not included in one of the three categories just mentioned, it is assumed they are not be imminently available for adoption.)

Two conclusions may be drawn from these data. First, half the children in the child welfare system may not be available for adoption (21,000 in out-of-home care awaiting final disposition and 16,000 not included in the statistics). Second, there is a difference between a child having a permanency plan for adoption and actually being available for adoption. Child welfare workers, on assessing a family, may record adoption as the permanency plan without adoption ever becoming a reality, leading to incorrect assumptions among the public and policymakers that children in such instances are actually available for adoption. Although these data are not restricted to children of color, they point to the inaccurate conclusions on which policy decisions may be made.

With regard to children with special needs, the Child Welfare League of America (1988) observed that "there is a surplus of potential parents seeking to adopt white infants and preschool children and a shortage of those applying for those children who are available and need families" (p. 5); available children are "minority, severely handicapped, . . . age 12 or over; and in foster care four or more years" (p. 5). Thus, although the latter children are heavily counted among those who are languishing in out-of-home care, they are not the children that potential parents are seeking to adopt. Transracial adoption laws that are more liberal would not be expected, therefore, to decrease the numbers of these children substantially.

Inequities in Services

Disparities related to ethnic group have been observed in the prevention and intervention services that children in the child welfare system receive (Barth, Courtney, Berrick, & Albert, 1994). The implication is that prevention and intervention services are associated with children's successful exit from the child welfare system, although the authors do not speak directly to this point.

Mech (cited in Gould, 1991) found that African American children "were more likely to have no contact with workers than were white or Hispanic children" (p. 64). Similarly, African American families studied in the first three months after placement of their children were found to have experienced a mean number of agency contacts of 2.9, compared with a mean of 7.2 for white families (Close, cited in Williams, 1991). In Connecticut, white children and foster families received more services and supports than children and foster families of color (Fein, Maluccio, & Kluger, cited in Barth, Courtney, Berrick, & Albert, 1994).

The issue of inequities in provision of services is especially important in family preservation, the process of providing intensive services and resources to families at risk of a child's removal from the home, usually because of real or threatened abuse or neglect. Williams (1991) noted that placement was avoided in more than three-fourths of families who received family preservation services and that children were able to safely remain in their own homes, for one year after intervention. Fraser, Pecora, and Haapala (1991) suggested that family preservation services may result in fewer placements for families of color compared to white families. Among families in Washington State, only 18.2 percent (10 of 55) of families of color who received family preservation services required the out-of-home placement of children, compared with 29.8 percent (75 of 252) of white families who received these services. These results suggest that intensive services can keep children of color out of out-of-home care.

Kinship Foster Care as Permanent Care

One of the most potentially misleading elements in the argument surrounding children of color in the out-of-home care system is the presentation of foster care statistics. Such statistics seldom distinguish kinship foster placements (placement of dependent children in the homes of relatives who have been formally approved, and subsidized, as foster parents for this purpose) from nonkinship foster placements. This distinction is important. Barth, Courtney, Berrick, Albert, and Needell (1994) noted that in California, two-thirds of the growth in the foster care caseload from 1984 to 1989 could be accounted for by the rise in kinship foster care. (This increase represents children who may otherwise have been placed in group homes or residential settings.) They also cite figures indicating that in 1990 kinship foster care accounted for 48 percent of all placements in New York (Meyer & Link, cited in Barth, Courtney, Berrick, Albert, & Needell, 1994). In New York City alone, the number of children in kinship foster homes rose from 151 in April 1985 to 14,000 in June 1989 (Thornton, 1991).

Children of color are widely represented in kinship foster placements. Forty-six percent of selected children in kinship foster care in California were African American, compared with 32 percent white children, 14 percent Hispanic children, and 9 percent children of other ethnic groups (Barth, Courtney, Berrick, & Albert, 1994). Ninety percent of kinship foster families in a Baltimore study were African American and 10 percent were white (Dubowitz, Feigelman, & Zuravin, 1993).

Two issues are important here. First, many kinship foster placements are considered permanent placements. In interviews with kinship foster parents in 20 homes, none of the children had a permanency goal of return to their parents (Thornton, 1991). In 19 of the 20 cases, the children were expected to be discharged to independent living when they became eligible (typically at age 17 or 18 years); in contrast, independent living was a goal for only 42 percent of children who were in nonrelative foster placements. When the kinship foster parents were asked "How long are you willing to provide care for your related foster child?" 100 percent of those who responded indicated they expected the children to remain with them until they were independent, until they no longer needed to be there, or as long as the foster parents were able to care for them. Similar findings were reported by Barth, Courtney, Berrick, Albert, and Needell (1994).

Second, kinship foster placements frequently do not result in formal adoption. Therefore, placement in relative foster care has consistently been linked to a corresponding decrease in the odds of adoption, especially for children of color, as if these were permanency failures. Barth, Courtney, Berrick, and Albert (1994) noted that "other things being equal, entering foster care under one year of age more than doubles a child's odds of being adopted but being placed initially in a kinship home cuts the odds by one-half" (p. 161). Thornton (1991) found that kinship foster parents were not interested in adopting the children in their care. Even when they were aware of available adoption subsidies, 85 percent of kinship foster parents stated that they would not adopt; one additional kinship foster parent stated that she would adopt only if she was pressured by the agency. Ninety-one percent of foster care caseworkers indicated awareness of this mindset on the part of kinship foster parents.

The reluctance to adopt formally among African American kinship foster caregivers is based in cultural definitions of family and attitudes about family relationships. For example, the reason given by 70 percent of kinship foster parents for their unwillingness to adopt was that they already considered the child and themselves as being a part of the same family and that it was therefore unnecessary to adopt and would be confusing to the child (Thornton, 1991). They were content to maintain a grandparent-to-grandchild caregiving relationship. (In most instances, kinship foster parents are grandparents or great aunts or uncles.) Also, 30 percent of kinship foster parents were concerned that adopting the child formally would result in conflict in their relationship with the child's biological parents.

In summarizing factors associated with the likelihood of being adopted, Barth, Courtney, Berrick, and Albert (1994) asserted that kinship foster care should not be considered a substitute for adoption. At the same time, they pointed out that it must, under law (Adoption Assistance and Child Welfare Act of 1980), be understood as an option for adoption. In spite of this, foster care statistics may continue to combine relative and nonrelative foster placements, inflating the number of children who are in out-of-home care and appear to be available for adoption. If kinship foster caregivers are accepted as a part of the child's family, and the child's planned long-term placement with them is considered an acceptable alternative to adoption, the numbers recorded for children who are available for or requiring adoption, especially children of color, should decrease dramatically.

Effects of Poverty

An overriding issue to be addressed is the circumstances that cause children of color to be in out-of-home placement in such large numbers. Living in poverty is one such circumstance, and it disproportionately affects children of color. Over 46 percent of all African American children lived in poverty in 1993, as did 41 percent of all Latino children; only 14 percent of white children lived in poverty

(Children's Defense Fund, 1995). Fifty-six percent of children living with their mothers only were poor, compared with 12 percent of those living with married parents, and children of color were more likely than white children to live in mother-only households.

Poverty has been linked to the circumstances that result in out-of-home placements. A recently released National Incidence Study of Child Abuse and Neglect ("Survey Shows," 1996) showed that "children from families with annual incomes below $15,000 were over 22 times more likely to experience maltreatment than children from families whose incomes exceeded $30,000. They were also 18 times more likely to be sexually abused, almost 56 times more likely to be educationally neglected, and over 22 times more likely to be seriously injured" (p. 3). Children of single parents had an 87 percent greater risk of being harmed by physical neglect and an 80 percent greater risk of suffering serious injury or harm from abuse and neglect. Thus, children of color may be at greater risk of abuse and neglect, which may be associated with the inadequate resources and resulting stresses their parents confront. Poor children are at risk of permanent removal from their families simply because of their economic position in society.

The direction of public policies currently is to speed up the transracial adoption of children of color without first correcting the resource deficiencies that cause the children to be in out-of-home care. Such policies ignore the complexities of this situation and risk giving one group (those desiring to adopt a young child) an advantage while failing to protect those who are among the most vulnerable (poor children and families). Social programs originating under the Family Preservation Act of 1992 (Omnibus Budget Reconciliation Act of 1993) are examples of corrective efforts. For example, most states have programs modeled after the original HomeBuilders, Inc., of Tacoma, Washington (Kinney, Madsen, Fleming, & Haapala, 1977). In such programs, child welfare workers are available to families on a 24-hour basis to provide immediate services and resources to facilitate the child's safe presence within the family. Wraparound programs (VanDenBerg & Grealish, 1996) coordinate the provision of services and resources to families, but on an ongoing rather than time-limited basis and as a collaborative community effort. These two programs are examples of how states may invest in families in attempting to prevent their breakdown.

SOCIAL WORK ORGANIZATION POSITIONS

The formal positions of social work and related organizations serve as a guide to social work practice in the context of considerations of race and ethnicity in adoption. There is some variability in these positions, and this chapter briefly summarizes several.

In its most recent policy statement, NASW (1997) included the following: "Placement decisions should reflect a child's need for continuity, safeguarding the child's right to consistent care and to service arrangements. Agencies must recognize each child's need to retain a significant engagement with his or her parents and extended family and respect the integrity of each child's ethnicity and cultural heritage" (p. 137). The policy statement continues, "The social work profession stresses the importance of ethnic and cultural sensitivity. An effort to maintain a child's identity and her or his ethnic heritage should prevail in all services and placement actions that involve children in foster care and adoption programs, including adherence to the principles articulated in the Indian Child Welfare Act" (p. 138). With regard specifically to principles related to adoption, the statement reads, "The recruitment of and placement with adoptive parents from each relevant ethnic or racial group should be available to meet the needs of children" (p. 140).

In the concluding paragraph to its current position statement, the NABSW (1994) states,

> In conclusion, family preservation, reunification and adoption should work in tandem toward finding permanent homes for children. Priority should be given to preserving families through the reunification or adoption of children with/by biological relatives. If that should fail, secondary priority should be given to the placement of a child within his own race. Transracial adoption of an African-American child should only be considered after documented evidence of unsuccessful same race placements has been reviewed and supported by appropriate representatives of the African-American community. Under no circumstance should successful same race placements be impeded by obvious barriers (i.e., legal limits of states, state boundaries, fees, surrogate payments, intrusive applications, lethargic court systems, inadequate staffing patterns, etc.). As such, it will be mandatory that national policies with adequate funding be adopted as part of any new legislation. (p. 4)

The most recent standards of the Child Welfare League of America (1988) include an emphasis on the preservation of the birth family:

> When children's rights to the care and protection of those who gave them birth are jeopardized, society should, through its appropriate designated agencies, provide support to birth parents to make it possible for children to remain in their own homes. Children should not be deprived of their birth parents solely because of economic need, or the need for other forms of community assistance to reinforce parental efforts to maintain a home for them. (p. 2)

With regard to the role of the extended family, the standards read, "When children's parents are unable or unwilling to rear them, efforts should be made to have members of the extended family assume the parenting role and responsibility, providing they can offer the care and protection that the children need and that this is the desire of the birth parents" (p. 3). Finally, with regard to considerations of race and ethnicity, "Children should not be deprived of the opportunity to have a permanent family of their own by reason of age, religion, racial, or ethnic group identification, nationality, residence, or handicap" (p. 4).

The standards include the clarification that federal legislation is perceived as safeguarding the rights of children.

The North American Council on Adoptable Children (NACAC) (Gilles & Kroll, 1991) has reaffirmed its original position, established in 1981, which stated as follows:

> Placement of children with a family of like ethnic background is desirable because such families are likely to provide the special needs of minority children with the strengths that counter the ill effects of racism. . . . The special needs of minority children who are of mixed ethnic background, school age, sibling groups or who have handicapping conditions should be considered in order to prevent unnecessary delays in placement. NACAC supports inclusion of multiethnic adoption as an option for children. (p. 37)

In 1988 NACAC (Gilles & Kroll, 1991), in addition to encouraging federal, state, and local officials to "fully utilize family resources in minority communities through aggressive and culturally sensitive recruitment and retention programs" (p. 38), decided to "direct [its] resources to the development, growth, and empowerment of minority adoptive parent groups" (p. 38). In 1990 it resolved the following: "Recognizing that fees charged prospective adoptive families present barriers to the most culturally appropriate placement for children in need of adoption, NACAC advocates that all child-placing agencies have as a goal working to develop alternative funding sources to cover all costs related to adoption services by working with both private and public sectors" (Gilles & Kroll, 1991, p. 38).

Five themes can be noted from among the position statements of these professional organizations regarding transracial adoption: (1) that ethnic heritage is important; (2) that children be raised preferably by their biological parents or, when not possible, by other biological relatives; (3) that economic need alone is not an acceptable reason for children to be deprived of their biological parents; (4) that efforts should be made to ensure that adoptive parents of the same race as the child are available and systemic barriers should not interfere; and (5) that placement with parents of a different race is acceptable and even preferable when the alternative means a child is deprived of a permanent home and family. It is important that social work organizations publicize these positions to their members and advocate for public policies that facilitate these themes.

CONCLUSIONS AND RECOMMENDATIONS

Inequities exist in the eligibility and recruitment of nonkin foster families and adoptive families of color, in services provided to children and families in the child welfare system, and in the increased tendency of poor children to be in out-of-home care. Statistics on the numbers and characteristics of children of color who are in foster care and who are available for adoption may be misleading. Public policies that disallow the consideration of race and ethnicity in adoption give an advantage to families who desire to adopt transracially.

At the same time, they fail to correct the circumstances that cause children of color to require out-of-home placement, and they fail to eliminate methods of maintaining or interpreting statistical data that may be misleading.

The following recommendations are made to lessen the need for transracial adoption. First, foster families of color should be actively recruited for kinship and non-kinship foster care and especially for participation in fost adoption programs, if such programs are to continue. Second, active and ongoing efforts to recruit and retain adoptive families of color should be increased so that the pool of available families equals or surpasses the number of children of color who are available for nonkin adoption. Third, creative strategies should continue to be developed to recruit adoptive families of color for "hard to place" children or children with special needs. Such children should continue to be placed according to their individual needs. Fourth, public policies and agency procedures should be established to require that children of color receive equitable services in all areas of the child welfare system. Fifth, statistics and outcome data relating to kinship foster care should be separated from those pertaining to nonrelative foster care; the benefits of the former as an acceptable permanent alternative to adoption should be evaluated. And sixth, policymakers should address the larger issues involved in ensuring that all children have access to the economic resources that can help them remain out of the child welfare system.

Social work has a central role to play in carrying out these recommendations. This role may include advocating in agencies for equitable (bias-free) selection; recruiting foster and adoptive families; orienting agency administrators, board members, and the general community regarding cultural definitions of "family"; conducting research that can scientifically inform public policy; participating in practice oriented to strengthening and unifying families while protecting children; and educating students and new professionals in the competent performance of such roles. A review of committee reports of the most recent adoption legislation (H. Rep. No. 104-542, 104th Congress, 2d Sess., 1996) demonstrates that statistical data, and the way they are collected and interpreted, play a primary role in the development of public policy. It is important, therefore, that social workers be actively involved in ensuring that complete and accurate research and numerical data are disseminated to public policymakers.

A limitation of this chapter is that in some instances the data were derived from studies of children in out-of-home care in a limited number of states. However, the consistency of the findings and the fact that research data on these topics are limited render available data useful in interpreting the state of the field and suggest directions for future research, policy, and practice.

Finally, seeking to solve the problems associated with the overrepresentation of children of color in the child welfare system by protecting transracial adoption is simplistic and fails to protect those who are most vulnerable in this society—the children dependent on

that society. A more responsible approach is to understand and eliminate the circumstances that constitute the base cause of this situation.
The most recent adoption legislation (Small Business Job Protection
Act of 1996) became effective only on January 1, 1997, so it is too early
to determine how adoption agencies will respond. However, this will
be an important area for review.

REFERENCES

Adoption Assistance and Child Welfare Act of 1980, P.L. No. 96-272, §473, 94 Stat. 500.

Adoption—Not just for Woody and Mia. (1992, September 23). *Wall Street Journal*,
p. A16.

Barth, R. P., Courtney, M., Berrick, J., & Albert, V. (1994). *From child abuse to permanency planning: Child welfare services pathways and placements.* New York: Aldine de
Gruyter.

Barth, R. P., Courtney, M., Berrick, J., Albert, V., & Needell, B. (1994). Kinship care:
Rights and responsibilities, services and standards. In R. P. Barth, M. Courtney,
J. Berrick, & V. Albert (Eds.), *From child abuse to permanency planning: Child welfare
services pathways and placements* (pp. 195–219). New York: Aldine de Gruyter.

Bartholet, E. (1991). Where do black children belong? The politics of race matching
in adoption. *University of Pennsylvania Law Review, 139,* 1163–1256.

Child Welfare League of America. (1988). *Child Welfare League of America standards for
adoption service.* Washington, DC: Author.

Children's Defense Fund. (1995). *The state of America's children yearbook: 1995.* Washington, DC: Author.

Courtney, M. E., Barth, R. P., Berrick, J. D., Brooks, D., Needell, B., & Park, L. (1996).
Race and child welfare services: Past research and future directions. *Child Welfare,
75,* 99–137.

Day, D. (1979). *The adoption of black children.* Lexington, MA: D. C. Heath.

Dubowitz, H., Feigelman, S., & Zuravin, S. (1993). A profile of kinship care. *Child
Welfare, 72,* 153–169.

Elias, M. (1991, August 15). Black kids, white parents: Debating what's best for the
kids. *USA Today,* p. 1D.

Flango, V. E., & Flango, C. (1994). *The flow of adoption information from the states* (Publication No. R-162). Williamsburg, VA: National Center for State Courts.

Folaron, G., & Hess, P. (1993). Placement considerations for children of mixed
African American and Caucasian parentage. *Child Welfare, 72,* 113–125.

Foster care and adoption statistics: Adoption and foster care analysis and reporting
system (1997, January 9). Available online at http://www.acf.dhhs.gov/
program/cb/stats.htm #AFCARS.

Fraser, M. W., Pecora, P. J., & Haapala, D. A. (1991). *Families in crisis: The impact of intensive family preservation services.* New York: Aldine de Gruyter.

Gant, L. M. (1984). *Black adoption programs: Pacesetters in practice.* Ann Arbor, MI: National Child Welfare Training Center.

Gilles, T., & Kroll, J. (1991). *Barriers to same race placement.* St. Paul: North American
Council on Adoptable Children.

Gould, K. H. (1991). Limiting damage is not enough: A minority perspective on
child welfare issues. In J. E. Everett, S. S. Chipungu, & B. R. Leashore (Eds.), *Child
welfare: An Africentric perspective* (pp. 58–77). New Brunswick, NJ: Rutgers University Press.

Hairston, C. F., & Williams, V. G. (1989). Black adoptive parents: How they view
agency adoption practices. *Social Casework, 70,* 534–538.

Hermann, V. P. (1993). Transracial adoption: "Child-saving" or "child-snatching"?
National Black Law Journal, 13, 147–164.

Herzog, E., Sudia, C., Harwood, J., & Newcomb, C. (1971). *Families for black children.*
Washington, DC: U.S. Government Printing Office.

Homes for Black Children: Hearing of the Senate Subcommittee on Children, Family, Drugs, and Alcoholism. (1993, July 15). Testimony of Sydney Duncan. 103d Congress, 1st Sess., 26–68.

Indian Child Welfare Act of 1978, §1214, 95th Cong., 2d Sess.

Jackson-White, G., Dozier, C. D., Oliver, J. T., & Gardner, L. B. (1997). Why African American adoption agencies succeed: A new perspective on self-help. *Child Welfare, 76,* 239–254.

Kinney, J. M., Madsen, B., Fleming, T., & Haapala, D. A. (1977). HomeBuilders: Keeping families together. *Journal of Consulting & Clinical Psychology, 45,* 667–673.

Mahoney, J. (1991). The black baby doll: Transracial adoption and cultural preservation. *University of Missouri–Kansas City Law Review, 59,* 487–501.

McRoy, R. G. (1989). An organizational dilemma: The case of transracial adoptions. *Journal of Applied Behavioral Science, 25,* 145–160.

McRoy, R. G. (1994). Attachment and racial identity issues: Implications for child placement decision making. *Journal of Multicultural Social Work, 3,* 59–74.

McRoy, R. G., Oglesby, Z., & Grape, H. (1997). Achieving same race adoptive placements for African-American children: Culturally sensitive practice approaches. *Child Welfare, 76,* 85–104.

Meezan, W., & Shireman, J. F. (1985). *Care and commitment: Foster parent adoption decisions.* Albany: State University of New York Press.

Multiethnic Placement Act of 1994, P.L. 103-382, §553, 108 Stat. 4057.

National Association of Black Social Workers. (1994). *Preserving African-American families: Position statement.* Detroit: Author.

National Association of Social Workers. (1997). *Social work speaks: NASW policy statements* (4th ed.). Washington, DC: NASW Press.

Omnibus Budget Reconciliation Act of 1993, P.L. 103-66, 107 Stat. 312.

Rezendes, M. (1994). Debate intensifies on adoptions across racial lines. *Boston Globe,* p. 1.

Richman, R. (1993, December 7). Transracial adoptions get vocal advocate. *Plain Dealer* (From the *Washington Post*), p. C6.

Silverman, A. R. (1993). Outcomes of transracial adoption. *Future of Children, 3,* 104–118.

Simon, R. J., & Alstein, H. (1977). *Transracial adoption.* New York: John Wiley & Sons.

Simon, R. J., & Alstein, H. (1987). *Transracial adoptees and their families: A study of identity and commitment.* New York: Praeger.

Small Business Job Protection Act of 1996, P.L. 104-188, §§ 1807–1808. http://web.lexis-nexis.com/eis/retrieve/document (1997).

Survey shows dramatic increase in child abuse and neglect, 1986–1993. Available: online at http://www.adv.dhhs.gov/news/press/1996/nis.htm.

Thornton, J. L. (1991). Permanency planning for children in kinship homes. *Child Welfare, 70,* 593–601.

VanDenBerg, J. E., & Grealish, M. (1996). Individualized services and supports through the wraparound process: Philosophy and procedures. *Journal of Child and Family Studies, 5,* 7–21.

Williams, C. C. (1991). Expanding the options in the quest for permanence. In J. E. Everett, S. S. Chipungu, & B. R. Leashore (Eds.), *Child welfare: An Africentric perspective* (pp. 266–289). New Brunswick, NJ: Rutgers University Press.

The author acknowledges Paula Allen-Meares and Kristine Siefert, University of Michigan School of Social Work, and Shelley MacDermid, Purdue University Department of Child Development and Family Studies, for their suggestions.

11 Mediation in Kinship Care:
Another Step in the Provision of Culturally Relevant Child Welfare Services

Maria Wilhelmus

Many pressing issues face the U.S. child welfare system. The system is being inundated with children in need of homes at a time when traditional foster placements are difficult to find (National Commission on Family Foster Care, 1991). An estimated 3.1 million children were reported to child protective services agencies as alleged victims of child maltreatment in 1995 alone, with 996,000 of this number eventually confirmed (based on data collected from 37 states and the District of Columbia; Daro, 1996). Child maltreatment reports also are increasing (Pear, 1996). Between 1994 and 1995, this increase was an average of 2 percent per state, with the total number of reports nationwide showing an increase of 49 percent since 1986 (Daro, 1996).

Not surprisingly, there has been a corresponding increase in the number of children entering foster care. From 1982 to 1992, there was a 62 percent increase in the number of children in out-of-home placements (U.S. Department of Health and Human Services, 1996). Finding homes for all the children in need of placement has become more difficult; the number of qualified foster homes has decreased 30 percent since 1984 (National Commission on Family Foster Care, 1991). Children of color are disproportionately represented in the foster care population (Davis, 1995; Hill, 1987), and there have been calls to increase "sensitivity to cultural context" in the delivery of child welfare services (Pinderhughes, 1991, p. 604).

KINSHIP CARE

To meet the challenges posed by the large numbers of children and limited nonrelative foster care placements, the child welfare system has begun to actively incorporate kinship care into its array of services (Berrick, Barth, & Needell, 1994; Gleeson, 1995). Although it is challenging to ascertain precise figures on a national level, in many jurisdictions it has been estimated that close to 50 percent of children removed from parental custody have been placed with relatives (Child

This chapter was originally published in the March 1998 issue of *Social Work*, Vol. 43, pp. 117–126.

Welfare League of America, 1994). *Kinship care* has been defined as "the full-time nurturing and protection of children who must be separated from their parents by relatives, members of their tribes or clans, godparents, step-parents, or other adults who have a kinship bond with a child" (Child Welfare League of America, 1994, p. 2). Kinship care has been further defined as being provided by either "kinship caregivers," who provide care that is not formally recognized by the foster care system, or "kinship foster parents," who are recognized by the foster care system (Berrick et al., 1994). This dual terminology used in kinship care captures the juxtaposition of a centuries-old tradition of extended family and community responsibility for the care of children and the modern child welfare system.

Years before the existence of kinship foster parents, there were kinship caregivers (Hill, 1987; National Commission on Family Foster Care, 1991; Stack, 1974). In a discussion of kinship care, Scannapieco and Jackson (1996) reviewed the literature detailing the historical response of African American families to separation and loss. From West African tradition to the pre–Civil War era, through Reconstruction and up to the modern day, the shared commitment to children, family, and community—as evidenced in the emphasis on kinship relationships—has been a great source of strength for African American families in the face of adversity. A modern example of the strength of African American kinship ties is evidenced in the current practice of African American midlife and older women stepping in to raise children left parentless by the crack cocaine epidemic (Minkler & Roe, 1993).

Even after recognition by the child welfare system, today's kinship foster families closely resemble the more informal kinship care relationships evidenced throughout history. Children in kinship foster care are predominantly African American (Berrick et al., 1994; National Commission on Family Foster Care, 1991; Thornton, 1991). In fact, a study in Baltimore found that 90 percent of kinship foster care families were African American (Dubowitz, Tepper, Feigelman, Sawyer, & Davidson, 1990), and a survey in Philadelphia found that 88 percent of kinship foster families were African American (Ingram, 1996).

Kinship caregivers tend to be low-income, older women of color (Thornton, 1987, 1991). A majority of kinship foster care families, including both biological parents and kin caregivers, have few financial resources (Berrick et al., 1994; Gleeson, 1996). Echoing the sentiments of kin caregivers throughout time, kinship foster caregivers are motivated primarily by a sense of familial responsibility to provide a nurturing environment for children in a time of stress (Minkler & Roe, 1993).

Growing Need for Culturally Responsive Child Welfare Services

It has been stated that the "ethnocentric design and implementation of the [child welfare] system, and its symbiotic relationship with the American legal system, are central to its failure to deliver culturally sensitive and relevant child welfare services" (Gleeson, 1995, p. 186). A quarter-century ago, Billingsley and Giovannoni (1972) expressed grave concerns regarding the effects of the child welfare system on African American children. More recently, a commentator on the child welfare system stated that the "changing demographics of our society require that we deal with our ever-increasing cultural diversity" (Pinderhughes, 1991, p. 604), and it has been asserted that "the cultural nuances of minority client populations are not fully accepted and are often misunderstood by child welfare administrators and practitioners" (Jackson, 1996, p. 597).

Arguably, the child welfare system has begun to move in a more culturally aware direction through the acknowledgment and support of kinship foster care, a practice with a rich cultural background. However, it remains to be seen what impact the formal recognition of kinship caregiving will have on the overall design and implementation of child welfare services. The foster care system was designed for nonrelative care, and questions have been raised whether "categorical models of service delivery that are designed for nonrelative care are a positive alternative for kinship families and children" (Jackson, 1996, p. 596).

Indeed, transforming child welfare policy and practice will most likely be a slow process. Currently, although all states treat kinship care as a kind of family foster care guided by federal policies on out-of-home placements (Gleeson & Craig, 1994), jurisdictions vary widely in their kinship care policies and practice. One of the major issues states face in developing new approaches to kinship care revolves around the traditional linkage that has existed between the level of support and the level of supervision for children and families in the system (Hornby, Zeller, & Karraker, 1996). The change from viewing relative caretaking "as an alternative to the child welfare system" to "a service encouraged and funded" is a dramatic one (Gleeson, 1995, p. 184) and has necessitated the redefinition of roles and relationships between the child welfare system and kinship foster families.

Sources of Conflict in Formalized Kinship Care

In kinship foster care policy and practice, controversy has erupted around the "factors that led to placement, internal family relationships, and family–agency relationships" (National Commission on Family Foster Care, 1991). Recently, Gleeson (1995) identified questions that are shaping national debate in this area: issues of family decision making, level of government intrusion into kinship networks, permanency concerns, and the financial responsibilities of the kinship members and the government.

At the policy level, the biggest question is whether children placed with kin will be included or excluded in the child welfare system. Hornby et al. (1996) asserted that this debate has special implications for families of color. For example, it may be anticipated that kin will take care of related children in need of placement because they are of the same family and ethnic identity. However, because most kinship families are families of color, a policy that attempts to include kinship caregivers in the child welfare system may arguably further the perception that families of color are unable to take care of their own children and thus need the intervention and supervision of the state. This viewpoint could be used to argue for exclusion of kinship care families from the system. In contrast, it can also be argued that deflecting kinship care families from the system is simply a way to withhold support from families of color, who are more likely to assume care for their related children than the larger community irrespective of assistance from the state (Hornby et al., 1996).

Family Perspective. At the practice level, policy questions and the systemic transition that is precipitating them often dissolve into conflict. For grandparents and other relative caretakers who step in to provide care for children, much stress is associated with the added responsibilities (Burton, 1992). However, the relatives who assume such duties are often the family members who have served as a family resource for years, successfully meeting various family crises and needs of children without the involvement of the child welfare system (Scannapieco & Hegar, 1996). For the relatives of a child in need of service, the child welfare system's broad policies and practices may seem ill fitted to the strengths and needs of individual families. This situation may be exacerbated by the fact that kinship foster parents have been found to be receiving considerably less (or even no) training to prepare for their new role as foster parents (Thornton, 1987), which can result in tension when child welfare workers operate under the assumption that standard foster parent interactions will be the norm. For example, the kinship caretaker may feel that "family knows best" and not understand and accept the agency's efforts on behalf of the child in placement.

Another cause of friction in agency–kinship foster family relations can be policies that result in kinship foster parents not being able to qualify for the higher foster care payments (Berrick et al., 1994). Kinship foster parents may also experience frustration at the child welfare system's emphasis on permanency planning, especially in cases where the child will not be reunified with the biological parent and adoption is the recommended goal; many kinship foster parents have mixed feelings regarding the termination of the biological parent's rights (Thornton, 1991). Also, even if there is no move to terminate parental rights, when a child's placement with kin is safe, stable, and ongoing, the kinship caregivers may resist the continued involvement of the child welfare agency in their lives.

There may also be resentment and frustration regarding child welfare workers' attempts to regulate and supervise visitation with the biological parent. This is a common cause of conflict between kinship caregivers and the agency, and one reason may be that there is simply more biological parent–child contact in kinship foster care situations. Berrick et al. (1994) found that not only is birth parent–child contact more frequent, it is also of a qualitatively different nature, with a more "informal" and "familylike" aspect to the visitations (p. 53). Also, conflicts between the agency and kinship caregivers can arise when the kinship placement occurred in a case where there was an "out-of-control parent," a "parent who is determined to reunite with the child by any means," or a "child who is determined to resist the placement" (Scannapieco & Hegar, 1996, p. 574).

Conversely, the kinship foster family may feel neglected and forgotten by the child welfare agency and feel that they are not getting the necessary services and expertise that a nonrelative foster care family might. Studies have shown that kinship care families receive less supervision than nonkin foster homes (Dubowitz et al., 1990). Berrick et al. (1994) found that services provided by placement agencies were much more likely to be offered to nonrelative foster parents than kinship foster parents. Although they found that kinship foster parents tended to report that they were pleased with their relationship with the agency social worker, over a third of the kinship foster parents stated that they would prefer more agency contact.

Scannapieco and Hegar (1996) discussed housing issues as another common source of agency–kinship family conflict. Many of the physical requirements for housing in the foster home certification process can pose problems for kinship caregivers and may require a flexible approach. Although some agencies may have extra funding to help kinship families meet the housing standards, others do not include such homes in the foster care program, even though children may be placed there without payment of the board rate for foster homes that pass the certification. Also, "there may . . . be occasions to relax requirements about separate sleeping space for boys and girls or number of children in a bedroom, depending on the ages, biological relationship, and accustomed sleeping patterns of the children involved" (Scannapieco & Hegar, 1996, p. 575).

Social Worker Perspective. When the placement is going well, the agency may be moved to question its ongoing role, especially regarding the quantity and quality of contact with the kinship foster family (Wilson & Chipungu, 1996). Unfortunately, there is no agreement among child welfare professionals whether kinship placements can be considered permanent placements, and this lack of consensus is reflected at the policy and practice levels, so this conflict will most likely continue (Hornby et al., 1996).

In other cases, child welfare workers may have concerns about the contact between the biological parent and the child that the kin foster parent is allowing to take place and may suspect that their directives on this subject are being circumvented. They may also believe that their authority and expertise in providing services to the child are undermined by the kin foster parent and find that they are in a more intense power struggle than previously experienced with nonrelative foster parents. Although the worker may agree that it is unfair that kinship care families receive less financial support than nonrelative foster families, he or she may believe that the kinship care family's anger is misdirected and may resent the overt anger at the worker and the agency over what the worker perceives to be a policy issue. The worker may have concerns that the kinship foster family produced the parent now deemed unfit to assume responsibility for the child in need of services (Gray & Nybell, 1990), and he or she may feel warranted in making greater intrusions into the kinship care foster family's life (one of the major arguments of opponents to formalized kinship care [Dubowitz, Feigelman, & Zuravin, 1993]).

Conversely, the worker may believe that relatives provide a more secure placement for foster children and feel warranted in providing less supervision. He or she may be unaware that the kinship foster family would actually prefer more visible agency involvement and support and that this laissez-faire approach, although it expresses confidence in the kinship foster family's abilities, is the cause of anxiety or frustration.

MEDIATION AS AN ALTERNATIVE METHOD OF RESOLVING DISPUTES

The response to escalating conflict in kinship foster care often entails turning to the judicial system for a resolution of the points in dispute. However, the failure of the child welfare system to deliver culturally relevant services has been linked to its inextricable ties to the courts (Gleeson, 1995). Child welfare programs exist within a legal environment that includes the legal system to "interpret legislation and define client rights" (Stein, 1991, p. 14). The courts' litigation process is bound by inflexible rules of procedure that dictate the format of information presented to the court, the parties who present the information, and when the dispute will be heard and resolved (Maresca, 1995). Even after a decision is rendered by a court of law, there may be continuing problems. The legal system is just not able to "supervise the fragile and complex interpersonal relationships between family members that may continue after their immediate dispute is resolved" (Folberg & Taylor, 1984, p. 35).

Particularly within the context of kinship foster care, which may involve the subtleties of cultural and ethnic implications, once affected subgroups have relinquished their authority to contribute to the resolution of the dispute, the final decision may not be perceived as fair or reflective of personal experience. The result may be feelings of powerlessness and frustration with the system, or even—if it was opposed in the hearing or trial by the kinship family and children— circumvention of the court order (Maresca, 1995). It is axiomatic that culturally relevant services for families and children must begin with input from the affected racial and ethnic groups.

As an alternative to the legal system in the resolution of disputes, mediation provides an opportunity for kinship foster families to have a voice in the development of meaningful interventions in child welfare. Social workers dealing with kinship care issues must develop the skills necessary to negotiate and resolve conflicts (Child Welfare League of America, 1994). Certainly such training is helpful to social workers in a multitude of settings. In fact, one of the functions of the social work profession has been described as mediating the conflicts that exist between individuals and society (Schwartz, cited in Compton & Galaway, 1989). However, this chapter proposes a more narrowly construed concept of mediation as a method of conflict resolution. Because of the unique historical and cultural context of kinship care and the gravity of the child protection issues involved, conflict in the family–agency relationship merits a nonadversarial approach to resolving disputes that incorporates concepts like respect and empowerment into its procedural mechanisms.

In an article on the function of minority group concerns in the development of mediation in Central and Eastern Europe, it was stated that "conflicts presented by minority groups in democratic society have the potential to create new norms, rules, and institutional structures that change consensual understandings concerning how the society functions" (Shonholtz, 1993, p. 235). To realize the potential of mediation in kinship foster care, a clear understanding of the procedure is necessary. *Mediation* has been defined as a process that

> offers an alternative to violence, self-help, or litigation [and] differs from the processes of counseling, negotiation, and arbitration. It can be defined as the process by which the participants, together with the assistance of a neutral person or persons, systematically isolate disputed issues in order to develop options, consider alternatives, and reach a consensual settlement that will accommodate their needs. Mediation is a process that emphasizes the participants' own responsibility for making decisions that affect their lives. It is therefore a self-empowering process. (Folberg & Taylor, 1984, p. 8)

With mediation, most disputes can be resolved in a half-day or one-day session (with the exception of divorce mediation). Mediation has proved successful in resolving a wide variety of interpersonal disputes. Guided by a few rules that are designed to protect confidentiality and to give all parties the opportunity to state their concerns and be heard, mediation typically involves an opening statement from the mediator, opening statements from all parties, a conference regarding the major issues in dispute, private caucuses where the mediator meets with each party separately to review strengths and weaknesses of the disputants' viewpoints and to brainstorm on ideas for settlement, and a final conference to work out any remaining differences. The settlement of the dispute may be reflected in an agreement that is signed by the parties. For the agreement to be legally enforceable, a court order can include the terms of the agreement, or the agreement can be written as a legal contract (Lovenheim, 1996).

Mediation and Cultural Tradition

Like kinship care, mediation has a rich historical tradition, with current mediation practice drawing from ancient Chinese, Japanese, and African cultures, among others. Within these cultures there was an emphasis on united efforts to resolve disputes. The processes of gathering information, presenting different aspects of a situation, and reaching equitable agreements were viewed as a collaborative effort that must necessarily be inclusive of the expertise of extended family and community (Folberg & Taylor, 1984).

In certain African communities, there is a cultural heritage involving the gathering of a "*moot*, or neighborhood meeting" when parties find themselves unable to resolve a disagreement (Gibbs, quoted in Folberg & Taylor, 1984, p. 2, italics added). The moot is presided over by a revered community member who facilitates the reaching of a consensual agreement. The actual composition of the moot may vary from one community to another, but there are certain underlying similarities. There is a presumption that a resolution can be reached through cooperative techniques. Also, decision-making power rests within the moot and is not transferred to an outside entity who has the authority to make a unilateral judgment and impose sanctions (Gibbs, cited in Folberg & Taylor, 1984).

It seems natural that in attempting to construct a practice response to concerns in the kinship foster care arena, there should be a return to the basic recognition that kin invested in an equitable and lasting resolution to a conflict involving their family may offer the most ingenious approach to seemingly intractable problems. At a minimum, mediation would provide a forum where the the voice of the kinship foster parent is not lost in the din of the often overpowering adversarial legal system. Mediation offers an alternative to the adversarial methods of dispute resolution where the final outcome involves the designation of winner and loser. With mediation, even if every aspect of the conflict in a kinship foster care situation cannot be settled, the issues that surround the dispute can be expressed and comprehended by the parties, thus breaking up the conflict into more easily tackled portions—a win–win situation (Folberg & Taylor, 1984).

Most important, when kinship foster families are families of color, the mediation process is uniquely designed to use "the values, norms, and principles of the participants" (Folberg & Taylor, 1984, p. 8). Nothing is more empowering to kinship foster care families of color than to have the ability to contribute ideas and plans that reflect their personal and cultural histories to the design of agreements that will guide future interactions with child welfare and legal authorities. In short, mediation can help "diminish obstacles to communication" between kinship foster care parents and the child welfare system, "maximize the exploration of alternatives" in this fast-growing area of child welfare, genuinely take into account "the needs of everyone involved," and create "a model for future conflict resolution" (Folberg & Taylor, 1984, p. 9).

Appropriateness of Mediation in Child Care

Although applying the process of mediation to the kinship care arena offers many advantages, there are two major issues that must be addressed. First, is it appropriate to mediate conflict in child welfare, where child protection is often at issue? Second, is there a power imbalance between kinship foster care families and the child welfare system such that the integrity of the mediation process is called into question? There is limited literature on the use of mediation to resolve disputes in the U.S. child welfare system (Kaminsky & Cosmano, 1990; Mayer, 1985, 1989). However, mediation has been used in child protective cases in Toronto with high levels of party agreement and child protection and considerable savings reported (Maresca, 1995). In Nova Scotia the development of a mediation program for child protection cases has resulted in a majority of the cases being mediated before resorting to court action (Savoury, Beals, & Parks, 1995). Significantly, Savoury et al. stated that child protection workers have typically received little, if any, training in dispute resolution and are often "in a vulnerable position in attempting to resolve conflict situations" (p. 745). As has been demonstrated in the United States, this vulnerability, combined with the vulnerability of the families in the child welfare system, usually lends itself to court involvement. Further research is needed within the context of the U.S. legal system to determine whether it is the exclusive province of the courts to offer justice to families in cases involving child protection issues.

Both Maresca (1995) and Savoury et al. (1995) addressed the issue of power imbalances between the parties to the child protection mediation (that is, kinship foster families and representatives of the child welfare agencies) and emphasized the importance of mediator training. Maresca listed some techniques the mediator can use to create an environment conducive to an equitable resolution of the conflict, including "translating professional jargon into accessible words, drawing out needs and interests and then summarizing them, giving parents an equal voice and validating their concerns, assisting the parties to generate different options for solutions, and ensuring that the parties have an opportunity to consult with others before committing themselves to any particular course of action" (p. 736). Kelly (1995) argued that a mediator can use "power-related interventions for vulnerable parties" to "temporarily" create an equal "negotiation field" that may represent the only chance an oppressed party may have "to express needs and interests" and "maximiz[e] options" (p. 88).

Obtaining Mediation Services

To prevent the mediation process from being viewed by the kinship foster families as simply an extension of the court's authority, the neutrality of the mediator is essential. Maresca (1995) stated that the "parties had to be confident that the mediator would be independent of any agency or identified interest group that might influence the mediator's response to any of the parties" (p. 736). How this can be accomplished within the context of the U.S. child welfare system warrants further exploration. This chapter proposes three alternatives: (1) public agencies contracting out for mediation services to a private mediator or community mediation center, (2) public agencies contracting with a private child welfare agency to deliver mediation services to families, and (3) public agencies supporting the training of community peer mediation groups, similar to the moots in African dispute resolution.

Private contractors can be used to conduct the mediation, but they can be costly, with one-hour sessions starting at about $125. Community mediation centers are typically independent, nonprofit organizations that get funding from state and local governments, and their services are either free or provided at a minimum cost (about $15 or $25). These community mediation centers are "an extremely cost-effective way" of resolving the kind of disputes "that often get lost in, or otherwise are not well served by, the local courts and criminal justice system," such as visitation access with the biological parent (Lovenheim, 1996, p. 3.11). The mediators at these centers are typically trained community volunteers, most are college educated, and they come from a variety of professional backgrounds (for example, teaching, social work, and law). There are about 400 such centers in the United States, and information about their services is available from the National Association for Community Mediation in Washington, DC (Lovenheim, 1996). It should be noted that the efforts of volunteer mediators have been discussed in the academic press, as evidenced in a successful dispute resolution on behalf of homeless populations (Nelson & Sharp, 1995).

In a discussion on service delivery in kinship care, Ingram (1996) detailed Philadelphia's practice of public agencies partnering with private agencies to provide supportive services to children and families. This collaboration is particularly successful because each of the private agencies is focused on a specific geographic area of the city, spurring greater use "of networks of community supports" and the development of "community peer groups among the kinship families" (Ingram, 1996, p. 562). Adding mediation to the listed services such private agencies provide may be another step in the provision of services within a community context. However, even though the services may be provided by the private agency, because authority and case management are retained by the public agency, there may be questions raised about the neutrality and possible bias of a mediator affiliated with a private agency that is in reality overseen by the public agency with whom the kin foster parent is in dispute. (Whether warranted or not, a perception of bias could undermine the mediation process.)

Another option in the application of mediation to resolve disputes in the kinship care arena would be for public agencies to train and supervise volunteer mediators drawn from the communities in which the kinship foster families reside. This arrangement would share the beneficial aspects of public and private agency partnership, because the decision-making process would occur at the community and neighborhood level, but there would be no doubt among kinship families about undue influence of the state on the mediator.

Like the concept of the moot, the mediator drawn from the community could involve the whole neighborhood in resolving the dispute. For example, if the agency is concerned that a foster grandmother is allowing the biological mother too much access to the children, the conflict may escalate for many reasons. Perhaps the foster grandmother feels too pressured by the biological parent to refuse access, or maybe she believes that the agency dictates are unfair, that the mother can be properly supervised, and that the grandmother's ability to handle the situation is being devalued. A trained mediator from the community has special knowledge and skills to apply to resolving the dispute and may even choose to include others from the neighborhood that have an active role in the lives of the children and family involved. This procedure would increase the likelihood of the conflict resolution process being culturally relevant by giving a voice to the community charged with raising the child and would thereby increase their level of investment in the outcome of the situation for the child and family.

CONCLUSION

Paradoxically, there are great obstacles and great opportunities in the provision of child welfare services. In part, the problems facing the foster care system have created an opportunity for the formal incorporation of kinship caretaking into the array of child welfare services. This formalization of relative caretaking has enriched the child welfare system with a service that has a long historical and cultural tradition. However, child welfare professionals have encountered some difficulties in an ethnocentrically designed system. Attempts to resolve these inherent conflicts present yet another opportunity for the growth of culturally relevant child welfare services.

The use of mediation, a method of nonadversarial dispute resolution with a strong cultural foundation, provides an empowering alternative for social workers and kinship foster families who are looking for solutions to problems in the child welfare system. Mediation offers a "swifter and more personally meaningful justice than the courts" and "complements social work values by empowering clients to plan for their future with a problem-solving focus" (Severson & Bankston, 1995, pp. 683–684). Severson and Bankston stated that social workers should suggest new areas where the process of mediation can be applied. Using mediation to resolve conflicts in kinship foster care is not only possible, it is arguably timely as well. Mediation represents yet another step toward the provision of culturally relevant social services.

REFERENCES

Berrick, J. D., Barth, R. P., & Needell, B. (1994). A comparison of kinship foster homes and foster family homes: Implications for kinship care as family preservation. *Children and Youth Services Review, 16*(1/2), 33–63.

Billingsley, A., & Giovannoni, J. (1972). *Children of the storm.* New York: Harcourt Brace Jovanovich.

Burton, L. M. (1992). Black grandparents rearing children of drug-addicted parents: Stressors, outcomes, and social needs. *Gerontologist, 32,* 744–751.

Child Welfare League of America. (1994). *Kinship care: A natural bridge.* Washington, DC: Author.

Compton, B. R., & Galaway, B. (1989). *Social work processes* (4th ed.). Belmont, CA: Wadsworth.

Daro, D. (1996). Current trends in child abuse reporting and fatalities: National Committee to Prevent Child Abuse (NCPCA)'s 1995 Annual Fifty State Survey. *American Professional Society on the Abuse of Children Advisor, 9*(2), 21–24.

Davis, R. (1995, April 13). Suits back interracial adoptions: Minority kids wait longer, groups say. *USA Today,* p. 3A.

Dubowitz, H., Feigelman, S., & Zuravin, S. (1993). A profile of kinship care. *Child Welfare 72,* 153–169.

Dubowitz, H., Tepper, V., Feigelman, S., Sawyer, R., & Davidson, N. (1990). *The physical and mental health and educational status of children placed with relatives: Final report.* Baltimore: University of Maryland School of Medicine.

Folberg, J., & Taylor, A. (1984). *Mediation: A comprehensive guide to resolving conflicts without litigation.* San Francisco: Jossey-Bass.

Gleeson, J. P. (1995). Kinship care and public child welfare: Challenges and opportunities for social work education. *Journal of Social Work Education, 31,* 182–193.

Gleeson, J. P. (1996). Kinship care as a child welfare service: The policy debate in an era of welfare reform. *Child Welfare, 75,* 419–449.

Gleeson, J. P., & Craig, L. C. (1994). Kinship care in child welfare: An analysis of states' policies. *Children and Youth Services Review, 16*(1/2), 7–31.

Gray, S. S., & Nybell, L. M. (1990). Issues in African-American family preservation. *Child Welfare, 69,* 513–523.

Hill, R. (1987, December). Building the future for black families. *American Visions,* pp. 16–25.

Hornby, H., Zeller, D., & Karraker, D. (1996). Kinship care in America: What outcomes should policy seek? *Child Welfare, 75,* 397–418.

Ingram, C. (1996). Kinship care: From last resort to first choice. *Child Welfare, 75,* 550–566.

Jackson, S. (1996). The kinship triad: A service delivery model. *Child Welfare, 75,* 583–599.

Kaminsky, H., & Cosmano, R. (1990). Mediating child welfare disputes: How to focus on the best interest of the child. *Mediation Quarterly, 7,* 229–234.

Kelly, J. B. (1995). Power imbalance in divorce and interpersonal mediation: Assessment and intervention. *Mediation Quarterly, 12,* 85–98.

Lovenheim, P. (1996). *How to mediate your dispute.* Berkeley, CA: Nolo Press.

Maresca, J. (1995). Mediating child protection cases. *Child Welfare, 74,* 731–742.

Mayer, B. (1985). Conflict resolution in child protection and adoption. *Mediation Quarterly, 7,* 69–81.

Mayer, B. (1989). Mediation in child protection cases: The impact of third party intervention on parental compliance attitudes. *Mediation Quarterly, 6,* 89–106.

Minkler, M., & Roe, K. M. (1993). *Grandmothers as caregivers: Raising children of the crack cocaine epidemic.* Newbury Park, CA: Sage Publications.

National Commission on Family Foster Care. (1991). *A blueprint for fostering infants, children, and youths in the 1990s.* Washington, DC: Child Welfare League of America, National Foster Parent Association.

Nelson, M. C., & Sharp, W. R. (1995). Mediating conflicts of persons at risk of homelessness: The Helping Hand project. *Mediation Quarterly, 12,* 317–325.

Pear, R. (1996, March 17). Many states fail to meet mandates on child welfare. *New York Times,* pp. 1, 14.

Pinderhughes, E. E. (1991). The delivery of child welfare services to African American clients. *American Journal of Orthopsychiatry, 61,* 599–605.

Savoury, G. R., Beals, H. L., & Parks, J. M. (1995). Mediation in child protection: Facilitating the resolution of disputes. *Child Welfare, 74,* 743–763.

Scannapieco, M., & Hegar, R. (1996). A nontraditional assessment framework for formal kinship homes. *Child Welfare, 75,* 567–582.

Scannapieco, M., & Jackson, S. (1996). Kinship care: The African American resilient response to family preservation. *Social Work, 41,* 190–196.

Severson, M. M., & Bankston, T. V. (1995). Social work and the pursuit of justice through mediation. *Social Work, 40,* 683–691.

Shonholtz, R. (1993). The role of minorities in establishing mediating norms and institutions in the new democracies. *Mediation Quarterly, 10,* 231–241.

Stack, C. (1974). *All our kin: Strategies for survival in a black community.* New York: Harper & Row.

Stein, T. J. (1991). *Child welfare.* White Plains, NY: Longman.

Thornton, J. L. (1987). *An investigation into the nature of kinship foster homes.* Doctoral dissertation, Wurzweiler School of Social Work, Yeshiva University, New York.

Thornton, J. L. (1991). Permanency planning for children in kinship foster homes. *Child Welfare, 70,* 593–601.

U.S. Department of Health and Human Services. (1996). *Child maltreatment 1994: Reports from the states to the National Center on Child Abuse and Neglect.* Washington, DC: U.S. Government Printing Office.

Wilson, D. B., & Chipungu, S. S. (1996). Introduction: Special issue on kinship care. *Child Welfare, 75,* 387–395.

Part III

EDUCATION AND YOUTHS

12 Reducing Racism in Schools:
Moving beyond Rhetoric

Michael S. Spencer

R acial prejudice has long been a part of human civilization. Although the United States maintains a goal of protecting human rights and promoting equality, there is an inconsistency between ideology and reality (Banks & Lynch, 1986). Historically, educational institutions have played an important part in responding to overt forms of racism. Educational reforms aimed at structural as well as curricular change have endured for much of the 20th century, despite controversy and opposition. More recently, there has been an increasing focus on curriculum development aimed specifically at reducing racial intolerance and the existing inequalities of the educational system (Banks & Lynch, 1986; Bennett, 1986; Leicester, 1989; Lynch, 1985; McCarthy, 1988; Mitchell, 1985, Mitchell, 1990; Pines & Hillard, 1990; Pipkin & Yates, 1992; Vincent, 1992).

Although the education system strives to meet the challenges of a multicultural society, it has become apparent that the goal of eliminating racism in schools is an immense task that requires the attention of all school personnel. School social workers are ideally suited to provide leadership in this area, because of their training in working with diverse and oppressed populations and their increasingly visible role in educational institutions.

This chapter addresses the problem of racism in schools and reviews some of the policies and programs aimed at reducing it from a historical perspective. The chapter also discusses the goals and objectives of programs such as multicultural education and antiracist education and the impact they have had on reducing racism and inequality. By understanding the problems of racism in schools and the philosophical underpinnings of existing programs, school social workers will be better able to identify and analyze current racism reduction efforts or the lack thereof in their schools. This chapter also discusses active roles and areas for school social worker involvement in reducing racism.

This chapter was originally published in the January 1998 issue of *Social Work in Education*, Vol. 20, pp. 25–36.

RACISM DEFINED

A working definition of racism is necessary to understand the problem in schools and the ways in which it can be addressed. The term "racism" became popularized in the late 1960s during the civil rights movement. Before this, Allport (1954/1979) used the term "ethnic prejudice," often cited as "an antipathy based upon faulty and inflexible generalization. It may be felt or expressed. It may be directed toward a group as a whole, or toward an individual because he (or she) is a member of that group" (p. 9). Allport's definition emphasizes ethnocultural differences and inaccurate stereotypic assumptions of groups and individuals on the basis of these differences. These assumptions can be either positive or negative.

Bennett (1986) provided a definition of racism that was more contemporary but not entirely different conceptually from that developed by Allport more than three decades earlier: "Racism is the belief that one's own race is superior to another. This belief is based on the erroneous assumption that physical attributes of a racial group determine their social behavior as well as their psychological and intellectual characteristics" (p. 31). Bennett's definition focused on phenotypic characteristics and related these physical differences to racist beliefs. It is through these types of beliefs that the racist legitimizes the inferior social treatment of others who are different from him or her.

Allport (1954/1979) also described five expressions of ethnic prejudice that demonstrate the range of intensity to which racism might be acted out:

1. antilocution, or verbally expressing one's negative feelings toward a particular group
2. avoidance of different groups at the expense of one's convenience
3. discrimination, where individuals or institutions reinforce their preconceived fears and prejudgments overtly or covertly through behaviors such as exclusion in employment, housing, education, or social privileges
4. physical attack on property and symbols of the differing group or direct physical violence against an individual of that group
5. extermination, including lynchings, assassinations, and programs of genocide.

Jones (1981) built on earlier definitions of ethnic prejudice and identified racism as "the transformation of race prejudice and/or ethnocentrism through the exercise of power against a racial group defined as inferior, by individuals and institutions" (p. 28). Jones introduced the concept of power as a mediator between individual or institutional racism and political or social action against individuals or groups. This action can be expressed through individual discriminatory behavior, institutional policies, or a value system that posits alternatives to the majority "model" as deviant and deficient (Ponterotto & Pedersen, 1993).

HISTORICAL PERSPECTIVE

The persistence of racism as a social problem can be partially attributed to its embeddedness in the socialization process of children and adults. These processes are rooted historically in racist beliefs motivated by greed and power that have, in turn, been justified by appeals to religion and science. Marsden (1990) cited Christian fundamentalist references to chapter 9 of Genesis, which tells the story of Noah and his three sons, Shem, Ham, and Japheth. From these three sons came the races of the earth, with Ham being the black race, Japheth being the white race, and Shem being the Arab peoples. It is claimed that God decreed Japheth's territories should be extended and that Ham's descendants should be the slaves of Japheth and Shem. Ham's son Canaan bore the curse of servitude for the offense of seeing his father naked.

Over the years, science has also made significant contributions to racist thinking, including studies that measured the shape and size of human skulls, noting that "the typical Negro is something between a child, a dotard and a beast" (Marsden, 1990, p. 338). By the late 1800s, Darwinism was gaining recognition for its ideas of order, equilibrium, and hierarchy, and the Social Darwinian concept of "survival of the fittest" had emerged as a means of justifying the treatment of primitive peoples and the colonization of their territories.

During the past few decades, the United States has seen a rise of new and the resurgence of old hate groups, including followers of "Christian Identity" theology, Aryan Nations, Covenant Sword and Arm of the Lord, Christian Patriots, and the Ku Klux Klan. Many of these groups justify their acts of violence and hate through the manipulation and reinterpretation of religious and scientific doctrines. In 1992 the Northwest Coalition against Malicious Harassment recorded 956 incidents such as racially motivated assaults, cross burnings, and vandalism in Idaho, Montana, Oregon, Washington, and Wyoming (Morelli & Spencer, 1994). Among youths, there has been an increase in the number of racist "skinhead" groups actively recruiting high school students. Struggling, disenfranchised youths in need of a haven from as well as a scapegoat for the problems they face are especially vulnerable to recruitment (Clark, 1992).

Racism in Schools

The educational experience of children throughout history also reflects a socialization to racial stereotyping and monoculturalism. In Colonial America, a primary goal of schools was to socialize new European immigrants to the dominant Anglo-European culture (Banks & Lynch, 1986). The education of people of color in this country consisted of a similar socialization pattern, often showing little respect or tolerance for their languages, cultures, or values. The socialization of children into a worldview of racism can also be traced to the literature and textbooks in which people of color were often characterized as wild, savage beasts, as in Ballantyne's *The Coral Island* (1897) or presented as simple and comical characters, as in Stowe's *Uncle Tom's Cabin.* Geography texts used the idea of environmental determinism, which interpreted climate as dictating not only pigment but also character and capacity for work (Marsden, 1990).

Although these texts are no longer used in schools, there is still evidence of racism in schools, both conscious and unconscious, at individual and institutional levels. Among students, racist attitudes are reflected in the use of racial slurs and slogans, in racial conflicts, and in physical assaults. Racism also is expressed more subtly among students through voluntary segregation by race, ethnicity, or language. As social institutions, schools propagate racism by teaching from a curriculum that is centered on Western civilization and that excludes the intellectual thought, contributions, and worldviews of people of color. This practice contributes to the destruction of the history and culture of ethnically diverse individuals, a history that has been rewritten to assert the claim of superiority of one race and class of people (Pines & Hillard, 1990).

Attitudes of teachers and school personnel can also affect children's motivation and capacity to learn. A national survey of high school biology teachers found that one in four respondents agreed that some races of people are more intelligent than others (Derman-Sparks, 1989). Educators who hold such beliefs may assign students of color to less challenging activities, refer students to remedial classrooms, or misinterpret students' behaviors such as nonassertiveness as a lack of ability or interest.

For children of color, racism can lead to a lack of affiliation or attachment to the school, loss of cultural identity, lower self-esteem and self-efficacy, or a decline in aspirations and hope, leading to increasing rates of drop out, suspension, and expulsion and to decreasing academic achievement (Pines & Hillard, 1990). Models of social development recognize these intermediate outcomes as risk factors for other problem behaviors, such as drug and alcohol problems, delinquency, and early sexual activity (Hawkins, Catalano, & Miller, 1992; Jessor & Jessor, 1977).

Racism in schools also has consequences for white children, who acquire a distorted sense of cultural superiority; continue to misunderstand, reject, or fear people of different cultures, languages, or cognitions; and are denied the full breadth of the human experience.

Education's Response

Although educational institutions have contributed their share to the socialization of racism in children, schools have also attempted to redress racial bias and inequality. Landmark court decisions, such as *Brown v. the Board of Education* (of Topeka, Kansas) in 1954, the legislation of the Civil Rights Act of 1964, and the Watts riots in August 1965 placed new demands on schools. These demands called for integrated textbooks reflecting diversity in the curriculum, more people of color hired as teachers and administrators, native languages legitimized, and more students of color admitted to colleges and universities.

Legislation was enacted at the state and federal levels in response to the ethnic revitalization movements of the 1960s, including the Title I Amendments to the Elementary and Secondary Education Act (ESEA) of 1965 (P.L. 89-750) (assistance to educational agencies for the education of low-income children), the 1988 Title VII amendment to the ESEA (the Bilingual Education Act, P.L. 100-297), and the Title IX amendment to the ESEA (ethnic heritage studies) (Banks & Lynch, 1986). A major goal of the ethnic revival movements was to remove barriers to education for students of color and to improve their chances in schooling and employment. Legislation, however, was often compensatory in nature, as it typically focused on assimilating children of ethnically diverse groups into mainstream society and was rarely designed to incorporate all students into the learning of cultures and histories of ethnically diverse children.

Later court decisions that further promoted equity within the school system included *Lau v. Nichols* in 1974, in which the Supreme Court ruled that the San Francisco school district denied Chinese students who did not speak English a meaningful opportunity to participate in the public education program, and *Martin Luther King, Jr., Elementary School Children v. Ann Arbor School District* (1979), in which the court ruled that the district must provide training for teachers to better understand black English (Banks & Lynch, 1986). Legislation and court rulings were instrumental in promoting educational equality and curricula reform. This effect was evidenced in November 1973 when the Board of Directors of the American Association of Colleges for Teacher Education adopted a policy statement on multicultural education, "No One Model American." The position statement endorsed multicultural education and described ways that schools could implement it (National Council for the Social Studies Task Force, 1976).

MULTICULTURAL EDUCATION

The movement toward multicultural education represents a major reform of the curriculum content and educative processes of the national education system (Banks, 1984). Multicultural education incorporates the study of racial and ethnic differences, as well as issues related to gender, age, socioeconomic status, and physical disabilities. The goals of multicultural education are to foster a sense of understanding and respect for differences, to overcome prejudice and discrimination and provide an understanding of the dynamics of racism, to replace historical and cultural misnomers with accurate information, and to ensure that all students receive equitable benefits from the education system (Drum & Howard, 1989). Advocates of multicultural education promote the personal development of students, particularly in the area of racial and ethnic identity and self-esteem, the use of fair and effective approaches to individual differences in learning styles believed to be linked to cultural influences, and the achievement of multicultural representation in the total school environment (Pipkin & Yates, 1992).

These principles suggest that racial biases and ethnic prejudices are inversely correlated with cognitive sophistication, moral development, social perspective taking, and receptivity toward ethnic and cultural pluralism (Gay, 1982). Therefore, the task of schools is to foster higher levels of cognitive and moral functioning consistently and continually in all subjects throughout the schooling of all children (Lynch, 1985).

In practice, the term "multicultural education" is used to describe a wide variety of school practices, policies, and programs designed to increase cultural awareness and educational equality. Although some programs are consistent with the goals of multicultural education as defined earlier, other programs amount to little more than rhetoric. For example, a study on the use of multicultural education materials in schools revealed that some teachers define lessons on the culture of Aztecs, Greeks, Vikings, and Spaniards as part of their multicultural efforts. In contrast, other teachers discussed the Jewish Holocaust in Europe and the internment of Japanese Americans in the United States during World War II to illustrate the consequences of racism and bigotry (Morelli & Spencer, 1994).

Banks (1984) explained that when educational innovations, such as multicultural education, arise and are in search of their raison d'etre, disparate programs and practices often emerge and claim the new title. These differences have ignited some concern and criticism.

Multicultural Education versus Antiracist Curriculum

Although some educators herald multicultural education as "the panacea to cure the ills that beset their educational systems" (Bullivant, 1986, p. 33), others feel multicultural education does little to promote the social, economic, and political rights of ethnic minority groups. Whereas multicultural education includes the reduction of prejudice and racism as one of its primary goals, there has been considerable debate as to whether this goal can be accomplished (Kalantzis & Cope, 1986; Mattai, 1992; Mitchell, 1990; Skelton, 1985; Vincent, 1992). Most educators would agree that multicultural education should promote tolerance and intercultural understanding.

However, critics of multicultural education state that teaching about different cultures still leaves students blind to the inequalities in society (Skelton, 1985). These critics, often described as "antiracist" theorists, argue that multiculturalism in schools has focused on the curriculum and the classroom at the expense of examining the wider social, political, and economic influences related to inequality and racism (Vincent, 1992). Furthermore, antiracists argue that multicultural curriculum neither addresses the elimination of racism directly nor provides strategies for empowering ethnically diverse groups to counteract racism (Mattai, 1992). Multiculturalism is thought to overemphasize ethnic differences in the hope that appreciation and tolerance will follow.

Critics of multicultural education contend that fostering feelings of difference may in fact increase racism and cultural chauvinism in some students and neglect the notion that everyone has a culture (Kalantzis & Cope, 1986). The following scenario illustrates the kinds of criticism antiracists have for multicultural programs: The setting is an ethnic food fair, one of the most popular events for promoting multiculturalism. Ethnic food fairs are typically social activities where students from different ethnic backgrounds bring food to share with one another. Before the fair, a white student was asked what kind of food she would be contributing. The student replied that she did not know what she could bring, because she was white and white people do not have a culture.

This example shows not only how some white Americans have historically assimilated the identity of being "white" as their race, but also demonstrates how some individuals fail to recognize that the white majority culture is "their culture." The inability to make this connection inhibits them from making further connections between the dominance of the white culture and its imposition on others. Without this level of understanding, the contributions of students of color to food fairs and other multicultural events may be viewed as anomalies or stereotypes and thus have little hope of reducing racism, if that is the goal.

Multicultural programs such as ethnic fairs often emphasize the notion that all cultures are equally valid. However, these programs often fail to include discussions of how cultures are not equally validated in reality. Derman-Sparks and the A.B.C. Task Force (1989) referred to this benign approach to multicultural programming as "tourist curriculum," which they stated can be patronizing—emphasizing the "exotic" differences between cultures—and trivializing—avoiding the reality of everyday problems and experiences people of different ethnicities face.

Antiracist theorists also argue that the research available on the functioning of multicultural programs and their outcomes is limited. The wide variation among multicultural education programs complicates the evaluation process. Antiracist theorists support curriculum and programs in schools that address racism and social injustice through discussions and analyses of the inequalities in power and economic status that determine race relations. Indeed, the most radical critiques of multicultural education have come from Great Britain, whereas critics in the United States have been less vocal. In fact, many of the programs well regarded among antiracist advocates in the United States, such as "Teaching Tolerance" published by the Southern Poverty Law Center and "Anti-Bias Curriculum: Tools for Empowering Young Children" published by the National Association for the Education of Young Children, are not easily distinguishable from comprehensive multicultural education programs such as "A World of Difference" by the Anti-Defamation League of B'nai B'rith

(Fisher, Green, & Maxie, 1990) and Project REACH (Respecting Our Ethnic and Cultural Heritage) (Krenek, 1994).

Some U.S. antiracist programs emphasize empowerment for children of color so that children develop both a strong self-identity and a strong group identity to help them withstand attacks of racism (Derman-Sparks & A.B.C. Task Force, 1989). Using an antiracist approach, children and teachers confront racist beliefs and acts rather than cover them up. Children learn about racism by thinking about it, making mistakes, and trying again. Examples of antiracist activities include learning to problem solve discriminatory behavior through role playing incidents of discrimination with male and female dolls from different ethnic backgrounds or promoting activism in children through letter-writing campaigns, speaking to public officials, or organizing community members around certain issues such as increasing bilingual materials in the classroom, replacing inadequate playground equipment in poor neighborhood schools, or selling dolls that demonstrate disabilities in toy stores (Derman-Sparks & A.B.C. Task Force, 1989).

Global Education

An outgrowth of multicultural and antiracist education discussed by Drum and Howard (1989) is "global education." Global education deals with diversity at the global level and focuses on the interrelated systems that affect the entire planet. The primary goal is to build understanding and respect for peoples and nations outside the United States. A global effort goes beyond the "Western-centric" curriculum pervasive in schools by providing an understanding of the dynamics of imperialism and oppression and creating an awareness of the earth as an interrelated holistic system. Students learn that their individual behavior and choices can have a global effect in an interdependent world. For example, discussions of conflicts in the Middle East might include an analysis of how U.S. citizens who are descended from people from this area are affected by these conflicts. The consequences of imperialism on native populations might also be analyzed, both historically and within the context of contemporary issues of native land rights, restitution, sovereignty, and independence.

CHALLENGES TO REDUCING RACISM IN SCHOOLS

Perhaps the greatest challenge to reducing racism in schools is the highly controversial and politicized nature of the problem. Discussions of racism and inequality evoke strong emotions and polarized opinions. Although there has been less criticism of multicultural education from antiracists in the United States, there has been growing opposition from conservatives and neoconservatives who prefer that multicultural education be eliminated. Banks (1984) summarized the conservative critique, which is typically grounded in a concern over the deteriorating quality of schools and a re-emphasis on teaching basic skills. This "back to basics" movement believes that programs and curricula aimed at reducing racism take valuable time away from subjects such as math, science, and English. Conservative critics also argue that students should develop knowledge and skills to participate in the shared national culture, promote the overarching ideals of the nation, and acquire competence in the national language (Banks, 1984). According to these critics, ethnic cultures and languages should not be taught in public institutions but at home instead.

Another major challenge is the lack of consistency and consensus about what programs belong under the label "multicultural education." Although the goals of multicultural education have been articulated by theorists, full implementation has been hampered by lack of knowledge of these goals by school personnel, lack of available and accessible resources, and lack of commitment to racism reduction, as well as resistance from conservative teachers, school officials, and community members. With these challenges in mind, it is becoming increasingly clear that multiculturalists and antiracists alike must work together to overcome these challenges, or they may be in danger of losing what ground has been gained. Although individual programs vary in the extent to which they deal with the problem of racism, comprehensive multicultural and antiracist programs share in a commitment to work for reform, equity, and justice. The profession is indebted to the multiculturalists who have laid the groundwork for later theorists to add to and improve on. These efforts often came at a great risk and struggle. Although it is clear that all multicultural efforts are not exemplary, this deficiency should not bias opinions against all endeavors.

ROLE OF SCHOOL SOCIAL WORKERS

There are many roles within the micro, meso, and macro systems in which school social workers can have a significant effect on reducing racism in schools. These roles may differ within the context of the school and community in which the social worker practices. Within a highly conservative environment, social workers may choose to begin at the micro level; they can provide services for students who are victimized by racism and students involved in or at risk of involvement in hate organizations. Social workers can also use multicultural and antiracist curricula in their own practice with individuals and groups. This may involve the empowerment of children by enhancing their self-identity and group identity or by teaching strategies for interrupting racism.

Promising innovations in the area of intergroup dialogues can also be used in practice as a means of empowering students as well as promoting social change. Intergroup dialogues provide a unique forum for students from different backgrounds and cultural identities to discuss commonalities, learn about differences, and address issues of conflict. Students learn about each other's histories and experiences, challenge stereotypes and misinformation, explore the sources of intergroup conflict, and identify ways of addressing institutional and individual forms of racism and discrimination (Nagda, Zuniga, & Sevig, 1995; Zuniga & Nagda, 1993). Intergroup dialogues have had a great deal of success with college students and may prove to be effective with younger students.

Beyond working with students, school social workers can work with teachers and school administrators in the areas of consciousness raising, in-service training, and resource acquisition. School social workers can play a vital role in stimulating and moderating discussions on the effectiveness of current multicultural efforts in their schools. In communities where these discussions are highly polarized, social workers can act as brokers among multiculturalists, antiracists, and conservatives within the school.

Efforts to improve teachers' in-service training are also needed. Rashid (1990) found that although a sample of teachers generally saw a need for multicultural education, many did not receive preservice training. Social workers in schools can be instrumental in providing the needed training or taking leadership in finding resources and people who can provide quality training for teachers and administrators.

Within an ecological school social work framework, practice efforts should include all systems that affect students' lives; social workers should intervene not only with students and teachers, but also with families, administrators, school boards, state- and district-level policymakers, and state and national officials. School social workers who focus only on counseling and treatment of students who are oppressed run the risk of "maintaining the status quo because their practice defines the locus of (the) problem within the micro system" (Clancy, 1995, p. 42). Social workers must emphasize the need for comprehensive and systemic approaches. This emphasis means moving beyond the individual and looking at issues such as

- issuing policy statements that cover broad school district philosophy, hiring practices, and the handling of bias-motivated incidents
- reporting and monitoring trends in racial attitudes
- checking textbooks and other resources for bias
- advocating the continued infusion of multicultural, antiracist, and global education into the curriculum
- involving parents and community members in these efforts (Mitchell, 1990; Pipkin & Yates, 1992).

Strong policy statements should reflect a commitment to reducing racism and include provision of a staff position to actualize the mission or an individual whose job it is to do so. There is also a need for rigorous research that evaluates the effectiveness of programs to eliminate racism and discrimination. Such research might involve examining the school's effectiveness in changing conflict levels and friendship patterns; monitoring changes in cultural awareness and appreciation; or analyzing disciplinary methods, student achievement, suspension and attendance rates, teacher absences, and parent participation (Pipkin & Yates, 1992). Short-term studies should be supplemented with longitudinal studies that have the ability to detect immediate as well as long-term effects.

Finally, in neighborhoods where conservative critics are influential, social workers may need to assume the roles of activist and community organizer, especially when potential supporters of racism reduction programs are silent or without power. School social workers who learn about the values of the community and build from the strengths of the existing community will be most successful in organizing and facilitating change (Gutierrez, Alvarez, Nemon, & Lewis, 1996).

Over two decades ago, Ehrlich (1973) stated that education and information can lead to changes in attitudes of racism but only through consistency, salience, and intensity. This statement is just as true today as we are about to embark on the 21st century. School social workers who are informed and committed to reducing racism in schools can have a major influence in this area. Unquestionably, the leadership of tomorrow is in the nation's schools. Social workers have the opportunity to provide children with a foundation that has escaped past generations, that of a world of racial harmony and tolerance.

REFERENCES

Allport, G. W. (1979). *The nature of prejudice.* Boston: Addison-Wesley. (Original work published 1954)

Ballantyne, R. M. (1897). *The Coral Island: A tale of the Pacific Ocean.* London: T. Nelson & Sons.

Banks, J. A. (1984). Multicultural education and its critics: Britain and the United States. *New Era, 65*(3), 58–65.

Banks, J. A., & Lynch, J. (1986). *Multicultural education in Western societies.* New York: Praeger.

Bennett, C. I. (1986). *Comprehensive multicultural education: Theory and practice.* Boston: Allyn & Bacon.

Bilingual Education Act, Title VII as added to P.L. 100-297, Title I, 102 Stat. 274 to 293 (1988).

Brown v. Board of Education, 347 U.S. 483 (1954).

Bullivant, B. M. (1986). Towards radical multiculturalism: Resolving tensions in curriculum and educational planning. In S. Modgil, G. K. Verma, K. Mallick, & C. Modgil (Eds.), *Multicultural education: The interminable debate* (pp. 33–47). London: Falmer Press.

Civil Rights Act of 1964, P.L. 88-352, 78 Stat. 241.

Clancy, J. (1995). Ecological school social work: The reality and the vision. *Social Work in Education, 17,* 40–47.

Clark, C. M. (1992). Deviant adolescent subcultures: Assessment strategies and clinical interventions. *Adolescence, 27,* 283–294.

Derman-Sparks, L. (1989, Winter). Challenging diversity with anti-bias curriculum. *School Safety,* pp. 10–13.

Derman-Sparks, L., & A.B.C. Task Force. (1989). *Anti-bias curriculum: Tools for empowering young children.* Washington, DC: National Association for the Education of Young Children.

Drum, J., & Howard, G. (1989, January). *Multicultural and global education: Seeking common ground* (Summary). Paper presented at a conference cosponsored by Las Palomas de Taos, REACH Center for Multicultural and Global Education, and the Stanley Foundation, Taos, NM.

Ehrlich, H. J. (1973). *The social psychology of prejudice.* New York: John Wiley & Sons.

Elementary and Secondary Education Act of 1965, Title I Amendments, P.L. 89-750, 80 Stat. 1196, 1199 to 1209.

Fisher, J. C., Green, M. B., & Maxie, A. (1990). *Making "a world of difference" in teacher education.* Los Angeles: California State University and the Anti-Defamation League of B'nai B'rith. (ERIC Document Reproduction Services No. ED 337 416)

Gay, G. (1982). Developmental prerequisites for multicultural education in the social studies. In L. W. Rosenweig (Ed.), *Developmental perspectives in the social studies* (Bulletin 66, pp. 67–81). Washington, DC: National Council for the Social Studies.

Gutierrez, L., Alvarez, A. R., Nemon, H., & Lewis, E. A. (1996). Multicultural community organizing: A strategy for change. *Social Work, 41,* 501–508.

Hawkins, J. D., Catalano, R. F., & Miller, J. Y. (1992). Risk and protective factors for alcohol and other drug problems in adolescence and early adulthood: Implications for substance abuse and prevention. *Psychological Bulletin, 112,* 64–105.

Jessor, R., & Jessor, S. L. (1977). *Problem behavior and psychosocial development: A longitudinal study of youth.* New York: Academic Press.

Jones, J. M. (1981). The concept of racism and its changing reality. In B. J. Bowser & R. G. Hunt (Eds.), *Impacts of racism on white Americans* (pp. 27–49). Beverly Hills, CA: Sage Publications.

Kalantzis, M., & Cope, B. (1986). *Pluralism and equitability: Multicultural curriculum strategies for schools* (NACCME Commissioned Research Paper No. 3). Woden, Australia: National Advisory and Coordination Committee on Multicultural Education.

Krenek, S. (1994). Project REACH (Respecting Our Ethnic and Cultural Heritage). *Writing Notebook: Visions for Learning, 11*(4), 23–24.

Lau v. Nichols, 414 U.S. 563, 94 S.Ct. 786 (1974).

Leicester, M. (1989). *Multicultural education: From theory to practice.* Windsor, England: Nfer-Nelson.

Lynch, J. (1985). Human rights, racism and the multicultural curriculum. *Educational Review, 37,* 141–152.

Marsden, W. E. (1990). Rooting racism into the educational experience of childhood and youth in the nineteenth and twentieth centuries. *History of Education, 19,* 333–353.

Martin Luther King, Jr., Elementary School Children v. Ann Arbor School District, 473 F. Supp. 1371 (E.D. Mich. 1979).

Mattai, P. R. (1992). Rethinking the nature of multicultural education: Has it lost its focus or is it being misused? *Journal of Negro Education, 61*(1), 65–77.

McCarthy, C. (1988). Rethinking liberal and radical perspectives on racial inequality in schooling: Making the case for nonsynchrony. *Harvard Educational Review, 58,* 265–279.

Mitchell, B. M. (1985). Multicultural education: A viable component of American education? *Educational Research Quarterly, 9*(3), 7–11.

Mitchell, V. (1990). *Curriculum and instruction to reduce racial conflict* (ERIC/CUE Digest No. 64). New York: ERIC Clearinghouse on Urban Education.

Morelli, P. T., & Spencer, M. S. (1994, August). *The NWCAMH Education Research Project: Existing anti-bigotry policies, curricula, and programs in Northwestern schools.* (Available from the Northwest Coalition against Malicious Harassment, P.O. Box 16776, Seattle, WA 98116)

Nagda, B. A., Zuniga, X., & Sevig, T. D. (1995). Bridging differences through peer-facilitated intergroup dialogues. In S. Hatcher (Ed.), *Peer programs on a college campus: Theory, training, and "voice of the peers"* (pp. 378–414). San Jose, CA: Resources Publications.

National Council for the Social Studies Task Force. (1976). *Curriculum guidelines for multiethnic education.* Washington, DC: Author.

Pines, G. J., & Hillard, A. G. (1990). Rx for racism: Imperatives for American schools. *Phi Delta Kappan, 71,* 593–600.

Pipkin, R., & Yates, D. (1992). Multicultural education: A middle school's approach to preparing tomorrow's leaders. *ERS Spectrum, 10*(4), 37–40.

Ponterotto, J. G., & Pedersen, P. B. (1993). *Preventing prejudice: A guide for counselors and educators.* Newbury Park, CA: Sage Publications.

Rashid, H. M. (1990). Teacher perceptions of the multicultural orientation of their pre-service education and current occupational settings. *Educational Research Quarterly, 14*(1), 2–5.

Skelton, K. (1985). *Development of curriculum strategies for schools in multicultural education* (NACCME Commissioned Research Paper No. 2). Woden, Australia: National Advisory and Coordination Committee on Multicultural Education.

Vincent, N. C. (1992, February). *The philosophy and politics of multicultural education and anti-racist education: An analysis of current literature.* Paper presented at the annual meeting of the National Association of Multicultural Education, Orlando, FL.

Zuniga, X., & Nagda, B. A. (1993). Dialogue groups: An innovative approach to multicultural learning. In D. Schoem, L. Frankel, X. Zuniga, & E. Lewis (Eds.), *Multicultural teaching in the university* (pp. 233–248). Westport, CT: Praeger.

The preparation of this chapter was partially supported by the Northwest Coalition against Malicious Harassment (NWCAMH) and the University of Michigan Social Work Research and Development Center NIMH Grant R24-MH51363. The author thanks Paula T. Morelli and Bill Wassmuth, executive director, NWCAMH, for their assistance.

13

Linking Schools, Human Services, and Community:
A Puerto Rican Perspective

Melvin Delgado

Urban-based school systems are playing an expanded role in providing education and human services (Behrman, 1992; Moroz & Segal, 1990; Wall, 1996; Zetlin, Ramos, & Valdez, 1996). In many instances these school systems have assumed a leadership role in the provision of social services (Chavkin & Brown, 1992; Dupper & Evans, 1996; Epstein, 1996). Puerto Ricans and other students of color are faced with tremendous challenges that go far beyond obtaining a formal education (Heath & McLaughlin, 1993; McLaughlin, 1993). Schools, as a result, are in a propitious position to play an active role in the life of a community because of their mission, geographic location, physical structure (often large enough to host social services programs), and nonstigmatizing climate (Davies, 1996; Delgado & Rivera, 1997).

School-linked literature has highlighted the promises and pitfalls of collaborative efforts (Aguirre, 1995; Dolan & Haxby, 1992; Kusserow, 1991). School-linked services have reduced dropout rates and absenteeism and have increased academic achievement (U.S. General Accounting Office [GAO], 1993). Collaboration offers many benefits for social services agencies as well:

> Community agencies and institutions also can benefit when they collaborate effectively with schools. They can reach more of their constituents, increase public support for their work, realize cost savings (sometimes), and gain access to school facilities and expertise. In some cases, this school-based collaboration may be an opportunity to coordinate their services with other community organizations. (Davies, 1996, p. 15)

School-linked partnerships, nevertheless, require considerable planning, clear communication, and time commitment to be successful. The professional literature rarely approaches this form of collaboration from a community perspective (Solo, 1992; Zetlin, Campbell, Lujan, & Lujan, 1994). The views of parents and their children represent a critical dimension that is often lost in the process of developing school-linked programs.

This chapter was originally published in the April 1998 issue of *Social Work in Education*, Vol. 20, pp. 121–130.

This chapter reports findings from a longitudinal study of Puerto Rican parents with children in a Boston elementary school bilingual program. Parents and their children were followed for $2^1/_2$ years. One of the goals of the study was to examine the views and suggestions of parents on how community (natural support systems), schools, and human services agencies can better collaborate to educate children. Recommendations are made to facilitate the development of closer collaboration among these systems.

REVIEW OF THE LITERATURE

The present-day concept of collaboration can be traced back to the 1970s, when a series of initiatives were promulgated by the U.S. Department of Health, Education, and Welfare (Baker, 1991). School-linked services have been proposed as a strategy to assist school-age children at risk of school failure. Critics note, however, that it is unfair for schools to be expected to deliver social services and that it is also detrimental to the educational process (Shaw & Replogle, 1995).

The term "school-linked" is generally preferred to the term "school-based" for the following reasons:

> We use the term "school-linked" instead of "school-based" to describe these collaborative programs because (1) schools are not always the initiators of programs but are among the key players responsible for planning and guiding the programs; (2) some services may be coordinated, but not actually delivered, at the school; and (3) school personnel are not typically providers of program services and may not be in the best position to lead collaborative efforts according to the literature. (GAO, 1993, pp. 2–3)

School linkage, although universally accepted, means many different things to many different parties, causing considerable confusion in the field. According to a recent GAO report (1993), there are a variety of school-linkage models: "Many different models exist for coordinating human services in schools, and no two are exactly alike. Each is shaped by (1) the unique needs of students likely to use the program and (2) community preferences and attitudes about the services to be offered" (p. 3).

School-linkage is intended to minimize fragmentation and duplication; to increase accountability; and to provide services in the areas of health, education, and job training. According to Zetlin et al. (1996),

> School-linked . . . service integration centers are emerging in which public and private community agencies work collaboratively with schools towards a shared goal of attending to the whole child. A comprehensive and integrated array of programs are made available as needed to promote healthy development and minimize barriers to learning in ways that address the whole family and its multiple problems and needs. (p. 98)

There are four critical elements that have been found in successful linkage efforts (GAO, 1993): (1) the presence of strong leadership was a common characteristic of the most comprehensive school-linked programs (serving to mobilize community and political support for programs); (2) program staff sought and valued school staff as important sources in both identifying and serving troubled youths; (3) programs favored the use of multidisciplinary teams to serve and connect youths with needed services; and (4) program staff placed tremendous value on following up referrals to ensure that services were provided and met presenting needs of children.

Definition of Key Concepts

This study used three key concepts in viewing community: (1) natural support systems (NSSs), (2) formal services, and (3) informal services. The study developed a definition of Puerto Rican NSSs based on a key informant survey of eight leaders in the field of education with special knowledge of Puerto Ricans. According to Delgado and Rivera (1997),

> Puerto Rican NSSs consist of an individual's familial and community networks that provide for their growth, welfare, safety, and development (human services providers, educators, and other "formal" helpers can become NSSs when they provide assistance that is widely considered outside of their job description and do so within a cultural-based context). NSSs play a crucial role in promoting a sense of identity, belonging, and self-esteem. These systems most often connote those needs that are met due to their membership in family or community grouping, as opposed to formal institutional and governmental arrangements. In essence, NSSs are socially created, organized experiences that facilitate the process of seeking assistance. (p. 84)

Consequently, the difference between formal and natural depends on the personality and qualities of the individual providing assistance (Delgado, 1992). A provider or educator can transcend to a natural support role if she or he is willing to go beyond a job description of activities and is trusted and respected. Teachers who display a willingness to visit a family at home, assist parents with translation of materials from English to Spanish, or provide advice that is not usually considered within their purview can become part of an NSS. Informal services, in turn, are provided by individuals who are willing to assist on a limited basis. Next-door neighbors, religious and community leaders, friends, and other individuals can be included in this group.

METHOD

Study Research Questions

The study consisted of four sets of interviews with parents, with each set of interviews focused on gathering information on specific subjects (all interviews were conducted in the participants' homes every six to eight months). The first interview provided baseline data and demographic information (socioeconomic status, migration history, and information concerning current community). The second interview focused on what constitutes support (natural, formal, or informal) and how to obtain it when needed (nature and extent of help-seeking patterns, composition of support system, and identification of unmet needs). The third interview, and the primary focus of this chapter, explored ways to improve collaboration among all parties (schools, agencies, and NSSs). The fourth and final interview gathered data on school–community relations and assessed the study's impact on the families; in addition, it captured what changes had transpired over the previous $2^1/2$ years.

Linkage-Specific Research Questions

The third interview consisted of 23 open-ended questions, 14 of which specifically addressed the subject of linkage. Questions gathered data on how collaboration could be initiated and facilitated, ways teachers could involve the community in educating children, and how community leaders and social services providers could be more actively involved in the school. Study questions were developed on the basis of input provided by parents during the first two interviews, meetings with teachers, and requests for specific information from the school principal, a key supporter of the study.

Sample Selection

The study was based in an elementary school in Boston. The school was selected because of its high concentration of Puerto Rican students and its geographic location within a predominantly Puerto Rican community. Two kindergarten and two first-grade bilingual teachers were asked to provide the names of all Puerto Rican families with children in their classrooms. Forty-five Puerto Rican families were selected as potential participants, with 24 (sample size) agreeing to participate.

Families were initially contacted by letter (in English and Spanish), followed by a telephone call to set up an appointment for a home visit. Each interview consisted of a series of open-ended questions and lasted approximately one hour. Twenty-two interviews were conducted in Spanish and two in English. Families were paid $25 per interview. The number of interviews in each stage of the study differed as a result of families moving and leaving no forwarding address. The second interview involved 18 families, with 16 and 13 participating in succeeding interviews.

Sample Description

The typical family in the sample was headed by a woman, average age 32.9, with three preschool- and elementary-age children. She was born in Puerto Rico and arrived in the United States (Boston) in 1974 and had been living in her current community 10 years. She did not finish high school and was receiving some form of public assistance. Her language preference for the interviews was Spanish.

The study sample did not differ dramatically from Puerto Ricans in Boston, with the exception of household type. The average family size was 3.37 people per household. Only 28.6 percent (seven parents), compared to 58 percent for all Puerto Ricans in the United States, had completed high school. The sample households were more than three times more likely to be headed by women, with no father present, which influenced the percentage of families on public assistance (17 of 24). Only one family had income above the poverty level ($16,000) for a family of four. Four families had one or both parents working outside of the home but still were below the poverty level, two received Supplemental Security Income, and one received social security benefits (Delgado & Rivera, 1997).

Analysis

The open-ended nature of the questions did not lend itself to quantitative analysis, with the exception of demographic characteristics. Qualitative analysis was undertaken using a three-step process: (1) identification of key points in responses to each question, (2) identification of key themes, and (3) grounding themes in the professional literature.

Study Limitations

Although the data obtained were very rich in detail, results cannot be generalized beyond the four classes. The sample of 24 is small and reflects only those families willing to participate in the study (21 families declined to participate). The drop off in sample size over the course of the study (from 24 to 13) further limits generalizability within the bilingual program of the school. The study focused primarily on adult perceptions, and minimal effort was made to assess actual support received. Children, the beneficiaries of education and services, were not interviewed. No effort was made to collect data on grades and test performances to measure support with school performance. Nevertheless, the study raised important considerations in the planning of school-linked services.

KEY FINDINGS

Although data were obtained on a multitude of topics, this section focuses on parent perceptions and recommendations for school-linked services. Parent experiences and recommendations for school-linked services are invaluable to the planning and delivery of such services and to attaining community support.

Support System Composition

The families in the study had a tremendous range of social and health needs that were not met by formal, natural, or informal systems. The average family had a support system (mostly family members) of 1.3 individuals (people they could turn to for any form of assistance). Nevertheless, Delgado (1997) found that families who indicated that they had relatives who could help with their child's homework if needed ($n = 7$) had, on average, a greater extensive support system (5.2 people) than those who indicated that an older sibling ($n = 8$) was the primary helper. Although they knew their next-door neighbors, most families (17 of 24) did not feel "comfortable" seeking their neighbor's assistance in time of need.

Minimal Utilization of Latino and Nonethnic Agencies

Parent involvement with formal services organizations (that is, Latino and non-Latino social services agencies) was limited. Parents ($n = 10$) indicated that Latino agencies were of limited assistance with issues regarding public assistance, advocacy, and "brokering" resources (assistance with English as a second language was considered to be their strength). Several respondents ($n = 4$) expressed fears that confidentiality could be breached because many staff members lived in their community.

Non-Latino agencies, in turn, were of limited assistance because of language and cultural barriers ($n = 14$). Respondents ($n = 12$) indicated a lack of "comfort" in visiting these agencies, particularly those providing public assistance. These organizations would be used only as a last alternative ($n = 12$). A sizable number of respondents ($n = 9$) indicated that when visiting these agencies, they often had to bring their own interpreters because of a lack of bilingual personnel.

Respondents ($n = 13$) expressed frustration with having to negotiate numerous agencies to have all of their needs met. This process of negotiation becomes an even greater challenge when a parent must rely on public transportation ($n = 9$). As a consequence, most parents ($n = 11$) were quick to recommend that these agencies come together in one place, preferably in a community location such as a school, where parents could drop off their children and obtain needed services.

Perceptions of School

All of the parents in the initial and subsequent interviews identified their child's elementary school as a major resource in their lives. It was not unusual to have parents refer to the school as part of their natural support system ($n = 11$). School personnel became part of the support system by going "above and beyond" their job responsibilities. Respondents ($n = 13$) said that school personnel played a prominent part in helping families address a multitude of needs. They assisted the families with interpreting government-related forms and letters ($n = 9$), obtaining winter clothing for themselves and their children ($n = 5$), providing opportunities for parents to get involved in the classroom with their children ($n = 4$), and making job referrals ($n = 3$). In short, school personnel respected, understood, and valued parents. A positive reputation serves to "invite" parents to visit and facilitate the attraction of agencies and other community resources.

Recommendations from Parents

When respondents were asked if they believed parents should be involved in the education of their children, all ($N = 16$) answered in the affirmative. Respondents indicated a need to know what their children were learning in school and cited the benefits of learning from their children. They noted that the school could make it easier to involve parents by providing social services on the premises ($n = 14$), increasing communication ($n = 13$), providing workshops ($n = 11$) on parenting ("being a parent is hard"), increasing parent–teacher conferences ($n = 9$), initiating festivals for parents and families ($n = 7$), and providing "special" services for single parents ($n = 5$).

Ten of 16 respondents indicated that community leaders and human services providers, too, must have a greater awareness and presence in the school. This participation could be accomplished by providing greater opportunities for community or parent leaders to be involved on committees and in other aspects of the school ($n = 8$). Human services providers could be encouraged to participate by providing them with space and opportunities to meet with parents and families ($n = 6$).

When asked for their recommendations concerning the provision of social and other services within the schools, all 16 parents indicated they liked that idea. Parents were very clear about the need for community, school, and human services organizations to better coordinate their activities. This coordination took on greater significance when parents could speak only Spanish, thereby limiting their access to agencies where staff spoke Spanish. Schools, they believed, were ideal settings to initiate and maintain such efforts. Parents ($n = 13$) expressed willingness to help if school personnel would take into consideration their schedules, child care situation, and transportation needs.

The following quotes from parents (translated from Spanish) raise the need for provision of school-linked services. One parent noted, "There needs to be a place where parents can get help for themselves and their children without running all over the city." Another parent said, "Schools must be a part of our 'world'; they cannot exist separate from the community. In fact, community and schools must be one." One parent noted why schools were the "perfect" place to seek help: "I like the idea that schools can provide more than education for our children. I feel very comfortable going there because everyone figures you are there to get education for your child. I always fear someone seeing me go to a counseling agency for help."

DISCUSSION

The results proved very revealing concerning the needs of Puerto Rican families and the limited options they perceive themselves to have in seeking assistance. Puerto Rican parents not only had a very limited support system, but also did not feel comfortable seeking assistance from Latino and non-Latino social services organizations. This finding was substantiated by another Boston-based study (Boston Persistent Poverty Project, 1989): "Hispanics who live in public housing seem particularly poorly connected. While about 25 percent of blacks and whites who live in public housing say they are familiar with community [social services] organizations, only eight percent of Hispanics in public housing give this answer" (p. 53). Barriers related to geography, culture, operational, and psychological factors severely limited getting help.

The limited scope of their NSSs may be the result of a number of factors: The uprootment from Puerto Rico to Boston resulted in extensive parts of the support system being left behind, the process of acculturation resulted in a devaluing of family helping each other, and the needs of support system members were too great to allow them to provide assistance to others in need. The interplay of these factors, in combination with limited access to formal services, increased the social isolation of the families.

The elementary school their children attended, however, proved to be one of the most important resources in their lives. This elementary school played a prominent role in their lives because it successfully addressed all four key aspects of accessibility: (1) geographic (it was located in the community); (2) cultural (personnel were bilingual and bicultural); (3) operational (the hours the school was open facilitated visits); and (4) psychological (parents felt welcomed and valued). Urban-based schools, contrary to popular belief, can fill an important vacuum in Latino communities; in so doing, they can attract other formal resources to help Latino families.

These findings raised the importance of school-linked services for low-income urban-based Latinos. These families face prodigious challenges in receiving culturally competent services. The provision of school-linked services provides schools with a role to monitor and influence the nature and quality of services. This "monitoring" role is often overlooked in the literature. Schools, as a condition of affiliation, are placed in the powerful position of dictating who is invited to provide school-linked services.

RECOMMENDATIONS

The following recommendations focus on the role school social workers can play in initiating, facilitating, and sustaining school-linked services:

- The development of an advisory committee consisting of parents and key school and human services personnel can play a critical role in providing advice, access to resources, and support for linkage-based services. Meetings, in turn, should rotate among schools, human services agencies, and community settings.

Every effort must be made to include Latino social services agencies in addition to nonethnic-focused agencies.

- School social workers must make a concerted effort to become members of community-based social services agency boards and advisory committees; in addition, they should play an active and highly visible role in community festivals and events. This participation minimizes distance between schools and communities and serves as a means of developing a better understanding of community resources and needs.

- School social workers must develop an "asset map" of Latino NSSs that can be used as resources in school-linked services (Delgado, 1996). They may even enlist the support of Latino students to conduct this asset assessment. Indigenous resources, in turn, can serve as referral agents, provide advice or suggestions for activities, or assist in the development of a sociocultural context to better inform linkage programmatic decisions.

- School-linked services do not have to be school-based to be considered school-linked. Schools can provide educational services in community-based human services agencies, indigenous settings like restaurants (space and location may make them more accessible), and in the parents' homes. For example, adult basic-education classes can be offered in the parents' homes, and each class session can rotate among participants' homes.

- School social workers can assist in the development of a resource directory of key human services organizations and important NSSs in the Latino community. This directory, in turn, can help schools decide who should be a part of school-linked services and identify indigenous resources that can serve in other capacities—resources for teachers, guest speakers, and so forth.

- The concept of school-linked services must be expanded beyond "traditional" services such as counseling, adult education, and so forth and must encompass innovative services such as health and nutrition, aerobics, music, computers, and others (Harkavy, 1990; Heleen, 1990).

These recommendations can be implemented only with the cooperation of all parties. And because school social workers have an indepth appreciation and understanding of the three major systems—schools, social services agencies, and community—they should perform optimally by identifying resources and brokering different parties.

CONCLUSION

There is little doubt that school social workers must play an active role in bringing together schools, social services agencies, and communities (Freeman, 1996). Their unique knowledge of these systems places them in the propitious position to create and help sustain these partnerships. However, it is of paramount importance to actively and meaningfully involve parents in school-linked collaborative initiatives. Parents and communities, too, are in unique positions of having contact with all three systems; their perspective, unfortunately, is frequently undervalued and overlooked.

Puerto Rican parents, as has been found in the Boston study, are keenly aware of the barriers Latino parents confront in seeking services and education for themselves and their children. Any partnership venture linking schools, agencies, and community will require their consent and cooperation. Their experiences, in turn, must not be lost in the process of developing school-linked services. These services must be culturally competent and address the most significant needs of the Latino community. School social workers, as a result, will serve as a bridge between what is often considered three distinctive and different worlds.

REFERENCES

Aguirre, L. M. (1995). California's efforts toward school-linked, integrated, comprehensive services. *Social Work in Education, 17,* 217–225.

Baker, F. (1991). *Coordination of alcohol, drug abuse, and mental health services.* Rockville, MD: U.S. Department of Health and Human Services.

Behrman, R. E. (1992). Introduction: School-linked services. *Future of Children, 2,* 6–7.

Boston Persistent Poverty Project. (1989). *In the midst of plenty: A profile of Boston and its poor.* Boston: Boston Foundation.

Chavkin, J., & Brown, K. (1992). School social workers building a multiethnic family–school–community partnership. *Social Work in Education, 14,* 160–164.

Davies, D. (1996). Partnerships for student success. *New Schools/New Communities, 12,* 14–21.

Delgado, M. (1992). *Natural support systems in Puerto Rican communities: A progress report.* Boston: Institute for Responsive Education.

Delgado, M. (1996). Community asset assessments by Latino youths. *Social Work in Education, 18,* 169–178.

Delgado, M. (1997). Puerto Rican elementary-age children: Assistance with homework as an indicator of natural support strengths. *Social Work in Education, 20,* 49–54.

Delgado, M., & Rivera, H. (1997). Puerto Rican natural support systems: Impact on families, communities, and schools. *Urban Education, 31,* 81–97.

Dolan, L. J., & Haxby, B. (1992). *The role of family support and integrated human services in achieving success for all in the elementary school.* Baltimore: Center for Research on Effective Schooling for Disadvantaged Students.

Dupper, D. R., & Evans, S. (1996). From band-aids and putting out fires to prevention: School social work practice approaches for the new century [Trends & Issues]. *Social Work in Education, 18,* 187–191.

Epstein, J. L. (1996). Advances in family, community, and school partnerships. *New Schools/New Communities, 12,* 5–13.

Freeman, E. M. (1996). The art of forecasting: Shaping the future of school social work [Editorial]. *Social Work in Education, 18,* 131–134.

Harkavy, I. (1990). Partnership produces comprehensive program in Philadelphia. *Equity and Choice, 6,* 13–15.

Heath, S. B., & McLaughlin, M. W. (1993). Building identities for inner-city youth. In S. B. Heath & M. W. McLaughlin (Eds.), *Identity and inner-city youth: Beyond ethnicity and gender* (pp. 13–35). New York: Teachers College Press.

Heleen, O. (1990). Community schools and service integration in New York. *Equity and Choice, 6,* 19–20.

Kusserow, R. P. (1991). *Services integration: A twenty-year perspective.* Washington, DC: U.S. Department of Health and Human Services, Office of Inspector General.

McLaughlin, M. W. (1993). Embedded identities: Enabling balance in urban contexts. In S. B. Heath & M. W. McLaughlin (Eds.), *Identity and inner-city youth: Beyond ethnicity and gender* (pp. 36–68). New York: Teachers College Press.

Moroz, K., & Segal, E. (1990). Homeless children: Intervention strategies for school social workers. *Social Work in Education, 12,* 134–143.

Shaw, K. M., & Replogle, E. M. (1995). Evaluating school-linked services. *Evaluation Exchange: Emerging Strategies in Evaluating Child and Family Services, 1,* 2–4.

Solo, L. (1992). Getting support from the community. *Principle, 71,* 26–27.

U.S. General Accounting Office. (1993). *School-linked human services: A comprehensive strategy for aiding students at risk of school failure.* Washington, DC: U.S. Government Printing Office.

Wall, J. C. (1996). Homeless children and their families: Delivery of educational and social services through school systems. *Social Work in Education, 18,* 135–144.

Zetlin, A., Campbell, B., Lujan, M., & Lujan, R. (1994). Schools and families working together for children. *Equity and Choice, 10,* 10–15.

Zetlin, A., Ramos, C., & Valdez, A. (1996). Integrating services in a school-based center: An example of a school–community collaboration. *Journal of Community Psychology, 24,* 97–107.

The research described in this chapter was funded through a grant from the U.S. Department of Education to the Institute for Responsive Education, Boston University School of Education (R117Q00031). The author was project director on this grant.

Promoting the Educational Achievement of Mexican American Young Women

Marian A. Aguilar

The Hispanic population increased from 14.6 million to a little more than 22 million between 1980 and 1990, an increase of 53 percent (Chapa & Valencia, 1993). The median age of the Hispanic population is 26, seven years younger than the white population (Perez & De La Rosa Salazar, 1993), indicating that Hispanics have higher fertility rates than other groups. In 1990 the percentage of the Latino population that were children ranged from 25 percent in Florida to a high of 45 percent in North Dakota (Children's Defense Fund, 1992).

The educational system has not been as successful in educating youths of color as in educating Anglo-American youths. Although there has been an increase in the enrollment of Hispanic students in the elementary grades, there has been a decrease in the upper-grade levels, confirming high dropout rates (Perez & De La Rosa Salazar, 1993). In some communities the dropout rate is as high as 85 percent (Perez & De La Rosa Salazar, 1993).

Dropout among Latino youths is a form of underachievement that has far-reaching consequences. Among the diverse ethnic groups in the United States, Mexican Americans have the highest dropout rates; youths who have dropped out are undereducated and ill prepared to perform tasks that require technical skills (Perez & De La Rosa Salazar, 1993). According to demographers, the work force will increasingly consist of people of color, with a large percentage of these being Hispanics. There are fears that without changes in the educational system, the future workforce will be largely illiterate and marginal (Perez & De La Rosa Salazar, 1993).

REVIEW OF THE LITERATURE

The literature on Mexican Americans in social work journals is sparse, and content on the educational achievement of Mexican Americans and the role of school social workers is all but nonexistent. Padilla (1990) examined reviews of literature about Mexican Americans in social work journals, reporting that they focused on practice and placed very little emphasis on the type of knowledge social workers needed for effective intervention with Mexican Americans.

This chapter was originally published in the July 1996 issue of *Social Work in Education*, Vol. 18, pp. 145–156.

McMahon and Allen-Meares (1992) conducted a content analysis of articles on intervention with people of color published between 1980 and 1989 in four social work journals: *Child Welfare, Social Casework, Social Work,* and *Social Service Review.* They found only 16 articles on Mexican Americans. They concluded that social work is racist because the articles focused on individual intervention; they gave little focus to institutional intervention and thus totally ignored the context in which people of color lived. McMahon and Allen-Meares further concluded that there was a reluctance among social work authors to undertake social action at the macro level.

Most of the social work literature on youths of color at risk of dropping out of school reflects a micro approach to intervention. Chavkin and Brown (1992) noted that intervention at the individual level is futile unless it is combined with a macro approach to reducing the barriers to retention and access at the systems level. The involvement of school social workers in the retention and achievement of culturally and racially diverse youths has not been fully addressed in the literature. In an editorial, Allen-Meares (1992) emphasized the need for social workers to have a cross-cultural perspective. She further stated that "teachers will need assistance in changing their perception of [racially diverse children] as a population at risk to one in which they see these students as children who have unique strengths on which they can build" (p. 4). Few studies focus on youths at risk who have succeeded. Most have focused on addressing the dropout problem after it has occurred, not on prevention.

A report published by the Texas Education Agency (1989) recognized that poverty and undereducation are both cyclical and interdependent. Rosenthal (1995) cited four variables identified in the literature that are positively associated with dropping out of school: low socioeconomic status, minority group status, increased household stress, and lack of social support. Chapa and Valencia (1993) added underachievement because of low expectations by the educational system. Nieto (1992), however, challenged the assertion that educational failure is caused by students' backgrounds and social characteristics, because some students with such characteristics are successful in the classroom. She further asserted that the role of racism and discrimination in the underachievement of youths of color cannot be discounted.

METHOD

To examine the pattern of educational achievement of a group of young women of color, a small pilot study was conducted with a sample of 84 Mexican American women who were the first in their families to attend college. The issue of achievement in education was considered from both a cultural and structural perspective. The strengths that allowed the participants to achieve were discussed. The literature on educational retention and achievement provides the framework from which to examine both the strengths and barriers identified by the participants.

The participants in the study came from backgrounds that placed them at risk of school dropout, yet these young women had succeeded in graduating from high school and entering college. Analyzing their pattern of achievement was helpful in exploring ways to retain Mexican American and other at-risk youths in school. Their responses provide a basis for developing social work interventions to reduce the dropout rate of these youths.

Participants

The participants for this basic exploratory study were recruited using a list of Hispanic female students enrolled at a small private university in the Southwest. The list was provided to the staff of the Center for Women in Church and Society, which is housed at the university. The center's function is to enhance the roles of women in the church and in society; it focuses on efforts to bring about interaction among varied groups of women and political organizations.

The university has a record of admitting at-risk students and moving them from a level of underachievement to a college-compatible level of achievement. The undergraduate enrollment of students of color is over 80 percent. Seventy-two percent of the student body is female; 75 percent are Hispanic and 5 percent are African American (Our Lady of the Lake University, 1994). The university is located in one of the poorest districts of the city, and a major part of the recruitment efforts are directed toward students of color.

Staff of the Center for Women in Church and Society mailed letters explaining the purpose of the study to all Hispanic female students and asking for volunteers who were the first in their families to attend college. The final sample consisted of 84 volunteers. Appointments for face-to-face interviews were made by the center staff who had helped develop and pretest the instrument. The term "Hispanic" is what the U.S. Bureau of the Census designates people who claim a Latin American background. It is an ascribed term. Some Hispanics prefer to be called either "Latino" or by their specific ethnic identity. For this reason, the terms "Latina" and "Mexican American" are used interchangeably when describing the women in this study.

Only women were used in the study because the staff of the center had undertaken a project to help women living in Catholic housing move toward economic independence. First, the staff felt the study could provide some guidelines for developing a training framework because the young women came from similar backgrounds that had elements not conducive to educational success.

Second, center staff recognized that women of color are the most adversely affected by undereducation and lack of marketable skills and that these deficits reduce the chances for economic self-sufficiency not only for themselves but also for their children. This is a critical issue because of the increasing percentage of Latino female-headed households living in poverty (46.3 percent) and requiring public assistance (Firestone & Harris, 1994). Firestone and Harris used the term "double jeopardy" in referring to individuals who endure two disadvantaged statuses at the same time (for example, male and African American, female and single head of household, Latino and undereducated). Latinas use the term "twice a minority" (Melville, 1980).

Measures

An instrument was designed and pretested to obtain data on those variables that the educational literature indicates have an effect on the school retention, dropout prevention, and educational achievement of youths. The variables cluster around six factors: (1) demographics, (2) the effects of growing up as a woman and a person of color on achievement (racism, sexism, parental attitudes), (3) cultural strengths, (4) personal strengths, (5) support systems, and (6) barriers. With the exception of the questions on demographics, the instrument contained open-ended questions to allow the participants the opportunity to elaborate. Demographic data were reported, and the open-ended questions were categorized and analyzed.

FINDINGS

Demographics

The majority of the 84 participants in this study were between the ages of 20 and 25 (72.6 percent). A little over half (56.0 percent) were college freshmen. Unlike most traditional college students, 14.2 percent of the participants were either married, divorced, or separated. A greater number (41.7 percent) were the oldest sibling (Table 14-1). The majority of the participants (58.3 percent) had fewer than four siblings. Eighty-eight percent ($n = 74$) were Catholic. Only seven of the women were born in Mexico; two were born in other countries (Japan and Germany), six were born in states other than Texas, and 69 were born in Texas. A small number of the women's parents were born in Mexico; both parents of 10 participants and one parent of 17 participants were born in Mexico.

When asked at what age they had decided on a career, 39.3 percent ($n = 33$) of the participants indicated that they had been between ages 16 and 20, 17.9 percent ($n = 15$) between ages five and 10, and 21.4 percent ($n = 18$) between ages 11 and 15; the remainder did not answer the question. All of the participants identified a profession and had career goals. The following were the most frequently mentioned professions to which the respondents aspired: attorney ($n = 14$), educator ($n = 14$), physician ($n = 9$), social worker ($n = 9$), psychologist ($n = 6$), and business woman ($n = 7$).

Growing Up a Latina

The responses to the question about what it was like growing up as a woman of color generated data that were broken down into two

Table 14-1

Demographic Characteristics of Respondents (*N* = 84)

Characteristic	*n*	%
Age		
19 and under	1	1.2
20–25	61	72.6
26–30	7	8.3
31–35	3	3.6
36–40	7	8.3
Over 40	5	6.0
College level		
Freshman	47	56.0
Sophomore	12	14.3
Junior	14	16.7
Senior	5	6.0
Graduate	6	7.1
Marital status		
Married	6	7.1
Divorced or separated	6	7.1
Never married	70	83.3
Other	2	2.4
Birth order		
Only child	1	1.2
Youngest	20	23.8
Middle	12	14.3
Oldest	35	41.7
Other position	16	19.0

categories for purposes of clarity: growing up as a woman and growing up as a person of color.

Sexism. Nearly one-half (48.8 percent, *n* = 41) of the respondents indicated that they experienced sexism. Some respondents felt that they experienced dual and conflicting expectations from within and outside their culture. Within their culture, their experience can be summed up by the following statement: Daughters were expected to assume traditional spousal roles, prepare for marriage, marry within their race, and bow to men. But their parents had different expectations of their brothers, who had more freedom to experiment, date, and leave home for college and had fewer family responsibilities.

Outside their culture, the women felt that they had to prove themselves. They felt that they had been held down by the school system, teachers, and employers because of their gender. They also reported having few role models.

Racism. Almost one-half (47.6 percent, *n* = 40) of the respondents reported that the educational system, their social environment, and other structures negatively influenced their experience of growing up as a person of color. The following statements capture their experiences:

- "We were physically punished for speaking Spanish."
- "I felt intimidated by the white students."
- "I felt I had to get rid of my accent."
- "I felt very much discriminated against."
- "The teachers [even teachers of color] said 'Why excel? You will get pregnant and have to marry.'"
- "I had to work twice as hard to prove myself."
- "I felt very, very lonely."
- "It was difficult not being able to express our heritage."
- "It was difficult; I could not identify with what was being taught."
- "I felt singled out, stereotyped."

Nearly one-third (28.6 percent, $n = 24$) of the participants reported being sheltered from discrimination because they lived in a predominantly Latino environment, went to predominantly Latino schools, or attended all-girls' schools or private (Catholic) schools. Over two-fifths (40.5 percent, $n = 34$) of the respondents stated that they were not aware of being in the minority until they moved out of their milieu to attend high school or college.

Parental Attitudes and Support. The young women used themselves as the basis of comparison in responding to the question about what their parents thought about the education of women. Many of the participants (71.4 percent, $n = 60$) said that both parents were supportive of their educational endeavors, 15 (17.9 percent) said the mother was more supportive than the father, and five (6.0 percent) said the father was the more supportive parent. In four instances the father was either absent or deceased. In three cases the father was totally against the daughter's pursuit of higher education, saying, "A girl does not need an education to get a job" or "You are going to get married anyway" or "I would rather provide the financial support for your brother." The fathers of three other girls were beginning to express support, gladness, and pride in their educational accomplishments.

Cultural Strengths

The responses to the question about the cultural factors that helped the participants reach their professional goals were broken down into five areas: family, beliefs, values, community, and negative aspects. Thirty-two (38.1 percent) of the respondents felt that family values such as unity, respect, support, parental expectations, and the ability to survive under adverse conditions including poverty were influential in helping them achieve their goals. Thirteen (15.5 percent) respondents felt that religious values (for example, faith, prayer, respect, the presence of God in the events of life) and traditional and nontraditional beliefs (for example, role expectations, the good of the family, family loyalty and support) were influential. Twenty-six participants (30.9 percent) were proud to be Mexican American, bicultural, and bilingual; were proud of their ethnicity; and expressed the desire to help others in their community.

Thirty-one (36.9 percent) felt that their own poverty and witnessing others' poverty influenced their educational pursuit and their desire to improve their communities and reduce the negative perceptions of Mexican Americans. The respondents were edified by the example of women in their communities who worked together and helped others. The young women also reported that teachers, counselors, and friends had given encouragement. Conversely, two women reported that the lack of community role models was the impetus they needed to pursue their goals.

Thirty (35.7 percent) respondents reported that their negative experiences served as a catalyst for achievement, including the Latino culture's lack of support of women, the social problems in their communities, not knowing successful Latina women, discrimination, the limited number of Latinas going to college, and family or community poverty. One respondent who mentioned being extremely poor said that this was the very experience that gave her the impetus to succeed; she was determined to get out of poverty.

Personal Strengths

The responses given by the participants to the question about their individual strengths were divided into five categories: cognitive, relational, emotional health, motivational, and socioecological. The cognitive strengths identified by the participants were bilingualism and biculturalism, academic skills, hard work, self-discipline, intelligence, multiple talents, and the ability to learn from their mistakes. The relational strengths identified by the participants were good communication skills; responsibility, reliability, and dependability; the ability to listen and get along; honesty; fairness; and a nonjudgmental nature. The characteristics identified by the respondents in the emotional health category were determination, perseverance, confidence, spiritual depth, faith, independence, anger, open-mindedness, strong will, belief in taking care of self, and enthusiasm.

Motivational strengths included being able to take on a challenge; being goal oriented, ambitious, aggressive, and assertive; being positive and visionary; and having a sense of calling and the desire to succeed. The socioecological strengths reported by the participants were the willingness to serve, ability to see the bigger picture, desire to be something different, dedication, cultural pride, sense of identity, and willingness to speak for others.

Support Systems

In responding to the question on who had supported their achievements, the majority of the respondents (83.3 percent, $n = 70$) identified family members or friends (parents, husband, siblings, aunts, boyfriends). In addition, 18 participants indicated that teachers (including nuns), mostly in high school, had been influential. Six said no one had helped them, one said that she had no role models, two said God had helped them, and two said they had female mentors.

Barriers

The barriers to educational success encountered by the young women were divided into the personal, the socioeconomic, the intracultural, and the extracultural. The personal barriers to goal achievement included lack of knowledge of how to achieve goals, low self-esteem, fear, stress, and self-doubt. The socioeconomic barriers most frequently mentioned were poverty, system-engendered lack of self-confidence, discrimination, difficulty speaking English, lack of knowledge of how to achieve goals, divorce or single parenthood, differences in lifestyle, poor education, sense of isolation, sexism, having to break from traditional values, and lack of family and cultural support. Intracultural barriers were lack of family support, family responsibilities, lack of someone to talk to, traditional values, and role expectations. Extracultural barriers included punishment for speaking Spanish, classmates' attitudes, discrimination, poor educational background, and teachers' attitudes and statements (for example, being told that they were not good enough).

FRAMEWORK FOR INTERVENTION

The responses of the 84 participants provide the basis for developing a framework that school social workers and educators can use in their efforts to retain youths at risk of dropping out and to promote educational achievement. On the basis of these findings, I propose a framework that integrates personal and cultural strengths in an effort to reduce the effects of the barriers on the achievement of Latinas. Four phases have been incorporated in the model: (1) awareness and recognition of the personal and cultural strengths and supports of students; (2) the recognition of barriers they face; (3) intervention at the micro and macro levels to promote changes that affirm diversity and integrate the cultural context of students; and (4) the removal of those structural and social barriers to educational achievement ingrained in school policy, curriculum, and resources. The insights discussed in the Findings section can help educators complete the first two phases; phases 3 and 4 constitute the intervention stage and are discussed next.

Affirming Diversity

The participants reported experiencing gender and racial and ethnic discrimination in numerous ways, such as being enrolled in remedial programs rather than learning programs, being isolated or ignored, receiving an inferior education, being punished for speaking Spanish, being placed in non–college preparatory courses (tracked), and having teachers expect less of them or not believe they were capable of academically demanding work. The literature confirms that racism and sexism are detrimental to achievement because they increase emotional stress and reduce motivation to learn.

Reducing Racism. In the past the prevailing method for increasing achievement levels was to devise ways of altering the personality, cognitive processes, and motivational dispositions of children (Boykin, 1986). In recent years this model of focusing on deficiencies has been sharply criticized; nonetheless, because this method is consistent with the underlying ideology of mainstream America, it persists (Boykin, 1986). For this reason teachers and social workers must re-evaluate their approach before beginning to make structural changes.

Both social workers and teachers need to be convinced not only that labeling, deficiency, and remediation practices hurt children of color, but also that the treatment of children of color as if they were culturally disadvantaged will persist unless helping professionals actively intervene (Boykin, 1986). These professionals are the ones who have the power to make positive structural changes. They can begin on a micro level by recognizing, affirming, and respecting diversity. Diversity is affirmed on a micro level when teachers and social workers acknowledge that being bilingual and bicultural are strengths.

Teachers and social workers must also take time to observe the incidents of discrimination and isolation of children of color that take place in the classroom, on the playground, and in all activities in which they choose to involve the children. They must demand that such practices be changed. Diversity is affirmed when a strategy for action, beginning with observation and a cultural assessment of each student, is undertaken by the teacher in coordination with the social worker (Delva-Tauili'ili, 1995). Teachers affirm diversity when they expect children of color to achieve and when they use the children's learning styles and cultural context in teaching.

Reducing Sexism. Nieto (1992) found that most schools are sexist in their organization, orientation, and goals. The school system is set up to serve the interests of the male student, and this message permeates school policy, instruction, and extracurricular activities. Studies indicate that boys receive more attention in the classroom, where the structure is competitive rather than collaborative.

Several studies, including Valenzuela's (1993), have found that single-sex schools are more conducive to learning for girls. They are more likely to develop girls' self-esteem and to encourage achievement and participation. Some of the young women in the present study noted that boys were called on more often, that less was expected of girls, and that a double standard existed. Those who attended private schools appeared to have fewer problems with self-esteem or achievement than those who attended public schools.

The implications of operating under a double standard need to be examined by both social workers and teachers to develop strategies to make changes at the macro level. Social work and teaching are professions where women predominate but men tend to set the policies and standards (Gibelman & Schervish, 1995; Huber & Orlando, 1995). A concerted strategic plan by teachers and social workers to ensure that women are placed in positions where they can influence decisions on curriculum, policies, and standards needs to be developed.

Integrating the Cultural Contexts of Students

Cultural Strengths. Every culture carries with it a rich legacy. The young women saw their culture, including family, beliefs, customs, language, and support systems, as a strength. The social and historical context from which children come, as well as ways of celebrating holidays and the history of the development of the neighborhood, need to be incorporated into the curriculum.

Stories of life, the immigrant experience, family experiences, and community heroes also need to be woven into the curriculum. Social workers have more access to the family and encounter many instances of heroic efforts to survive in the midst of adversity.

Culturally Sensitive Teaching. Children should not have to choose between family and school, between a sense of belonging and a sense of succeeding. According to the participants the stress involved in balancing these choices leads to low self-esteem, shame, and isolation. The promotion of diversity by social workers leads to the enhancement of learning for both teachers and students.

Because school social workers are more attuned to the effects of the school system on young women and social and economic influences on student learning and retention, they have the tools to document and report the need for individual and structural changes. School professionals need to systematically study and experience how children of color learn. For example, many studies in the education literature document the use of an experiential contextual approach to learning for children of color, but this approach has not been adequately explored by teachers or school systems (Mestre & Royer, 1991; Trueba, 1989).

Social workers and teachers should become familiar with the use of the Internet and other visual and interactive aids as learning tools. The media are teaching and learning tools. Drawing examples of role models from television, magazines, and online services for discussion when teaching or running groups can be a very effective teaching device.

When Selena Quintanilla, the popular Tejano singer, was murdered in March 1995, the press carried her story for many days after her funeral. Some radio and television stations played her music or carried her story nonstop. Music stores all over the country quickly ran out of her compact discs and cassettes. Many young and old Mexican Americans considered this 23-year-old a role model, because she made them proud of being Mexican American. She affirmed that being Mexican American was good. She probably did more for the self-esteem of young children than many social workers or teachers. As unfortunate as her death was, the subsequent attention it received was a perfect example of a teachable moment, a moment in which a successful role model could be discussed.

Parental Support and Involvement. Parents were on the whole very supportive of the participants' educational goals. Yet a primary complaint of school officials is that parents tend to be only minimally involved with the school. Several respondents said that their parents had a very limited education or none at all. Some parents spoke only Spanish. Others were very poor and did not know where to look for resources or opportunities. Nonetheless, all of these parents wanted their daughters to get at least a high school education.

According to Mestre and Royer (1991), the literature indicates that Mexican American families do not differ from Anglo-American families in educational values and aspirations, only in educational attainment. For this reason Mexican American parents may be unable to translate encouragement into concrete actions such as helping with homework.

Parents of color have not been adequately tapped by most school systems. Social workers can enhance parental involvement by reinforcing a sense of ownership of the schools their children attend. The schools belong to the communities, and as residents of those communities parents need to believe they have a say in the education of their children.

It is preposterous to say that most parents of color do not care. I have observed several examples of the actions of poor women of color who, when they witnessed the violence in their neighborhoods, organized to reclaim their communities. They have held candlelight processions through their neighborhoods. They have formed neighborhood safety patrol groups. They have come together to strategize about the removal of drugs from their community. In a successful retention project sponsored by a large university and the Junior League, Mexican American mothers walked with their daughters through workshops, classes, and career fairs as the daughters learned how to study, think of career options, and select a college.

Removing Structural and Social Barriers

Both students and teachers have limited opportunities to provide input into a school system's structure, texts, and curriculum. Systems generally support student organizations that are mostly social or educational in nature but do not provide an arena for more substantive input. The school social worker can recommend the establishment of student–teacher exchange forums that provide a mechanism for teachers and students to express their ideas about changes in curricula, policies, and texts. During these forums participants can examine issues, problems, learning styles, and concerns related to discrimination.

Because students need role models, the interaction between teachers and students is important. Through such sessions students can see that teachers are normal human beings and that many of them have the best interests of their students at heart. Teachers, on the other hand, can use forum time to learn where the students are coming from and why they make the choices they do.

The elimination of poverty is not within the direct domain of the instructor or school social worker. Nonetheless, two issues can be extrapolated from the study. First, the participants recognized that

Table 14-2
Removing Barriers to Educational Achievement in Youths of Color

Barrier	Type of Intervention
Socioeconomic	Distribution of resources through dissemination of information
Personal	Recognition and affirmation of students' strengths
Intracultural	Active encouragement of family involvement in the schools
Extracultural	Improved educational opportunities through greater teacher and social worker awareness of cultural diversity, history, and customs
Racism	Changes in educational policies, practices, and administration; changes in teachers' sensitivity and expectations
Sexism	Changes in male-oriented classroom practices, changes in educational policies that favor boys, changes in teachers' behavior

education reduces the likelihood of poverty in the future. For this reason retention efforts should seek to increase the awareness of the community that education potentially reduces poverty. Second, many school districts with a majority of students of color have limited resources for improving the teacher pool and acquiring high-tech hardware and expertise (Perez & De La Rosa Salazar, 1993). The issue of resources is highly relevant to the retention and achievement of students of color. Social workers can use their expertise in assessing resources and helping administrators set goals for the acquisition of human and material resources. The barriers to educational success identified by the participants in the study and the types of interventions that would be appropriate are listed in Table 14-2.

DISCUSSION

School reform is just as urgent as health and welfare reform. Social workers must be part of the solution, which requires commitment and creativity more than a major influx of funding. The proposed framework for retention of students of color facilitates social workers' interventions with individuals, families, teachers, support staff, and the system as a whole. Without intervention, the price that society pays when youths drop out of school will multiply when these youths enter the nonskilled workforce. The failure to affirm diversity in the nation's schools will result in a less productive economy.

The embryonic framework presented here may be limited and needs testing. Although the sample in the present study was small, the data confirm what others have identified as issues and barriers to educational achievement. The framework can provide the impetus and foundation for intervention and further study.

In affirming diversity, there is an underlying assumption that individuals who are culturally and socially diverse vary in the way they learn, think, and make decisions. The effect and interplay of culture and language in the cognitive performance of children of diverse backgrounds need to be closely examined, discussed, and integrated into the continuing education of school social workers, teachers, and their aides (Perez & De La Rosa Salazar, 1993).

Many young lives are being wasted because of lack of reform of a school system that is becoming increasingly diverse. Gunn-Allen (1989) asserted that the "materials, values, cultural expression forms, models and techniques, science, facts and thinking processes taught are all cut from the Anglo-American model" (p. 15). She further stated, "Children who resist this intense, compulsory indoctrination are punished in a variety of ways: flunked out, forced out (or graduated illiterate in a society that requires literacy as the price of dinner), shamed, coerced, beaten, . . . denied, discounted, and thrown away, as though human beings were yesterday's leavings" (p. 15). Despair, shame, grief, and inexpressible fury are the terms she used to describe experiences of the American Indians living on reservations and in urban enclaves. The same can be said of Hispanic and African American youths who have dropped out of school.

Social workers and teachers cannot prevent all students from dropping out, but they can do a great deal more than is currently being done. They can reduce the dropout rate by setting retention goals. They can approach the issue from a strengths perspective. At the point of intersection where people and programs are linked, the strengths perspective becomes critical in terms of retention and achievement. Very little has been documented about the effects of using a strengths perspective, although the development of cognitive, emotional, social, and motivational skills has been recognized by educators as important to the retention of youths (Texas Education Agency, 1989).

CONCLUSION

Language, culture, family, and personal characteristics have not been identified as strengths in youths at risk. Neither have the roles of poverty and discrimination in the retention of students been adequately addressed. Parents and at-risk youths possess strengths that have not been called forth or even acknowledged. If inroads are going to be made in retention, a strengths perspective in formulating any curriculum or structural changes is imperative. Through the recognition and the affirmation of students and involvement in activities that remove structural and social barriers in the educational system, teachers and social workers will witness the reduction of the attrition rate of students of color and an increase in the level of their achievement.

REFERENCES

Allen-Meares, P. (1992). Prevention and cross-cultural perspective: Preparing school social workers for the 21st century. *Social Work in Education, 14,* 3–5.

Boykin, W. (1986). The triple quandary and the schooling of Afro-American children. In U. Neisser (Ed.), *The school achievement of minority children: New perspectives* (pp. 57–92). Hillsdale, NJ: Lawrence Erlbaum.

Chapa, J., & Valencia, R. (1993). Latino population, demographic characteristics, and educational stagnation: An examination of recent trends. *Hispanic Journal of Behavioral Sciences, 15,* 165–187.

Chavkin, N., & Brown, K. (1992). School social workers building a multiethnic family–school–community partnership. *Social Work in Education, 14,* 160–164.

Children's Defense Fund. (1992). *The state of America's children, 1992.* Washington, DC: Author.

Delva-Tauili'ili, J. (1995). Assessment and prevention of aggressive behavior among youths of color: Integrating cultural and social factors. *Social Work in Education, 17,* 83–91.

Firestone, J., & Harris, R. (1994). Hispanic women in Texas: An increasing portion of the underclass. *Hispanic Journal of Behavioral Sciences, 16,* 176–184.

Gibelman, M., & Schervish, P. (1995). Pay equity in social work: Not! *Social Work, 40,* 622–630.

Gunn-Allen, P. (1989). Introduction. In P. Gunn-Allen (Ed.), *Spider woman's granddaughters* (pp. 1–25). New York: Fawcett Columbine.

Huber, R., & Orlando, B. (1995). Persisting gender differences in social workers' incomes: Does the profession really care? *Social Work, 40,* 585–594.

McMahon, A., & Allen-Meares, P. (1992). Is social work racist? A content analysis of recent literature. *Social Work, 37,* 533–538.

Melville, M. (1980). *Twice a minority.* St. Louis: C. V. Mosby.

Mestre, J., & Royer, J. (1991). Issues in Latino testing. In G. Keller, J. Deneen, & R. Magallan (Eds.), *Assessment and access: Hispanics in higher education* (pp. 39–46). Albany: State University of New York Press.

Nieto, S. (1992). *Affirming diversity: The sociopolitical context of multicultural education.* New York: Longman.

Our Lady of the Lake University. (1994, Fall). *Demographics* (IR Report No. 008-01). San Antonio, TX: Author.

Padilla, Y. (1990). Social science theory on the Mexican American experience. *Social Service Review, 64,* 261–275.

Perez, S., & De La Rosa Salazar, D. (1993). Economic, labor force, and social implications of Latino educational and population trends. *Hispanic Journal of Behavioral Sciences, 15,* 188–229.

Rosenthal, B. (1995). The influence of social support on school completion among Haitians. *Social Work in Education, 17,* 30–39.

Texas Education Agency. (1989). *Successful schooling for economically disadvantaged at-risk youths.* Austin: Author, Publications Distribution Office.

Trueba, H. (1989). Creating success in a border school: Culture and literacy in the empowerment of Hispanic high school students. *Estudios Fronterizos, 8,* 68–82.

Valenzuela, A. (1993). Liberal gender role attitudes and academic achievement among Mexican-origin adolescents in two Houston inner-city Catholic schools. *Hispanic Journal of Behavioral Sciences, 15,* 310–323.

A paper based on the data was presented at the conference on New Directions in Education V, Texas A&M University, June 1994, Bryan College Station, TX.

15 Puerto Rican Elementary School–Age Children:
Assistance with Homework as an Indicator of Natural Support Strengths

Melvin Delgado

The educational challenges facing Puerto Rican children and their families have been well documented in the professional literature (Hidalgo, Siu, Bright, Swap, & Epstein, 1995; Kozol, 1991). Puerto Rican children have an exceedingly high probability of failing one or more grades, of being placed in special education, and of dropping out of school before graduation (Children's Defense Fund, 1991; Irvine & York, 1993; Perez & Martinez, 1993). The lack of educational achievement represents a serious threat to the emotional, economic, and social well-being of the Puerto Rican community (Solis, 1995).

School recognition of cultural strengths, in this case natural support systems, is one method of fostering an environment based on mutual understanding and respect (Delgado & Rivera, 1997). If formal educational success is to be achieved, it will necessitate collaboration among schools, families, and community: "Research in this field [families, schools, and communities] is still in its infancy. Although based on a long tradition of research on families and on schools studied separately, attention to issues of 'partnership' is relatively new" (Hidalgo et al., 1995, p. 498).

This chapter addresses the role of natural support systems as a resource for helping Puerto Rican children with homework. The identification of who and how many people help a child with homework is a low-labor-intensive means of focusing on strengths and cultural resources. This resource, however, has implications beyond homework.

A 2$^1/_2$-year study of 24 Puerto Rican families in an urban elementary school uncovered attitudes, aspirations, and coping strategies contrary to the stereotypes of low-income Puerto Rican families commonly portrayed in the mass media. These families had high educational expectations for their children. The findings have practice implications for school social workers in elementary schools in their quest to develop meaningful partnerships among schools, families, and communities (Delgado, 1996b).

This chapter was originally published in the January 1998 issue of *Social Work in Education*, Vol. 20, pp. 49–54.

LITERATURE REVIEW

A review of the literature on elementary school–age Puerto Rican children did not identify an extensive coverage of the topic. The few scholarly articles on this topic generally touched on issues related to uprootment, low test scores, and the importance of school personnel understanding and building on Puerto Rican culture (Condon, Peters, & Sueiro-Ross, 1979; Walsh, 1991).

Diaz-Soto's (1988, 1989, 1990) research of Puerto Rican families dispelled the myth that Puerto Rican children are low achievers. She found that parents who were "high achievers" communicated with children in both English and Spanish, had high career aspirations, and both disciplined and protected their children from environmental harm. Volk (1992) found that Puerto Rican families initiate in-home learning activities with their children. Diaz-Soto (1992) stressed the importance of assessing learning activities within a social–cultural context—varied learning contexts and multiple significant players, some of whom are extended family members, neighbors, family friends, and religious leaders.

Few scholars, however, have viewed natural support systems as a vehicle for helping children by bringing together school, family, and community (Nadal & Morales-Nadal, 1993). The identification of a natural support system lends itself to a strengths perspective in viewing Puerto Rican youths and their families and communities (Delgado, 1996a).

METHODS

Forty-five Puerto Rican families were selected as potential participants. Their children were in two kindergarten and first-grade bilingual classes in a Boston elementary school. Teachers in these classrooms were approached to help with recruiting. From lists provided by the teachers, 24 families (sample goal) agreed to participate, for which they received $25 per interview; there were four interviews over a 30-month period. Families were visited in their homes by bilingual and bicultural (Puerto Rican) interviewers; each visit lasted approximately one hour, during which the interviewer asked a series of open-ended questions about family history, culture, community, and school. Each set of interview questions was informed by answers to the previous set of questions.

The study examined four dimensions of natural support systems (Delgado & Humm-Delgado, 1982): (1) extended family; (2) religion (Catholic, Pentecostal, Jehovah's Witnesses, and Seventh Day Adventist); (3) folk healers (herbalist, Santeria, spiritist, and Santiguador); and (4) merchant and social clubs (grocery stores, botanical shops, and hometown clubs).

The study also undertook a key informant survey of "experts" on Puerto Rican educational issues as a means of laying out a consensal definition of natural support systems. Eight educators and scholars from three eastern states were selected because of their publications and experience with educating Puerto Rican elementary school–age children.

The following definition of Puerto Rican natural support systems was used to analyze the study participants' responses. It is a composite of input from the eight experts in educating Puerto Rican children and provides a social–cultural context from which to assess family resources:

> Natural support systems (NSS) represent institutions, individuals, and a perspective on viewing life when in time of need. These systems mediate day-to-day contingencies within a cultural context (physical and metaphysical). NSS are those systems that are sought instinctively; these systems have been useful in the past and are not created by the host culture. NSS consist of an individual's familial and community networks that provide for their growth, welfare, safety, and development. (Human service providers, educators, and other "formal" helpers *can* become natural support systems when they provide assistance that is widely considered outside of their job description and do so within a cultural-based context.) NSS play a crucial role in promoting a sense of identity, belonging, and self-esteem. These systems most often connote those needs that are met due to their membership in family or community groupings, as opposed to formal institutional and governmental arrangements. (Delgado & Rivera, 1997, p. 84)

In essence, natural support systems are socially created organized experiences that facilitate the process of help seeking. The definition captures the importance and potential of these systems in helping Puerto Rican children succeed in school and the community. Thus, school personnel, particularly social workers, are in an excellent position to assess these systems and involve them in the educational process.

FINDINGS

Five key findings from this study identified the potential of support systems and schools working together to better educate Puerto Rican children. First, the natural support systems of families in this study were limited, averaging 1.3 persons per family. This low number was unexpected. Most of the families did not have extensive social support even when faced with tremendous need. This finding has important practice implications for school social workers in their quest to help students who are having academic problems.

Second, when parents were asked what was the most important way they could help with their children's education, they most frequently cited helping with homework ($n = 13$), followed by attending school activities ($n = 6$) and communicating with school personnel whenever there was a concern ($n = 5$). However, families who indicated they had relatives who could help with their child's homework if needed ($n = 7$) had on average (5.2) a greater extensive support system than families who indicated that an older sibling ($n = 8$) was the primary helper. Families with a more extensive support system also were more likely to indicate being very religious and to attend religious services.

Third, families had very high expectations for their children's achievement in school and in postsecondary education. The overwhelming majority of families (n = 14 of 18) wanted their children to graduate from high school and obtain a college education. Families were quick to identify their children's strengths (academically and socially) and the importance of homework; in addition, they were cognizant of the barriers their children faced in obtaining a quality education in public schools.

Fourth, not all aspects of a Puerto Rican's natural support system play an influential role in educating children (Delgado & Humm-Delgado, 1982). There is no doubt that *la familia* is central to any effort, followed by religion. However, neighbors, folk healers, merchant or social clubs, and indigenous leaders were not active in helping with homework or achievement in school.

Finally, the 24 Puerto Rican families identified the neighborhood school as a major resource in their lives. The school was considered by many (n = 20) as an active and influential part of their support system. School personnel (all Puerto Rican), most notably the principal, teachers, and teacher aides, were identified as receptive, caring, and knowledgeable about their children's strengths and needs. They became part of a natural support system by going beyond their job descriptions.

IMPLICATIONS FOR SCHOOL SOCIAL WORK PRACTICE

Teachers and social workers can collaborate in obtaining information on who helps children with homework. This information should be gathered early in the academic year and should play a role in helping decide who should be invited to teacher–parent conferences in general and when there is an academic problem.

Information on who helps children with homework can help teachers and social workers link tutors with appropriate children early in an academic year. The students fortunate enough to have an extensive network to help them with homework can also benefit from having these "helpers" receive acknowledgment of their work and assistance in becoming better helpers. School social workers can help communicate with these helpers and perhaps set up workshops on the basis of identified needs of the support system.

Social workers can play an influential role in having outside speakers meet with parents. These speakers, preferably Puerto Rican or Latino, can offer advice to parents on how to ensure that their children get a college education. Parents should not have to wait until their children are in high school to get this type of support and guidance.

Because the Puerto Rican families viewed the school as a major resource, school social workers are in an excellent position to broker outside resources to help these families and their children. Social workers not only must endeavor to attract resources but also must ensure that the school is welcoming to these "guests," never an easy task.

CONCLUSION

The findings highlight the importance of schools in the lives of young Puerto Rican children and their families. They also stress the need to identify who is involved with helping a child with homework, including the nature and extent of a support system.

School personnel should not overlook the presence or absence of a support system to help Puerto Rican young people with homework. Parents were not averse to attending workshops on helping children with homework and developing good study habits or meeting with teachers or other personnel to further improve their children's education. However, I recommend that any efforts to help parents be better "teachers" must also involve older siblings, other family members (as determined by parents), and other significant individuals. In short, the definition of family must be broadened.

The findings also stress the interconnectedness of school-related work and other aspects of a family's life. In this case, assistance with homework, an often overlooked dimension of education, provided a window into the extent of support a family can count on when in need.

REFERENCES

Children's Defense Fund. (1991). *America's Latino children.* Washington, DC: Author.

Condon, E. C., Peters, J. N., & Sueiro-Ross, C. (1979). *Special education and the Hispanic child: Cultural perspectives.* Philadelphia: Temple University.

Delgado, M. (1996a). Community asset assessments by Latino youths. *Social Work in Education, 18,* 169–178.

Delgado, M. (1996b). A guide for school-based personnel collaborating with Puerto Rican natural support systems. *New Schools, New Communities, 12,* 38–42.

Delgado, M., & Humm-Delgado, D. (1982). Natural support systems: Source of strength in Hispanic communities. *Social Work, 27,* 83–89.

Delgado, M., & Rivera, H. (1997). Puerto Rican natural support systems: Impact on families, communities, and schools. *Urban Education, 32,* 81–87.

Diaz-Soto, L. (1988). The home environment of higher and lower achieving Puerto Rican children. *Hispanic Journal of Behavioral Sciences, 10,* 161–167.

Diaz-Soto, L. (1989). Relationship between home environment and intrinsic versus extrinsic orientation of higher achieving and lower achieving Puerto Rican children. *Educational Research Quarterly, 13,* 22–36.

Diaz-Soto, L. (1990). *Families as learning environments: Reflections on critical factors affecting differential achievement.* (ERIC Document Reproduction Service No. ED 315 498).

Diaz-Soto, L. (1992). Success stories. In C. Grant (Ed.), *Research and multicultural education* (pp. 153–164). London: Falmer Press.

Hidalgo, N. M., Siu, S. F., Bright, J. A., Swap, S. M., & Epstein, J. L. (1995). Research on families, schools, and communities: A multicultural perspective. In J. A. Banks & C. A. McGee-Banks (Eds.), *Handbook of research on multicultural education* (pp. 498–524). New York: Macmillan.

Irvine, J. J., & York, D. E. (1993). Teacher perspectives: Why do African-American, Hispanic, and Vietnamese students fail? In S. W. Rothstein (Ed.), *Handbook of schooling in urban America* (pp. 161–173). Westport, CT: Greenwood Press.

Kozol, J. (1991). *Savage inequalities: Children in America's schools.* New York: Harper
    Perennial.
Nadal, A., & Morales-Nadal, M. (1993). Multiculturalism in urban schools: A Puerto
    Rican perspective. In S. W. Rothstein (Ed.), *Handbook of schooling in urban America*
    (pp. 145–159). Westport, CT: Greenwood Press.
Perez, S. M., & Martinez, D. (1993). *State of Hispanic America 1993: Toward a Latino an-*
    tipoverty agenda. Washington, DC: National Council of La Raza.
Solis, J. (1995). The status of Latino children and youth: Challenges and prospects. In
    R. E. Zambrana (Ed.), *Understanding Latino families: Scholarship, policy, and practice*
    (pp. 62–81). Thousand Oaks, CA: Sage Publications.
Volk, D. (1992, June). *A case study of parental involvement in the homes of three Puerto Ri-*
    can kindergartners. Paper presented at the annual meeting of the American Educa-
    tional Research Association, San Francisco.
Walsh, C. E. (1991). *Pedagogy and the struggle for voice: Issues of language, power, and*
    schooling for Puerto Ricans. New York: Bergin & Garvey.

---

*The research reported in this chapter was supported by Grant No. R117000031
from the U.S. Department of Education, Office of Educational Research, in
cooperation with the U.S. Department of Health and Human Services.*

16 Violence among Urban African American Youths:
An Analysis of Environmental and Behavioral Risk Factors

James Herbert Williams, Arlene Rubin Stiffman, and John L. O'Neal

The level of violence in U.S. society is a significant social problem, challenging social scientists to develop effective prevention strategies and programs. The levels of participation in violent acts diverge across race, ethnicity, and gender groups (Prothrow-Stith & Weissman, 1991), with African American adolescents increasingly involved with and exposed to acts of violent behavior (Fitzpatrick & Boldizar, 1993). Thus, understanding the role of ethnicity is important to develop prevention strategies.

Arrest rates, victimization rates, and risk factors all demonstrate disproportionate involvement for African Americans. Although African Americans constitute 12 percent of the population, 46 percent of those arrested in 1993 for violent crimes were African American. Juvenile arrest rates for African Americans are of particular concern because they are 50 percent of the arrests for violent crimes, and the arrest rates for African American youths were five times that of white youths (1,429 per 100,000 compared to 274 per 100,000). These differences are evident in arrests for the most serious violent crimes. The juvenile murder arrest rate for African American youths was 7.5 times that of white youths (47.3 per 100,000 compared to 6.3 per 100,000). The juvenile rape arrest rate for African American youths was 4.3 times higher than that of white youths (66.3 per 100,000 compared to 15.4 per 100,000). And finally, the juvenile robbery arrest rate for African American adolescents was 8.7 times higher than that of white youths (644 per 100,000 compared to 74 per 100,000) (U.S. Department of Justice, 1993). Note that these data indicate differences in arrest rates, which may not accurately reflect actual levels of prevalence.

Williams, Ayers, Abbott, and Hawkins (1997) found that young African American females had higher initiation rates of violence and aggressive acts than young white females. They also found that African American female adolescents had higher levels of juvenile justice involvement than white female youths. When comparing race

This chapter was originally published in the March 1998 issue of *Social Work Research*, Vol. 22, pp. 3–13.

and gender differences in initiation of violence and juvenile justice system involvement, only African American and white male youths have higher rates of prevalence than African American female adolescents (Williams et al., 1997).

Victimization by violence disproportionately affects the young (ages 16 to 19) and African Americans (Fingerhut, Ingram, & Feldman, 1992a, 1992b; O'Donnell, 1995; Stiffman, Elze, Dore, Chen, & Cheng, 1996). Between 1979 and 1989, firearm-related homicide doubled for African American males between ages 15 and 19 (Fingerhut et al., 1992a). Fingerhut et al. (1992a) found that African American male adolescents had $2\frac{1}{2}$ times the rate of deaths from the use of firearms than white youths (48 percent compared to 18 percent) and that African American female adolescents, whose rates were notably lower than males, had twice the rate of white female adolescents (17 percent compared to 8 percent).

Risk factors for violent behavior differ across racial groups (Barnes & Farrell, 1992; Matsueda & Heimer, 1987; Williams, 1994; Williams, Ayers, & Arthur, 1997). Earlier research shows that structural conditions, such as income inequality, are predictors of violence for white youths but not for African American youths (Harer & Steffensmeier, 1992). Consistent with this research, Shihadeh and Steffensmeier (1994) found that intraracial income inequality was more highly correlated with juvenile violence than interracial income inequality.

RESEARCH LITERATURE ON ADOLESCENT VIOLENCE

Extensive research has identified other risk factors for crime and violence. Earlier research on adolescent violent behavior suggested that abuse of alcohol, marijuana, and cocaine contributes to the prevalence of adolescent suicide, homicide, robbery, rape, and assaults (Johnston, O'Malley, & Bachman, 1993; Kandel, 1982; Newcomb & Bentler, 1988). Studies have also shown that a child witnessing or being a victim of violence increases the risk of the child developing aggressive behavior patterns and being violent during childhood, adolescence, and early adulthood (Rivera & Wisdom, 1990; Salzinger, Feldman, & Hammer, 1993). Lack of parental supervision, parental conflict, marital discord, aggressive behavior in childhood, academic failure, and association with peers who engage in violent behavior are also considered predictors of adolescent violent behavior (Cairns & Cairns, 1992; Elliott, Huizinga, & Ageton, 1985; Farrington, 1991; Loeber & Dishion, 1984).

Whether overt (aggressive), covert (concealing), or both, the delinquent activities of most youths follow a common pattern of initiation, escalation, de-escalation, and desistance, with less serious behaviors generally preceding more moderate and serious ones (Elliott, Huizinga, & Menard, 1989; Loeber, Stouthamer-Loeber, Van Kammen, & Farrington, 1991; Loeber et al., 1993). Reviewing the literature, Loeber (1988) concluded that evidence supports a dual pathway model with an aggressive–versatile pathway (aggressive and concealing behavior) and a nonaggressive–antisocial pathway (nonaggressive, covert behavior only). More recently, in their longitudinal study of boys, Loeber et al. (1993) used reports from the children and their caretakers to identify three distinct developmental pathways young people take to problem behavior and serious, violent, and chronic offending: (1) authority conflict pathway—a progression from stubborn behavior to authority avoidance, (2) covert pathway—a progression from minor covert behaviors to serious delinquency, and (3) overt pathway—a progression from minor aggression to more serious violence. Loeber et al.'s results indicated minor differences between white youths and African American youths. White youths started the overt pathway at an earlier point than African American youths. Other research has clearly determined that aggression in childhood and the early onset of conduct disorder is highly correlated with deviance in adulthood (Farrington, 1991; Offord, Boyle, & Racine, 1991).

Ecological Approach

Few studies explore an ecological approach to understanding violent behavior among African Americans, yet we know the importance of the interdependence of individuals and their physical (geographical and spatial) and social (peers and groups) environments (Longres, 1995). Previous research provides evidence that early exposure to violence is related to violent behavior in children and adolescents (DuRant, Cadenhead, Pendergrast, Slavens, & Linder, 1994; Stiffman et al., 1996). In their studies of 225 African American youths in a mid-sized southern city, DuRant, Cadenhead, et al. (1994) and DuRant, Pendergrast, and Cadenhead (1994) investigated the social and psychological risk factors associated with violent behavior in youths residing in urban housing projects. Environmental risk factors such as exposure to violence, personal victimization, family conflict, school grades, unemployed head of household, and physical punishment significantly predicted the youths' self-reported violent behavior and frequency of physical fighting. They also found that behavioral risk factors such as levels of depression and hopelessness accounted for a significant portion of the variation in physical fighting (DuRant, Pendergrast, & Cadenhead, 1994).

Although there is considerable debate as to the causes of violence among youths, to develop intervention programs society must continue to build a knowledge base concerning the causal factors associated with violence in African American adolescents. The analyses in this chapter expand earlier work by studying African American youths from an urban area with a high per capita crime rate and by using an ecological approach to understanding violence. Thus, our research provides additional empirical evidence on which environmental and behavioral risk factors explain the involvement in violent behavior of African American youths.

METHOD

Design

The Youth Services Project at Washington University, funded by the National Institute of Mental Health, interviewed youths from the city of St. Louis who had received services from one of the following gateway services sectors: health care, juvenile justice, child welfare, and education. These services sectors were all in a position to screen youths for behavioral and mental health problems and to provide mental health services or referrals to services elsewhere. The Youth Services Project interviewers recruited youths (with the aid of service providers) by approaching them in service sector waiting rooms and by sending letters and mounting posters requesting volunteers for a study of adolescents' needs for social and mental health services. No records were kept of specific refusal or volunteer rates by sector because there was no way to measure the numbers of youths exposed to posters or contacted by service providers. Direct refusal to interviewers recruiting in waiting rooms was less than 2 percent.

The Youth Services Project examined adolescents' exposure to violence and their emotions or behaviors that might limit their future opportunities: feelings of hopelessness; failure to set future goals; high-risk behaviors such as sexual risk taking, substance abuse, suicidality, or violence toward others; and mental disorders. (The measurements discussed in this chapter were only a small part of the overall assessment.) Trained professional interviewers administered individual interviews, averaging 58 minutes in length. Interviewers obtained informed consent from all youths and their guardians.

A confidentiality certificate protected information about illegal behavior. Also, a procedure for breaking confidentiality and obtaining help for youths who might be abused or suicidal was described in the consent form and was implemented twice. Fewer than 1 percent of the youths skipped or refused to answer any questions. Debriefing procedures following the interview showed that 86 percent of the youths found it interesting and 42 percent felt more comfortable after the interview, with 58 percent reporting that they felt the same. When possible, the interviewer completed the interview on site, immediately before or after services were obtained; otherwise, the interviewer arranged an appointment for a future interview in the youth's home or at a mutually acceptable site. Interviewers and subjects were not matched for gender or race because most interviews occurred when the youths were recruited on site.

Participants

The total sample consisted of 796 adolescents between the ages of 14 and 17, with a mean age of 15.3 years. Eighty-six percent were African American, 13 percent were white, and 1 percent were members of other ethnic groups. Forty-three percent of the sample were male and 57 percent were female. The occupation of the parent who provided the most financial support to the family over the past six months was used as a determinant of socioeconomic status (Hollingshead, 1975). The socioeconomic composition of the respondents' parents was as follows: 15 percent were on public assistance, 33 percent were laborers or semiskilled workers, 23 percent were blue-collar workers, 14 percent were white-collar workers, and 9 percent were professionals. Fifty-three percent of the adolescents lived in female-headed households, 14 percent in two-parent households, 15 percent in foster or group care, 12 percent with nonparental relatives, and 6 percent elsewhere.

Comparisons with tallies of the demographics of adolescents using the four gateway arenas found that the sample was representative of adolescent service sector users. Adolescents interviewed from the child welfare and educational sectors did not differ in race, gender, or age from other adolescents using those respective service sectors. However, respondents interviewed in the health sector were, on average, three months younger than adolescents using that provider. There were fewer males among youths interviewed from the juvenile justice sector, and the average age was two months younger than other adolescents using that sector. Although the total sample is not representative of the population of the city of St. Louis, which is approximately 47 percent African American and 50 percent European American, it appears representative of public service sector users. To investigate risk factors associated with violence in African American youths, only the 684 African American youths from the sample were used in this study.

Structured interviews were used to collect information about involvement in violent behavior, exposure to violence, deteriorated neighborhoods, deteriorated schools, family instability, negative peer environment, traumatic experiences, alcohol use, other substance use, and posttraumatic stress symptoms.

Dependent Variable: Involvement in Violent Behavior

The dependent variable was measured by an index of 13 categorical items summing the different types of violent behavior engaged in by the respondent. The items were taken from the Diagnostic Interview Schedule for Children—Revised (Shaffer, Schwab-Stone, Fisher, & Cohen, 1993) section on conduct disorder. Example of items measuring violent behaviors are

1. Has your behavior ever caused someone's death or injury?
2. In the past six months have you
   a. snatched someone's purse?
   b. held someone up or robbed someone?
   c. threatened someone in order to steal from them?
   d. hurt or injured an animal on purpose?
   e. forced someone to do something sexual with you against their will?

f. been in any serious physical fights where there was punching or hitting?

g. ever used a weapon in a fight, like a bat, or a brick, or a bottle, or a knife, or a gun?

h. ever been physically cruel to someone or tried to cause them pain?

i. threatened or hurt other young people who didn't fight back?

j. ever gotten into fights after drinking?

k. ever gotten into fights after using drugs?

l. ever been put into jail for any of the previous questions that you answered yes to?

Independent Variables: Environmental

Exposure to Violence. This variable was measured by items culled from various parts of the structured interview that asked about family, neighborhood, or traumatic events. Sample items of this measure are as follows: (1) Have you had any of the following events happen to you: being physically attacked or beaten, seeing a person killed or being seriously hurt, having a family member or friend attempting or committing suicide? (2) Over the past six months, has there been much quarreling or fighting in the home where you have lived? Has anyone hurt or threatened to hurt another member of your household? Has anyone you know well been beaten up or killed? Has anyone hurt or threatened to hurt you? (3) Over the past six months, how much of the following has been in your neighborhood: shootings, murders? in your school: shootings or knifings, teachers injured by students?

Construct validity is demonstrated by the index's high correlation with violent behavior and mental health problems (Stiffman et al., 1996). Note that engagement in violent behaviors may lead to actual exposure to more violence, in that youths engaging in a fight might be more likely to report being beaten. Yet the engagement and exposure items clearly came from two different instruments in the interview—one asking about participation, the other about passive experience. There is no way, however, to specifically disaggregate the two.

Deteriorated Neighborhoods. This variable was measured by a five-item scale assessing the character of the respondent's neighborhood. Examples of items included in this scale are as follows: In the past six months, how much drug dealing has been in your neighborhood? None, some, a lot. In the past six months, how many homeless people were in the streets in your neighborhood? None, some, a lot. In the past six months, how many abandoned buildings were there in your neighborhood? None, some, a lot. Factor analysis indicated this scale had only a single factor (Hadley-Ives, Stiffman, & Dore, 1997). Cronbach's alpha is .76. Validity was demonstrated by this scale's strong correlation with census indicators of neighborhood poverty and housing deterioration.

Deteriorated Schools. This independent variable was measured by a three-item scale assessing the environment of the respondent's school. Items used in this scale were rated on a scale of none, some, or a lot: In the past six months, how much drug dealing was going on in your school? In the past six months, how much of the school equipment was damaged in your school? Cronbach's alpha was .59. Although the alpha was low as a result of the few items, the scale items showed high loadings on a single factor and demonstrated validity through negative correlations with other items related to school quality (Hadley-Ives et al., 1996).

Family Instability. The scale measuring respondent's family situation consisted of four items: (1) respondent currently lives with biological parents, (2) respondent lives in a foster or group home, (3) respondent has lived in current situation less than one-half of life, and (4) respondent has lived with biological parents only part of life. Cronbach's alpha is .88.

Negative Peer Environment. This factor was measured by a seven-item scale that assessed the respondent's peer environment. Items were rated as none, a few, about half, most, or all. Examples of the items are as follows: How many of the people you know who are about your age use drugs or marijuana? How many of the people you know who are about your age have been in trouble with the police or a juvenile officer? How many of the people you know who are about your age are not in school or training and don't have a job? Cronbach's alpha is .77.

Traumatic Experiences. The eight-item index measuring this variable was summed from traumatic events listed in the posttraumatic stress questions from the Diagnostic Interview Schedule (DIS) (Robins, 1985; Robins, Helzer, Croughan, & Ratcliff, 1981). Examples of items from the DIS are as follows: Have you ever had any of the following events happen to you: serious accident from an auto crash, a fire, or something like that; forced separation from your home; family member or friend die? Construct validity is demonstrated through the index's high correlation with mental health problems and specifically symptoms of posttraumatic stress (Stiffman et al., 1996).

Independent Variables: Behavioral

Measures of mental health problems and alcohol and drug abuse or dependence were adapted from the Diagnostic Interview Schedule for Children–Revised (DISC–R) (Shaffer et al., 1993). The DISC–R allows two separate operationalizations of mental health problems: (1) a diagnosis of disorders on the basis of computer algorithms that combine symptoms according to the criteria in DSM-IV (American Psychiatric Association, 1994) or (2) a count of significant symptoms (lasting two weeks or more, or which interfere significantly with the youth's life). For this chapter, we present symptoms counts for alcohol dependence and abuse, substance dependence and abuse, and posttraumatic stress.

Alcohol Dependence and Abuse. The index measuring alcohol dependence and abuse consists of 21 items. Examples of the items are as follows: Did your grades go down or did you have problems doing your job because of drinking? Did it seem you could drink more and more before you got drunk? Did drinking cause any problems with how you got along with family members or friends? Did you ever wake up the day after drinking and discover you couldn't remember what you had said or done while you were drunk? Cronbach's alpha is .90.

Substance Dependence and Abuse. The index measuring substance dependence and abuse consists of 18 items. Examples of the items are as follows: Did you often take or use more of the drugs than you thought you would? Did you spend a lot of time thinking about or planning how you would get hold of the drugs? Did you ever go to school or work when you were high on the drugs? Did it seem you could take or use more and more of the drugs before they had an effect on you? Cronbach's alpha is .90.

Posttraumatic Stress Symptoms. This variable was measured by an eight-item index assessing the respondent's symptoms related to posttraumatic stress. Measures of posttraumatic symptoms were modified from the DIS (Robins, 1985; Robins et al., 1981). Examples of the items are as follows: Because of the (list of traumatic experiences participants had previously identified had happened to them) in the past six months, do you keep remembering it even when you don't want to? Because of the (list of traumatic experiences) in the past six months, do you have trouble sleeping? Because of the (list of traumatic experiences) in the past six months, have you had nightmares or felt like you were living through it again? Cronbach's alpha is .76.

ANALYSIS STRATEGY

We used hierarchical regression analysis by regressing the dependent variable—involvement in violent behavior—on six environmental variables (exposure to violence, deteriorated neighborhoods, deteriorated schools, family instability, negative peer environment, and traumatic experiences) and three behavioral variables (symptoms of alcohol dependence and abuse, symptoms of substance dependence and abuse, and posttraumatic stress symptoms). Other studies have found that environmental factors (for example, exposure to violence and victimization) and behavioral factors (for example, fighting and depression) were both significant predictors of involvement in violent acts, with environmental factors explaining the larger portion of the variance (DuRant, Cadenhead, et al., 1994; DuRant, Pendergrast, & Cadenhead, 1994; Salts, Lindholm, Goddard, & Duncan, 1995). In an effort to build on these previous models, environmental factors were entered into the model first, followed by behavioral factors (Cotten et al., 1994; DuRant, Cadenhead, et al., 1994; Hausman, Spivak, & Prothrow-Stith, 1994; Salts et al., 1995). We conducted separate regressions for males

Table 16-1

Means and Standard Deviations among Environmental and Behavioral Factors Predicting Violent Behavior among African American Adolescents

Variable	Range	All Respondents (N = 594)		Males (n = 268)		Females (n = 326)	
		M	SD	M	SD	M	SD
Violent behavior (dependent variable)	0–13	1.58	1.75	2.03	2.02	1.22	1.42
Environmental factor							
Exposure to violence	0–11	3.76	2.24	4.04	2.36	3.54	2.12
Deteriorated neighborhoods	0–10	4.56	2.71	4.80	2.79	4.37	2.63
Deteriorated schools	0–6	2.23	1.58	2.25	1.66	2.22	1.51
Family instability	0–4	1.05	1.52	1.11	1.58	1.01	1.47
Negative peer environment	0–25	9.33	5.22	9.10	5.27	9.51	5.18
Traumatic experiences	0–6	2.00	1.38	2.32	1.39	1.76	1.32
Behavioral factor							
Alcohol use	0–16	0.98	2.43	1.46	3.04	0.61	1.73
Substance use	0–16	0.94	2.40	1.54	3.07	0.47	1.54
Posttraumatic stress symptoms	0–8	2.78	2.22	2.47	2.04	2.99	2.34

and females to investigate possible gender differences. Analysis was performed using SPSS Regression (SPSS, 1994) with an assist from SPSS Frequencies in evaluation of assumptions. Because of positively skewed data, logarithmic transformations $[\log^{10}(X_j + 1)]$ were used on all scales to reduce the level of skewness of the data (Tabachnick & Fidell, 1996). This transformation gave the distributions more symmetry with a reduction in the size of standard deviations, reduced the number of outliers, and improved the normality and linearity.

RESULTS

Reported involvement in violence was fairly low, with a mean of less than two incidents per person (Table 16-1). However, consistent with other studies, males reported higher rates of participation in violence than females (Chesney-Lind & Shelden, 1992; Eisenman & Kritsonis, 1993; Farnworth, 1984). Males also had higher levels of exposure to violence, and females reported a higher mean number of posttraumatic stress symptoms. The mean use of alcohol and other illegal substances was higher for males than females by a 2 to 1 ratio. Males had a higher mean number of traumatic experiences than females.

Predictors of Violence for African American Adolescents

The first set of columns in Table 16-2 presents the full ecological model (N = 594). A combination of environmental and behavioral

Table 16-2

Hierarchical Regression of Environmental and Behavioral Factors on Violent Behavior for African American Adolescents, by Gender

Variable	All Respondents (N = 594)			Males (n = 268)			Females (n = 326)		
	B	β	sr²	B	β	sr²	B	β	sr²
Environmental factor									
Exposure to violence	0.235	0.19	.20*	0.312	0.26	.27*	0.157	0.14	.14*
Deteriorated neighborhoods	0.041	0.04		-0.003	.00		0.92	0.10	
Deteriorated schools	0.111	0.09	.02*	0.066	0.06	.02*	0.160	0.15	.03*
Family instability	0.011	0.01		-0.064	-0.06		0.072	0.08	.02*
Negative peer environment	0.016	0.01	.01*	0.055	0.05	.03*	-0.013	-0.01	
Traumatic experiences	0.273	0.18	.06*	0.107	0.07	.02*	0.324	0.23	.07*
Behavioral factor									
Alcohol use	0.174	0.19	.08*	0.135	0.17	.08*	0.198	0.19	.05*
Substance use	0.186	0.20	.02*	0.173	0.22	.02*	0.173	0.14	.02*
Posttraumatic stress symptoms	0.027	0.30		0.153	0.15	.02*	-0.029	-0.03	
Intercept	-0.1063			-0.0577			-0.1168		
	$R^2 = .41$			$R^2 = .46$			$R^2 = .32$		
	Adjusted $R^2 = .40$			Adjusted $R^2 = .45$			Adjusted $R^2 = .32$		
	$R = .64$			$R = .68$			$R = .58$		

*$p < .01$.

predictors accounted for 40 percent of the variance in violent behavior [$F(9, 584) = 44.97, p < .01$]. Four of the six environmental risk factors explained 29 percent of the variance in the full model. Exposure to violence explained a unique 20 percent of the variance [$F(1, 592) = 152.50, p < .001$]; deteriorated schools explained 2 percent [$F(1, 592) = 14.71, p < .001$]; negative peer environment explained 1 percent [$F(1, 592) = 9.79, p < .01$], and traumatic experiences explained 6 percent [$F(1, 592) = 53.93, p < .001$]. Deteriorated neighborhoods and family instability were the only environmental variables that did not significantly contribute to the prediction of violent behavior.

Two of the three behavioral risk factors explained 10 percent of the variance in the model. Symptoms of alcohol dependence and abuse explained 8 percent of the variance [$F(1, 592) = 73.20, p < .001$], and symptoms of substance dependence and abuse explained 2 percent [$F(1, 592) = 24.04, p < .001$]. Symptoms of posttraumatic stress were the only behavioral variable that did not contribute significantly to the prediction of violent behavior.

Predictors of Violence for African American Males

The second set of columns in Table 16-2 presents the ecological model when applied only to African American males ($n = 268$). A combination of environmental and behavioral predictors accounted for 45 percent of the variance [$F(9, 258) = 24.97, p < .01$] in males. The four environmental risk factors that were significant for the full sample explained 34 percent of the variance in violence for African American male adolescents. Exposure to violence explained 27 percent of the variance [$F(1, 266) = 99.26, p < .001$]; deteriorated schools explained 2 percent [$F(1, 266) = 7.94, p < .01$]; negative peer environment explained 3 percent [$F (1, 266) = 11.89, p < .001$]; and traumatic experiences explained 2 percent [$F(1, 266) = 6.94, p < .01$]. Again deteriorated neighborhoods and family instability did not make a significant contribution to the prediction of violent behavior.

For males, all three of the behavioral risk factors significantly contributed to the variance in their violence, explaining 12 percent. Symptoms of alcohol dependence and abuse explained 8 percent of the variance [$F(1, 266) = 36.98, p < .001$]; symptoms of substance dependence and abuse explained 2 percent [$F(1, 266) = 11.84, p < .001$]; and symptoms of posttraumatic stress explained 2 percent [$F(1, 266) = 8.02, p < .01$].

Predictors of Violence for African American Females

The third set of columns in Table 16-2 presents the ecological model when applied only to violent behavior in African American female adolescents ($n = 326$). A combination of environmental and behavior predictors accounted for 32 percent of the variance in violent behavior [$F(9, 316) = 18.33, p < .01$] in females. Four of the original six environmental risk factors explained 26 percent of the variance for

African American females. Three of those variables were the same as for males. Exposure to violence explained 14 percent of variance [$F(1, 324) = 53.68, p < .001$]; deteriorated schools explained 3 percent [$F(1, 324) = 10.74, p < .01$]; and traumatic experiences explained 7 percent [$F(1, 324) = 33.12, p < .001$]. In contrast with the results for males, where negative peer environment was significant but family instability was nonsignificant, for females, family instability explained 2 percent of the variance [$F(1, 324) = 6.96, p < .01$], but negative peer environment was nonsignificant. For both females and males, deteriorated neighborhoods did not significantly contribute to the prediction of violent behavior.

Two behavioral risk factors explained 7 percent of the variance for female adolescents. Symptoms of alcohol dependence and abuse explained 5 percent of the variance [$F(1, 324) = 25.39, p < .001$]; and symptoms of substance dependence and abuse explained 2 percent [$F(1, 324) = 8.13, p < .01$]. Unlike the model for males, symptoms of posttraumatic stress for females did not contribute significantly to the prediction of violent behavior.

DISCUSSION

This study's results indicate that both environmental and behavioral variables are directly related to involvement in violent behavior among African American youths and that exposure to violence, deteriorating neighborhoods, deteriorating schools, negative peer environments, personal traumatic experiences, posttraumatic stress, and alcohol and substance abuse are significant predictors of violent behavior in male and female adolescents, although a stronger case is made for males than for females. These gender differences may be related to higher levels of participation by males in violent behavior (Fitzpatrick & Boldizar, 1993) and to their higher levels of exposure to violence. In this study, males witnessed more violence and were more likely to be victims of violence than females (Stiffman et al., 1996).

Environmental Predictors

The results of our study indicate a strong relationship between many of the environmental factors and involvement in violent behavior for African American youths. These results are consistent with earlier research indicating that factors such as exposure to violence and fighting are significant predictors of involvement in violent behavior for males and females (DuRant, Cadenhead, et al., 1994; Fitzpatrick & Boldizar, 1993; Stiffman et al., 1996). Interestingly, the experiences of either purposeful or accidental trauma in the environment of African American male youths were related to violence, but the experience of traumatic events (either as witness or victim) explained a larger amount of the variance for females. A disorganized school environment also consistently predicted violence for both genders. Males and females did differ in the importance of two environmental predictors. Family instability was a significant predictor for female violence, but not for male violence. In contrast, negative peer environment was significant for males, but not for females.

Behavioral Predictors

The results of our study also indicate a relationship between behavioral factors and involvement in violent behavior for African American male and female youths (DuRant, Cadenhead, et al., 1994; Elliott et al., 1985). Our study reveals that alcohol abuse and dependence and the abuse of other illicit substances were significantly associated with African American youths' involvement in violent behavior. Males and females did differ in the importance of one behavioral factor: symptoms of posttraumatic stress were a significant predictor of violence for males, but not for females.

Limitations of the Study

Although our findings support the comprehensive nature of environmental and behavioral factors in involvement in violent behaviors for African American youths, the study has several limitations. Many of the African American adolescents in this study reside in neighborhoods characterized by high levels of crime and violence. We found that self-reported use of violence by these adolescents was significantly correlated with exposure to violence. Because these data were collected in a cross-sectional survey, we can only assume an association between exposure to violence and African American adolescents' reported use of violence and cannot imply a causal relationship. The relationship between exposure to violence and use of violence may be covariational in nature. Although previous studies in public health and psychology have strongly supported a possible causal relationship between exposure to violence and involvement in violence (Cotten et al., 1994; DuRant, Cadenhead, et al., 1994; Fitzpatrick & Boldizar, 1993), there is a continual need for violence research to determine a better discernment of the temporal ordering of these events. A more comprehensive examination of the covariation between exposure to violence and involvement in violent acts will minimize any possible conceptual overlap.

Because all the youths who participated in this study were taken from a sample of gateway sectors in only one midwestern city, they may not be generally representative of urban African American adolescents or inner-city African American adolescents. African American adolescents in other U.S. cities not using gateway sector services may experience different rates of involvement in violence, and the factors predicting their behavior may differ from those used as predictors in this study. Nevertheless, anonymous tallies kept by the gateway service providers indicate that the youths in the sample are representative of adolescents using gateway sectors in St. Louis (Stiffman et al., 1996). Given our sampling methods, we have no knowledge of prior services received to ameliorate previous or current problems related to delinquency, substance use, or mental health.

Despite these limitations, our study demonstrates a conclusive association between various environmental and behavioral risk factors and violent behavior. These data also suggest that being a victim of violence will probably increase the risk of involvement in violence. It appears that other contextual (for example, school and family) and interpersonal (for example, alcohol and substance use) risk factors are related to this antisocial behavior among African American youths. The results of our study underline the necessity of future research for investigating the longitudinal effects of environmental and behavior variables on violent behavior and the need to understand protective factors within African American communities.

IMPLICATIONS FOR SOCIAL WORK

Our study supports the need to develop comprehensive prevention strategies that involve many components of an adolescent environment. Interventions should be focused on all social domains (for example, individual, family, peers, and schools) (Hawkins, Catalano, & Brewer, 1995). Individual intervention should include clinical strategies that are implemented in educational and community mental health settings and that can provide effective treatment for the behavioral risk factors of alcohol use, substance use, and symptoms of posttraumatic stress (Fitzpatrick & Boldizar, 1993). It is apparent that African American youths are exposed to high levels of violent acts (that is, perpetrator or victim) in their environments (Stiffman et al., 1996; Williams et al., 1997). We propose that interventions focused on the prevention and reduction of violent behavior among African American youths should provide them with skills for using a more self-directed approach to their behavior.

Interventions focused on the family and individual should address risk factors such as poor family management practices and family conflict. A large body of research literature indicates that family interventions such as parent training, intensive family preservation services, and family therapy are effective in reducing family conflict, decreasing children's antisocial behavior, and improving family management practices (Dumas, 1989; Henggler & Borduin, 1990; Henggler, Melton, & Smith, 1992; Rossi, 1992; Shadish, 1992). Parent training approaches consist of teaching parents specific child management skills. Dumas (1989) concluded that parent skills training has been shown to be effective in the reduction of childhood antisocial behavior and improvement of family management practices.

The evaluation of parent training programs indicate that they are a more effective approach when used in collaboration with other interventions (Satterfield, Satterfield, & Schell, 1987). Although the evaluations of the effectiveness of intensive family preservation services have reported mixed results regarding the success of decreasing out-of-home placements or child maltreatment, other studies have suggested that such services may reduce risk of violence and delinquency

(Walton, Fraser, Lewis, Pecora, & Walton, 1993). Research studies also have found that family therapy programs have demonstrated long-term preventive effects on antisocial behaviors among adolescents (Shadish, 1992; Szapocznik et al., 1989).

Intervention strategies focused at the peer and school domains are numerous. These interventions focus on the development of social skills, enhancing conflict resolution abilities, anger management, and the teaching of violence avoidance. These curricula are usually administered in a school or other group setting. Many such curricula have been extensively evaluated. Results of these studies indicate some effectiveness, but more studies are needed to address cultural relevance. Various programs (for example, Think First, Fighting Fair, Positive Adolescents Choices Training) have shown effectiveness in decreasing problem behaviors in the school setting, decreasing physical and verbal aggression, and lowering rates of juvenile court-recorded offenses among program participants (Hammond & Yung, 1993; Larson, 1992; Marvel, Moreda, & Cook, 1993). These strategies may also be indirectly effective as an environmental strategy by decreasing the youths' exposure to violence.

REFERENCES

American Psychiatric Association. (1994). *Diagnostic and statistical manual of mental disorders* (4th ed.). Washington, DC: Author.

Barnes, G. M., & Farrell, M. P. (1992). Parental support and control as predictors of adolescent drinking, delinquency, and related problem behaviors. *Journal of Marriage and the Family, 54,* 763–776.

Cairns, R. B., & Cairns, B. D. (1992). Social cognition and social networks: A developmental perspective. In D. Pepler & K. H. Rubin (Eds.), *The development and treatment of childhood aggression* (pp. 249–278). Hillsdale, NJ: Lawrence Erlbaum.

Chesney-Lind, M., & Shelden, R. G. (1992). *Girls, delinquency and juvenile justice.* Pacific Grove, CA: Brooks/Cole.

Cotten, N. U., Resnick, J., Browne, D. C., Martin, S. L., McCarraher, D. R., & Woods, J. (1994). Aggression and fighting behavior among African-American adolescents: Individual and family factors. *American Journal of Public Health, 84,* 618–622.

Dumas, J. E. (1989). Treating antisocial behavior in children: Child and family approaches. *Clinical Psychology Review, 9,* 197–222.

DuRant, R. H., Cadenhead, C., Pendergrast, R. A., Slavens, G., & Linder, C. W. (1994). Factors associated with the use of violence among urban black adolescents. *American Journal of Public Health, 84,* 612–617.

DuRant, R. H., Pendergrast, R. A., & Cadenhead, C. (1994). Exposure to violence and victimization and fighting behavior by urban black adolescents. *Journal of Adolescent Health, 15,* 311–318.

Eisenman, R., & Kritsonis, W. (1993). Race, sex, and age: A nationwide study of juvenile crime. *Psychology, 30*(3–4), 66–68.

Elliott, D. S., Huizinga, D., & Ageton, S. (1985). *Explaining delinquency and drug use.* Beverly Hills, CA: Sage Publications.

Elliott, D. S., Huizinga, D., & Menard, S. (1989). *Multiple problem youth: Delinquency, substance use, and mental health problems.* New York: Springer-Verlag.

Farnworth, M. (1984). Male–female difference in delinquency in a minority-group sample. *Research in Crime and Delinquency, 21,* 191–212.

Farrington, D. (1991). Childhood aggression and adult violence. In D. Pepler & K. H. Rubin (Eds.), *The development and treatment of childhood aggression* (pp. 5–29). Hillsdale, NJ: Lawrence Erlbaum.

Fingerhut, L. A., Ingram, D. D., & Feldman, J. J. (1992a). Firearm and nonfirearm homicide among persons 15 through 19 years of age: Differences by level of urbanization, United States, 1979 through 1989. *JAMA, 267,* 3048–3053.

Fingerhut, L. A., Ingram, D. D., & Feldman, J. J. (1992b). Firearm homicide among black teenage males in metropolitan counties. *JAMA, 267,* 3054–3058.

Fitzpatrick, K. M., & Boldizar, J. P. (1993). The prevalence and consequences of exposure to violence among Africa American youth. *Journal of American Academy of Child and Adolescent Psychiatry, 32,* 424–430.

Hadley-Ives, E., Stiffman, A. R., & Dore, P. (1996). *The development and use of two scales to measure neighborhood and school quality.* Unpublished manuscript.

Hammond, W. R., & Yung, B. R. (1993). Preventing violence in at-risk African American youth. *Journal of Health Care for the Poor and Underserved, 2,* 359–373.

Harer, M. D., & Steffensmeier, D. L. (1992). The differing effects of economic inequality on black and white rates of violence. *Social Forces, 70,* 1035–1054.

Hausman, A. J., Spivak, H., & Prothrow-Stith, D. (1994). Adolescents' knowledge and attitudes about and experience with violence. *Journal of Adolescent Health, 15,* 400–406.

Hawkins, J. D., Catalano, R. F., & Brewer, D. D. (1995). Preventing serious, violent, and chronic delinquency and crime: Effective strategies from conception to age 6. In J. C. Howell, B. Krisberg, J. D. Hawkins, & J. J. Wilson (Eds.), *A sourcebook on serious, violent, and chronic juvenile offenders* (pp. 47–60). Thousand Oaks, CA: Sage Publications.

Henggler, S. W., & Borduin, C. M. (1990). *Family therapy and beyond: A multisystemic approach to treating the behavior problems of children and adolescents.* Pacific Grove, CA: Brooks/Cole.

Henggler, S. W., Melton, G. B., & Smith, L. A. (1992). Family preservation using multisystemic therapy: An effective alternative to incarcerating serious juvenile offenders. *Journal of Consulting and Clinical Psychology, 60,* 953–961.

Hollingshead, A. B. (1975). *Four-Factor Index of Social Status.* New Haven, CT: Yale University.

Johnston, L. D., O'Malley, P. M., & Bachman, J. G. (1993). *National survey results on drug use from the Monitoring the Future Study, 1975–1992: Volume 1.* Rockville, MD: National Institute on Drug Abuse.

Kandel, D. (1982). Epidemiological and psychosocial perspectives on adolescent drug use. *Journal of American Academy of Child Psychiatry, 21,* 328–347.

Larson, J. D. (1992). Anger and aggression management techniques through the Think First Curriculum. *Journal of Offender Rehabilitation, 18,* 101–117.

Loeber, R. (1988). Natural histories of conduct disorder, delinquency, and associated substance use: Evidence for developmental progressions. In B. B. Lahey & A. E. Kazdin (Eds.), *Advances in clinical child psychology* (Vol. 11, pp. 73–124). New York: Plenum Press.

Loeber, R., & Dishion, T. J. (1984). Boys who fight at home and school: Family conditions influencing cross-setting consistency. *Journal of Consulting and Clinical Psychology, 52,* 759–568.

Loeber, R., Stouthamer-Loeber, M. S., Van Kammen, W., & Farrington, D. P. (1991). Initiation, escalation, and desistance in juvenile offending and their correlates. *Journal of Criminal Law and Criminology, 82,* 36–82.

Loeber, R., Wung, P., Keenan, K., Giroux, B., Stouthamer-Loeber, M., Van Kammen, W. B., & Maughan, B. (1993). Developmental pathways in disruptive child behavior. *Development and Psychopathology, 5,* 103–133.

Longres, J. F. (1995). *Human behavior in the social environment.* Itasca, IL: F. E. Peacock.

Marvel, J., Moreda, I., & Cook, I. (1993). *Developing conflict resolution skills in students: A study of the Fighting Fair Model.* Miami, FL: Peace Education Foundation.

Matsueda, R. L., & Heimer, K. (1987). Race, family structure, and delinquency: A test of differential association and social control theories. *American Sociological Review, 52,* 826–840.

Newcomb, M., & Bentler, P. (1988). *Consequences of adolescent drug use: Impact on the lives of young adults.* Newbury Park, CA: Sage Publications.

O'Donnell, C. R. (1995). Firearm deaths among children and youth. *American Psychologist, 50,* 771–776.

Offord, D. R., Boyle, M. H., & Racine, Y. A. (1991). The epidemiology of antisocial behavior in childhood and adolescence. In D. J. Pepler & K. H. Rubin (Eds.), *The development and treatment of childhood aggression* (pp. 31–54), Hillsdale, NJ: Lawrence Erlbaum.

Prothrow-Stith, D., & Weissman, M. (1991). *Deadly consequences: How violence is destroying our teenage population and a plan to begin solving the problem.* New York: HarperCollins.

Rivera, B., & Wisdom, C. S. (1990). Childhood victimization and violent offending. *Violence and Victims, 5,* 19–35.

Robins, L. N. (1985). Epidemiology: Reflections on testing the validity of psychiatric interview. *Archives of General Psychiatry, 42,* 918–924.

Robins, L. N., Helzer, J. E., Croughan, J., & Ratcliff, K. S. (1981). The NIMH Diagnostic Interview Schedule: Its history, characteristics and validity. *Archives of General Psychiatry, 38,* 318–389.

Rossi, P. H. (1992). Assessing family preservation programs. *Children and Youth Services Review, 14,* 77–97.

Salts, C. J., Lindholm, B. W., Goddard, H. W., & Duncan, S. (1995). Predictive variables of violent behavior in adolescent males. *Youth & Society, 26,* 377–399.

Salzinger, S., Feldman, R. S., & Hammer, M. (1993). The effects of physical abuse on children's social relationships. *Child Development, 64,* 169–187.

Satterfield, J. H., Satterfield, B. T., & Schell, A. M. (1987). Therapeutic interventions to prevent delinquency in hyperactive boys. *Journal of the American Academy of Child and Adolescent Psychiatry, 26,* 56–64.

Shadish, W. R., Jr. (1992). Do family and marital psychotherapies change what people do? A meta-analysis of behavioral outcomes. In T. D. Cook, H. Cooper, D. S. Cordray, H. Hartmann, L. V. Hedges, R. J. Light, T. A. Louis, & F. Mosteller (Eds.), *Meta-analysis for explanation: A casebook* (pp. 129–208). New York: Russell Sage Foundation.

Shaffer, D., Schwab-Stone, M., Fisher, P., & Cohen, P. (1993). The Diagnostic Interview Schedule for Children–Revised version (DISC–R): Preparation, field testing, interrater reliability, and acceptability. *American Academy of Child and Adolescent Psychiatry, 32,* 643–650.

Shihadeh, E. S., & Steffensmeier, D. J. (1994). Economic inequality, family disruption, and urban black violence: Cities as units of stratification and social control. *Social Forces, 73,* 729–751.

SPSS, Inc. (1994). *SPSS base system syntax reference guide* (Release 6.1). Chicago: Author.

Stiffman, A. R., Elze, D., Dore, P., Chen, L., & Cheng, Y. (1996). *Truncated future life opportunities and adolescent exposure to violence in families, neighborhoods, and schools.* Unpublished manuscript.

Szapocznik, J., Rio, A., Murray, E., Cohen, R., Scopetta, M., Rivas-Vazquez, A., Hervis, O., Posada, V., & Kurtines, W. (1989). Structural family versus psychodynamic child therapy for problematic Hispanic boys. *Journal of Consulting and Clinical Psychology, 57,* 571–578.

Tabachnick, B. G., & Fidell, L. S. (1996). *Using multivariate statistics.* New York: HarperCollins.

U.S. Department of Justice, Federal Bureau of Investigation. (1993). *Uniform crime reports for the United States.* Washington, DC: U.S. Government Printing Office.

Walton, E., Fraser, M. W., Lewis, R. E., Pecora, P. J., & Walton, W. K. (1993). Inhome family-focused reunification: An experimental study. *Child Welfare, 72,* 473–487.

Williams, J. H. (1994). *Understanding substance use, delinquency involvement, and juvenile justice involvement among African American and European American adolescents.* Unpublished doctoral dissertation, University of Washington, Seattle.

Williams, J. H., Ayers, C. D., Abbott, R. D., & Hawkins, J. D. (1997). *Initiation of adolescent problem behavior: A logit analysis of race and gender differences.* Unpublished manuscript.

Williams, J. H., Ayers, C. D., & Arthur, M. W. (1997). Risk and protective factors in the development of delinquency and conduct disorder. In M. W. Fraser (Ed.), *Risk and resilience in childhood: An ecological perspective* (pp. 140–170). Washington, DC: NASW Press.

This research was supported by grant no. R24 MH50857-02 from the National Institute of Mental Health. This chapter is based on presentations given at the annual meeting of the Midwestern Criminal Justice Association, October 1995, Chicago, and the World Congress on Violence and Human Coexistence, August 1997, Dublin, Ireland.

Turning Points in the Lives of Young Inner-City Men Forgoing Destructive Criminal Behaviors: A Qualitative Study

Margaret Hughes

Youths and young adults represent the largest population of property and violent crime arrests in the United States. The 1993 crime statistics show that juveniles younger than 18 years accounted for 41 percent of arrests for all serious crimes, of which 18 percent were for murder and nonnegligent manslaughter and 20 percent were for aggravated assault. Young adults ages 18 to 24 accounted for 26 percent of arrests for all serious crimes, of which 41 percent were for murder and nonnegligent manslaughter and 27 percent were for aggravated assault. These arrest rates are alarmingly disproportionate for African Americans and Latinos (U.S. Bureau of the Census, 1996). The arrest rates should alert researchers to the critical need to find solutions to these problems.

Most research has focused on the causes of criminal behavior. However, understanding the causal factors of crime is only half of the solution; the other half is to understand what makes young men forgo crime. Examining life courses of individuals has uncovered important information about how attitudinal and behavioral changes develop. Elder (1985) defined the life course as a pathway differentiated by age: "Movement through the age-graded life course in each [institutional] sphere may correspond with social expectations or depart markedly from them" (p. 30). The concepts of trajectories and transitions are unifying themes. A *trajectory* is defined as "a lifeline or career, a pathway over the life span. The pathway may be psychological . . . or social. Worklife, marriage, and parenthood represent multiple, interlocking social trajectories" (pp. 17–18). A pathway of criminal activity would also be considered a trajectory. *Transitions* are "changes in state" and are "embedded in trajectories; the latter give meaning and shape to the transition experience" (p. 18). Whether a transition is present or absent may be reflected in the choices made by the individual. First significant job, committed relationship, and childbirth are examples of transitions. Several studies have used the life course perspective in an effort to understand how transitions affect a trajectory of crime (Caspi, Elder, & Herbener, 1990; Laub &

This chapter was originally published in the September 1998 issue of *Social Work Research*, Vol. 22, pp. 143–151.

Sampson, 1993; Loeber & Stouthamer-Loeber, 1996; Macmillan, 1995).

Sampson and Laub's (1993) secondary data analysis of Glueck and Glueck's (1950, 1968) longitudinal study of 500 delinquents and 500 controls found evidence that "childhood pathways to crime and conformity over the life course are significantly influenced by adult social bonds" (p. 243). The authors emphasized "the quality and strength of social ties more than the occurrence or timing of life events" (p. 246). Strong marital attachment and job stability were two transitions related to desistance from crime. These transitions are proposed as informal social bonds and forms of social capital that can facilitate positive change in behavior despite deviant trajectories from early childhood. Macmillan (1995) studied the changes that three life course transitions (marriage, living at home, and labor force participation) had on crime rates among youths and young adults ages 15 to 24. Using a time series analysis of Canadian property crimes, Macmillan found significantly lower crime rates for youths and young adults in his sample who were married, lived at home, or were employed.

The uniform crime reports show a positive correlation between age and desistance from crime. Shover and Thompson (1992) offered several explanations as to why deviance desists with age, including loss of interest, ability to understand consequences of a criminal lifestyle, degree of payoff, disenchantment with a criminal lifestyle, and fear of consequences. The "differential expectations" influence individuals engaged in a criminal lifestyle to desist. These explanations suggest an age of maturation at which individuals reach a cognitive developmental stage that acts as a transition from a criminal trajectory. Gove (1985) suggested the age–criminal desistance correlation is influenced, in part, by normative, socially structured transitions (for example, marriage and childbirth). The adolescent and early adult years are ages when anomie, or normlessness, is most apt to occur, in part because of a lack of socially structured roles and uncertainty about the future. Gove argued that "if social roles change and life takes on structure and meaning, then deviance should decline accordingly" (p. 126).

Loeber and LeBlanc (1990) argued for a developmental approach—developmental criminology—to the study of delinquency. One focus of this approach is "the identification of explicative or causal factors which predate behavioral development and have an impact on its course" (Loeber & Stouthamer-Loeber, 1996, p. 13). This approach can also be used to study desistance from delinquency by identifying factors that affect decisions to turn from delinquency. This chapter describes a study that explored the lives of previously delinquent young men to uncover factors that facilitated their decisions to desist from criminal activity.

THE STUDY

This study contributes to the literature by focusing on African American and Latino American young men who are desisting from crime after long criminal histories; one white young man who grew up in a predominantly African American community and who associated solely with African American youths was interviewed and used as a comparison. The study used primary data collection methods. One limitation of the study was its reliance on self-reported histories. Longitudinal panel studies like Glueck and Glueck's (1950, 1968) are ideal because they increase reliability; however, such studies are rare because of time, money, and attrition. Some findings in this study matched transitions leading to desistance found in other studies, that is, marriage, childbirth, and labor force participation (Macmillan, 1995; Sampson & Laub, 1993). However, variations of these transitions as well as transitions not previously noted in the literature were found.

Participants

Twenty young adult, inner-city men made up the sample population in this exploratory study. Demographics of the participants were diverse, particularly with respect to age, ethnicity, education, and city of residence. There were nine (45 percent) African Americans, three (15 percent) Mexican Americans, four (20 percent) Puerto Ricans, three (15 percent) Jamaicans, and one (5 percent) white young man who grew up in an inner-city community with a predominantly African American and Latino population. The participants ranged in age from 18 to 27. Throughout most of their adolescent years, they resided in Boston, New York, San Francisco, Philadelphia, or Chicago. Only two participants were married; however, seven (35 percent) had children. Two other participants considered themselves fathers but were not the biological parent. Their educational backgrounds were less than high school, seven (35 percent); high school graduate, four (20 percent); general equivalency diploma, three (15 percent); trade school in addition to high school, three (15 percent); and some college, three (15 percent).

Criteria

The following criteria were used to choose the sample: male between the ages of 18 and 28, history of destructive behavior (that is, individual and group participation in violent acts, property crimes, other crimes against people, illegal drug marketing, and illegal drug use), evidence of efforts to make positive life changes (for example, legal employment; participation in programs emphasizing positive change; and self-reports indicating they no longer participated in acts of violence, illegal drug marketing and use, and other criminal activities), and evidence of positive involvement in the community (for example, mentoring other youths at risk of engaging in destructive behaviors, volunteering with organizations promoting community improvement, volunteering with recreational programs for youths, and speaking against destructive behaviors in schools and other centers serving youths).

Data Collection

Data collection began with open selection by convenience. I selected the initial group of participants (five) from an intervention program I had worked with as a volunteer mentor for the preceding two years. Through information obtained from the program staff as well as personal knowledge from direct contact with some of the young men, I determined that each participant met the criteria for the study.

Intervention program directors, community leaders, and pastors identified the remaining participants using the study's criteria. Nine participants were part of a residential program that accepted young men from across the United States. Three participants were identified by pastors of local churches, and three were identified by community leaders.

I collected data over a two-year period. I conducted in-depth interviews with each participant, each lasting approximately 90 minutes. I contacted 16 participants a second time, either by telephone or in person, for a shorter interview; four participants had moved and could not be contacted. I used data from the second interviews to validate interpretations and information, to obtain any missing information, and to include the sample as active participants in the study's analysis. In addition, I made ethnographic observations of some participants from the first group over the two-year period.

Interviews took place in offices or the participants' homes with no other people present. The interviews began by my verifying that each participant met the criteria. Then I collected demographic data (age, ethnicity, marital and parental status, education level attained, employment status, and place of residence). The remainder of the first interviews focused on open-ended, topical questions concerning experiences with family, school, law enforcement and criminal justice, significant people, intervention programs, community, street group affiliation (if applicable), and significant life events. I chose these topics to ensure that the participants covered significant life stages and agents contributing to their socialization. I asked the participants to detail those periods and events related to their decisions to make positive changes in their life course.

Data Analysis

I transcribed each taped interview verbatim. I then used the computer program, *Qualitative Solutions and Research, Non-numerical Unstructured Data Indexing, Searching, and Theorizing 3.0* (1994) to manage and analyze the interviews. Analytic conclusions can be formulated by coding and then categorizing similar statements of experiences from data.

When examining the outcomes of individuals using Elder's (1985) Life Course Dynamics model, it is important to consider the trajectories taken by other agents who influence the individual's life. It is also important to examine the "connections between widely separated events and transitions, as in the relation between young adulthood and old age" (Elder, 1985, p. 34). A list of codes was predetermined that described phenomena related to me during the interviews and during my previous work as a mentor. The list contained codes describing influential agents in the participants' lives (family, school, church, law enforcement, employers, peers, and role models), developmental periods (childhood, adolescence, and young adulthood), and phenomena connected to the onset of trajectories of criminal activity and desistance from crime. I subsequently read each transcript and categorized passages using these codes. The coded passages were analyzed to determine which were related to participants' decisions to make positive changes in their behaviors. These passages were grouped and recategorized as factors facilitating positive change. Conclusions were drawn from these factors (Strauss & Corbin, 1990).

FINDINGS

Conclusions drawn from the categorized passages indicated four significant factors: (1) respect and concern for children, (2) fear of physical harm or incarceration, (3) contemplation time, and (4) support and modeling. These factors are reported in summary form.

Respect and Concern for Children

The many crises faced, the all-too-frequent need to self-nurture because of absent parents, perilous environments requiring development of survival techniques, and a shortage of characteristics of a healthy childhood (for example, play, laughter, wonderment, pleasurable experiences, and feelings of security, love, and worth) give rise to an atypical childhood for many poor youths in the inner cities. Data revealed that these unhealthy childhood experiences were typical for participants throughout their juvenile and adolescent years. Perhaps because of their unhealthy experiences, these young men sensed the critical importance of a healthy childhood. Participants revealed the development of a deep-seated respect and concern for children. They alluded to experiences involving children as playing a role in their decision to change.

Six participants indicated that love for their own children was a factor leading to their decision to change. Ronnie stated that a traumatic incident involving his son led to his decision to change:

> I robbed this dude one day, and I was high, and I had my son. He might have been like six months. He [the victim] ran up on me with a gun, and he said, "I won't kill you right now because your son's in the carriage, but next time I see you man, it ain't no tellin' what I'll do." So after that, I was like man I can't do this anymore. I can't do this. My son coulda got hurt. You know bullets don't have no name.

The incident also evoked memories of his childhood pain from an absent father:

> Sometimes I feel like I'ma die not knowing who my father is. So
> do I wanna go on not letting my kids know? It's like a vicious cy-
> cle; it's going on and on and on. Now somebody's gonna have to
> change that. And you know, I'm steppin' off the merry-go-round.
> I mean this is in my whole family, the lifestyle . . . I feel like I'm a
> young man. I got a lot to live for. I'm steppin' off the merry-go-
> round. I'm going to make things happen. You know, things ain't
> happening when you keep going around in circles. That's what I
> want to do for mine.

George stated, "What's workin' for me now, and what will work
for me in the long run, I have a son. Without a doubt, I don't want
him to grow up and I don't be around." A similar statement was
made by Michael: "But pretty much now, I'm just tryin' to establish
with my daughter. I'd say that was the number one reason, other than
me just wanting to get out of it [drug dealing and drug abuse], the
number one motive to do the right thing." Other participants made
statements indicating their own children gave them a feeling of
worth. Daniel stated,

> Sometimes I look back at all the things I've done, and I be like, I
> knew there was some kind of plan that God had for me, and when
> I first moved up here, I said, "Look, I know I've been through a
> war." I been shot and stabbed and beat down and all this. I said,
> "You gotta have something better. You gotta have something bet-
> ter." I guess this is it, and I got a little girl. I'm tryin', a black man
> trying to get custody of his child. I could never see myself saying,
> wow, I'm really trying to get custody of a child, you know. But the
> good thing about it is that I'm able to do it.

For one respondent, observing the dangerous situation his drug
marketing exposed a child to influenced him to change. John recounted,

> I went into a house one day. This dude owed me my money. So
> me and my boy Earl, my boy James, we went into this house. And
> then I never got my money, but I went in the house. I saw the con-
> dition of the house. It was disgusting. It was like it had never been
> cleaned for the past two years and a crib over in the corner with a
> little baby in the crib in this nasty, filthy, stinky house. And I just
> stood there, and I couldn't believe that this had happened. It was
> a crack house. Everyone in that house was usin'. That was one of
> our biggest buyers. And I saw. I was so devastated just to see
> what the drugs had done. I mean I really started to feel for them.
> Before, I would just be a heartless person with no conscience. I
> had no conscience. Oh yeah, just to see that little baby. The baby
> had sores all over his body. He was in the crib, and no one was
> taking care of him. You could tell he had gone to the bathroom in
> his diaper. Ahhhh! And no one was taking care of the child. So I
> made it a point, and I just called DSS [Department of Social Ser-
> vices]. I told 'em there was a baby in that house, and no one was
> taking care of him. DSS checked on the baby, checked on the
> apartment. By me being able to do something like that, I just
> couldn't go on. I just couldn't.

Three other participants stated it bothered them when they realized children were being affected by their drug marketing. They felt that parents using Aid to Families with Dependent Children money to buy drugs was wrong and that they were neglecting their children by getting high.

Fear of Physical Harm, Incarceration, or Both

Participants reported that the longer they remained active in the street life, the greater the probability of their being physically harmed. They attributed this increased danger to an increase in the number of peer enemies and new competition in the drug market trying to take over their established territory.

John explained about the time limits as well as the dangers of the drug business for young men like him:

> It was knuckled up in spots. It got to the point when we were blowing people away when I got 19, and I had two more years left in the streets. 'Cause it's known that you're only large [real successful] in the streets for six years. If you work you figure if you get into the game at six years, you work for two or three years, then you get some money. And then, if you're smart you invest your money in more drugs and have people buying and selling for you. That's how you get large. You have a total of six years 'cause that crop of young boys is comin' up. And that's where the violence started comin' into play. Everybody wants to knock this dude off, knock this dude off and get his territory. Get what he had. You either get what you want and realize you have enough to get out or you can stay there, fight for your territory, and eventually die. I know a lot of guys who eventually died 'cause they gunna stay and fight for their territory. That's why there's so many young people in jail for killing someone. Chances are, they shot someone older than them 'cause they want what they had.

Vicente recounted being shot by a competitor while making a drug deal. He described being double-crossed by the other person in the deal. He emphasized the need to always be on the alert. "I did business with him before, you see. So I didn't expect that, but I always brought along a gun because you know things happen. Expect the unexpected, and this was what happened." Other participants talked about times when drug deals went bad and they felt their lives were endangered.

Data revealed that participants reached a point at which the fear of physical harm, particularly death, had a significant influence on their leaving the street life. Allen stated, "If you gonna be true to it, you wanta be on the streets, you should be true to it. But I don't think I want to be true to the streets. There ain't nothin' out there but jail or death. I got too much life to live." Laron recounted what it was like once he tried to make a positive change:

> Man, I been carrying a weapon ever since. Since this year, I ain't had a gun on me. I ain't had a gun on me, not a piece on me since

this fall, this whole '94 year. This is my first shot ever from '86 to now. This is my first year that I didn't have a gun. As a matter of fact, I got shot at the most this year out of my whole life. That's why I came to [this program].

Although the street life, especially in connection with drug dealing, was perceived by respondents to have become more dangerous as they got older, other factors influenced their fear. Eighty percent of these young men recounted experiences of being shot or stabbed. In some cases, these experiences had occurred more than once. Many had sustained critical injuries. The longer they continued in the street life, the more enemies they gained and, as a result, the more they felt their lives were in danger. All but one participant stated he had been incarcerated more than once as a juvenile and some as an adult. They stated that it was not a big deal as a juvenile because they received short sentences, but that as adults they would receive longer, harsher sentences. Most of those who had served sentences as adults, which ranged from one to three years, indicated that their experiences were unbearable and that they were afraid of having to serve any more time. Some circumstances of their incarceration that they felt made it unbearable included sexual assaults, physical assaults, and unlivable prison conditions.

Contemplation Time

A significant factor in participants' decisions to change destructive behaviors was time away from their chaotic environments to contemplate their lives. Eleven participants indicated that during this time they were able to understand more clearly the progression their lives had taken and what circumstances led to that progression. They also indicated realizing that only they could change their life course. The critical aspect of this factor was the time away from those environments that fostered destructive behaviors, not the site where contemplation occurred.

The nine participants who made changes in their behavior while participating in the previously mentioned residential program underwent a very intensive and disciplined regime. They were not permitted to leave the facility for an initial three-month period except during program-supervised outings. The staff worked on instilling new values and building self-esteem and self-worth. The participants involved in this program all described it as hard because of the regimentation and consistency of expectations of them. They also commented that they were forced to live 24 hours a day, seven days a week with what they termed bad attitudes. Although they encountered bad attitudes in the streets, at the facility they were unable to deal with these attitudes in a manner counterproductive to the program's purpose. Although support was an additional significant factor in this program (see "Support and Modeling" section), participants indicated by their statements that the contemplation time the program offered them was a separate influence.

Devon stated his initial reason for coming to this program was the $5,000 stipend it offered at the end of three years. He had no desire to change his street life behavior before coming to the program. He recounted,

> I wanted the $5,000 that I heard they was supposed to give you. But then after awhile, I was like, I'm liable to stay 'cause I need a change. Let me see, let me mess with myself a little bit. Let me see what'll happen on the other side of the fence. So I tried, and I like it.

Relocation allowed other participants the opportunity to contemplate and decide to make changes. Jay recounted several experiences of short incarcerations in detention facilities and jail and indicated that his behavior worsened after these confinements. However, at age 18, he left his neighborhood environment, where he had engaged in illegal drug marketing and armed robberies. It was during this time that he began to experience changes in his behavior and way of thinking. He stated,

> I came to Boston. I came here and spent the summer here and got away from Philadelphia for the rest of the summer. I ended up going to Nantucket, where I went to school, and I ended up like just removing myself from Philadelphia. And then, from then, that's when I started doing some of my growing, and I started re-examining some of my values. And I was like, what's going on in my life?

Gilberto indicated he began thinking about change after a period he spent in Mexico. He went to live in Mexico to escape problems with the law. Recounting what occurred on returning, he stated,

> This was the summer when I had barely came back from Mexico. And after that I was trying to get out of it [participating in destructive behaviors]. I was working at the letter company, which was real good. I was working there and then I was going to school at night.

Four participants made the decision to change their behavior while incarcerated. They indicated that incarceration gave them time to think about where their lives were going. Allen clearly described this experience:

> When I got arrested the last time, and I had a lot of time to think in jail. That's when we usually do it. And I was just thinking. I was like just sayin', "What if?" Well, being behind bars, my freedom is worth more than this. And I just want to change my life. And I just thought about it.

Ricardo expressed deep feelings about his two-year prison experience, stating,

> Honestly, I didn't think I could make it in prison. Prison wasn't for me. Prison was not what changed me. What it was, I had [realized] that I was wrong. Prison was that, yo, you need to chill. But you could have stuck me anywhere for a week and same thing. I didn't need to do that.

Ricardo also spoke about the significance of getting out of his chaotic environment:

> I go to church to get down on my knees an' thank God for my life. And to me church is the most peaceful thing in the world. People never realize that you can go to church and stop the whole world from affecting you. No one ever realizes that you can stop the whole world. 'Cause you don't hear nothin'. You don't hear brothers swearing. You don't hear brothers killin' each other. You don't hear ambulances. You don't hear cops. You just hear yourself.

None of those who had been incarcerated indicated that the harsh treatment gave rise to thoughts of change. Instead they mentioned feelings of anger and hatred because of such treatment. It was at those times in prison when they were alone to think without the mind-cluttering, punitive conditions when they thought of change.

Support and Modeling

All 20 participants associated the support of a consistently dedicated person with their ability to make changes in their lives, although none felt that this alone was the influential change factor. The kinds of support participants described as influential in their decisions to change included unconditional acceptance of them, particularly at times of relapse into destructive behavioral patterns; availability on a consistent basis when they needed advice, counseling, or just someone to talk to; involvement with them in activities that were recreational and gave a feeling of "family"; assistance with job training and placement or educational attainment; and instillation of self-worth and self-esteem.

The most commonly reported quality of effective support people was genuine concern and caring. Gilberto described one woman whom he felt especially influenced him to change:

> She's been working for about three years, and it's only her by herself. It's just one lady. And what's weird is that her sons and daughters are never been in gangs, never been in problems, but she's still working in the community. 'Cause usually what happens, a mother gets involved after her son gets killed and stuff like that. And this lady doesn't have nothin' like that.

Another participant, Jesus, also mentioned this same woman as an influential support person. He stated, "She's the one that got me in this program [the residential program] 'cause she knew me and my friend, and she knew that we could make something better of our life than being gang bangers."

Several support people reported by participants as influential in their decisions to change were women. In addition to the woman described by Gilberto and Jesus, two young men from the program for which I mentored reported female mentors were a factor in their decisions to change. Five participants indicated that they experienced their greatest support from an intimate female. They talked about feeling, particularly in childhood and early adolescence, that no one really cared for or loved them. They stated that the young women whom they dated were only with them for material gain (clothes, jewelry, and entertainment they bought for them). Gilberto described the supportive feeling his girlfriend gave him: "My girlfriend showed me that she did care, so then I figured there is someone out there that cares. She totally changed my life around, showed me that there actually are people who care." Jerome identified his wife, a girlfriend at the time, as the person who most influenced him to get out of the street life and return to school. Vicente described a time when he felt that he had relapsed by hanging around with an old friend and connecting the friend with a drug dealer. He said that he later cried because he felt he had let down all those who had helped him. It was his girlfriend who was most supportive at this time:

> That's right, and my girl was the one that supported me so much in this, 'cause she gave me a lot of counseling, personal counseling you know. And she pointed out all the things that I've achieved and all the people that supported me and started naming things and names. I was like, I can't do this, and that was why I got my act together. I have to straighten up. And now I'm like more serious.

Other participants talked about the importance of intimate young women who supported them and who they felt genuinely loved them.

Data indicate that the important aspect of support is its consistency. These young men have typically experienced interactions with people earlier in their lives that resulted in their perception that adults cannot be counted on. This feeling of not being able to trust was very apparent to me as a mentor. The young men I worked with required long-term evidence of my sincerity and commitment before an indication of trust evolved.

David's experiences with individuals he felt were very instrumental in his desire to change showed the importance of the support being consistent and unconditional. David experienced a relapse in his effort to change because of the traumatic loss of his grandmother, who had raised him. This relapse unfortunately ended in years of incarceration. Yet, as he recounted, the support people continued to be there for him throughout his prison term and after his release. David at present works as a mentor in a program assisting other young men like himself. He is also in a premed program.

One particularly striking finding was that seven participants reported that seeing a change in the behavior of their previously drug- and alcohol-addicted parents motivated them to change their own lives. Allen reported that seeing his mother become active in the community had a big influence on him. This finding indicates the power of resilience, parental attachment, and positive role modeling, despite severe childhood abuse. Only one of the seven participants indicated that his parent made a conscious effort to encourage positive behavior changes in his life.

CONCLUSION

The notion that young men like the participants in this study are a lost generation is far too terminal. Findings indicate survival, strength, and determination among the sample population and suggest that young men moving along a trajectory or pathway of criminal activity can make transitions to pathways of desistance from crime. The turning points for the participants were facilitated by four significant factors: (1) respect and concern for children, (2) fear of physical harm or incarceration, (3) contemplation time, and (4) support and modeling.

Respect and concern for children appeared to be the most significant factor, because it is the only one that is an unselfish motive. The data indicated that these young men experienced great difficulty in caring for and trusting others. Given their early childhood experiences of abuse, it is no wonder. Children may represent a safe population for these participants—a population they view as less likely to disappoint them. Social workers can use this factor as a healing tool with similar young men. Connecting troubled young men with programs that give them the opportunity to help troubled children can develop their feelings of worth. Also, social workers can make an effort to develop meaningful relationships and contacts among troubled young men and their children. They can advocate for policy changes so that visitation programs for incarcerated fathers can take place in secured, children-centered sections of prisons where fathers can spend quality time with their children.

The high percentage of participants from the study active in intervention programs suggests that these programs are effective arenas for addressing aspects of young men's lives indicated by the sample as facilitating their decisions to change. Intervention programs can promote the powerful bond young men reported feeling for their children through focus groups, such as the Men as Teachers group formed by Fagan and Stevenson (1995), which allows open discussion about issues of parenthood, counseling to assist young parents in overcoming the social and personal forces that act as barriers to good parenting practices, and modeling of positive parent–child relationships by mentors who are parents. Fostering functional, cooperative male–female relationships, particularly those in which children are present, is another area in which intervention programs could place emphasis. Including significant women in focus group discussions and counseling sessions when topics address such issues as parenting, social and environmental stressors, and relationship stressors may build the kind of supportive male–female bonds reported by the participants as influential in their decisions to change. These strong bonds could be a preventive measure against raising another generation of children that engage in destructive behaviors.

The fear of physical harm and incarceration was reported by some participants as influential in their decisions to change their destructive behavioral patterns. However, participants also reported that time away from their chaotic and often dangerous environments, either in residential programs in their own communities or in other locations, had the same effect. Programs that offer a residential component need to be evaluated to assess whether the residential component makes a significant difference in outcome. If this component is found to be an effective intervention, courts, as an alternative to imprisonment, could offer placement in residential programs to offenders as a last step before imprisonment, especially for first-time and nonviolent offenders.

Further research that continues to explore and test factors leading to positive changes in behavior is of utmost importance. Findings from such research will be useful to program directors, social services providers, and policymakers. The population of young men attempting to desist from previous delinquent behaviors is also more accessible to researchers, as this study's findings seem to indicate, because this population participates in community assistance programs.

Investments in human capital that we as a society make in these young men will determine the future stability of our inner cities. Participants in this study demonstrate the success of such investments as they return to their communities to "give back." They become social capital where little is found.

REFERENCES

Caspi, A., Elder, G., & Herbener, E. (1990). Childhood personality and the prediction of life course patterns. In L. Robins & M. Rutter (Eds.), *Straight and devious pathways from childhood to adulthood* (pp. 13–35). Cambridge, England: Cambridge University Press.

Elder, G. (1985). *Life course dynamics.* Ithaca, NY: Cornell University Press.

Fagan, J., & Stevenson, H. (1995). Men as teachers: A self-help program on parenting for African American men. *Social Work with Groups, 17,* 29–42.

Glueck, S., & Glueck, E. (1950). *Unraveling juvenile delinquency.* New York: Commonwealth Fund.

Glueck, S., & Glueck, E. (1968). *Delinquents and nondelinquents in perspective.* Cambridge, MA: Harvard University Press.

Gove, W. (1985). The effect of age and gender on deviant behavior: A biopsychosocial perspective. In A. S. Rossi (Ed.), *Gender and the life course* (pp. 115–144). New York: Aldine de Gruyter.

Laub, J., & Sampson, R. J. (1993). Turning points in the life course: Why change matters to the study of crime. *Criminology, 31,* 301–325.

Loeber, R., & LeBlanc, M. (1990). Toward a developmental criminology. In N. Morris & M. Tonry (Eds.), *Crime and justice* (pp. 375–473). Chicago: University of Chicago Press.

Loeber, R., & Stouthamer-Loeber, M. (1996). The development of offending. *Criminal Justice and Behavior, 23,* 12–24.

Macmillan, R. (1995). Changes in the structure of life courses and the decline of social capital in Canadian society: A time series analysis of property crime rates. *Canadian Journal of Sociology, 20,* 51–79.

Qualitative Solutions and Research, Non-numerical Unstructured Data Indexing, Searching, and Theorizing 3.0 [Computer software]. (1994). Victoria, Australia: La Trobe University.

Sampson, R., & Laub, J. (1993). *Crime in the making: Pathways and turning points through life.* Cambridge, MA: Harvard University Press.

Shover, N., & Thompson, C. (1992). Age differential expectations and crime desistance. *Criminology, 30,* 89–104.

Strauss, A., & Corbin, J. (1990). *Basics of qualitative research.* Newbury Park, CA: Sage
    Publications.
U.S. Bureau of the Census. (1996). *Statistical abstract of the United States: 1996* (116th
    ed.). Washington, DC: U.S. Government Printing Office.

---

*This chapter is based on a doctoral dissertation (UMI Microfilm No. 9537820).
A related publication can be found in* Smith College Studies in Social Work,
67(3).

Part IV

COMMUNITIES

18 Murals in Latino Communities: Social Indicators of Community Strengths

Melvin Delgado and Keva Barton

The professional literature on Latinos has generally focused on the socioeconomic challenges facing this community. Latinos consistently have a disproportionate number of families in poverty; high rates of school dropout; alcohol, tobacco, and other drug abuse; and HIV/AIDS, to list just four social problems (Chachkes & Jennings, 1994; Holmes, 1996; Mayers, Kail, & Watts, 1992). They generally reside in sections of urban areas that are often referred to as "ghettos," "barrios," "slums," or "inner cities" or that are euphemistically called "distressed." Social workers and other helping professionals quickly learn to identify social indicators related to "urban despair," for example, billboards selling alcohol and tobacco, large numbers of bars and liquor establishments, vacant lots, boarded-up buildings, abandoned cars, and so forth.

Although the concept of strengths and assets has emerged slowly in the professional literature (Delgado, 1997a, 1998, in press; Logan, 1996; McKnight & Kretzmann, 1991; Saleebey, 1992a, 1992b), not enough attention has been paid to indicators of community health. A social–political appreciation of murals can help social workers and other helping professionals better understand Latino communities from an asset perspective. According to Holscher (1976–77), "Murals . . . are newspapers on walls and a wealth of information is contained in them. They can be valuable to educators, politicians, sociologists, political scientists, architects and planners" (p. 45). Social workers can also be added to Holscher's list.

Diego Rivera, arguably the most famous muralist in the Western hemisphere, summed up the importance of murals quite well: "Mural painting must help in [a person's] struggle to become a human being, and for that purpose it must live wherever it can; no place is bad for it, so long as it is there permitted to fulfill its primary functions of nutrition and enlightenment" (Rivera & Wolfe, 1934, p. 13).

This chapter provides social workers with a multifaceted perspective on Latino murals and the important functions they serve for youths and their community. It is critical for social workers to view murals from an asset perspective to better understand the strengths

This chapter was originally published in the July 1998 issue of *Social Work*, Vol. 43, pp. 346–356.

of community and the issues and struggles of its residents. For community revitalization, for example, social workers must systematically consider the role murals can play in bringing a community together (Herszenhorn & Hirsh, 1996). This chapter presents and analyzes a case study, drawing on themes and competencies social workers can translate into strategies for community (youth) participation.

CONCEPT OF FREE SPACE AND STRENGTHS

The theoretical work by Evans and Boyte (1986) and Saleebey (1992a, 1992b) set an excellent foundation from which to analyze the importance of murals in Latino and other communities of color across the United States. Evans and Boyte developed the concept called "free spaces" to explain places where community residents can come together and articulate common concerns, hopes, and shared values:

> The central argument . . . is that particular sorts of public places in the community, what we call free spaces, are the environments in which people are able to learn a new self-respect, a deeper and more assertive group identity, public skills, and values of cooperation and civic virtue. Put simply, free spaces are settings between private lives and large-scale institutions where ordinary citizens can act with dignity, independence, and vision. (p. 17)

Applying the concept of free spaces to Latino communities highlights numerous institutions and places controlled by and for the community. These places can be beauty or barber shops, grocery stores, social clubs, fundamentalist houses of worship, and parks, to list but a few types (Delgado, 1996, 1997b). Free spaces vary according to the community. However, the question is not whether they exist but how they are manifested in the community.

Building walls—interior and external—must also be considered free spaces. Murals are very often painted on the free spaces found in urban communities. Some are painted in "official" buildings such as schools, police stations, and other public buildings. However, most are painted on building walls that have been "claimed" by the community as their own, even though they are not owned by community residents. These spaces are transformed from their original purpose as part of a building structure to a message board for the internal and external community to see, read, and learn from. These spaces, as noted by Cooper and Sciorra (1994), are a canvas for expression: "The energy is still there—energy to create, energy to be seen, energy to be heard" (p. 9).

Saleebey (1992a) is widely credited with popularizing the concept of strengths in social work practice. A strengths perspective stresses five key elements for social work practice (Saleebey, 1992b): (1) unquestioned respect for a client's abilities, innate resources, and perspectives; (2) use of strengths as a central theme in any intervention; (3) stress on collaboration among clients, their communities, and providers; (4) avoidance of using a "victim" mind-set throughout a professional relationship; and (5) use of indigenous community resources whenever possible in assessment and development of interventions. The concepts of free space and strengths form the basis for analyzing murals within communities of color.

REVIEW OF THE LITERATURE

The topic of murals (sometimes referred to as "spraycan art") in Latino communities, with few exceptions, has not been addressed in the professional literature (Chalfant & Prigoff, 1987; Drescher & Garcia, 1978; Holscher, 1976, 1976–77; Treguer, 1992). The press, however, has been quick to understand the significance of murals in urban communities ("California Town Hopes," 1996; Madden, 1996). There is recognition that murals represent much more than a community's effort to find artistic expression.

Graffiti, a popular art form often covered in the popular press, is commonly referred to as "tagging." This form of artistic expression is usually initiated by individuals rather than groups or communities and is not restricted to communities. Tagging can be manifested on subway trains, doors, mailboxes, and other less significant locations. The messages contained in graffiti art generally reflect the struggles associated with urban living and issues of oppression (Ferrell, 1995). Murals differ from tagging by their coordinated effort at involving a community, the nature and extent of project planning, and the location in communities (Cooper & Chalfant, 1984; Kurlansky, Naar, & Mailer, 1974; Walsh, 1996).

On the East Coast, especially in New York City, there is an art form involving memorial murals (Cooper & Sciorra, 1994). This art form involves the use of aerosol paint cans by artists who are commissioned by an individual or group of community residents. In short, murals represent a community effort, whereas tagging is a much more individualized effort at creative expression. In addition, murals represent one dimension, although a significant one, of urban arts projects that also encompass other forms of expression such as sculptures.

For murals to have cultural meaning and impact, they must target the internal audience, namely the community (Treguer, 1992). It would be simplistic to think that murals can easily be classified into categories: "One is impressed by the heterogeneity of the mural styles, subjects, and locations. The typical mural does not exist. There are too many of them, depicting numerous ideas and themes, painted in literally hundreds of different places, to allow us to form an unsophisticated conclusion about the reasons for their existence" (Holscher, 1976, p. 25). Drescher and Garcia (1978) examined Latino murals (primarily focused in Los Angeles) from an artistic and social (historical, political, and economic) perspective. Treguer (1992) considered murals as a cultural-based form of self-expression for communities that have few unregulated outlets for their public voices. As noted by Jon Pounds, "Murals express more than ethnic pride. It's about people expressing what their own issues are" (personal communication, 1996). Holscher (1976–77), one of the few social scientists to study this phenomenon, identified the sociopolitical value murals play in undervalued communities.

This art form takes on added significance because of the limited market for artists of color. Some geographic areas of the country are fortunate because there are centers devoted to this art form, as is the case in Chicago (Chicago Public Art Group), Los Angeles (Social and Public Art Resource Center), and San Francisco (Precita Eyes Mural Arts Center). However, these centers are rare in other cities across the United States. Murals provide many artists with an opportunity to earn a living and serve as socially constructive outlets for their art. Artists have a community-sanctioned medium for expressing their emotions and communicating those of the community. Latinos generally do not control media outlets such as radio stations, newspapers, and television stations. Consequently, messages specifically developed by and targeting their community are lacking.

Although there is no typical mural, a content analysis of Latino murals will generally uncover seven key themes that communicate a central message and the importance of this art form to the community. Each of the following themes has implications for social work practice: symbols of ethnic and racial pride, religious symbols, issues related to social justice, decorative symbols, homages to national and local heroes, memorials commissioned by local residents, and symbolic locations.

Symbols of Ethnic and Racial Pride

Themes related to ethnic and racial pride can be manifested in a variety of ways (Coleman, 1994; Drescher & Garcia, 1978; Holscher, 1976–77; Laird, 1992; Treguer, 1992). Treguer (1992) stated, "Pre-Colombian themes, intended to remind Chicanos of their noble origins, are common. There are motifs from the Aztec codices, gods from the Aztec pantheon, allusions to the Spanish conquest and images of the Virgin of Guadalupe, a cherished Mexican icon" (p. 23). Cooper and Sciorra's research (1994) in New York City also noted the importance of ethnic and racial pride among Puerto Rican and other Latino groups.

Cultural pride serves as a cornerstone of culturally competent social work practice. Cultural competence, in turn, relies on a strengths perspective toward individuals and communities (Delgado, 1997a, 1997b). Consequently, murals provide a "canvas" for Latinos to demonstrate knowledge of their history and pride in their cultural heritage, as well as to articulate their struggles against oppression.

Religious Symbols

Spirituality, in the form of religion and folk beliefs, plays an important role in the lives of Latinos (Coleman, 1994; Cooper & Sciorra, 1994; Treguer, 1992). Religious and spiritual symbols often represent a community's hopes for the future, its history and, depending on the symbols, the value it places on the metaphysical. These symbols are not uncommon in Latino murals. Mexican American communities very often have the Virgin of Guadalupe, an important Mexican icon. Cooper and Sciorra (1994) commented on the mixture of images and symbols of memorial artists in New York City: "Drawing from sources sacred and profane, memorial artists creatively juxtapose an array of images and symbols in their work. Their innovative mix allows for individual input while establishing the parameters of this recent genre of graffiti art" (p. 17).

The subject of spirituality is slowly being recognized within the social work profession (Bullis, 1996). Spirituality, which can be manifested in beliefs and in organized religion, plays an important role in communities of color, Latinos being no exception. In the form of organized religion, spirituality can also serve as a method for bringing people together in an affirming activity. Social work agencies can develop collaborative relationships with houses of worship to better serve communities that may be reluctant to use formal social services. Space can be used, social work staff can be located, and workshops can be held in community-based religious institutions.

Issues Related to Social Justice

There is no escaping the toll oppression has extracted on the Latino community (Chalfant & Prigoff, 1987; Coleman, 1994; Dowdy, 1995; Holscher, 1976; Valdes, 1995). Murals, as noted by Holscher (1976), are a natural form for expression of protest: "The concept of art as a revolutionary tool, as a weapon in a propaganda campaign against the oppressor, or as revolution itself has been carried over into the murals by Chicano artists in Los Angeles today" (p. 27).

In some Latino communities, scenes of police brutality, arson, alcohol and other drug abuse, prison, U.S. imperialism (particularly related to government-sponsored terrorism in the Caribbean and Latin America), and infant mortality are commonplace: "These neighborhood billboards are used to elicit critical examination of the root causes and solutions to the daily onslaught against inner-city youth . . . documenting community life and . . . to kindle discussion on the untimely deaths of neighborhood residents" (Cooper & Sciorra, 1994, p. 14). In essence, mural scenes are based on historical events and are a daily reminder of the trials and tribulations of being Latino in this country and of the search for social justice.

Issues of oppression and social justice are central to social work's mission. A content analysis of murals can assist social workers in developing a more in-depth, locale-specific understanding of the issues the community considers of importance. This understanding should translate into interventions that address these concerns. Themes related to historical events, police–community relations, the impact of crime and drugs, and so forth will emerge, highlighting priority areas for intervention.

Decorative Symbols

Murals do not have to have significant social meaning to be important to a community ("California Town Hopes," 1996; Chalfant &
Prigoff, 1987; Coleman, 1997; Fishman, 1996; Treguer, 1992). According to Treguer, murals translate commonplace or even unsightly areas
into memorable spaces: "What had been a hideous forest of concrete
pillars soon became a pleasant and attractive place, a park decorated
with paintings of remarkable beauty whose subject matter was critical, even subversive" (p. 24). Fishman (1996) reported on a mural project combining environmental concerns and art. Patricia Rose stated it
eloquently: "A blank wall is just waiting for something" (personal
communication, 1997).

The decorative dimension of murals is well illustrated in Twenty-
nine Palms, California, a town seeking to make itself the "Mural
Capital of America," although it is estimated that Los Angeles has
more than 1,000 murals ("California Town Hopes," 1996). A large
public works campaign is under way in an effort to make the town
more appealing to tourists; murals are viewed as windows to the
town's history.

Social work interventions stressing murals can serve as a means to
rally a community to take pride in its environment. Murals, when
combined with community gardens, are an excellent means of involving a community in projects that are nonstigmatizing and a way
to engage a community in dialogue and mutual planning.

Homages to National and Local Heroes

Murals, if they are to be accepted by the community, must be painted
by residents and must involve the community in all stages of the
process (Coleman, 1997; Cooper & Sciorra, 1994). One mural artist
noted that mural themes are influenced by whether the artist is internal or external to the community and whether the artist shares the
same ethnic or racial background as the residents:

> There's a certain stereotype perpetuated by some of the white
> artists doing public works projects....You see the same thing over
> and over again: Say no to drugs, stop the violence. I wanted to do
> a mural that reflects us as we really are. We don't just kill each
> other and sell drugs. We have other aspects to our lives. We need
> a variety of murals and public arts projects. (Valdes, 1995, p. 54)

Latino and other communities of color rarely have the opportunity to honor their own. Unlike national heroes such as the Rev. Martin
Luther King, Jr., Malcolm X, and Cesar Chavez, many local heroes
never make it into history books. Consequently, murals provide local
residents with opportunities to validate their experiences through
their heroes. School social workers, for example, can help teachers
develop projects that use local heroes in their assignments. Murals

can make excellent schoolwide and agency projects for involving students, parents, and other interested community residents.

Memorials Commissioned by Local Residents

Residents may commission a mural for a dead relative, close friend, or gang member (Cooper & Sciorra, 1994). Gonzalez (1994) focused most of his article on murals commissioned by local residents:

> The walls, sometimes playful in spirit and other times dripping with menace, are also a visual chronicle of each beleaguered neighborhood's history. Played out from block to block, the results of bad luck, bad health, or just plain badness are etched onto brick and concrete looming as a cautionary backdrop for those who survive another day, an uneasy reminder of how chaotic city life has become . . . death is the ultimate scene stealer. (pp. 67–68)

The rituals associated with murals honoring the dead are very elaborate and symbolic: "The idea of honoring the dead and remembering is very visual. . . . People watch while the murals are painted; they have a ceremony at the end. It's a way for the community as a whole to deal with these losses" (Gonzalez, 1994, p. 68). In situations such as these, murals help residents mourn and honor their dead in a public arena.

The number and extent of murals dedicated to community residents who have died can be an excellent indicator of key issues within the community. The assessment can provide important data on gender, age, and cause of death, as well as other information. Support groups can be developed when the themes and numbers warrant such an intervention.

Symbolic Location of Murals

Content represents one very important dimension of a mural. The location of a mural adds a different, yet equally important, dimension. There are three perspectives concerning location: (1) limited audience exposure—small public places such as alleys or infrequently traveled areas, (2) targeted audience exposure—inside select buildings such as schools and police stations, and (3) maximum audience exposure—public areas with a high volume of traffic. Murals in maximum-audience-exposure locations and high-profile buildings provide the greatest prestige for the paintings and have the highest potential for conveying a message about the community.

Murals in places with limited audience exposure do not have a great impact on a community but still represent an effort to convey a message. This message, however, may not have wide salience, or the group seeking to send it may not have sufficient status to warrant a high-exposure location. Memorial murals, however, must take into consideration another factor, namely, location of where the deceased person died, lived, or congregated with friends.

Social workers can play an instrumental role in helping communities negotiate with government authorities and private parties for the painting of murals using their spaces. Murals in prime locations can serve to empower communities to organize to seek services and other resources to help them develop their capacities to help themselves.

DEVELOPMENT OF COMPETENCE IN YOUTHS

Murals also provide an outlet for educating youths on a variety of topics that can be transferred to school and other arenas. School social workers and others working with Latino youths can use murals to enhance youth and community capacities. Mural development necessitates the development or enhancement of 11 knowledge and skill areas, each of which is discussed in this section.

Research Skills

Research skills are necessary in the development of murals. Youths must develop ways of seeking input from community residents and other stakeholders. They must also undertake library research to learn more about cultural symbols (Fishman, 1996). For many Latino youths this experience in learning more about their cultural history represents the first and only instance of studying their history. Few urban-based public schools provide Latino students with an opportunity to learn about Caribbean and Latin American history. Ethnic pride may be an important secondary gain in mural painting. Youths must present their ideas to the group and the community and be prepared to explain why a certain design has historical and cultural meaning. They are then entrusted with the role of educator for youths who are not part of the project.

Social workers can facilitate this research process by brokering with school officials to sponsor murals within their schools. Agency-based social workers can help organize mural festivals, walking tours, and other activities that stress development of research skills. Youths who have participated in mural painting can be used as mentors for younger children who are just learning the art.

Negotiation Skills

Murals cannot be painted without an extensive period of negotiation and dialogue involving multiple sectors of a community. This negotiation takes on added significance if bringing a community together in pursuit of a common goal is a desired objective (Dowdy, 1995; Drescher & Garcia, 1978; Fishman, 1996): "Many admirers of subway graffiti found the appropriation of city property a particularly alluring and provocative feature of the art form. Memorial artists, on the other hand, are more inclined to seek permission for coveted wall space" (Cooper & Sciorra, 1994, pp. 12–13). Numerous numbers of meetings are required involving individuals and small and large groups. Youths must exercise negotiation skills that later can be easily transferred to other situations. Negotiation skills play a critical role in conflict resolution. The impact of violence on the lives of Latino youths is overwhelming, particularly youth-on-youth violence. Thus, negotiation skills transfer very well to everyday life. Social workers can take the lessons learned from negotiating murals and directly apply them to violence prevention.

Safety Consciousness and Following Rules

Murals require participants to be acutely aware of safety concerns. There are too many points in a mural project where participants can be hurt if they do not follow safety procedures. The preparation of the surface to be painted and the application of paint, as well as falling from scaffolds, can result in serious harm. Consequently, participants must be totally aware of the rules and prepared to follow established procedures, for their good as well as that of their team members.

Development of safety consciousness translates well to everyday life. Latino youths can take the lessons learned about safety and the importance of following rules and apply them to their homes, schools, and communities. Social workers can take the subject of environmental safety and make it relevant to the Latino community through workshops, demonstrations, discussions at local health fairs, and so forth.

Teamwork

Murals should never be an individual project; successful murals involve countless numbers of participants (Fishman, 1996). Skills related to effective teamwork must be stressed throughout an entire project's existence. The research phase, for example, necessitates a team of participants taking individual or small group assignments to study particular aspects of a symbol or theme. Upon completion of the task, participants must reassemble and compare notes. Failure on the part of an individual results in a delay of the project. If the project is being undertaken during the summer months, then there is not very much time to waste. Similar challenges are also applicable to the other phases of a mural project. A team approach also allows for members to find their individual voices and to use their unique talents and abilities, making for a successful team effort (A. Lopez, personal communication, 1997).

The lessons learned from teamwork will serve Latino youths the rest of their lives. Social workers can use Latino youths who have worked on murals to teach other youths the advantages and challenges of teamwork. Youths become an indigenous resource in helping their school and community. Adults can also learn about the importance of teamwork, and youths can serve as models on how this goal can be accomplished.

Starting and Completing a Project

An often overlooked experience in mural painting is the starting and completion of a project. As already noted, much planning and research goes into a mural before painting commences. Youths, as a result, develop an appreciation for the importance of planning and the compromises that are associated with implementation. Furthermore, the experience of completing a project provides youths with an opportunity to showcase their talents before the community. There generally is a ceremony for unveiling a mural, and this is an opportunity for the community to come together with its youth to celebrate this accomplishment.

The importance of planning and completing a mural is also applicable to other projects. Social workers working with youths can help them develop problem-solving skills and greater self-awareness of how they cope with frustrations in all aspects of a project. These lessons can translate very well to school assignments or to starting community initiatives involving youths.

Work Habits

The development of proper work behavior enhances the value of murals. Youths must be able to work together; this can be accomplished only if members can rely on each other. Thus, attendance and punctuality are critical. Members who are absent must inform their supervisors; members who must leave early must take into account how their departure will affect the production schedule. The development of a mural can be thought of as an art project; it can also be thought of as a job. These two ways of viewing murals are not mutually exclusive and can serve to teach youths the necessary skills for employment.

Social workers assisting with murals must endeavor to reinforce the importance of good work habits and the importance of following through. These lessons not only help Latino youths involved with murals, but also help their friends and siblings who are not part of this venture. The responsibility that goes with good work habits will assist youths in all aspects of their lives.

Communication Skills

The importance of communication cannot be overemphasized. Communication entails oral and written skills. Youths need to assess the sentiments of the community to better design a mural. They also have to express themselves within the group throughout all phases of a project. Failure to communicate clearly can create misunderstandings and hard feelings. Furthermore, failure to communicate effectively can result in accidents during the painting process, which often requires youths to paint at different heights simultaneously. Falling from a high height onto painters at lower levels can be dangerous.

Good communication skills do not just happen. Consequently, social workers must stress all aspects of communication in the process of developing murals. Written and oral communication skills are necessary in all aspects of an individual's life. However, they take on greater significance for youths in their efforts to navigate many of life's challenges, in and out of school. Social workers can help youths develop a better appreciation of how important good communication skills are in group and community projects.

Knowledge of Math and Chemistry

The roles of math (primarily geometry and use of scales) and chemistry (mixing of paints) are central to a mural project. Youths not only must understand these principles, but also must be able to apply them in real-life situations. For some youths these principles are well understood; for others, they are not. As a result, youths must teach youths. The role of teacher is one that must be carried out in a sensitive and supportive manner to foster team spirit. Murals provide an excellent mechanism for the teaching of academic concepts.

Few topics can turn young people off as much as mathematics and chemistry. Social workers, particularly those in school settings, can help translate how math, chemistry, and other subjects that are essential for murals can be relevant in other aspects of life. The teaching of academic subject matter does not have to be boring and irrelevant. When academic subjects are made relevant and fun, learning is not a struggle. Thus, social workers can also consider themselves to be teachers in their quest to help youths with mural painting.

Working across Generations

Murals require several generations working together (Coleman 1994; Dowdy, 1995). Youths not only work with other youths, but also with community residents and local stakeholders, who invariably are adults. Sometimes these parties come together and form advisory groups for a mural project. Youths also have to enlist the support of individuals responsible for the space on which a mural will be painted. Adults, in turn, must trust youths and turn over space for murals. Sometimes adults must be prepared to accept a concept that may be presented orally or, in some instances, as a sketch. Communities consist of multiple generations; mural projects, as a result, must also involve multiple generations.

The negotiation skills Latino youths learn through murals can also be used in working with adults. Cross-generational work takes on great importance for youths, because a great deal of power resides with adults. Social workers can help Latino youths better understand the challenges and rewards of convincing adults about the merits of a mural. These lessons, however, can have tremendous benefits in other dealings with adults.

Budgeting and Scheduling Abilities

Murals are not inexpensive community projects. It is generally estimated that the creation of a "typical" mural costs approximately
$20,000 and can cover a period of eight weeks (N. Abbate, personal
communication, 1996; Fishman, 1996). Youths are forced to comparison shop for materials, estimate costs according to the phases of development of a mural, and develop timelines. The length of time associated with painting murals, combined with the importance of
proper weather conditions, makes murals excellent projects for summer employment (Dowdy, 1995).

An understanding of money and scheduling is as essential to mural projects as it is to any other aspect of life. Social workers must endeavor to translate how budgeting and scheduling apply in other situations, and there are countless opportunities to do so during a
mural project. This should not prove too challenging if placed within
the context of a goal, be it individual or group.

Contribution to the Community

Murals provide youths with an opportunity to be constructive members of the Latino community. There are few opportunities for
youths to collaborate with each other and with the community. Murals provide youths with a chance to make a lasting, highly visible
contribution to the community. A group of youths is no longer
viewed as a gang; youths contribute to the physical and social fabric
of the community.

Social workers must stress how youths can make contributions to
their community once a mural is completed. Although mural painting brought together a certain group of youths, there are other ways
the youths can contribute, which serves not only to empower them
but also to empower the community.

CASE STUDY: HOLYOKE, MASSACHUSETTS

The city of Holyoke is located approximately 100 miles west of Boston.
Its mills played an instrumental role in the Industrial Revolution. In
1990 Holyoke had a population of 44,000, of which 12,700 (28.9 percent) were Latino. Puerto Ricans are the largest Latino group, representing 93.5 percent of the Latino community (Gaston Institute, 1992,
1994).

Holyoke's Puerto Rican community has a disproportionate number
of families living below the poverty level (59.1 percent); of high
school dropouts (60.0 percent); and of people who are not part of the
labor force, with 27.1 percent unemployment (Gaston Institute, 1994).
Approximately 5.2 percent of Latino households own their home,
compared with 50.3 percent of white, non–Puerto Rican households;
3.1 percent of black households; and 59.4 percent of Asian households
(Gaston Institute, 1994). The Puerto Rican community is primarily

located within several distinct geographic sections of the city, with the South Side (the focus of this case study) having the highest concentration.

The following is based on events surrounding a mural project in Holyoke involving 20 Puerto Rican youths ages nine to 17 years. The project, as well as the resulting events, symbolized much more than a painting on a wall. As with many murals in Latino communities, this project brought together a community and effectively depicted the conflicting values between internal and external communities. This case study can easily be titled "En Busca de Unidad" (Hard Lessons Learned by Holyoke Latino Youths).

In the spring of 1996, El Arco Iris (the Rainbow), an after-school program of Nueva Esperanza (New Hope), a local community-based organization, received funds to create a mural (Gomez, 1996; Plaisance, 1996; Woods, 1996). After receiving permission from the owner of an abandoned building that faces a vacant lot that was to be used as a community garden, the youths painted a mural of a nature scene. Included in the mural was a painting of two flags (those of Puerto Rico and the United States), as a representation of the youths' two communities. Shortly thereafter, a controversy ensued when several veterans voiced their discontent to a councilwoman. Their discontent focused on the mural showing the U.S. flag upside down and below the Puerto Rican flag. The councilwoman and veterans threatened to paint over the mural. After much debate that touched the entire Holyoke community, the youths decided to paint over the U.S. flag by extending the Puerto Rican flag.

Ironically, this mural project was the youths' attempt to show unity between Puerto Rico and the United States. It was their way of showing how they negotiate the two communities in which they exist. This unfortunate event helped to perpetuate the very alienation and oppression the youths were challenging. Fortunately, a positive experience arose from this struggle. The obstacles faced in doing this mural project galvanized the Puerto Rican community. They came together as adults and youths to fight for their beliefs and to strengthen their voice within the community. Youths developed a better understanding of how change within a community context tested all of the lessons learned in the process of painting a mural. They also witnessed the importance of a community acting in unison. The leadership and bravery demonstrated by the youths was widely recognized within and outside the community. Ultimately, the lessons learned went beyond the painting of a picture. If it is true that a painting speaks a thousand words, then the mural painted by these youths will be speaking for years to come.

If one of the goals of a mural is to encourage community participation, it will also serve to unify Latino communities in search of social and political justice. The incident sparked by the mural in this case study served as a valuable lesson for the internal and external community. If one of the primary goals of a mural is to cause thought and dialogue, then the Holyoke mural exceeded the artists' expectations. The incident served to promote dialogue within and between communities. In short, no sector of the city was untouched by the mural.

CONCLUSION

The presence and role of murals in Latino communities and other communities of color are often overlooked or misunderstood by the external world. Murals, as this chapter points out, represent a lens through which social workers and other helping professionals can better understand and appreciate the Latino community's strengths and struggles for social justice. No two murals are ever alike, yet their role and function within communities generally address several major themes.

Holscher (1976), commenting on Chicano murals, summed up the importance of this art form for other Latino groups:

> In a sociological sense, it is difficult to assess the murals from the artist's perspective. . . . What does exist in the murals by Chicano artists is a common bond based on language and on points of view which have been tempered by direct and indirect experiences with Mexico and by the situations that Chicanos have encountered in the United States. (p. 28)

This art form also serves important functions that go far beyond communication. Murals teach youths many skills that can be transferred to school and work arenas. The social work profession, with an emphasis on community and undervalued groups, is in a strategic position to use murals to bring greater community participation, to help inculcate valuable academic lessons, and to help foster this form of artistic expression. Viewing murals as a sign of the strength of the Latino community represents a dramatic departure from prevailing deficit perspectives. Such a change in paradigms also facilitates the engagement of Latino communities by better conveying an inventory of their resources, history, and needs to the external community.

REFERENCES

Bullis, R. K. (1996). *Spirituality in social work practice.* Washington, DC: Taylor & Francis.

California town hopes eye-catching murals will put it on map. (1996, November 10). *New York Times*, p. 24.

Chachkes, E., & Jennings, R. (1994). Latino communities: Coping with death. In B. O. Dane & C. Levine (Eds.), *AIDS and the new orphans: Coping with death* (pp. 77–99). Westport, CT: Auburn House.

Chalfant, H., & Prigoff, J. (1987). *Spraycan art.* London: Thames & Hudson.

Coleman, S. (1994, December 11). Mission's marvelous murals if you go. . . . *Boston Globe*, p. B1.

Coleman, S. (1997, January 25). Taking it to the walls: The expressive mural. *Boston Globe*, pp. C1, C7.

Cooper, M., & Chalfant, H. (1984). *Subway art.* New York: Henry Holt.

Cooper, M., & Sciorra, J. (1994). *R.I.P. memorial wall art.* New York: Henry Holt.

Delgado, M. (1996). Puerto Rican food establishments as social service organizations: Results of an asset assessment. *Journal of Community Practice, 3*, 57–77.

Delgado, M. (1997a). Strength-based practice with Puerto Rican adolescents: Lessons from a substance abuse prevention project. *Social Work in Education, 19*, 101–112.

Delgado, M. (1997b). Role of Latina-owned beauty parlors in a Latino community. *Social Work, 42*, 445–453.

Delgado, M. (1998). *Social work practice in non-traditional urban settings.* New York: Oxford University Press.

Delgado, M. (in press). *Community social work practice in an urban context: A capacity enhancement perspective.* New York: Oxford University Press.

Dowdy, Z. R. (1995, August 7). Art with an urban edge: Teacher helps graffiti masters transform drab city spaces. *Boston Globe*, p. 13.

Drescher, T., & Garcia, R. (1978). Recent Raza murals in the U.S. *Radical America, 12*, 14–31.

Evans, S. M., & Boyte, H. C. (1986). *Free spaces: The sources of change in America.* New York: Harper & Row.

Ferrell, J. (1995). Urban graffiti: Crime, control, and resistance. *Youth & Society, 27*, 73–92.

Fishman, S. (1996, November 24). Eco-artists gather at the river: Environmental science and art meld. *Boston Globe* [City Section], pp. 15, 18.

Gaston Institute. (1992). *Latinos in Holyoke.* Boston: University of Massachusetts.

Gaston Institute. (1994). *Latinos in Holyoke: Poverty, income, education, employment and housing.* Boston: University of Massachusetts.

Gomez, G. (1996, October 28). Flag issue's really cultural confusion [Letter to the editor]. *Union News*, p. A6.

Gonzalez, D. (1994). Death along New York's bloodiest blocks, graffiti memorials to the departed are the latest refinement of ghetto art. *VIBE, 2*, 65–71.

Herszenhorn, D. M., & Hirsh, S. (1996, December 8). Helping neighborhoods with comprehensive community building. *New York Times*, p. 61.

Holmes, S. A. (1996, October 13). For Hispanic poor, no silver lining. *New York Times*, p. E5.

Holscher, L. M. (1976). Artists and murals in East Los Angeles and Boyle Heights: A sociological observation. *Humboldt Journal of Social Relations, 3*, 25–29.

Holscher, L. M. (1976–77). Tiene arte valor afuera del barrio [Art has value outside of the community]: The murals of East Los Angeles and Boyle Heights. *Journal of Ethnic Studies, 4*, 42–52.

Kurlansky, M., Naar, J., & Mailer, N. (1974). *The faith of graffiti.* New York: Praeger.

Laird, R. (1992, March). Local mural walks convey pride and sense of history. *San Francisco Peninsula Parent*, pp. 17, 22.

Logan, S. (Ed.). (1996). A strengths perspective on black families: Then and now. In S. L. Logan (Ed.), *The black family: Strengths, self-help, and positive change* (pp. 8–20). Boulder, CO: Westview Press.

Madden, J. (1996, November 14). Offending art: Graffiti on Beverly wall attracts attention, criticism. *Salem Evening News*, pp. A1, A10.

Mayers, S. R., Kail, B. L., & Watts, T. D. (Eds.). (1992). *Hispanic substance abusers.* Springfield, IL: Charles C Thomas.

McKnight, J. L., & Kretzmann, J. (1991). *Mapping community capacity.* Evanston, IL: Northwestern University, Center for Urban Affairs Policy and Research.

Plaisance, M. (1996, October 25). Hispanics to rally against councilor. *Union News*, p. B1.

Rivera, D., & Wolfe, B. D. (1934). *Portrait of America.* New York: Covici-Friede.

Saleebey, D. S. (1992a). Introduction: Beginnings of a strengths approach to practice. In D. S. Saleebey (Ed.), *The strengths perspective in social work practice* (pp. 41–44). New York: Longman.

Saleebey, D. S. (Ed.). (1992b). *The strengths perspective in social work practice.* New York: Longman.

Treguer, A. (1992). The Chicanos—Muralists with a message. *UNESCO Courier, 45*, 22–24.

Valdes, A. (1995, August 18). Creating a "Black family." *Boston Globe*, p. 54.

Walsh, M. (1996). *Graffito*. Berkeley, CA: North Atlantic Books.

Woods, J. (1996, October 30–November 5). Kos-Lecca, Mayor swap charges on "unity" mural. *Holyoke Sun*, pp. 3, 8.

The authors thank Nancy Abbate, Jon Pounds, Ana Lopez, Patricia Rose, and Maria Salgado for their time and insights on murals. This chapter was made possible through funding from the Carlisle Foundation, Framingham, MA.

"Gathering the Spirit" at First Baptist Church: Spirituality as a Protective Factor in the Lives of African American Children

Wendy L. Haight

Spiritual socialization can be central to children's healthy development. In the following narrative fragment, Mrs. H, a 73-year-old
African American woman, spontaneously recounted to me her
experiences as a seven-year-old child walking to a segregated school.

"The whites would be walking one way, and we'd be walking the
other. They'd yell at us, 'You dirty, black niggers! We hate you! We
hate you!' I'd go to Mama and ask her, 'Why do they hate us?' She'd
always take me to the Bible. She taught me that God loves us all.
God is the judge. She taught me not to take hate inside of myself."
Mrs. H went on to explain that when we hate, we destroy that part
of God that he left inside each of us when he created us. Thus, from
the perspective taught to her by her mother, Mrs. H was not the victim of this story; rather, her taunters were.

My research on the spiritual socialization of African American
children is informed by the concept of resilience. Investigators of resilience attempt to understand individuals like Mrs. H, who have developed well despite profound, ongoing stressors (see, Fraser, 1997).
Unfortunately, very little systematic research has explored the
strengths of African American children, their families, and their communities, including the ways in which African American adults like
Mrs. H socialize resilience. Rather, research focuses on social problems such as educational underachievement, poverty, teenage pregnancy, drug use, and crime. Thus, the first goal of this chapter is to
describe effective socialization contexts and practices that support
children's healthy development in an African American community.

Identifying sources of resilience has become a basic component of
assessment and intervention in social work practice with children
(Maluccio, 1995). Ethnographic methods represent one important
strategy for developing such knowledge in ethnically diverse communities (Devore & Schlesinger, 1996). Although ethnographic methods
are receiving growing acceptance and appreciation within social work
(see, McRoy, 1995), there remain relatively few examples of their application to the generation of knowledge in social work practice. Thus,

This chapter was originally published in the May 1998 issue of *Social Work*, Vol. 43,
pp. 213–221.

the second goal of this chapter is to provide a model of the use of ethnographic strategies to generate knowledge of an African American community.

Although understanding ethnographic methods is important, it is not sufficient for effective social work practice. Social workers must go one step further than the ethnographer to apply their knowledge of diverse cultures to their own practices (Thornton & Garrett, 1995). Thus, the third goal of this chapter is to demonstrate how knowledge generated from ethnographic strategies was used to generate ethnic-sensitive social work interventions in an African American community.

CHILDREN'S SPIRITUAL SOCIALIZATION IN AFRICAN AMERICAN SUNDAY SCHOOLS

The church has been discussed as a potential community-level source of protective factors (Masten, Best, & Garmesy, 1990). Throughout its history the African American church has played a significant role in the provision of social support and services (see, for example, Franklin, 1980). Unfortunately, almost no research has investigated the role of the church in the socialization of competence (Ogbu, 1985) or resilience in African American children. Available empirical evidence suggests a relationship between socialization experiences emanating from the African American church and a number of positive developmental outcomes. For example, Brown and Gary (1991) found that self-reports of church involvement were positively related to educational attainment among African American adults. In an interview study of African American urban male adolescents, Zimmerman and Maton (1992) found that youths who left high school before graduation and were not employed, but who attended church, had relatively low levels of alcohol and drug abuse. In a questionnaire administered to African American adults (Seaborn-Thompson & Ensminger, 1989), 74 percent responded "very often" or "often" to the statement "The religious beliefs I learned when I was young still help me." On the basis of data from the 1979–80 National Survey of Black Americans, Ellison (1993) argued that participation in church communities is positively related to self-esteem in African American adults.

One of the mechanisms through which the African American church may promote resilience is through the nurturance of spirituality (Hill-Lubin, 1991). Among peoples of African descent, spirituality—that is, an acceptance of a nonmaterial higher force that pervades all of life's affairs—has been identified as a common cultural value (Boykin, 1994; Schiele, 1996). Hale-Benson (1987) characterized the spirituality of African Americans as a key factor in coping with stressful events. The importance of spirituality also is reflected in numerous biographies and autobiographies. For example, Comer (1988) begins the biography of his mother, Maggie, at the doorway of a black Baptist church. In Maya Angelou's (1969) autobiography, the spirituality of African American women sustains families and is a source of creativity.

Despite a resurgence of interest in spirituality in the field of social work (see Bullis, 1996), relatively little attention has been paid to children's spirituality. Similarly, relatively little systematic research exists within the fields of developmental psychology and education, although the development of religious knowledge (that is, age-related changes in understanding and reasoning within particular religious traditions) has received some attention (see Oser, 1991). Werner (1990) observed that resilient children from a variety of backgrounds and communities have in common religious beliefs that provide stability and meaning to their lives, especially in times of hardship. Coles (1990) described spirituality as an important tool on which African American children relied to survive racial hatred during forced school desegregation. In the words of an eight-year-old North Carolina girl in 1962,

> I was all alone, and those people [segregationists] were screaming, and suddenly I saw God smiling, and I smiled. . . . A woman was standing there [near the school door] and she shouted at me, "Hey, you little nigger, what are you smiling at?" I looked right at her face and I said, "At God." Then she looked up at the sky, and then she looked at me, and she didn't call me any more names. (Coles, 1990, pp. 19–20)

Within the church, Sunday school is a particularly important context for children. Mitchell (1986) observed that

> Many a mature Black still remembers with pride an Easter recitation or a Christmas play which awakened his or her first conscious awareness of personal dignity and worth. . . . Perhaps the crowning contribution of the Sunday schools would have to be the tremendous percentage of Black adult church persons whose sense of identity with and commitment to Jesus Christ was evidenced and symbolized in a conversion experience during childhood or youth. Almost all of these were directly or indirectly the result of the love, concern and influence of teachers in the Sunday schools, and the joyous activities associated with this program. (p. 109)

According to Brown and Gary (1991), however, "The absence of research in this area represents a glaring gap in the existing body of knowledge on African American social and cultural life" (p. 423). Thus, this chapter summarizes an ethnographic study of Sunday school relevant to the socialization of resilience in African American children (Haight, 1998).

STUDYING SPIRITUAL SOCIALIZATION: AN OVERVIEW OF THE SUNDAY SCHOOL PROJECT

The ethnographic study spanned a continuous, four-year period from 1991 to 1995 (see Haight, 1998) at First Baptist Church in Salt Lake City, Utah. First Baptist Church emerged approximately 103 years ago from a "Baptist Prayer Band," a group of African Americans who, excluded from worshipping in the white churches, met in one another's homes. At the time of the study, First Baptist Church had approximately 300 members and was the largest predominantly African American church in Utah. When questioned, African American educators in Salt Lake City consistently indicated First Baptist Church as a center of the African American Utahn community.

To identify indigenous socialization practices, a participant–observer audiotaped and took notes in a total of 40 1½-hour Sunday school classes for children ages three to 16. From these materials, verbatim transcripts of Sunday school classes and descriptions of nonverbal contexts were reconstructed and analyzed in the tradition of language socialization (for example, Haight & Miller, 1993), paying particular attention to how children and adults interacted—for example, the ways in which adults prompted and elaborated on children's stories.

To understand the cultural meanings of socialization practices, interviews were conducted with the adults in charge of Sunday school: the pastor, the Sunday school superintendent, and four Sunday school teachers. Each informant was formally interviewed on at least two occasions and by at least two independent interviewers. These interviews yielded nearly two hours of audiotaped recordings for each informant. In the tradition of topic-focused ethnography, the interview included both open-ended and more focused questions on spiritual socialization. From these interviews verbatim transcripts were reconstructed. These transcripts were analyzed in the tradition of interpretive psychology (see Gaskins, Miller, & Corsaro, 1992) to yield a description of major themes.

To more fully understand the cultural bases of socialization practices as well as their relationship to the larger context, other contexts were observed and described in fieldnotes and sometimes audiotaped. These included key yearly events such as vacation Bible school, monthly events such as baptisms, weekly events such as "children's story time" during regular church services, and a variety of informal social occasions. These observations served as critical checks to discipline emerging interpretations of observational and interview data.

SUMMARY OF MAJOR FINDINGS

Social Context of First Baptist Church

The African American community in Salt Lake City displays both similarities to and differences from other African American communities. African American Utahns, like African Americans in other parts of the country, experience racial discrimination in employment, housing, education, and everyday social interactions (Coleman, 1981). In addition, the overwhelming majority of African Americans in Utah also find themselves within the religious minority. In contrast to the predominantly Baptist African American community, most of the population of Utah belong to the Church of Jesus Christ of Latter-Day Saints. This Mormon community is close-knit, and members typically enjoy a variety of social and cultural programs.

The informants, as well as European Americans who are not Mormon, commented on feelings of isolation. This situation is particularly difficult for children who may feel that they routinely are left out of the after-school activities of their Mormon classmates.

The conditions of African Americans in Utah also may be unique in the extent to which they are isolated from one another daily on their jobs, at school, and in their neighborhoods. In Utah, African Americans make up 0.7 percent of the total population (Nakoryakov, 1994), and there are no predominantly African American neighborhoods. Even in the most diverse neighborhoods, people of color, including Asians, Pacific Islanders, and Hispanics, as well as African Americans, make up only 36 percent of the population (Mathews & Wright, 1994). Thus, First Baptist Church, one of the few public institutions run by and for African Americans, and relatively independent of Mormon culture and religion, is viewed by many African Americans as a haven, a center of community, and one of the few contexts in which they may interact with other African American Baptists.

Key Cultural Concepts Relevant to Children's Socialization

Adult informants expressed a number of similar beliefs relevant to children's socialization. First, every one of the informants placed the development of African American children within a social and cultural context that they viewed as negligent at best and virulently racist at worst. Every informant spontaneously reported incidences involving discrimination, and they all directly or indirectly discussed the detrimental effects of racism on children's development. Although active forms of hostile racism were described, the main forms of racism discussed in reference to children growing up in Salt Lake City today were negative expectations for African American children by European American educators in the public schools. Informants felt that racism contributed to children's feelings of inferiority and not belonging, which adversely affected their motivation in school. For example, in discussing sources of underachievement in African American children, one Sunday school teacher explained, "They excludes the black children. You know? They don't fit in. It's hard to try to fit in somewhere everybody else . . . is Mormons, and they gonna . . . put you down." In response to my probe regarding her advice to European American teachers educating African American children, she responded, "Don't be so quick to judge us. Have that patience the same way they would with their own race. If you just look at teaching a child right here in Sunday school class—I can't say, 'OK, because you're this color, and you're that color, you sit over there, and—you know—God don't love you, and God love you.'"

Second, church was described by all the informants as a haven in which children could learn about their heritage from other African Americans who valued and nurtured them. Through the church, children are exposed to the hopeful, loving, and egalitarian message of the Christian gospels. In commenting on her own experiences as a child at church, one teacher described her relationship with adult members: "I gathered my spirit from them. I saw what they did. I saw them pray. I saw what they were going through. I saw them read the Bible. I saw them sing, and they would sing joyously."

Third, among the informants, spirituality is perceived as protective. It is a lifeline, most important to eternal life through belief in Jesus, but it is also a healthy way of coping with the trials of everyday life. The observation of one teacher that "the reason that most blacks survive is because of religion" was echoed by others in more than one sense. "Christian" beliefs and conduct were seen by our informants as physically protective and, most important, as spiritually protective. For example, during a sermon, the pastor noted the importance of parents disciplining their young children strictly and lovingly, so that the children did not err in public and give "The Man" an opportunity to harm them. Also, as one informant commented, "you can't take hate inside of yourself" because to do so is spiritually devastating.

SOCIALIZATION PRACTICES AT FIRST BAPTIST CHURCH

Observations of Sunday school and other church contexts, as well as interviews, identified several specific beliefs and practices associated with children's socialization. Because of space constraints, this summary focuses on general patterns. As with any community, there was intracultural variation in socialization beliefs and practices. Also, as with any socialization context, not all practices necessarily were effective. This summary focuses on what I perceive to be general practices relevant to the socialization of resilience.

The following excerpt, from an audiotaped Sunday school class for eight- to 12-year-old children, illustrates several key characteristics of socialization practices at First Baptist Church.

> *Teacher:* They [the apostles] were supposed to be waiting for Jesus. Alright?... Peter got impatient and decided he was gonna go fishing.... Now I'm gonna explain this part of the story because I want you guys to put it in modern-day times as far as this lesson goes, OK? So Peter, he gets this attitude. It's like, "Look, Jesus ain't comin' back. He ain't gonna show up, you know?" So they said, "Well, we better go back and do what we been doing, right?" Which they—what were they all before they became disciples?
>
> *Class (in chorus):* Fishermen.
>
> *Teacher:* So they just decided, "OK. No more Jesus." Peter said, "No more Jesus. We ain't gonna see him again. Let's go back to being fishermen. Let's go fishing." And they were supposed to be waiting for him! They, they were being disobedient.... Then they get out there and they don't catch anything all night long, right?
>
> *Class:* Umhm.
>
> *Teacher:* Being hard headed. Being hard headed, OK? So then, finally, what happens is, Jesus finally appears to them. And,

alright, they got their—their net cast out on the left side of the boat. What did he tell them to do? Pull it in and do it on what?

Class: Right side! . . . *(They discuss the double meaning of "right side.")*

Teacher: Alright. Let's see where I'm going with this.

Class: OK! *(Laughter)*

Teacher: What—when Jesus went to the disciples because they were fishermen, he said, "I'm gonna make you fisher's of—" You know that blank? Fill in the blank. They were fisher-?

Class: Men!

Teacher: OK. But, when he recruited them—as they say in modern days—to become disciples, he said, "Instead of being fishermen, I'm going to make you fishers of !?" Say the word.

Class: Men!

Teacher: OK. Tell me what they difference between that is? OK. Fishermen, or fishers of men.

Child: Oh! One means you *cast out,* and one means using the net, right?

Teacher: Wait, wait, wait a minute! Back up now. One more time. Listen now. Listen. OK. I'm gonna throw the net in. . . . I'm a fisherman. *(Enacts fishing)* And what am I catching?

Child: Fish.

Teacher: Yeah. I'm catching fish. Right? Right?

Class: Mmm. *(Children are nodding.)*

Teacher: OK. Now I'm part of the crusade that Jesus has. Jesus has picked me and said, "You will no longer be a fisher*man,* you're gonna be a fisher of men." What am I trying to say today? Instead of catching fish, what are these disciples gonna be catching? With the word of Jesus?—People, think! If you get this you're heading in the right direction! Think! Think! He don't want them catching fish no more. What does he want them to catch?

Child 1: Holy fish?

Child 2: Catch the word of God.

Teacher: OK! *(Excited, nodding approval of child 2's response)* They're out there casting the word of God. Casting the word of God. *(Writes that on the board.)* OK. Alright. And who, who do you think would get caught with this? Not *fi—sh!* Who?

Class: Men!

First, the excerpt illustrates positive and accepting adult–child relationships. Resilience research consistently identifies positive relationships with responsible adults as a protective factor (for example, see Fraser, 1997). In our example, the teacher and children respond warmly to one another. They are very animated and accepting. At one point the teacher stumbles in her explanation, "Let's see where I'm going with this," and the children laugh and shout "OK!" In discussing socialization, both in the church and in other contexts, all adult informants stressed a positive personal relationship between adults and children in which children feel a sense of belonging and of being valued and accepted. For example, in discussing the qualities of a good teacher, no informant discussed pedagogical theory, higher education, or other intellectual characteristics. Good teachers love their children. They are sensitive to children's emotional needs and concerned about their well-being within and outside school.

Second, the excerpt also illustrates the importance attached to helping children understand the relevance of, and then apply, biblical concepts to their own lives. Adults are convinced that the lessons children learn in Sunday school are relevant to developing effective strategies for coping with stressors in their everyday lives. In our example, the teacher explicitly asked the children to relate the story to their own experiences, for example, "I want you guys to put it in modern-day times as far as this lesson goes." Although the members of First Baptist Church view the Bible as the sacred word of God, learning about the scriptures is not viewed as a passive process involving only the simple absorption of facts. Rather, the Bible is viewed as a living word, central to modern life, and each individual also must find his or her own meaning in the scriptures.

The importance of finding personal meaning in the scriptures was redundantly conveyed during interviews and observations in various contexts. For example, the teacher of the young adult Sunday school class admonished her students not to simply listen to the pastor, an individual highly respected both for his spirituality and his biblical knowledge, but to go home and read the scriptures and meditate on them for themselves.

One of the ways in which biblical concepts are personalized for children is through storytelling. In our example, the methods used by the teacher seemed to encourage the children's identification with the story. She relied on her considerable storytelling abilities, quoting the disciples in modern-day black English—for example, "So Peter, he gets this attitude. It's like, 'Look, Jesus ain't comin' back...'"—and engaging in role play as an apostle. For example, in trying to explain the metaphor "fisher of men," the teacher briefly "becomes" an apostle, "I'm gonna throw the net in.... I'm a fisherman.... Now I'm part of the crusade that Jesus has." I also observed this teacher and other teachers actually assign children roles to act out as the teacher retold the stories. For example, in retelling Judas's betrayal, this teacher instructed 10-year-old Geoffrey "You be Judas." To which Geoffrey replied, "I don't want to be that dude." And the teacher responded, "But, how do you think he felt? And how would you feel if that was you?"

Observations in other contexts revealed that the importance of teaching through stories is explicitly taught to members of First Baptist Church. For example, one of the topics of the young adult Sunday school class was teaching through stories in which Jesus's use of parables as a pedagogical tool was elaborated. Storytelling also was mentioned by informants as a unique characteristic of African American teachers.

Third, our excerpt also illustrates that children are encouraged to be actively engaged with their peers in responding to the material. For example, children are responsive as members of the class chorus during call-and-response sequences. For example, when the teacher said that they would no longer be fishermen, but that they would be fishers of —?, the class responded that they would be fishers of men. Call-and-response sequences were mentioned specifically by the pastor as educational tools that help children to speak up, in contrast to the more competitive practice in public schools of requiring children to raise their hands to be recognized individually.

A number of socialization themes complementary to and redundant of Sunday school emerged from the examination of diverse material from other church contexts. For example, activities centered in the larger church community also emphasize the relevance of spirituality to everyday life. In these contexts, however, spiritual concepts often are extended from the personal to a broader community context. For example, during the regular Sunday services, the pastor invites all the children to come to the front of the church where they are told a story, for example, a traditional African folktale. That story is then related to biblical texts. In vacation Bible school, adults discuss with children African American history and culture in relation to biblical themes. Thus, in Sunday school children may be stimulated to reflect on spiritual beliefs as they relate to themselves as individuals, whereas in the big church, they are encouraged to relate spiritual beliefs to themselves as members of a larger African American community.

DEVELOPMENT OF A SOCIAL WORK INTERVENTION: THE COMPUTER CLUB

In collaboration with leaders from First Baptist Church, we developed an intervention, informed by knowledge generated through the ethnographic study, to support the development of children's resilience. From an ecological systems perspective (Norton, in press), we shared two major concerns. First, we were concerned that the professionals supporting the development of local African American children, including educators, social workers, and health care providers, were poorly prepared to assume these responsibilities. Indeed, within the local community, helping professionals were predominantly European American, middle class, and living in highly segregated neighborhoods. We intended to provide European American students entering social work, psychology, education, and health care with meaningful, personal contact with members of the local African American community. Second, we were concerned that the linkages between the local state university and the local African American community were very weak. African American children and youths typically were not taking advantage of the resources available at the local university. For example, only rarely did college-bound African American seniors choose to attend the local university, and the university had little outreach involvement in the African

American community. We hoped that by supporting relationships between members of the university and church communities, linkages between these communities would be strengthened.

The context of our intervention was the "Computer Club." Consistent with ethnographic materials generated in other African American communities (Williams, 1994), our informants both prioritized educational achievement and identified school as problematic for African American children. In particular, the pastor and other adults at First Baptist Church viewed the development of children's computer literacy as a specific area of need, and learning more about computers as an opportunity that children and families would embrace. Indeed, during the final three years of the ethnographic fieldwork, the Computer Club was used regularly by approximately 50 children ages three to 18. Although the focal activities of the Computer Club were educational computer games, university student mentors engaged children in a variety of activities, including picnics, parties, outdoor games, field trips to the local university, and the production of several computer-generated art shows. Students and children also participated together in a variety of church-sponsored activities, including African dance and the children's gospel choir. University students facilitated children's acquisition of basic computer literacy skills and their positive learning experiences, but more important, students and children developed relationships in which perspectives and experiences were shared.

An understanding of indigenous socialization beliefs and practices informed the development of the Computer Club at all levels. Perhaps most significant, our ethnographic materials informed our choices of how to conduct the intervention. Consistent with other reports (for example, Boykin, 1994; Schiele, 1996), our informants emphasized the centrality of cooperative social relationships. Indeed, positive adult–child relationships were emphasized as a prerequisite to learning. Thus, in supervising our university student mentors, we emphasized warm rather than aloof "professional" relationships, and we worked with children within small, cooperative groups. We sought out materials allowing cooperation rather than competition among children (for example, *Oregon Trail*, a game in which several pioneers attempt to reach Oregon against natural odds, was very popular) and, of course, materials emphasizing spiritual themes (for example, the computer game *Bible Trivia*). In addition, consistent with other reports (for example, Gates, 1989; Heath, 1983; Williams, 1994), storytelling emerged as an important tradition within this African American community. Thus, we encouraged mentors to share their own educational experiences with children, as well as eliciting such stories from children.

CONCLUSION

Knowledge of human behavior in cultural context, including the ways in which adults socialize resilience, is the source from which all ethnic-sensitive social work practice emerges. Ethnographic research at First Baptist Church revealed a variety of beliefs and socialization practices consistent with previous work in other African American communities, including the importance of church as a center of community (for example, Frazier, 1988) and Sunday school as a context for children's socialization (Mitchell, 1986), the values of spirituality and interdependent relationships (for example, Boykin, 1994; Schiele, 1996), and the centrality of storytelling (Gates, 1989; Heath, 1983; Williams, 1994). Ethnographic research also revealed a variety of other socialization practices emerging from the unique social and historical context of First Baptist Church, including tensions between Baptist and Mormon religious beliefs. The ability of social workers to develop knowledge of cultural beliefs and practices relevant both to African American communities in general and to the unique African American communities in which they are practicing is critical to the development of ethnic-sensitive social work interventions such as the Computer Club.

REFERENCES

Angelou, M. (1969). *I know why the caged bird sings*. New York: Random House.

Boykin, W. (1994). Harvesting talent and culture: African American children and educational reform. In R. Rossi (Ed.), *Schools and students at risk: Context and framework for positive change* (pp. 116–138). New York: Teachers College Press.

Brown, D. R., & Gary, L. E. (1991). Religious socialization and educational attainment among African Americans: An empirical assessment. *Journal of Negro Education, 3*, 411–426.

Bullis, R. (1996). *Spirituality in social work practice*. Washington, DC: Taylor & Francis.

Coleman, R. (1981). Blacks in Utah history: An unknown legacy. In H. Z. Papanikolas (Ed.), *The peoples of Utah* (pp. 115–140). Salt Lake City: Utah State Historical Society.

Coles, R. (1990). *The spiritual life of children*. Boston: Houghton Mifflin.

Comer, J. (1988). *Maggie's American dream: The life and times of a black family*. New York: Plume.

Devore, W., & Schlesinger, E. (1996). *Ethnic-sensitive social work practice* (4th ed.). Boston: Allyn & Bacon.

Ellison, C. (1993). Religious involvement and self-perception among black Americans. *Social Forces, 71*, 1027–1055.

Franklin, J. (1980). *From slavery to freedom: A history of Negro Americans* (5th ed.). New York: Alfred A. Knopf.

Fraser, M. (Ed.). (1997). *Risk and resilience in childhood: An ecological perspective*. Washington, DC: NASW Press.

Frazier, E. F. (1988). *The Negro church in America*. New York: Schocken Books.

Gaskins, S., Miller, P., & Corsaro, W. (1992). Theoretical and methodological perspectives in the interpretive study of children. In W. Corsaro & P. Miller, (Eds.), *Interpretive approaches to children's socialization* (New Directions in Child Development, Series No. CD 58). San Francisco: Jossey-Bass.

Gates, H. L. (1989). Introduction. In L. Goss & M. E. Barnes (Eds.), *Talk that talk: An anthology of African American storytelling* (pp. 15–19). New York: Simon & Schuster.

Haight, W. (1998). *"Gathering the spirit": Children's spiritual socialization within an African American church*. Unpublished manuscript.

Haight, W., & Miller, P. (1993). *Pretending at home: Early development in a sociocultural context*. Albany: SUNY Press.

Hale-Benson, J. (1987, December 8–11). *The transmission of faith to young black children*. Paper presented at the Conference on Faith Development in Early Childhood, Henderson, NC.

Heath, S. (1983). *Ways with words: Language, life, and work in communities and classrooms*. Cambridge, England: Cambridge University Press.

Hill-Lubin, M. A. (1991). The African American grandmother in autobiographical works by Frederick Douglass, Langston Hughes, and Maya Angelou. *International Journal of Aging and Human Development, 33*, 173–185.

Maluccio, A. (1995). Children: Direct practice. In R. L. Edwards (Ed.-in-Chief), *Encyclopedia of social work* (19th ed., Vol. I, pp. 442–447). Washington, DC: NASW Press.

Masten, A., Best, K., & Garmesy, N. (1990). Resilience and development: Contributions from the study of children who overcome adversity. *Development and Psychopathology, 2*, 425–444.

Mathews, A., & Wright, L. (1994, March 20). Utah's people of color: The east-west wall hasn't fallen in racially divided S.L. valley. *Salt Lake Tribune*, p. A1.

McRoy, R. G. (1995). Qualitative research. In R. L. Edwards (Ed.-in-Chief), *Encyclopedia of social work* (19th ed., Vol. III, pp. 2009–2015). Washington, DC: NASW Press.

Mitchell, E. P. (1986). Oral tradition: Legacy of faith for the black church. *Religious Education, 81*, 93–112.

Nakoryakov, M. (1994, April 22). Utah population, ethnic diversity to keep climbing through 2020. *Salt Lake Tribune*, p. D1.

Norton, D. (in press). *Plurality and ecology: Beyond the dual perspective*. Alexandria, VA: Council on Social Work Education.

Ogbu, J. U. (1985). A cultural ecology of competence among inner-city blacks. In M. Spencer, G. Brookins, & W. Allen (Eds.), *Beginnings: The social and affective development of black children*. Hillsdale, NJ: Lawrence Erlbaum.

Oser, F. (1991). The development of religious judgment [Monograph]. *New Directions in Child Development, 52*, 5–26.

Schiele, J. (1996). Afrocentricity: An emerging paradigm in social work practice. *Social Work, 41*, 284–294.

Seaborn-Thompson, M., & Ensminger, M. E. (1989). Psychological well-being among mothers with school age children: Evolving family structures. *Social Forces, 67*, 715–730.

Thornton, S., & Garrett, K. (1995). Ethnography as a bridge to multicultural practice. *Journal of Social Work Education, 31*, 67–74.

Werner, E. (1990). Protective factors and individual resilience. In S. Meisels & J. Shonkoff (Eds.), *Handbook of early childhood intervention* (pp. 97–116). New York: Cambridge University Press.

Williams, K. (1994). *The socialization of literacy in black middle-class families*. Unpublished doctoral dissertation, University of Chicago.

Zimmerman, M. A., & Maton, K. I. (1992). Life-style and substance use among male African American urban adolescents: A cluster analytic approach. *American Journal of Community Psychology, 20*, 121–138.

This study was generously supported by the National Academy of Education. The author thanks Pallassana Balgopal, David Dupper, Jill Kagle, and John Poertner for their helpful comments.

Part V

HEALTH

20 Politically Correct or Culturally Competent?

Dennis L. Poole

I am writing this in Chalma, Mexico. Just a few feet from the tiny restaurant where I sit flows a steady stream of people down the steep pathway to the *Sancturario de Señor de Chalma*. Millions of pilgrims flock to this important Catholic shrine every year. They journey to give thanks to *Señor de Chalma*, to fulfill vows previously made, or to ask for divine favor in the case of illness or other problems.

Somewhere along the pathway they will rub shoulders with social work students from the United States. These students have come to Chalma for a different purpose. They are taking a two-week cultural immersion course in Mexico, which I lead. I hesitate to use the word "teach," because I am learning as well. We are living with Mexican families, learning the Spanish language, visiting health and social services providers, and touring important cultural sites. In the case of Chalma, we have come to observe firsthand the central role of religion in Mexican culture, especially among rural Mexicans, who have a high migratory tradition to the United States. We recognize the need for greater competence in our efforts to serve this population.

This is the second year I've brought students to Mexico. My guess is that this year's group will leave the country as the other one did—more informed, less biased, and more skilled in their work with people of Mexican heritage. At the same time, I recognize that the challenges that these students face in social work practice extend beyond any one cultural group. This brief respite in Chalma gives me time to reflect on what it is I am trying to accomplish here and how I can best prepare my students for competent practice in our increasingly pluralistic society.

POLITICAL CORRECTNESS

This much is clear. I do not want my students to be politically correct. "Political correctness," Drucker (1998) observes, "is a purely totalitarian concept" (p. 380). Stalinists first made use of the term in the late 1930s and early 1940s. They used intimidation, character assassination, and denial of freedom of thought and speech to suppress all but the "party line." Current use of the term is different. Political groups use political correctness to denigrate people who have a progressive

This chapter was originally published in the August 1998 issue of *Health & Social Work*, Vol. 23, pp. 163–166.

orthodoxy on issues involving race, gender, sexual orientation, and the rights of marginalized people.

I object to any form of political correctness—Left or Right—that attempts to limit deep and thoughtful examination of complex cultural issues. Having been in social work education for many years, I know how tempting it is for faculty to make their students politically correct when students do not conform to ideological fashion. Students become reticent at speaking out or taking positions on these issues for fear of alienating faculty or offending their colleagues.

Take religion, for example. In the culture of science, complex cultural issues involving spirituality seldom receive adequate attention in social work education. This is odd. Many of the most thoughtful men and women of the world believe in divine providence. And most people served by social workers believe that spirituality affects their health and well-being. Still, it is not politically correct to discuss—with openness and intelligence—issues of spirituality in social work education.

Chalma reminds me of this fact. Mountain water collects in a deep basin beside the *Sanctuario de Señor de Chalma*. Pilgrims believe this water is holy and miraculous. Last year more than half of my students—20 in all—placed their hands or feet in the basin. One stripped to his shorts, then dove headfirst into the frigid water. Mexican pilgrims watched in amazement. Perhaps this student wanted healing head to toe, body and soul.

I later asked this group of students two questions: Is spirituality a major concern in your life? Have faculty ever asked you to discuss your personal spirituality in class? Nearly all of the students answered "yes" to the first question and "no" to the second one. They said that they avoided sharing spiritual issues in the classroom because faculty and students might ridicule or harass them for their views. How unfortunate! How can social workers provide culturally competent services in, say, matters of death and dying without having first examined their own spiritual views on these matters, not to mention those of their clients?

There are other complex cultural issues related to ethnicity, gender, and sexual orientation. These, too, need to be examined openly, allowing room for diversity of viewpoints. Open and free debate, after all, is one of the best antidotes to oppression, discrimination, and stereotyping. It is also our nation's best hope for building a "viable cultural agenda" (Berger, 1998). Political correctness undervalues human variety; closes the American mind; and drives people into separate, hostile communities.

CULTURALLY COMPETENT

Providing an open, vibrant, and intellectually challenging atmosphere for my students is the first challenge. The second is equipping them for culturally competent practice. Culturally competent professionals recognize similarities and differences in the values, norms, customs, history, and institutions of groups of people that vary by ethnicity, gender, religion, and sexual orientation. They recognize sources of comfort and discomfort between themselves and clients of similar or different cultural backgrounds. They understand the impact of discrimination, oppression, and stereotyping on practice. They recognize their own biases toward or against certain cultural groups. And they rely on scientific evidence and moral reasoning to work effectively in cross-cultural situations.

Chalma reminds me of cultural incompetence in the field of health. Even though people of Mexican heritage represent one of the fastest growing groups in the United States, the U.S. health care system has done little to adapt to this group's cultural beliefs, rituals, and pathways of care, which is one reason why this population underutilizes professional health services in the United States (Estrada, Trevino, & Ray, 1990; Flaskerud & Calvillo, 1991; Mikhail, 1994; Sue, Chun, & Gee, 1995).

To help remedy the situation, my students need to be culturally competent in at least five areas. The first is knowledge. They need to understand the relationship between what they are observing now in Chalma—acts of faith, sacrifice, penance, and devotion to God, the Virgin, and the saints—and the perceived health of many Mexicans that migrate to the United States. They need to know the powerful influence of the family and social networks on health care behavior (Flaskerud & Calvillo, 1991; Frenks, Campbell, & Shields, 1992) and the roles that traditional healers (for example, *curanderos, herbalistas,* and *inyeccionistas*) play in Mexican pathways to care (Chavez, 1984; Lozano-Applewhite, 1995; Mas-Condes & Caraveo, 1991; Salgado de Synder, de Jesus Diaz-Perez, & Bautista, 1998; Slesinger & Richards, 1981).

Cultural competence also requires knowledge of the varied elements within the larger cultural matrix of a society and those of other societies. For example, it is important for my students to know that what they are observing today in Chalma is not representative of all Mexicans, that health beliefs and practices vary greatly among people of different social strata in Mexico (Diaz-Guerrero, 1995). It is equally important for them to understand similarities and differences in the ethnopsychology of Mexicans and North Americans. According to Diaz-Guerrero and Szalay (1993), the concept of self among Mexicans is based on a culture of love, whereas that of North Americans is based on a culture of power.

The second area of cultural competence is skill. My students need to be able to make adjustments to work effectively in cross-cultural situations. One adjustment is knowing how to intervene early in a client's normal pathway to care. Salgado de Synder and her colleagues (1998) reported that the typical pathway to mental health care for rural Mexicans with a high migratory tradition to the United States proceeds from self-care ⇒ social networks ⇒ informal services ⇒ physicians ⇒ specialists. Few make it to physicians and specialists, except in emergency situations. Skilled social workers can help remedy the situation by developing partnerships with social networks and traditional healers along the person's normal pathway to care.

Adjustments in diagnosis and treatment are needed as well. Cultural biases in the interpretation of psychosocial functioning can result in conflicting and oppressive treatment modalities. Given the importance of *la familia* in Mexican culture, involving extended family in counseling and treatment can improve clinical outcomes. Genograms can be helpful as well; they show the client and family that the social worker respects tradition. Tying rituals and spiritual aspects to treatment plans also can improve clinical outcomes and keep people in treatment (Fernando, 1995; Rosado & Elias, 1993).

My students also need cultural competence in the area of policy. Although scholars have only begun to explore the policy dimension of culturally competent practice, we know that hiring staff that can respond effectively to client culture is critical. Hispanic and bilingual staff that believe in natural support providers and have the willingness to accept these providers as peers are usually most helpful. Using natural helpers and traditional healers to train professional staff in culturally competent practice can be helpful as well (Fernando, 1995; Rosado & Elias, 1993).

Moreover, for social workers and other professionals to form partnerships with natural support systems, agency policy must allow them to leave their offices and enter the great "out-thereness" of the community. This is no small challenge under conditions of managed care. Nevertheless, some progress is being made toward the establishment of formal and informal partnerships in the social networks and informal service providers of different cultural groups (Daley & Wong, 1994; Delgado, 1997; Poole & Van Hook, 1997).

Fourth, it is clear that my students need to be culturally competent in research, a difficult area to address in social work education. Despite the long history of recommendations concerning cultural competencies and standards in the service professions, little attention has been given to the development of sound and conceptually anchored instrumentation for evaluating cultural competence (Ponterotto, Rieger, Barrett, & Sparks, 1994). Nevertheless, some helpful instruments are available to my students, including the checklist for cultural competence in agencies developed by Dana, Behn, and Gonwa (1992). Other instruments include the Cultural Self-Efficacy Scale (Bernal & Froman, 1993) and the Multi-Cultural Awareness, Knowledge, and Skills Survey (D'Andrea, Daniels, & Heck, 1991). Students in clinical practice also can benefit from the Cross-Cultural Counseling Inventory–Revised (LaFromboise, Coleman, & Hernandez, 1991) and the Multicultural Counseling Inventory (Sodowsky, Taffe, Gutkin, & Wise, 1994).

The fifth area of cultural competence relates to values. Fortunately, my students can turn to the *NASW Code of Ethics* (NASW, 1996) for help in this area. The *Code* offers several useful guidelines and standards that directly or indirectly deal with culturally competent practice.

But personal judgment is needed as well. It is often said that culturally competent practitioners "accept and value" cultural differences. But this definition of cultural competence is too broad, too politically correct. It falls into the camp of cultural relativism. There are good and bad traits in every culture. I want to encourage my students to lean toward tolerance but not to accept or value cultural traits that harm or oppress people. Chalma should help them recognize the difference.

REFERENCES

Berger, P. L. (1998). The culture of liberty: An agenda—Issues that arouse cultural conflicts. *Society, 35,* 407–416.

Bernal, H., & Froman, R. (1993). Influences on the cultural self-efficacy of community health nurses. *Journal of Transcultural Nursing, 4,* 24–31.

Chavez, L. R. (1984). Doctors, curanderos, and brujas: Health care delivery and Mexican immigrants in San Diego. *Medical Anthropology Quarterly, 15,* 31–37.

Daley, J. M., & Wong, P. (1994). Community development within emerging ethnic communities. *Journal of Community Practice, 1,* 9–24.

Dana, R. H., Behn, J. D., & Gonwa, T. (1992). A checklist for the examination of cultural competence in social service agencies. *Research on Social Work Practice, 2,* 220–233.

D'Andrea, M., Daniels, J., & Heck, R. (1991). Evaluating the impact of multicultural training. *Journal of Counseling and Development, 70,* 143–150.

Delgado, M. (1997). Making the case for culturally appropriate community services: Puerto Rican elders and their caregivers. *Health & Social Work, 22,* 246–256.

Diaz-Guerrero, R. (1995). Origins and development of Mexican ethnopsychology. *World Psychology, 1,* 49–67.

Diaz-Guerrero, R., & Szalay, L. B. (1993). *El mundo subjetivo de Mexicanos y Norteamericanos* [The subjective world of Mexicans and North Americans]. Mexico, DF: Trillas.

Drucker, P. F. (1998). Political correctness and American academe. *Society, 35,* 380–385.

Estrada, S. L., Trevino, F. M., & Ray, L. A. (1990). Health care utilization barriers among Mexican Americans: Evidence from HHANES 1982–84. *American Journal of Public Health, 18,* 27–31.

Fernando, S. (Ed.). (1995). *Mental health in a multi-ethnic society: A multidisciplinary handbook.* New York: Routledge.

Flaskerud, J. H., & Calvillo, E. R. (1991). Beliefs about AIDS, health, and illness among low-income Latina women. *Research in Nursing and Health, 14,* 431–438.

Frenks, P., Campbell, T. L., & Shields, C. G. (1992). Social relationships and health: The relative roles of family functioning and social support. *Social Science and Medicine, 34,* 779–788.

LaFromboise, T. D., Coleman, H., & Hernandez, A. (1991). Development and factor structure of the Cross-Cultural Counseling Inventory–Revised. *Professional Psychology: Research and Practice, 22,* 380–388.

Lozano-Applewhite, S. (1995). *Curanderismo:* Demystifying the health beliefs and practices of elderly Mexican Americans. *Health & Social Work, 20,* 247–253.

Mas-Condes, C., & Caraveo, J. (1991). La medicina folklorica: Un estudio sobre la salud mental [Folkloric medicine: A study of mental health]. *Revista Interamericana de Psicologia, 25,* 147–160.

Mikhail, B. I. (1994). Hispanic mothers' beliefs and practices regarding selected children's health problems. *Western Journal of Nursing Research, 16,* 623–638.

National Association of Social Workers. (1996). *NASW code of ethics*. Washington, DC: Author.

Ponterotto, J. G., Rieger, B. P., Barrett, A., & Sparks, R. (1994). Assessing multicultural counseling competence: A review of the instrumentation. *Journal of Counseling and Development, 72*, 316–322.

Poole, D. L., & Van Hook, M. (1997). Retooling for community health partnerships in primary care and prevention [Editorial]. *Health & Social Work, 22*, 2–5.

Rosado, J. W., & Elias, M. J. (1993). Ecological and psychocultural mediators in the delivery of services for Cuban, culturally diverse Hispanic clients. *Professional Psychology: Research and Practice, 24*, 450–459.

Salgado de Synder, V. N., de Jesus Diaz-Perez, M., & Bautista, E. M. (1998). *Pathways to mental health services among inhabitants of a Mexican village with high migratory tradition to the United States.* Unpublished manuscript, Mexico Institute of Psychiatry, Mexico, DF.

Slesinger, D. P., & Richards, M. (1981). Folk and clinical medical utilization patterns among Mejicano migrant farmworkers. *Hispanic Journal of Behavioral Sciences, 3*, 59–73.

Sodowsky, G. R., Taffe, R. C., Gutkin, T. B., & Wise, S. L. (1994). Development of the Multicultural Counseling Inventory: A self-report measure of multicultural competencies. *Journal of Counseling Psychology, 41*, 137–148.

Sue, S., Chun, C. A., & Gee, K. (1995). Ethnic minority intervention and treatment research. In J. F. Aponte, R. Y. Rivers, & J. Wohl (Eds.), *Psychological interventions and cultural diversity* (pp. 266–282). Needham Heights, MA: Allyn & Bacon.

Alternative Health Practices in Ethnically Diverse Rural Areas:
A Collaborative Research Project

Gerald W. Vest, John Ronnau,
Belinda R. Lopez, and Gloria Gonzales

Concern is growing about the nationwide increase in diabetes and in stress, obesity, and hypertension, which have been cited as contributing factors. In addition, it is believed that stress plays a significant role in all illness. Skillful touch, long overlooked by health care practitioners, has been documented by several research institutions as promoting the healing process (Eidelman, 1990).

Poor diabetic health status among poor populations and people of color has been attributed to three factors (Auslander, Anderson, Bubb, Jung, & Santiago, 1990). First, little preventive care is available. Second, there is little knowledge of proper management among those with the disease. Third, few support networks are available for individuals with diabetes and their families.

This chapter describes a study of the impact of alternative medicine and health practices on the physical symptoms of people with diabetes and their families. Traditional medical treatment, as well as holistic health approaches including acupressure, breathing techniques, and lifestyle training, were provided to the target group and their families.

METHOD

Setting

An innovative and collaborative health project was implemented by a university social work health promotion team and a rural medical clinic in response to the high incidence of diabetes among Mexican Americans in southern New Mexico. This clinic is one of four facilities in a private, nonprofit health corporation partially funded by the U.S. Department of Health and Human Services and located in southern New Mexico less than 50 miles from the Mexican border. The organization's mission is to promote the health and well-being of people in rural communities through the cost-effective use of available resources to provide comprehensive, family-centered, culturally

This chapter was originally published in the May 1997 issue of *Health & Social Work*, Vol. 22, pp. 95–100.

appropriate health and human services in partnership with the community served (La Clinica de Familia, 1992).

At the time of the study (1994), there were 10,000 registered consumers in the corporation's service area, and 75 percent were of Mexican descent. New Mexico is one of the most culturally diverse states in the nation; 50 percent of the population is white, 9 percent is Native American, 2 percent is African American, and 38 percent is Hispanic American (Williams, 1986). The southern New Mexico county served by the health clinic where this research was carried out is similarly diverse. In addition to being only a few miles from Mexico, 52 percent of the county's population is Hispanic (Williams, 1986). Five hundred low-income Hispanic consumers are diagnosed with diabetes. Many of these individuals suffer from stress and hypertension, which greatly increase the risk of gradual damage to small blood vessels, resulting in impaired circulation. Drugs are helpful only to a limited degree. Research indicates that certain relaxation techniques increase the blood's circulation. Meeting the needs of this group is the motivating factor for the clinic's interest in researching alternative methods for controlling this disease.

Research Design

This exploratory study used a pre-experimental one-group, pretest–posttest design (Cook & Campbell, 1979). The study was designed to answer the question, In what ways does the alternative health practice known as the "15-Minute Stressout Program" (Vest, 1995) affect people diagnosed with diabetes?

Two social work students, one graduate level and one bachelor's level, were chosen to jointly conduct this pilot research study at health clinics in San Miguel, New Mexico. To initiate this research project, holistic health practices were introduced to staff and consumers from the various clinics. Education provided to the staff and consumers included skillful and respectful touch, instruction in the art of acupressure and breathing techniques, and lifestyle training including stress management.

Independent Variable: The 15-Minute Stressout Program. Since 1992 the 15-Minute Stressout Program has been used for health promotion and prevention on university campuses, in public schools, and in several major regional industries (for example, NASA, the White Sands Test Facility, a U.S. Army base) in numerous states and internationally (Israel, Mexico) (Vest, 1983; Vest & Ronnau, 1993). Trained volunteers have administered more than 4,000 "Stressouts" free of charge. A videotape was produced to demonstrate this stress management approach (Vest, 1995). However, although much anecdotal information has been accumulated regarding the benefits of the program, no formal evaluations have been conducted. This exploratory research is a first step toward assessing the impact of this innovative alternative health practice (Vest, 1983; Vest & Ronnau,1993).

The use of touch for promoting health, wellness, and disease prevention is an ancient approach to medicine that was introduced over 2,000 years ago in China. According to Eisenberg (1993), "Millions of Americans are already using massage, meditation, acupuncture, and herbal remedies of all kinds, without their doctors' recommendations" (p. 306). These alternative health practices are used not only for stress reduction but also for relief of pain, heart disease, anxiety, and inability to sleep. Furthermore, in his dialogue with Bill Moyers in *Healing and the Mind*, Eisenberg suggested that in the Chinese culture, it is believed that how you live ultimately influences your health: "It's not just diet or exercise; it's also a spiritual or emotional balance that comes from the way you treat people and the way you treat yourself. And since that's the basis of their culture, it spills over into their medicine" (p. 308).

Kabat-Zinn (1990) described the use of a whole range of holistic Eastern and Western interventions to promote health and restore well-being in a program of the stress reduction clinic at the University of Massachusetts Medical Center. Patients' pain and symptoms diminished as they learned to be mindful and to maintain an "awareness of the breath," commonly referred to as "meditation":

> One of the most healing things you can do for your body during the day is to use your breath periodically to penetrate the pain and help it to soften in the same way that we use it in the body scan. . . . You can do this by consciously directing your breath in to the painful region, feeling it as it moves into your back and then visualizing the pain softening and dissolving as you relax and let go into each outbreath. (p. 303)

Not unlike the experience of mindfulness, the 15-Minute Stressout Program incorporates the use of acupressure with the awareness of the breath by both giver and receiver. The vitality of the breath connected to the power of touch produces a relaxation response that helps patients and others maintain a balance of body, mind, and emotions.

Learning to appropriately touch is rarely, if ever, a subject for discussion in the home, school, medical setting, or workplace. Professional social workers and other allied health professionals traditionally establish physical boundaries that limit opportunities for participants to learn effective touch in fostering and nurturing relationships. Yet many parents, social workers, and teachers know that a loving touch produces a healing response to a child's physical, mental, or emotional distress.

Obviously, there are serious considerations for being circumspect and skillful in offering touch as a conscious intervention in the workplace or in a family environment. Guidelines for the safe use of touch include

- providing the option for participants to self-administer the program
- having participants sign a release of liability form

- receiving permission to touch and reminding participants that contact is always in safe areas
- having witnesses or partners present
- teaching the activity to others so that they can be the givers of the Stressout
- encouraging participants to use the teaching video and study guide (Vest, 1995) if the worker chooses not to make physical contact.

Skillful, appropriate, and safe touch can be introduced as a means for teaching physical communication as a respectful alternative to violence and stress. Social workers are professionally trained to holistically assess and improve their clients' health, to enable their clients to provide self-care to prevent impairment, and to include the whole family in their use of communication, including touch.

In the 15-Minute Stressout Program (Vest, 1995),

- The giver and the receiver maintain a focus on the breath throughout the experience of the touch so that emotions are balanced and empathy is sustained.
- The giver applies a systematic process of touch that includes several techniques that remain within safe boundaries: feathering the back, shoulders, and arms; squeezing the arm muscles; stretching and spreading the hands; and gripping the wrists and fingers.
- The giver applies pressure-point massage or acupressure to selected points on the hands, shoulders, back, neck, and head.

Use of this intervention involves an important assumption related to holistic health: The improved health of one member of a family can be an improvement for the entire family. Thomas Delbanco, head of the Picker/Commonwealth Program for Patient-Centered Care in Boston, recognized that "families can interfere with medicine or they can be the medicine. . . . Respecting and facilitating family bonds may be more crucial to a patient's survival than the latest diagnostic procedure or therapeutic innovation" (Delbanco, 1993, p. 4). Kelly (1985) identified nine assumptions or variables related to family preservation and holistic health practice values:

1. People who live together influence each other's health.
2. The concepts of holistic health can be used both to evaluate and to improve the quality of family wellness.
3. The quality of health of the family as a whole tends to indicate the general quality of the health of its members.
4. Some family members (adults) have more responsibility for family wellness than other members (children), but this difference is merely relative within the responsibility of the family as a whole.
5. Children need wellness supervision and education.
6. A member who is in poor health depresses the quality of health for the family as a whole.

7. To recover health, a person needs the cooperation and support of the family.
8. The various elements that make up family life affect both individual and family wellness.
9. Family health is an ongoing process that changes as the members change and that fluctuates with environmental pressures. (p. 295)

Dependent Variables. The three dependent variables assessed in this study were stability of metabolic control, persistence of physical symptoms, and self-perception of well-being. Fasting blood sugar and random blood sugar were used to assess stability of metabolic control. Fasting blood sugar was measured pre- and postintervention during the first and final sessions. Random blood sugar was assessed at the outset of each treatment session. It was measured both pre- and postintervention during sessions 2, 4, and 6.

Persistence of physical symptoms was assessed using the Dartmouth COOP Charts (Nelson et al., 1987). The COOP Charts were developed as practical and easy-to-administer measures of health and functioning. The charts are designed in a clear and concise manner and include "a nontechnical title, a straightforward question referring to the past month, and five response choices. Each response is illustrated with a drawing that graphically represents the equivalent level of a five-point ordinal scale. High scores always represent unfavorable scores on the measure" (Nelson et al., 1987, p. 565). The three COOP charts used to assess persistence of physical symptoms in this study were Physical Fitness, Level of Pain, and Change in Health Status. The three charts were administered at the beginning of each treatment session.

The participants' perceptions of well-being were assessed using three sets of data collection tools. The first of these were three COOP charts—Quality of Life, Daily Activities, and Feelings—that were administered at the outset of each session. Second, the team administered focused, open-ended postintervention interviews. The interviews were initiated by two questions: (1) In what way has this experience changed the way you feel about yourself? and (2) Will your health habits change because of this experience? The respondents were encouraged to provide additional comments.

In addition, the "Stressout Survey" (Vest & Ronnau, 1993) was administered postintervention. This survey comprises four sections: individual benefits, family and friends, work environment, and additional comments. Each of the sections except the last lists potential benefits of the intervention and asks the respondents to check yes, no, or not applicable.

Population

The incidence of diabetes is rising at an alarming rate, particularly among Hispanics, for whom diabetes borders on epidemic proportions. This overrepresentation of diabetes in one population is disturbing to the medical community. National, state, and local statistics (De La Rosa, 1989) concerning diabetes suggest that

- The incidence of diabetes is more than three times higher in Hispanics than in non-Hispanic populations.
- Low-income Hispanic women have a prevalence of diabetes four times higher than the total Hispanic population.
- The incidence of diabetes among low-income Hispanic women may be caused by poor diet and eating habits.

Local public health clinics such as La Clinica provide diabetic health care to a majority of Hispanic families.

Sample

The challenges researchers face in recruiting participants in innovative health care projects are numerous. It is human nature to be hesitant about offering oneself for experimentation. The challenges were even more daunting in this evaluation research project; the rural, traditional, first- and second-generation Hispanic American people who used clinics services were hesitant to participate in a project carried out by "outsiders." For these reasons, the sample size is small, although useful for an exploratory study. The respondents' participation is a testament to their trust in clinic staff and the sincerity of the researchers.

Forty-six announcements were mailed out to randomly selected patients with diabetes. These announcements described the intervention and the project as a collaborative effort with a land grant university and rural health clinics. The research team explained that they would follow up by telephone during the next week to find out if the patients would be interested in participating in the six-week project. Forty-one telephone contacts were made. Seventeen consumers with diabetes were scheduled to start their six weekly sessions. Out of the 17, 12 kept their appointments. Six participants completed all six sessions (five women and one man), four completed five sessions, and two completed four sessions.

RESULTS

The average score on the initial random blood glucose pretest was 214. The average final posttest score was 191. The average pretest score for sessions 2, 4, and 6 was 188. The posttest scores for those same sessions averaged 172.

On average, fasting blood sugar pre-to-post results dropped from 170 to 154 points. Seven of the 12 participants experienced a drop in values; five increased. The greatest drop was 284 points (385 to 101). The largest increase was 95 (212 to 307).

Persistence of Physical Symptoms

Physical Fitness, Level of Pain, and Change in Health Status COOP charts all registered a drop in average scores across participants from session 1 to session 6. Although interesting, no claim is made of statistical significance. A pre-to-post change score of 2 or more is considered noteworthy. The scores of most respondents fluctuated, at most, up or down one to two points per session, with some notable exceptions. One participant dropped three points on the Physical Fitness chart. The Pain chart registered the highest number of notable change scores. Four participants dropped between four and three points. On the Change in Health Status chart, three participants dropped their scores two to three points. It should be noted that two of the charts, Physical Fitness and Change in Health Status, each registered one participant whose pre-to-post scores increased by two points.

Self-Perception of Well-Being

The Quality of Life and Daily Activities charts reflected a slight pre-to-post drop in average scores across participants. A slight rise in average scores occurred on the Feelings chart. One participant registered a notable (two points) increase in scores on both the Feelings and Quality of Life charts. The qualitative measures reflected the most dramatic impact of the intervention.

Table 21-1 shows the number of participants who reported experiencing each of the benefits listed on the Stressout Survey. Most of the participants reported tangible benefits from the intervention. Although the research methodology does not rule out intervening

Table 21-1

Number of Participants Who Reported Experiencing Each of the Benefits Listed on the 15-Minute Stressout Program Survey

Benefit	Yes	No	NA
Individual			
Anxiety reduced	12	0	0
Improved sleeping habits	12	0	0
Asthma attacks reduced	2	0	10
Migraine and sinus headaches relieved	7	1	4
Reduced swelling in joints	8	0	4
Improved breathing	12	0	0
Less anger	12	0	0
More at ease with self and others	12	0	0
More relaxed	12	0	0
Family and friends			
Improved relationship with spouse or significant other	11	0	1
Improved relationship with children and friends	12	0	0
Work environment			
Reduced stress	12	0	0
More positive about work	12	0	0
Increased creativity and productivity	11	1	0

NOTE: NA = not applicable.

variables as possible explanations, it is noteworthy that the participants indicated such dramatic effects.

In response to the question, "In what way has this experience
changed the way you feel about yourself?" several respondents expressed emotional relief—that is, less anger, depression, and anxiety
and higher levels of tranquility, energy, and vitality. Others commented on the physical aspects of the experience—that is, less pain and the
lessening of arthritic symptoms. The participants were also asked,
"Will your health habits change because of this experience?" Several
reported walking and exercising more as a result of less pain, and
others spoke of plans to continue exercises, massage, and diet.

Limitations

The limitations of quasi-experimental designs, and especially one-
group pretest–posttest designs, are numerous (Cook & Campbell,
1979). The validity and reliability threats to this study are many,
prominent among them the potential for interference of intervening
variables. The method did not allow us to claim that the intervention
alone caused the benefits listed. The quantitative results are, overall,
not remarkable, and no claim of statistical significance is made. These
limitations notwithstanding, the authors believe there is sufficient evidence to suggest that this alternative health practice holds promise
for this population and warrants further study.

CONCLUSION

Cousins (1981) observed, "I have learned never to underestimate the
capacity of the human mind and body to regenerate—even when the
prospects seem most wretched" (p. 48). The results of this research
project support the need to integrate holistic health concepts and
practices into rural area health care systems. Questions and insights
with patients who have diabetes and other consumers have been
generated to justify further and more extensive studies.

The practice methods designed for this project will be further tested for their efficacy with a diverse population and a variety of health
settings. This project has already made a significant contribution to
collaborative relationships with other health care professions and
furthered the health and well-being of the culturally diverse population in this border state and with our neighbors in Mexico.

REFERENCES

Auslander, W. F., Anderson, B. J., Bubb, J., Jung, K. C., & Santiago, J. V. (1990). Risk
    factors to health in diabetic children: A prospective study from diagnosis. *Health
    & Social Work, 15,* 133–142.
Cook, T., & Campbell, D. (1979). *Quasi-experimentation design and analysis issues for
    field settings.* Boston: Houghton Mifflin.
Cousins, N. (1981). *Anatomy of illness as perceived by the patient.* New York: W. W.
    Norton.
De La Rosa, M. (1989). Health care needs of Hispanic Americans and the responsive-
    ness of the health care system. *Health & Social Work, 14,* 104–113.

Delbanco, T. (1993). The art of healing. In B. S. Flowers & D. Grubin (Eds.), *Healing and the mind: Bill Moyers* (pp. 2–5). New York: Doubleday.

Eidelman, W. S. (1990, July–August). The emerging science of bioenergy therapy. *New Frontier, 11–12,* 45–46.

Eisenberg, D. (1993). Another way of seeing. In B. S. Flowers & D. Grubin (Eds.), *Healing and the mind: Bill Moyers* (pp. 305–322). New York: Doubleday.

Kabat-Zinn, J. (1990). *Full catastrophe living.* New York: Bantam.

Kelly, A. (1985). Evaluating and improving family health. In S. Bliss, E. Bauman, L. Piper, A. Brint, & P. Wright (Eds.), *The holistic health handbook* (pp. 294–295). Berkeley, CA: Stephen Green.

La Clinica de Familia. (1992). *La Clinica de Familia's clinical policies and procedures manual.* Las Cruces, NM: Author.

Nelson, E., Wasson, J., Kirk, J., Keller, A., Clark, D., Dietrich, A., Stewart, A., & Zubkoff, M. (1987). Assessment of function in routine clinical practice: Description of the COOP Chart method and preliminary findings. *Journal of Chronic Diseases, 40,* 555–635.

Vest, G. (1983). The holistic health team: An alternative social group work approach. *Reaping from the Field: From Practice to Principle, 1,* 312–325.

Vest, G. (Producer), KRWG Studio (Director). (1995). *15-Minute Stressout Program* [Videotape with English/Spanish study guide]. (Available from Family Preservation Institute, New Mexico State University, Box 30001, Dept. 3SW, Las Cruces, NM 88003-8001.)

Vest, G., & Ronnau, J. (1993). [15-Minute Stressout Program survey]. Unpublished raw data. Las Cruces: New Mexico State University, Department of Social Work.

Williams, J. L. (Ed.). (1986). *New Mexico in maps.* Albuquerque: University of New Mexico Press.

The authors acknowledge with sincere appreciation the contributions of Dr. Michael Stehney and his staff of La Clinica de Familia.

22 Promoting Breast Cancer Screening in Rural, African American Communities:
The "Science and Art" of Community Health Promotion

Mary Altpeter, Jo Anne L. Earp, and
Janice H. Schopler

Comprehensive community health promotion models typically combine community organization and citizen participation principles with behavioral theories to address ways to generate change at the individual and policy levels (Bracht, 1990). Social workers new to community practice struggle with the complex interplay of these theories and the need to develop skills necessary for working successfully with diverse community groups. Using an eight-year cancer prevention project, the North Carolina Breast Cancer Screening Program (NC-BCSP), as a case study, this chapter describes both the "science and art" (Greenwood, 1961) of conducting a successful community health promotion program. It examines how social ecological theory, social work community organization models, and principles underlying institutionalization of health promotion programs form the conceptual foundation for NC-BCSP. The chapter also provides examples illustrating the "art" of generating participation by both lay and professional individuals to make community health promotion efforts succeed in a seemingly resource-poor, rural area. Although the project's objectives are specific to increasing breast cancer screening rates among older African American women in rural North Carolina, many of our "lessons learned" could apply to other health or mental health promotion programs. The chapter concludes with guidelines for social workers who plan to conduct their own community health promotion programs.

BACKGROUND: THE PROBLEM AND THE SETTING

Breast cancer incidence in North Carolina, as it is nationally, is higher in white women; however, African American women have a 28 percent higher breast cancer mortality rate (Leserman et al., 1993).

This chapter was originally published in the May 1998 issue of *Health & Social Work*, Vol. 23, pp. 104–115.

Higher mortality rates result, in part, from diagnosis at a later stage of disease. African American women are more likely to be diagnosed with late-stage disease than are white women (45 percent compared with 33 percent) (Leserman et al., 1993). Later diagnosis is related to lower rates of regular breast cancer screening. In one study in rural eastern North Carolina, half as many African American women (27 percent) as white women (54 percent) reported having had a mammogram in the past year (Fletcher et al., 1993). The differences between these groups in mortality, stage of diagnosis, and screening rates are particularly disturbing given the estimated 30 percent of breast cancer deaths that could be prevented if women over the age of 50 were screened in accordance with published guidelines (Hamblin, 1991).

Given these disparities, researchers have underscored the need for comprehensive community-oriented interventions to increase breast cancer screening rates in African American communities (Fletcher et al., 1993; Haynes & Mara, 1993; Worden et al., 1994; Zapka, Stoddard, Maul, & Costanza, 1991). NC-BCSP is one such program. The program is based in five rural, low-income, medically underserved counties in eastern North Carolina (Earp, Altpeter, Mayne, Viadro, & O'Malley, 1995). These counties encompass 1,200 square miles and are sparsely populated; only two towns have populations that exceed 5,000. African Americans are a larger portion of the total population than in North Carolina as a whole, ranging from 30 percent to 60 percent across the five counties. About 6,500 African American women over age 50 live in this region. Poverty rates are 50 percent to 100 percent higher than for the state as a whole, with older African American women two to three times more likely to be poor than white women (U.S. Bureau of the Census, 1993). Access to health care in these rural counties is limited. There is only one physician for every 1,300 people (North Carolina Department of Environment, Health, and Natural Resources, 1992), and two counties have been designated as "areas having difficulty in obtaining accessible screening services for breast cancer" by the state's Division of Adult Health Promotion.

NC-BCSP CONCEPTUAL ROOTS AND PROGRAM DESIGN

NC-BCSP's community health promotion approach is based on several related and reinforcing theoretical constructs. These include the social–ecological theory of health promotion, two complementary community-organizing models (locality development and social planning), and principles for institutionalizing health programs. The social–ecological perspective of community health promotion emphasizes the need for coordinated interventions targeted at several levels of the community, ranging from individuals and their social networks to institutions and policymakers (Anderson & O'Donnell, 1994; McLeroy, Bibeau, Steckler, & Glanz, 1988; Stokols, 1992, 1996). This perspective recognizes that for health-related behaviors to change, community interventions designed to increase breast cancer screening rates among older African American women in rural areas must promote complementary "linkages" among women, their social networks, their health care providers, and the community agencies and institutions that serve them.

Locality development is a community-organizing model used in neighborhoods or rural counties to enhance the capacity of community members to improve the quality of their own lives (Rothman, 1979; Rothman & Tropman, 1987; Weil & Gamble, 1995). The model uses social workers or others as coaches or teachers who help organize local efforts and provide technical assistance or training as needed for developing the community participants' skills. The social planning model complements the lay orientation of locality development by focusing on the problem-solving skills of the professional community, such as health care providers, to help meet the community's service needs. Using social workers as planners, proposal writers, or managers who help identify and integrate the needs of underserved constituents into service planning, it aims to improve service delivery, particularly for marginal or at-risk groups (Pilisuk, McAllister, & Rothman, 1996; Rothman, 1979; Rothman & Tropman, 1987; Weil & Gamble, 1995).

The NC-BCSP program design incorporates the social–ecological approach and these community-organizing approaches within three interventions: (1) OutReach, (2) InReach, and (3) Access. OutReach targets individual women and the community networks to which they belong. This intervention incorporates locality development approaches with a focus on building the capacity of local leadership to promote and advocate for breast cancer screening. Three groups play key roles in the OutReach intervention: agency-based "community outreach specialists," county-based community advisory groups, and an extensive network of volunteers that spans the project's five-county region.

The InReach and Access interventions both incorporate the social planning model. InReach enhances service delivery through a range of activities, including restructuring clinic policies and procedures to increase the efficiency with which preventive services are delivered, offering provider education on breast cancer topics, and helping agencies implement community outreach efforts that are customized to older African American women. Health care providers are key players in each county. They include physicians in private practice, radiology centers, county health departments, and federally funded rural health centers. The Access intervention promotes accessible, equitable care by helping overcome institutional-level barriers (for example, cost, transportation, and mammography quality assurance) that prevent low-income, rural African American women from getting mammograms. Key Access intervention players include state and local agencies responsible for financing or delivering needed services.

While designing the interventions, NC-BCSP staff also formulated a plan that over time could institutionalize the program's successes.

The plan relied on multiple strategies proposed by Goodman and Steckler (1989) for institutionalizing health promotion programs. These strategies include developing "program champions," working with multiple subsystems, and establishing an organizational "niche." *Program champions* are individuals who can influence their organization's policies with respect to the newly created health promotion program. First, NC-BCSP cultivated positive relationships within state and local agencies, laying the groundwork for the creation of program champions who would advocate for improving breast cancer screening services. Institutionalization also requires strong "multiple subsystems" in both organizations and the community that can adopt the newly developed program changes. Second, NC-BCSP established relationships with local health departments, rural health clinics, radiology centers, and physicians to ensure that the proposed program changes meshed with the "systems" already in place in the local organizations. Third, to ensure longevity, new programs must fit a "niche" within an organization. Hence, NC-BCSP staff established the goal of helping local agencies and the African American community uncover existing grassroots community linkages that could firmly establish a comprehensive system of accessible, available, and affordable breast cancer screening and treatment options for all women in the counties.

THE PROCESS

The NC-BCSP program design represents a blend of strategies for health promotion and program institutionalization as well as social work community practice models. Its complexity required that it be implemented in sequential phases. The first phase, infrastructure development, involved engaging key agencies at the state and regional level, establishing the local staffing structure to serve the counties, recruiting local leaders, and creating the volunteer outreach networks. The second phase focused on forming community linkages at multiple levels within the infrastructure and seeking resources that supported the program's activities over time. The third phase entailed sustaining the infrastructure by monitoring and providing feedback to maintain its linkages, build resources, and increase the program's scope and responsiveness. The second and third phases, once initiated, have been ongoing.

Infrastructure Development

Engaging Key Agencies. The social–ecological theory of health promotion programs requires targeting all levels of the community, including those institutions that regulate or plan health care delivery. Thus, at the beginning of the project, NC-BCSP staff engaged the participation of several state-level organizations with a variety of objectives in mind. First, these agencies needed to become aware of the disparities in rates of breast cancer screening, diagnosis, and treatment that existed between African American and white women and, in the spirit of the social planning model, assume responsibility for closing existing gaps in services. Second, the organizations needed to become familiar with NC-BCSP's mission, particularly areas of existing mutual interests or commonalities that could help improve cancer prevention services for rural and African American populations. Third, it was important to determine whether these organizations could support NC-BCSP's mission through concrete means such as technical assistance or fiscal resources. Finally, NC-BCSP staff began planning with these key agencies to help institutionalize NC-BCSP's program successes after the project's grant funding ended.

A major part of the central plan was to create a program advisory committee. The list of organizations invited to join that committee included the North Carolina Division of Adult Health Promotion (DAHP), which administers the Breast and Cervical Cancer Control Program funded by the U.S. Centers for Disease Control and Prevention (CDC); the North Carolina Office of Rural Health, which directs services planning for underserved rural counties; the North Carolina Primary Care Association, which oversees the state's federally funded neighborhood rural health centers; the North Carolina Division of the American Cancer Society (ACS); and the Leo Jenkins Cancer Center, which is part of East Carolina University's School of Medicine and is a tertiary care center located in a county adjacent to the project's target counties.

The establishment of the program advisory committee proved beneficial for the agencies as well as for NC-BCSP. For example, North Carolina Equity, an advocacy organization for women and minority health issues, was drawn to NC-BCSP's social action focus on improving the quality of life for underserved African American women. The Primary Care Association was interested in NC-BCSP's InReach plans to work with local community providers. Some agencies saw that by becoming formally involved with NC-BCSP, their own program missions could be enhanced or they could benefit from the links or program structures that NC-BCSP had implemented. For example, DAHP shares the goal of increasing breast cancer screening for older women. By linking with NC-BCSP, the division could obtain assistance in designing outreach programs for hard-to-reach, at-risk women. The mission of the North Carolina Office of Minority Health (OMH) was to provide cultural-sensitivity training in the local health departments. Because NC-BCSP had already formed working relationships with the local health departments to provide continuing education programs about breast cancer screening for public health nurses, OMH was able to use these connections to launch its own training agenda.

NC-BCSP benefited in a number of ways, too. For example, DAHP helped in the early stages of building NC-BCSP's infrastructure by agreeing to create, through a subcontract with NC-BCSP, a nurse regional coordinator position. This position oversees the project's

10-county target region and helps plan, implement, coordinate, and evaluate project activities at the county level. The Leo Jenkins Cancer Center offered to house the nurse regional coordinator in office space, which enabled NC-BCSP to establish a strong presence in the target region. DAHP also assisted with NC-BCSP's early data collection efforts. Specifically, DAHP helped assess the distribution of capitated funds for the delivery of breast cancer screening as well as county-specific annual patient demographic and services data on breast cancer services (for example, number of women over age 50 receiving clinical breast examinations or mammography referrals). Such data helped NC-BCSP InReach staff formulate service planning initiatives with the local county health departments. Together, the DAHP and the Leo Jenkins Cancer Center also coordinated provider skills assessments and training to help enhance the delivery of breast cancer screening services.

Establishing the Local Staffing Infrastructure. The next phase of the process entailed establishing the local staffing infrastructure. Consistent with locality development objectives, NC-BCSP created "community outreach specialist" positions to be filled by indigenous workers. These individuals could help link the health care system with local African American communities and generate a sense of community caring about the breast cancer screening needs of older African American women. Four county-based community outreach specialist positions were established in local health departments and rural health centers and funded by NC-BCSP to serve the five-county intervention region. Because a paucity of older African American women in the target region had the desired training in health education and community health promotion interventions, NC-BCSP staff worked with the local health care agencies in all five counties to identify older women "through the grapevine." The identified individuals had been serving on the boards of directors of various health care agencies, were known as long-time residents of and volunteers in their counties, or had community leadership roles through their professional experiences in teaching, social work, or library science.

Once the community outreach specialists were hired, NC-BCSP staff trained them in practical community-organizing skills. The specialists learned to assess the resources and needs for breast cancer screening services in their counties. They also became acquainted with materials and resources about breast cancer and breast cancer screening at the state and national levels. They learned strategies for enlisting the interest of citizen leaders to advocate for breast cancer screening services, as well as for building and reinforcing a sense of community mobilization directed at older African American women. In addition, they were guided in developing local plans (for example, mammography screening advocacy during Mother's Day events) for breast cancer screening promotion campaigns and educational activities. This learning process enabled the specialists to become, within several months, "experts" on breast cancer services in their communities.

The supervision for the community outreach specialists was intentionally designed to be jointly provided by NC-BCSP's nurse regional coordinator and unit directors based in the local health care agencies. This "supervisory linkage" was established for the mutual benefit of the local agencies and NC-BCSP. It provided local health care agencies with a formalized connection to the NC-BCSP team, thus facilitating agency participation in the project's outreach program planning. It also allowed the NC-BCSP team to gain insights into each agency's service planning processes, intraorganizational and community challenges, and daily operations.

Recruiting Local Leaders. The community outreach specialists, with assistance from NC-BCSP staff, coordinated the next phase of the process. This entailed the establishment of five county-based community advisory groups composed of African American community leaders. Ranging in size from six to 13 members and including 60 individuals, these groups expanded the community-organizing capacity of the specialists. Specifically, the advisory groups helped identify and "convene" each county's intrinsic resources, coordinated the natural helping that occurs among individuals in neighborhoods, and promoted community ownership of the project (Collins & Pancoast, 1976; Eng & Smith, 1995). Diverse in professional training, the advisory group members were active and retired teachers, school principals, health care providers, business executives, members of the clergy, mayors, and county commissioners. The majority (81 percent) had resided in their communities their entire lives.

After forming the community advisory groups, the community outreach specialists conducted orientations about the project's goals and intervention design and their county's specific needs for breast cancer screening and treatment. The training set the tone for NC-BCSP's desire to promote citizen participation and to develop a "grassroots linkage" in which each advisory group would recognize and, through their own strengths, develop methods for addressing the service needs in their county (Bracht, 1990; Hatch & Earp, 1976).

In addition to this type of capacity building, locality development also entails assigning discrete tasks to the local leadership (Weil & Gamble, 1995). The community advisory groups accepted this charge and have been highly effective in helping NC-BCSP implement its OutReach intervention. For example, the advisory group members helped with the next phase of infrastructure development by identifying local women who could serve as NC-BCSP outreach volunteers. They assisted with a number of logistics related to the planning and delivery of the training sessions for the volunteers. They also helped NC-BCSP staff design tailored, county-specific educational brochures used to promote screening among older women. Finally, and perhaps most important, community advisory group members have provided credibility to NC-BCSP's OutReach efforts among local health care providers and African American communities in the region, laying the foundation for institutionalizing the most successful community advocacy efforts.

Creating the Volunteer Outreach Networks. The next phase of the process entailed the creation of the volunteer networks. Numerous community-oriented cancer prevention studies focus on social support models in which outreach workers or lay helpers provide one-on-one counseling and assistance to increase use of breast cancer screening within communities of African American women and other culturally diverse communities (Brownstein, Cheal, Ackermann, Bassford, & Campos-Outcalt, 1992; Eng, 1993; Eng & Parker, 1994; Erwin, Spatz, & Turturro, 1992; Kang, Bloom, & Romano, 1994; Skinner, Strecher, & Hospers, 1994; Suarez, Lloyd, Weiss, Rainbolt, & Pulley, 1994; Tessaro, Eng, & Smith, 1994). The lay health adviser model, which reflects one mechanism to deliver social support, depends on individuals who offer help naturally and spontaneously and are the types of people to whom others routinely turn for advice and support (Earp et al., 1997; Eng & Young, 1992; Israel, 1985; Service & Salber, 1979). Lay health advisers can help break through many of the barriers that prevent low-income women from obtaining mammograms. They can help women change their attitudes toward and beliefs about breast cancer risk, view mammograms more positively, and alter their screening behavior. Lay health advisers also can help logistically by providing transportation to mammography centers or notifying women when a mobile mammography van is scheduled to be in town.

Over a 14-month period, the outreach specialists and advisory groups recruited and trained more than 150 volunteers to become lay health advisers to provide outreach to older women in the community. They recruited women who were interested in helping others and who were demographically similar to the NC-BCSP's target population. Socioeconomic status and place of work also were factors. Once recruited, the advisers participated in NC-BCSP training sessions designed to broaden their health knowledge and more precisely target their social networking skills.

Locality development is a process of "creating a web of continuing relationships so that people may indeed come together, share their supportive attentions and resources, and experience a sense of belonging to their community" (Pilisuk et al., 1996, p. 17). The lay health advisers, in tandem with the community outreach specialists and community advisory groups, have carried out outreach activities far exceeding NC-BCSP's original projections. On average, all five advisory groups oversee at least one community campaign each month; each outreach specialist makes approximately three community presentations per month, and each lay health adviser typically averages two one-on-one contacts with women each week. They also have developed a variety of creative outreach educational and promotional materials about breast cancer screening that target women at different stages in their decision making. These materials include church fans and bulletins, county-specific posters and brochures, and greeting cards customized to the target population.

Forming Community Linkages at Multiple Levels

Linkages between Volunteers and Providers. Rothman and Tropman (1987) noted that community practice often entails the "phasing in" or "meshing" of several approaches as a community builds interest and skills in problem solving and creating new services. As the intervention activities have been implemented and relationships with the African American lay community and the local health care provider system have developed, NC-BCSP has begun to phase in elements of a "functional community organizing approach" (Weil & Gamble, 1995). In this second phase of NC-BCSP's implementation process, the emphasis has been on bringing together like-minded groups representing various facets of the community to pool social advocacy and policy–planning efforts to address inadequacies in services. In addition, NC-BCSP began to identify program champions and community subsystems that could be tapped to help initiate the institutionalization process. NC-BCSP staff thus began to facilitate numerous community-based linkages to counter shared concerns about the unavailability or inaccessibility of breast cancer screening services for older African American women. These efforts also fostered institutionalization of newly created services.

The 14-month period of the lay health adviser training sessions provided ample opportunities for such linkages. Health and human services professionals in each county were asked to serve as trainers for the health knowledge modules in the lay health adviser training sessions. Such lay–professional interaction helped the advisers recognize that their volunteer efforts as breast care advocates for community women were perceived as important to local health care providers. These linkages also enhanced the "community competence" (Cottrell, 1976) or "cultural competence" (Ager & Colindres, 1994) of the health care providers by helping them become better informed about the service needs and barriers that older African American women in these counties experienced. As a result, some of the providers began implementing their own culturally sensitive outreach materials and programs.

Linkages among Provider Groups. The NC-BCSP team has also built linkages among provider groups in the counties to promote social planning. For example, in one county four entities provide health care, including a group of seven private physicians' practices, the federally funded rural health center, the county health department, and the local hospital. Despite the fact that three of these providers were located only half a mile from each other, they had never coordinated breast cancer screening efforts before. As the first step in building these provider linkages, NC-BCSP endorsed an application to a private foundation so the hospital could buy a mammography unit, thus eliminating the need for county women to travel an hour or more to get screening mammograms. NC-BCSP staff next worked with the four sets of providers to form a consortium of all-county services. The consortium's first project was to apply for the CDC Breast and

Cervical Cancer Control Program funds that pay for screening and for state Cancer Control Program funds that pay for breast cancer treatment and follow-up if screening detects cancer. As a result of these collective efforts, and partly through the work of NC-BCSP, all health care providers in this county now are linked to provide subsidized cancer screening and treatment for low-income women.

Linkages between State and Local Entities. NC-BCSP staff also have built linkages with state and local entities to help provide funding or in-kind support to lay the foundation for and eventually institutionalize intervention activities. At the state level the DAHP annually contributes funding to help support one of the community outreach specialist positions. The North Carolina Division of the ACS provides funding for projects such as training of African American cosmetologists to participate (for the first time ever in the five intervention counties) in the ACS's Look Good, Feel Better Program. Locally, the county health departments and community health centers provide office space, equipment, and supervision at no cost for the project's community outreach specialists. Finally, churches, public agencies, restaurants, and small businesses donate meeting space and refreshments for the local advisory committees and lay health advisers.

Monitoring and Providing Feedback to Maintain the Infrastructure

"Action research" is a natural extension of community organizing that helps integrate theory and practice (Pareek, 1990; Smith, Pyrch, & Lizardi, 1993) and promote collaboration, cooperation, and co-learning and capacity-building among community participants (Flynn, Ray, & Rider, 1994; Pareek, 1990; Sarri & Sarri, 1992). Sharing assessments of program progress reinforces the efforts of local participants and helps them recognize whether their organizing efforts are beginning to achieve success. Thus, the last phase of this community health promotion process entails evaluation strategies to monitor changes in screening rates and mortality among African American women, plus feedback mechanisms to share progress made or setbacks encountered with the local providers and community leaders.

NC-BCSP's outcome evaluation is a panel study with three data collection times over an eight-year period that track overall differences in breast cancer screening attitudes, beliefs, and behaviors between white and African American women. A quasi-experimental, pre- and posttest research design is used to survey a cohort of 2,000 rural women (1,000 white, 1,000 African American) over age 50, randomly selected from the five intervention counties and five comparison counties. The outcome evaluation allows comparisons to be made in screening rates between the two racial groups and between intervention and comparison counties.

At the beginning of the project, prior to the baseline (time 1) data collection, NC-BCSP staff conducted a small orientation conference for the local health care agencies in the five intervention and five comparison counties. The goals were to acquaint all participants with the research questions and study design and to explain how the data collected would benefit their service planning and delivery. Project staff also explained the plans for the OutReach, InReach, and Access interventions. By sharing the overall plan with the local agencies and encouraging them to ask questions and make suggestions early on about program implementation, staff were able to motivate agencies to participate in the program.

Results from the time 1 data collection were shared at a second provider conference conducted six months after the preliminary data analysis was completed. Nearly 40 health professionals in key administrative positions from the 10 counties attended. Conference participants heard the preliminary findings from the cohort survey and suggested ways these findings could inform efforts to provide optimum breast cancer screening for women in their catchment areas.

To complement the outcome data, the NC-BCSP team also implemented a process evaluation plan to measure shorter-term achievements and to make comparisons across and within counties from the perspective of the lay health advisers, community women, providers, and agencies (Viadro, Earp, & Altpeter, 1997). Because NC-BCSP's program objectives center on reducing barriers to obtaining mammography screening and on strengthening the factors that lead women to obtain screening mammograms, many of the instruments pertain to providers' health care knowledge and practices and women's experiences with the health care system. Data collected from these instruments also were shared at the provider conference. NC-BCSP staff presented the data to the group in aggregate form to ensure confidentiality about behaviors of specific providers. Staff also cautioned participants about the limitations of the process evaluation findings (that is, small sample sizes and convenience rather than random sampling). Nevertheless, participants were eager to discuss, and sometimes refute, the findings, stimulating lively discussions about breast cancer screening service gaps and agency limitations in the respective counties. These discussions were viewed by NC-BCSP as a positive step in generating interest in social planning at the agency level that could address the status of breast cancer services in the county.

NC-BCSP staff devised a monthly reporting system for the community outreach specialists to monitor their numerous countywide activities. Among many items, the reporting system tracks the number and location of community campaigns (for example, health fairs at senior centers, mobile van days, testimonies at churches, and so forth) conducted by the lay health advisers. The community outreach specialists also record the type and number of presentations they make on their own (for example, presentations at staff meetings and health fairs). The form also includes lists of the number of outreach materials distributed and to what sites (for example, Mother's Day and Valentine's cards at senior citizen centers).

In the spirit of "empowerment evaluation" that is "with the community, not on the community" (Grills, Bass, Brown, & Akers, 1996, p. 130), NC-BCSP staff showed the community outreach specialists how the data were summarized and presented in grant reports. Along with reporting these quantitative data, staff also included many salient anecdotes that the community outreach specialists had shared in the open-ended sections of their monthly reports. Stories were selected if they helped convey the poignancy of the project's one-on-one intervention efforts to reach out to older African American women. Seeing how their reports were used in grant writing motivated the community outreach specialists to keep accurate and comprehensive records and especially to write relevant and compelling accounts of the numerous ways women had been helped.

NC-BCSP staff also wanted to collect lay health adviser activity data that would help the advisers gauge their influence on women in the communities. A dilemma, however, was how to collect information about the lay health advisers' activities when their activities were, by definition, natural and spontaneous. How does one formally collect information about an informal process? And how does one motivate "natural helpers" to invest in the evaluation process? To tackle this problem, the NC-BCSP staff conducted focus groups with all the leaders of the lay health adviser groups (12 women) and their respective community outreach specialists. Questions raised in the focus groups generated ideas for obtaining accurate and representative evaluation data, finding out what information was useful to the advisers and developing a system of data collection that could be institutionalized. The groups also discussed how research and community interests differed. These interactions created the same dynamic as those conducted with the community outreach specialists; the advisers responded positively to the NC-BCSP staff's interest in their viewpoints and consequently became more personally interested in the data collection effort.

PRACTICE IMPLICATIONS

The lessons we learned about the art of engaging players in the community, although simple and straightforward, are nonetheless fundamental to successful program implementation. These basic insights can serve as useful guidelines for social work practitioners interested in developing or establishing other community-based initiatives focusing on health or mental health issues.

Learn about the Community Where the Interventions Will Take Place

To be effective community organizers, social workers must take time to listen carefully to the perspectives of the central as well as the peripheral members of the target community before proceeding with a full-scale intervention. Because NC-BCSP's "community" encompassed five counties, staff learned about them from multiple sources. They spent many hours talking individually with staff of the key state agencies that ultimately joined the program advisory committee. Although all these organizations were geographically peripheral to the target region, they nevertheless had experience with community interventions; had worked with rural, underserved, marginalized, or at-risk groups; or had access to databases that provided information about the availability of and gaps in breast cancer screening services in the region.

NC-BCSP staff also made multiple local site visits to county health departments and rural health centers to observe clinic operations, learn staff perspectives and opinions about their client populations, and ask about assets and constraints in the counties that affected the delivery of breast cancer services. The community outreach specialists corroborated or refuted this information by performing their own county needs assessments and providing anecdotal information about the reputations and relationships of these health care agencies in the African American communities. The community advisory groups and lay health advisers offered their viewpoints on what types of breast cancer screening campaigns should be mounted for older African American women. Learning these community perspectives helped the project staff better recognize and use the available resources and, later, manage the political issues that arose in each county. For any community intervention program, this assessment task is ongoing and cannot be rushed or skipped.

Educate the Community Players about the Intervention Plans

Social workers should take time to explain precisely what the planned community health promotion program is intended to accomplish and be prepared to repeat that explanation often. In the case of this project, the local communities seemed to have difficulty distinguishing NC-BCSP from the state-operated Breast and Cervical Cancer Control Program. The community outreach specialists and project staff had to conduct multiple group presentations to clarify the two related but distinct programs. Using a variety of media (video, slides, overheads, pictures, display boards), multiple presentations were made at the program advisory committee meetings as well as at the local community advisory group meetings. Audiovisual aids helped portray the project's mission in an engaging way. The use of attractive materials also conveyed the sophistication of the project and the desire of project staff to put its "best foot forward" for this cause.

In addition to group presentations, articles were placed in daily and weekly papers to showcase project activities or local participants (agency staff, lay health advisers, community advisory group members) or to provide a more general overview of the NC-BCSP mission. In one year alone, 24 newspaper and magazine articles were published about NC-BCSP and its local participants and activities. This type of publicity helps build awareness of the program in both the lay and professional communities, generate interest among potential volunteers, and develop the community's investment and pride in the program's accomplishments.

Actively Communicate with Community Participants

To maintain community involvement, social workers must find ways to continuously cultivate and nurture that interest. The NC-BCSP staff used several methods to sustain involvement with the project. One method was the publication of project newsletters. Produced by the NC-BCSP central project office staff, the main newsletter reaches a variety of audiences (state and local agencies, community groups, breast cancer advocacy organizations, project participants, other researchers). Each issue generally features an overall theme such as the role of volunteers in the project, the efforts of local participating agencies, or the variety of outreach materials NC-BCSP has developed to target older African American women. A second newsletter, produced by the regional office, is intended to link the lay health advisers and community advisory groups in the five intervention counties. Its themes showcase successful community- or county-level outreach activities and credit those lay health advisers or advisory groups that have made significant contributions to their communities. This monthly communication also provides a venue for the volunteers to share motivational stories, healthy recipes, or other items of personal interest.

The NC-BCSP staff also produced a number of "holiday" one-page letters for local volunteer networks, state and county agencies, researchers, and funders. The letters provided updates of the year's accomplishments and also thanked community participants for their support of NC-BCSP.

A third way NC-BCSP has fostered communication with the counties is through a variety of meetings. As noted earlier, the project has held "provider conferences" to explain research objectives and to report preliminary findings. The lay health advisers also hold an annual conference for all advisers and community advisory group members to hear about what each county is doing and to share accomplishments. During the conference, they also learn new skills about lay health advising techniques and hear updates from NC-BCSP staff about the project's accomplishments and program plans.

Maintain Flexibility in Responding to the Community's Changing Role

Although an overall plan is essential before proceeding with a community-based project, social workers must be willing to let program activities evolve naturally. They must also be prepared to relinquish some control over program activities as the community becomes actively engaged and invested in the project. For NC-BCSP, the community advisory groups and lay health adviser networks were established to have specific roles in carrying out the OutReach intervention. As this intervention was implemented, it became clear that the advisory groups and lay health advisers were far more willing to invest their time and energy in creating community-oriented breast cancer screening education and promotional strategies than the project staff originally anticipated. As part of their investment, they actually exerted significant control over the kinds of educational or promotional materials they thought should be developed and the types of messages they believed would be most salient to older African American women.

For example, the volunteers decided that church fans would be a practical outreach tool, particularly in the many non–air-conditioned churches in the region. They designed fans that contained breast cancer screening promotional messages on one side and religious pictures on the other side. This design was appropriate for where the fans were going to be used, but the inclusion of religious symbolism created a problem with the project's funders. The funders (private foundations and the federal government) needed to disassociate themselves from the appearance of religious favoritism and to maintain "separation of church and state." Initially, NC-BCSP staff objected but ultimately complied with the funders' positions and advised the volunteers to substitute a simple country scene for the religious picture. However, the next year the volunteers persisted with their desire to use religious imagery on a new batch of church fans. This time, the NC-BCSP staff reached a compromise with the funders that advocated for the volunteers' efforts to carry out the intended mission of the project, that is, to reach out to marginal women through messages that genuinely "spoke" to them in their terms, not in the project's or the funders' terms. As a result, the funders agreed to provide the fiscal support to cover the church fan production expense, but requested that acknowledgment of their support not be printed on the fans.

Acknowledge Community Involvement

Another way social workers can foster community investment and allegiance to the community health promotion program is through participant recognition awards. Each year, at the annual Lay Health Advisor Conference, an award is given to a lay health adviser judged by the community outreach specialists and NC-BCSP regional office staff to have made a significant contribution to breast cancer screening and advocacy. The major criteria for selection are regular attendance at local lay health adviser meetings, timely submission of activity reports, creativity in seeking ways to promote breast cancer screening messages, service on committees established by community outreach specialists, and willingness to offer transportation to women needing assistance in getting to providers for breast health care or mammograms. The award serves as a subtle method of reinforcing the desired behaviors of lay health advisers, encouraging them to maintain routine involvement in campaign activities, one-on-one advising, and regular activity reporting. Annual appreciation dinners also are held in each county to thank community advisory groups for their participation in the program. NC-BCSP staff prepare press releases for the local papers to recognize the lay health adviser awards and the community advisory group appreciation dinners. These types of recognition, although relatively low cost, are important to, and well received by, the volunteers.

CONCLUSION

NC-BCSP's experience illustrates the complex interplay between the "science" of health promotion through community development and the "art" of successfully engaging community members, both lay and professional, in generating individual and institutional change. Social workers have opportunities through classroom instruction and an extensive literature base to be trained in the theoretical aspects of community health promotion and community organization models; however, they have limited occasions to observe, learn, or practice the skills that make such models successful. By illustrating successful "real-life" approaches and actual "field" methods that can be applied to a variety of complex health issues of hard-to-reach groups with whom social workers practice, we believe this description of a breast cancer screening program in eastern North Carolina targeted at older African American women helps fill this gap.

REFERENCES

Ager, S., & Colindres, M. (1994). *The North Carolina Latino cultural competency training curriculum.* Raleigh: North Carolina Department of Environment, Health, and Natural Resources, Women's Preventive Health Branch.

Anderson, D., & O'Donnell, M. (1994). Toward a health promotion research agenda: "State of the science" reviews. *American Journal of Health Promotion, 8,* 462–465.

Bracht, N. (Ed.). (1990). *Health promotion at the community level.* Newbury Park, CA: Sage Publications.

Brownstein, J. N., Cheal, N., Ackermann, S. P., Bassford, T. L., & Campos-Outcalt, D. (1992). Breast and cervical cancer screening in minority populations: A model for using lay health educators. *Journal of Cancer Education, 7,* 321–326.

Collins, A., & Pancoast, D. (1976). *Natural helping systems.* Washington, DC: NASW Press.

Cottrell, L. S. (1976). The competent community. In B. Kaplan, R. Wilson, & A. Leighton (Eds.), *Further explorations of social psychiatry* (pp. 195–209). New York: Basic Books.

Earp, J. L., Altpeter, M., Mayne, L., Viadro, C. I., & O'Malley, M. S. (1995). The North Carolina Breast Cancer Screening Program: Foundations and design of a model for reaching older, African-American, rural women. *Journal of Breast Cancer Research and Treatment, 35*(1), 7–22.

Earp, J. A., Viadro, C. I., Vincus, A. A., Altpeter, M., Flax, V., Mayne, L., & Eng, E. (1997). Lay health advisors: A strategy for "getting the word out" about breast cancer. *Health Education and Behavior, 24,* 432–451.

Eng, E. (1993). The Save Our Sisters Project: A social network strategy for reaching rural black women. *Cancer, 72*(Suppl.), 1071–1077.

Eng, E., & Parker, E. (1994). Measuring community competence in the Mississippi delta: The interface between program evaluation and empowerment. *Health Education Quarterly, 12,* 81–92.

Eng, E., & Smith, J. (1995). Natural helping functions of lay health advisors in breast cancer education. *Journal of Breast Cancer Research and Treatment, 35*(1), 23–29.

Eng, E., & Young, R. (1992). Lay health advisors as community change agents. *Family Community Health, 15,* 24–40.

Erwin, D. O., Spatz, T. S., & Turturro, C. L. (1992). Development of an African-American role model intervention to increase breast self-examination and mammography. *Journal of Cancer Education, 7,* 311–319.

Fletcher, S. W., Harris, R. P., Gonzalez, J. J., Degnan, D., Lannin, D. R., Strecher, V. J., Pilgrim, C., Quade, D., Earp, J. A., & Clark, R. L. (1993). Increasing mammography utilization: A controlled study. *Journal of the National Cancer Institute, 85,* 112–120.

Flynn, B. C., Ray, D. W., & Rider, M. S. (1994). Empowering communities: Action research through healthy cities. *Health Education Quarterly, 21,* 395–405.

Goodman, R. M., & Steckler, A. (1989). A model for the institutionalization of health promotion programs. *Family Community Health, 11,* 63–78.

Greenwood, E. (1961). The practice of science and the science of practice. In W. G. Bennis, K. Benne, & R. Chin (Eds.), *The planning of change* (pp. 73–82). New York: Holt, Rinehart & Winston.

Grills, C. N., Bass, K., Brown, D. L., & Akers, A. (1996). Empowerment evaluation: Building upon a tradition of activism in the African American community. In D. M. Fetterman, S. J. Kaftarian, & A. Wandersman (Eds.), *Empowerment evaluation: Knowledge and tools for self-assessment and accountability* (pp. 123–140). Thousand Oaks, CA: Sage Publications.

Hamblin, J. E. (1991). Physician recommendations for screening mammography. *Journal of Family Practice, 32,* 472–477.

Hatch, J., & Earp, J. A. (1976). Consumer involvement in the delivery of health services. In E. Hassinger & L. Whiting (Eds.), *Rural health services and use* (pp. 243–259). Ames: Iowa State University Press.

Haynes, S. G., & Mara, J. R. (Eds.). (1993). *The picture of health: How to increase breast cancer screening in your community.* Washington, DC: U.S. Department of Health and Human Services.

Israel, B. (1985). Social networks and social support: An overview of research, practice, and policy implications. *Health Education Quarterly, 12,* 81–92.

Kang, S. H., Bloom, J. R., & Romano, P. S. (1994). Cancer screening among African-American women: Their use of tests and social support. *American Journal of Public Health, 84,* 101–103.

Leserman, J., Cilenti, D., Hall, S. P., Hamby, S. L., Murphy, C. E., & Berkman, N. D. (1993). *In sickness and in health: The status of women's health in North Carolina.* Raleigh: North Carolina Equity.

McLeroy, K. R., Bibeau, D., Steckler, A., & Glanz, K. (1988). An ecological perspective on health promotion programs. *Health Education Quarterly, 15,* 351–377.

North Carolina Department of Environment, Health, and Natural Resources, State Center for Health and Environmental Statistics. (1992). *NC chartbook on population and health: 1990.* Raleigh: Author.

Pareek, U. (1990). Culture-relevant and culture-modifying action research for development. *Journal of Social Issues, 46,* 119–131.

Pilisuk, M., McAllister, J., & Rothman, J. (1996). Coming together for action: The challenge of contemporary grassroots community organizing. *Journal of Social Issues, 52,* 15–37.

Rothman, J. (1979). Three models of community organization practice: Their mixing and phasing. In F. Cox, J. L. Erlich, J. Rothman, & J. E. Tropman (Eds.), *Strategies of community organization* (3th ed., pp. 25–45). Itasca, IL: F. E. Peacock.

Rothman, J., & Tropman, J. E. (1987). Models of community organization and macro practice perspectives: Their mixing and phases. In F. Cox, J. L. Erlich, J. Rothman,

& J. E. Tropman (Eds.), *Strategies of community organization* (4th ed., pp. 3–24). Itasca, IL: F. E. Peacock.

Sarri, R. C., & Sarri, C. M. (1992). Organizational and community change through participatory action research. *Journal of Administration in Social Work, 16,* 99–122.

Service, C., & Salber, E. J. (1979). *Community health education: The lay health advisor approach.* Durham, NC: Duke University Health Care System.

Skinner, C. S., Strecher, V. J., & Hospers, H. (1994). Physician's recommendations for mammography: Do tailored messages make a difference? *American Journal of Public Health, 84,* 43–49.

Smith, S. E., Pyrch, T., & Lizardi, A. O. (1993). Participatory action-research for health. *World Health Forum, 14,* 319–324.

Stokols, D. (1992). Establishing and maintaining healthy environments: Toward a social ecology of health promotion. *American Psychologist, 47,* 6–21.

Stokols, D. (1996). Translating social ecological theory into guidelines for community health promotion. *American Journal of Health Promotion, 10,* 282–298.

Suarez, L., Lloyd, L., Weiss, N., Rainbolt, T., & Pulley, L. V. (1994). Effect of social networks on cancer-screening behavior of older Mexican-American women. *Journal of the National Cancer Institute, 86,* 775–779.

Tessaro, I., Eng, E., & Smith, J. (1994). Breast cancer screening in older African-American women: Qualitative research findings. *American Journal of Health Promotion, 8,* 286–293.

U.S. Bureau of the Census. (1993). *Census of population and housing, 1990: Summary tape file 4* (NC) (machine-readable data files). Suitland, MD: Author.

Viadro, C. I., Earp, J. A., & Altpeter, M. (1997). Designing a process evaluation for a comprehensive breast cancer screening intervention: Challenges and opportunities. *Evaluation and Program Planning, 20,* 237–249.

Weil, M., & Gamble, D. (1995). Community practice models. In R. L. Edwards (Ed.-in-Chief), *The encyclopedia of social work* (19th ed., Vol. 1, pp. 577–594). Washington, DC: NASW Press.

Worden, J. K., Mickey, R. M., Flynn, B. S., Costanza, M. C., Vacek, P. M., Skelly, J. M., Lloyd, C. M., Landis, D. C., Myer, D. M., & Noonan, M. A. (1994). Development of a community breast screening promotion program using baseline data. *Preventive Medicine, 23,* 267–275.

Zapka, J. G., Stoddard, A., Maul, L., & Costanza, M. E. (1991). Interval adherence to mammography screening guidelines. *Medical Care, 29,* 697–707.

The authors thank the National Cancer Institute, which funds the Specialized Program of Research Excellence (SPORE) in Breast Cancer of which the North Carolina Breast Cancer Screening Program (NC-BCSP) is a part (No. 1-P50-CA5). They also thank the Susan G. Komen Breast Cancer Foundation (No. 9512), the Avon Breast Health Access Fund, the Kate B. Reynolds Charitable Trust (No. 95-123), The Pittsburgh Foundation (No. N8344), and the UNC Lineberger Comprehensive Cancer Center, which have provided the NC-BCSP with additional funding. Additional thanks go to Richard L. Edwards, Cheryl Moyer, Caroline Bishop, and Ellen Smolker for their valuable suggestions. This chapter is dedicated to the memory of Janice Schopler, who died in December 1997.

23 Mothers' Satisfaction with Medical Care: Perceptions of Racism, Family Stress, and Medical Outcomes in Children with Diabetes

Wendy F. Auslander, Sanna J. Thompson, Daniele Dreitzer, and Julio V. Santiago

Medical outcomes, such as adherence to prescribed regimens and patient's health, are greatly influenced by patient satisfaction with health care services. With the advent of managed care and health maintenance organizations, patient satisfaction has become a specific organizational goal and is used as an indicator of provider performance. Results from surveys of patient satisfaction have been used by managed care companies to determine how well providers deliver medical services. These data have also been used to predict patient behavior patterns, because differences in satisfaction predict where patients choose to get treatment and the extent to which they comply with medical recommendations (Ware & Davies, 1983).

Satisfaction with medical care is a multidimensional concept defined as the "personal evaluation of health care services and providers" (Ware, Snyder, Wright, & Davies, 1983, p. 247). It is related to patients' expectations of health services based on their sense of what they deserve or the level of participation they have in decision making (Golin, DiMatteo, & Gelberg, 1996). It has been conceptualized by Ware and colleagues (1983) to include eight areas: provider's interpersonal manner, technical quality of care, accessibility and convenience, finances, physical environment, availability, continuity of care, and efficacy or outcome of care.

Pressure for public accountability and consumer control has generated an increasing interest in patient satisfaction (Proctor, Morrow-Howell, Albaz, & Weir, 1992; Strasser, Aharony, & Greenberger, 1993). Investigators have found that patients' satisfaction with their doctors and medical treatment has emerged as an important determinant of patient commitment to and compliance with recommended treatment (Lewis, Scott, Pantell, & Wolfe, 1986). The literature suggests that patient satisfaction is largely a result of the physician's

This chapter was originally published in the August 1997 issue of *Health & Social Work*, Vol. 22, pp. 190–199.

interpersonal manner (verbal and nonverbal communication) when interacting with the patient (Buller & Buller, 1987).

One type of interpersonal communication that is strongly linked with satisfaction is exemplified by clear, comprehensive explanations and actions that demonstrate an interest in the patient. Satisfaction is increased when physicians are attentive, give patients the chance to relay information in their own way, provide more information, and share control of the termination of the medical interaction (Anderson, 1990). In one study, mothers at a pediatric facility were more satisfied with physicians who addressed their concerns by answering questions and expressing warmth and empathy (Korsch, Gozzi, & Francis, 1986). In general, practitioners who use a more companionable communicative style characterized by warmth, empathy, genuineness, and a nonjudgmental attitude rather than a controlling, authoritative style receive more favorable evaluations by patients.

CONCEPTUAL FRAMEWORK

An ecological framework (Bronfenbrenner, 1979; Germain, 1991) highlights the importance of environmental factors on health behaviors and beliefs. Within this ecological approach, individual health behaviors and cognition about medical care (that is, satisfaction) are influenced by the physical contexts surrounding the individuals' beliefs and behaviors, such as the family and community (Auslander & Corn, 1996). Previous research investigating predictors of patient satisfaction have focused primarily on individual predictors such as age, gender, education, income, and other demographic variables, although findings have been inconsistent. For example, many studies have determined that income, age, gender, education, and race significantly predict patient satisfaction (Hall, Irish, Roter, Ehrlich, & Miller, 1994; Sherbourne, Hays, Ordway, DiMatteo, & Kravitz, 1992; Zastowny, Roghmann, & Cafferata, 1989); however, some studies contradict these findings (Hsieh & Kagle, 1991; Ross, Steward, & Sinacore, 1993). Review of these studies indicates that little attention has been directed toward examining the environmental contexts that frame individuals' responses to their medical care. Inconsistency in previous findings related to demographics led us to explore other predictors associated with satisfaction with medical care and to use the ecological framework to examine how family and community contexts may predict satisfaction with medical care.

DIABETES IN CHILDREN AND ADOLESCENTS

Insulin-dependent diabetes mellitus (IDDM) is one the most common chronic childhood diseases, with incidence rates more than four times higher than any other chronic disease of children and adolescents (for example, cystic fibrosis, muscular dystrophy, leukemia, arthritis, AIDS). The prevalence rate of IDDM in youths under age 19 is estimated to be 1.7 per 1,000 (LaPorte, Matsushima, & Chang, 1995). Diabetes is managed primarily by the patient with frequent consultations with health care providers. It is the responsibility of the child and family to perform the necessary daily tasks to maintain normal or near-normal blood glucose levels. This maintenance entails making clinical decisions about insulin dosages on the basis of observations of the child to prevent episodes of high and low blood glucose levels. Insulin injections, exercise, diet, and glucose testing must be coordinated into a regular daily routine. Failure to follow this complex regimen exposes patients and their families to long-term complications such as loss of vision, renal failure, and amputations.

The purpose of the study discussed in this chapter was to determine the extent to which variables from the individual (demographics), family, and community contexts are predictors of mothers' satisfaction with medical care of their children with diabetes and to determine whether mothers' satisfaction with medical care is significantly associated with medical outcomes such as adherence to treatment regimens and the health status of their children with diabetes.

METHOD

Participants

The participants in the present study were 158 children with diabetes and their mothers or female guardians. The children were receiving medical treatment at outpatient diabetes clinics of two university-affiliated pediatric hospitals in St. Louis and had been diagnosed with diabetes at least one year before the study. The demographics for the sample are shown in Table 23-1. Socioeconomic levels of the mothers were determined using the Hollingshead (1975) Four-Factor Index, which takes into account education, occupation, marital status, and number of wage earners in the family.

Procedures

Children and adolescents who had been diagnosed with diabetes at least one year previously and their mothers or female caretakers were invited to participate in the study. Children were excluded if they had any other chronic illness or were older than age 18. The mothers completed interviews and questionnaires regarding family and community stressors, adherence, and satisfaction with medical services. Children age nine and older completed interviews and questionnaires assessing their adherence to medical regimens and their perceptions of family interactions. Blood samples were drawn at the time of the interview to determine the children's health status (metabolic control).

Measures

Satisfaction with Medical Care. The mothers' satisfaction with their children's medical care was measured with the Patient Satisfaction Questionnaire developed by Ware and colleagues (1983). The scale, a

Table 23-1
Demographic Characteristics of the Sample (N = 158)

Characteristic	n	%	
Gender of child			
Female	80	50.6	
Male	78	49.4	
Race			
African American	55	34.8	
White	103	65.2	
Family status			
Two parents	104	65.8	
Single parent	54	34.2	
Receive Medicaid			
Yes	31	19.6	
No	127	80.4	
Education level of mother			
Some high school	12	7.6	
High school graduate	42	26.6	
Some college	60	38.0	
College graduate	31	19.6	
Graduate school	13	8.2	
	M	*SD*	**Range**
Age (years)			
Child	12.6	3.5	3–18
Mother or female caregiver	39.3	7.2	21–80
Socioeconomic status[a]	37.5	14.1	6.0–63.5

[a]As measured by the Hollingshead (1975) Four-Factor Index.

69-item self-report instrument that measures attitudes toward doctors and medical care, includes eight subscales that measure dimensions of medical care (Table 23-2). For our analyses, we computed a total satisfaction score for mothers and two subscale scores: total access (accessibility or convenience of care and finances) and total doctor's manner and competence (interpersonal manner and technical quality). Validity of the scale has been demonstrated in reports by Ware and colleagues (1983). Reliability analyses for the present sample indicated Cronbach's alpha coefficients in the acceptable range (total access, .81; total doctors' manner and competence, .87; and total patient satisfaction, .92).

Patients' Adherence to Medical Regimen. The Adherence and IDDM Questionnaire–R (Hanson, Henggeler, & Burghen, 1987a) was used to assess the degree to which the youths followed medical advice in several areas. The questionnaire was administered in face-to-face interviews with the mothers and youths. The initial questionnaire consisted of 15 items measuring adherence to blood glucose testing and urine testing for ketones (three items), diet (nine items), and treatment of hypoglycemia (three items).

Table 23-2

Dimensions of Patient Satisfaction

Dimension	Definition
Interpersonal manner	Amount of caring physician shows toward patient in terms of friendliness, concern, patience, and respect
Technical quality of care	Providers' ability, experience, thoroughness, attention to detail, and clear explanations
Accessibility and convenience	Ease of arranging appointments, distance from sites, hours in which care can be received, waiting times, and access to care by telephone or from home
Finances	Cost of care, flexibility of payments, and comprehensiveness of insurance coverage
Physical environment	The particular site of care, including the pleasantness of the atmosphere, comfort of seating, clarity of signs and directions, cleanliness, and access to equipment
Availability	Medical providers' availability in geographic area
Continuity of care	The regularity of care in a particular facility or location, and whether patients see the same provider on consecutive visits
Efficacy or outcome of care	Whether providers are able to cure patients, prevent disease, and relieve suffering

SOURCE: Ware, J. E., Snyder, M. K., Wright, R. W., & Davies, A. R. (1983). Defining and measuring patient satisfaction with medical care. *Evaluation and Program Planning, 6,* 247–263.

For the present sample the total scale and subscales were revised and items dropped on the basis of reliability analyses for parents and youths. This analysis resulted in the following internal consistency reliability coefficients for the subscales and total scale according to parent and child reports, respectively: glucose and urine testing (two items, .78, .65), diet (nine items, .65, .52), and total adherence (combining adherence to blood glucose and urine ketone testing, diet, and hypoglycemia treatment) (14 items, .70, .70). The hypoglycemia subscale was not used separately in the analyses because the Cronbach's alpha was too low (<.50).

Neighborhood Stressors. A portion of Dressler's (1991) Survey Interview Schedule was used to assess neighborhood stressors. Eight items were used to measure participants' ratings of their neighborhood in the following areas: police protection, neighborhood cooperation, protection of property, personal safety, friendliness, delivery of goods and services, cleanliness, and quietness. Respondents rated their neighborhoods on these areas using a four-point scale ranging from 1 = bad to 4 = very good. Items were reverse scored so that higher scores connote higher neighborhood stressors. The Cronbach's alpha coefficient for this scale was .85.

Perception of Racism. Dressler's (1991) Perception of Racism section of the Survey Interview Schedule was modified to measure perceptions of unfair treatment on the basis of race by city officials, restaurant workers, health care providers, and school teachers.

Participants responded to six items using a four-point Likert scale ranging from 1 = strongly disagree to 4 = strongly agree. The Cronbach's alpha coefficient was .78 for this scale.

Family Stress. The Family Inventory of Life Events and Changes (FILE) (McCubbin & Patterson, 1987) is a 71-item self-report instrument designed to record normative and nonnormative family demands and strains (Cronbach's alpha = .76). The scale consists of nine subscales that include intrafamily strains, marital strains, pregnancy and childbearing strains, finance and business strains, work or family transitions, illness and family care strains, family losses, family transitions, and family legal violations. The validity of the instrument has been demonstrated in several reports (McCubbin & Patterson, 1987). In the present study, the mothers completed the FILE.

Family System Resources. The Family Inventory of Resources for Management, developed by McCubbin and Comeau (1987), is a 69-item self-report instrument that measures the family system resources in four areas: family esteem and communication, sense of mastery and health, financial well-being, and extended family social support. A score for total family resources is derived from summing these four subscales. Internal consistency reliability for the subscales and total inventory were considered adequate to good in previous reports (McCubbin & Comeau, 1987). For the present study, the Cronbach's alpha coefficient for total family resources was .92.

Youths' Health Status. The youths' health status was measured by testing their level of metabolic control using a glycosylated hemoglobin blood test, or HbA_1c. HbA_1c provides an estimate of blood glucose control during the preceding six to eight weeks (Epstein et al., 1981). Reports indicate that HbA_1c is a reliable and valid measure of metabolic control when correlated with physicians' clinical ratings of patients and fasting blood glucose levels (Gonan, Rubenstein, Rochman, Tanega, & Horwitz, 1977). During the past 20 years, HbA_1c has become the "gold standard" for determining level of metabolic control and a predictor of health status among individuals with diabetes. Higher HbA_1c values are associated with more long-term diabetic complications, and sustained reductions in HbA_1c are associated with reduced risk for long-term complications.

RESULTS

The means, standard deviations, and ranges for mother's satisfaction with medical care, family stress and resources, neighborhood stressors, perception of racism, adherence to medical regimen, and child's health status are shown in Table 23-3. The health status of the youths with diabetes who participated in this study, as measured by HbA_1c, ranged from 6.1 percent to 14.0 percent ($M = 9.2$, $SD = +1.8$). Values below 9 percent have been classified as good control and those under 8 percent as excellent (White & Henry, 1996).

Family stress levels as reported by mothers were in the moderate range as determined by the normative data from the developers of

Table 23-3

Means and Standard Deviations of Key Variables

Variable	M	SD	Range
Mother's satisfaction with medical care			
Total patient satisfaction	176.6	17.3	122–228
Doctor's manner and competence	55.4	6.8	34–75
Access and cost of care	44.3	6.1	25–58
Family variable			
Family stress	422.0	291.1	0–1,818
Family resources	112.0	20.7	54–149
Community variable			
Neighborhood stressors	14.7	3.7	8–27
Perception of racism	10.7	2.8	6–19
Adherence—Parent's report			
Total	24.1	5.9	5–36
Diet	15.6	5.0	1–26
Glucose testing	4.1	1.4	0–5
Adherence—Child's report			
Total	22.6	5.5	8–32
Diet	14.9	4.4	4–23
Glucose testing	4.0	1.4	0–5

the scale. Family resource levels reported by mothers in this study were comparable to a normative sample of families with a chronically ill child (McCubbin & Thompson, 1987).

Using bivariate and multivariate methods, we analyzed demographic, family, and community variables to predict mother's satisfaction with medical services. Mothers' satisfaction with medical services was analyzed as a predictor of two medical outcomes: (1) adherence to the diabetes treatment regimen and (2) children's health status.

Demographic, Family, and Community Predictors of Patient Satisfaction

The relationships between predictor variables and patient satisfaction were examined using Pearson product-moment correlations between satisfaction with medical care and demographic, family, community, and health status variables. Because of the number of correlations performed at the bivariate level (13), Bonferroni's correction was used, and only those correlations with significance levels less than .004 were used in multivariate analyses.

Contrary to findings from previous studies with adults that show demographic and socioeconomic correlates of patient satisfaction (Hall et al., 1994; Sherbourne et al., 1992; Zastowny et al., 1989), none of the demographic variables were associated with access and cost of care, doctor's manner and competence, or total patient satisfaction (Table 23-4). In contrast, family variables demonstrated consistent significant relationships with access and cost of care, doctor's manner and competence, and total patient satisfaction. Mothers who reported a higher level of family stress were less satisfied with access and cost of care ($r = -.32, p < .001$), doctor's manner and competence ($r = -.36, p < .001$), and total satisfaction with medical care ($r = -.33, p < .001$). Having fewer family resources was significantly associated with less satisfaction with access and cost of care ($r = .27, p < .001$), doctor's manner and competence ($r = .32, p < .001$), and total satisfaction with medical care ($r = .31, p < .001$).

Community-level variables such as neighborhood stressors and perception of racism were significantly associated with dissatisfaction with medical care. Mothers who perceived high levels of neighborhood stress reported significantly greater dissatisfaction with access and cost of care ($r = -.21, p < .01$), doctor's manner and competence ($r = -.21, p < .01$), and total patient satisfaction ($r = -.24, p < .01$). A similar pattern of results was found with perception of racism, in that a greater perception was associated with dissatisfaction with doctors' manner and competence ($r = -.31, p < .001$) and with total patient satisfaction ($r = -.30, p < .001$).

Multiple regression analyses with simultaneous entry of independent variables were performed to determine the demographic, family, and community predictors of patient satisfaction. Variables that

Table 23-4

Single-Order Correlations among Demographic, Family, Community, and Patient Satisfaction Variables

Predictor Variable	Total Patient Satisfaction	Doctor's Manner and Competence	Access and Cost of Care
Demographic characteristic			
Age of child	−.07	−.01	−.02
Age of mother	.15	.14	.17
Gender of child	.04	.00	.11
Race			
(1 = white, 2 = black)	−.08	.02	−.05
Family income	.03	−.03	.06
Mother's marital status			
(0 = single, 1 = married)	.04	.01	.06
Education of mother	−.07	−.02	−.06
Medicaid use			
(1 = yes, 2 = no)	.11	.09	.02
Employment status	−.11	−.08	−.09
Family variable			
Family stress	−.33**	−.36**	−.32**
Family resources	.31**	.32**	.27**
Community variable			
Neighborhood stressors	−.24*	−.21*	−.21*
Perception of racism	−.30**	.31**	−.17

*$p < .01$, two-tailed. **$p < .001$, two-tailed.

were significantly correlated with patient satisfaction significance levels at less than the .004 level in the bivariate analyses, as determined by Bonferroni's correction, were included in the multiple regression analyses. We performed simultaneous entry of variables so that the significance of the unique variance of each variable could be determined. The *unique variance* is defined as the increment of proportion of variance contributed by a variable when it is entered last in the model (Pedhazur, 1982). Standardized regression coefficients were computed to compare the relative influence of each variable in the model.

Separate models were generated to predict total patient satisfaction, doctor's manner and competence, and access and cost of care (Table 23-5). Results from the regression analysis to predict total patient satisfaction indicated that family stress and perception of racism remained significant in a model that accounted for 20 percent of the variance [$F(3, 134) = 11.04, p < .0001$]. Similar results were found in a multiple regression to predict doctor's manner and competence in that family stress and perception of racism remained the strongest predictor variables in a model that accounted for 22 percent of the variance [$F(3, 131) = 12.18, p < .0001$]. Results of the multiple regression analysis to predict access and cost of care indicated that family stress remained significant in a model that accounted for 11 percent of the variance [$F(2, 135) = 8.31, p < .001$].

Patient Satisfaction as a Predictor of Adherence and Health Status

To determine whether patient satisfaction was a significant predictor of medical outcomes such as adherence to the diabetes treatment regimen and health status, we performed bivariate analyses using Pearson

Table 23-5

Reduced Regression Models for Predicting Total Patient Satisfaction, Doctor's Manner and Competence, and Access and Cost of Care

Dependent Variable and Predictor	R^2	Beta[a]	p
Total patient satisfaction	.20		
Family stress		.238	.01
Family resources		.086	NS
Perception of racism		−.247	.004
Doctor's manner and competence	.22		
Family stress		−.236	.01
Family resources		.100	NS
Perception of racism		−.271	.001
Access and cost of care	.11		
Family stress		−.222	.02
Family resources		.157	NS

NOTE: NS = not significant.
[a]Standardized regression coefficient.

Table 23-6

Single-Order Correlations among Patient Satisfaction, Adherence, and Metabolic Control Variables

Predictor Variable	Total Patient Satisfaction	Metabolic Control
Youth's report		
Adherence to diet	.23**	−.15
Adherence to glucose testing	.07	−.35***
Total adherence	.22*	−.26**
Mother's report		
Adherence to diet	.07	−.28***
Adherence to glucose testing	.03	−.26***
Total adherence	.08	−.33***
Total patient satisfaction		−.11

*$p < .05$, two-tailed. **$p < .01$, two-tailed. ***$p < .001$, two-tailed.

product-moment correlations. Results indicated that patient satisfaction was significantly associated with dietary adherence (Table 23-6). Mothers who reported greater overall satisfaction with medical care had children who reported greater adherence to diet ($r = .23$, $p < .01$). Furthermore, greater adherence was significantly associated with better health status of the children. Mothers' reports of adherence to diet ($r = −.28$, $p < .001$), adherence to glucose testing ($r = −.26$, $p < .001$), and total adherence ($r = −.33$, $p < .001$) were associated with better metabolic control (lower Hb_1c values indicate better metabolic control). Similarly, children who reported greater adherence to glucose testing, ($r = −.35$, $p < .001$) and total adherence ($r = −.26$, $p < .01$) had better metabolic control.

In conclusion, mothers' satisfaction with medical care was a significant predictor of adherence, and adherence significantly predicted the child's level of metabolic control. However, there was no significant relationship found between mothers' satisfaction and the children's level of metabolic control.

DISCUSSION

Results of the study indicate that mothers' perception of racism was the strongest predictor of their satisfaction with the doctor's interpersonal manner and competence and overall satisfaction with medical care. Mothers who believed that their racial background had a negative influence on how they were treated in general and in the community (by city officials, school personnel, health care workers, restaurant workers) were more dissatisfied with their medical care. Recent research has provided empirical evidence for the negative influence of racism on health among African Americans (Jackson et al., 1996). The present study builds on this literature by providing evidence for a possible pathway by which racism influences health—through patient–practitioner communication. Mothers who were more likely to perceive greater racism were more dissatisfied with their practitioners' interpersonal manner than mothers who were more satisfied. One may hypothesize that mothers who perceive that they are treated unfairly because of their race may be more sensitive to a health care system that is inherently biased toward the majority culture. The greater the cultural distance between mother and provider, the poorer the communication and the more likely mothers will be dissatisfied with medical care.

Findings also indicate that family stress was a significant predictor of mothers' satisfaction with medical care for their children with diabetes. Mothers who reported greater family stress were significantly less satisfied overall with their medical care and specifically less satisfied with their doctor's interpersonal manner and competence than mothers from less stressful environments. Mothers who reported greater family stress were also less satisfied with access and cost of medical care. One explanation for these findings is that mothers of chronically ill children who come from highly stressful family environments may have greater medical and mental health needs and subsequently higher expectations of their health care providers than mothers with less stress. Dissatisfaction among these mothers suggests that they were experiencing a "pileup" of stressors (McCubbin & Patterson, 1987) and had inadequate resources for coping. Their high level of psychosocial needs may have led to less satisfaction with health care providers.

Findings confirm the importance of patient satisfaction as a predictor of adherence to the treatment regimen as evidenced by the significant association between mother's satisfaction with medical care and dietary adherence reported by their children with diabetes. These results are consistent with another study that found that youths' adherence was significantly associated with the mother's, father's, and youth's satisfaction with health care (Hanson et al., 1988). Our findings highlight the significance of patient satisfaction as a critical indicator of dietary adherence. These results are important because adherence to dietary guidelines is the most difficult area for youths with diabetes to follow and often causes conflict between mothers and youths. It is not clear from the present study of cross-sectional data whether greater satisfaction among mothers leads to greater adherence to treatment among the youths or whether greater adherence of the youths leads to more satisfied mothers. Most likely, there are reciprocal influences between satisfaction with medical care and medical outcomes such as adherence to treatment regimens. Mothers who are satisfied with medical care may be also satisfied with their child's management of diabetes, which in turn influences how a child reacts to an imposed dietary regimen.

Finally, there was no significant association between mothers' satisfaction with medical care and the children's level of metabolic control or health status. This finding is again consistent with research by Hanson and colleagues (1988), who found no significant relationship between mothers' and fathers' satisfaction with medical care and youths' health status. Metabolic control, a biochemical estimate of the health status of children with diabetes, is likely to be influenced by multiple behavioral, psychosocial, and hormonal factors. The data in the present study indicate a strong relationship between adherence and health status, which suggests a chain of influence whereby patient satisfaction affects adherence, which in turn affects the child's health status.

Contrary to previous research, our results did not indicate that demographic variables of the mothers and children were significant predictors of satisfaction with medical care. One explanation for inconsistencies in findings concerns the methodological differences that exist between this study and previous research. For example, there have been differences in the measurement of satisfaction with medical care with various studies using different scales. Some studies used adult participants or groups that included patients with diseases other than diabetes (for example, Hsieh & Kagle, 1991; Sherbourne et al., 1992). Still other studies sampled the patients themselves (for example, Hsieh & Kagle, 1991; Zastowny et al., 1989) rather than reports from mothers, as was done in the present study.

IMPLICATIONS FOR SOCIAL WORK

Dissatisfaction with medical care is an indicator of ineffective communication between patients and providers. Ineffective communication can be caused by a lack of sensitivity to the cultural values, norms, and environmental contexts of patients of races or ethnicities other than that of the provider. Previous discussions in the literature have identified strategies that social workers or other health care providers can use to improve communication with patients and their families (Auslander, Bubb, Rogge, & Santiago, 1993; Auslander, Thompson, & Dreitzer, 1996). These strategies include providing patients and their families with culturally relevant information in a clear and concrete way, eliciting the concerns of patients and their families, assessing and understanding the patients' family and cultural contexts, encouraging patients and their family members to be more actively involved in decisions about treatment, and developing shared expectations with patients and their families. This study indicates the need for social workers to advocate for culturally diverse patients within health care settings who perceive that they are treated differently because of their racial background or stressful family life situations.

Dissatisfaction with medical care also may be an indicator of unmet family needs and expectations. Social workers should identify family needs and expectations so that they can be addressed in routine outpatient clinic visits. One strategy that may improve satisfaction with health providers is to have social workers meet with mothers and their children to elicit their needs and expectations before they meet with the physician. Mothers experiencing high levels of family stress may be less likely to be organized and prepared with questions for the physician. Helping the family identify questions or concerns that they have immediately before meeting with the physician and encouraging the family members to ask questions during the medical visit may increase their satisfaction.

The data from the present study support an ecological framework that emphasizes the influence of environmental factors on individuals' cognitive beliefs, such as satisfaction with medical care and adherence behaviors. Previous studies with diabetic youths have focused primarily on the family context (Auslander et al., 1993; Hanson, Henggeler, & Burghen, 1987b). Our findings provide support for the importance of perceptions of racism and family stress on how medical care is perceived. Finally, this study suggests that increased satisfaction with medical care may improve patient adherence to medical regimens, a medical outcome that is important for improving the health status of children with diabetes.

REFERENCES

Anderson, L. A. (1990). Health-care communication and selected psychosocial correlates of adherence in diabetes management. *Diabetes Care, 13* (Suppl. 2), 66–76.

Auslander, W. F., Bubb, J., Rogge, M., & Santiago, J. V. (1993). Family stress and resources: Potential areas of intervention in recently diagnosed children with diabetes. *Health & Social Work, 18,* 101–113.

Auslander, W., & Corn, D. (1996). Environmental influences to diabetes management: Family, health care system, and community contexts. In D. Haire-Joshu (Ed.), *Management of diabetes mellitus: Perspectives of care across the lifespan* (pp. 513–526). St. Louis: C. V. Mosby.

Auslander, W., Thompson, S., & Dreitzer, D. (1996). Patient satisfaction: Impact on adherence and medical outcomes. *Practical Diabetology, 15*(2), 8–13.

Bronfenbrenner, U. (1979). *The ecology of human development.* Cambridge, MA: Harvard University Press.

Buller, M. K., & Buller, D. B. (1987). Physicians' communication style and patient satisfaction. *Journal of Health and Social Behavior, 28,* 375–388.

Dressler, W. W. (1991). *Stress and adaptation in the context of culture.* New York: State University of New York Press.

Epstein, L., Beck, S., Figueroa, J., Farkas, G., Kazdin, A., Danema, D., & Becker, D. (1981). The effects of targeting improvements in urine glucose on metabolic control in children with insulin dependent diabetes. *Journal of Applied Behavior Analysis, 14,* 364–375.

Germain, C. B. (1991). *Human behavior in the social environment: An ecological view.* New York: Columbia University Press.

Golin, C. E., DiMatteo, M. R., & Gelberg, L. (1996). The role of patient participation in the doctor visit. *Diabetes Care, 19,* 1153–1164.

Gonan, B., Rubenstein, A. H., Rochman, H., Tanega, S. P., & Horwitz, D. L. (1977). Hemoglobin A1: An indicator of the metabolic control of diabetic patients. *Lancet, 2,* 734–736.

Hall, J. A., Irish, J. T., Roter, D. L., Ehrlich, C. M., & Miller L. H. (1994). Satisfaction, gender, and communication in medical visits. *Medical Care, 32,* 1216–1231.

Hanson, C. L., Henggeler, S. W., & Burghen, G. A. (1987a). Model of the associations between psychosocial variables and health outcome measures in adolescents with IDDM. *Diabetes Care, 6,* 752–758.

Hanson, C. L., Henggeler, S. W., & Burghen, G. A. (1987b). Social competence and parental support as mediators of the link between stress and metabolic control in adolescents with insulin-dependent diabetes mellitus. *Journal of Consulting and Clinical Psychology, 55,* 529–533.

Hanson, C. L., Henggeler, S. W., Harris, M. A., Mitchell, K. A., Carle, D. L., & Burghen, G. A. (1988). Associations between family members' perceptions of the health care system and the health of youths with insulin-dependent diabetes mellitus. *Journal of Pediatric Psychology, 13,* 543–554.

Hollingshead, A. B. (1975). *Four-Factor Index of social status.* Unpublished manuscript, Yale University, New Haven, CT.

Hsieh, M., & Kagle, J. D. (1991). Understanding patient satisfaction and dissatisfaction with health care. *Health & Social Work, 16,* 281–290.

Jackson, J. S., Brown, T. N., Williams, D. R., Torres, M., Sellers, S. L., & Brown, K. (1996). Racism and the physical and mental health status of African Americans: A thirteen year national panel study. *Ethnicity and Disease, 6,* 132–147.

Korsch, B. M., Gozzi, E. K., & Francis, V. (1986). Gaps in doctor–patient communication. *Pediatrics, 42,* 855–871.

LaPorte, R. E., Matsushima, M., & Chang, Y. (1995). Prevalence and incidence of insulin-dependent diabetes. In National Diabetes Data Group (Ed.), *Diabetes in America* (NIH Publication No. 95-1468, 2nd ed., pp. 37–45). Washington, DC: National Institute of Diabetes and Digestive and Kidney Diseases.

Lewis, C. C., Scott, D. E., Pantell, R. H., & Wolfe, M. H. (1986). Parent satisfaction with children's medical care: Development, field test, and validation of a questionnaire. *Medical Care, 24,* 209–215.

McCubbin, H. I., & Comeau, J. K. (1987). Family inventory of resources for management. In H. I. McCubbin & A. I. Thompson (Eds.), *Family assessment inventories for research and practice* (pp. 169–188). Madison: University of Wisconsin.

McCubbin, H. I., & Patterson, J. M. (1987). Family inventory of life events and changes. In H. I. McCubbin & A. I. Thompson (Eds.), *Family assessment inventories for research and practice* (pp. 26–47). Madison: University of Wisconsin.

McCubbin, H. I., & Thompson, A. I. (Eds.). (1987). *Family assessment inventories for research and practice.* Madison: University of Wisconsin.

Pedhazur, E. J. (1982). *Multiple regressions in behavioral research: Explanation and prediction.* New York: Harcourt Brace College.

Proctor, E. K., Morrow-Howell, N., Albaz, R., & Weir, C. (1992). Patient and family satisfaction with discharge plans. *Medical Care, 30,* 262–275.

Ross, C. K., Steward, C. A., & Sinacore, J. M. (1993). The importance of patient preferences in the measurement of health care satisfaction. *Medical Care, 31,* 1138–1149.

Sherbourne, C. D., Hays, R. D., Ordway, L., DiMatteo, M. R., & Kravitz, R. L. (1992). Antecedents of adherence to medical recommendations: Results from the medical outcomes study. *Journal of Behavioral Medicine, 15,* 447–468.

Strasser, S., Aharony, L., & Greenberger, D. (1993). The patient satisfaction process: Moving toward a comprehensive model. *Medical Care Review, 50,* 219–248.

Ware, J. E., & Davies, A. R. (1983). Behavioral consequences of consumer dissatisfaction with medical care. *Evaluation and Program Planning, 6,* 291–297.

Ware, J. E., Snyder, M. K., Wright, R. W., & Davies, A. R. (1983). Defining and measuring patient satisfaction with medical care. *Evaluation and Program Planning, 6,* 247–263.

White, N. H., & Henry, D. N. (1996). Special issues in diabetes management. In D. Haire-Joshu (Ed.), *Management of diabetes mellitus: Perspectives of care across the life span* (2nd ed., pp. 342–404). St. Louis: C. V. Mosby.

Zastowny, T. R., Roghmann, K. J., & Cafferata, G. L. (1989). Patient satisfaction and the use of health services: Explorations in causality. *Medical Care, 27,* 705–723.

This research was supported in part by grant no. DK20579 from the National Institute of Diabetes and Digestive and Kidney Diseases to the Diabetes Research and Training Center of Washington University, and by U.S. Public Health Service grant no. M01 RR06021 awarded to the Pediatric General Clinical Research Center at Washington University. Portions of this chapter were presented at the annual meeting of the American Diabetes Association, June 1995, Atlanta.

24 Immunization among African American Children: Implications for Social Work

Valire Carr Copeland

H ealth care services for poor children have historically been inadequate. Over the past decade the percentages of children living in poverty, children with no health insurance, and children who lacked access to medical care services increased (Harvey, 1991; National Center for Children in Poverty [NCCP], 1990). Although childhood immunizations are one of the most effective ways to prevent and control infectious and communicable diseases, thousands of preschool children are not being adequately immunized (Centers for Disease Control and Prevention [CDC], 1994a; National Commission on Children [NCC], 1991; National Vaccine Advisory Committee [NVAC], 1991; Orenstein, Atkinson, Mason, & Bernier 1990; U.S. Department of Health and Human Services [DHHS], 1991). Immunization of preschool children is a function of the interrelationship among the health-seeking behaviors of parents of young children, financial and nonfinancial barriers to health care, and provider practices that inhibit appropriate immunization. Low rates of immunization are an especially critical problem for inner-city African American preschool children from economically disadvantaged families.

BACKGROUND

Because immunizations provide both individual and group immunity, the goal is to have the greatest possible proportion of the entire population immunized. If a high percentage of the population is immunized, the likelihood that the disease will be introduced into the community and infect unimmunized individuals is minimized. Immunization is incomplete when an insufficient percentage of the total population is immunized or when significant numbers of critical segments of the population, such as children, lack partial or complete immunization protection (Interagency Committee to Improve Access to Immunization Services [ICI], 1992). Childhood immunizations are one of two well-child care services (newborn screening is the other) that have been unequivocally demonstrated as an effective method of intervention, and the cost-effectiveness of childhood immunizations

This chapter was originally published in the May 1996 issue of *Health & Social Work*, Vol. 21, pp. 105–114.

has been demonstrated repeatedly (Kotch, Blakely, Brown, & Wong, 1992).

A child is fully immunized when the recommended schedules for active immunizations have been met (Miller, Fine, & Adams-Taylor, 1989). Current recommendations suggest that children receive between 11 and 15 vaccines, many in combination form and all requiring more than one dose, for a total of five immunizations by age two (CDC, 1995b; DHHS, 1991, 1994; ICI, 1992). A child who begins receiving immunizations by 10 months of age should be able to complete the full series of individual immunizations by his or her second birthday (DHHS, 1994; Klein, 1991). By school entry, state legislation usually requires the immunization of children against polio, diphtheria, pertussis (whooping cough), tetanus, measles, rubella, mumps, hepatitis B, and Haemophilus B conjugate. This accounts for the higher rates of immunization among kindergarten and first-grade children than among younger children (Hinman, 1990; ICI, 1992; Novello, 1991; Orenstein et al., 1990). Compulsory immunization for school entry is widely supported by health and welfare officials because immunization rates are a good predictor of long-term changes in the incidence of disease (Miller et al., 1989).

However, there is no universal approach to immunizing all children, and the current childhood immunization system lacks national coordination. Although the actual vaccine delivery system is the responsibility of state and local governments (Orenstein et al., 1990), the past success of childhood immunization programs has been a direct result of the partnership among local, state, and federal governments. About half of U.S. children receive their immunizations from private pediatricians, and the other half receive their immunizations in the public sector through public health departments and community health centers (*Childhood Immunizations*, 1992; DHHS, 1994; Hinman, 1990; NVAC, 1991). The latter half are likely to be children of color and disadvantaged socioeconomically (Hinman, 1990). Since 1963 federal immunization grants have been provided to states and some large cities and counties to supplement efforts to provide immunization through local public health programs. With the help of federal immunization grants, the widespread use of vaccines has resulted in the eradication of smallpox and declines in the incidence of measles, mumps, and whooping cough (Klerman, 1991; Orenstein et al., 1990).

Although some states have statewide integrated tracking, outreach, and education systems, most do not have comprehensive systems to identify and notify the parents of children who are due for vaccinations. The lack of a uniform data system to identify children who need to be vaccinated, the missed opportunities to offer immunizations when children have unrelated health care visits, the failure to assess the immunization status of younger siblings when school-aged children are vaccinated, and the overinterpretation of contraindications are among the service delivery system factors that negatively influence immunization (*Childhood Immunizations*, 1992;

DHHS, 1994; Hinman, 1991; ICI, 1992; NVAC, 1991; Orenstein et al., 1990). A *contraindication* is a medical illness that prevents a child from being vaccinated while receiving medical care. In some facilities mild conditions such as a minor trauma, a temperature not exceeding 100.9° F, or an upper respiratory tract infection were incorrectly referred to as contraindications (Hutchins et al., 1993).

DECLINE IN IMMUNIZATION RATES

The proportion of American preschoolers immunized against routine childhood diseases fell to fewer than half during the 1980s (Liu & Rosenbaum, 1992). As a result, communicable diseases such as measles among preschool populations are on the rise. Key reasons for the decline in immunization include the increase in vaccine cost, rising child and family poverty rates, an increasing number of children without health insurance, inadequate access to health care, and underfunding of public health programs. In addition, many parents are unaware that 80 percent of immunizations are needed by age two, and many policy-related administrative barriers exist within the health care system (Children's Defense Fund [CDF], 1992; DHHS, 1994; Kotch & Barber-Madden, 1992; Kotch et al., 1992; Liu & Rosenbaum, 1992; Schiff, 1992).

Many parents and providers have become indifferent or resistant to immunization. Some parents are unaware of the importance of immunizations or have too many other competing priorities (Kleigman, 1992; Marwick, 1991; Orenstein et al., 1990). Because people no longer see the epidemics that immunizations were developed to control (for example, polio and smallpox), parents and providers have become less sensitive to their threat. In addition, current immunization systems are not user friendly. The regular hours of both physicians and clinics require many working parents to take unpaid leave to have their children vaccinated (DHHS, 1994; NVAC, 1991; Orenstein et al., 1990).

Despite national efforts to improve the vaccine delivery system, vaccination levels for two-year-olds remain low (CDC, 1994a). In fact, immunization surveys by state health departments indicate that the percentage of two-year-olds appropriately immunized ranges from a low of 30 percent in Texas to a high of 84 percent in Vermont. The majority of states report vaccination coverage levels below 60 percent (CDF, 1992; *Childhood Immunizations*, 1992). According to the CDF (1994), "only about 55 percent of two year olds are fully immunized, and in many cities the proportion is much smaller" (p. 5). Data from the 1985 National Immunization Survey (the most recent source of national data on immunization status) showed that among children younger than five, 21.2 percent were not immunized against measles; 24.3 percent were inadequately protected against polio; and 13 percent were inappropriately protected against diphtheria, pertussis, and tetanus (Perrin, Guyer, & Lawrence, 1992). The discontinuation of nationwide data collection on immunization by the Reagan administration in 1985 (CDF, 1991a; NCC, 1991; Novello, 1991) probably accounts for some of the variability in reported statistics.

MEASLES: A PREVENTABLE EPIDEMIC

As a result of insufficient vaccine delivery to preschool children, the number of reported measles cases increased to epidemic proportions during 1989 and 1990 (CDF, 1991a; Liu & Rosenbaum, 1992; Novello, 1991; NVAC, 1991; Orenstein et al., 1990). In 1990, 27,786 cases of measles and nearly 100 measles-related deaths were reported (Atkinson, Hadler, Redd, & Orenstein, 1992; ICI, 1992; Marwick, 1991). These figures represent the largest epidemic of measles in over 10 years and the most measles-related deaths in 20 years. Because measles is more readily transmitted than other childhood infections (Marwick, 1991), this epidemic was one of the first signs that the nation's immunization system was failing. There was a general fear that serious outbreaks of rubella, mumps, and pertussis would follow if children were not properly immunized (ICI, 1992; NVAC, 1991). An analysis of 88 percent of the reported measles cases in 1990 found that the percentage of cases in preschool children of color grew from 37 percent in 1989 to 50 percent in 1990 (Hinman, 1990; Marwick, 1991).

When health officials reviewed immunization records of children entering school in Chicago in 1990, they found that most children had been immunized by school entrance regardless of race. However, the age at actual vaccination time did vary by race. In schools attended primarily by black and Hispanic children, only 50 percent had been immunized for measles by age two. In the predominantly white schools, 80 percent of the students had been vaccinated by age two. Before school entry, 7 percent of the students in the predominantly white schools needed measles vaccinations, whereas 27 percent and 29 percent of black and Hispanic students needed vaccinations, respectively. When 75 percent or more of the students in the predominantly white schools were vaccinated by their second birthday, virtually no measles were reported in the communities served by these schools. In contrast, when only 45 percent to 55 percent of the students in the predominantly black and Hispanic schools were vaccinated by their second birthday, higher incidence rates for measles were reported (Hinman, 1990; Orenstein et al., 1990).

By 1990 it was estimated that approximately 60 percent of preschool children nationwide were vaccinated against measles. In 1991 more preschool children had been vaccinated, and the number of reported measles cases decreased from 27,786 in 1990 to 9,643 in 1991 (Atkinson et al., 1992; CDF, 1992; Liu & Rosenbaum, 1992). Nevertheless, the 1991 figure was still significantly higher than the annual number of reported cases during most of the 1980s. As a result of the nationwide effort to increase vaccination levels following the measles resurgence between 1988 and 1991, the number of reported measles cases decreased to a historic low of 312 in 1993 (CDC, 1994a, 1995a).

BARRIERS TO IMMUNIZATION FOR
AFRICAN AMERICAN CHILDREN

On many occasions, poor families face a combination of barriers when trying to obtain quality, comprehensive health care. For the most part, these barriers fall into one of three categories: information barriers, financial barriers, and systemic barriers.

Information Barriers

Like other child health status indicators, the percentage of preschool children who are adequately immunized and who have a regular source of preventive care varies considerably by race and income. For example, black preschool children from low-income families are seven times as likely to get measles as white preschool children from low-income families (CDC, 1994a; Harvey, 1991; ICI, 1992; Kleigman, 1992; Miller, Coulter, Fine, Adams-Taylor, & Schorr, 1985; NVAC, 1991; Perrin et al., 1992; St. Peter, Newacheck, & Halfon, 1992). Black preschool children from low-income families have more limited access to preventive services; their parents may have skeptical attitudes or cultural beliefs about health care (for example, a disbelief in their susceptibility to disease) (Perrin et al., 1992; Riddiough, Willems, Sanders, & Kemp, 1981) or may feel powerless to prevent disease (Perrin et al., 1992; Riddiough et al., 1981; Wessner, 1992). In addition, low maternal educational levels are associated with lack of mothers' clear understanding that vaccines are needed, which reduces the demand for services as well as the levels of immunization (ICI, 1992; Perrin et al., 1992; Racine, Joyce, & Grossman, 1992).

Financial Barriers

Health insurance coverage has a significant effect on children's use of health services (Harvey, 1991; ICI, 1992; St. Peter et al., 1992), and low parental income lessens a child's chances of having a regular source of health care. Black children whose parents are employed are significantly more likely than white children to have parents with low annual incomes and no employer health coverage (CDF, 1991a; Danziger & Stern, 1990; NCC, 1991; Newacheck & Halfon, 1988). They are also more likely than white children to be uninsured and to have separate and unequal sources of health care (St. Peter et al., 1992). Uninsured children have fewer physician visits for particular acute illnesses and are less likely to be adequately immunized than children with public or private insurance.

Because health insurance reduces out-of-pocket costs of health care at the time when services are received, health insurance, private or public, has a crucial role in facilitating access to health services. Depending on the breadth of services covered, health insurance coverage does have some influence on immunization protection (Lewit, Larson, Gomby, Shiono, & Behrman, 1992). Although most private insurance programs cover illnesses for children, many do not cover

the cost of preventive services such as immunizations, forcing pediatricians and other physicians to pass on costs to parents or refer parents to already overburdened public clinics (NVAC, 1991; Perrin et
al., 1992; Skolnick, 1991). Health maintenance organizations and preferred provider organizations typically cover the costs of preventive
care for children. The increased cost of vaccines—from $11 in the
mid-1970s to $235 in 1994, excluding the cost to administer the shots
(CDF, 1994)—has made it difficult for many low- and middle-income
families to receive immunization for their children from private
providers.

Systemic Barriers

Because of higher rates of poverty, black children, including those in
working families, depend on Medicaid to a higher degree than white
children (CDF, 1991b). Medicaid pays for preventive care, including
immunizations (Liu & Rosenbaum, 1992; NVAC, 1991; Perrin et al.,
1992; Skolnick, 1991), but the low reimbursement rates and the absence of follow-up care have created serious problems for poor children enrolled in Medicaid programs. Medicaid children between six
months and five years of age are less likely to have a regular source
of health care than older Medicaid children (Hutchins et al., 1993)
and are thus less likely to be monitored for immunizations. Children's immunization rates appear higher when cases are monitored,
when there is a usual source of routine care, when immunization
records are kept for future retrieval, and when children are enrolled
in organized community health care programs or child care programs with health care components (Gemperline, Brockert, & Osborn, 1989; Hinman, 1990; Marsh & Channing, 1987; McDaniel, Patton, & Mather, 1975; Miller et al., 1985; St. Peter et al., 1992). For the
program year ending 1983, 93.5 percent of children in Head Start had
complete or up-to-date immunizations. Despite the broad range of
preventive and primary health services available to Medicaid-eligi-
ble children through the Early and Periodic Screening Diagnosis and
Treatment (EPSDT) program, over half of all black preschool children were inadequately immunized against various preventable
childhood diseases in 1981 (Rosenbaum & Johnson, 1986). In Michigan in 1983, Medicaid children participating in the EPSDT program
achieved immunization levels of 82.0 percent, compared with the
state average of 68.6 percent (Miller et al., 1985).

IMPLICATIONS FOR SOCIAL WORK

Social workers are intervening with families to prevent the future
onset of illness by integrating education and support into traditional services for children who have already been infected as a result of
no immunization (Ell & Northen, 1990). As child health advocates,
social workers educate parents about the nature of preventable disease, support and encourage parents to seek assistance from local

immunization programs, and clarify and help anticipate problems parents may face in seeking assistance. Social workers who have joined forces with public health agencies are targeting traditional public welfare populations and encouraging cooperative working relationships that focus on public health concerns. Personnel from agencies that administer Title XIX (Medicaid) and Title V (Maternal and Child Health Services Programs) funds are jointly sponsoring health education and health behavior programs for hard-to-reach populations (Evans, 1991; Hill & Breyel, 1991; Johnson & Shearer, 1992; Machala, 1992). They are seeking the help of and providing support to health care providers for the development of culturally sensitive health promotion programs that focus on immunization and other preventive health measures for families of color. Public health social workers are supporting strategies that link immunization services with federal assistance programs so that the opportunities to vaccinate at-risk preschool children are increased.

Social workers who provide services to families and children are on the front line in improving health services utilization. Through professional collaboration with local public health departments, social workers are involved in community initiatives for which the primary goals are health care prevention, health education, and health promotion services (Auslander, Haire-Joshu, Houston, & Fisher, 1992; Baily, 1992; Evans, 1991; Johnson & Shearer, 1992; Machala, 1992; Smyly, McCluskey, & Umolu, 1992). Immunization can be increased by improving access to community outreach programs, facilitating community organization efforts, assisting communities through self-help and mutual-aid initiatives, and supporting national efforts to improve immunization status among poor children.

Community Outreach Programs

Studies show that the educational level of parents, the use of multiple providers, large family size, socioeconomic status, race, parental age, single parent status, and lack of prenatal care are likely to influence immunization (CDC, 1994a; *Childhood Immunizations*, 1992; Cutts, Orenstein, & Bernier, 1992; Hutchins et al., 1989; Klerman, 1992; Markland & Durand, 1976; Marks, Halpin, Irvin, Johnson, & Keller 1979; Orenstein et al., 1990; Perrin et al., 1992; Woodard, 1987). These are factors to consider when designing programs to improve the rate at which poor parents seek immunization for their children. Immunization education for parents of well children through well-child care clinics, schools, child care and Head Start programs, and religious organizations provides an opportunity for social work and public health collaboration. Participation in prenatal care programs provides an occasion for mothers to learn about the value of immunization. Fortunately, there are also many other approaches for helping families increase immunization for their children.

Community outreach programming is an effective method for reaching underserved and low-income populations. These programs encourage the use of a regular source of health care, disseminate health-related information about the presenting problem, and educate parents about immunization at strategic times, such as during prenatal visits, during health risk assessments, and during eligibility determination for public welfare programs. Such programs also encourage record keeping and build reminder systems into institutions such as clinics, community centers, child care settings, the workplace, and school and at redetermination of eligibility (Auslander et al., 1992; DHHS, 1994; Evans, 1991; Johnson & Shearer, 1992; Machala, 1992; Smyly et al., 1992).

For example, in the Perinatal Community Initiatives Program, a joint program of the Massachusetts Department of Public Health and Massachusetts Department of Public Welfare Medicaid Program (Johnson & Shearer, 1992), parents, guardians, and caregivers are informed about government-sponsored health and welfare programs that are available to meet the immunization needs of low-income families. Participants are encouraged to enroll their children in well-child care clinics, Maternal and Child Health Services Programs, the EPSDT program, and so forth. For fiscal year 1992, 99 percent of the infants graduating from the Perinatal Community Initiatives Program had completed their first pediatric visit, which included the first of a series of childhood immunizations. The program is now being adapted to track the immunization status of children by following them through their first year of life. Through community-based initiatives like this, parents increase their knowledge base and their awareness of the value of preventive health care for their children.

Joint ventures involving social workers and public health agencies increase access to both clinical preventive and primary health care services for those who are most in need of such services. The U.S. Department of Health and Human Services and the Centers for Disease Control and Prevention have chosen six geographic areas that are representative of the many without adequate childhood immunization to develop immunization plans as part of a national drive to ensure that children are appropriately immunized by two years of age (Woods & Mason, 1992). The six areas are Dallas; Maricopa County, including Phoenix, Arizona; South Dakota; Detroit; San Diego; and Philadelphia. As a whole, the immunization action plans include, but are not limited to, establishing tracking systems for Medicaid and EPSDT participants in need of immunizations and providing adequate reimbursement for services. Medicaid eligibility workers will assess immunization levels of clients served by individual providers as a measure of quality and to ensure compliance with federal EPSDT requirements. State EPSDT programs will make aggressive efforts to comply with federal guidelines to enroll eligible families, to recruit and retain health care providers, to provide appointment scheduling and transportation assistance, and to establish the well-child visit schedule recommended by the American Academy of Pediatrics. In addition, state officials will establish coordinated systems, particularly in large urban areas, to support the determination of the immunization status of children who receive services from other public health and welfare programs such as the Special Supplemental Food Program for Women, Infants, and Children; Aid to Families with Dependent Children; Healthy Mothers/Healthy Babies; and Healthy Start (American College of Obstetricians and Gynecologists, 1993; ICI, 1992; NVAC, 1991). These programs offer an opportunity for additional collaboration between health and social services delivery systems.

Community Organization

For poor and underserved communities, broadening the traditional relationship between social work and public health for improved health service delivery is imperative if immunization is to be increased. Social workers can encourage, organize, and educate community participants, but they cannot do it alone. The goal is to empower the community and its residents to set an agenda for change in health behavior through health awareness and health care utilization (Auslander et al., 1992; Braithwaite, Murphy, Lythcott, & Blumenthal, 1989; DHHS, 1994; NVAC, 1991).

Subcommittees of the Immunization Education and Action Committee of the Healthy Mothers/Healthy Babies coalition are determining the feasibility of the use of volunteers in providing professional and support services to local health departments, working with community leaders and national leaders to identify strategies to eliminate gaps in immunization service delivery, and working with local health departments to ensure that the immunization service and delivery needs of children of color are given a high priority (American College of Obstetricians and Gynecologists, 1993). Immunization programs that are designed to meet the health needs of low-income children from African American families must be developed by extending programs and services in the communities where these children live. It is essential that both the program development efforts and the health interventions that emerge be culturally sensitive to African American families (Auslander et al., 1992; Baily, 1992; Braithwaite et al., 1989; DHHS, 1994) and age appropriate for the defined parental group. By capitalizing on existing public health and social welfare resources, community participants are mobilized to problem solve through self-help and empowerment.

For example, in some areas, community outreach workers have been organized to do more targeted, door-to-door case-finding projects. Women in the community volunteer, or are employed, to make scheduled periodic home visits to young expectant mothers and their children up to the first year of life (Hill, 1992; Hutchins & Walch, 1989). These volunteers act as role models and mentors by providing information on immunizations and other preventive health measures. In other areas, community outreach workers meet with both young mothers and fathers and their children at designated community sites that are frequented by community residents (Hutchins & Walch, 1989). The primary goals are to provide information, encourage women to receive adequate and appropriate prenatal and postnatal care, reduce the incidence of low birthweight babies, and increase participation in preventive health services including childhood immunizations. Using community outreach workers that have the same racial, ethnic, or cultural background as the participants has had some success in several health promotion programs (Auslander et al., 1992; Baily, 1992; Hutchins & Walch, 1989; Stewart & Hood, 1970). However, accurate data demonstrating the extent of their success are extremely hard to come by, and therefore some observers question the cost-effectiveness of this extremely staff- and labor-intensive strategy (Hill, 1992; Hutchins et al., 1989).

Nevertheless, given the present social, political, and economic climate, it is critical that collaborative relationships with agencies, individuals, and groups capable of performing social welfare functions in the community be established. The potential benefits of such relationships among public health, social work, and the community lie in the development of immunization programs specifically designed to improve the health of underserved black children. The challenge is to design partnership models for collaboration that maximize the potential for community participation (Auslander et al., 1992; DHHS, 1994).

Self-Help and Mutual Aid

Black self-help has been defined as mutual-aid initiatives that black people are responsible for developing, implementing, and directing (Hill, 1989). Among the self-help institutions in the black community—churches, fraternal organizations, voluntary associations, neighborhood groups, and extended families (Hill, 1989)—the church, the cornerstone of the community, deserves special note. The church emphasizes a range of religious, social, educational, and cultural programs directed toward strengthening families and enhancing positive development in children and youths (Hill, 1989), and it is the natural locus for the delivery of preventive health services.

In Atlanta, a Special Project of Regional and National Significance grant was awarded to reduce infant mortality. The program uses churches as the key mechanism for reaching at-risk groups. Local church women are trained as "resource mothers" to help pregnant women negotiate the health care and social services systems. The Resource Mothers Development Project is a nationally coordinated approach for implementing home visiting programs aimed at reducing infant mortality, low birthweight, and other health risks facing young families. As volunteers, resource mothers teach young women how to cope with barriers that prevent optimum maternal and child health care and educate them about existing health care resources, including immunizations, and how to use them. With the assistance of public health social workers, black churches with existing child care programs have the opportunity to seek funding and increase their resources to develop special immunization projects for their preschool community.

National-Level Efforts

Social services and public health leaders are being encouraged to support national efforts that address ways to support the following priorities that have been identified by the NVAC: simplify the way in which some vaccines are administered and develop ways to combine others; reduce the number of visits or injections required for a full series of immunizations, which might improve parental compliance; combine the four inactivated antigen vaccines (diphtheria–tetanus–pertussis, inactivated polio, Haemophilus B, and hepatitis B); combine the four live vaccines (measles, mumps, rubella, and varicella); and produce new formulations of vaccines.

The NVAC has also recommended that additional federal support, adequate insurance, and Medicaid coverage be provided; that physicians make immunizations available on request without requiring routine examinations or using enrollment in day care or public assistance programs to screen or deliver immunizations; that surveillance of vaccine-preventable diseases and more research into vaccine delivery be enhanced; that public awareness be increased; and that long-term planning for immunization needs be developed to increase the immunization of underserved populations (CDF, 1991b; ICI, 1992; NVAC, 1991). These recommendations are consistent with those of other health care providers who call for local-level policy changes with respect to the way in which immunizations are administered (Hinman, 1990; Orenstein et al., 1990; Zylke & Marwick, 1991) and for additional federal and state support to health and welfare departments to enhance the vaccine- delivery infrastructure at the local level.

President Clinton's fiscal year 1994 budgetary proposals aimed to assist families in getting their children immunized. The Clinton administration proposed a comprehensive immunization strategy, with a $326.5 million increase to fund immunization plans in states and cites. These funds would be used to hire more public health nurses and open more public health clinics, educate parents, and coordinate immunization services with other children's programs funded by federal and state monies (CDF, 1993). In October 1994 the federal government made free pediatric vaccines available to all children who are uninsured, are enrolled in Medicaid, or are American Indians or Alaska Natives, thus shifting the responsibility of immunization to state and local health officials. The Childhood Immunization Initiative launched by the Clinton administration has focused on improving the quality and quantity of vaccination delivery services; reducing vaccine costs for parents; increasing community participation, education, and partnership; improving health care systems to monitor diseases and vaccinations; and improving vaccines and vaccine use (CDC, 1994b).

In addition, social workers should support state legislators who are trying to require that private insurers provide or reimburse providers for immunizations as part of their basic health benefits package and that all managed health care systems provide routine vaccination services. Finally, if America's children are to benefit from the best the U.S. health care system has to offer, immunizations should be given as part of a comprehensive child health program. Universal strategies should be developed to ensure that every eligible child is immunized at the right time. Unfortunately, the delivery of immunizations, our most effective health service, cannot wait for the development of an ideal universal and comprehensive child health program. Essential changes that target all children and especially those at greatest risk should be made now (DHHS, 1994; Harvey, 1991; NVAC, 1991). All sectors of the public and private health care system must be partners in sharing the responsibility for ensuring that all of the nation's children are appropriately immunized. By engaging in active efforts at each level of service, social workers can play a crucial role in ensuring that all children are immunized against preventable diseases.

REFERENCES

American College of Obstetricians and Gynecologists. (1993, Spring). Immunization education and action committee. *Healthy Mothers/Healthy Babies*, p. 2.

Atkinson, W. L., Hadler, S. C., Redd, S. B., & Orenstein, W. A. (1992). Measles surveillance—United States, 1991. *Morbidity and Mortality Weekly Report, 41*(6), 1–12.

Auslander, W. F., Haire-Joshu, D., Houston, C. A., & Fisher, E. D. (1992). Community organization to reduce the risk of non-insulin-dependent diabetes among low-income African-American women. *Ethnicity and Disease Journal, 2*, 176–184.

Baily, E. J. (1992, November). *Community health care worker: The key to prenatal health care programs for African American women.* Paper presented at the annual meeting of the American Public Health Association, Washington, DC.

Braithwaite, R. L., Murphy, F., Lythcott, N., & Blumenthal, D. S. (1989). Community organization and development for health promotion within an urban black community: A conceptual model. *Health Education, 20*(5), 56–60.

Centers for Disease Control and Prevention. (1994a). Vaccination coverage of 2-year-old children—United States, 1991–1992. *Morbidity and Mortality Weekly Report, 42*(51 & 52), 985–988.

Centers for Disease Control and Prevention. (1994b, August 9). *Vaccines for Children Program* (CDC Fax Information, Document No. 240022). Atlanta: Author.

Centers for Disease Control and Prevention. (1995a). Measles—United States, 1994. *Morbidity and Mortality Weekly Report, 44*(26), 486, 487, 493–494.

Centers for Disease Control and Prevention. (1995b). Recommended childhood immunization schedule—United States, January 1995. *Morbidity and Mortality Weekly Report, 44*(RR-5), 1–9.

Childhood Immunizations: Opportunities to Improve Immunization Rates at Lower Cost. Hearings Before the Senate Committee on Finance, Subcommittee on Health for Families and the Uninsured, 102d Cong., 2d Sess. 1–6 (1992) (testimony of Mark V. Nadel).

Children's Defense Fund. (1991a). *Child poverty in America.* Washington, DC: Author.

Children's Defense Fund. (1991b). *The health of America's children.* Washington, DC: Author.

Children's Defense Fund. (1992). *The health of America's children 1992.* Washington, DC: Author.

Children's Defense Fund. (1993, May). Budget proposes funding boost for children. *CDF Reports,* p. 4.

Children's Defense Fund. (1994, May). Immunizations. *CDF Reports,* p. 5.

Cutts, F. T., Orenstein, W. A., & Bernier, R. H. (1992). Causes of low preschool immunization coverage in the United States. *Annual Review of Public Health, 13,* 385–398.

Danziger, S., & Stern, J. (1990). *The causes and consequences of child poverty in the U.S.* Unpublished manuscript.

Ell, K., & Northen, H. (1990). *Families and health care: Psychosocial practice.* New York: Aldine de Gruyter.

Evans, C. A. (1991, November). *Self-help programs.* Paper presented at the annual conference of the American Public Health Association, Atlanta.

Gemperline, P., Brockert, J., & Osborn, L. M. (1989). Preventive health care utilization. *Clinical Pediatrics, 28*(1), 34–37.

Harvey, B. (1991). Why we need a national child health policy. *Pediatrics, 87,* 1–6.

Hill, I. T. (1992). The role of Medicaid and other government programs in providing medical care for children and pregnant women. *Future of Children, 2*(2), 134–153.

Hill, I. T., & Breyel, J. M. (1991). *Caring for kids.* Washington, DC: National Governors Association.

Hill, R. (1989). Self-help groups in the African-American community: Current organization and services. In A. E. Johnson (Ed.), *The black experience workshops: Collected papers* (Vol. 2, pp. 193–209). Chapel Hill: University of North Carolina Press.

Hinman, A. R. (1990). Immunizations in the United States. *Pediatrics, 86*(6, Pt. 2), 1064–1066.

Hinman, A. R. (1991). What will it take to fully protect all American children with vaccines? *American Journal of Diseases of Children, 145,* 559–562.

Hutchins, S. S., Escolan, J., Markowitz, L. E., Hawkins, C., Kimbler, A., Morgan, R. A., Preblud, S. R., & Orenstein, W. A. (1989). Measles outbreak among unvaccinated preschool-age children: Opportunities missed by health care providers to administer measles vaccine. *Pediatrics, 83,* 369–374.

Hutchins, S. S., Gindler, J. S., Atkinson, W. L., Mihalek, E., Ewert, D., LeBaron, C. E., Swint, E. B., & Hadler, S. C. (1993). Preschool children at high risk for measles: Opportunities to vaccinate. *American Journal of Public Health, 83,* 862–867.

Hutchins, V., & Walch, C. (1989). Meeting minority health needs through special MCH projects. *Public Health Reports, 104,* 621–626.

Interagency Committee to Improve Access to Immunization Services. (1992). The public health service action plan to improve access to immunization services. *Public Health Reports, 107,* 243–251.

Johnson, A., & Shearer, B. (1992). *Perinatal community initiatives program.* Boston: Massachusetts Department of Public Health, Bureau of Family and Community Health, Division of Perinatal and Child Health.

Kleigman, R. M. (1992). Perpetual poverty: Child health and the underclass. *Pediatrics, 89,* 710–713.

Klein, J. O. (1991). Immunizations. *Current Problems in Pediatrics, 21,* 381–386.

Klerman, L. V. (1991). *Alive and well.* New York: Columbia University Press.

Klerman, L. V. (1992). Nonfinancial barriers to the receipt of medical care. *Future of Children, 2*(2), 171–185.

Kotch, J. B., & Barber-Madden, R. (1992). The case for universal maternity care. In J. B. Kotch, C. H. Blakely, S. S. Brown, & F. Y. Wong (Eds.), *One pound of prevention: The case for universal maternity care in the U.S.* (pp. 252–270). Washington, DC: American Public Health Association.

Kotch, J. B., Blakely, C. H., Brown, S. S., & Wong, F. Y. (Eds.). (1992). *One pound of prevention: The case for universal maternity care in the U.S.* Washington, DC: American Public Health Association.

Lewit, E. M., Larson, C. S., Gomby, D. S., Shiono, P. H., & Behrman, R. E. (1992). Analysis. *Future of Children, 2*(2), 7–22.

Liu, J. T., & Rosenbaum, S. (1992). *Medicaid and childhood immunizations: A national study.* Washington, DC: Children's Defense Fund.

Machala, M. (1992, November). *Piecing together the crazy quilt of prenatal care*. Paper presented at the annual meeting of the American Public Health Association, Washington, DC.

Markland, R. E., & Durand, D. E. (1976). An investigation of socio-psychological factors affecting infant immunization. *American Journal of Public Health, 66,* 168–170.

Marks, J. S., Halpin, J. J., Irvin, J. J., Johnson, D. A., & Keller, J. R. (1979). Risk factors associated with failure to receive vaccinations. *Pediatrics, 64,* 304–309.

Marsh, G. N., & Channing, D. M. (1987). Comparison in use of health services between a deprived and an endowed community. *Archives of Disease in Childhood, 62,* 392–396.

Marwick, C. (1991). Measles eradication? Data suggest reaching goal will be a challenge. *JAMA, 265,* 2163.

McDaniel, D. B., Patton, E. W., & Mather, J. A. (1975). Immunization activities of private practice: A record audit. *Pediatrics, 56,* 504–507.

Miller, C. A., Coulter, E. J., Fine, A., Adams-Taylor, S., & Schorr, L. B. (1985). 1984 update on the world economic crisis and the children: A United States case study. *International Journal of Health Services, 15,* 431–449.

Miller, C. A., Fine, A., & Adams-Taylor, S. (1989). *Monitoring children's health* (2nd ed.). Washington, DC: American Public Health Association.

National Center for Children in Poverty. (1990). *Five million children*. New York: Columbia University Press.

National Commission on Children. (1991). *Beyond rhetoric: A new American agenda for children and families*. Washington, DC: U.S. Government Printing Office.

National Vaccine Advisory Committee. (1991). *The measles epidemic: The problems, barriers, and recommendations*. Atlanta: Centers for Disease Control.

Newacheck, P. W., & Halfon, N. (1988). Preventive care use by school-aged children: Differences by socioeconomic status. *Pediatrics, 82*(3, Pt. 2), 462–468.

Novello, A. (1991). The past, present, and future of children at risk. *Journal of Health Care for the Poor and Underserved, 2,* 1–6.

Orenstein, W. A., Atkinson, W. A., Mason, D., & Bernier, R. H. (1990). Barriers to vaccinating preschool children. *Journal of Health Care for the Poor and Underserved, 1,* 315–330.

Perrin, J., Guyer, B., & Lawrence, J. M. (1992). Health resources for children and pregnant women. *Future of Children, 2*(2), 58–77.

Racine, A. D., Joyce, T. J., & Grossman, M. (1992). Health services for children and adolescents. *Future of Children, 2*(2), 40–57.

Riddiough, M. A., Willems, J. S., Sanders, C. R., & Kemp, K. (1981). Factors affecting the use of vaccines: Considerations for immunization program planners. *Public Health Reports, 96,* 529–535.

Rosenbaum, S., & Johnson, K. (1986). Providing health care for low-income children: Reconciling child health goals with child health financing realities. *Milbank Quarterly, 64,* 442–478.

Schiff, D. W. (1992). Health consequences of inadequate access to maternity and infant health care. In J. B. Kotch, C. H. Blakely, S. S. Brown, & F. Y. Wong (Eds.), *One pound of prevention: The case for universal maternity care in the U.S.* (pp. 108–124). Washington, DC: American Public Health Association.

Skolnick, A. (1991). Should insurance cover routine immunizations? *JAMA, 265,* 2453–2454.

Smyly, V., McCluskey, T., & Umolu, I. (1992, November). *Promoting community leadership on black infant health*. Paper presented at the annual meeting of the American Public Health Association, Washington, DC.

Stewart, J. C., & Hood, W. R. (1970). Using workers from "hard-core" areas to increase immunization levels. *Public Health Reports, 85,* 177–185.

St. Peter, R. F., Newacheck, P. W., & Halfon, N. (1992). Access to care for poor children: Separate and unequal? *JAMA, 267,* 2760–2764.

U.S. Department of Health and Human Services. (1991). *Healthy people 2000: National health promotion and disease prevention objectives*. Washington, DC: U.S. Government Printing Office.

U.S. Department of Health and Human Services. (1994). *HHS fact sheet: The Childhood Immunization Initiative.* Atlanta: CDC Press Office.

Wessner, C. (1992). Measles outbreaks on the rise: Childhood diseases on the rebound? *State Health Notes: Intergovernmental Health Policy Project, 13*(142), 1, 8.

Woodard, H. B. (1987). Some factors associated with non-immunization. In L. Leathers (Ed.), *Proceedings of the 21st Immunization Conference* (pp. 67–69). Atlanta: Centers for Disease Control, Center for Prevention Services, Technical Information Services.

Woods, D. R., & Mason, D. D. (1992). Six areas lead national early immunization drive. *Public Health Reports, 107,* 252–256.

Zylke, J. W., & Marwick, C. (1991). Vaccine challenges. *JAMA, 266,* 1322.

This chapter was written when the author was on the School of Social Work faculty at the University of Michigan. The author would like to thank Kristine Siefert for her comments. An earlier version was presented at NASW's Annual Meeting of the Profession, November 1993, Orlando, Florida.

25 Asian and Pacific Islander Cultural Values: Considerations for Health Care Decision Making

Linda A. McLaughlin and Kathryn L. Braun

By the end of the century, almost 30 percent of U.S. residents will be people of color, that is, non-Caucasian; by the year 2050, this proportion is expected to reach almost 50 percent (Day, 1996). The level of diversity is even greater in Hawaii, where 71 percent of the population is of Asian or Pacific Islander ancestry and only 27 percent of the population is white (Yatabe, Koseki, & Braun, 1996). However, the medical standards of today's health care system are based on Western values promulgated through such organizations as the Joint Commission for the Accreditation of Healthcare Organizations, the American Medical Association (AMA), and the American Hospital Association (AHA). Conflicts that reach hospital ethics committees are resolved based on a Western model of ethics that includes four principles: autonomy, beneficence, nonmaleficence, and justice (Beauchamp & Childress, 1983). This chapter looks primarily at the principle of autonomy and the health care conflicts that can arise when it is applied to cultures that are more collectivist than individualist (Barker, 1994). In further exploration of these issues, the chapter discusses the individualist value base that supports current U.S. health care policies; examines collectivist decision-making norms, with examples from six Asian and Pacific Islander cultures; considers specific problems in health care when culture and policy clash; and presents implications for practice and research.

HEALTH CARE DECISION MAKING IN THE UNITED STATES

It may surprise many Americans that before 1960, health care decision-making practices in the United States were often paternalistic (Novack et al., 1979). Deference to doctors' health care decisions was commonplace, although there are reports that patients were uncomfortable with their sole dependence on physicians to disclose their true diagnosis (Edge & Groves, 1994). Even when informed consent became an ethical obligation in 1957 (as articulated in the codes of ethics of the AMA and the AHA), physicians still resisted telling patients about serious illness, especially if the prognosis was terminal (Feifel,

This chapter was originally published in the May 1998 issue of *Health & Social Work*, Vol. 23, pp. 116–126.

1990; Novack et al., 1979). For example, Oken (1961) found that only 12 percent of physicians surveyed in 1960 said they would tell patients of a diagnosis of incurable cancer.

Originating in the consumerism movement of the 1960s and 1970s was the increased demand for the right of autonomous health care decision making in the United States. Advances in medical technology resulted in increased treatment options that provided consumers with more choices (Edge & Groves, 1994). To help judge whether they were receiving the best course of treatment, many people demanded more knowledge about their diagnosed condition, the treatment options, and the benefits and risks associated with each option. With increased discretionary spending ability, some people also exercised this demand through their pocketbooks, preferring to buy services from professionals who provided more information and options. In other cases, people sued their physicians for withholding information or not allowing patients to choose their course of treatment (Edge & Groves, 1994). It was not until 1973 that the Patient's Bill of Rights was passed; it elevated patient self-determination from an ethical concern to a legal obligation for physicians (Edge & Groves, 1994; Foster & Pearman, 1978; Hattori et al., 1991). A big change in practice resulted, as evidenced by a 1977 follow-up to Oken's (1961) study. Of the physicians surveyed in 1977, 97 percent said that they would tell patients their true diagnosis, even if the prognosis was terminal (Novack et al., 1979). The Patient Self-Determination Act (PSDA) of 1990 (P.L. 101-508) furthered the individual's right to self-determination in health care decision making by requiring that health care institutions follow patient preferences for medical treatment as outlined in advance directives.

According to Ewalt and Mokuau (1995), self-determination is regarded by Americans as freedom from group expectations, and self-reliance is regarded as a sign of strength. It is not surprising then, that the United States would develop moral and legal mandates for physicians to follow on the basis of individualist expectations, such as the Patient's Bill of Rights and the PSDA. In effect, individualist health care decision making in the United States is the result of dissatisfaction with medical paternalism, and the value implicit in the right to self-determination has become embedded in American health care policy.

TWO INDIVIDUALIST HEALTH CARE CONCEPTS

Informed Consent

Two health care concepts that specifically reflect this individualist value base are medical informed consent and advance directives. The medical informed consent process requires physicians to communicate to patients their diagnosis, prognosis, and alternatives for treatment. Information must be communicated in a way that patients can understand, even if it requires the use of an interpreter. Patients must then make a decision about how to proceed with treatment. From a legal perspective, informed consent can be viewed as a mechanism for adjusting a historically uneven relationship, with a shift in authority from physician to patient (Cotsonas, 1991).

Advance Directives

How does the right to self-determination work for people who are no longer able to make decisions for themselves? Advance directives allow individuals to influence their course of treatment when incapacitated and unable to express their wishes directly (DeSpelder & Strickland, 1996). The two most common types of advance directives are the living will and the durable power of attorney for health care decisions. A *living will* is a document in which an individual states the kinds of medical treatment he or she wants or does not want in case of disability so severe that the individual cannot communicate his or her desires. The *durable power of attorney for health care decisions* is a written document in which an individual designates another person to make crucial health care decisions in the event of incapacitation. According to the PSDA, health care providers who receive federal Medicare funds must ask patients if they have an advance directive and if the patient does, must request a copy for the medical record or, if the patient does not, must offer the patient information about advance directives and how they can be completed (Miles, Koepp, & Weber, 1996).

COLLECTIVE DECISION MAKING IN ASIAN AND PACIFIC ISLANDER CULTURES

When discussing Asian and Pacific Islander (API) Americans, it is important to remember that this label encompasses over 30 distinct cultural and linguistic groups (Tanjasiri, Wallace, & Shibata, 1995). The largest Asian American groups are Japanese, Chinese, Filipino, Korean, and East Indian, and the largest Pacific Islander groups are Native Hawaiian, Samoan, Guamanian, and Micronesian (Zane, Takeuchi, & Young, 1994). Although each group has its own language, culture, and history in the United States, there is a growing literature that suggests that the API cultures are more collectivist than individualist (that is, these cultures tend to downplay the goals of individuals in favor of those of the group) (Hattori et al., 1991; Hofstede, 1980; Kitano & Kimura, 1980; Long & Long, 1982). A number of concepts emerge in the literature that are relevant to understanding decision making in collectivist societies.

Shared or Deferred Decision Making within Families

In collectivist societies, many decisions are not made by individuals, but by families and groups, presumably with the larger good in mind. For example, in focus groups in Hawaii, physicians said they modified their approach to families on the basis of their understanding of cultural decision-making norms. Unlike the custom among white people, for whom the individual patient is the decision maker, many Japanese and Chinese families assign decision-making duties to the eldest son. In Pacific Islander families, it may be less obvious who the decision maker is. A member may be designated as decision maker, and others are assigned to other duties (for example, bringing food, telling stories, and running errands). Regardless of role, all family members customarily receive the same level of detail about the patient's diagnosis, prognosis, and treatment options (Braun, Mokuau, & Tsark, 1997).

Filial Piety

Filial piety refers to the obligation of family members to care for each other, with a particular obligation for the younger generation to care for the older generation and family ancestors. Thus, children must ensure that parents are well cared for in old age, and the family feels great shame if they cannot. In a health care context, decisions about placing an elderly patient in a nursing home, for example, may be somewhat simplified by the cultural norm to keep the elderly relative at home (Long & Long, 1982). On the other hand, it can cause conflict in families that are unable to arrange schedules, finances, and assistance to provide home-based care. This value may also result in a reluctance to tell an older family member his or her true diagnosis and prognosis, as the younger person has an obligation to protect the older person from upsetting news (Tamura, 1994).

Silent Communication

A collectivist style of silent communication relies on an implied understanding between people of that culture. Because of cultural norms, implicit concerns are not allowed to be expressed verbally. For example, it would be improper for a son or daughter to discuss issues of death and dying with parents, yet concern by either party may be expressed by nonverbal cues such as bowing of the head or eye contact. When dealing with Western health care workers, implicit understandings are not overtly stated. Unless the health care provider understands the culture so well that he or she can address the unspoken, this valuable information is lost and can lead to a misunderstanding about family–patient dynamics and agreement with the plan of care (Marsella, 1993).

Preservation of Harmony

The concept of preservation of harmony affects health care decision making in several ways. People from collectivist societies may be less willing to share bad news within the group, because it may disrupt the harmony of the group. They may also be less likely to question the decisions made by the family, feeling that the decision was made for the overall good of the family. As revealed in Honolulu-based focus groups, families may also be less inclined to question decisions made by health care professionals who have the harmony of the health system to maintain. Finally, they may be more likely to endure hardship and pain, and they are more likely to keep their wishes silent, especially if they believe their true desires would inconvenience another person or disturb the group (Saldov, Kakai, & McLaughlin, 1997).

Health Care: Delayed Access but Great Respect

Societies with a high reliance on their own social group or community for care may delay their use of Western medicine, especially preventive services. Rather there is an expectation that minor ailments will be cared for within the family or social unit, and Western medicine will be used only if emergency care is needed. Once inside the health care system, however, those from collectivist cultures may abdicate decision making to the physician, who is seen as a wise and benevolent authority figure. This approach to decision making does not allow for individual choice in medical care. Instead, physicians are expected to make decisions that are in the best interest of the greatest number of people involved with the patient. The physician also serves as a buffer so that individual family members are not at risk of being blamed for poor decisions (Feldman, 1985).

SPECIFIC CULTURAL NORMS

Japanese

In Japan the concept "amae" refers to four principles that guide decision making in traditional Japanese families: (1) collective family interests take priority over the interests of individuals, (2) harmony must be preserved, (3) the family is responsible for caring for its elders, and (4) family members are interdependent (Hattori et al., 1991). Caring for parents must be done with feelings of deep gratitude and happiness that the children are able to return the caring that their parents gave them. Not acting accordingly brings great shame to the family name (Takamura, 1991). In terms of help seeking, there is an expectation that all help will be provided from within the family and there will be resistance to obligating oneself to an outside provider of help (Fujita, Ito, Abe, & Takeuchi, 1991).

In the traditional culture, Japanese people attach stigma to emotional and mental problems, which are attributed to genetics, punishment for past behavior (karma), or poor guidance from the family unit (Shon & Ja, 1982). Such problems are often denied and the affected family member hidden. Talking to an outsider would make the person stand out even more and would cause the family to "lose face." Once in the health care system, however, physicians' decisions are respected, and lawsuits for wrongful health care decisions are extremely rare (Long & Long, 1982).

An analysis of the Japanese saying "born Shinto, die Buddhist" exemplifies a way in which the effect of religion influences collectivist decision making. The significance of this phrase is that Shinto believe in life and light and consider the mention of death taboo (Freund &

Ikeuchi, 1995). Therefore, Shintoism does not deal with death and dying, and its followers believe that even speaking words related to terminal illness can cause *kegare*, which translates as "contamination or spiritual pollution" (Long & Long, 1982). Buddhism, on the other hand, regards death as a natural life process, and Buddhists believe that the soul continues beyond death (Braun & Nichols, 1997). Thus, many traditional Japanese turn to Buddhism in later life. The continuation of life after death comes in the form of rebirth, determined by good or bad karma accrued during life. These two beliefs, *kegare* and karma, allow for an interpretation of health care issues that is often contrary to Western medicine. First, *kegare* creates a situation in which it is not advisable to discuss terminal illness, death, or dying. This precept conflicts with informed consent procedures in the United States that mandate that diagnosis and prognosis be discussed by patient and physician. Second, the idea of karma adds to the collectivist concept of continuation of life after death, implying that present actions will affect what happens to the individual in another lifetime. Therefore, it is prudent to make decisions that serve society. For example, a person may decide to take care of elderly or sick individuals, believing that he or she will be well cared for when needed. Or one might decide to take an action that would relieve one's family or society of a burden. The idea of making a decision on the basis of personal desires may seem unnecessary or unethical to traditional Japanese people.

Chinese

Based on centuries of Confucian thought and an agrarian lifestyle, traditional Chinese beliefs center around the harmony, unity, and survival of the family. Hierarchical family relationships take priority over spousal relationships and friendships. Family members have prescribed roles according to gender, age, and birth order; for example, women are subordinate to men, children obey and care for their parents without question or resentment, and the first-born son has the greatest authority and responsibility. Elder care usually is provided by the wife of the first-born son, but all children are expected to "repay parental sacrifice via filial piety" (Huang, 1991, p. 84; see also Char, Tseng, Lum, & Hsu, 1980).

Specific to decision making, elders must be treated with respect, which may result in protecting them from bad news about diagnosis and prognosis, as well as reluctance to place them in a nursing home. The concept of karma is also important in the Chinese culture and affects views of death, dying, and decision making. For example, many traditional Chinese people feel that it is bad luck to talk about illness or death because talking about it can cause it to happen. An early death is often interpreted as punishment for bad deeds performed in this lifetime or in a past lifetime (Braun & Nichols, 1997).

Traditional Chinese people believe that spirits and fate influence health, as well as self-control. Thus, moderation is a common practice to avoid the excesses that cause illness, including moderation in eating and drinking and suppression of strong negative feelings like anger and expressions of pain (Lasky & Martz, 1993). The traditional culture also believes that personal mistakes or outcries can reflect badly on the entire family and cause shame. Thus, traditional Chinese families may keep private concerns within the family, rather than talking about them with outsiders (Lin, 1985; Ryan, 1985). Instead, they might rely on more passive forms of coping, such as keeping busy, looking the other way, and not thinking too much (Huang, 1991). They may also treat themselves with herbs and other Chinese approaches to healing (Char et al., 1980). Barker (1994) found that some Chinese patients have been labeled noncompliant as a result. Although use of traditional remedies does not specifically represent a collectivist means of decision making, it does affect Chinese willingness to make use of Western health care. If traditional Chinese people are not using Western health care, they will be less knowledgeable of policies designed to enhance individual rights in these settings. However, once in the health care system, physicians are seen as authority figures, and traditional Chinese families are likely to defer to the physician about treatment recommendations.

Vietnamese

The Vietnamese have been influenced by several sets of religious beliefs that reflect on end of life and health care decision making. With strong emphasis on Buddhism, the concept of karma can lead to fatalistic attitudes toward illness and death (Lasky & Martz, 1993). Among Vietnamese in Hawaii, there is a notion that karma determines longevity (Braun & Nichols, 1997). Thus, there is little sense in completing advance directives, as they imply that the individual can have control over his or her life span. Family unity and filial piety are also important, requiring that children care for their elders and ancestors who, in turn, watch over the family. These notions work in tandem; as interviews in Hawaii suggested, when children take good care of the parents, both parents and children will be reborn at a higher level in the next lifetime (Braun & Nichols, 1997).

Taoism is also a prevalent religion among Vietnamese (and Chinese) people. This philosophy stresses that when things are permitted to assume their natural course, they move toward perfection and harmony (Hoang, 1985). To facilitate harmony, Vietnamese will frequently use traditional healing medicines, either before seeking Western medicine or while being treated by physicians. Like the Chinese, the Vietnamese are hesitant to allow any procedure that cuts the flesh because of a fear of disrupting harmony (Nguyen, 1985). They may also be reluctant to say "no" to a physician or health care worker because this would be disrespectful and may also create disharmony (Nguyen, 1985). However, Nguyen found that Vietnamese families want to be involved in major decisions concerning the health care of an individual family member, which is in line with a collectivist culture.

Filipino

Although there are limited studies available on Filipino decision making about health care, filial piety is clearly an influence. Barker (1994) cited an example of an elderly Filipino man who had inoperable cancer. The hospital staff wanted to make a referral to a hospice. Although the daughter concurred, she insisted that the doctor tell the patient that it was the hospital's decision to have her father admitted to a hospice rather than her decision. The shame experienced by the daughter in needing help to care for the father was more than she could bear.

Many in the traditional Filipino culture believe that illness is caused by an imbalance in spirit or morals. Baysa, Cabrera, Camilon, and Torres (1980) found that many Filipinos believe that most people get what they deserve and that if people behave badly, bad things will happen to them. Filipinos may delay seeking treatment and attempt to care for themselves until there are signs of bleeding or extreme weight loss and then present at a hospital emergency room as a last resort. Filipinos are similar to the Chinese and Vietnamese in that they believe invasive medical procedures that puncture the skin can cause "bad things" to happen to the body.

Filipinos expect family members to care for them in the event of illness, and within the family it is quite common to freely express pain and suffering (Frank-Stromborg & Olsen, 1993). However, Filipinos are hesitant to express signs of suffering in front of strangers or to discuss emotions with health care workers (Baysa et al., 1980). They also may avoid seeking help because they do not want to be a burden. Once health care is obtained, Filipinos tend to be compliant because of deference toward physicians. The exception is cases in which the patient or family do not understand what is being said but are reluctant to ask for clarification. Our personal experience working with members of this group in Honolulu suggests that patients may not be compliant if a health care worker disregards other family members' opinions.

Hawaiian

In traditional Hawaiian culture, there was a tendency to accept medical conditions and adjust to unpleasant symptomatology without complaint. This was, in part, a result of the fact that traditionally health practices were integrated with daily religious and social practices and emphasized the spiritual unity of the individual with the environment. Added to tradition is a Hawaiian view of Western medicine as autocratic and in conflict with the Hawaiian culture's more holistic approach (Braun et al., 1997; Frank-Stromborg & Olsen, 1993). Thus, it is not surprising that Hawaiians may avoid Western medical services or use them only when experiencing severe conditions or advanced stages of illness (Native Hawaiian Health Research Consortium, 1985).

Families provide care for sick or disabled members, and this caregiving is regarded with spiritual significance and importance (Braun et al., 1997). This practice may lead to a seeming lack of concern about performing preventive health behaviors; Hawaiians know that their families will care for them and that there is significant value attached to this caregiving. Hawaiians also may not feel a need to plan for future functional incapacitation by completing personal advance directives. One of the best examples of collectivism in Hawaiian culture is the frequently used term *kokua,* defined as mutual support and interdependence (Braun et al., 1997). Implied in *kokua* is a collectivist belief that family members are expected to anticipate each other's needs and help each other without being asked.

Hawaiians also believe in a continuation between this life and the next (Nichols & Braun, 1996). People in this life are expected to have cared for those who have died, and those who have died watch over the living. In hospice, Hawaiian patients are calmed by the notion that spirits of the dead are present to help them move to the other world when it is time. Again, a collectivist theme emerges. If an individual adheres to this belief, he or she is less likely to use medical care or to assert individual desires about health care. Rather, the person is apt to take the path that will result in the greatest harmony with family members (living and dead), society, and nature.

Samoan

According to Markoff and Bond (1980), who studied Samoans residing in Hawaii, traditional social structure in Samoan society is hierarchical, yet collectivist. The extended family is responsible for mutual support, and communities care for their members. As in the Hawaiian culture, a specific decision maker may be designated; for example, the first author was working with a Samoan patient in hospice who was the widow of a former chief. All questions about treatment had to be presented to a designated person within the extended family, who then discussed them privately with the patient's sons. Once a decision was made, this decision maker relayed it to the social worker. Although this arrangement was time-consuming and led to delays in treatment, the family insisted on it. For major decisions, the chief may be asked to listen to the case and make a judgment.

Gaining access to Western medical care appears to be problematic for Samoans living in Hawaii. Not only is it expected that injured or ill family members will be cared for at home, but also there appears to be a mistrust of Western medical care (Fiatoa & Palafox, 1980). The exception is when a loved one is in need of emergency care, at which time Western health care is sought. Western health care workers, with their emphasis on prevention, often have difficulty coping effectively with Samoans in a health care setting because of what they may perceive as a lack of regard for preventive health care. However, Samoans tend to regard the authority of a doctor with great respect and do not want their doctor to waiver on treatment decisions. Traditional Samoans also do not want to be asked what their preferences for health care might be (Fiatoa & Palafox, 1980). They want their physician to be directive, and if trust is established, compliance will follow. Young female physicians may have the most difficult time in establishing trust and achieving compliance with Samoan patients, because of paternalistic views of the physician–patient relationship.

CONFLICTS WITH U.S. HEALTH CARE POLICIES

Because of cultural differences in decision making, conflict or misunderstanding can result when non-Western patients are asked to make independent health care decisions. In many cases, the patient's dilemma goes unnoticed by health care workers, and the patient who has difficulty making independent decisions is labeled as noncompliant.

Medical Informed Consent

An aspect of collectivist cultures is to maintain harmony and further the goals of the group; therefore, it is not difficult to envision cases in which patients may sign documents because they feel it is expected by the doctor or family members. It is also easy to understand that these patients would be uncomfortable telling their physician what they want to have done medically. A study in Hawaii that investigated problems with obtaining informed consent from elderly Japanese oncology patients illustrates these problems. Preliminary findings suggest that these patients have internal conflicts about signing consents but that the health care workers are largely unaware that their Japanese elderly patients are in conflict. The hesitancy in signing the consent form results in treatment delays, but the delays are not attributed to value conflicts. Rather, health care workers attribute delays to the patient being elderly or noncompliant or having a language barrier (Saldov et al., 1997).

Another difficult culturally based problem is that of disclosure of the true diagnosis to the patient, particularly if the diagnosis is terminal (Blackhall, Murphy, Frank, Michel, & Azen, 1995). In many API traditions, a terminal diagnosis is withheld. Reasons for this may be that the family does not want the patient to become disheartened and give up on living, that the family feels it is disrespectful to speak of such things to an elder, or that talking about death is "polluting" or will cause bad luck. Family members, however, are generally told of the terminal diagnosis by the physician. If the patient is aware of his or her fate, the patient does not let family members know it. Therefore, medical informed consent practice, which is required in the United States, poses ethical dilemmas for physicians when family members ask them not to disclose the true diagnosis to the patient. How can the physician obtain consent to proceed with treatment if the patient is not told his or her true diagnosis and treatment options? To insist that the patient be told, however, causes conflict within the family and between patient and family.

Advance Directives

Advance directives are another area where conflict often occurs between API and Western cultures. Health care facilities are required by law to approach patients for copies of advance directives. However, it is well documented in the literature on traditional Hawaiian, Chinese, and Japanese cultures that if one talks about death, one may bring on death or, at least, spiritual pollution. It may also seem pointless to have written instructions about what to do after death because, in collectivist cultures, decisions about property and funeral services are already known within families (Nichols & Braun, 1996).

A Buddhist belief in fate and karma also adds to the dilemma for some API patients. If a patient adheres to a belief that illness and death can occur because of the way in which he or she has lived (either in this life or a past life), then there is little to be gained from trying to interfere with the course life and death may take. If patients and family members from collectivist cultures do not see a need for asserting health care directives in advance of incapacitation, there is also little need to designate a person to make those decisions. The Western rationale for assigning someone to make decisions for an incapacitated individual is based on a mistrust of the health care system (Cotsonas, 1991). From a collectivist viewpoint, individuals feel secure that in the event of incapacitation, family members and physicians will make the best possible decision for everyone concerned.

Decisions about Nursing Home Placement

When individuals can no longer live independently because of impairments and disabilities, they may need to be moved to institutional settings that provide 24-hour assistance with daily living. For API families, stress associated with caregiving is unlikely to be expressed to health care workers. In line with the concept of filial piety, a female family member (often the daughter-in-law) is expected to accept the burden of caregiving without complaint. In Hawaii, where two incomes are often needed to make financial ends meet, the stress associated with caregiving for elderly parents, working a full-time job, and caring for one's own family are more than can be tolerated. On the other hand, to express distress or need for help would trigger feelings of shame and failure. Thus, whereas a Western family may make a decision for nursing home placement early in the stress cycle, a traditional API family may wait until the situation is extremely difficult before seeking assistance and placement.

In addition, there are cultural variations as to the acceptability of family members dying at home, which also influence placement decisions. Westerners tend to be more reluctant to have a death take place in the home and may make a decision about nursing home placement early enough to avoid this occurrence. In contrast, many traditional API cultures expect death to occur at home and have mourning traditions that involve keeping the body at home for a number of days before burial (Nichols & Braun, 1996). The possibility of a death occurring in the home in a traditional household may not even be an issue in terms of making a decision for nursing home placement.

DISCUSSION

When considering health care options, there are always decisions to be made. The answer to the question "who decides" is based largely on cultural values. In the United States, the individual patient is empowered to make his or her own health care decisions. This value has been codified into a number of documents that are standard in American health care institutions, including medical informed consent and the advance directive. Alternatively, in many API cultural traditions, the individual may have (and want) little input into the decision-making process; rather, health care decisions may be decided by the family as a whole or relegated to the patient's doctor (Hattori et al., 1991; Long & Long, 1982).

The primary recommendation for cross-cultural practice is for increased sensitivity on the part of health care workers (see, for example, Brislin, 1993; Koenig, 1997; Mokuau & Shimizu, 1991). We agree with this and encourage universities and health care settings to provide education and training that promote understanding and appreciation of diverse cultures. On the basis of our work in Honolulu, we suggest the following strategies for helping professionals who work cross-culturally:

- Learn about the cultural traditions of the groups you are working with.
- Pay close attention to body language, lack of response, or feelings of tension that may signify that the patient or family is in conflict but perhaps hesitant to tell you.
- Ask the patient and family open-ended questions to elicit more information about their assumptions and expectations.
- Remain nonjudgmental when provided with information that reflects values that differ from your own.
- Follow the advice given to you by your clients about appropriate ways to facilitate communication within families and between families and other health care providers.

Although we support an increased understanding of ethnically diverse cultures, we also realize that the study of cultural variations and health care decision making is in its infancy. More research is needed on how illness and death are perceived and discussed in different cultures, how and when help is sought, and how decision making may be delegated or shared (Koenig, 1997). For API Americans, some of the same values outlined in this chapter may complicate research in this area; for example, if the culture places a high value on harmony, respondents may tell you what they believe you want to hear. Severity of pain and suffering may be underreported for similar reasons or because it may not be thought to be appropriate to share feelings with strangers. Fears of contamination and bringing bad luck on the self also create problems for health care professionals and researchers who want to ask questions about personal health and advance planning. A way to overcome these problems in data collection is to use projective-type questioning (for example, reading a scenario about a hypothetical family and asking respondents how they think that family would respond).

At both the practice and policy levels, our findings tend to support the notion that the current U.S. system of using advance directives to determine how patients want to be treated in end-of-life situations is, in itself, biased and ineffective. As other researchers have found, it appears that advance directives have more appeal to educated, insured, middle-class white people than to the country's various populations of color (Eleazer et al., 1996; Hanson & Rodgman, 1996; Randall, 1994; Sulmasy, Song, Marx, & Mitchell, 1996). Other researchers have found that even when advance directives have been made available to health care professionals, they may have little effect on use of life-sustaining treatment at the end of life (Jacobson et al., 1996; Johnson, Baranowski-Birkmeier, & O'Donnell, 1995; Teno et al., 1997). Thus, there is a call to begin addressing end-of-life planning issues with whole families (not just individual patients) earlier in the life course (rather than waiting until the end) and in nonhospital venues (Braun & Kayashima, in press; Heffner, Fahy, & Barbieri, 1996; Johnston, Pfeifer, & McNutt, 1995; Teno et al., 1997).

These findings also support further exploration into family-centered, rather than patient-centered, models of medical decision making (Blackhall et al., 1995). In fact, the law on informed consent currently gives physicians some leeway in their interpretation of how to obtain informed consent and does not negate use of a family-centered model (Cotsonas, 1991). Support for shared decision-making mechanisms comes from DeSpelder and Strickland (1996) as well, who argued that many health care decisions are too big for any single person to make, regardless of their ethnicity. Moody (1992) concurred and called for further exploration of the concept and practice of "negotiated consent" as a middle ground between paternalist and autonomous decision making in nursing homes. A process to obtain a negotiated consent recognizes the legitimacy of multiple views (for example, of the resident, family, health care providers, and the institution) and supports open communication and increased understanding as the parties move toward fair decisions.

CONCLUSION

The United States is becoming more ethnically and culturally diverse. To help health care workers increase their awareness of different cultures and to reduce potential conflict, more research is needed on how different cultural groups approach end-of-life decision making. The study of more collectivist cultures may also shed light on the use and usefulness of shared or negotiated decision-making models. Given that our current system of health care decision making, which is based on patient autonomy, does not appeal to all Americans (Koenig, 1997) and may not work well in the context of long-term care and end-of-life care (Moody, 1992), study of collectivist cultures may help the U.S. medical community develop a more effective model for decision making in these situations.

REFERENCES

Barker, J. (1994). Recognizing cultural differences: Healthcare providers and elderly patients. In D. Wieland, D. Benton, B. Kramer, & G. Dawson (Eds.), *Cultural diversity and geriatric care* (pp. 9–21). Binghamton, NY: Haworth Press.

Baysa, E., Cabrera, E., Camilon, F., & Torres, M. (1980). The Filipinos. In N. Palafox & A. Warren (Eds.), *Cross-cultural caring: A handbook for health care professionals in Hawaii* (pp. 197–231). Honolulu: Transcultural Health Care Forum.

Beauchamp, T. L., & Childress, J. F. (1983). *Principles of biomedical ethics.* New York: Oxford University Press.

Blackhall, L., Murphy, S., Frank, G., Michel, V., & Azen, S. (1995). Ethnicity and attitudes toward patient autonomy. *JAMA, 274,* 820–845.

Braun, K. L., & Kayashima, R. (in press). Death education in churches and temples. In B. DeVries (Ed.), *End-of-life issues: Interdisciplinary and multidimensional perspectives.* New York: Springer.

Braun, K. L., Mokuau, N., & Tsark, J. (1997). Cultural themes in health, illness, and rehabilitation for Native Hawaiians: Observations of rehabilitation staff and physicians. *Topics in Geriatric Rehabilitation, 12,* 19–37.

Braun, K. L., & Nichols, R. (1997). Death and dying in four Asian cultures. *Death Studies, 21,* 327–360.

Brislin, R. (1993). *Understanding culture's influence on behavior.* Orlando, FL: Harcourt Brace.

Char, W. F., Tseng, W. S., Lum, K. Y., & Hsu, J. (1980). The Chinese. In J. F. McDermott, W. S. Tseng, & T. W. Maretzki (Eds.), *People and cultures of Hawaii: A psychocultural profile* (pp. 53–72). Honolulu: University Press of Hawaii.

Cotsonas, C. (1991). The law and the limits of the law of informed consent. *Family Systems Medicine, 9,* 307–312.

Day, J. C. (1996). *Population projections of the United States by age, sex, race, and Hispanic origin: 1995 to 2050* (Current Population Reports, P-251130). Washington, DC: U.S. Government Printing Office.

DeSpelder, L., & Strickland, A. (1996). *The last dance.* Mountain View, CA: Mayfield.

Edge, R. S., & Groves, J. R. (1994). *The ethics of health care: A guide for clinical practice.* Albany, NY: Delmar.

Eleazer, G. P., Hornung, C. A., Egbert, C. B., Egbert, J. R., Eng, C., Hedgepeth, J., McCann, R., Strothers, H., Sapir, M., Wei, M., & Wilson, M. (1996). The relationship between ethnicity and advance directives in a frail older population. *Journal of the American Geriatrics Society, 44,* 938–943.

Ewalt, P., & Mokuau, N. (1995). Self-determination from a Pacific perspective. *Social Work, 40,* 168–175.

Feifel, H. (1990). Psychology and death: Meaningful rediscovery. *American Psychologist, 45,* 537–543.

Feldman, E. (1985). Medical ethics the Japanese way. *Hastings Center Report, 155,* 21–24.

Fiatoa, L., & Palafox, N. (1980). The Samoans. In N. Palafox & A. Warren (Eds.), *Cross-cultural caring: A handbook for health care professionals in Hawaii* (pp. 250–271). Honolulu: Transcultural Health Care Forum.

Foster, M. G., & Pearman, W. A. (1978). Social work, patient rights, and patient representatives. *Social Casework, 59,* 89–100.

Frank-Stromborg, M., & Olsen, S. J. (1993). *Cancer prevention in minority populations: Cultural implications for health care professionals.* St. Louis: C. V. Mosby.

Freund, A., & Ikeuchi, F. (1995). A Japanese Buddhist hospice and Shunko Tashiro. In D. Chappel (Ed.), *Living and dying in Buddhist cultures* (p. 8). Honolulu: University of Hawaii, Buddhist Studies Center.

Fujita, S., Ito, L., Abe, J., & Takeuchi, D. (1991). Japanese Americans. In N. Mokuau (Ed.), *Handbook of social services for Asians and Pacific Islanders* (pp. 61–77). Westport, CT: Greenwood Press.

Hanson, L. C., & Rodgman, E. (1996). The use of living wills at the end of life: A national study. *Archives of Internal Medicine, 156*, 1018–1022.

Hattori, H., Salzberg, S. M., Kiang, W. P., Fujimiya, T., Tejima, Y., & Furuno, J. (1991). The patient's right to information in Japan: Legal rules and doctor's opinions. *Social Science and Medicine, 32*, 1007–1016.

Heffner, J. E., Fahy, B., & Barbieri, C. (1996). Advance directive education during pulmonary rehabilitation. *Chest, 109*, 373–379.

Hoang, G. (1985). Cultural barriers to effective medical care among Indochinese patients. *Annual Review of Medicine, 36*, 229–239.

Hofstede, G. (1980). *Culture's consequences: International differences in work-related values.* Newbury Park, CA: Sage Publications.

Huang, K. (1991). Chinese Americans. In N. Mokuau (Ed.), *Handbook of social services for Asians and Pacific Islanders* (pp. 79–96). Westport, CT: Greenwood Press.

Jacobson, J. A., Kasworm, E., Battin, M. P., Francis, L. P., Green, D., Botkin, J., & Johnson, S. (1996). Advance directives in Utah: Information for death certificates and informants. *Archives of Internal Medicine, 156*, 1862–1868.

Johnson, R. F., Baranowski-Birkmeier, T., & O'Donnell, J. B. (1995). Advance directives in the medical intensive care unit of a community teaching hospital. *Chest, 107*, 752–756.

Johnston, S. C., Pfeifer, M. P., & McNutt, R. (1995). The discussion about advance directives: Patient and physician opinions regarding when and how it should be conducted. *Archives of Internal Medicine, 155*, 1025–1030.

Kitano, H., & Kimura, A. (1980). The Japanese American family. In R. Endo, S. Sue, & W. Wagner (Eds.), *Asian Americans: Social and psychological perspective* (Vol. 2, pp. 32–48). Palo Alto, CA: Science & Behavior Books.

Koenig, B. A. (1997). Cultural diversity in decision making about care at the end of life. In Institute of Medicine (Ed.), *Approaching death: Improving care at the end of life* (pp. 363–382). Washington, DC: National Academy Press.

Lasky, E., & Martz, C. (1993). The Asian/Pacific Islander population in the U.S.: Cultural perspectives and their relationship to cancer prevention and early detection. In M. Frank-Stromborg & S. Olsen (Eds.), *Cancer prevention in minority populations* (pp. 26–50). St. Louis: C. V. Mosby.

Lin, T. Y. (1985). Mental disorders and psychiatry in Chinese culture. In W. S. Tseng & D.Y.H. Wu (Eds.), *Chinese culture and mental health* (pp. 369–393). San Diego: Academic Press.

Long, S., & Long, B. (1982). Curable cancers and fatal ulcers: Attitudes toward cancer in Japan. *Social Science and Medicine, 16*, 2101–2108.

Markoff, R., & Bond, J. (1980). The Samoans. In F. McDermott, W. S. Tseng, & T. W. Maretzki (Eds.), *People and cultures of Hawaii: A psychocultural profile* (pp. 250–271). Honolulu: University Press of Hawaii.

Marsella, A. J. (1993). Counseling and psychotherapy with Japanese Americans: Cross-cultural considerations. *American Journal of Orthopsychiatry, 63*, 200–208.

Miles, S. H., Koepp, R., & Weber, E. P. (1996). Advance end-of-life treatment planning: A research overview. *Archives of Internal Medicine, 156*, 1062–1068.

Mokuau, N., & Shimizu, D. (1991). Conceptual framework for social service for Asian and Pacific Islander Americans. In N. Mokuau (Ed.), *Handbook of social services for Asians and Pacific Islanders* (pp. 21–36). Westport, CT: Greenwood Press.

Moody, H. R. (1992). *Ethics in an aging society.* Baltimore: Johns Hopkins University Press.

Native Hawaiian Health Research Consortium. (1985). *E Ola Mau: The native Hawaiian health needs study* (Medical task force report). Honolulu: Alu Like, Inc.

Nguyen, M. (1985). Culture shock: A review of Vietnamese culture and its concept of health and disease. *Western Journal of Medicine, 142,* 409–412.

Nichols, R., & Braun, K. L. (1996). *Death and dying in five Asian and Pacific Islander cultures: A preliminary study.* Honolulu: University of Hawaii, School of Public Health, Center on Aging.

Novack, D., Plumer, R., Smith, R. L., Ochitill, H., Morrow, G. R., & Bennett, J. M. (1979). Changes in physician's attitudes toward telling the cancer patient. *JAMA, 241,* 897–900.

Oken, D. (1961). What to tell cancer patients: A study of medical attitudes. *JAMA, 175,* 1120–1128.

Randall, V. R. (1994). Ethnic Americans, long-term health care providers, and the Patient Self-Determination Act. In M. B. Kapp (Ed.), *Patient self-determination in long-term care.* New York: Springer.

Ryan, A. S. (1985). Cultural factors in casework with Chinese-Americans. *Social Casework, 66,* 333–340.

Saldov, M., Kakai, H., & McLaughlin, L. (1997). *Obtaining informed consent from traditional Japanese elders for treatment in oncology: Final report.* Honolulu: University of Hawaii, School of Social Work.

Shon, S. P., & Ja, D. A. (1982). Asian families. In M. McGoldrick, J. K. Pearce, & J. Giordano (Eds.), *Ethnicity and family therapy* (pp. 208–228). New York: Guilford Press.

Sulmasy, D. P., Song, K. Y., Marx, E. S., & Mitchell, J. M. (1996). Strategies to promote the use of advance directives in a residency outpatient practice. *Journal of General Internal Medicine, 11,* 657–663.

Takamura, J. C. (1991). Asian and Pacific Islander elderly. In N. Mokuau (Ed.), *Handbook of social services for Asians and Pacific Islanders* (pp. 185–202). Westport, CT: Greenwood Press.

Tamura, E. H. (1994). *Americanization, acculturation, and ethnic identity: The Nisei generation in Hawaii.* Chicago: University of Illinois Press.

Tanjasiri, S., Wallace, S. P., & Shibata, K. (1995). Picture imperfect: Hidden problems among Asian and Pacific Islander elderly. *Gerontologist, 35,* 753–760.

Teno, J. M., Lynn, J., Wenger, N., Phillips, R. S., Murphy, D. P., Connors, A. F., Desbiens, N., Fulkerson, W., Bellamy, P., & Knaus, W. A. (1997). Advance directives for seriously ill hospitalized patients: Effectiveness with the Patient Self-Determination Act and the SUPPORT intervention. *Journal of the American Geriatrics Society, 45,* 500–507.

Yatabe, S., Koseki, L., & Braun, K. (1996). *Asian and Pacific Island elders: An educational training module.* Honolulu: University of Hawaii, School of Public Health, Center on Aging.

Zane, N.W.S., Takeuchi, D. T., & Young, N. J. (1994). *Confronting critical issues of Asian and Pacific Islander Americans.* Thousand Oaks, CA: Sage Publications.

We thank Dr. Morris Saldov, who inspired investigation of medical decision making through his research on informed consent with Japanese elder cancer patients, and his research assistant, Hisako Kakai, who researched the Japanese-language literature for concepts that were incorporated into this chapter. We also thank Carol Matsumiya and Kim Sugawa-Fujinaga of the Center on Aging for their editorial assistance and Virginia Tanji, School of Public Health, University of Hawaii, for assistance with the literature review.

26 Health Care Needs of Medically Underserved Women of Color: The Role of the Bureau of Primary Health Care

Marilyn H. Gaston, Sharon E. Barrett,
Tamara Lewis Johnson, and Leonard G. Epstein

The hypotheses, studies, programs, and approaches discussed in this and other chapters in this book are familiar to social workers in a variety of educational and practice settings. The respective helping professions and the Bureau of Primary Health Care (BPHC) have known and worked closely together with women from Native American, Hispanic American, African American, and Asian American and Pacific Islander backgrounds for decades. The bureau has recently developed a specialized program, the Office of Minority and Women's Health (OMWH), to help address some of the unmet health care needs of women of color. This new program and its conceptualization have been based on our mutual knowledge that women of color (particularly in the lowest income group) and their children have not received the level of access or quality of physical and mental health care that they require to sustain themselves (Adams, 1995; Bayne-Smith, 1996; Center for Health Economics Research, 1993; Salganicoff, 1997; Schoen, 1997; U.S. Department of Health and Human Services [HHS], 1985; Weaver, 1976; Weiss, 1997). The difficult task for the helping professions and for government has been to determine and agree on the most effective policies, services, and conceptual approaches to support and implement in this new and fluid managed health care environment. However, during the past several years, our knowledge of successful model programs that solve and prevent some health problems has increased significantly (BPHC, 1996a). A number of successful programs developed by BPHC have been based on a clearer understanding of the relationship between the culture of a community and its health status. At the close of the 20th century, we know more about how to assist medically underserved women than ever before (Adams, 1995; Bayne-Smith, 1996). But the research challenge remains urgent to identify more specifically what works well and with which women, under what conditions and in what amounts, to prevent poor health, illness, and early death. These are critical issues in our current health care

This chapter was originally published in the May 1998 issue of *Health & Social Work*, Vol. 23, pp. 86–95.

environment, where human and fiscal resources are limited and where access, cost, quality, and utilization are being managed by new processes (Mauer, Jarvis, Mockler, & Trabin, 1995).

The intent of this chapter is to describe the roles of BPHC and OMWH and their legislative mission to enhance the health status of underserved and vulnerable women and their children; to briefly review some of the background data on the medically underserved and the particular status of women of color within that population; to identify a series of questions to help frame the policy dialogue for developing services to medically underserved women of color; and to invite dialogue, feedback, and participation with social workers around a number of these key questions and issues that can help guide our collective vision and health care initiatives for the medically underserved population over the next several years.

BPHC MISSION

One of the most significant problems for underserved populations is their inability to obtain health care services in the marketplace. Where access is severely limited, "people use fewer health services and have worse health outcomes" (Center for Health Economics Research, 1993, p. 6). The limited access of medically underserved and vulnerable populations is reflected in their higher mortality rates and increased rates of cancer, heart disease, stroke, and dental disease (Center for Health Economics Research, 1993).

BPHC was developed by the Public Health Service to increase access to comprehensive primary and preventive health care and to improve the health status of populations defined as medically underserved (BPHC, 1996b). Generally, the *medically underserved population* in the United States is defined as individuals and families who lack adequate "access to primary care" (Hawkins & Rosenbaum, 1993, p. 49). Multiple barriers to access exist: low income, lack of health insurance, old age, poor health outcomes, inadequate health infrastructure, and insufficient supply of primary physicians, as well as cultural, attitudinal, and linguistic differences (Hawkins & Rosenbaum, 1993). When gender is added to these characteristics, the risk of limited access increases. A medically underserved woman encounters additional barriers to health care access that result from any combination of the following characteristics including, but not limited to, poverty: race, ethnicity, and culture; state of mental or physical health; geographic location; and sexual orientation (BPHC, 1996b).

When the definition of medically underserved is operationalized to include 12 health status variables (see Hawkins & Rosenbaum, 1993) designed to measure the extent and distribution of vulnerability in state and county populations, the results show that approximately 43 million Americans fall into this category. Of these 43 million who lack access to a primary care physician, the majority are poor, female, young, and uninsured (BPHC, 1996b). Furthermore, survey research shows that these medically underserved populations are found in each state, although the proportionate distribution varies by state and to some extent by region. Proportionately more (eight of 12) of the southern states have populations that are medically underserved compared with other regions of the country. Only seven states have populations in which fewer than 10 percent are medically under-served, whereas 15 states have medically underserved populations that range between 21 percent and 46 percent of the overall popula-tion. In 28 states between 11 percent and 20 percent of the popula-tions are medically underserved (BPHC, 1996b).

Under the Public Health Service Act, BPHC does not provide di-rect services to people in local communities, but rather assists local communities in identifying populations at risk of poor health out-comes and then helps these communities in four primary ways:

1. helps establish and support the Community and Migrant Health Centers and Health Care Programs for people who are homeless and for residents of public housing
2. operates the National Health Services Corps, which provides financial support for training and education of culturally com-petent health care providers in exchange for their provision of health care services in rural and urban areas, where there is a shortage of health care professionals
3. identifies and disseminates information about creative and suc-cessful health care programs that serve as nationwide models for replication
4. works directly with local communities to establish and build primary care systems and recruit health care clinicians.

BPHC's 1998 budget appropriation of $977 million supports 17 pro-gram initiatives in more than 746 local nonprofit health clinics, in 4,500 related programs, and for more than 5,000 health care providers throughout the United States. Nearly 85 percent of the total appropri-ation to the bureau is used to support local nonprofit community health centers. The remaining 16 percent is used to support the Na-tional Health Services Corps and programs for a number of special-ized diseases—black lung, Hansen's, and Alzheimer's. The 746 non-profit health centers provide true safety-net services to the medically underserved population without regard for their ability to pay or the availability of health insurance.

Services Supported

BPHC supports primary and preventive health care for 10.3 million of the 43 million medically underserved Americans. In the period be-tween 1990 and 1996, the nonprofit health centers increased the number of uninsured people receiving plenary health care by 46 per-cent, whereas there was an increase of only 16 percent in the number of uninsured people receiving similar care nationally from other health care providers (BPHC, 1996b). Between 1995 and 1996, the number of uninsured people receiving primary care from nonprofit health centers increased by nearly 4 million, and the number of Medicaid-insured people receiving care from the health centers declined by almost 3 million. Overall, health centers supported by the bureau had over 33 million total visits in 1996.

The 17 program initiatives supported by the bureau at the local level are designed to enhance the health status of the following underserved populations: uninsured people; underserved mothers and children; inner-city, elderly poor people; women and people of color living in poverty; high-risk pregnant women; homeless families and individuals; people in rural and frontier areas; Native Hawaiians and Pacific Islanders; school children in poor communities; residents of public housing; people who are substance abusers; new immigrants and detained aliens; adolescents; people with Hansen's disease; migrant farm workers; people with Alzheimer's disease; and people with HIV/AIDS-related disorders.

Local community health centers supported by BPHC provide primary and preventive care, outreach, and dental care to these populations. In addition, the health centers offer a range of ancillary health services to the medically underserved population, including laboratory testing, environmental health, pharmacy services, health education, transportation, translation services, and prenatal care. The health centers also establish collaborative linkages with welfare agencies, Medicaid, substance abuse treatment services, the Supplemental Food Program for Women, Infants, and Children, and related state and local services and agencies. In addition, more than 350 health centers are contractually linked to managed care organizations, HMO primary care networks, and state Medicaid managed care networks in their efforts to provide quality care to the medically underserved population.

Population Served

Analysis of user data shows that low-income women of color are the major recipients of services provided in almost all 746 local health centers supported by BPHC (BPHC, 1996b). Of the people served directly in local health center programs, 57 percent are low-income women of color (32 percent are of childbearing age), and 42 percent are children. Slightly more than 65 percent of the total population served are people of color, and 85 percent of these are poor, near poor, and among the sickest and most isolated in the nation (BPHC, 1996b). The remaining 35 percent are white and have incomes that are between 100 percent and 200 percent above the poverty line. Almost 41 percent of the clients served in local health centers are uninsured. Nearly one-third of all health center clients have Medicaid coverage, whereas fewer than 8 percent have Medicare benefits. Fewer than 15 percent have private insurance benefits but have limited options for obtaining quality services in their geographic areas.

The proportion of medically underserved males and females receiving services across all local health center program initiatives is evenly distributed up to age 12. However, between ages 13 and 64, the frequency of service utilization by women almost doubles that of men. Similarity in utilization rates by gender is not noted again until both groups exceed age 85.

Women older than age 15 make up 27 percent of the clients served by the Health Care for the Homeless Program. Of the women served in this program, 40.0 percent are African American, 36.0 percent are white, 14.0 percent are Hispanic, 2.3 percent are Asian or Pacific Islander, and 2.1 percent are Native American (BPHC, 1994a, 1994b). In the HIV Early-Intervention Program, 15,000 women over age 13 received services in 1994. Of this number, a disproportionate percentage (51.7) were African American, whereas African American women make up only 6 percent of the total population of the United States (U.S. Bureau of the Census, 1995). Nearly 20 percent of the HIV Early-Intervention Program recipients were white women, and 25 percent were Hispanic. Together, African American and Hispanic women were 77 percent of all of the women older than age 13 treated by local health services for HIV in 1994.

In each key health status initiative offered by local health care centers, the frequency of service utilization by women of color exceeded the expected frequency based on this group's relatively small representation in the general population. Clearly, the local nonprofit health center programs supported by BPHC constitute the primary health care service system for low-income women and their children who have been medically underserved for a variety of interrelated personal, organizational, financial, and bureaucratic reasons. Although BPHC can and does address the health disparities that affect the lives of low-income women and their children, these disparities are only symptomatic of more entrenched causes. The frequency of use and the persistence of wide health disparities between low-income women of color and others in the community support the need for a specialized initiative to examine, evaluate, and strategically plan how to reach and provide primary health care to this segment of the population.

OMWH: Formulating a Vision

One of the newest initiatives within BPHC is the development of the Office of Minority and Women's Health in 1994. OMWH's mission is to develop and promote specific activities that help reduce the disparities in the health status of women of racial and ethnic minority populations. In addition, OMWH was designed to develop collaborative partnerships to ensure that health services are coordinated and reflective of the cultural and linguistic needs of the population of culturally diverse women that are served. OMWH uses three related strategies to move toward achievement of its mission:

1. promotion of strategies to improve access of members of ethnic minority groups and women to health care

2. development of collaborative linkages between public and private organizations to encourage the sharing of resources
3. gathering and dissemination of information on the health status of women of color and model programs that have been successful in eradicating barriers to health care.

Beginning in 1991 BPHC developed a Women's Health Workgroup to examine the health status of women of color and the continued disparities in their access to primary health care. The workgroup was asked to review background data on the current health status and access of women of color, identify and evaluate research studies and reports on the health condition of this population, explore historical trends in access and their relationship to the health risks of this population, and examine existing health services programs that have achieved a measure of success in getting women of color access to primary care. The workgroup was also asked to help develop a comprehensive strategic plan by spring 1998 for increasing the access of women of color to primary care.

One of the first tasks for the workgroup was to review existing reports on the disparities in health status and access of women of color to primary care. Several studies over the past 13 years showed clearly the dilemmas of obtaining access to health care and the added risks when the population is poor, of color, and female. Three of these reports were of particular relevance to our strategic planning process.

Research on Underserved Populations

The Heckler Taskforce. One of the first comprehensive reports on the health status of people of color and their children was issued by HHS in 1985. Margaret Heckler, then secretary of HHS, recognized in her annual report to Congress what she termed "a continuing disparity in the burden of death and illness experienced by black and other minority Americans as compared with our nation's population as a whole" (p. x). Heckler established a national taskforce and asked that it examine four interrelated areas of health care for black and other populations of color: (1) current health status, (2) access to the health care system, (3) actual use of health care services, and (4) factors related to disparities in health status.

The taskforce structured its methods and data analysis around the concept of excess deaths to show the extent of differences in health status by income, color, and gender. *Excess deaths* were defined operationally as the number of deaths that would not have taken place had the rates for the ethnic minority populations been equal to the rate of white Americans. The taskforce found that 80 percent of the excess deaths in these populations resulted from six causes: (1) cancer, (2) cardiovascular disease and stroke, (3) chemical dependency, (4) diabetes, (5) homicide and accidental injuries, and (6) infant mortality. The actual rankings within each population of color varied. The report showed that overall the rates of excess mortality for African American, Native American, and Hispanic American (Mexican origin) females greatly exceeded that of white females. However, data on Asian American female populations indicated an absence of excess deaths in this population. In fact, the rates of actual deaths were significantly lower than for white females in every category.

When the specific causes of death were examined comparatively by group, African American females were at considerably higher risk in every category. The risk of excess mortality for African American females from infant mortality, tuberculosis, hypertension, homicide, and diabetes was consistently higher than for all other groups of females. The risk of excess deaths for African American females from tuberculosis was 15 times greater, and their risk of death from hypertension was 13 times greater than the risk for white females. The highest risk of excess deaths for Native American females was from cirrhosis, tuberculosis, and renal disease (HHS, 1985).

On the basis of this report, Heckler proposed a series of national policy strategies that would "end the health disparity" between Americans (HHS, 1985, p. x):

1. an outreach strategy to disseminate health information to increase early detection, health promotion, and intervention
2. development of specific efforts to educate patients and health care providers about the links between health risks and culture
3. development and implementation of flexible models of health care that are culturally competent
4. development of methods to increase the availability of health care programs in ethnic minority communities
5. discovery of ways to increase collaboration within and across various federal branches and departments that affect the availability of health professions in underserved areas
6. an increase in the capacity of the nonfederal sector to address the health problems of people of color
7. improvement in and facilitation of the use of available sources of data
8. development and fostering of a research agenda to ensure health issues of ethnic minority populations are studied scientifically.

Studies by the Robert Wood Johnson Foundation. A second major effort to document the health status of populations of color was conducted by the Robert Wood Johnson Foundation between 1991 and 1993. The foundation commissioned three related studies of secondary health care data that included sampling of African American and Hispanic populations. The first report (Robert Wood Johnson Foundation, 1991) focused on health status, human resources, and availability of hospital and nursing home beds. Although the report noted that life expectancy of women of color (particularly African American women) had increased relative to men, the range of disparities by race and Hispanic origin noted in the Heckler report (HHS, 1985) remained. The report cited distressingly high rates of infant mortality, neonatal mortality, low-birthweight babies, deaths from addictive substances, and lower annual physician visits by race and

Hispanic origin. The most significant new data in the 1991 report was information on the development and spread of AIDS: The risk of new cases of AIDS was most pronounced among African American and Hispanic women and their infants.

The second Robert Wood Johnson report (Institute for Health Policy, 1993) focused on substance abuse, with fewer indicators of linkages by race and Hispanic origin. Although the rate of death from the ingestion of alcohol and illicit drugs was considerably greater for African American men, the rate of death for African American women (4 per 100,000) noted in the report was two times greater than the rate for white women. Deaths from alcohol use were found to be lower generally among white, African American, and Hispanic women than men. Data and information on other ethnic groups was not included in the analysis.

The third Robert Wood Johnson report (Center for Health Economics Research, 1993) focused on the relationship between access to health care and health status. The foundation concluded that although the United States had made major gains in health care delivery that were reflected in advances in the health status of the population as a whole, these advances had not trickled down to lower-income African Americans and Hispanics. Data were not available on Native American and Asian American populations.

This third report identified a number of factors related to access to health care. Most notable among the factors that determined both limited access to health care and poor health status were low income, the maldistribution of health services in the community, absence of culturally competent services providers, and the unavailability of health insurance. The report noted that the uninsured tend to be young, low-income African American and Hispanic women and their children. In addition, the data showed that there were limited improvements or changes in several areas of health care noted in the Heckler report (HHS, 1985): continued high rate of neonatal deaths, low-birthweight babies, and limited access to prenatal care for most underserved women of color. Furthermore, the report found that although more than 75 percent of white women obtained prenatal care, only 65 percent of African American and Hispanic women received such care. Part of the reason for the differences in access to prenatal and postnatal care by race and Hispanic origin is the difficulty Hispanic and African American women reported in obtaining care and the limited number of health care providers located in their communities or the limited number who accepted Medicaid payments. Overall, the report concluded that a central issue that continued to produce negative health outcomes for women of color was limited access to quality health care.

Studies on Asian and Pacific Islander Populations. Few of the research reports produced over the past several decades provide adequate data on Asian American and Pacific Islander populations and issues of health care. Where data have been available, the quality of the data has been questioned (Zane, Takeuchi, & Young, 1994).

Gardner (1994) provided an overview of critical health care issues for Asian American and Pacific Islander populations that allowed for comparisons with white, African American, and Hispanic populations on key causes of mortality. Gardner examined crude death rates for various populations between 1940 and 1980. The rates for Asian American and Pacific Islanders for all causes of death were lowest. Recent figures (Gardner, 1994) on life expectancy show that Asian American and Pacific Islander populations tend to have life spans equal to those of white and African American females. Infant mortality rates and the proportion of low-birthweight babies of Asian American, and Pacific Islanders are the lowest of all population groups in the United States. Although Asian American and Pacific Islander women die from the same six causes as women in other populations, the rates and percentages of death by cause are lower than for other groups of American women. For example, whereas the death rate from all causes per 100,000 for white females in 1980 was 405 and the rate for African American women was 611, the rate for Asian American women was only 244 per 100,000 (Gardner, 1994). The leading causes of death for Asian American women in 1980 were cancer and heart disease. However, these rates per 100,000 population were twice as low as those for other female populations.

Conclusions of the Women's Health Workgroup

The Women's Health Workgroup concluded from its review of studies that one primary cause of dismal health outcomes for low-income women of color was limited access to primary health care at critical stages of their lives. Low-income women of color in many underserved areas have great difficulty finding day-to-day health care for themselves and their families. The reasons for this situation are both complex and long-standing.

The workgroup believed that a special initiative aimed at women of color, supported by BPHC and implemented at the local level, could increase access to primary care by low-income women of color and their families. The workgroup noted that experiences in delivering health care to these populations at the local level over the past several years suggested that such an approach could be successful. Progress in two health care indicators was cited as an example. In their efforts to eliminate systemic barriers to care, health center programs supported by BPHC have developed and implemented innovative primary and preventive services for underserved women in their own communities. These health center programs have exceeded two Healthy People 2000 objectives (mammograms and Pap smears) for women and surpassed national averages, despite the challenges inherent in serving predominantly underserved populations. Compared with the general population, women who received health care services from health centers supported by BPHC had more up-to-date Pap smears and mammograms and prenatal care. These local health center programs have been successful in getting high-risk women into care and maintaining their linkages because these programs meet their needs and help reduce barriers to health care and related services.

Despite these and related achievements, the workgroup noted that the majority of BPHC health services and health data collected on women served by BPHC programs focused primarily on women in their reproductive years and less on the broader range of systemic health and social issues that women experience throughout their lives (for example, women and health issues across the life cycle and gender and ethnocultural issues and their relationship to access). The workgroup believed that additional efforts and resources must be made to address life span issues for women of color. It is important to recognize that many of the underlying social and health issues that negatively affect the lives of these women have existed for decades (HHS, 1985; Rice & Jones, 1990).

Although women of color are more likely than men of color to receive medical and mental health care, the workgroup noted they are underrepresented in all aspects of biomedical research (Glied & Kofman, 1995). There is an even greater shortage of research data on the health status of underserved women and women of color (Weiss, 1997). In many instances the workgroup noted that the nation and the helping professions are unclear about how low-income women of color conceptualize health or disease or what factors determine how they decide when and how to seek help for themselves or their children. Consequently, the workgroup concluded that there is not sufficient information on many important aspects of the health status of women of color and the methods of intervening early to prevent ill health or disease.

The workgroup also noted that there is an urgent need to broaden the scope of women's health research and services to include programs, services, and data that will have a more effective and lasting impact on the health status of underserved women. The group recognized that to truly improve the health status of underserved women, it is necessary to develop and implement services that address related gender and psychosocial factors within the individual's culture that have an influence on women's health status.

OMWH and the Women's Health Workgroup are attempting to develop a policy and program agenda that flows from a set of experiential principles concerning women's health needs, their caregiving roles and responsibilities, and their health practices. In the past, the failure to articulate the values that women bring to health care has produced policies and programs that impair rather than improve the health of underserved women. The following 10 basic questions form the foundation of the strategic planning proposals for women's health policy and program development:

1. How do we address women's health issues throughout their life span?
2. How do we integrate knowledge and understanding of culture and gender roles into effective health services delivery for women?

3. How can BPHC advocate for health promotion and for prevention and treatment of disease for all underserved populations?
4. How does the bureau incorporate the diverse values of women into service design and delivery?
5. What role can complementary and alternative medicine play in helping underserved women promote and maintain health and wellness?
6. How can BPHC-supported programs forge partnerships with the women they serve, providing care with, not for, their clients?
7. How do we integrate a holistic, biopsychosocial approach to health care in the lives of underserved women and avoid the isolation of medical issues?
8. How do we collect, analyze, and disseminate information and knowledge about this underserved population?
9. What kind of leadership strategies are needed to develop and move new policies and services that preserve the viability of bureau programs and other safety-net providers for underserved women?
10. How do we link our efforts with those of social work practitioners and professional schools?

The Women's Health Workgroup also proposed that cultural competence, as defined by Cross, Bazron, Dennis, and Isaacs (1989), be considered as a conceptual framework for organizing services to the large number of racial, ethnic, and linguistic minority groups that receive services from BPHC-funded agencies. The shortage of linguistically and culturally appropriate services for ethnically, racially, and culturally diverse populations is a significant health disparity issue for these populations in the continental United States and U.S.-associated jurisdictions (Davis, 1997). Although many Americans receive linguistically and culturally appropriate health services as a matter of course, a sizable proportion do not. Title VI of the Civil Rights Act and the Disadvantaged Minority Health Improvement Act of 1990 (P.L. 101-527) mandate that HHS provide equal access to its programs and services to ethnically, racially, and culturally diverse populations and to people with limited English skills. Americans whose language and culture of orientation are not within the dominant Western–European American mainstream experience severe health service disparities. As a result, the workgroup believes that cultural competence offers health services an overarching conceptual frame of reference to organize the delivery of services to the underserved populations (Davis, in press).

The strategic planning process established by OMWH is ongoing. The Women's Health Workgroup will continue to meet to develop and help implement a series of steps at the local level to remove the barriers to care that have been a consistent impediment to access for low-income women of color.

IMPLICATIONS FOR SOCIAL WORK

Although social workers and many other professions have known about and worked for decades to resolve the disparities in health status that mark communities of color, it is clearer than ever before that women of color continue to die at unexpectedly higher rates than other populations from new and old diseases: AIDS, violence, breast cancer, cervical cancer, liver cancer, cardiovascular disease, and cirrhosis. Their risk of excess death is higher. Their resources and choices of care are lower. The children of low-income women of color, too, continue to die at rates that are more expected in countries of lesser wealth than the United States. Some of the implications of these disparities for the nation as a whole and for health care professionals and universities are obvious.

To reduce and eventually resolve these disparities and the factors that have sustained them for decades requires that the nation and the helping professions collaborate in efforts to put the health of ethnic minority populations in all of its forms (physical, mental, and social) high on the national agenda, high on the agenda of social workers, and high on the agendas of the president of the United States and Congress.

In one of his weekly radio addresses, President Clinton (1998) pointed out the disturbing presence of major disparities in health status for African Americans, Asian Americans, Hispanic Americans, and Native Americans compared with other Americans. He indicated that although the reasons for these disparities may not be as clear as we as a nation would like, it is clear that "racial and ethnic disparities in health are unacceptable in a country that values equality and equal opportunity for all" (p. 2). In response to these issues, the president established the following goal: "By the year 2010, we must eliminate racial and ethnic disparities in health status" (p. 2). To work toward this goal, Clinton earmarked $400 million in his 1998 budget submission to Congress for this purpose. Clinton's goal identifies the second implication for social work: Social workers must identify how the profession will contribute to achieving this most important national social justice goal to equalize health status and access.

The social work profession must help find ways to assist the health care industry in recognizing and valuing the central role culture plays in women's health-related behavior. Cultural diversity has a pervasive influence on the level and quality of health care services provided to women of color, who represent some of the most underserved populations, by local health care and assistance programs. Racism affects both the resources devoted to serving women and the willingness of women to seek care. Culture, language, and gender affect all facets of health status for underserved women, from personal health behaviors to the shortage of health resources in medically underserved communities. The cultural diversity and cultural competence of administrators and providers influence both the quality of and access to care.

Social workers need to strengthen the emphasis on prevention in the social work curriculum. Many illnesses prevalent among women today are preventable, either through changes in lifestyle (for example, improved diet, increased exercise, or smoking cessation) or preventive health care (for example, mammograms and Pap smears). Programs that enhance women's understanding of the effects of their own behavior can result in dramatic improvements in health outcomes. Assessing women's knowledge of daily life skills is important in understanding healthy behavior.

Lifestyle issues are particularly relevant for teenagers, pregnant women, and older women. Good health care choices must also be woven into the cultural traditions of a people. Intergenerational improvement of health behaviors may also serve to ameliorate persistent health beliefs and practices that are deleterious to women's health. Women gather strength and resilience from relationships, and those relationships are central to encouraging women to lead healthy lifestyles, seek appropriate health services, and work with clinicians to manage illness. Health promotion and illness prevention and treatment programs need to recognize the importance of establishing relational ties with the women they want to serve and of nurturing those relationships that lead to prevention.

There are clear implications that social workers must continue to gather and use information and data about the medically underserved to engage policymakers and government representatives in the development of legislation and policies that show promise of increasing low-income women's access to primary care. Part of this data gathering and analysis can and should be done by social work scholars in collaboration with BPHC and its hundreds of local programs.

CONCLUSION

The major disparities in health care that pervade the lives of medically underserved women of color, their families, and communities have plagued the United States and all health care professions for decades. The brief overview of data on this population here and in some other chapters in this book makes clear the continuing dilemma the nation faces: Although women are central figures in maintaining the health of their families and communities, medically underserved women are less likely to be able to fulfill this role. Women of color are often unable to carry out this critical role in their families and communities for a variety of reasons: racist, economic, bureaucratic, institutional, cultural, and political, as well as scientific. Medically underserved women need the human services professions to assist in removing fundamental barriers that restrict their ability to maintain their health and the health of their families and communities. Part of that responsibility rests with BPHC and OMWH.

The bureau and its programs have a critical role to play in researching and analyzing health care outcomes in relation to underserved women. The bureau must work in partnership with other federal agencies as well as state and local agencies and private, nonprofit, and community-based organizations to promote and support research programs that seek to improve health care services and health outcomes for underserved women. Here, too, there are important roles for social work schools and researchers. Collaborative efforts between BPHC, the hundreds of local programs it supports, and the field of social work can and should identify existing national- and state-based data sources and areas where additional data collection is needed. More than any other factor, it may be our ability to collaborate that will allow us as a nation and as professional groups to help mitigate the numerous problems and barriers that have caused and sustained the unjust disparities in health care for medically underserved women, their families, and communities.

There is also a need to work with other partners who have established relationships with women, such as schools, faith-based organizations, and social services agencies, to draw women into the health care system and provide comprehensive care. The role women play in caring for their families and their communities must be recognized, supported, and nurtured. At the same time, women must be empowered to care effectively for themselves, something that women may neglect while caring for others. Healthy women build healthy communities.

REFERENCES

Adams, D. (1995). *Health issues for women of color: A cultural diversity perspective.* Thousand Oaks, CA: Sage Publications.

Bayne-Smith, M. (1996). *Race, gender and health.* Thousand Oaks, CA: Sage Publications.

Bureau of Primary Health Care. (1994a). *Women and primary care.* Bethesda, MD: U.S. Department of Health and Human Services, Health Resources and Services Administration.

Bureau of Primary Health Care. (1994b). *The women we serve.* Bethesda, MD: U.S. Department of Health and Human Services, Health Resources and Services Administration.

Bureau of Primary Health Care. (1996a). *Models that work: Compendium of innovative primary health care programs for underserved and vulnerable populations.* Bethesda, MD: U.S. Department of Health and Human Services, Health Resources and Services Administration.

Bureau of Primary Health Care. (1996b). *Uniform data system: Changes in the uninsured, 1990–1996.* Bethesda, MD: U.S. Department of Health and Human Services, Health Resources and Services Administration.

Center for Health Economics Research. (1993, November). *Access to health care: Key indicators for policy.* Princeton, NJ: Robert Wood Johnson Foundation.

Clinton, W. J. (1998, February 21). *Saturday radio address by the President to the nation* [Transcript]. Washington, DC: White House, Office of the Press Secretary.

Cross, T. L., Bazron, B., Dennis, K., & Isaacs, M. (1989). *Toward a culturally competent system of care.* Washington, DC: Georgetown University, Child Development Center, CCASSP Technical Assistance Center.

Davis, K. (1997). *Exploring the intersection between cultural competency and managed behavioral health care: Implications for state and county mental health agencies.* Alexandria, VA: National Technical Assistance Center for State Mental Health Planning.

Davis, K. (in press). Race, unemployment, managed care and cultural competency. In F. Brisbane (Ed.), *Cultural competency series*. Bethesda, MD: U.S. Department of Health and Human Services, Center for Substance Abuse Prevention.

Disadvantaged Minority Health Improvement Act of 1990, P.L. 101-527, 104 Stat. 2311.

Gardner, R. (1994). Mortality. In N.W.S. Zane, D. T. Takeuchi, & L.N.J. Young (Eds.), *Confronting critical health issues of Asian and Pacific Islander Americans* (pp. 53–104). Thousand Oaks, CA: Sage Publications.

Glied, S., & Kofman, S. (1995, March). *Women and mental health: Issues for health reform*. New York: Commonwealth Fund Commission on Women's Health.

Hawkins, D. R., & Rosenbaum, S. (1993). *Lives in the balance: The health status of America's medically underserved populations*. Washington, DC: National Association of Community Health Centers.

Institute for Health Policy. (1993, October). *Substance abuse—The nation's number one health problem: Key indicators for policy*. Princeton, NJ: Robert Wood Johnson Foundation.

Mauer, B., Jarvis, D., Mockler, R., & Trabin, T. (1995). *How to respond to managed behavioral health care*. Tiburon, CA: Centralink.

Rice, M. F., & Jones, W. (1990). *Health of black Americans from post-Reconstruction to integration, 1871–1960*. Westport, CT: Greenwood Press.

Robert Wood Johnson Foundation. (1991). *Challenges in health care: A chartbook perspective, 1991*. Princeton, NJ: Author.

Salganicoff, A. (1997). Medicaid and managed care: Implications for low-income women. *Journal of the American Medical Women's Association, 52*(2), 78–80.

Schoen, C. (1997, September). Insurance matters for low-income adults: Results from the Kaiser Commonwealth Foundation Five-State Low Income Survey. *Health Affairs, 16*, 163–171

U.S. Bureau of the Census. (1995). *Census of the United States update*. Washington, DC: U.S. Department of Commerce.

U.S. Department of Health and Human Services. (1985, August). *Report of the Secretary's Task Force on Black and Minority Health: Volume 1*. Washington, DC: Author.

Weaver, J. B. (1976). *National health policy and the underserved: Ethnic minorities, women, and the elderly*. St. Louis: C. V. Mosby.

Weiss, L. D. (1997). *Private medicine and public health: Profit, politics, and prejudice in the American health care enterprise*. Boulder, CO: Westview Press.

Zane, N.W.S., Takeuchi, D. T., & Young, L.N.J. (Eds.). (1994). *Confronting critical health issues of Asian and Pacific Islander Americans*. Thousand Oaks, CA: Sage Publications.

27 The Well: A Neighborhood-Based Health Promotion Model for Black Women

Karin A. Elliott Brown, Frances E. Jemmott,
Holly J. Mitchell, and Mary L. Walton

The Well is a community-based drop-in, self-help wellness center located in a high-quality low-income housing complex in Los Angeles. It represents an empowerment approach to developing culturally appropriate neighborhood-based health promotion for black women. *Wellness* is defined by Well members as achieving and maintaining physical, emotional, and spiritual well-being. In this chapter, the term *black women* refers to African American women and all other women of African descent whose citizenship or ethnic identification is not American (for example, black women from the Caribbean, Africa, or Europe). This chapter describes the process of development and current characteristics of The Well and presents suggestions for replicating this process in other communities.

Although black women constitute only 7 percent of the women in California, they experience disproportionately poorer health outcomes than other female population groups. A profile of women's health status in California from 1984 to 1994 indicates that black women had the shortest life expectancy, the highest levels of mortality at every age, the highest mortality from heart disease and stroke, the highest prevalence of hypertension and obesity, the highest mortality rates from homicide and AIDS, and the highest incidence of other sexually transmitted diseases (Nelson & Dumbauld, 1997).

Black women between 15 and 34 years of age are more likely to be victims of unintentional injury and homicide; are involved in domestic violence; report low self-esteem, increased depression, anxiety, substance abuse, and eating disorders; experience higher rates of infant mortality and low-birthweight babies; and experience problems with reproductive health and obesity compared to white and Latina women residing in the state (California Women's Health Project, 1993).

For black women between ages 35 and 64, the effects of alcohol and tobacco, a sedentary lifestyle, and nutritional imbalances influence poor health status. This age cohort is marked by the development of chronic major illnesses that span a significant portion of a woman's life. Cancer, particularly lung cancer, is the leading cause of

This chapter was originally published in the May 1998 issue of *Health & Social Work*, Vol. 23, pp. 146–152.

death for this group of black women. Despite higher rates of screening, mammography, and self-examination, black women experience higher rates of death from breast cancer than women of other ethnicities. They also experience higher rates of death from cervical cancer, heart disease, liver disease, stroke, and diabetes (California Women's Health Project, 1993).

Black women ages 65 years and older are at greater risk of death from heart disease than from cancer. Diabetes, pneumonia, influenza, and coronary obstructive pulmonary disorder are the leading causes of death among this group of black women, as well as other populations in this age cohort.

THE WELL: GETTING STARTED

The Well was established by the California Black Women's Health Project (CBWHP) in 1994. CBWHP serves as the statewide coordinating arm of the National Black Women's Health Project (NBWHP), a self-help and health advocacy organization founded in 1983 to promote the health of black women through community-based, grassroots initiatives. In 1994 the NBWHP contracted with the University of California, Los Angeles (UCLA), Psychology Department to help develop the statewide organization. The James Irvine Foundation, as part of its Women's Health Initiative, funded the development of the CBWHP.

The vision of The Well emerged at a planning retreat attended by 40 black women to develop a vision and action plan to promote their wellness and to improve their health status. The planners were invited to participate on the basis of their prior involvement with the NBWHP and their record of community activism on women's issues.

Participants engaged in a group process where they shared personal and community issues, concerns, and goals regarding health and wellness. In sister circles and in the larger group, they discussed personal efforts to achieve and maintain wellness and identified potential barriers to success. The idea of The Well emerged as one of several health promotion strategies discussed during the retreat.

THE WELL: AN OVERVIEW

The Well is located in a 48-unit low-income housing complex built to provide affordable housing for the working poor. It is located in Service Planning Area 6 (SPA 6), a subregion of the Southeast Health District in Los Angeles County. SPA 6 represents a population of 987,271, composed primarily of African American (41 percent) and Latino (54 percent) residents (Los Angeles County Children's Planning Council, 1996). Over 500,000 of the residents are living below the poverty level, and nearly 400,000 are receiving some type of public assistance.

The physical space housing The Well is a 1,650-square-foot unit located on an accessible and visible first-floor corner in the housing complex. The space serves as a meeting room, exercise and fitness room, and lounge/library, with a partitioned examination room and nurse practitioner's office. The nurse practitioner's office houses a database and computerized system for scheduling visits with affiliated hospitals and clinics.

For the most part, Well participants are drawn from members of the Southern California Chapter of the NBWHP, residents of the housing complex, women from the immediate neighborhood who walk to The Well, and women who come to The Well for a specific service or activity and then learn about other Well-sponsored programs and events.

Participation in most Well activities and services is open to all women with health needs. The sister circles are primarily self-help groups for and about black women. Members from each sister circle can determine if they want to open their circle to women from other ethnic groups. Although the majority of Well participants are black women, we found that Latina women are more likely to ask about reproductive health information and contraceptives from the John Wesley Community Health (JWCH) Institute Family Planning Program housed at The Well.

Well Activities

This model of neighborhood-based health promotion for black women can be depicted as a wheel, with The Well located in the center hub (see Figure 27-1). The Well offers several wellness and health promotion activities sponsored by the CBWHP located on site, such as self-help groups and sister circles, exercise classes, Walking for Wellness programs, Facts and Feelings workshops, a Community Health Education campaign, and other health advocacy activities. The model also includes community health programs jointly sponsored with other health promotion organizations (spokes) and important partnerships with supporting community organizations (other spokes).

Affiliated Services and Jointly Sponsored Programs

Current affiliated services and jointly sponsored programs include the LA Birthing Project, the JWCH Institute Family Planning Program, Fitness Funatics, Prototypes, the Dunbar Economic Development Corporation, and Partners in Prevention. These alliances create multiple community linkages that increase the accessibility of comprehensive health services, information, and support to promote wellness.

The LA Birthing Project is a local chapter of Birthing Project USA, a national model that facilitates better birth outcomes by using volunteers (known as "sister-friends"). Sister-friends provide practical and emotional support to women during pregnancy and for one year after the birth of their child. Assistance can include identifying and coordinating health and social services; attending childbirth preparation and parenting classes; and being a birth partner, if appropriate (Birthing Project USA, n.d.).

Figure 27-1
California Black Women's Health Project

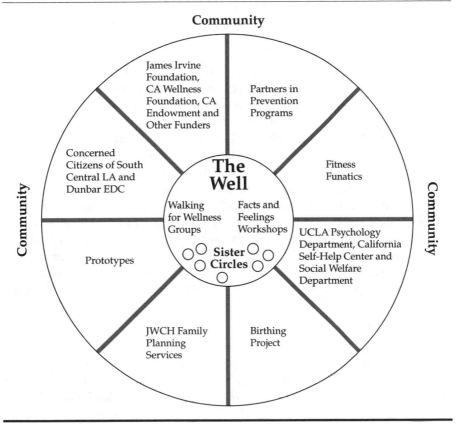

NOTES: The California Black Women's Health Project is an affiliate of the National Black Women's Health Project. CA = California; LA = Los Angeles; UCLA = University of California, Los Angeles; EDC = Economic Development Corporation; JWCH = John Wesley Community Health.

The CBWHP partnered with the JWCH Institute, Inc., to establish the JWCH Institute Family Planning Program at The Well. The program seeks to improve access to nonclinical family planning services for low-income women by making services available in community-based settings. It provides pregnancy testing, counseling, and referral; high blood pressure screening; breast examinations and breast self-exam instruction; limited referrals for other medical and social services; and scheduled appointments to a full-service clinic for a complete physical exam (JWCH Institute, n.d.).

Fitness Funatics is a community-level fitness promotion intervention of the Charles R. Drew University of Medicine and Science focused on urban Los Angeles African Americans and Latinos. The Well serves as one of more than 15 southern Los Angeles sites where Fitness Funatics has established at least weekly exercise sessions. The CBWHP plans to continue to provide free fitness classes at The Well when the funding period for Fitness Funatics has ended.

Prototypes provides substance abuse outreach and HIV/AIDS ed-ucation, prevention, and intervention to women and their families. A team of three to five outreach workers staff The Well three days each week. The Dunbar Economic Development Corporation (Dunbar EDC) has developed three Section 8 housing complexes on Central Avenue. The Well has a collaborative relationship with the Dunbar EDC for Girl Talk, a teenage sister circle, and the Partners in Preven-tion weight loss program. Partners in Prevention represents an orga-nizational entrée, where proposals for establishing new community partnerships are written and reviewed. For example, the California Endowment Community Health Investment Program recently fund-ed the first CBWHP Partners in Prevention Weight Control program to provide black women and girls with education and awareness, life skills development, social and emotional support, and a community infrastructure to minimize the conditions or risk of obesity and relat-ed poor health outcomes. Program activities include a self-report health screening, weigh-in and measuring, blood pressure readings, cholesterol count, a medical clearance to participate in nonaerobic fit-ness groups, Fitness Funatics, nutrition and cooking class, age appro-priate self-help support groups, Walking for Wellness, and field trips.

Supporting Organizations

Important supporting organizations include several funders, universi-ties, the landlord of the housing project, the Southern California Chap-ter of the NBWHP, and the NBWHP. To date, the various funders of Well health promotion programs include the James Irvine Foundation, the Wellness Foundation, and the California Endowment. The Well benefits from other funding sources that provide financial support to affiliated programs. For example, the JWCH Institute Family Planning Program is funded by the California Department of Health Services, Office of Family Planning, Expanded Clinic Access Demonstration Project. The March of Dimes provided seed money for the LA Birthing Project.

Supportive university affiliations can strengthen community-based health promotion programs in a number of important ways. In this case, the former California Self-Help Center in the UCLA Department of Psychology provided sponsorship and technical assistance with proposal development for initial funding. The Self-Help Center also provided the research and theory that guided and supported the pro-gram model. A faculty member from the Department of Social Wel-fare, UCLA School of Public Policy and Social Research, currently provides The Well with consultation and technical assistance with program evaluation.

The Well's landlord, Concerned Citizens of South Central, is a community-based organization committed to the development of af-fordable quality housing for low-income families. There is a recipro-cally supportive relationship between The Well and its landlord. For example, the executive director of Concerned Citizens of South

Central sits on the Board of Directors for the CBWHP. In addition, The Well offers health promotion services to housing residents, and residents volunteer to help with Well activities and generally welcome and support Well staff. Similarly, the Southern California chapter of the NBWHP is integrally involved in Well activities. Chapter members serve as both voluntary providers and as consumers of Well programs. Last, as the parent organization, the NBWHP provides The Well with a guiding philosophy and mission statement to promote health and empowerment among black women.

STRENGTHS AND POTENTIAL PITFALLS AND BARRIERS

Strengths of the Model

On the basis of our collective reflection on The Well as a community-based health promotion model, five strengths emerged: (1) the empowerment process, (2) shared ownership, (3) community-based location, (4) relationship with a university, and (5) community partnerships.

The idea of The Well was based on an empowerment process from its conception. The planning retreat brought together the experiences and voices of a richly diverse group of black women from California. NBWHP members and program participants are regularly involved in the decision-making process and planning regarding Well programs and community-based collaborations. Shared ownership is a Well philosophy and practice that keeps health promotion efforts responsive to individual-, group-, and community-identified health needs, concerns, and resources. The philosophy is promoted through membership outreach and maintenance, particularly by encouraging active involvement in a range of health-promoting activities.

Our community-based location increases accessibility to health prevention and treatment services, fosters indigenous self-help and mutual support to determine and achieve wellness goals, and demonstrates our commitment to community-driven health promotion. Also, the establishment of a supportive partnership or association with a nearby university is very important. Most funders want to be sure their grant resources are well managed, supported programs are informed by a well-conceptualized theoretical base, and program managers have access to professional consultation (for example, evaluation research expertise) and technical support. Universities are well equipped and designed to provide this kind of professional support to community organizations. Finally, community partnerships increase access and utilization of a range of health services.

Potential Pitfalls and Barriers and Remedies

Successful implementation of any community-based health promotion effort must seriously and realistically consider potential pitfalls and barriers to community access, utilization, and active participation. Five potential pitfalls or barriers were identified as CBWHP began to engage our diverse community of women in health promotion activities at The Well:

1. lack of anonymity or privacy for some housing residents and chapter members
2. the question of membership versus service organization (for and by black women)
3. need for sufficient staffing to avoid dependency on volunteers for maintenance of administrative duties
4. shared space not being synonymous with shared identity or ownership
5. need to actively foster unity while maintaining respect for and understanding of diversity among black women.

Perceived and actual lack of anonymity or privacy for some housing residents and chapter members of the NBWHP became an obvious issue when sister circles were formed. Personal stories shared by women in sister circles can be highly emotional and intimate. Although each woman chooses her level of personal disclosure, some new participants appear overwhelmed or uncomfortable with intimate discussions of personal experiences. This discomfort can come from fears of having to reciprocate the sharing of deeply personal experiences or feelings or from lack of trust that "personal business" will be kept confidential. Also, some women are hesitant to, or have made a clear decision not to, share intimately in a support circle when they are familiar with other participating women (for example, sister, mother, child, coworker, employer, supervisor, or neighbor) to avoid compromising or changing existing relationships (that is, power shifts, loss of valued images, violation of personal or professional boundaries).

Relatedly, women participating in workshops may be hesitant to ask questions for fear of embarrassment or a desire to conceal ignorance about a particular health issue. Also, a woman's privacy can easily be compromised if neighbors and friends observe her entering The Well for family planning services. Strategies to address these realistic barriers to participation include the following:

1. Hold a group discussion to review benefits and potential concerns of group support with known and unknown participants, so that each woman can make an informed decision before joining a sister circle at each event or workshop.
2. Emphasize the need for and value of privacy and involve the group in a verbally stated shared commitment to confidentiality.
3. Circulate a question box before or during workshops to provide an opportunity for participants to raise their questions anonymously.
4. Provide a telephone number on all printed information about health services offered at The Well that prospective participants concerned about privacy can call for an off-site referral or to schedule a visit at a time when they would feel less vulnerable.

The NBWHP began as and still remains a membership organization for and about black women. Expanding the scope of the organization to include the provision of a range of health services has raised a critical question regarding the identity of the CBWHP (a statewide extension of the NBWHP) and the operation of The Well as a membership versus a service organization. We had to ask the following questions: Are our participants primarily members, service recipients–clients, or both? When participants hold a combined role as service providers and recipients, how do we determine responsibility and accountability within the organization? These questions have been and will continue to be discussed during quarterly membership meetings and meetings held by the CBWHP board of directors.

Initially, The Well relied heavily on volunteer service provided by chapter members to perform many administrative tasks. The Well learned quickly that dependence on volunteers for maintenance of administrative duties was an unfair and insufficient approach to responding promptly and effectively to the administrative demands of an evolving community-based organization. Insufficient staffing of a membership organization is an avoidable pitfall that can be remedied by securing funds and including hired staff in the annual budget, even though volunteer services are available and can be incorporated in the planning and implementation process of all health promotion activities.

The observation that shared space does not equal shared identity or ownership is another "lesson learned" that can lead to internal conflict if left unattended. The benefits of forming community-based partnerships to provide on-site health promotion services are great and well worth the effort required to negotiate competing needs and interests among program components. It can be very challenging to coordinate activities and establish priorities within the realistic limits of a small physical space and a shared pool of program participants.

The greatest complication in forming partnerships and then coordinating on-site health promotion activities is that many of the service organizations that have engaged in a partnership with The Well already have established identities in California as independent community-based organizations. A potential conflict can arise when determining which organization should be identified to accept funds for jointly sponsored prevention programs. What happens when both The Well and the partnering service organization are soliciting funds from the same source? Confusion or conflicts in program implementation and identity are inevitable if working relationships are not clearly defined during the formation of the partnership and jointly monitored (if agreed) over the course of the program.

To overcome these conflicts, annual "community building" retreats or regularly scheduled workshops and meetings can be planned for those who staff partnership programs housed at The Well. The goals are to foster the development and maintenance of supportive relationships, clear communication, and effective collaboration for Well activities.

Finally, black women do not represent a monolith; we are richly diverse in belief systems, life experiences, formal education, physical appearance, age, religious affiliations, and a host of other personal characteristics. The power of sister support is drawn from our common experiences, shared health concerns, and collective interests. However, at times our differences can generate distrust, miscommunication, and emotional distancing. The Well has responded to these potential barriers by actively fostering unity while maintaining respect for and understanding of diversity among black women. Facts and Feelings workshops have been offered to provide black women with a forum to discuss, develop an understanding of, and share feelings about differences that may separate us (for example, classism, homophobia, and differences in religious beliefs and practices). Also, self-help group facilitators are provided with training and support to model and promote active listening and nonjudgmental acceptance toward all women who share in their sister circles.

PROGRAM EVALUATION

The health promotion and wellness activities sponsored by The Well are currently being evaluated. Indicators of success included in the evaluation design are increases in projected number of self-help groups; evidence of strengthened California chapters of the NBWHP; changes in women's knowledge, attitudes, and behaviors regarding personal health and wellness based on pre–post participant feedback; feedback from community partners regarding their collaboration with The Well; and additional change data from women who participate in the Partners in Prevention Weight Loss project, including preprogram and postprogram weight, blood pressure, body dimensions, and cholesterol count.

POTENTIAL FOR REPLICATION

To develop a model for neighborhood-based health promotion that is most responsive to the needs of community participants, one must replicate the process rather than adopt the exact program components of The Well. The model must reflect the various cultural beliefs of the community regarding health and wellness and address community-specific needs and concerns affecting health and well-being. With this in mind, we believe that six key components of the process and resulting health promotion model can be replicated:

1. Begin with a shared vision of health concerns.
2. Use self-help support circles to serve as the mechanism for enhancing personal and collective empowerment.
3. Develop health education and promotion workshops that actively involve participants, allowing them to share experiences in support circles at some point in the program.
4. House the program in an accessible and welcoming space in the community (that is, "location, location, location").

5. Provide on-site exercise classes and equipment.
6. Establish and maintain supportive and collaborative community linkages and partnerships.

CONCLUSION

The Well as a model of neighborhood-based health promotion is best conceptualized as a process model that can inspire community change. The mission of The Well is to promote health-enhancing change through mutual support, personal growth, community education, and collective action toward empowering ourselves and our communities to invest in wellness. This process allows us to embrace our strengths as black women, heal our hurts, seek wellness, and raise our collective voice to draw attention to and change our health status.

REFERENCES

Birthing Project USA. (n.d.). *The underground railroad for new life* [Pamphlet]. Sacramento, CA: Author.

California Women's Health Project. (1993). *Health status of women in California: Reproductive health, occupational health, mental health, and physical health* (Four reports to Governor Pete Wilson). Sacramento, CA: Author in collaboration with the California Research Bureau.

JWCH Institute. (n.d.). *The Well: Offering family planning services by JWCH Institute, Inc.* [Pamphlet]. Lynwood, CA: Author.

Los Angeles County Children's Planning Council. (1996, May). *Profiles of Los Angeles County Services Planning Area resources for children, youth and families.* Los Angeles: County Board of Supervisors.

Nelson, M., & Dumbauld, S. (1997, March). *Profile of women's health status in California, 1984–1994* (Report to Governor Pete Wilson). Sacramento, CA: Office of Women's Health and the Center for Health Statistics.

An earlier version of this chapter was presented at the conference "Psychosocial and Behavioral Factors in Women's Health: Research, Prevention, Treatment, and Service Delivery in Clinical and Community Settings," sponsored by the American Psychological Association and other health-related organizations, September 1996, Washington, DC.

28 Racial Differences in Discharge Planning

Nancy Morrow-Howell, Letha A. Chadiha,
Enola K. Proctor, Maggie Hourd-Bryant, and
Peter M. Doré

D ischarge from the hospital is an important transition in the continuum of care for elderly patients, with discharge planning as the critical process for meeting patients' needs in the posthospital environment. In preparation for discharge, the social worker, patient, and family pursue options and make decisions about posthospital care. Most patients discharged from the hospital enter home care and receive a mix of informal and formal services. Patients not going home are likely to enter some form of institutional care.

Studies show that African American and white older adults differ in their use of institutional and noninstitutional care (see Belgrave, Wykle, & Choi, 1993), including informal and formal services received following hospitalization (Chadiha, Proctor, Morrow-Howell, Darkwa, & Dore, 1995; Morrow-Howell & Proctor, 1994). In spite of evidence of racial differences in posthospital service utilization, virtually no empirical study has examined racial differences in the discharge planning processes used by the social worker, patient, and family to pursue and develop various options for posthospital care.

Several investigators have conceptualized discharge planning in terms of decision making, demonstrating that outcome is enhanced by patient and family perceptions of a range of alternatives and involvement in the decision-making process (Abramson, 1990; Arenth & Mamon, 1985; Dunkle, Coulton, MacKintosh, & Goode, 1982; Morrow-Howell, Proctor, & Dore, 1993; Proctor, Morrow-Howell, Albaz, & Weir, 1992). In taking steps toward eventual care arrangements, discharge planners may assess a variety of patient needs and strive to meet them by organizing health and social services (Arenth & Mamon, 1985). Ideally, the patient and family members along with the discharge planner are involved in assessing needs and deciding options for posthospital care plans (Dunkle et al., 1982).

The study discussed in this chapter approached discharge planning as a decision-making process in which social workers, patients, and families discussed, pursued, and selected potential alternatives for posthospital care. Because cases varied in terms of the eventual

This chapter was originally published in the May 1996 issue of *Health & Social Work*, Vol. 21, pp. 131–139.

discharge plan, it was assumed that the number of options pursued; the extent to which patients, families, and the social worker discussed alternative options; and the reasons for finally selecting one option varied also. Given reported racial differences in the actual arrangements for posthospital care, this analysis focuses on differences in the care options pursued by patients, family members, and discharge planners. It also examines whether African American and white older adults showed different preferences for nursing home care in discharge planning. Because the discharge planner has an integral role to play in assisting families with options and decision making about the care of their elderly relatives, findings from this study will provide social work discharge planners with new knowledge about possible racial differences in this decision-making process.

LITERATURE REVIEW

The literature documenting racial differences in service utilization, including institutional and noninstitutional care, informed this study. Use of medical and supportive services is viewed as important to both health and social outcomes, particularly for sick older adults in the vulnerable period following hospitalization (Andersen, 1995). Yet the literature indicates consistently that African American families may underuse services that could enhance the quality of their care.

Institutional Care

African American elderly people use nursing home care less than white people, as evidenced by their underrepresentation in nursing homes (U.S. Department of Health and Human Services, 1990; Yeo, 1993). Racial differences in nursing home use have been documented consistently for over a decade. For example, the percentage of African Americans in nursing homes in 1980 was 3 percent for those age 65 and over and 12 percent for those 85 and older, compared with 5 percent for white people age 65 and over and 23 percent for those 85 and over (Yeo, 1993). Findings from the 1982–84 National Long-Term Care Survey show that only 22.5 percent of African Americans resided in nursing homes at some time between age 65 and death, compared with 37.9 percent of white people and those of other races (Murtaugh, Kemper, & Spillman, 1990). In addition, when longevity and gender are controlled, elderly African Americans had a significantly lower rate of nursing home use than white elderly people of comparable ages.

Data from the 1984–85 National Health Survey and Supplement on Aging showed that functionally dependent elderly people of color (10 percent) were less likely than white elderly people (17 percent) to reside in a nursing home (U.S. Department of Health and Human Services, 1990). When medical, social, and financial factors were controlled, older African Americans were significantly less likely than older white people to enter nursing homes after hospitalization;

however, no racial differences were found in the use of rehabilitation units (Morrow-Howell & Proctor, 1994).

Noninstitutional Services

Although most functionally dependent noninstitutionalized elderly people receive the bulk of their home care through informal sources (U.S. Department of Health and Human Services, 1990), elderly African Americans rely heavily on informal rather than formal supports. Older adults in a national survey of African Americans were recipients of informal care provided by a highly responsive extended support system (Chatters, Taylor, & Jackson, 1986; Gibson & Jackson, 1989).

Comparative studies of elderly African American and white people report racial differences in types of services used. Elderly African Americans in a community-based study used low levels of formal services and relied heavily on informal assistance from family, friends, and others (Spence & Atherton, 1991). Mindel, Wright, and Starrett (1986) found racial differences in the support systems of older adults, with African Americans using the formal system less than white people when income was controlled. Mui and Burnette (1994) reported that frail elderly African Americans used fewer in-home and nursing home services than their white counterparts; African Americans relied more heavily on informal helpers.

African American and white elderly patients entering home care following hospitalization differed in amounts of informal and formal services received; African Americans received significantly fewer hours of formal care per week and more hours of informal care per week from their primary caregiver (Chadiha et al., 1995).

STUDY HYPOTHESES

The present study sought to increase understanding of factors underlying previously reported findings of racial differences in the use of posthospital care. Accordingly, the study focused on the process by which posthospital care is arranged. Racial differences in this process were hypothesized to exist and thereby offer partial explanation for differences in posthospital care.

The following hypotheses were tested:

- Hypothesis 1: Discharge planning with African American patients and families involves more pursuit of informal care arrangements than discharge planning with white patients and families.
- Hypothesis 2: Discharge planning with African American patients and families involves less pursuit of formal care than discharge planning with white patients and families.
- Hypothesis 3: Discharge planning with African American patients and families involves less pursuit of institutional care than discharge planning with white patients and families.

■ Hypothesis 4: African American patients are more likely to rule out nursing home placement because of patient and family preference than white patients.

METHOD

Sample

Data were derived from a study of discharge planning for 369 elderly patients at a large, urban teaching hospital in the Midwest. All patients who met the selection criteria from June 1, 1988, to February 1, 1989, were approached for the study; 95 percent consented to participate. Selection criteria included Medicare coverage; a diagnosis of congestive heart failure (CHF), cerebrovascular accident (CVA), or hip fracture; and participation in discharge planning with a member of the hospital social work department. Using a stratified sampling procedure, we obtained approximately 100 patients in each diagnostic group. In addition, for one month (September 1988), all Medicare patients on the general medicine unit were included regardless of diagnosis.

CHF, CVA, and hip fracture were selected as target diagnoses because of their frequent occurrence among elderly people and because patients in these diagnostic groups are discharged to a variety of posthospital destinations—usually home, nursing home, or rehabilitation units. Because the three diagnoses are among the most common reasons for hospital admission among elderly people (May, Kelly, Mendlein, & Garbe, 1991), the selection of these diagnoses enhances the generalizability of the findings. The medicine unit participants hospitalized during September 1988 had been diagnosed with more than 25 medical problems, primarily pneumonia, renal failure, and chronic obstructive pulmonary disease. This group was included to further increase generalizability.

Patients were referred to the discharge planners through routine hospital practice, primarily physician or nurse referral, or team conferences that included social workers who identified high-risk patients. Given the study's focus on discharge planning, it was essential that all patients in the study receive discharge planning.

Data Collection

Data for this study are based on social workers' reports about the discharge planning process. Trained research assistants screened social worker caseloads daily. Social workers with patients identified as meeting the study criteria and whose clients provided informed consent were interviewed by the research assistants within 48 hours following the patient's discharge. The social workers' recall of case details was enhanced by the immediacy of the interview, the use of a structured interview schedule, and the use of case notes during the interview. Sixteen social workers contributed data; most had a master's degree, and they had an average of eight years of experience in hospital social work.

Dependent Variables

Dependent variables were developed to reflect the extent to which various alternative care arrangements were pursued and the reasons for ruling out potential discharge destinations.

Extent of Pursuit. During the postdischarge interview, research assistants asked social workers to rate for each patient the extent to which the social worker, patient, and family pursued a particular option for posthospital care. Extent of pursuit was rated as follows: 1 indicated no conversation with patient or family, 2 indicated that the option was ruled out quickly after conversation with patient or family, 3 indicated serious discussion of the option with patient or family but no steps taken toward arrangement, 4 indicated serious discussion with patient or family and some time invested in making arrangements, and 5 indicated a great deal of time invested in making arrangements. Dependent variables were measured by the extent to which each of the following five discharge options were pursued: (1) home with informal care only, (2) home with both informal care and formal care (for example, home health nursing aide), (3) rehabilitation unit, (4) intermediate care facility (ICF), and (5) skilled nursing facility (SNF).

Nursing home care is classified as intermediate or skilled depending on the type of care provided and the level and training of the personnel. ICFs address more chronic needs of daily living, such as bathing, feeding, and medicine administration; requirements for staff education and staffing levels are lower. Medicare does not cover intermediate care. SNFs require higher levels of nursing staff and provide care for acute medical needs such as wound care, intravenous medications, and feeding tubes. Medicare covers skilled nursing care.

Extent of pursuit was analyzed only on care options actually discussed. Thus, if the social worker and patient or family did not discuss a particular option, the case was excluded from the analysis on that discharge option. This process ensured that only the discharge planning process that actually occurred with patient and family involvement was subject to analysis. Social workers, rather than patients, rated extent of pursuit, because many of their efforts beyond the initial conversation to explore or arrange various options were not apparent to patients. For example, the social worker made calls and sought information about care options when working away from the patient's room. In addition, given the necessity of timely discharge as soon as the patient was medically ready, the investigators agreed with hospital administrators that querying patients directly about alternative placements might threaten the preparation for discharge. It should be noted, however, that although the social worker is the source of information, the information itself relates to the extent to which patient, families, and discharge planners pursued discharge options.

Ruled Out Because of Preference. We constructed a dependent variable to discern why the patient did not go to an SNF after hospital discharge. Several potential reasons were assessed including "not acceptable to patient or family," which directly reflects preference. We developed a code to reflect whether SNF was ruled out because of patient or family preference: 0 = not ruled out because of patient or family preference (ruled out for other reasons, such as finances not available or medical needs outweighed) and 1 = ruled out because of patient or family preference. We constructed a second dependent variable to discern why the patient did not go to an ICF after hospital discharge using the same coding scheme: 0 = not ruled out because of patient or family preference and 1 = ruled out because of patient or family preference. It should be noted that the social worker is the source of information for this measure, but the information relates to patient or family preference expressed during the discharge planning process.

Independent and Control Variables

The only independent variable in this study, race, was coded dichotomously (white = 0 and African American = 1).

The effects of several variables that might affect discharge destination, and thus the discharge planning process, were controlled. These variables were selected because earlier studies had demonstrated their effect on discharge destination (Morrow-Howell & Proctor, 1994) and on health services utilization (Andersen, 1975; Wolinsky, 1990). Control variables were measured as follows: living alone before hospitalization (1 = lived alone, 0 = did not live alone), Medicaid recipient (1 = Medicaid recipient, 0 = not a Medicaid recipient), cognitive status (1 = not impaired, 2 = mildly impaired, 3 = severely impaired), and functional dependency (range 0 to 24, with higher scores reflecting greater dependency).

The social worker rated patient cognitive status at the time of discharge on the basis of observation of and interaction with the patient. Functional dependency was ascertained from nursing notes using a rating scale developed by Northwest Oregon Health Systems (Coe, Wilkenson, & Patterson, 1986); the scale measures the extent to which patients need human assistance with activities of daily living and medical regimens. A nurse trained in this measurement protocol abstracted medical records using information from nursing notes about mobility; bathing and hygiene needs; route and number of medications; and procedures such as tube feeding, catheter, or ostomy care.

Analyses

Descriptive statistics were produced to describe the patients in the study. To test the hypotheses about extent of pursuit, a series of ordinal probit regressions were conducted to determine the effect of race on the five dependent variables. Probit regression, which uses maximum likelihood estimation, is more appropriate than ordinary least-squares regression, because the dependent variables have a limited number of ordered categories (Maddala, 1983; Miller, 1991). Four control variables were included in each model, and the parameter estimate on the race variable indicated the independent contribution of race to the prediction of the dependent variable. The test statistic for the parameters is Wald's chi-square.

To test the hypotheses about ruling out options for nursing home placement because of patient or family preference, logistic regression was used, given the dichotomous dependent variables. In logistic regression, maximum likelihood estimation is used to produce parameter estimates that represent the change in log odds for the dependent variable associated with a unit change in the independent variable. These log odds can be transformed into odds ratios, which lend themselves to a more straightforward interpretation.

FINDINGS

The patient sample was one-third (35.0 percent) African American and almost two-thirds (65.0 percent) white (Table 28-1). Nearly two-thirds (63.7 percent) of the 369 patients lived alone before hospitalization. Most patients were cognitively intact (64.5 percent), although the sample as a whole was moderately functionally dependent at discharge ($M = 13.5$, $SD = 5.99$, range 0 to 24). Only 16.3 percent of the patients were Medicaid recipients.

Table 28-2 presents the distribution of the extent to which social workers, patients, and family members pursued five discharge options. Sometimes the social worker did not discuss discharge to certain

Table 28-1
Characteristics of the Sample (N = 369)

Characteristic	n	%
Race		
African American	129	35.0
White	240	65.0
Lived alone before discharge		
Yes	235	63.7
No	134	36.3
Cognitive status		
Not impaired	238	64.5
Mildly impaired	99	26.8
Severely impaired	32	8.7

	M	SD	Skewness	Range
Functional dependency	13.5	5.99	.13	0–24

destinations with patients or family members. For example, in 60.7 percent of the cases, there was no discussion about discharge to an ICF; in 66.4 percent of the cases, there was no conversation about discharge to a rehabilitation unit. Such lack of conversation reflects the fact that for certain medical conditions, some options for posthospital care are unnecessary and others are not feasible. Yet for the destination of home with formal and informal care, social workers had no discussion with only 16.0 percent of patients, reflecting both the frequency of this option as well as the patient's and family's desire to pursue such arrangements.

Patients and families with whom social workers had no conversation about a particular option were eliminated from subsequent analysis about the option; the number excluded for each option is reflected in Table 28-2 in the first row, which specifies the percentage of cases where there was no conversation. Chi-square tests were conducted on no conversation versus some pursuit by patient race; none were significant, confirming that one racial group was not differentially excluded from conversations about the discharge option.

Table 28-3 reports the findings of probit regressions on the extent of pursuit of posthospital care options. Based on social workers' reports, discharge planning for African American and white patients did not differ in the extent to which going home with only informal care was pursued. Yet a racial difference was found for pursuit of going home with formal care. Discharge planning with the African American patients and families involved significantly greater pursuit of formal home care services. No racial difference was found in the extent of pursuit of rehabilitation units. The extent to which social workers pursued an ICF approached significance ($p = .09$), with discharge planning with African Americans tending to involve less pursuit of this option. Discharge planning with African Americans involved significantly less pursuit of posthospital skilled nursing home care.

Table 28-4 reports findings from the logistic regressions on the dependent variables about ruling out nursing home placement because of patient or family preference. African American patients were significantly more likely than white patients to rule out intermediate nursing care because of patient or family preference; however, African American and white patients did not differ in the probability of ruling out skilled nursing home care because of patient or family preference.

DISCUSSION

This study has several limitations. Because only one discharge planner knew the details of the discharge planning process with a particular patient, it was not possible to establish interrater reliability on the dependent measures. However, we have subsequently developed other measures of social work activities and discharge planning processes that are similar to these two measures; test–retest

Table 28-2
Extent of Pursuit of Posthospital Care Options (N = 369)

Extent of Pursuit	Home Informal Care Only		Home Formal and Informal Care		Rehabilitation Unit		Intermediate Care Facility		Skilled Nursing Facility	
	n	%	n	%	n	%	n	%	n	%
No conversations with patient or family	166	45.0	59	16.0	245	66.4	224	60.7	182	49.3
Ruled out quickly after conversation with patient or family	130	35.2	58	15.7	44	11.9	69	18.7	76	20.6
Discussed seriously but did not take steps toward arranging	34	9.2	64	17.3	9	2.4	28	7.6	33	8.9
Invested some time in arranging	36	9.8	137	37.1	40	10.8	21	5.7	37	10.0
Invested a great deal of time in arranging	3	0.8	51	13.8	31	8.4	27	7.3	41	11.1

Table 28-3
Probit Regression Results: Effect of Race on Extent of Pursuit of Posthospital Care Options

Independent Variable	Home Informal Care Only (n = 200)		Home Formal and Informal Care (n = 302)		Rehabilitation Unit (n = 120)		Intermediate Care Facility (n = 142)		Skilled Nursing Facility (n = 183)	
	Estimate	χ^2	Estimate	χ^2	Estimate	χ^2	Estimate	χ^2	Estimate	χ^2
Living alone	-.13	.53	.30	4.92*	.07	.11	-.12	.28	-.44	5.24*
Cognitive status	.07	.16	-.17	2.39	.19	.82	.10	.42	.31	5.30*
Medicaid	-.18	.34	-.14	.56	-.40	1.51	.86	12.48*	.48	4.10*
Functional dependency	-.06	10.48*	-.05	15.42*	.01	.40	.01	.34	.07	16.29*
Race	-.22	1.16	.30	4.48*	-.34	2.11	-.38	2.86**	-.88	17.92*

*p < .05. **p = .09.

Table 28-4

Logistic Regression Results: Effect of Race on Ruling out Nursing Home Care Because of Patient or Family Preference

Independent Variable	Intermediate Care Facility Classification[a] (n = 319)			Skilled Nursing Facility Classification[b] (n = 295)		
	Parameter Estimate	SE	Odds Ratio	Parameter Estimate	SE	Odds Ratio
Medicaid	−.11	.44	.90	−1.12	.47	.33**
Functional dependency	.01	.02	1.01	.14	.03	1.16*
Race	.92	.30	2.52*	.26	.03	1.30

[a]0 = not ruled out for reason of preference (80.6 percent); 1 = ruled out for reason of preference (19.4 percent).
[b]0 = not ruled out for reason of preference (74.6 percent); 1 = ruled out for reason of preference (25.4 percent).
*$p = .00$. **$p = .02$.

reliabilities are acceptable, with weighed kappas over .80 (Proctor, Morrow-Howell, & Chadiha, 1993). The lack of a direct measure of cultural preference for the pursuit of an option or the elimination of nursing home placement is another weakness of this study. Racial differences (after controlling for socioeconomic and health status) do not solely reflect cultural characteristics, so further research is needed to draw conclusions about cultural preferences.

Finally, because of constraints in data collection in the hospital setting and patients' and families' lack of awareness of many discharge planning efforts, social workers were the source of information about the discharge planning process. However, patients' and families' perspectives on the discharge planning processes warrant further investigations. Although variables were constructed to capture the realities of patient and family involvement in the discharge planning processes, we cannot completely rule out racial bias in the reporting of this information by the discharge planners.

The findings are significant for their potential to shed light on the determinants rather than just the patterns of care. Earlier studies of service utilization (for example, Kemper & Murtaugh, 1991; Murtaugh et al., 1990) were limited to who goes to nursing homes, not the reasons for selecting that care option and ruling out others. Even studies that focused on cultural explanations of differential patterns of service utilization base those explanations, at best, on indirect measures such as nursing home utilization rates (Belgrave et al., 1993; Yeo, 1993). However, the present data reflect the processes of decision making involving social workers as well as patients and families, enabling us to more directly test explanations for service utilization, particularly reasons for ruling out an option on the basis of preference for alternative sites of care.

Institutional Care

The findings support the study's conceptualization of racial differences in discharge planning processes as a potential explanation of posthospital service utilization differences. Before discharge, African American patients, their families, and the discharge planners pursued to a lesser extent nursing home placements as an option for posthospital care. Furthermore, at the same level of functional dependency and Medicaid status, African Americans were significantly more likely to rule out ICF placements because of patient or family preference.

These findings help explain earlier service utilization and posthospital care findings that African American patients are less likely to use nursing home care than white patients. This study offers insight into this phenomenon by demonstrating that African Americans with comparable levels of cognitive and physical functioning and Medicaid eligibility are more likely than white people to rule out nursing home care because it is not acceptable to the patient or family. Correspondingly, the discharge planning process involving African American patients and families involves less pursuit of options for nursing home care.

Earlier work (Belgrave et al., 1993) invoked a cultural preference explanation for African Americans' underuse of nursing home care based only on observed differences in use. This study represents an improvement in that racial differences in patient or family preferences for nursing home care are addressed directly. However, evidence of racial differences in ruling out nursing home care because of patient or family preference still may not constitute evidence of a cultural preference explanation. Further development of direct measures of cultural preference are needed.

It is important to note that although African Americans ruled out ICFs because of patient or family preference more often than their white counterparts, they did not do so more often for SNFs. This likely reflects the fact that SNFs are often viewed and used as extensions of acute care; SNFs are covered by Medicare and are geared toward treatment of acute conditions and the recovery of the patient. The potential of a short-term stay and discharge to the community is quite good, especially when compared with ICFs, where longer-term stays are needed to attend to the patient's chronic care needs. Thus, to an elderly African American and his or her family, discharge to an SNF may be more acceptable than discharge to an ICF.

This explanation probably holds for the finding that no racial differences were observed in the pursuit of rehabilitation unit options. Discharge to rehabilitation is viewed as temporary, geared toward recovery, and covered by Medicare. Although rehabilitation units are institutional and represent a high level of formal care, this discharge option is also seen as an extension of acute care. Morrow-Howell and Proctor (1994) found no racial differences in frequency of actual discharge to a rehabilitation unit, and the present study suggests that the discharge planning process underlying this discharge also does not differ by race.

Noninstitutional Care

Compared with planning with white patients and families, discharge planning with African American patients and their families involved a greater pursuit of discharge to home with formal care arrangements. No racial difference was found in the extent to which social workers, patient, and family pursued discharge to home with informal care only. These findings do not support the study's hypotheses that discharge planning with African American patients and their families would involve more pursuit of informal care in the home than planning by white patients (hypothesis 1) and less pursuit of formal care than white patients (hypothesis 2).

Because the health status control variable in the present study captures functional ability more than sickness, it may not control all of the variance in the dependent variables because of differential health status between African American patients and white patients. Evidence that African Americans enter home care sicker and more functionally dependent is reported elsewhere (Proctor, Morrow-Howell, & Chadiha, 1993). Thus, African American patients and families may desire discharge home with informal care only, but social workers may invest time in trying to help them accept formal services in the home. The measure of extent of pursuit reflects the activity of the social worker, patient, and family but does not permit distinction among the social worker's, patient's, and family members' efforts. The findings may also reflect the fact that with African American patients, greater efforts were required to make formal home care possible (for example, more discussions of who would provide what care, more discussions of what agencies could provide the needed level of skilled care).

IMPLICATIONS FOR SOCIAL WORKERS

The findings have a number of implications for social workers and other health professionals involved in discharge planning for posthospital care. They suggest that discharge planning demands culturally sensitive assessment and intervention. African American patients and families appear to prefer home care to institutional care. Yet given African American patients' poorer health and higher needs for care, the ability of family and friends to meet their needs must be carefully explored. As long as no harm will ensue from a discharge home to informal care, professionals need to respect and foster client self-determination (Proctor, Morrow-Howell, & Lott, 1993). When medical needs demand formal home care, professionals need to anticipate possible patient and family reluctance based on a preference for informal care. Such reluctance might require more thorough, painstaking discussion of options for formal in-home care.

Risk is compounded by evidence that the home care of elderly African Americans tends to be less adequate than that provided for other groups (Chadiha et al., 1995). Research documents that professionals viewed institutional settings as more adequate to meet patient needs (Morrow-Howell, Proctor, & Mui, 1991). Concern has been raised that African American patients who avoid institutional care in favor of home care may have their needs met less well than if they had gone to nursing homes.

When nursing home placements are medically necessary, discharge planners need to anticipate, appreciate, and respond to patient and family reluctance. Theories of decision making posit that exploring a wider range of options increases the quality of an eventual decision, enhances confidence in the decision, and increases satisfaction (Janis & Mann, 1982). Pursuing an optimum number of feasible alternatives may enhance family satisfaction with discharge planning (Proctor et al., 1992). Time spent exploring the risks and limits of home care might help reluctant patients and families accept the need for higher levels of care provided in institutional placements. If a patient goes to a nursing home after expressing clear reluctance, intervention is needed around issues of adjustment and acceptance. In addition, racial discrimination in certain nursing homes must be addressed, given its possible contribution to African Americans' reluctance to enter nursing homes (Belgrave et al., 1993).

This study begins the exploration of factors that explain differential service utilization among elderly African Americans by focusing on the discharge planning processes that underlie posthospital care arrangements. Findings confirm that racial differences exist in discharge planning processes. These differences may partially account for the differences in care arrangements previously noted in the literature. Specifically, this study demonstrates that African American patients and families rule out institutional care for reasons of preference and that discharge planning with African American patients and families involves less pursuit of nursing home placements and more pursuit of formal services in the home. Further research is clearly needed, because service arrangement and utilization are complex phenomena; several explanatory factors are probably operating, including cultural preference, service system bias, and socioeconomic status. Although this study advances the measurement of cultural preference and presents empirical evidence of its operation in discharge planning, more work is needed to directly measure the attitudes and preferences of clients of color regarding health and social services.

REFERENCES

Abramson, J. S. (1990). Enhancing patient participation: Clinical strategies in the discharge planning process. *Social Work in Health Care, 14*, 53–71.

Andersen, R. (1975). Health service distribution and equity. In R. Andersen, J. Kravits, & O. W. Anderson (Eds.), *Equity in health services: Empirical analyses in social policy* (pp. 9–32). Cambridge, MA: Ballinger.

Andersen, R. (1995). Revisiting the behavioral model and access to medical care: Does it matter? *Journal of Health & Social Behavior, 35,* 1–10.

Arenth, L. M., & Mamon, J. A. (1985). Determining patient needs after discharge. *Nursing Management, 16,* 20–24.

Belgrave, L. L., Wykle, M. L., & Choi, J. M. (1993). Health, double jeopardy, and culture: The use of institutionalization by African Americans. *Gerontologist, 33,* 379–385.

Chadiha, L. A., Proctor, E. K., Morrow-Howell, N., Darkwa, O., & Dore, P. (1995). Post-hospital care for African-American and white elderly. *Gerontologist, 35,* 233–239.

Chatters, L. M., Taylor, R. J., & Jackson, J. S. (1986). Aged blacks' choices for an informal helper network. *Journal of Gerontology, 41,* 94–100.

Coe, M., Wilkenson, A., & Patterson, P. (1986). *Preliminary evidence on the impact of DRGs: Dependency at discharge.* Beaverton: Northwest Oregon Health Systems.

Dunkle, R., Coulton, C., MacKintosh, J., & Goode, R. (1982). Factors affecting the posthospital care planning of elderly patients in an acute care setting. *Journal of Gerontological Nursing, 4*(3–4), 95–106.

Gibson, R. C., & Jackson, J. S. (1989). The health, physical functioning, and informal supports of the black elderly. In D. P. Willis (Ed.), *Health policies and black Americans* (pp. 421–454). New Brunswick, NJ: Transaction.

Janis, I., & Mann, L. (1982). A theoretical framework for decision making. In I. Janis (Ed.), *Counseling on personal decisions: Theory and research on short-term helping relationships* (pp. 47–72). New Haven, CT: Yale University Press.

Kemper, P., & Murtaugh, C. M. (1991). Lifetime use of nursing home care. *New England Journal of Medicine, 324,* 595–600.

Maddala, G. (1983). *Limited-dependent and qualitative variables in econometrics.* Cambridge, England: Cambridge University Press.

May, D., Kelly, J., Mendlein, J., & Garbe, P. (1991). Surveillance of major causes of hospitalization among the elderly, 1988. *Morbidity and Mortality Weekly Report, 40*(SS-1), 7–21.

Miller, L. (1991). The relationship between social support and burnout: Clarification and simplification [Methodological Note]. *Social Work Research & Abstracts, 27*(1), 34–47.

Mindel, C., Wright, R., & Starrett, R. (1986). Informal and formal health and social support systems of black and white elderly: A comparative cost approach. *Gerontologist, 26,* 279–285.

Morrow-Howell, N., & Proctor, E. K. (1994). Discharge destinations of Medicare patients receiving discharge planning: Who goes where. *Medical Care, 34,* 486–497.

Morrow-Howell, N., Proctor, E. K., & Dore, P. (1993). *Adequacy of care: The concept and its measurement.* Paper presented at the Annual Scientific Meeting of the Gerontological Society of America, New Orleans.

Morrow-Howell, N., Proctor, E. K., & Mui, A. C. (1991). Adequacy of discharge plans for elderly patients. *Social Work Research & Abstracts, 17*(1), 6–13.

Mui, A. C., & Burnette, D. (1994). Long-term care service by frail elders: Is ethnicity a factor? *Gerontologist, 34,* 190–198.

Murtaugh, C. M., Kemper, P., & Spillman, B. C. (1990). The risk of nursing home use in later life. *Medical Care, 28,* 952–962.

Proctor, E. K., Morrow-Howell, N., Albaz, R., & Weir, C. (1992). Patient and family satisfaction with discharge plans. *Medical Care, 30,* 262–275.

Proctor, E. K., Morrow-Howell, N., & Chadiha, L. (1993). *The adequacy of care plans for chronically ill elderly: Final report* (Submitted to the Agency for Health Care Policy and Research in fulfillment of grant requirement). St. Louis: Washington University, George Warren Brown School of Social Work.

Proctor, E. K., Morrow-Howell, N., & Lott, C. L. (1993). Classification and correlates of ethical dilemmas in hospital social work. *Social Work, 38,* 166–177.

Spence, S. A., & Atherton, C. R. (1991). The black elderly and the social service delivery system: A study of factors influencing the use of community-based services. *Journal of Gerontological Social Work, 16,* 19–35.

U.S. Department of Health and Human Services. (1990). Long-term care for the functionally dependent elderly. In *Vital and health statistics* (Series 13, No. 104, Publication No. PHS 90-1765). Hyattsville, MD: Author.

Wolinsky, F. D. (1990). *Health and health behavior among elderly Americans: An age stratification perspective.* New York: Springer.

Yeo, G. W. (1993). Ethnicity and nursing homes: Factors affecting use and successful components for culturally sensitive care. In C. M. Barresi & D. E. Stull (Eds.), *Ethnic elderly and long-term care* (pp. 161–177). New York: Springer.

This work was supported by grant no. 2RO1-HS06406 from the Agency for Health Care Policy and Research.

Part VI

LONG-TERM CARE

29 Navajo Elderly People in a Reservation Nursing Home: Admission Predictors and Culture Care Practices

Susan O. Mercer

The aging of the American Indian population presents many of the same challenges for long-term care provision as does that of the general U.S. population. Manson and Callaway (1988) suggested that planning for long-term care among American Indians is less often discussed and more uncoordinated than care for other elderly people. Furthermore, the Indian Health Service (IHS) has emphasized children and family concerns more than those of older Indians.

Unlike the general U.S. population, which has more than 19,000 nursing homes available, American Indian communities on reservations have few skilled- and intermediate-care facilities. Most elderly Indians who require nursing home care must leave the reservation and their families. About 4,600 elderly Indians reside in non-Indian nursing homes (Manson & Callaway, 1988; Mercer, Garner, & Leon, 1991), which rarely employ Indian staff, serve traditional foods, or encourage traditional customs. These voids can lead to social isolation, loneliness, depression, and diminished quality of life and health status (Mick, 1983).

Few researchers have done in-depth studies of American Indian nursing homes (Mick, 1983), and no major social work journal has published an article on Indian elders in nursing homes in more than 15 years. Research on the reasons Indians use nursing homes, including events and circumstances that heighten vulnerability to placement, and on culture-specific caregiving practices does not exist.

Because of their cultural uniqueness, American Indian nursing homes deserve closer attention. This chapter describes ethnographic research conducted at the Navajo Nation nursing home in Chinle, Arizona, and answers two research questions: What primary events and circumstances result in nursing home placement? What culturally sensitive care principles and practices exist in the nursing home?

BACKGROUND

Navajo History

Early Spanish colonizers in North America referred to the Navajos as *Apache de Navaho* (strangers of the cultivated fields). Navajos called

This chapter was originally published in the March 1996 issue of *Social Work*, Vol. 41, pp. 181–189.

themselves *Diné* (pronounced DEE-neh, meaning "The People") and called their beloved land *Dinehtah* (Gilpin, 1968; Locke, 1989; Suppee, Anderson, & Anderson, 1990).

Navajo tradition says that generations of ancestors wandered through inhospitable country, eventually coming together to settle the fifth world (the fourth world in some tellings) of their mythology. This land was bounded by Blanco Peak (*Sisnaajiní*) to the east in Colorado, Mt. Taylor (*Tsoodzil*) to the south in New Mexico, San Francisco Peak (*Dook'o'oosliid*) to the west in Arizona, and Mt. Hesperus (*Dibé Nitsaa*) to the north in Colorado. The mountains were the source of ritually required herbs, communal strength, and traditional legends. When and exactly how the Navajos arrived in this land is still conjecture. It is possible that they have lived in the southwestern United States for at least 1,000 years.

The Navajos were influenced by the neighboring Pueblo or village-dwelling Indians who shared weaving, the making of painted pottery, and agricultural skills. Spanish colonizers introduced silversmithing as well as horses, sheep, and goats, changing the Navajo lifestyle and economy (Kluckhohn & Leighton, 1974; Locke, 1989; Seymour, 1988). The Spanish colonizers established settlements among the Pueblo Indians in New Mexico beginning in 1568. For the next 200 years, the Navajos existed uneasily with their neighbors, alternating between raiding and trading with other tribes and warring over land and resources with Spanish and Mexican colonizers. In turn, the colonizers and Pueblo Indians raided the Navajo settlements for slaves.

When Anglo-Americans arrived on the land in the 19th century, the land was opened for settlement. Continuing raids and military retaliations eventually led the U.S. government to send Kit Carson in 1863 to Canyon de Chelly to subjugate the Navajos. The Navajos were skilled warriors who used the canyons, mountains, and desert to their advantage, but Carson's tactics of burning their homes and crops and destroying their livestock subdued them in less than a year.

In what is now called the "Long Walk," thousands of Navajos were marched by U.S. soldiers over 300 miles to Fort Sumner in eastern New Mexico. The number of Navajos involved in the four-year relocation totaled more than 8,000, although thousands more remained hidden within their land. Hundreds escaped from Fort Sumner and survived the journey home. This incarceration and experiment in forced acculturation failed. The Navajos suffered deprivation, diseases, starvation, and death, but they outlasted the patience and resources of their Anglo-American captors and in 1868 negotiated a treaty to return to their land (Barker, 1992; Trimble, 1993).

Navajo Religion

Traditional Navajo religion deals with controlling the many supernatural powers in the Navajo world. Earth Surface People (living and dead humans) and Holy People (supernatural beings) interact. A series of Lower Worlds existed before the present one, and activities and travels of the Holy People are paramount in these legends. No hierarchy exists among the Holy People; of major importance are Changing Woman, First Woman, the Hero Twins, Monster Slayer, Born-for-Water, Talking God, White Corn Boy, Yellow Corn Girl, Corn Pollen Boy, and Corn Beetle Girl. Changing Woman is the only deity with consistent exemplary behavior. The other Holy People are unpredictable; they can harm as well as help humans. Holy People are "holy" in the sense of being powerful and belonging to the sacred world (Frisbie, 1987; Kluckhohn & Leighton, 1974; Locke, 1989; Seymour, 1988).

Navajos abide by prescriptions and proscriptions (taboos) given by the Holy People to maintain harmony with others, nature, and supernatural forces. Ideal harmony (*hózhó*) includes universal beauty and happiness and manifests itself in good health, peace, balance, and positive events in the lives of self and relatives. The goal of traditional Navajo life is to live in harmony and die of old age. If one indulges in excesses, has improper contacts with dangerous powers, or deliberately or accidentally breaks other rules, then disharmony, conflict, evil, sickness of body and mind, misfortune, and disaster result.

A fine line exists between good and evil, positive and negative. Witches, either men or women, are frequently referred to as "wolves" or "skinwalkers" (they dress in wolf or coyote skins). Witches are capable of causing harm, sickness, and death. During the night witches are thought to transfer "corpse poison" to a victim, utter spells over an object closely associated with a victim (hair or clothing), and "shoot" a small object (bone or ash from a home where someone has died) into a victim. In the past witchcraft beliefs served as a form of social control. If a person was too rich or too selfish, he or she was accused of being a witch.

When an imbalance in harmony occurs, the afflicted person's family discusses the etiology of the illness, including infection by animals, natural phenomena, or evil spirits such as ghosts (*chindi*) and witches. The afflicted person and family also turn to hand tremblers, star gazers, crystal gazers, and water gazers for diagnosis and recommendations to re-create harmony. Ceremonies deal with the cause of the illness and involve the relevant Holy People in the restoration of harmony. Ceremonies work simultaneously in the physical, mental, spiritual, and social realms (Frisbie, 1987).

Preventive ceremonies maintain and reinforce harmony, invoke blessings, and avert misfortune. Wyman and Kluckhohn's (1938) classification system identified six major groups of song ceremonials. For example, Blessingway can bless pregnant women, departing and returning travelers, ceremonial paraphernalia, and new leaders or can remove the dead's contamination of the living. Each ceremony is associated with certain Holy People, etiological factors, and specific illnesses. Ceremonies vary in length from one to nine nights and are seasonally timed (Frisbie, 1987).

Ceremonies are led by medicine men or women, also called Singers *(hataali)*. A Singer apprentices to an experienced healer for years of training, specializing in only two or three complex ceremonies. Each rite combines the use of many elements: ritual and sacred items from the medicine bundle *(jish)* such as prayersticks, sacred stones, corn pollen, and herbs; songs, chants, prayers, and dances; body painting; sweating and emesis with purification functions; and sacred dry-paintings (sandpaintings). Selection of these and other elements and their orderly combination create an effective ceremony (Reichard, 1977).

As major social and religious events involving entire communities, ceremonies are a major investment of time and resources for the afflicted person, extended family, and clan. All who attend the ceremony are fed, and the Singer, dancers, and other helpers are compensated with sheep, cloth, and cash. Cooperative efforts focus on butchering sheep and goats, cooking, hauling wood and water, and washing dishes. The final day and night of a ceremony may be attended by more than 100 people. A nine-night ceremony such as the Night Chant *(Yeibichai)* may cost a family thousands of dollars (Lamphere, 1989; Locke, 1989).

Navajo Family

"I was born to the Towering House clan [mother's side] and born for the Many Goats clan [father's side]. My maternal Grandmother's clan is Bitter Water; my paternal Grandfather's clan is Edgewater." This is a typical introduction for a traditional Navajo. There are more than 60 clan-based kinship groups. An extended Navajo family has a much larger membership than most families.

Lineage, like inheritance, is traced through the mother. A Navajo will refer to her mother's sister's son as a brother, when an Anglo-American would refer to him as a first cousin. A Navajo may call a male friend who is a member of her Grandfather's clan "Grandfather," even when there is no blood connection (Gilpin, 1968; Reichard, 1977).

Family and clan determine economic and social obligations as well as privileges and restrictions. It is forbidden (and can lead to emotional and physical sickness) for Navajos to marry within their clans. It is taboo for clan members to touch or look at the nude bodies of relatives, particularly their brothers and sisters. In the past the clan was a source of social control of irresponsible or illegal activity; all members of a clan were responsible for the debts and crimes of other members (Kluckhohn & Leighton, 1974).

Navajo Homes

A *hogan* ("the place home"), a traditional Navajo home, is the center of traditional Navajo life and is considered a sacred place, a gift from the Holy People. A typical *hogan* on the reservation today evolved from a forked-stick, mud-covered dwelling to a circular or eight-sided domed-roof structure with cribbed horizontal logs chinked with adobe, clay, or mortar. Logs are laid so they converge in a central smoke hole. The door faces east to greet the morning sun and new day. Once a *hogan* is completed, a Blessingway is performed, and the Holy People are asked to make the home a happy one.

A heating and cooking stove, often an adapted metal drum, is placed in the center with the stove pipe extending through the smoke hole in the roof. Positions of possessions and people are prescribed in the legends; the south side belongs to women and the north side to men. If the *hogan* is struck by lightning or a death occurs inside, the structure is considered *chindi,* or "witched," and is abandoned.

Traditionally, an entire Navajo family lived in a *hogan* about 25 square feet in size. Anglo-American–style houses or mobile homes are common today, but most families build a *hogan* nearby for ceremonial purposes. Many Navajos have both summer and winter homes. Water supply, weather, and available grazing and farm lands play a role in this mobility (Gilpin, 1968; Locke, 1989; Reichard, 1977; Wyman, 1970).

Navajo Reservation

The Navajo reservation land is beautiful, rugged, and immense, spanning more than 25,000 square miles, an area equivalent in size to West Virginia. The reservation is situated in the south central area of the Colorado Plateau and extends into New Mexico, Arizona, and Utah. Much of the sparsely populated reservation is arid grasslands, deep canyons, and mountains. Navajos live in small clusters referred to as "extended family camps." Relative isolation because of geography and lifestyle is further compounded by a webbing of dirt roads that frequently are impassable during inclement weather (Goodman, 1982; Wainapel, 1989).

Delivering in-home care in this environment is difficult. The Navajo Division of Social Services and Division on Aging have a meals-on-wheels program, in-home public health nurse care through the IHS, community health representatives, and adult in-home care that provides assistance with activities of daily living. Staff may travel through rough terrain 30 miles or more round-trip to serve one household.

Navajo Nation

The 1990 census counted 1,959,000 American Indians (Reddy, 1993). The Navajo Nation is the largest U.S. reservation-based tribe, with a reservation population of more than 155,000 and a yearly growth rate of about 3 percent.

Demographically and economically, American Indians differ from the general U.S. population in a number of ways that negatively affect health. For example, 47 percent of Navajos live below the poverty level, 51 percent have no piped water or indoor toilet facilities, 46 percent lack electric lighting, and 80 percent do not have telephones. The 1988 per capita income was $4,344 (compared to the general population's $8,012). The rural reservation has a population density of 6.9 people per square mile. Only 40 percent of Navajo families live within 30 miles of any health care facility, and 32 percent must drive more than one hour to receive health care. The median age is 18.7 years, and about 5 percent of Navajos are age 60 or older. The average Navajo has a life expectancy of 73.7 years (compared to 76.0 years for the general population) (Navajo Area Indian Health Service, 1992).

The Navajo Nation's two nursing homes, Chinle (79 beds) and Toyei (64 beds), cannot provide care for all Navajo elders who need it. About 300 Navajo elders reside in nursing homes off the reservation. The Navajo Division of Health has estimated that 150 additional nursing home beds are needed (personal communication with staff at the Area Agency on Aging, Window Rock, AZ, September 1994). The number of Navajo elders is projected to grow by 3 percent a year.

METHOD

Data in this qualitative study were extracted from ethnographic research conducted during the fall of 1993 at the Chinle Nursing Home in the heart of the Navajo reservation. I lived five weeks on the reservation with the nursing home's Navajo administrator, a social worker with an MSW. I was present in the facility each workday and frequently on weekends and spent informal time with the residents, their families, and staff members to help establish trust and gain acceptance into the nursing home community. For example, I worked beside staff and residents during a clean-up day outside the nursing home and also took saunas with some of the Grandmothers, who sang traditional songs for their benefit and mine.

Ten Navajo elders, referred to as "Grandparents," and their family members were chosen for interviews because of their representativeness (that is, the participants were balanced according to gender, age, and length of residency) and sufficient cognitive capacity to be engaged directly or through a translator. Staff members and one Grandmother served as translators. I recorded observations, interactions, and events in a field diary. The primary criteria for data analysis were credibility, dependency, recurrency, and saturation. Dependency and credibility were established through the use of Navajos as translators and being open to a variety of stimuli. As interviews and chart reviews were completed, they were summarized, and emerging patterns and themes were discussed with key informants in the setting to assess reliability of the information. Drafts of the manuscript were critiqued for general accuracy by Navajo and Anglo-American anthropologists familiar with the Navajo culture.

Data collection methods included record review, which yielded medical and social history information; semistructured interviews with key nursing staff to identify culturally sensitive care practices; semistructured interviews with key administrative staff to identify issues facing Navajo Grandparents, including circumstances leading to nursing home placement; semistructured interviews with Grandparents and families; observation and participation in all weekly care conferences (where families were frequently present), resident council meetings, and key staff meetings; and participation in all activities of the nursing home.

FINDINGS

Facility

Opened in 1971, the Chinle Nursing Home, not licensed by the state of Arizona, is operated by Navajolands Nursing Homes, Inc., a nonprofit organization with an all-Navajo board of directors. With 79 beds divided between two wings (one for men and one for women), the facility provides intermediate care for reservation residents older than 16. A majority of the rooms have four beds, and a small number are private or two-bed rooms. The facility had a 98 percent occupancy rate in the last six months of the study. A modern 60-bed IHS hospital (adult, pediatric, and obstetrics) with an emergency room, renal dialysis unit, and outpatient psychiatric services is within walking distance.

The medical director of the nursing home was an Anglo-American physician from the IHS. Other staff included an administrator and assistant administrator; a director of nursing (a registered nurse), five licensed practical nurses, and 28 certified nurse's aides; a dietary supervisor; a maintenance and housekeeping supervisor; a social worker; an activity director; two physical therapist assistants; and support staff for housekeeping, maintenance, laundry, and dietary services. All staff were Navajo except for one Anglo-American and one Hopi licensed practical nurse.

The annual budget, provided to the Navajo Division of Social Services (DSS) and then submitted to the BIA, was about $1,350,000 in 1993. Per diem rates, including room and board, ranged from $43.83 to $58.56. After review and approval by the BIA, funds were sent to the tribe and then distributed to the nursing home. Resident monies generally came from Supplemental Security Income. DSS paid the residential portion of the per diem rate; IHS paid the medical portion. Grandparents received a maximum of $35 monthly on an as-needed basis for personal use, with the monies negotiated through the facility's social worker.

Reasons for Admission

Grandparents were referred for admission to the nursing home by themselves, family members, IHS staff, the tribal community, or a public health worker. Before admission each Grandparent and his or her family members were interviewed (including a home visit if appropriate) by a social worker from the DSS, who assessed the situation, explored options with the family, and determined the elder's eligibility. Recommendations about admission were made to the tribe. Meetings were held with the facility's administrative staff, including the social worker, if the final recommendation was for admission. If no bed was available at Chinle, the Grandparent could choose an off-reservation facility or be placed on the waiting list. In either case, the family was encouraged to visit the facility.

Primary reasons for nursing home admission include the following (no numbers or percentages are given because most overlap):

- The Grandparent's health care needs, primarily in the area of physical functioning, were too great for the family (usually the youngest daughter) and community support system to provide.
- The Grandparent's home was unsafe, unsanitary, or otherwise inadequate (for example, no running water, electricity, or indoor bathroom).
- The Grandparent's home was too isolated and transportation unavailable or difficult to manage, particularly in the winter.
- The Grandparent's financial income was inadequate, perhaps compounded by the traditional Navajo way of sharing income and resources with all in the family.
- The Grandparent's family members worked off the reservation and were unavailable to assist, or they were out of the home all day, leaving the Grandparent at risk.
- The Grandparent lived alone and had no relatives to provide care.
- Neglect or physical abuse of the Grandparent by children or grandchildren was either confirmed or suspected.
- Alcoholism by the Grandparent or family member made the home unsafe.

The following case vignettes demonstrate the most common circumstances that led to nursing home placement of Navajo elders:

- L, age 84, suffered from partial blindness, depression, anemia, and hypothyroidism. She was cognitively alert but required limited help with activities of daily living, which she was not receiving in her home. She lived with her sons in a frame house that had no indoor plumbing or electricity and had a wood stove for heat. L was admitted to the nursing home from an acute care hospital because of physical abuse by a son who abused alcohol. Following the abuse, she had been taken to the emergency room by another son, who did not return for her.
- K, age 85, was unable to be cared for by her daughter after she fractured her pelvis. Her husband died in 1969, and she had eight surviving children. Ten people lived in K's home, a small trailer with no water or electricity.
- C, age 79 and a widow for 16 years, had eight children and numerous grandchildren. The family members rarely visited, did not help with chores such as hauling water and wood, and were verbally abusive. She reported that a grandson hit her in the

head during a fight about money, and this injury resulted in mental confusion. Family members abused alcohol and demanded money from her. C attempted suicide four times by overdosing on pills and ingesting rubbing alcohol.

- P, age 78, had cognitive and functional disabilities and no one to care for her. Her husband had physically assaulted her, resulting in severe cognitive and linguistic deficits. She and her husband, both Singers of ceremonies, had eight children, with five surviving. The family reported that both P and her husband were involved in witchcraft based on events that took place in the community.

- M, age 69, was diagnosed with a cerebrovascular accident, hypertension, and diabetes mellitus. He became unable to care for himself because of his physical condition and abuse of alcohol. His daughter cared for him for four months before requesting placement. He often left the daughter's home in his wheelchair, went to the local grocery store, and drank with friends. The Navajo police often brought him home.

- J, age 71, was diagnosed with diabetes mellitus, hypertension, and a cerebrovascular accident. A medicine man and sheepherder, he never formally married and had no children. He requested admission because of chronic diarrhea and dehydration and because "no one was committed to caring for him." A sister lived nearby and helped some, but because of traditional Navajo beliefs and taboos about touching a sibling, she was unwilling to change his clothes and bathe him.

Care Principles and Practices

Cultural care can be defined as the learned and transmitted values and beliefs that enable people to maintain their well-being and health and to deal with illness, disability, and death (Leininger, 1990, 1992). Major themes and principles related to culturally sensitive care practices emerged in interviews with the Navajo Grandparents, their families, and staff members, including communication; clan associations and social structure; personal space, modesty, privacy, and cleanliness; traditional foods; dying and death; and cultural rituals.

Communication. Few of the Navajo Grandparents spoke English with any fluency; the majority spoke their own language. The Navajo language reflects the concept of a universe that is always in motion. For example, whereas an English speaker says, "I got dressed," the Navajo speaker says, "I moved into my clothes." Furthermore, the Navajo language does not always have one single word that is similar to an English word. These language differences highlight the importance of using a translator and have obvious implications for the sometimes daunting tasks of completing an assessment, interpreting a diagnosis, and establishing goals and interventions (Giger & Davidhizar, 1991).

Listening and not interrupting are strongly held values in Navajo etiquette. Navajos consider it rude to interrupt anyone when he or she is speaking, and frequently a Navajo listener waits a short period before speaking to make certain the other person has completed a statement (Dawson, 1994; Giger & Davidhizar, 1991).

Clan Associations and Social Structure. When introducing themselves, Navajos traditionally state their clan associations and where they are from before giving their own names. Navajos are very family oriented, and the extended biological family is the center of the social structure. To Navajos the real measure of poverty is to be without family (Hanley, 1991).

It was not uncommon for many members of the extended family to visit the Grandparents at the nursing home. Staff were sensitive to the fact that some family traveled from great distances and made significant financial sacrifices to make the journey.

Personal Space, Modesty, Privacy, and Cleanliness. Personal space is important to Navajos, and some have difficulty adapting to spaces and people with whom they are not familiar (Hanley, 1991). Traditional Navajos sleep on mattresses or sheep skins stacked on the floor. The Grandparents were not accustomed to the high hospital bed with railings and often wanted to move the mattress to the floor, a request honored by staff. The Grandparents gradually became comfortable with sleeping in the beds.

Navajos' modesty and strong sense of privacy create problems around showering communally or being touched by strangers. Also, most Navajo elders are more accustomed to having sweat baths. One Grandmother said that a sweat bath with prayers and songs "cleans you inside and outside spiritually" and that she did not feel clean after a regular shower. Both wings of the nursing home have a sauna that simulates a sweat bath. Showers were offered two times a week.

The Navajos also have religious prescriptions for bathing and cleanliness. Traditional Navajos use yucca roots to wash their hair; some Grandparents reported that their hair did not feel clean when washed with regular shampoo.

Traditional Grandparents were accustomed to sleeping in their regular clothes and felt naked in night clothes. Staff permitted the Grandparents to sleep in whatever they chose; most eventually adapted to the night clothes.

Traditional Foods. Older Navajos have specific food and beverage preferences: grilled mutton, mutton stew, fry bread, corn, fried potatoes, and coffee. The nursing home's kitchen served roasted mutton and mutton stew (actually lamb because it is easier to chew and digest and has less fat) three times a month and baked most of the breads. Family members were encouraged to bring traditional foods if the Grandparent's diet was not restricted.

Some foods are restricted following a traditional healing ceremony. These dietary admonitions and instructions were understood and respected by the dietary staff.

Dying and Death. Traditional Navajos have many restrictions regarding contact with the dead. They do not talk about death, believing that discussing death may "bring it to you." A family will move a dying member to a brush shelter nearby to avoid a death in the *hogan*. A *hogan* in which someone has died is usually abandoned and in some way destroyed to signal avoidance to others. No traditional Navajo would seek shelter in or use the wood from such a place.

In the past, two or three adults were chosen to clean and dress the body after death, taking care to avoid taboos. The body was carried to the final resting place, perhaps buried in a high rock crevice and covered with deadwood as a protection against predators. Jewelry or other items were buried with the body. Families mourned for four days and ritually washed themselves. If proper precautions were not taken, the *chindi* could return to avenge some neglect or offense. Names of the deceased are not used again, because the *chindi* may hear the calling and return to make the "caller" sick. Four days of mourning are not necessary for those who die of old age, are stillborn, or are infants who do not live long enough to utter a sound, because they do not produce *chindi* (Kluckhohn & Leighton; 1974; Lamphere, 1989; Locke, 1989).

Today, most Navajos die in a hospital, and their bodies are taken to the funeral home (Lamphere, 1989; Locke, 1989; Reichard, 1977). Nevertheless, a majority of the Grandparents and staff did not want to touch a dead body or personal clothing of the dead person. Traditional beliefs are responsible for the lack of acceptance of advance directives such as living wills or health care powers of attorney. No Grandparents had signed advance directives, and the social worker did not pressure them to do so. Furthermore, nursing staff said that it is "almost taboo" to perform cardiopulmonary resuscitation (CPR) on a person, because if that person dies he or she "takes your breath to the grave," and a ceremony is necessary to "bring the breath back to the living person." Navajos who have converted to Christianity are more likely to have performed CPR.

Any Grandparent near the last stage of an illness was transferred to the IHS hospital so he or she would not die in the nursing home. If there was a death in the nursing home, a Singer performed a cleansing ceremony before the room was used again. A ceremony was done preventively for the entire facility.

Cultural Rituals. A traditional *hogan* was built adjacent to the nursing home and was available to the Grandparents, their families, and staff. Ceremonies, prayers, and associated practices were an integral part of the Grandparents' daily life.

DISCUSSION AND CONCLUSION

Although the recent advent of nursing homes in American Indian communities recognizes a previously unmet need, the care of Indian elders still presents a pressing social and health issue. The constant care demands of a frail, impaired older adult can strain even an Indian family system, and the IHS and the tribes will not have the resources to meet the service demands of elderly Indians projected over the next several decades (Manson & Callaway, 1988). It is likely, therefore, that more Indian elders will reside in non-Indian nursing homes, requiring knowledge-building efforts by non-Indian social workers and other health care providers. Perhaps it is time to "anthropologize" the social work curriculum to broaden the belief that ethnic diversity is stimulating and precious (Cerroni-Long, 1993; Leininger, 1992).

Culture care practices will be required in all aspects of the care process—assessment and intervention, staff selection and training, policy and procedure implementation, and facility location and design. Culturally sensitive care requires accommodation and negotiation with clients as partners in the process and attention and sensitivity to what is in their best interests, requiring frequent rechecks of their values, beliefs, and practices (Leininger, 1978). It is easy to comprehend why elder Navajos who live off the reservation reported loneliness, depression, and isolation, whereas the Grandparents at the nursing home appeared to be content, satisfied, and "at home." Principles of care at the Chinle Nursing Home can be applied to other American Indian elders and nursing homes.

An extreme level of poverty, lack of basic resources and in-home health and social services, difficulty traveling within the reservation during inclement weather, and rural isolation contributed to Navajo elders' nursing home placement. Many non-Indians referred to the reservation as a Third World country within the United States; traditional Navajos generally do not agree with this assessment because of their value of nonmaterialism (Dawson, 1994). However, younger generations struggle with the contrast between the reservation and Anglo-American worlds; they try to maintain traditional ways, including respecting and caring for their elders, but also seek employment off the reservation that may provide a better life. Furthermore, the extent to which alcoholism plays such a major role in the reason for nursing home placement is unlikely to be duplicated in any Anglo-American nursing home. To what extent these findings are comparable to other Indian nursing homes on reservations is largely unknown, and more systematic studies are needed of appropriate interventions.

Ewalt (1994) stated that too often pre-existing Western European influences dominate social work practice theories. If this chapter conveys the importance of cultural mindfulness (Cerroni-Long, 1993) and listening to and learning from clients and finding ways to act on this knowledge (Davis & Gelsomino, 1994), then its goals have been achieved.

REFERENCES

Barker, R. (1992). *The broken circle.* New York: Simon & Schuster.

Cerroni-Long, E. L. (1993). Ethnicity in the USA: An anthropological model. *Anthro Notes, 15*(3), 4–6.

Davis, L. E., & Gelsomino, J. (1994). An assessment of practitioner cross-racial treatment experiences. *Social Work, 39,* 116–123.

Dawson, S. (1994). Fieldwork among the Navajo: Implications for social work research and practice. *Journal of Multicultural Social Work, 3,* 101–111.

Ewalt, P. L. (1994). Visions of ourselves [Editorial]. *Social Work, 39,* 5–7.

Frisbie, C. J. (1987). *Navajo medicine bundles or jish: Acquisition, transmission, and disposition in the past and present.* Albuquerque: University of New Mexico Press.

Giger, J. N., & Davidhizar, R. E. (1991). *Transcultural nursing: Assessment of intervention.* St. Louis: C. V. Mosby.

Gilpin, L. (1968). *The enduring Navajo.* Austin: University of Texas Press.

Goodman, J. M. (1982). *The Navajo atlas.* Norman: University of Oklahoma Press.

Hanley, C. E. (1991). Navajo Indians. In J. N. Giger & R. E. Davidhizar (Eds.), *Transcultural nursing assessment and interventions* (pp. 215–238). St. Louis: C. V. Mosby.

Kluckhohn, C., & Leighton, D. (1974). *The Navajo* (rev. ed.). Cambridge, MA: Harvard University Press.

Lamphere, L. (1989). *To run after them: Cultural and social bases of cooperation in a Navajo community.* Tucson: University of Arizona Press.

Leininger, M. M. (1978). *Transcultural nursing: Concept, theories and practices.* New York: John Wiley & Sons.

Leininger, M. M. (1990). Historic and epistemologic dimensions of care and caring with future directions. In J. Stevenson (Ed.), *American academy of nursing* (pp. 19–31). Kansas City, MO: American Nurses Association Press.

Leininger, M. M. (1992). *Cultural care diversity and universality: A theory of nursing* (Publication No. 15-2401). New York: National League for Nursing Press.

Locke, R. F. (1989). *The book of the Navajo* (4th ed.). Los Angeles: Mankind.

Manson, S. M., & Callaway, D. G. (1988). Health and aging among American Indians: Issues and challenges for the biobehavioral sciences. In S. M. Manson & N. G. Dinges (Eds.), *Behavioral health issues among American Indians and Alaska Natives: Explorations on the frontiers of biobehavioral sciences* (pp. 160–210). Denver: University of Colorado, Health Sciences Center.

Mercer, S. O., Garner, J. D., & Leon, J. (1991). *Geriatric case practice in nursing homes.* Newbury Park, CA: Sage Publications.

Mick, C. (1983). *A profile of American Indian nursing homes.* Tucson: University of Arizona, Long-Term Care Gerontology Center.

Navajo Area Indian Health Service. (1992). *Area profile.* Window Rock, AZ: Author, Office Program Planning and Development.

Reddy, M. A. (1993). *Statistical record of native North Americans.* Detroit: Gale Research.

Reichard, G. A. (1977). *Navajo religion: A study of symbolism.* Princeton, NJ: Princeton University Press.

Seymour, T.V.N. (1988). *When the rainbow touches down.* Seattle: University of Washington Press.

Suppee, C., Anderson, D., & Anderson, B. (1990). *Canyon de Chelly: The story behind the scenery.* Las Vegas: KC Publications.

Trimble, S. (1993). *The people.* Santa Fe, NM: School of American Research.

Wainapel, S. F. (1989). *Institutional long-term care of American Indian elderly: Results of a survey of nursing homes on the Navajo and Laguna reservations.* Unpublished manuscript.

Wyman, L. C. (1970). *Blessingway.* Tucson: University of Arizona Press.

Wyman, L. C., & Kluckhohn, C. (1938). *Navajo classification of their song ceremonials* (American Anthropological Association Memoirs No. 50). New York: American Anthropological Association.

The author extends her appreciation to the Navajo Grandparents and her Navajo colleagues and friends LuCinda Morris, LaVerne Thomas-Wyaco, Anita Etsitty-Draper, Rita Wagner, Harriet John, Eddie Laneman, Laura Thompson, Donna Platero, Frank Begay, Franklin Goldtooth, Paul Jumbo, Mary James, Tom James, Gladys Ambrose, and Ruthe Hunter, without whom this research would not have been possible. May they walk in hózhó *all of their days.*

30 Puerto Rican Sons as Primary Caregivers of Elderly Parents

Melvin Delgado and Sharon Tennstedt

Elders' long-term care needs are the subject of considerable attention in the United States, with controlling government spending on this population at the forefront of the debate. Numerous studies attest to the importance of family in providing care for elders and to the need for formal organizations to support them in the caregiving role (Bass & Noelker, 1987; Horowitz, 1985; Horowitz & Shindelman, 1983; Weeks & Cuellar, 1981). Therefore, health care providers should never lose sight of the family in the caregiving process: "However comprehensive the network of services for the elderly, the family as the second target population will continue to have unique needs. Programs that provide individual and group counseling, skills training, and in-home and institutional respite will remain important" (Horowitz, 1985, p. 233).

Reliance on family as primary caregivers can prove troubling for elders (Winbush, 1993):

> Families today are faced with numerous new challenges not evident in the past, which raise questions about the families' ability to overcome—and to overcome without assistance. For example, family caregiving today is taking place in a societal setting characterized by changes in family composition, technology and social advances, life-threatening health problems, and a devalued attitude towards family. (p. 131)

These societal changes require that social workers develop innovative ways to reach out to and support "new" caregivers.

LITERATURE REVIEW

The role of women, particularly daughters, as primary caregivers is well documented (Baum & Page, 1991; Chappell, 1989; Cicirelli, 1993; Noelker & Bass, 1994; Pratt, Jones, Shin, & Walker, 1989; Tennstedt & McKinlay, 1989). Historically, women have been the primary and often only caregivers. As a result, most social services organizations have developed services, expertise, and comfort with female caregivers as the beneficiaries. The fields of social work and gerontology have not paid sufficient attention to the role of sons as primary caregivers. When addressed in the professional literature, sons

This chapter was originally published in the March 1997 issue of *Social Work*, Vol. 42, pp. 125–134.

have received minimal attention; often only their numerical presence in a caregiving system is mentioned.

Nevertheless, a few publications have examined sons' presence, roles, and unique issues in fulfilling caregiving roles (Coward & Dwyer, 1990; Dwyer & Coward, 1991; Dwyer & Seccombe, 1991; Stoller, 1990):

> There is evidence that growing numbers of men are becoming elder caregivers, yet little is known about their unique needs, experiences, and contributions. As men are called on to assist, augment, or replace the caregiving efforts of women, it is crucial to understand the particular stresses and gratifications this task holds for them and to study their specific coping strategies. (Kaye & Applegate, 1990, p. 289)

The needs of elders of color and their caregivers are expected to grow in importance and priority as this group increases in population and continues to age at a rapid pace (Hayes-Bautista, 1992; Treas, 1995). During the past decade social services organizations have been paying close attention to Latino elders in the United States (Bastida & Leuders, 1994; Lockery, 1992; Sotomayor & Curiel, 1988). The professional literature on Latino elders has portrayed a group that is becoming more diverse and that has tremendous social services needs because of the effects of poverty and racism and high levels of functional disabilities (Castex, 1994; Espino, 1993). A reconceptualization is needed of who can provide informal care to this population: "The research findings highlight that both structural and dynamic forces are important in understanding the variation in family caregiving to the frail elderly. The strongest influence on behaviors and experiences of families is the caregiving context itself" (Horowitz, 1985, p. 225). Culture represents an important component of context, influencing caregiving expectations and behavior.

Although Latino elders have a high need for social services, they have not gained access to these resources, relying instead almost exclusively on the assistance of informal caregivers (Applewhite, 1995; Bartlett & Font, 1994; Delgado, 1995, 1996b; Delgado & Tennstedt, 1996; Mendoza, 1981; Sotomayor & Curiel, 1988). Unfortunately, there is still a dearth of research on Puerto Rican and other Latino informal caregivers (Bartlett & Font, 1994; Becerra & Shaw, 1984; Cox & Monk, 1993; Delgado & Tennstedt, 1996; Sotomayor & Randolph, 1988). The literature has highlighted the importance of family, primarily daughters and women, as caregivers (Delgado & Tennstedt, 1996). The role of Puerto Rican sons as caregivers has received little attention. For example, studies of Puerto Rican caregivers in the United States (Bastida, 1988; Sanchez-Ayendez, 1992; Sotomayor & Randolph, 1988) and Puerto Rico (Cruz-Lopez & Pearson, 1985; Sanchez, 1990) have consistently reported the role of daughters as caregivers for disabled parents. Some studies (Bastida, 1988; Sotomayor & Randolph, 1988) have reported the predominant source for various types of care; sons were described as not being the primary providers of most types of care and, when they were mentioned, provided gender-oriented types of help such as home or car repairs (Sotomayor & Randolph, 1988).

Latino sons, similar to sons of other racial and ethnic groups, rarely have been identified as primary providers and usually have been relegated to secondary caregiving status (Dwyer & Coward, 1991; Lee, Dwyer, & Coward, 1993). Yet for reasons cited earlier, as well as increasing evidence of changing demands on Puerto Rican women that might limit their availability to provide care (Ortiz, 1995), more attention should be given to the involvement of sons as caregivers for their parents.

METHOD

Research Questions

We asked the following research questions:

- What is the profile of a disabled elder who has a son as a primary caregiver? How is this profile similar to or different from an elder who has a daughter as a caregiver?
- What is the profile of a caregiving son? How is this profile similar to or different from that of a daughter?
- Under what circumstances have sons assumed primary caregiving roles?
- What types of care do sons provide? Do they assume responsibility for a wide range of elder care needs, or do they provide gender-specific assistance?

The answers to these questions have important implications for how social workers engage and assist Puerto Rican and other Latino elders and their caregivers.

Sample

The sample of Puerto Rican elders was drawn from the Springfield Elder Project, a comparative observational study of African American, Puerto Rican, and non-Latino white elders ages 60 and older. The primary objective of the study was to investigate the needs for assistance with activities of daily living and the sources and patterns of assistance within and between the three groups. The study was conducted in Springfield, Massachusetts, about 100 miles west of Boston, because of the availability of sufficient numbers of older people in the three ethnic groups. In addition, the Latino population was predominantly Puerto Rican, which allowed for focus on one Latino subgroup to avoid differences that could result from variability in Latino culture.

Because of the limited number of older Puerto Ricans in Springfield, we attempted a complete enumeration of the population using the local annual census. Because race and ethnicity are not included on the list, Latino surnames were identified by the staff of a local Latino service and advocacy agency. People identified as potentially

Puerto Rican were screened for ethnicity (for example, self-reported as Puerto Rican) at first contact, and 772 Puerto Rican elders were identified. Of this number, 617 were located and determined eligible for the study. There were 368 respondents who were disabled. Of these, 206 reported having a caregiver. Interviews were completed with 192 caregivers. We report data for 106 caregivers (17 sons and 89 daughters).

Data Collection

Interviews with the Puerto Rican elders were conducted most often by telephone in English or Spanish. English–Spanish equivalents of the survey instruments were developed using back translation techniques (Becerra & Shaw, 1984; Lindholm, Marin, & Lopez, 1980). In-home interviews were conducted when necessary (31 percent of the Puerto Rican cases), typically for those with a nonpublished telephone number or without a telephone. Proxy interviews were conducted when the elder was functionally or cognitively impaired. Both in-home and proxy interviews were conducted more frequently with Puerto Rican respondents than with respondents in the other two ethnic groups.

A two-stage field design was used. In the first stage, data were collected from the respondents, who were first screened for functional disability. For elders who were not disabled, a brief interview collected sociodemographic data and information about their natural support system. Elders identified as functionally disabled received a more extensive interview to collect data about their informal caregiving network, the help provided by these caregivers, and their use of formal long-term services. For a respondent receiving informal care, the name, address, and telephone number of the person providing the most help (the primary caregiver) were sought.

In the second stage, telephone interviews were conducted with the primary caregiver to collect data about the type and amount of help provided. Sociodemographic data about the primary caregiver and other caregivers, cultural factors, motivation for providing care, and the impact of the care on their lives were collected also.

A variety of qualitative methods were used to develop a context for examining quantitatively derived data. An elder advisory committee provided guidance and helped interpret the findings (Delgado, 1996a). In addition, key informants, focus groups, and a community forum aided all aspects of the study (Delgado, in press).

Data Analysis

To describe the population of Puerto Rican caregiving sons and daughters and their caregiving situations, univariate (frequency distributions, means) and bivariate (chi-square, t-tests, Wilcoxon rank-sum tests) statistics were used. Further multivariate analyses were precluded because of the small sample size.

Variables considered in the analysis included caregiver and care recipient sociodemographic characteristics and several aspects of the caregiver situation: duration of care, number of caregivers, reasons for becoming and continuing to be a caregiver, and the negative effects of providing care. The hours per week of care were collected for several types of informal care and community services. Services purchased privately in addition to those provided by public and private agencies were considered formal services to capture more completely the use of formal care. Hours per week for each type of informal care and formal services were summed to obtain total hours per week for both.

FINDINGS

Care Recipients

The majority of the Puerto Rican elders were mothers ages 70 to 73 (Table 30-1). Although almost two-thirds lived with others, a substantial number lived alone. Few elders were married and living with a spouse. However, the elders cared for by sons were more likely than those cared for by daughters to be married but not living with a spouse (11.8 percent versus 5.6 percent, respectively) or to be divorced (29.4 percent versus 5.6 percent, respectively). Although the elders had an average of eight children, few were reported to be less

Table 30-1

Characteristics of Care Recipients

Characteristic	Caregiving by Sons (n = 17)	Caregiving by Daughters (n = 89)
Gender (% female)	88.2	77.5
Age (mean years)	69.9	73.3
Lives alone (%)	41.2	41.6
Marital status (% married, living with spouse)	5.9	5.6
Number of children	7.8	8.3
Children less than one hour away		
Number of sons	2.0	1.4
Number of daughters	1.2	2.1
Extent of disability (mean)		
Total (range 0–13)	6.8	7.1
Help with ADLs (range 0–5)	1.9	2.0
Help with IADLs (range 0–6)	3.2	3.7
Mobility (range 0–2)	1.6	1.5
Perceived health status		
Excellent/very good	0	3.4
Good	11.8	10.1
Fair/poor	88.2	86.5

NOTES: ADLs = activities of daily living; IADLs = instrumental activities of daily living.

than one hour away. Further, elders cared for by sons reported more sons nearby, whereas the opposite pattern was reported by elders cared for by daughters, suggesting that proximity and availability influence selection of a primary caregiver. Finally, the elders reported extensive disabilities and poor health. Sons and daughters cared for similarly disabled elders.

Caregivers

The Puerto Rican sons were somewhat younger than the daughters and much less likely to be married (Table 30-2). Probably related to their marital status, the sons were more likely to live with the care recipient or alone. Although the sons were more likely to be employed than the daughters, more than half of the sons were not working. Both sons and daughters were not likely to be acculturated; the majority of both groups were born in Puerto Rico, and although most had lived in the United States for more than 10 years, few reported English as their language of use.

Caregiving Situation

The sons were more likely to assume a caregiving role because other family members did not live close by (Table 30-3). The proportion of sons citing emotional attachment to the elder was similar to that for daughters. Sons, however, were more likely than daughters to cite filial responsibility as the primary motivation for providing the care and to state that there was no limit to what they would do for their parent. Formal service use by elders cared for by sons was less frequent and lower than the use by elders cared for by daughters.

Table 30-2
Characteristics of Primary Caregivers

Characteristic	Sons (n = 17)	Daughters (n = 89)
Average age (years)	38.6	42.1
Marital status (% married)*	17.6	33.6
Employed (%)	41.2	36.0
Coresidence with elder (%)	47.1	31.5
Lives alone (%)	29.4	3.4
Birthplace (% Puerto Rico)	76.5	88.8
Years in the United States (% < 10 years)	5.9	13.5
Language of use (% English)	5.9	10.1
Perceived health status		
Excellent/very good	29.4	38.2
Good	23.5	24.7
Fair/poor	47.1	37.1

*p < .05.

Table 30-3
Characteristics of the Caregiving Situation

Characteristic	Sons (*n* = 17)	Daughters (*n* = 89)
Duration of caregiving (mean years)	7.0	6.9
Average number of caregivers	1.8	1.7
Relationship of secondary caregivers: % siblings	100.0	62.5
Reason for becoming caregiver		
No one else was available	11.8	25.6
Proximity to elder	47.1	17.4
Emotional attachment	41.1	45.4
Other	0.0	11.6
Motivation for providing care		
Filial responsibility	70.6	59.6
Love	0.0	12.4
Both responsibility and love	23.5	13.5
Other	5.9	14.5
Any limit to providing care: No*	100.0	79.8
Elder uses formal services (%)	23.5	41.6
Formal service use (hours/month)[a]	8.9	24.6

[a]Geometric means reported because of skewness of hours.
*$p < .05$.

Both sons and daughters provided a wide range of assistance to their parents (Table 30-4). Daughters more frequently provided personal care, whereas sons more frequently provided financial management and transportation. However, sons provided more help with housekeeping and shopping, usually considered female activities. Overall the sons provided similar amounts of informal care as the daughters. However, that the elders cared for by sons used far

Table 30-4
Types and Hours of Care Provided

Care	Sons (*n* = 17)		Daughters (*n* = 89)	
	% Provides	Hours/Month	% Provides	Hours/Month
Personal care	11.8	0.2	32.6	4.9
Medications	35.3	0.6	46.1	2.3
Housekeeping	82.4	21.4	79.8	15.1
Meal preparation	52.9	13.8	64.0	16.4
Shopping	100.0	7.1	86.5	4.7
Financial management	82.4	1.2	51.7	0.8
Arranging services	29.4	1.1	41.6	1.1
Transportation	76.5	6.4	61.8	3.7
Total hours of care[a]	34.2		40.2	

[a]Geometric means are reported because of skewness of hours.

fewer formal services than those cared for by daughters suggests that caregiving demands are greater for sons than for daughters.

Impact of Providing Care

The vast majority of the caregivers reported no negative consequences of their caregiving role (Table 30-5). Further, the likelihood of experiencing specific negative effects was similar for sons and daughters. However, the sons were less likely than the daughters (52.9 percent versus 68.5 percent, respectively) to report having someone to turn to for assistance or emotional support, and the sons were more likely to be the sole caregiver and to have less assistance from other caregivers (Table 30-3). The data suggest that the sons might be at higher risk for experiencing caregiving stress.

DISCUSSION

Implications for Service Delivery

The findings of this study raise important implications for gerontological social work (Schlesinger, 1985). Although the sons were providing caregiving for almost the same amount of time as the daughters, the sons were younger and cared for a parent who was younger. As a result, the sons could expect to continue the caregiving role for a longer time. The sons were expected to carry out activities different from those of the daughters. However, in contrast to Bastida's (1988) study of Puerto Rican caregivers in Hartford, Connecticut (about 60 miles south of Springfield), that found strikingly different results between the caregiving activities of sons and daughters, the Springfield study found sons assisting with a wide range of activities. Although the sons provided about 30 percent fewer hours of caregiving than the daughters, they essentially fulfilled all the same caregiving responsibilities as the daughters.

Table 30-5

Negative Impacts of Caregiving

Negative Impacts	Sons (n = 17)	Daughters (n = 89)
Personal/leisure time	23.5	25.8
Personal privacy	11.8	15.7
Financial situation	11.8	12.5
Managing own household	17.6	20.2
Health	11.8	23.6
Sleep	23.5	24.7
Relationship with spouse	0.0	13.2
Relationship with children	7.7	7.5
Employment	18.8	23.1

The sons had limited outside responsibilities and sources of financial support. More than half were unemployed. The majority had never married, and the few who had were divorced or separated. These situations, combined with a tendency to be living alone or with a frail parent, raise important considerations for the sons' needs. When asked who else was involved in caring for their parent, all of the sons who indicated another caregiver identified their siblings. In contrast, the daughters mentioned a wide range of individuals including their spouses and children, suggesting a more extensive network. The sons, like the daughters, were not seeking formal services for their parents or themselves. Therefore, the sons seem to have minimal support in their role. This isolation may be fostered by cultural expectations of women as primary caregivers, further compounding any efforts by the sons to seek assistance from others.

The sons assumed the caregiver role out of a "sense of responsibility" and because there were no other potential caregivers or others lived far away. Filling this type of void may not be an unusual need now or in the future. About 42 percent of the elders in this study with at least one functional disability did not have a primary caregiver. As a result of structural demands on Puerto Rican families, daughters may not automatically assume culturally dictated roles as caregivers. Daughters may have their own families, employment outside of the home, and other demands that limit the time and energy needed to care for frail parents.

Consequently, Puerto Rican sons may become caregivers without adequate preparation and support. Sons without employment or their own families to assist with the care may have little choice but to become caregivers. The sons in this study were not likely to report any negative effects associated with caregiving and also noted that there were no limits to the amount of caregiving they could provide. This, in combination with a reluctance to place their parents in nursing homes, will have consequences for them as their parents continue to age and become more disabled.

Puerto Rican sons living with their frail parents benefit economically from the caregiving arrangement. The sons' lack of employment, limited command of English, and lack of familial responsibilities make the care of elder parents beneficial to both. As a result, the provision of care by sons can take on the elements of a social and economic exchange of services. This exchange, however, does not negate the needs sons have while helping their parents.

Implications for Practice

The absence of research on Latino men filling the roles of fathers, husbands, natural support providers, and elder caregivers has contributed to the lack of development of appropriate and acceptable social services and support programs. Knowledge of how Latino men fulfill support roles must be used in the planning and development of services. Services must consider approaches to helping that are compatible with men's problem-solving strategies and ways of relating to others (Powell, 1995). In addition, services must consider a series of cultural and structural factors.

Service programs would benefit by employing men with caregiving experience to serve as role models. The paucity of men in social work and gerontology necessitates hiring and retention strategies to recruit and retain them. Programming and outreach must consider caregiver feelings of awkwardness associated with assuming a cultural role normally fulfilled by women. Male social workers can acknowledge that this role historically has been fulfilled by women and identify the special challenges inherent for sons as caregivers.

Changes in society may result in more and more sons assuming primary caregiving responsibilities, and every effort must be made to provide them with instrumental and expressive support. For this to be accomplished, sons must expand their social networks to involve other caregivers. Consequently, sons can be helped to identify potential caregivers, including relatives, close family friends, neighbors, religious institutions, and other natural supports (Delgado, 1995). Social workers can broker these supports. As a result, social workers must have an in-depth knowledge of the resources of the Latino community.

Social services providers can also help sons accept formal and informal services for themselves and not feel inadequate as caregivers by doing so (Chappell & Blandford, 1991). However, sons must first feel comfortable with seeking individual or group assistance and be assured that seeking help does not reflect negatively on their capabilities for providing care (Toseland, Rossiter, Peak, & Smith, 1990; Whitlatch, Zarit, & von-Eye, 1991). Sons can be encouraged to join support groups of other male caregivers as a means of obtaining expressive and instrumental assistance in carrying out their responsibilities (Simoni & Perez, 1995). Support groups, although difficult to establish for men of any racial and ethnic background (Gregory, Peters, & Cameron, 1990), may prove more challenging for Puerto Rican and other Latino groups because of language and cultural factors (Monahan, Greene, & Coleman, 1992). However, these groups, if successful, can offer the greatest potential benefit for male caregivers.

Sons can obtain training in various caregiving responsibilities to better prepare them for their role (Calvano, 1991). Training will have an impact within and outside the family. These caregivers may be in a position to help other caregivers, men and women, who live in the community (Sanchez, 1987). Finally, social workers can help Puerto Rican elders who have daughters as primary caregivers explore the potential role that sons can play in caregiving (Gelfand, 1994). As shown by the data in this study, sons can and are willing to be involved in a variety of caregiving activities.

CONCLUSION

The recommendations in this chapter increase the likelihood that sons will be open to receive and benefit from informal and formal services. Cox and Monk (1993) summed up the influence of Latino culture on help-seeking and the role of social workers:

> Throughout this process, there needs to be a constant reaffirmation of both strengths and limitations of caregivers and the appropriate use of formal assistance. This affirmation should include a discussion of . . . acceptable care alternative(s). However, in these discussions, social workers must be sensitive to Hispanic values and the sense of guilt that may be experienced when the values are perceived as being violated. (p. 99)

Puerto Rican sons can fulfill unique roles within the Puerto Rican community, and their circumstances must be considered in the planning and implementation of support services. These caregivers may represent a greater segment of informal Latino caregiving in the future, and social work is in the unique position to ensure that quality services are available for both elder and caregiver to prevent the institutionalization of elders. As for other ethnic and racial groups (Horowitz, 1985), support from family members is critical to maintaining the independence of a parent and preventing or postponing nursing care placement (Espino, 1993).

REFERENCES

Applewhite, S. L. (1995). Demystifying the health beliefs and practices of elderly Mexican Americans. *Health & Social Work, 20,* 247–253.

Bartlett, M. C., & Font, M. E. (1994). Hispanic men and long-term care: The wives' perspective. *Journal of Multicultural Social Work, 3,* 77–88.

Bass, D. M., & Noelker, L. S. (1987). The influence of family caregivers on elders' use of in-home services: An expanded conceptual framework. *Journal of Health and Social Behavior, 28,* 184–196.

Bastida, E. (1988). Reexamining traditional assumptions about extended familism: Older Puerto Ricans in a comparative perspective. In M. Sotomayor & H. Curiel (Eds.), *Hispanic elderly: A cultural perspective* (pp. 163–183). Edinburg, TX: Pan American University Press.

Bastida, E., & Leuders, L. (1994). Hispanic elderly health: An overview of the literature. In C. M. Barresi (Ed.), *Health and minority elders: An analysis of applied literature, 1980–1990* (pp. 77–97). Washington, DC: American Association of Retired Persons.

Baum, M., & Page, M. (1991). Caregiving and multigenerational families. *Gerontologist, 31,* 762–769.

Becerra, R. M., & Shaw, D. (1984). *The Hispanic elderly: A research guide.* Lanham, MD: University Press of America.

Calvano, S. (1991). A project to teach basic nursing skills to caregivers of elders. *Gerontology and Geriatrics Education, 11,* 77–87.

Castex, G. M. (1994). Providing services to Hispanic/Latino populations. *Social Work, 39,* 288–296.

Chappell, N. L. (1989). Health and helping among the elderly—Gender differences. *Journal of Aging and Health, 1,* 102–120.

Chappell, N. L., & Blandford, A. (1991). Informal and formal care: Exploring the complementary. *Aging and Society, 11,* 299–317.

Cicirelli, V. G. (1993). Attachment and obligation as daughters' motives for caregiving behavior and subsequent effect on subjective burden. *Psychology and Aging, 8,* 144–155.

Coward, R. T., & Dwyer, J. W. (1990). The association of gender, sibling network composition, and patterns of parent care by adult children. *Research on Aging, 35,* 209–217.

Cox, C., & Monk, A. (1993). Hispanic culture and family care of Alzheimer's patients. *Health & Social Work, 18,* 92–100.

Cruz-Lopez, M., & Pearson, R. E. (1985). The support needs and resources of Puerto Rican elders. *Gerontologist, 25,* 483–487.

Delgado, M. (1995). Puerto Rican elders and natural support systems: Implications for human services. *Journal of Gerontological Social Work, 24,* 115–130.

Delgado, M. (1996a). Aging research and the Puerto Rican community: The use of an advisory committee of intended respondents. *Gerontologist, 36,* 406–408.

Delgado, M. (1996b). Puerto Rican elders and botanical shops: A community resource or liability? *Social Work in Health Care, 23,* 67–81.

Delgado, M. (in press). Interpretation of Puerto Rican elder research findings: A community forum of research respondents. *Journal of Applied Gerontology.*

Delgado, M., & Tennstedt, S. (1996). *Making the case for culturally appropriate community services: Puerto Rican elders and their caregivers.* Unpublished manuscript.

Dwyer, J. W., & Coward, R. T. (1991). A multivariate comparison of the involvement of adult sons versus daughters in the care of impaired parents. *Journals of Gerontology, 46,* S259–S269.

Dwyer, J. W., & Seccombe, K. (1991). Elder care as family labor—The influence of gender and family position. *Journal of Family Issues, 12,* 229–247.

Espino, D. V. (1993). Hispanic elderly and long-term care: Implications for ethnically sensitive services. In C. M. Barresi & D. E. Stull (Eds.), *Ethnic elderly and long-term care* (pp. 191–212). New York: Springer.

Gelfand, D. E. (1994). *Aging and ethnicity: Knowledge and services.* New York: Springer.

Gregory, D. M., Peters, N., & Cameron, C. F. (1990). Elderly male spouses as caregivers—Toward an understanding of their experience. *Journal of Gerontological Nursing, 16,* 20–34.

Hayes-Bautista, D. E. (1992). Young Latinos, older Anglos, and public policy: Lessons from California. In E. P. Stanford & F. Torres-Gil (Eds.), *Diversity: New approaches to ethnic minority aging* (pp. 73–80). Amityville, NY: Baywood.

Horowitz, A. (1985). Family caregiving to the frail elderly. In N. P. Lewron & G. Maddox (Eds.), *The annual review of gerontology and geriatrics* (pp. 194–246). New York: Springer.

Horowitz, A., & Shindelman, L. W. (1983). Reciprocity and affection: Past influences on current caregiving. *Journal of Gerontological Social Work, 5,* 5–20.

Kaye, L. W., & Applegate, J. S. (1990). Men as elder caregivers: Building a research agenda for the 1990s. *Journal of Aging Studies, 4,* 289–298.

Lee, G. R., Dwyer, J. W., & Coward, R. T. (1993). Gender differences in parent care: Demographic factors and same-gender preferences. *Journal of Gerontology, 48,* S9–S16.

Lindholm, K. J., Marin, G., & Lopez, R. E. (1980). *Fundamentals of proposal writing: A guide for minority researchers.* Rockville, MD: National Institute of Mental Health.

Lockery, S. A. (1992). Caregiving among racial and ethnic minority elders: Family and social supports. In E. P. Stanford & F. M. Torres-Gil (Eds.), *Diversity: New approaches to ethnic minority aging* (pp. 113–122). Amityville, NY: Baywood.

Mendoza, L. (1981). Los servidores: Caretakers among the Hispanic elderly. *Generations, 5,* 24–25.

Monahan, D. J., Greene, V. L., & Coleman, P. D. (1992). Caregiver support groups: Factors affecting use of services. *Social Work, 37,* 254–260.

Noelker, L. S., & Bass, D. M. (1994). Relationships between the frail elderly's informal and formal helpers. In E. Kahana, D. E. Biegel, & M. L. Wykle (Eds.), *Family caregiving across the lifespan* (pp. 356–381). Thousand Oaks, CA: Sage Publications.

Ortiz, E. (1995). The diversity of Latino families. In R. Zambrana (Ed.), *Understanding Latino families: Scholarship, policy, and practice* (pp. 18–39). Thousand Oaks, CA: Sage Publications.

Powell, D. R. (1995). Involving Latino fathers in parent education and support programs: Development of a program model. In R. E. Zambrana (Ed.), *Understanding Latino families: Scholarship, policy, and practice* (pp. 85–106). Thousand Oaks, CA: Sage Publications.

Pratt, C. C., Jones, L. L., Shin, H. Y., & Walker, A. J. (1989). Autonomy and decision making between single older women and their caregiving daughters. *Gerontologist, 29,* 792–797.

Sanchez, C. D. (1987). Self-help: Model for strengthening the informal support system of the Hispanic elderly. *Journal of Gerontological Social Work, 9,* 117–130.

Sanchez, C. D. (1990). Sistemas de apoyo informal de viudas mayores de 60 anos en Puerto Rico [Informal systems of support for widows 60 years or older in Puerto Rico]. *Revista Salud y Cultura, 12,* 101–115.

Sanchez-Ayendez, M. (1992, October). *Older and middle-aged Puerto Rican women: Cultural components of support networks.* Paper presented at the Annual Meeting of the American Anthropological Association, San Francisco.

Schlesinger, E. G. (1985). *Health care and social work practice: Concepts and strategies.* St. Louis: Times/Mirror/Mosby.

Simoni, J. M., & Perez, L. (1995). Latinos and mutual support groups: A case for considering culture. *American Journal of Orthopsychiatry, 65,* 440–445.

Sotomayor, M., & Curiel, H. (Eds.). (1988). *Hispanic elderly: A cultural signature.* Edinburg, TX: Pan American University Press.

Sotomayor, M., & Randolph, S. (1988). A preliminary review of caregiving issues among Hispanic elderly. In M. Sotomayor & H. Curiel (Eds.), *Hispanic elderly: A cultural signature* (pp. 137–160). Edinburg, TX: Pan American University Press.

Stoller, E. P. (1990). Males as helpers: The role of sons, relatives, and friends. *Gerontologist, 30,* 228–235.

Tennstedt, S., & McKinlay, J. (1989). Informal care for the frail older person. In M. Ory & K. Bond (Eds.), *Aging and health care* (pp. 145–166). New York: Routledge.

Toseland, R. W., Rossiter, C. M., Peak, T., & Smith, G. C. (1990). Comparative effectiveness of individual and group interventions to support family caregivers. *Social Work, 35,* 209–217.

Treas, J. (1995). Older Americans in the 1990s and beyond. *Population Bulletin, 50,* 2.

Weeks, J. R., & Cuellar, J. (1981). The role of family members in the helping networks of older people. *Gerontology, 21,* 388–394.

Whitlatch, C. J., Zarit, S. H., & von-Eye, A. (1991). Efficacy of interventions with caregivers: A reanalysis. *Gerontologist, 31,* 9–14.

Winbush, G. B. (1993). Family caregiving programs: A look at the premises on which they are based. In L. Burton (Ed.), *Families and aging* (pp. 129–133). Amityville, NY: Baywood.

This project was funded through National Institute on Aging grant no. AG11171.

Making the Case for Culturally Appropriate Community Services:
Puerto Rican Elders and Their Caregivers

Melvin Delgado and Sharon Tennstedt

The number of Latino elders is projected to increase significantly in the next two decades (Treas, 1995). Not only are Latino elders dispersed throughout the country, but there is increasing diversity within the group, with Latino elders coming from all Caribbean and Latin American countries (Castex, 1994). In contrast to elders in other ethnic minority groups and to non-Latino white elders, Latino elders have been reported to be in poorer health and to have higher rates of functional disability (Hing & Bloom, 1990; Wallace, Campbell, & Lew-Ting, 1994). These differences suggest that because of their disadvantaged status, Latino elders are likely to have a greater need for long-term care than other elderly people. Generally, there are two sources of long-term care—formal services provided by community agencies (such as home health aides, homemakers, and home-delivered meals) and nursing homes and informal (unpaid) care by family members and friends.

TRENDS THAT AFFECT CAREGIVING

Families are the primary source of long-term care for elderly people with functional disabilities, and women family members provide the vast majority of this care (Doty, 1986; Stone, Cafferata, & Sangl, 1987; Tennstedt, Sullivan, McKinlay, & D'Agostino, 1990). It is commonly assumed that Latinos have a strong commitment to family and thus are highly likely to provide care for their elderly family members who are disabled. The fact that Latinos report little use of formal community services (Burnette & Mui, 1995; Greene & Ondrich, 1990; Wallace, Levy, & Ferguson, 1995) seems to support the assumption that care is provided informally. However, there is evidence that the structure of Latino families and the social roles of Latino women (Delgado & Tennstedt, 1997; Ortiz, 1995) are changing and hence that women may not be as available as before to provide such care.

This chapter was originally published in the November 1997 issue of *Health & Social Work*, Vol. 22, pp. 246–255.

Puerto Ricans began migrating to the continental United States in large numbers in the late 1940s for economic reasons. Therefore, the current cohort of elders has been on the mainland for approximately 30 or more years, and their offspring, if not born on the mainland, have spent most of their lives here. Among the Puerto Ricans who migrated to the mainland, there is clear evidence of socioeconomic adaptation with associated changes in family structure and roles. These individuals left Puerto Rico for plentiful, low-skill manufacturing jobs in New York City. With the decline of these jobs, many then moved to Connecticut and Massachusetts to work as seasonal farm laborers, typically at low wages. The combination of Puerto Rican men earning lower wages (Reimers, 1984) and economic necessity (Ortiz, 1995) has resulted in more Puerto Rican women working to help support their families.

Other social trends that influence the availability of Puerto Rican families, particularly women, to care for their disabled elders also are evident. As Ortiz (1995) noted, "Puerto Rican women have experienced the most dramatic changes in marital and family status over the last 30 years. They are less likely to be married, more likely to head families on their own, and more likely to have children at younger ages and prior to marriage" (p. 35). In sum, as Puerto Rican families continue to adapt to the changing socioeconomic context of life in the continental United States, it cannot be assumed that they will be available and able to provide care for their elderly disabled members.

There is a wealth of empirical data on caregiving systems for non-Latino white people (Horowitz, 1985; Tennstedt & McKinlay, 1989) and a growing body of literature on such systems for African Americans (Chatters, Taylor, & Jackson, 1985, 1986; Keith, 1987; Miller et al., 1995; Miller, McFall, & Campbell, 1994; Taylor, 1985; Taylor & Chatters, 1991). However, relatively little is known about Latinos (Bartlett & Font, 1994; Becerra & Shaw, 1988; Sotomayor & Randolph, 1988). Most of what is known has come from studies with small or nonprobability samples. Furthermore, the information is generally consistent with what has been reported for non-Latino white populations; for example, the structure of caregiving networks is hierarchical, with one family member having the primary responsibility for care (Roberto, 1993). As with other ethnic populations, studies have reported that the majority of caregivers are women—particularly daughters (Bastida, 1988; Cruz-Lopez & Pearson, 1985; Sanchez, 1990; Sanchez-Ayendez, 1992; Sotomayor & Randolph, 1988). The gender division in caregiving activities reported in most studies to date was also reported for Latinos by Sotomayor and Randolph (1988) and by Bastida (1988). These studies were limited, however, in that they did not gather detailed data on the amounts of care provided or on the concurrent use of home and community services.

This chapter reports on a study of the caregiving arrangements for a population of disabled Puerto Rican elders in Springfield, Massachusetts, a large northeastern city. In addition to describing the characteristics of the recipients of care and the caregivers, it identifies the types and amounts of informal care that were provided, the factors associated with the amount of care that was provided, and the use of formal community services by these elders.

METHODS

Sample

The sample of Puerto Ricans used in the study was drawn from the Springfield Elder Project, a comparative observational study of the needs of African American, Puerto Rican, and white elderly people, ages 60 and over, for assistance with activities of daily living (ADLs) and the sources (both informal and formal) and patterns of this help within and among these groups. The study was located in Springfield for several reasons: the elderly population is socioeconomically diverse; the city has sufficient populations of older African Americans and Latinos; and Puerto Ricans make up almost all the Latino population in the city, because it is a major point of population dispersal for them. The latter reason permitted the authors to focus on one Latino subgroup to avoid obscuring any between-group differences that could result from variations among Latino cultures (Solis, Marks, Garcia, & Shelton, 1990).

Because of the limited number of elderly Puerto Ricans in Springfield, the authors attempted to enumerate the population using the annual local census list. Because race and ethnicity are not included in this list, the staff of a local Latino services and advocacy agency identified Latino surnames manually. People who were thought to be Puerto Rican were screened for ethnicity on the first contact with them; that is, they reported themselves to be Puerto Rican. The number of people identified as Puerto Rican and eligible for inclusion in the study was 772. Of this number, 591 (76.6 percent) were interviewed; 16 people (2.0 percent) refused to be interviewed, and 165 (21.4 percent) could not be contacted or had moved out of the study area before the authors attempted to contact them.

Data Collection

Interviews with the respondents were conducted primarily by telephone in either English or Spanish. English–Spanish equivalents of the survey instruments were developed using back-translation techniques (Becerra & Shaw, 1988; Lindholm & Lopez, 1980). In-home interviews were conducted when necessary (in 31 percent of the cases), typically for those without telephones or with nonpublished telephone numbers. The only differences between the respondents who were interviewed at home and those who were interviewed by telephone were that the former were more likely to live alone and were less disabled ($p < .001$). Proxy interviews were conducted for 51 (8.6 percent) of the elders who were too functionally or cognitively impaired to complete the interviews; in almost all these cases, the proxy interviewees were the primary caregivers for the respondents. Both in-home and proxy interviews were conducted more frequently ($p < .01$) with the Puerto Rican respondents than with the African American and non-Hispanic white respondents in the larger study.

A two-stage field design was used. In the first stage, data were collected from the elderly respondents, who were first screened for functional disability with measures used in the 1984 and 1986 National Longitudinal Study on Aging (Fulton, Katz, & Hendershot, 1989). For each of 13 ADLs—personal (eating, bathing, dressing, bed transfers, and toileting), instrumental (using the telephone, doing heavy housework, preparing meals, shopping, managing money, and doing light housework), or mobility (walking, going outside)—the respondents were asked, "Because of a health or physical problem, do you have difficulty performing _____?" The respondents who reported having some difficulty were also asked, "By yourself and without using special equipment, how much difficulty do you have performing _____: some, a lot, or are you unable to do it?" A respondent was considered disabled when he or she reported more than some difficulty with at least one of the 13 activities.

If the respondents were not disabled, 15-minute interviews were conducted in which sociodemographic data and information on their natural support systems were collected to investigate potential sources of informal care. Elders who were identified as functionally disabled ($n = 368$; 62.3 percent of the respondents) received more extensive interviews (30 minutes), in which data on their informal caregiving networks (the number, relationships, ages, genders, and proximity of the caregivers), the help these caregivers provided (the types and hours of care), and the respondents' use of formal long-term care services (the types and hours) were gathered. If a respondent was receiving informal care, the name, address, and telephone number of the person providing the most help (the primary caregiver) were obtained. Of the 214 disabled elders (56 percent) with caregivers, 206 provided the names of their caregivers. In the second stage, 50-minute telephone interviews were conducted with 194 primary informal caregivers (response rate 94.2 percent). These interviews yielded detailed data on the types and amount of help provided, as well as sociodemographic data about the primary caregivers and other (secondary) caregivers, cultural factors, the motivation for providing care, and the impact of this care on their lives.

Variables

To describe this population of Puerto Rican caregivers and their caregiving arrangements, univariate (frequency distributions and means) and bivariate (chi-square) statistics were used. Variables that were considered in the analyses included the following characteristics of elders: age, gender, disability (number of personal ADLs, instrumental ADLs, and mobility tasks with which an elder reported more than some difficulty), residence (with caregiver or not), and socioeconomic status. The last variable was measured by the Nam-Powers

Socioeconomic Index (Nam & Powers, 1983), which ranks primary occupation on a scale of 1 to 100 on the basis of the level of education and average income associated with that occupation, as derived from census data. The characteristics of caregivers included relationship to elder, gender, marital status, and employment status. In addition, the following characteristics of the caregiving situation were considered: number of caregivers, reasons for assuming and continuing in the caregiving role, and number of potential caregivers. Finally, the hours per week of care were collected from the caregivers for several types of informal care and community services (personal care, medications, housekeeping, shopping, meals, transportation, financial management, and arranging services). Services purchased privately in addition to those provided by public and private agencies were considered formal services to capture more completely the use of formal care. Hours per week for each type of informal care and formal service reported by the caregivers were summed to determine the total hours per week of informal and formal care, respectively.

To identify the correlates of the total hours of informal care provided, the authors used direct-entry multivariate regression modeling with total hours of informal care as the dependent variable. Because of skewness of the dependent variable, the log transform of total hours of care was used. The covariates in the regression model were those that were previously identified from preliminary univariate analyses, as well as from related work (Tennstedt, McKinlay, & Crawford, 1993; Tennstedt et al., 1990): the level of functional disability, elder's socioeconomic status, caregiver's gender, caregiver's–elder's relationship, and elder's residential status (with the caregiver or not). An interaction term was constructed to measure coresidence and the relationship of the caregiver to the recipient of care because of previously reported differences in the amount and type of care provided on the basis of residency status versus relationship status (Tennstedt et al., 1990). This interaction term was coded coresident offspring, noncoresident offspring, coresident other relative or nonrelative, and noncoresident other relative or nonrelative. It was assumed that all spouse caregivers were coresidents for this sample of community-dwelling elders.

RESULTS

Who Receives Care

The Puerto Rican elders who were receiving informal care were quite disabled (particularly in performing instrumental ADLs) and generally perceived their health as fair to poor (Table 31-1). Their living arrangements were consistent with their marital status. Despite their level of disability, only half lived with their caregivers, although those who were disabled lived in close proximity to them; 96 percent lived within 15 to 30 minutes of them, and 77 percent said that they saw them at least daily.

Table 31-1

Characteristics of Care Recipients (*N* = 214)

Characteristic	*n*	%	*M*	*SD*
Gender				
Female	134	62.6		
Male	80	37.4		
Age (range 60–105)			70.7	8.1
60–64	41	26.2		
65–74	107	50.0		
75 and over	66	23.8		
Marital status				
Unmarried	146	68.2		
Married	68	31.8		
Socioeconomic status				
(range 0–100)[a]			27.5	19.3
Total number of disabilities				
(range 0–13)			6.8	3.2
Number of personal				
disabilities (range 0–5)			1.9	1.6
Number of instrumental				
disabilities (range 0–6)			3.5	1.6
Number of mobility				
disabilities (range 0–2)			1.5	0.8
Health status				
Very good or good	18	8.4		
Fair	119	55.6		
Poor	77	36.0		
Coresident status				
Resides with caregiver	103	48.1		
Does not reside with caregiver	111	51.9		
Years in continental United States				
Fewer than 10	30	14.1		
10–30	99	46.5		
More than 30	85	39.4		
Primary occupation				
Manual labor	184	86.0		
Other	30	14.0		

[a]Measured by Nam-Powers (1983) Socioeconomic Index, which ranks primary occupation on a scale of 1 to 100 on the basis of level of education and average income associated with that occupation, as derived from census data.

Who Provides Care

The majority of elders (58 percent) who reported at least one functional disability had caregivers. As with other populations, women were the most frequent caregivers of the Puerto Rican respondents, and consistent with other groups, daughters and wives were most often identified as the primary caregivers (Table 31-2). However,

Table 31-2

Characteristics of Caregivers (*N* = 194)

Characteristic	*n*	%	*M*	*SD*
Gender				
Female	155	79.9		
Male	39	20.1		
Age (range 18–85)			47.6	14.1
Relationship to elder (*N* = 194)				
Spouse	51	26.3		
Daughter	89	45.9		
Son	17	8.8		
Other relative	28	14.4		
Nonrelative	9	4.6		
Marital status				
Not married	98	50.5		
Married	96	49.5		
Employment status				
Unemployed	145	74.7		
Employed	49	25.3		
Duration of caregiving (years)			7.1	7.6
Number of caregivers				
One	99	51.0		
Two	41	21.2		
Three or more	54	27.8		

unlike other populations of caregivers reported previously (see Horo-witz, 1985; Stone et al., 1987; Tennstedt & McKinlay, 1989), about half were not married and about three-quarters were not employed. With an average age of 47.6 years, they began providing care at a relatively early age; the average duration of caregiving was 7.1 years (although, on the basis of the standard deviation of 7.6, there was considerable variation in duration of caregiving).

Over half the caregivers were the only people providing help. Most caregivers said they provided help because of love or a sense of responsibility; however, 50 percent said that their initial reason for providing care was not love or a sense of responsibility, but simply that they were available to help. Nevertheless, 76.8 percent stated that there was no limit to the amount of help they would provide. Furthermore, of those who stated that there was a limit to the help they would provide, 64.4 percent cited their own health—not the elder's—as the reason. Most caregivers (60 percent) also said that if they were not available, care could be provided by other family members; few would resort to formal services (13.7 percent) or nursing home care (4.2 percent). However, 14.7 percent of the caregivers identified no alternative other than themselves to provide help to their elderly relatives.

Table 31-3

Receipt of Informal Care and Formal Services as Reported by Caregiver

Informal Care	*n*	%	Formal Service	*n*	%
Personal care	70	36.1	Home health aide	31	16.1
Medications	94	48.5	Homemaker	32	16.6
Housekeeping	155	79.9	Meals	13	6.7
Meals	126	64.9	Transportation	12	6.2
Shopping	168	86.6	Financial management	—	—
Transportation	103	53.1	Case management	16	8.5
Financial management	104	53.6	Adult day care	5	2.6
Arranging services	81	41.8			

Care Provided

The caregivers provided a wide range of help with personal and instrumental ADLs (Table 31-3). Consistent with the types of disabilities of the elders they were caring for, they provided help most frequently with the instrumental tasks of shopping, housekeeping, meal provision, transportation, and financial management and less frequently with personal care and medications. A substantial number of the caregivers also had helped the elders obtain social and health services.

With regard to how much care the caregivers provided, the results of the multivariate regression model indicated that the total hours of informal care were associated with the number of disabilities the elder had, the caregiver's gender and relationship to the elder, and the coresidence (Table 31-4); that is, older Puerto Ricans who were more disabled and had female caregivers received greater amounts of informal care. With the exception of noncoresiding offspring caregivers,

Table 31-4

Correlates of Total Hours of Care: Results of the Multiple Regression Model

Variable	Estimate	SE
Intercept	2.83	0.27
Number of disabilities	0.06**	0.02
Elder's socioeconomic status	0.006	0.004
Caregiver's gender (female)	0.57***	0.17
Caregiver's relationship × coresidence		
Coresiding offspring	0.27	0.20
Noncoresiding offspring	−0.44*	0.19
Coresiding other relative	−0.29	0.32
Noncoresiding other relative	0.28	0.25
Coresiding spouse	0.00	

*$p < .05$. **$p < .01$. ***$p < .001$.

the amount of informal care provided generally was not associated with the caregiver's relationship to the elder or whether the caregiver lived with the elder, factors that were associated with the amount of care in previous studies of non-Hispanic older people (Horowitz, 1985; Tennstedt & McKinlay, 1989; Tennstedt et al., 1990, 1993). In this sample, offspring caregivers who did not live with the recipients of care provided less care than did other groups of caregivers.

Use of Formal Services

These Puerto Rican elders and their caregivers used few community long-term care services (see Table 31-3). Of those who used such services, the ones mentioned most frequently were homemaker and home health aide services. The fact that these two services are widely available through a publicly funded home care program probably accounts for their more frequent use. However, given the elders' great need for help with these tasks, the low level of use of such services is especially noteworthy. None of the caregivers used services such as respite care that are designed specifically to help them. Furthermore, only 9.3 percent of the caregivers indicated that they knew of such services.

DISCUSSION

This study investigated the need among older Puerto Ricans for assistance with ADLs and the sources of such assistance to understand the challenges of delivering services to this population. Although this group of Puerto Rican elders had severe disabilities, the majority lived alone and received most of the care they needed from family members rather than from community agencies. A wide range of care was provided, often by only one person per elder. Elders who were more disabled and had female caregivers received the most care. These findings substantiate a number of key conclusions reached by other researchers, both in Puerto Rico and the United States. However, several findings raise questions about the virtual absence of nonfamily caregivers and have important implications for how social services should be developed to reach Puerto Rican elders and their caregivers.

Of the frameworks proposed for understanding attitudinal and behavioral changes in the family lives of Latinos, one of the most promising is social adaptation (Vega, 1990), a structural approach in which increased attention is paid to the social situations and contexts that affect Latino families. This framework considers the connection between the internal dynamics of family life and external conditions, such as changing labor markets and political systems, rather than the dominant culture and family structure, as the normative benchmark for changes in attitudes and behavior used by the previously dominant framework of assimilation (Gordon, 1964). According to Zinn (1995), this approach is particularly relevant, given the current historical context (the restructuring of the U.S. economy and the conservative political climate, including the backlash against immigrants).

The structural adaptation approach recognizes that family diversity is a legitimate adaptation to the socioeconomic context. Increased structural diversity among Latino families, such as more single-parent families, blended families, and cohabiting adults, can be expected to influence the current and future caregiving of elders. The study's findings that the majority of Puerto Rican elders had severe disabilities, lived alone, and had a limited number of current or potential caregivers indicate the importance of using a structural adaptation framework for analyzing these unexpected results.

There is no question that the family is still the principal source of caregiving for Puerto Rican elders, given that daughters were the most frequent caregivers in this study, a finding that is consistent with those of earlier studies (Bartlett & Font, 1994; Bastida, 1988; Sanchez, 1987, 1990; Sanchez-Ayendez, 1989, 1992). However, the level of involvement of sons (8.8 percent) in this study was the lowest of any previous study; for example, Bastida (1988) found that sons represented 20.6 percent of the caregivers in Hartford, Connecticut. Other natural support systems, such as religious groups, friends, and neighbors, were not as active and influential in the caregiving networks of the elders in this study, which is also consistent with the findings of other studies in the United States (Bartlett & Font, 1994) and in Puerto Rico (Cruz-Lopez & Pearson, 1985).

The high proportion of elders who lived alone and had a limited number of caregivers is contrary to what was reported in other studies. However, this high rate of living alone may be specific to these older Puerto Ricans living in Springfield, Massachusetts. The majority of these elders (86 percent) had been farmworkers or laborers who left Puerto Rico for the mainland for employment and often moved from place to place, depending on the availability of work. Therefore, their living arrangements may have been the result of an interplay of any one or a combination of factors.

First, a pattern of geographic moves from the island to the mainland and back (Angel & Angel, 1992) may have reduced the number of people available to provide support, particularly if it involved multiple moves and uprootings, in which potential caregivers were left behind. That is, every subsequent uprooting may have further eroded the elders' support systems. This erosion may have started in Puerto Rico as the elders migrated from rural to urban areas because of urbanization and industrialization and continued on the mainland as they moved from New York City to Hartford and Springfield.

Second, potential caregivers may have either "acculturated or adopted" a new value system that minimizes familial responsibilities, particularly to parents. Third, potential caregivers, especially men, themselves may be struggling economically and socially and hence may not have the resources, energy, time, or willingness to accept the responsibilities that go with being caregivers. Furthermore, this factor is supported by the finding that noncoresiding offspring caregivers (those with competing responsibilities) provided less care than did other caregivers.

The Puerto Rican elders in this study were severely disabled and, as was found in other studies (Burnette & Mui, 1995; Starrett, Decker, Araujo, & Walters, 1989; Wallace et al., 1995), were not receiving an extensive array of formal services. The provision of informal care has been found to mediate the use of formal services (Greene & Ondrich, 1990; Wallace et al., 1995). Indeed, the caregivers provided a wide variety of help to these elders and for a considerable length of time. Notably, they reported frequent involvement in "arranging services" that the elders rarely used. It is possible that this informal assistance, necessitated by language barriers (94 percent of the elders spoke only Spanish), extended to acute care and other services not covered by this study.

It is also noteworthy that although the caregivers arranged for services for the elders, they did not use services (like respite care) designed for themselves. The caretakers may not have used such services because they were uncomfortable admitting that they needed help, were not aware that such services exist, were concerned that they would have to pay for these services, or were worried that relatives and friends might question their ability or willingness to care for the elders if they used services. The latter is an important point. Cox and Monk (1993) found that Hispanics believe that the use of formal services means that the caregivers are not properly assuming responsibility for those for whom they are caring.

Because of this belief, involving caregivers in planning and delivering services will go a long way toward helping both frail elders and their caregivers. Sanchez (1987) recommended that efforts to reach Puerto Rican elders be broadened to reach caregivers as well: "The primary component of the natural support system of the elderly—relatives, friends, and neighbors—provides an array of services that are ongoing, generally non-technical in nature (such as providing emotional support), [and that involve] a long-term commitment. The challenge to providers of social services is to enhance and sustain this network" (p. 118). As a result, caregivers must be considered active and invaluable team members with providers of formal services. They must come to see that the use of formal services is a helpful adjunct to meeting, rather than shirking, their responsibilities. Because daughters are the most frequently identified caregivers, they are in a position to play an active role in the provision of formal services to elders. Consequently, agencies should target daughters as a means of facilitating access to Puerto Rican elders. However, it is important to consider that efforts to provide formal services may undermine the role of daughters in their families. Furthermore, daughters' ability to fulfill this "traditional" role will be much more difficult in the future as Puerto Rican women continue to enter the work force in greater numbers. Balancing the roles of breadwinner and caregiver will no doubt result in increased stress for both elders and their daughters because of role conflict.

Involving caregivers in planning services to complement and support their efforts also may relieve the sense of burden they may feel in providing for their elderly relatives. The caregivers in this study viewed the act of helping as their responsibility and part of their culture. The majority stated that there was no limit to what they would do for the elders and indicated that the concept of mutuality was present in the relationship with the recipients of care—that is, that the act of giving and receiving was either equal, or that they received more than they gave. This perception may mediate any negative consequences that caregivers may experience caring for elders.

Most Puerto Rican caregivers (and probably most caregivers of other ethnic or racial groups) do not have an abundance of financial resources at their disposal. Limited formal education and incomes below the poverty level, combined with a clear preference for the Spanish language, may make these caregivers a population in need of various social services themselves. However, the lack of bilingual and bicultural services makes seeking help just as difficult for them as for elders. In essence, caregivers' tremendous responsibilities could be shared with appropriate agencies if the agencies offered culturally sensitive and specific services.

Health and social services agencies can reach out to elderly Puerto Rican people with disabilities and their caregivers by actively involving Latino community-based agencies in the process, placing public service announcements in the Spanish media, appointing elders to advisory committees so they can participate in the design of services, and hiring staff who are Latino (Delgado, 1996). These measures will increase the likelihood that services will meet the special needs of this population. The social work profession is in an excellent position to help elderly Puerto Rican people and their primary caregivers, who require providers who both understand and value the participation of members of the community in planning and delivering services. Social workers can serve as a bridge between Puerto Rican and other Latino communities and the agencies that serve them, but they can do so only when they understand the unique circumstances and challenges that these groups face in this society.

REFERENCES

Angel, J., & Angel, R. J. (1992). Age at immigration, social connections, and well-being among elderly Hispanics. *Journal of Aging and Health, 4*, 480–499.

Bartlett, M. D., & Font, M. E. (1994). Hispanic men and long-term care: The wives' perspective. *Journal of Multicultural Social Work, 3*, 77–88.

Bastida, E. (1988). Re-examining traditional assumptions about extended familism: Older Puerto Ricans in a comparative perspective. In M. Sotomayor & H. Curiel (Eds.), *Hispanic elderly: A cultural signature* (pp. 153–183). Edinburg, TX: Pan American University Press.

Becerra, R. M., & Shaw, D. (1988). *The Hispanic elderly: A research reference guide.* Lanham, MD: University Press of America.

Burnette, D., & Mui, A. C. (1995). In-home and community-based service utilization by three groups of elderly Hispanics: A national perspective. *Social Work Research, 19*, 197–205.

Castex, G. M. (1994). Providing services to Hispanic/Latino populations. *Social Work, 39*, 288–296.

Chatters, L. M., Taylor, R. J., & Jackson, J. S. (1985). Size and composition of the informal helper networks of elderly blacks. *Journal of Gerontology, 40,* 605–614.

Chatters, L. M., Taylor, R. J., & Jackson, J. S. (1986). Aged blacks' choice for an informal helper network. *Journal of Gerontology, 41,* 94–100.

Cox, C., & Monk, A. (1993). Hispanic culture and family care of Alzheimer's patients. *Health & Social Work, 18,* 92–100.

Cruz-Lopez, M., & Pearson, R. E. (1985). The support needs and resources of Puerto Rican elders. *Gerontologist, 25,* 483–487.

Delgado, M. (1996). Puerto Rican elders and gerontological research: Avenues for empowerment and research. *Activities, Adaptation & Aging, 21,* 77–89.

Delgado, M., & Tennstedt, S. (1997). Puerto Rican sons as primary caregivers of elder parents. *Social Work, 42,* 125–134.

Doty, P. (1986). Family care of the elderly: The role of public policy. *Milbank Quarterly, 64,* 34–75.

Fulton, J., Katz, S., & Hendershot, G. (1989). *Physical function of the aged: United States, 1984* (Vital and Health Statistics, Series 10, No. 167). Washington, DC: National Center for Health Statistics.

Gordon, M. (1964). *Assimilation in American life.* New York: Oxford University Press.

Greene, V. L., & Ondrich, J. I. (1990). Risk factors for nursing home admissions and exits: A discrete-time hazard function approach. *Journal of Gerontology: Social Sciences, 45,* S250–S258.

Hing, E., & Bloom, B. (1990). *Long-term care for the functionally disabled* (Vital and Health Statistics, Series 13, No. 104). Hyattsville, MD: U.S. Public Health Service.

Horowitz, A. (1985). Family caregiving to the frail elderly. In N. P. Lewron & G. Maddox (Eds.), *The annual review of gerontology and geriatrics* (pp. 194–246). New York: Springer.

Keith, V. M. (1987). Long-term care and the black elderly. In W. Jones, Jr., & M. F. Rice (Eds.), *Health care issues in America: Politics, problems, and prospects* (pp. 173–209). Westport, CT: Greenwood Press.

Lindholm, M. G., & Lopez, R. (1980). *Fundamentals of proposal writing: A guide for minority researchers.* Rockville, MD: National Institute of Mental Health, Center for Minority Group Mental Health Programs.

Miller, B., Campbell, R. T., Davis, L., Furner, S., Giachello, A., Prohaska, T., Kaufman, J. E., Li, M., & Perez, C. (1995). Minority use of community long-term care services: A comparative analysis. *Journal of Gerontology: Social Sciences, 51,* S70–S81.

Miller, B., McFall, S., & Campbell, R. T. (1994). Changes in sources of community long-term care among African-American and white frail older persons. *Journal of Gerontology: Social Sciences, 49,* S14–S24.

Nam, C., & Powers, M. (1983). *The socioeconomic approach to status measurement.* Houston: Cap and Gown Press.

Ortiz, V. (1995). The diversity of Latino families. In R. E. Zambrana (Ed.), *Understanding Latino families: Scholarship, policy, and practice* (pp. 18–39). Newbury Park, CA: Sage Publications.

Reimers, C. (1984). The wage structure of Hispanic men: Implications for policy. *Social Science Quarterly, 65,* 401–416.

Roberto, K. A. (1993). *The elderly caregiver: Caring for adults with developmental disabilities.* Thousand Oaks, CA: Sage Publications.

Sanchez, C. D. (1987). Self-help: Model for strengthening the informal support system of the Hispanic elderly. *Journal of Gerontological Social Work, 9,* 117–131.

Sanchez, C. D. (1990). Sistemas de apoyo informal de viudas mayores de 60 años en Puerto Rico (Systems of informal support for widows 60 years or older in Puerto Rico). *Revista Salud y Cultura, 12,* 101–115.

Sanchez-Ayendez, M. (1989). Puerto Rican elderly women: The cultural dimension of social support networks. *Women & Health, 14,* 239–252.

Sanchez-Ayendez, M. (1992, October). *Older and middle-aged Puerto Rican women: Cultural components of support networks.* Paper presented at the annual meeting of the American Anthropological Association, San Francisco.

Solis, J. M., Marks, G., Garcia, M., & Shelton, D. (1990). Acculturation, access to care, and Hispanics' use of preventive health services. *American Journal of Public Health, 80*(Suppl.), 11–19.

Sotomayor, M., & Randolph, S. (1988). A preliminary review of caregiving issues among Hispanic elderly. In M. Sotomayor & H. Curiel (Eds.), *Hispanic elderly: A cultural signature* (pp. 137–160). Edinburg, TX: Pan American University Press.

Starrett, R. A., Decker, J. T., Araujo, A., & Walters, G. (1989). The Cuban elderly and their service use. *Journal of Applied Gerontology, 8,* 69–85.

Stone, R., Cafferata, G. L., & Sangl, J. (1987). Caregivers of the frail elderly: A national profile. *Gerontologist, 27,* 616–626.

Taylor, R. J. (1985). The extended family as a source of support to elderly blacks. *Gerontologist, 25,* 488–495.

Taylor, R. J., & Chatters, L. M. (1991). Extended family networks of older black adults. *Journal of Gerontology: Social Sciences, 46,* S210–S217.

Tennstedt, S. L., & McKinlay, J. B. (1989). Informal care for frail older persons. In M. Ory & K. Bond (Eds.), *Aging and health care* (pp. 145–166). London: Routledge.

Tennstedt, S. L., McKinlay, J. B., & Crawford, S. (1993). Kinship tie vs. coresidence: Predictors of patterns of care. *Journal of Gerontology: Social Sciences, 48,* S74–S83.

Tennstedt, S. L., Sullivan, L. M., McKinlay, J. B., & D'Agostino, R. B. (1990). How important is functional status as a predictor of service use by older people? *Journal of Aging and Health, 2,* 439–461.

Treas, J. (1995). Older Americans in the 1990s and beyond. *Population Bulletin, 50,* 2.

Vega, W. A. (1990). Hispanic families in the 1980s: A decade of research. *Journal of Marriage and the Family, 52,* 1015–1024.

Wallace, S. P., Campbell, K., & Lew-Ting, C. Y. (1994). Structural barriers to the use of formal in-home services by elderly Latinos. *Journal of Gerontology, 49,* S253–S263.

Wallace, S. P., Levy, L., & Ferguson, L. R. (1995). Access to paid in-home assistance among disabled elderly people: Do Latinos differ from non-Latino whites? *American Journal of Public Health, 85,* 970–975.

Zinn, M. B. (1995). Social science theorizing for Latino families in the age of diversity. In R. Zambrana (Ed.), *Understanding Latino families: Scholarship, policy, and practice* (pp. 177–189). Thousand Oaks, CA: Sage Publications.

The study on which this chapter is based was supported by grant no. AG11171 from the National Institute on Aging.

Part VII

MENTAL HEALTH AND SUBSTANCE ABUSE

32 Cultural Diversity and Mental Health: The Haudenosaunee of New York State

Kathleen A. Earle

ntil 1970 it was widely thought that American Indians had no mental health needs or resources (Attneave, 1984). Mental health care for native people was not officially addressed until the Mental Health Office of the Indian Health Service was established in 1965 (Nelson, McCoy, Stetter, & Vanderwagen, 1992). Meanwhile, despite the encroachment of European settlers on native lands and psyche, native people apparently managed to deal with problems of adjustment or serious mental disorder within their own society. Many of these traditional approaches, including the use of indigenous healers, or "medicine men" (Attneave, 1984; LaFromboise, 1988; Lejero, Antone, Francisco, & Manuel, 1988; Williams & Ellison, 1996) have recently been revived.

Among the Iroquois of New York State, traditional healing rituals such as the "False Face" ceremony are still used for mental health problems (Earle, 1996). This ceremony has been described by anthropologist Wallace (1959) as a ritualized purging of an individual's mental illness and by Fenton (1987) as a public or private ceremony to rid a community, household, or individual of disease.

Although the literature suggests that American Indians need a unique mental health approach based on different cultural norms, research supporting this hypothesis is rare (Blount, Thyer, & Frye, 1992; Manson, Tatum, & Dinges, 1982). The research presented in this chapter is a necessary precursor to comparative studies of different approaches with indigenous people. The hypothesis of this study was that American Indian and white, non-Hispanic mental health care recipients differ in demographic characteristics, services received, and attitudes toward mental health. If so, this may indicate the need for an alternative therapeutic approach for Native Americans.

APPROPRIATE THERAPEUTIC APPROACH

Various elements of an appropriate therapeutic approach have appeared in the literature. The need to assess degree of acculturation is a crucial part of the treatment of American Indians (Trimble, Manson, Dinges, & Medicine, 1984; Williams & Ellison, 1996). Growing

This chapter was originally published in the June 1998 issue of *Social Work Research*, Vol. 22, pp. 89–99.

up or being educated on or near a reservation, having social activities primarily with other American Indians, being involved in religious or tribal activities, having an extended family orientation, and knowing about native culture are indications of cultural identification with a native group (Sue & Sue, 1990).

Once an identification with a native culture is found, a nondirective, facilitative approach is advocated by Blount et al. (1992) and by Greene, Jensen, and Jones (1996). This approach was defined even more narrowly by Good Tracks (1973) as one of "noninterference." Good Tracks stated that overzealous social workers who want to "rescue" their clients are overstepping a boundary they may not even know exists.

According to Sue and Sue (1990), native cultures do not emphasize self-revelation, making face-to-face individual treatment difficult. As Laine (WICHE, 1993) noted in reference to her brother, diagnosed with schizophrenia: "Our people are taught to keep feelings to themselves or within the family, so typical day programs are not conducive to helping him be as well as he can be" (p. 18).

Many authors stress the need for a family or group approach for American Indians (Blount et al., 1992; Edwards & Edwards, 1984; Lefley, 1990). An American Indian whose personal experience has been primarily as part of a group may appear passive or hostile when seen for individual counseling because he or she does not know what is expected (Blount et al., 1992). Group treatment (Owan, 1982; Red Horse, 1980) or family treatment (Joe & Malach, 1992; Red Horse, 1980, 1982) are more in keeping with the existing tribal structure.

A therapist may consider the optional use of Native American healers, a preference for some (LaFromboise, 1988), when counseling a Native American person or family (Jilek, 1971; Joe & Malach, 1992). This must be done with caution, respecting the privacy of ceremonies that are frequently closed to outsiders (Joe & Malach, 1992).

Some authors address specific aspects of Indian culture that may affect a therapeutic encounter. These include differences in conceptions of time for many American Indians (Joe & Malach, 1992; McShane, 1987; Sue & Sue, 1990). Respecting this difference may require waiting for what the client or family perceives is a good time for a meeting rather than sticking to rigid schedules. Differences in body language, such as reluctance to make eye contact (Sue & Sue, 1990) or a preference for periods of silence (Joe & Malach, 1992) also need to be accepted. Readers are cautioned, however, against generalizing these traits to all American Indians. There are wide discrepancies between tribes and within tribes (Gross, 1995; Jarvenpa, 1985; Williams & Ellison, 1996).

BACKGROUND

There are between 1 million and 2 million American Indians living in the United States, making up less than 1 percent of the population (Joe & Malach, 1992; Nelson et al., 1992). The National Plan for American

Indian Mental Health Services (U.S. Department of Health and Human Services [HHS], 1989) reported that American Indians have much more serious and numerous mental health problems than the general population, although rates were not included.

Apart from small-scale studies of specific populations, data on actual prevalence of mental illness among American Indians is difficult to find. This may be partially the result of problems of diagnosis among Western therapists and of definition among American Indians.

Problems of Diagnosis

O'Nell (1989) reported that styles of presentation such as "flat affect," "hallucinations involving spirits," and "prolonged mourning" are more frequent among Native Americans than among the general population. However, symptoms such as these do not necessarily indicate psychopathology (Manson, Shore, & Bloom, 1985; Price-Williams, 1987). For example, episodes of prolonged, ardent, and emotionally fraught mourning, which are part of a ritual ceremony prescribed by the Iroquois Constitution (Parker, 1968; Wallace, 1959), can be misdiagnosed as signs of severe depression requiring psychiatric hospitalization (Perkins, 1927).

Problems of Definition

In addition, there are reports of emotional difficulties among American Indians that are not defined in the general culture (Johnson & Johnson, 1965; Lewis, 1975; Manson et al., 1985; Matchett, 1972; O'Nell, 1989; Trimble et al., 1984). These disorders include, for example, *pibloktoq* (arctic hysteria [Trimble et al., 1984, p. 209]), *iich'aa* (moth sickness, which is said to be caused by brother–sister incest [Trimble et al., 1984, p. 204]), *windigo* (delusion of transformation into a *witiko* who has a fear of ice [Trimble et al., 1984, p. 202]), *wacinko* (when people pout when they do not get what they want or when the situation is unbearable [Lewis, 1975, p. 754]), and *tawatl ye sni* (O'Nell, 1989). *Tawatl ye sni*, translated as "totally discouraged, was reported by Johnson and Johnson (1965) among the Dakota Sioux on the Standing Rock reservation. The authors identified a specific syndrome among members of the tribe that included "(1) conditions of present deprivation; (2) the traveling of one's thoughts to the dwelling place of dead relatives, the ghost camp; (3) an orientation to the past as the best time; (4) thoughts of death; (5) facilitating a move to the death camp by willing death, threatening or committing suicide, or drinking to excess; (6) being preoccupied with ideas of ghosts or spirits; and (7) expression that present actions are blocked, like in the statement 'There's nothing he can do. It's hopeless.' "(O'Nell, 1989, p. 59). Although these symptoms would appear to fit Western definitions of depression, O'Nell stated that "it is clear that the cultural meanings of these categories are sufficiently different from depressive disorder . . . to warn against drawing facile equations across these systems of thought" (p. 60).

Definition of an American Indian

The definition of who is an American Indian may also affect the accuracy of data regarding prevalence of mental illness. The U.S. Constitution describes American Indian tribes as sovereign nations who deal directly with the federal government. Specific Indian nations must apply to the U.S. government to be recognized as such. Individual tribal membership, or "enrollment" in an Indian tribe or nation, is based on percentage of American Indian blood and either patrilineal or matrilineal descent (Prucha, 1990). On the basis of earlier history, many American Indian people do not trust the U.S. government and are not federally enrolled (Schaaf, 1990). Also, many people who are biracial but who do not meet enrollment criteria may identify themselves as American Indian on standard surveys and official records and in census data.

The Haudenosaunee

The Iroquois Indians of New York State were chosen as a population for analysis. The Haudenosaunee, also called Iroquois, consist of six nations (Mohawk, Oneida, Onondaga, Cayuga, Seneca, and Tuscarora) allied into a confederacy. In September 1994 there were approximately 18,000 enrolled members of the Iroquois Confederacy. These included 6,469 Seneca, 1,050 Tonawanda Seneca, 462 Cayuga, 6,140 St. Regis Mohawk, 1,200 Tuscarora, 1,694 Onondaga, and 1,109 Oneida (personal communication with the Eastern Area Office of the U.S. Bureau of Indian Affairs [BIA], Buffalo, NY, November, 1994). About half of the Iroquois live on or near one of the seven reservations located in central, western, and northern New York State. Members of the Confederacy may be found anywhere in the United States and Canada.

METHOD

Using New York State data, two research questions were addressed: First, do American Indian recipients differ in demographic and service variables from white, non-Hispanic recipients of mental health services? And second, do American Indian recipients of services have different attitudes toward mental health than white recipients? A multisite descriptive design using two comparisons between two groups was undertaken.

Comparison of Demographic and Services Variables

The first part of the study compared American Indian and white, non-Hispanic people who received mental health services (outpatient, inpatient, or residential) from the New York State Office of Mental Health (OMH) between January and October 1994. Counties in upstate, central, and western New York, which contained or were adjacent to the seven Iroquois reservations were included in the study. Information was obtained from the OMH's Department of Mental Hygiene Information System (DMHIS).

The DMHIS is based on data from forms completed when a person is admitted to, released from, or transferred within an OMH-operated program. It includes information such as age, gender, ethnicity, education, religion, legal status, county of residence, marital status, diagnosis, household composition, type of residence, source of referral, veteran status, type of income, presence of a significant problem (for example, alcohol, substance abuse, mental health, mental retardation or developmental disability, physical disability), time since last service, program site, and type of service received.

Initial analyses compared all available data for the two groups using chi-square tests. After differences among white, non-Hispanic, and American Indian recipients were identified, logistic regression was used to predict native ethnicity based on these differences. Of 90 Native Americans receiving mental health services, one-half were treated by OMH clinics attached to prisons. These 45 recipients were dropped from the study because of the unavailability of data from the DMHIS in crucial areas. For example, the DMHIS lists under "county of residence" the county where the prison is located rather then the county where the person lived before he or she was in prison. Adult respondents were the focus of the study.

To control for gender, program, and age when performing the logistic regression analysis, the 45 American Indians were matched to 45 white, non-Hispanic recipients. Although there were over 6,000 white recipients of services on which to match, matches by specific program site, age, and gender yielded at most two possible matches, in which case the first one was chosen.

Comparison of Attitudes

The second part of the study compared attitudes toward mental health of American Indian and white recipients of mental health care. Copies of the Mental Health Values Questionnaire (MHVQ) (Tyler, Clark, Olson, Klapp, & Cheloha, 1983; Tyler & Suan, 1990) were left to be anonymously completed by a convenience sample of people at or near an outpatient site identified in the first part of the study as serving 14 (31 percent) of the 45 American Indians.

The MHVQ (Tyler et al., 1983; Tyler & Suan, 1990) was developed at the University of North Dakota to measure attitudes toward mental health. The authors first defined the domain of good mental health by asking groups of patients, professionals, mental health workers, and college students to generate a pool of traits indicative of good mental health. Factor analysis was used to construct a questionnaire using these traits, and the instrument was administered to groups of respondents with other standard scales to determine reliability and validity of the instrument (Tyler et al., 1983).

The MHVQ asks respondents to rate statements such as "The person is happy most of the time" as indicating good or poor mental health on a five-point scale, where 1 = very poor mental health, 2 = poor mental health, 3 = neutral, not related to mental health, 4 =

good mental health, and 5 = very good mental health. The reliability coefficients of the eight factor subscales (self-acceptance, negative traits, achievement, affective control, good interpersonal relations, untrustworthiness, religious, and unconventional reality) ranged from .76 to .88.

The authors later administered the MHVQ to 93 white and 66 American Indian undergraduates at the University of North Dakota and found that the "unconventional reality" subscale discriminated between the two groups. The most important finding of the study was that white students were significantly more likely to associate unconventional experiences (having visions, communicating with spirits of the dead, guiding one's life according to spirits, seeing things others do not see, and hearing things others do not hear) with poor mental health than were the American Indian students. The American Indian students reported a neutral relationship of such experiences to mental health (Tyler & Suan, 1990).

We distributed 180 copies of the MHVQ to clinic, continuing treatment, or residential clients from October 1995 through February 1996. Each form had a dollar bill attached and a stamped envelope addressed to the researcher. The majority of forms were handed out randomly to white clients and specifically to any Native American clients by receptionists or staff of the programs. During the last month of the study, some forms were distributed to American Indians by an American Indian who was a member of the consumer advisory board, at the suggestion of the primary site director. All forms were handed out with no instructions other than those written on the first page. Demographic data such as gender, age group, ethnic type of white (French, German, and so forth) or American Indian identity (specific tribe or nation), and federal enrollment (yes or no) for American Indian respondents were included. As shown in Table 32-1, the respondents in part 1 of the study and the respondents in part 2 were similar in gender and age breakdown, the only two variables that the two samples had in common.

RESULTS

Differences in Demographic and Services Variables

Initial analyses found that the 45 American Indian recipients of services differed significantly from the 6,064 white, non-Hispanic recipients on average age; the average was 40 for white clients and 33 for American Indians [$F(1, 6,108) = 9.447, p < .005$]. Nearly half (49 percent) of the American Indians specified a religion other than Catholic or Jewish, compared with 18 percent of white people [$\chi^2(3, N = 6,109) = 23.01, p < .001$]. American Indians had higher reported rates of an alcohol-related diagnosis: 27 percent of American Indians and 9 percent of white clients [$\chi^2(1, N = 6,109) = 13.49, p < .001$]. Over four-fifths (84 percent) of American Indians and 69 percent of whites were single or divorced or separated [$\chi^2(3, N = 6,109) = 8.27, p < .05$]. Forty-two percent of American Indians and 23 percent of white clients

Table 32-1

Comparison of American Indian Respondents from Part 1 and Part 2 of Study

Characteristic	Part 1: DMHIS (N = 38)		Part 2: MHVQ (N = 14)	
	n	%	n	%
Gender				
Male	18	47	6	43
Female	20	53	8	57
Age (years)				
18–20	1	3	2	14
21–30	7	18	1	7
31–40	14	37	4	29
41–50	8	21	4	29
51–60	6	16	2	14
61–70	0		1	7
71 or older	2	5	0	

NOTE: DMHIS = Department of Mental Hygiene Information System (New York). MHVQ = Mental Health Values Questionnaire (Tyler, Clark, Olson, Klapp, & Chelona, 1983; Tyler & Suan, 1990).

were seen for outpatient admission rather than for inpatient admission, screening, or termination [$\chi^2(6, N = 6{,}109) = 23.56, p < .001$].

The 45 cases were then matched with 45 white, non-Hispanic cases by age, gender, and specific program site. Dropping from the analysis six children under 18 and one case with too few data elements to match yielded 38 white and 38 American Indian adult respondents. To increase the power of the logistic regression analysis, all variables of interest were dichotomized into characteristic "yes" or characteristic "no/unknown." Lumping "unknown" with "no" is the most rigorous approach, as some of the unknowns may be a desirable "yes" for these variables.

After the groups were matched by age, gender, and program, the only variables that differed significantly using chi-square analysis were time since last visit and significant alcohol problem; American Indians were less likely to have been last seen over a year ago [$\chi^2(1, N = 76) = 3.71, p < .05$] and more likely to report a significant alcohol problem [$\chi^2(1, N = 76) = 3.71, p < .05$]. (The DMHIS allows people completing Form OMH 725 to check under significant problems any of the following that apply: mental illness, alcohol, mental retardation/developmental disability, substance abuse, significant physical impairment, or other specified problem.) Data on diagnosis for this study showed proportionately fewer American Indians (89.5 percent) had diagnoses of severe mental illness (defined as "significant mental illness" on OMH Form 725) compared with whites (97.4 percent), although these results were not statistically significant. Other variables that were not significant but yielded relatively high chi-square values were included in the logistic regression analysis: education less than high school and significant substance abuse problem.

Religion other than Christian or Jewish, living with relatives, and unemployment were included as well. Religion had a high chi-square value in the original comparison of white people and American Indians [$\chi^2(3, N = 6,109) = 23.01, p < .01$] and was felt to be related to the second half of the study in that "having visions" and so forth may be related to religion. Living with relatives, an indication of a possible extended family, was included because it is considered by many authors as central to American Indian lifestyle (Joe & Malach, 1992; Red Horse, 1980, 1982; Wilkinson, 1980). Lack of employment was included both because it has been found to be a fact of life for many American Indians (Blount et al., 1992; Nelson et al., 1992; HHS, 1989) and because it may be related to lack of success as defined by the dominant culture, also described as characteristic of American Indians (Dykeman, Nelson, & Appleton, 1995; Joe & Malach, 1992; Sue & Sue, 1990). A "yes" response to all of these dichotomized variables except for "last visit over one year ago" was expected for the American Indian clients. (Because the desired response for this variable was no, lumping "no" with "unknown" weakens the analysis.) Marital status and type of visit were not entered into the model because their chi-square values were low when the groups were matched.

Logistic regression analysis allows the researcher to determine the combined influence of several variables on an independent variable and to use these variables to predict membership in a dichotomized group. The group in this case was American Indian: yes–no. The following variables were chosen by the model as predictors of membership in the Indian/yes group: alcohol problem/yes; last seen over one year ago/no; education less than high school/yes; specific religion other than Christian or Jewish/yes. This model correctly predicted ethnicity 63.2 percent of the time.

Using Cohen's kappa yields a value of $r = .26$. This statistic and its level of significance [$\chi^2(71, N = 76) = 94.7, p = .03$] indicate the variables chosen by the model (time since last service, alcohol problem, education level, and religion) are responsible for 26 percent of the difference above chance between the two groups. This is a moderate-to-strong effect size. Although power is difficult to calculate in a logistic regression, by using regression as a proxy measure, it was found that this analysis had a power of 80 percent (Cohen, 1988).

Differences in Attitude

Of the 180 copies of the MHVQ distributed, 47 were returned. Seven were not completed correctly or were missing demographic information, leading to a return rate of 22 percent. Those that were complete were from 26 white and 14 American Indian respondents.

The low response rate to the survey may have been affected by two unexpected occurrences at the time of the study: (1) The primary outpatient program's parent office began a major reorganization in 1995–96 in which many outpatient programs were told they might be closed. (2) There was a major internal disruption at the Iroquois reservation adjacent to the study site right before the beginning of data collection. Several months after this study was completed the outpatient program director was laid off as part of OMH's downsizing of state-operated programs.

The disruption at the reservation was the result of differences between members of the traditional, clan-based culture and the elected leaders and led to a fatal shooting. There was a resulting lack of communication with people or agencies outside the reservation for a number of months while the tribal members attempted to restore unity and internal order. These unrelated factors may have affected both the numbers of people attending the state mental health programs and the willingness of people to complete the survey.

Because of both the low response rate and the implausibility of assumptions regarding normality, the Mann-Whitney U and Kruskal-Wallis statistical tests for ordinal data were used (Kenny, 1987). Initial comparisons (using t-test and chi-square analysis) between 26 white and 14 American Indian anonymous respondents to the survey were made on demographic variables (age, gender) to ensure the two groups were equivalent. The Mann-Whitney U test was then used to compare responses of the two groups on each of the 99 questions and the eight subscales designed by the authors of the questionnaire (Tyler et al., 1983).

Most white respondents checked membership in more than one ethnic group. The most commonly checked groups were German (46 percent), English (46 percent), and Irish (35 percent). American Indian respondents included 11 people (79 percent) who were federally enrolled members of the Seneca Nation and three people—a Cherokee, a Shoshone, and a white/Mohawk/Blackfoot/Cheyenne—who were not enrolled in their tribe/nation. The white/Indian person was treated as an American Indian in the analysis.

Attitudes toward what constitutes good or poor mental health differed significantly between white and American Indian respondents on seven specific items and on one of the subscales, "unconventional reality," as shown in Table 32-2. The first four items after the "unconventional reality" subscale are part of this scale, as defined by the original authors (Tyler et al., 1983). The American Indian respondents reported that having visions, seeing things others do not see, and guiding one's life according to spirits are not related to either poor or good mental health. White recipients reported these statements were indicative of poor mental health. These responses were similar to those of the students at the University of North Dakota for these items in the original study using the MHVQ.

In the original study the importance to mental health of "viewing things differently at different times" did not differ significantly between the two groups (Tyler & Suan, 1990). In this study, white recipients reported that viewing things differently at different times

Table 32-2

**Differences in Responses between White and American Indian
Respondents to the Unconventional Reality Subscale of the MHVQ,
1995–96**

Response on Subscale	Average Score		Z Score	Mann-Whitney Two-Tailed *p*
	White	Native American		
Unconventional reality	2.2	2.8	−2.4095	.02
The person has visions.	2.0	3.0	−2.5224	.01
The person sees things that others do not see.	1.8	2.9	−2.4741	.01
The person guides his/her life according to spirits.	2.2	3.0	−2.3813	.02
The person views things differently at different times.	3.0	3.7	−1.9675	.05
The person is bored most of the time.	2.0	2.8	−2.3234	.02
The person attempts to improve himself or herself.	4.5	4.1	−2.1340	.03
The person communicates directly and honestly with others.	4.5	4.1	−2.7055	.01

NOTES: MHVQ = Mental Health Values Questionnaire (Tyler, Clark, Olson, Klapp, & Chelona, 1983; Tyler & Suan, 1990). 1 = very poor mental health, 2 = poor mental health, 3 = neutral, not related to mental health, 4 = good mental health, 5 = very good mental health.

was not related to good or poor mental health, whereas the American Indian response was closer to "good mental health." The flexibility of response indicated by the assignment of "good" mental health to the ability to change one's mind may be a reflection of the importance of individual decision making among the Haudenosaunee. This was chronicled as early as 1884 in the *Annual Reports of the Trustees of the Peabody Museum* as follows:

> Ostensibly the supreme power of the tribe was vested in a council composed of chiefs and elders, though there is reason to believe that in all they did they acted as attorneys for the women rather than independently and of their own volition. As a rule their decisions were respected though this was not always the case; and in the event of opposition on the part of any individual, he was at liberty to follow the bent of his own inclination. (Carr, 1984, p. 30)

Responses to three items not included in the "unconventional reality" subscale were also found to differ significantly between the two groups. As with the first three statements, being bored showed "poor" mental health for white respondents but was closer to neutral for American Indians. Making attempts to improve oneself and communicating directly and honestly with others were rated as showing "good" mental health by American Indians but rated closer to "very good" mental health by whites. Tyler and Suan (1990) reported different results.

Differences among Native American Responses to the MHVQ

Federal enrollment in the Seneca Indian Nation was used as a proxy for lack of assimilation into the mainstream culture. The use of enrollment as a proxy for lack of acculturation is based on discussion in the literature indicating that ties of location and kinship to an American Indian reservation community connote adherence to American Indian cultural tradition. Eleven of the 14 Indian respondents were federally enrolled Seneca Indians living on or near the Seneca Cattaraugus Reservation. Analysis of variance was undertaken using the Kruskal-Wallis test to gauge the effects of Seneca enrollment (see Table 32-3 for results). The results of the Kruskal-Wallis test for the direction and relative size of mean rank indicate the effect of enrollment in the Seneca Nation on the variable of interest. These data show that the enrolled Seneca Indians were largely responsible for differences from whites on statements related to having visions and seeing things others do not. The nonenrolled Indians from other tribes were most responsible for the differences from whites on statements related to being bored, improving self, and communicating directly and honestly.

These results suggest the possibility that the three nonenrolled American Indians fit the "pan-Indian" profile. Among pan-Indians the lines dividing specific native cultures are blurred and traits attributed primarily to the Plains Indians become symbolic of a generic Indian identity (Jarvenpa, 1985; Nagel & Snipp, 1993). According to

Table 32-3

Differences in Responses among White (Group 1), Nonenrolled American Indian (Group 2), and Enrolled American Indian (Group 3) Recipients of Mental Health Services, 1995–96 (Kruskal-Wallis analysis of variance)

	Mean Rank				
Variable	Group 1	Group 2	Group 3	χ^2	p
Unconventional reality subscale	15.33	23.67	24.25	5.813	.05
Has visions	15.81	16.33	27.45	8.976	.01
Sees things others do not see	17.31	20.33	28.09	7.268	.03
Guides life according to spirits	17.06	26.00	25.85	5.671	NS
Views things differently at different times	17.94	17.33	27.41	5.778	NS
Is bored most of the time	17.17	32.27	23.55	7.059	.03
Makes attempt to improve himself or herself	23.02	9.83	17.45	5.877	.05
Communicates directly and honestly	23.75	9.00	15.95	8.384	.02

NOTE: NS = not significant.

Williams and Ellison (1996), pan-Indians are likely to avoid activities of the dominant culture and to adopt the traditions of various American Indian groups. In so doing, it is possible that many of the American Indian stereotypes as described by Mander (1991) and others (Joe & Malach, 1992; Sue & Sue, 1990) may be evident. These include a de-emphasis on time or schedules (being bored is not a problem), sharing rather than acquiring (personal success is less important), and primary allegiance to the American Indian group (communicating directly and honestly is less important with members of the dominant culture) (Mander, 1991).

Limitations of the Study

Each part of this study had its own limitations. Part 1 was affected by the limitations of the DMHIS database. These include lack of information that may have been important to the study as well as gaps in information that was available. Part 2 was limited because participation was voluntary. The convenience sample of people who completed the forms may have differed in terms of motivation, mental disability, education, and other traits from people who did not take part in the survey. The lack of consistency in distribution of the questionnaires may also have affected the results.

Sampling is an issue for both parts of the study. Because part 1 was used to identify a site for part 2 of the study, some of the participants for the two parts of the study may be the same, further limiting an already small sample size. The small sample size limits the generalizability of the findings to other Native American groups.

IMPLICATIONS FOR PRACTICE

To be effective with American Indian clients, a social worker must first decide which culture the client belongs to. Williams and Ellison (1996) noted the following factors as indications that a client is acculturated to Western norms: high level of formal education, generations of removal from a reservation, low family affiliation, lack of current contact with a reservation, and previous personal or family experience with Western health care.

The results of this study support earlier literature regarding the possible effects of traditional Native American religious beliefs on attitudes toward mental health (LaFromboise, 1988; Lejero et al., 1988; O'Nell, 1989; Tyler & Suan, 1990). For the Seneca Indian clients, such attributes as having visions and guiding one's life according to spirits may incorrectly appear to be symptoms of a serious mental disorder such as schizophrenia.

If identification with a Native American culture has been ascertained, the worker may want to use American Indian healers as an adjunct to treatment. Although some authors suggest joint treatment, many attempts at collaboration fail because of confusion about issues of billing, credibility, and expectations of both the therapist and client (LaFromboise, 1988). Among the Haudenosaunee, involvement of a clinician in a traditional rite such as those performed by the False Face Society would be prohibited. The referral to traditional ceremonies has been successfully used by at least one director of a mental health program that serves members of the Iroquois Confederacy (personal communication with Rob Higgens, director, St. Regis Mohawk Mental Health Services, St. Regis Reservation, Hogansburg, NY, May 1997).

This study found that American Indians were less likely to have been seen at an outpatient program over a year ago and more likely to have an alcohol problem when compared with white clients. These factors may be related because people appearing at a New York State–operated mental health clinic with a primary alcohol diagnosis would be referred to another program, and people with a chronic mental illness would be seen over a period of years. With an American Indian client who has a dual mental health/alcohol abuse diagnosis, the skilled therapist must be attuned not only to standard treatment for alcohol abuse but also to cultural aspects of intervention. The clinician should know, for example, that among many groups of Native Americans, including the Haudenosaunee, the adherence to a traditional religion requires abstention from alcohol (Choney, Berryhill-Paapke, & Robbins, 1995; Earle, 1996).

When setting goals with a Native American client, a therapist needs to be aware that the client's goals may not be those of members of the dominant culture. One implication of this study, found in the literature as well, is that American Indians may be less likely than members of the general population to have achieved educational success (Blount et al., 1992; LaFromboise, 1988; Marshall, Martin, Thomason, & Johnson, 1991; McShane, 1987) or to value individual success as defined by the dominant culture (Dykeman et al., 1995; Sue & Sue, 1990; Wilkinson, 1980). Rather than attending a conventional college, for example, a more relevant goal for a traditional American Indian client may be to learn his or her own native language or to attend a tribal college or American Indian Studies program (Wollock, 1997).

AVENUES FOR FURTHER STUDY

This study raised some intriguing and important questions. To expand information found about mental health services provided by New York State, this study used an additional database. Data from all (federal, state, local, private, and proprietary) mental health programs in the identified counties were compared to census data to obtain a comparative rate of service. Program data were from the Patient Characteristics Survey completed every two years by OMH and accessible to the author. The rates, which included data from four federal mental health clinics operated on Iroquois reservations by the Indian Health Service, were one service per 100 population for American Indians and 11 services per 100 population for white people during a two-week period.

Because Native Americans in these areas of New York State are receiving standard services at a much lower rate than white people, where, if at all, are American Indians getting mental health services? Are people receiving traditional American Indian mental health healing rituals in lieu of standard services? It is not known, for example, how many members of the Haudenosaunee use traditional healing for personal problems.

The clinic that was the primary site for part 2 of the study served about one-third of the Native Americans receiving services from OMH in part 1. It thus differs from other services in upstate, central, and western New York. The next highest number of American Indian clients seen at one site was five.

The study site was adjacent to an Iroquois reservation and the program director had grown up in a white family on the grounds of another Iroquois reservation. At the program director's initiative, clinic staff had received ongoing training from from experts in American Indian culture at a nearby university.

Another question raised is, Why were half the Native Americans who received OMH services in these areas of New York receiving them in prison? According to Bloom, Manson, and Neligh (1980), the difficulties of obtaining emergency psychiatric commitment of American Indians when needed for "danger to self or others" may lead to the inappropriate use of jails, a common response of a community to disruptive or aberrant behavior. The difficulty of commitment is the result primarily of the unique relationship of Native American tribes with the federal government rather than the state governments, leading to possible disagreements about jurisdiction in matters of psychiatric commitment for American Indians (Bloom et al., 1980; Lejero et al., 1988).

CONCLUSION

This study suggests that there may be important differences between white and American Indian clients in demographic and service variables and attitudes toward mental health that require a different therapeutic approach for American Indians. I hope that this analysis of the primarily Iroquois people of New York State will provide some direction for future study and some limited assistance to any social worker who treats American Indian clients. The need for additional research is indicated in this difficult but interesting area.

REFERENCES

Attneave, C. L. (1984). Themes striving for harmony: Conventional mental health services and American Indian traditions. In S. Sue & T. Moore (Eds.), *The pluralistic society: A community mental health perspective* (pp. 149–191). New York: Human Services Press.

Bloom, J. D., Manson, S. M., & Neligh, G. (1980). Civil commitment of American Indians. *Bulletin of the American Academy of Psychiatry and the Law, 8,* 1–10.

Blount, M., Thyer, B. A., & Frye, T. (1992). Social work practice with Native Americans. In D. F. Harrison, J. S. Wodarski, & B. A. Thyer (Eds.), *Cultural diversity and social work practice* (pp. 107–134). Springfield, IL: Charles C Thomas.

Carr, L. (1984). On the social and political position of women among the Huron–Iroquois tribes. In W. G. Spittal (Ed.), *Iroquois women: An anthology* (pp. 9–36). Ontario, Canada: Iroqrafts.

Choney, S. K., Berryhill-Paapke, E., & Robbins, R. R. (1995). The acculturation of American Indians: Developing frameworks for research and practice. In J. G. Ponterotto, J. M. Casas, L. A. Suzuki, & C. M. Alexander (Eds.), *Handbook of multicultural counseling* (pp. 73–92). Thousand Oaks, CA: Sage Publications.

Cohen, J. (1988). *Statistical power analysis in the behavioral sciences.* Hillsdale, NJ: Lawrence Erlbaum.

Dykeman, C., Nelson, J. R., & Appleton, V. (1995). Building working alliances with American Indian families. *Social Work in Education, 17,* 148–158.

Earle, K. A. (1996). Working with the Haudenosaunee: What social workers should know. *New Social Worker, 3,* 27–28.

Edwards, E. D., & Edwards, M. E. (1984). Group work practice with American Indians. *Social Work with Groups, 7,* 7–21.

Fenton, W. N. (1987). *The false faces of the Iroquois.* Norman: University of Oklahoma Press.

Good Tracks, J. G. (1973). Native American noninterference. *Social Work, 18,* 31–35.

Greene, G. J., Jensen, C., & Jones, D. H. (1996). A constructivist perspective on clinical social work practice with ethnically diverse clients. *Social Work, 41,* 172–180.

Gross, E. R. (1995). Deconstructing politically correct practice literature: The American Indian case. *Social Work, 40,* 206–213.

Jarvenpa, R. (1985). The political economy and political ethnicity of American Indian adaptations and identities. *Ethnic and Racial Studies, 8,* 29–48.

Jilek, W. G. (1971). From crazy witch doctor to auxiliary psychotherapist—The changing image of the medicine man. *Psychiatria Clinica, 4,* 200–220.

Joe, J. R., & Malach, R. S. (1992). Families with Native American roots. In E. W. Lynch & M. J. Hanson (Eds.), *Developing cross-cultural competence: A guide for working with young children and their families* (pp. 89–115). Baltimore: Paul H. Brookes.

Johnson, D. L., & Johnson, C. A. (1965). Totally discouraged: A depressive syndrome of the Dakota Sioux. *Transcultural Psychiatric Research Review, 2,* 141–143.

Kenny, D. A. (1987). *Statistics for the social and behavioral sciences.* Boston: Little, Brown.

LaFromboise, T. D. (1988). American Indian mental health policy. *American Psychologist, 47,* 388–396.

Lefley, H. P. (1990). Culture and chronic mental illness. *Hospital and Community Psychiatry, 41,* 277–285.

Lejero, L., Antone, M., Francisco, D., & Manuel, J. (1988). An indigenous community mental health service on the Tohono O'odham (Papago) Indian reservation: Seventeen years later. *American Journal of Community Psychology, 16,* 369–379.

Lewis, T. (1975). A syndrome of depression and mutism in the Ogala Sioux. *American Journal of Psychiatry, 132,* 753–755.

Mander, J. (1991). *In the absence of the sacred: The failure of technology and the survival of the Indian Nations.* San Francisco: Sierra Club Books.

Manson, S. M., Shore, J. H., & Bloom, J. D. (1985). The depressive experience in American Indian communities: A challenge for psychiatric theory and diagnosis. In A. Kleinman & B. Good (Eds.), *Culture and depression: Studies in anthropology and cross-cultural psychiatry of affect and disorder* (pp. 331–368). Berkeley: University of California Press.

Manson, S. M., Tatum E., & Dinges, M. G. (1982). Prevention research among American Indian and Alaskan natives. In S. M. Manson (Ed.), *New directions in prevention with American Indians* (pp. 11–62). Portland: Oregon Health Services.

Marshall, C. A., Martin, W. E., Thomason, T. C., & Johnson, M. J. (1991). Multiculturalism and rehabilitation counselor training: Recommendations for providing culturally appropriate counseling services to American Indians with disabilities. *Journal of Counseling and Development, 70,* 225–234.

Matchett, W. F. (1972). Repeated hallucinatory experiences as part of the mourning process among Hopi Indian women. *Psychiatry, 35,* 185–194.

McShane, D. (1987). Mental health and North American Indian/native communities: Cultural transactions, education, and regulation. *American Journal of Community Psychology, 15,* 95–115.

Nagel, J., & Snipp, M. (1993). Ethnic reorganization: American Indian social, economic, political, and cultural strategies for survival. *Ethnic and Racial Studies, 16,* 203–235.

Nelson, S. H., McCoy, G. F., Stetter, M., & Vanderwagen, W. C. (1992). An overview of mental health services for American Indians and Alaska natives in the 1990s. *Hospital and Community Psychiatry, 43,* 257–261.

O'Nell, T. D. (1989). Psychiatric investigations among American Indians. *Culture, Medicine and Psychiatry, 13,* 51–87.

Owan, T. C. (1982). Neighborhood-based mental health: An approach to overcome inequities in mental health services delivery to racial and ethnic minorities. In D. E. Biegel & A. J. Naperstek (Eds.), *Community support systems and mental health: Practice, policy, and research* (pp. 282–300). New York: Springer.

Parker, A. C. (1968). *Parker on the Iroquois.* Syracuse, NY: Syracuse University Press.

Perkins, A. E. (1927). Psychoses of the American Indians admitted to Gowanda State Hospital. *Psychiatric Quarterly, 1,* 335–343.

Price-Williams, D. (1987). Summary: Culture, socialization, and mental health. *Journal of Community Psychiatry, 15,* 357–361.

Prucha, F. P. (1990). *Documents of United States Indian Policy.* Lincoln: University of Nebraska Press.

Red Horse, J. (1980). Family structure and value orientation in American Indians. *Social Casework, 61,* 462–467.

Red Horse, J. (1982). Clinical strategies of American Indian families in crisis. *Urban and Social Change Review, 15,* 17–19.

Schaaf, G. (1990). *Wampum belts and peace trees.* Golden, CO: Fulcrum.

Sue, D. W., & Sue, D. (1990). *Counseling the culturally different: Theory and practice.* New York: John Wiley & Sons.

Trimble, J. E., Manson, S., Dinges, G., & Medicine, B. (1984). American Indian concepts of mental health: Reflections and directions. In P. B. Pederson, N. Sartorius, & A. J. Marsella (Eds.), *Mental health concepts: The cross cultural context* (pp. 199–220). Beverly Hills, CA: Sage Publications.

Tyler, J., Clark, J. A., Olson, D., Klapp, D. A., & Cheloha, R. S. (1983). Measuring mental health values. *Counseling and Values, 27,* 20–31.

Tyler, J. D., & Suan, L. V. (1990). Mental health values differences between Native American and Caucasian American college students. *Journal of Rural Community Psychology, 11,* 17–29.

U.S. Department of Health and Human Services, U.S. Indian Health Service. (1989). *National plan for Native American mental health services* (Draft document).

Wallace, A.F.C. (1959). The institutionalization of cathartic and control strategies in Iroquois religious psychotherapy. In M. K. Opler (Ed.), *Culture and mental health: Cross-cultural studies* (pp. 63–96). New York: Macmillan.

Western Interstate Commission for Higher Education. (1993). *The journey of Native American people with serious mental illness.* Boulder, CO: WICHE Publications.

Wilkinson, G. T. (1980). On assisting Indian people. *Social Casework, 61,* 451–454.

Williams, E. E., & Ellison, F. (1996). Culturally informed social work with American Indian clients: Guidelines for non–Indian social workers. *Social Work, 41,* 147–151.

Wollock, J. (1997). Protagonism emergent: Indians and higher education. *Native Americans, 14,* 12–23.

The author thanks Alan Ackley, director, Zoar Valley Clinic, for his assistance in completing this study.

33 Depression among Elderly Chinese Immigrants:
An Exploratory Study

Ada C. Mui

etween 1980 and 1990, the Asian American population in the United States increased by 107.8 percent (from 3,500,439 to 7,273,662), compared with 6 percent for whites, 13 percent for blacks, and 53 percent for Hispanics (U.S. Bureau of the Census, 1991). The Asian American population is composed of more than two dozen ethnic groups from Asia and the Pacific Islands, including Chinese, Koreans, Filipinos, Japanese, Asian Indians, Vietnamese, Thais, Hmong, Laotians, and many others. For Chinese Americans and Chinese immigrants specifically, the growth rate was about 104 percent (from 806,040 to 1,645,472). Data from the 1990 census also show that one-third of Asian American elderly people are Chinese and that over 85 percent of these older Chinese are foreign born (U.S. Bureau of the Census, 1991).

Although there are an increasing number of Asian and other ethnic groups and immigrants in the population, there are substantial knowledge gaps regarding the state of ethnic groups in America, especially the elderly populations, because of a lack of empirical research (LaVeist, 1995). Researchers with the Gerontological Society of America's Minority Task Force noted that numerous medical, psychological, social, and biological research questions remain unanswered because of the unavailability of data on this population (Gibson, 1989; Jackson, 1989).

In a survey of ongoing aging-related data sources supported by U.S. federal agencies, LaVeist (1995) found that for the white elderly population, all available national data sets were large enough to conduct analysis, and a majority of the data sets were large enough for research on the African American elderly population. However, Asian American and other ethnic elderly groups were rarely included in sufficient numbers to enable meaningful statistical analysis. In this study, the author has attempted to fill this gap by conducting an empirical study to understand factors associated with depression among elderly Chinese immigrants in a major U.S. metropolitan region.

This chapter was originally published in the November 1996 issue of *Social Work*, Vol. 41, pp. 633–645.

MENTAL HEALTH STATUS OF ELDERLY CHINESE IMMIGRANTS

Of all the psychological problems that affect elderly people, depression is the risk factor most frequently associated with suicide (Lapierre, Pronovost, Dube, & Delisle, 1992). One-fifth of all late-life suicides are due to depression (American Psychiatric Association, 1988). There is evidence that Chinese Americans have a higher rate of suicide than white Americans (Yu, 1986). Compared with other groups, the suicide rate for older Chinese women has been much higher than for their white counterparts. In 1980, the suicide rate for elderly Chinese immigrants was almost three times higher than the rate for U.S.-born older Chinese Americans (Yu, 1986). Because suicide attempts and suicide are considered manifestations of mental disorder and because suicide is more likely among people who are depressed, the mental health status of elderly Chinese immigrants deserves careful evaluation and attention so that culturally appropriate intervention programs can be developed.

Depression may occur frequently in elderly immigrants because they have limited resources and yet must deal with physical losses and stressful life events (Gelfand & Yee, 1991). Despite substantial prevalence rates, symptoms of depression often go unrecognized, undiagnosed, and untreated due to patient- and health care–related barriers and problems in the organization and financing of mental health services for older adults (Gottlieb, 1991). Studies also suggest that Chinese immigrants tend to underuse mental health services, even though the prevalence and types of reported psychological disorders are similar to those in the white population (Loo, Tong, & True, 1989; Snowden & Cheung, 1990). Depressive symptoms do not tend to remit spontaneously in older adults (Allen & Blazer, 1991), and undiagnosed and untreated depression in late life causes tremendous distress for older adults, their families, and society.

Research suggests that older Chinese Americans and older Chinese immigrants are at higher risk of depression than older white people (Ying, 1988). The most common risk factors for depression—poverty, low educational attainment (Ross & Huber, 1985), poor physical health (National Institute of Aging, 1990), and high rates of family disruption—are prevalent among ethnic elders, including older Chinese Americans and new immigrants (New York Center for Policy on Aging of the New York Community Trust, 1993). The stresses of immigration and acculturation pose additional risks for situational stress and somatic symptoms, often when family supports are weakened or unavailable (Gelfand & Yee, 1991). However, depressed Chinese elders are less likely than white elders to be identified by service providers and less likely to receive treatment (Chi & Boey, 1993).

Although depression is the most common psychological problem among elderly people of all nationalities, few researchers have studied depression in older Chinese Americans or immigrants. In addition, the possibility of cultural effects in measuring depression has complicated the accurate assessment of depression in this population.

Some instruments for measuring depression may not be culturally suited to assess the mental health of Chinese American elderly people. Recently, Chinese researchers in Hong Kong have used the Geriatric Depression Scale (GDS) to study the mental health status of the Chinese elderly population in Hong Kong. Chiu and his colleagues (1993) did a cross-cultural validation study to establish the reliability and validity of the 30-item GDS among both normal and depressed Chinese elders in Hong Kong. In the United States, epidemiological studies have examined the prevalence of depressive symptoms in communities using a variety of self-rating scales and interviews. Depending on the selected cutoff points and instruments, Blazer et al. (1988) reported the prevalence of depression among those over 65 living in the community as ranging from 2 percent to 5 percent for major depressive disorders to as high as 44 percent to 50 percent for depressive symptoms.

Previous research has shown that older people are more likely to be depressed if they are female, have poor self-rated health, are living alone, and have poor quality of social support (Burnette & Mui, 1994; Mui, 1993). A preponderance of studies of white and other ethnic elders have shown that elderly women are more depressed than elderly men (see Mui, 1993, for a review of these studies). Other researchers have found that family and social support are associated with less depression; social support can mediate the impact of stress among elderly people (Husaini et al., 1990; Krause, 1986). Furthermore, it is not the size of the support network but the perceived satisfaction with family help that has been associated with less depression (Borden, 1991; Mui, 1992; Wethington & Kessler, 1986). There is also evidence of cultural and ethnic differences in family support. For example, Cantor (1979) found that Hispanic elders consistently had higher levels of support from their children than either black or white elders. Compared with white elders, both black and Hispanic elders were disproportionately poor and underserved by mental health systems (Butler, Lewis, & Sunderland, 1991; Mui & Burnette, 1994b). Some differences in family support among ethnic groups can be attributed to culture, socioeconomic status, and immigration patterns (Linn, Hunter, & Perry, 1979; Markides & Mindel, 1987).

Previous studies on both white and ethnic elders found that older people who rated their health as poor were more likely to be depressed (Burnette & Mui, 1994; Kemp, Staples, & Lopez-Aqueres, 1987; Mahard, 1988; Mui, 1993). The issue of the coexistence of depression with physical illness is important and complex (Ouslander, 1982). Depressive symptoms are natural responses to physical illness. Furthermore, some of the depressive symptoms, such as sleep disturbance and fatigue, can result from physical illnesses or from drug treatments for those illnesses. A wide variety of physical illnesses can be accompanied by depressive symptoms in elderly people (Ouslander, 1982; Reifler, 1991).

Recent research suggests that living alone is associated with more depression because it increases the risk of social isolation (Mui,

1993). For example, a study using the 1992–94 National Long-Term Care Channeling Demonstration database found that despite having fewer physical, cognitive, and functional impairments, elders who lived alone had significantly higher rates of depression and lower levels of life satisfaction than did study counterparts who lived with others (Mui & Burnette, 1994a). Living alone may engender social isolation, especially if social contacts are not maintained.

In the present study the author asked the question, What is the impact of age, gender, self-rated health, living arrangements, and perceived family support on the level of depression among elderly Chinese immigrants?

METHOD

Participants were 50 elderly Chinese immigrants living in a major U.S. metropolitan region who volunteered for the study. Community-dwelling Chinese elderly immigrants were approached and interviewed by the author at senior centers and congregate meal sites in a Northeast metropolitan area from September 1994 to January 1995. Elders were included in the study when judged to be without psychiatric or memory problems as determined by the Chinese version of the Short Portable Mental Status Questionnaire (Chi & Boey, 1993). No one was screened out by this procedure, and the response rate was 89 percent. Because a fifth of the participants were not able to read in any language, and because the researcher desired a consistent procedure, all respondents were administered the questionnaire through face-to-face interviews. The author administered a Chinese-language questionnaire developed to assess sociodemographics, informal support system, self-rated health status, stressful life events, and depression. All data collection was conducted by the author, who is a native speaker of Chinese.

Depression Measure: GDS

The GDS, the dependent variable, was used to measure depression. The GDS was chosen because it is one of the most widely used and highly recommended screening measures for depression in older adults (Olin, Schneider, Eaton, Zemansky, & Pollock, 1992; Thompson, Futterman, & Gallagher, 1988). It is a 30-item inventory that takes 10 to 15 minutes to administer. Previous study populations have included psychiatric and medical patients and normal elders. The GDS has excellent reliability and validity (test–retest reliability = .85; internal consistency = .94). The GDS has been validated against Research Diagnostic Criteria (Spitzer, Endicott, & Robins, 1978) and is able to discriminate among normal and mildly and severely depressed adults. It performs as well as the DSM-III-R symptoms checklist in predicting clinical diagnoses (Parmelee, Lawton, & Katz, 1989).

The assessment of depression in an elderly population is more difficult than in a younger population because of the higher prevalence of somatic complaints, genuine physical problems, and medication use. One of the strengths of the GDS is that it contains no somatic items that can introduce age bias into the depression screening scale and inflate total scores among the elderly population (Berry, Storandt, & Coyne, 1984; Kessler, Foster, Webster, & House, 1992). Another strength of the GDS is its simple yes-or-no response format for symptom endorsement. This is preferable for participants with limited formal education (Olin et al., 1992).

Translation and Back-Translation of the GDS

The GDS has been translated into many languages, including Spanish, Hebrew, Russian, and Yiddish. In this study, the GDS was translated into Chinese and was back-translated from Chinese to English using techniques consistent with the literature to ensure that items would be understandable and culturally meaningful (Brislin, 1986; Mui, 1996b). The GDS was translated into Chinese by a bilingual mental health professional and then translated back into English by three other bilingual mental health professionals. This back-translation was then translated (for a second time) into Chinese and compared with the original Chinese translation. During this process, the team of four bilingual professionals compared the various translations to ascertain that the items were culturally valid and matched the intent of the original instrument. The final Chinese version of the GDS was compared to the GDS Chinese version done in Hong Kong (Chiu et al., 1993). There were slight discrepancies between our Chinese translation and the Hong Kong Chinese version. A decision was made to select wordings that were easier to understand and yet would be consistent with the intent of the original instrument. Content and face validity of the GDS Chinese version were established through intensive review of the instrument by the panel of four bilingual experts to ascertain and confirm its vocabulary and syntax.

Measures of other major independent variables were as follows: Family support was operationally defined by three questions: size of social network, help provided by family members, and satisfaction with the quality of family help. Respondents were asked to answer three sets of questions: (1) Who are you living with, and how many? In general, how well do you get along with each of these people? (2) In general, do your family members provide assistance to you? (3) At present, are you satisfied with your family and the help you receive? Answers ranged on a four-point scale from 1 = very dissatisfied to 4 = very satisfied.

Health conditions were measured by self-report of the following conditions: high blood pressure, heart disease, stroke, diabetes, arthritis, osteoporosis, eye problems, stomachaches, fatigue, chest pain, unusual cough, and frequent headaches. Respondents rated their perceived health status on a four-point scale ranging from 1 = excellent to 4 = poor.

Stressful life events were measured by asking respondents to answer yes or no to the following question: In the past three years, did you experience the following events? The events were children moved out, serious illness or injury, robbed or home burglarized, birth or immigration of a new family member, death of a spouse, death of a family member or good friend, divorce or separation, illness or injury of a family member, change in residence, family discord, and change in financial status. These stressful life events were selected because they were used in previous research with Chinese elders (Chi & Boey, 1993). Sociodemographic variables (age, gender, marital status, language spoken, religion, income, education, length of stay in the United States, literacy, and living arrangements) were also measured.

RESULTS

Sample Characteristics

The mean age of the respondents was 75.1 years (SD = 6.5 years) (Table 33-1); ages ranged from 62 to 91 years. Almost 82 percent (n = 41) of the respondents were 70 years and older. All were participants in senior centers and congregate meal sites, and the majority had only a grade-school level of education. Close to half (48.9 percent, n = 24) were married, 38.8 percent (n = 19) were widowed, and 12.3 percent (n = 6) were divorced or separated. More than 20 percent (n = 10) of respondents were unable to read at all, 77.6 percent (n = 38) were able to read Chinese only, and one person (2.0 percent) knew English. The average length of stay in the United States was 19.1 years, and all respondents were born in Asian countries. Perhaps because of their low levels of education, their income levels were also low, with 81.6 percent (n = 40) receiving less than $500 a month from either social security or Supplemental Security Income.

Social Network and Life Events

About one-third of the respondents (n = 18) lived alone, similar to the white elderly population in general (Burnette & Mui, 1994) (Table 33-2). Remaining respondents lived with spouses, children, both spouses and children, or other relatives. There were no gender differences in terms of social network characteristics in this sample. The average number of adult children of the Chinese respondents was 2.7. About two-thirds of families provided emotional support, and somewhat fewer than half provided financial support. Family members spent more leisure time with the female respondents (60.9 percent) than with their male counterparts (36.0 percent). About one-third of respondents received help with decision making, activities of daily living, medical care, and transportation. Most respondents (63.8 percent) seemed to be satisfied with the help they got from family members. However, 36.2 percent expressed some dissatisfaction with the quality of help they received.

A significant portion of respondents had experienced difficult times in the three years before the interview; 28.2 percent had children move out, 23.1 percent had a serious illness or injury, 15.4 percent were robbed or burglarized, 25.6 percent had a new family member born or immigrate, and 10.3 percent had an ill or injured family member. The data suggest that some respondents had to make many adjustments in the previous year because of these life events.

Health Status

This study included questions on three measures of physical health: (1) self-rated health, (2) physical symptoms and diseases, and (3) extent to which daily activities were affected by health problems. Results indicate that the Chinese men tended to rate their health as better than the women (Table 33-3). Among the diseases reported, the women tended to have more diabetes and arthritis than the men. For both groups, fatigue was a major problem. The daily activities of the women tended to be more affected by their poor health. The men may have been less likely to admit that they were affected, or they actually may have been healthier than the women.

Depressive Symptomatology

The GDS measures depression, with scores ranging from 0 to 30 representing the total number of depressive symptoms. According to Brink and his colleagues (1982), those who report 10 or fewer symptoms are considered normal, those who report 11 to 20 symptoms are considered mildly depressed, and those who report 21 or more symptoms are considered moderately to severely depressed. Using this sample, the alpha coefficient of the Chinese-language GDS was .90, which indicates good internal consistency and reliability of this scale. The split-half reliability of the GDS was .86. With few exceptions, there were few gender differences in GDS depression scores (Table 33-4). With regard to the first question on satisfaction with life in general, the older men appeared to feel better than the older women. However, the older men felt worse in terms of a sense of helplessness, had a harder time starting new projects, and felt that their situation was hopeless. The overall mean for both gender groups was about the same (7.2), which is considered normal. Using the Brink et al. cutoff points, 18 percent of the respondents were mildly to severely depressed. Although these data are not intended as population estimates, the rate of depression in this community sample was similar to that found in other community samples of elderly people (Rankin, Galbraith, & Johnson, 1993).

To examine factors that were associated with depression in these elderly Chinese immigrants, a regression analysis was conducted, and five independent variables (age, gender, self-rated health, living alone, and perceived satisfaction with family help) were included because these variables were important predictors in other studies (Mui, 1993). Stressful life events were not entered into the regression model, because the number count of these stressful life events was highly correlated with the perceived dissatisfaction with family help.

Table 33-1
Elderly Chinese Sample Characteristics

Characteristic	Women				Men				Total			
	%	n	M	SD	%	n	M	SD	%	n	M	SD
Age (years)			76.6	7.1			73.6	5.6			75.1	6.5
60–69	16.7	4			20.0	5			18.4	9		
70–79	50.0	12			60.0	15			55.1	27		
80 and older	33.3	8			20.0	5			26.5	13		
Marital status*												
Married	37.5	9			60.0	15			48.9	24		
Widowed	58.3	14			20.0	5			38.8	19		
Divorced	4.2	1			16.0	4			10.2	5		
Separated	0	0			4.0	1			2.1	1		
Language spoken												
English	4.4	1			0	0			2.1	1		
Cantonese	47.8	11			68.0	17			58.3	28		
Toishanese	34.8	8			28.0	7			31.3	15		
Other	13.0	3			4.0	1			8.3	4		
Education												
No education	25.0	6			4.0	1			14.3	7		

	%	n	%	n	%	n
Grade school	58.3	14	56.0	14	57.2	28
High school	4.2	1	16.0	4	10.2	5
Some college	8.3	2	16.0	4	12.2	6
Other training	4.2	1	8.0	2	6.1	3
Religion						
No religion	25.0	6	8.0	2	16.3	8
Buddhist	4.2	1	0	0	2.1	1
Catholic	25.0	6	16.0	4	20.4	10
Protestant	45.8	11	76.0	19	61.2	30
Income						
Less than $500 per month	79.2	19	84.0	21	81.6	40
$501–$1,000 per month	20.8	5	16.0	4	18.4	9
Years of stay in the United States	18.8	10.0	20.7	15.3	19.1	12.2
Born overseas	100	24	100	25	100	49
Literacy*						
Not able to read	33.3	8	8.0	2	20.4	10
Able to read Chinese	66.7	16	88.0	22	77.6	38
Able to read English and Chinese	0	0	4.0	1	2.0	1

NOTE: Chi-square statistics were used.
*p < .05.

Table 33-2
Social Network and Stressful Life Events of the Sample

Characteristic	Women				Men				Total			
	%	n	M	SD	%	n	M	SD	%	n	M	SD
Living arrangement*												
Living alone	37.5	9			36.0	9			36.7	18		
With spouse	33.3	8			28.0	7			30.6	15		
With spouse and children	0	0			28.0	7			14.3	7		
With children	29.2	7			4.0	1			16.3	8		
With other relatives	0	0			4.0	1			2.1	1		
Family network												
Number of adult children			3.0	2.4			2.6	2.2			2.7	2.6
Number of sons and daughters-in-law			2.0	1.8			1.4	2.2			1.8	1.3
Number of grandchildren			4.5	4.5			2.2	3.8			3.3	4.4
Number of other relatives[a]			1.1	1.7			1.0	1.4			1.0	1.5
Assistance provided by family members												
Emotional support	69.6	16			56.0	14			62.5	30		
Financial support	47.8	11			44.0	11			45.8	22		
Help with decision making	39.1	9			37.5	9			38.3	18		
Help with activities of daily living	34.8	8			38.0	9			35.4	17		
Help with medical care and medication	30.4	7			36.0	9			33.3	16		

	%	n	%	n	%	n
Entertainment in leisure*	60.9	14	36.0	9	47.9	23
Transportation or escort	47.8	11	32.0	8	39.6	19
Perceived satisfaction with family help						
Very dissatisfied	22.7	5	8.0	2	14.9	7
Dissatisfied	13.6	3	28.0	7	21.3	10
Satisfied	22.7	5	44.0	11	34.0	16
Very satisfied	40.9	9	20.0	5	29.8	14
Stressful life events						
Children moved out	31.3	5	26.1	6	28.2	11
Serious illness or injury	25.0	4	21.7	5	23.1	9
Robbed or home burglarized	6.3	1	21.7	5	15.4	6
Birth or immigration of a new family member	37.5	6	17.4	4	25.6	10
Death of a spouse	12.5	2	4.4	1	7.7	3
Death of a family member or good friend	6.3	1	8.7	2	7.7	3
Divorce or separation	0	0	4.4	1	2.6	1
Illness or injury of a family member	25.0	4	0	0	10.3	4
Change in residence	12.5	2	0	0	5.1	2
Family discord	6.3	1	8.7	2	7.7	3
Change in financial status	6.3	1	8.7	2	7.7	3

NOTE: Chi-square statistics were used.
[a]Including nephew or niece, nephew- or niece-in-law, and sibling.
*p < .05.

Table 33-3
Physical Health Conditions and Health Status of the Sample

Condition or Status	Women %	Women n	Men %	Men n	Total %	Total n
Physical condition						
High blood pressure	28.6	6	32.0	8	30.4	14
Heart disease	4.8	1	12.0	3	8.7	4
Stroke	4.8	1	0	0	2.2	1
Diabetes*	23.8	5	12.0	3	17.4	8
Rheumatoid arthritis*	52.4	11	20.0	5	34.8	16
Osteoporosis	14.3	3	0	0	6.5	3
Eye problems	14.3	3	4.0	1	8.7	4
Stomachaches	9.5	2	12.0	3	10.9	5
Fatigue	42.9	9	32.0	8	37.0	17
Chest pain	19.1	4	4.0	1	10.9	5
Unusual cough	14.3	3	8.0	2	10.9	5
Frequent headaches	9.5	2	16.0	4	13.0	6
Self-rated health*						
Excellent	19.0	4	16.0	4	17.4	8
Good	23.8	5	28.0	7	26.1	12
Fair	28.6	6	48.0	12	39.1	18
Poor	28.6	6	8.0	2	17.4	8
Activity affected by health*						
Not at all	52.4	11	72.0	18	63.0	29
A little bit	47.6	10	24.0	6	34.8	16
A great deal	0	0	4.0	1	2.2	1

NOTE: Chi-square statistics were used.
*$p < .05$.

Results indicate that the model explains 49 percent of the variance in depression (Table 33-5). Three variables were significant in predicting depressive symptoms: poor self-rated health ($\beta = .44$), living alone ($\beta = .36$), and perceived dissatisfaction with family help ($\beta = -.29$). The predictive power of poor health and living alone is consistent with the findings of earlier studies using white and other ethnic elderly populations (Burnette & Mui, 1994; Mui, 1993).

DISCUSSION AND IMPLICATIONS

Elderly Chinese respondents in the present study admitted to depressive symptoms at a rate that is lower than that found in other research on this group (Kuo, 1984). On the other hand, a study done in the Los Angeles area found that elderly Chinese immigrants showed greater moderation and reported fewer physical and mental health problems than white American elders (Raskin, Chien, & Lin, 1992). Therefore, it is possible that my findings underestimated these elderly Chinese immigrants' mental health problems.

Table 33-4

Percentage of Respondents Agreeing with Geriatric Depression Scale (GDS) Items

Item	Women (n = 23)[a]	Men (n = 24)[b]	Total (N = 47)[c]
1. Satisfied with life*	5.3	20.8	13.9
2. Dropped activities and interests	26.3	27.3	26.8
3. Life is empty	38.9	35.0	36.8
4. Often get bored	31.6	26.1	28.6
5. Hopeful about the future	41.2	52.3	47.6
6. Obsessive thoughts	22.2	33.3	27.5
7. In good spirits	27.8	17.4	22.0
8. Fear bad things	38.9	22.7	30.0
9. Happy most of the time	38.9	17.4	26.8
10. Often feel helpless*	5.6	26.1	17.1
11. Often get restless	16.7	26.1	21.9
12. Prefer to stay home	44.4	60.8	53.7
13. Worry about the future	16.7	22.7	20.0
14. Problem with memory	50.0	45.5	47.5
15. Wonderful to be alive	22.2	14.3	17.9
16. Feel downhearted and blue	17.6	22.7	20.5
17. Feel worthless	27.8	17.4	22.0
18. Worry about the past	16.7	9.1	12.5
19. Life is exciting	21.7	31.8	30.0
20. Hard to start new projects*	12.5	47.6	32.4
21. Full of energy	33.3	18.8	25.0
22. Situation hopeless*	11.1	34.8	24.4
23. Others are better off	37.5	39.1	38.5
24. Upset over little things	11.1	22.8	17.5
25. Feel like crying	11.1	8.7	9.8
26. Trouble concentrating	11.1	23.8	17.8
27. Enjoy getting up in the morning	23.5	9.1	15.4
28. Avoid social gatherings	22.2	17.4	19.5
29. Easy to make decisions	11.1	14.3	12.8
30. Mind as clear as it used to be	44.4	31.8	37.5
Diagnosis			
Normal (0–10)	84.0	80.0	82.0
Mildly depressed (11–20)	12.0	20.0	16.0
Moderately to severely depressed (21–30)	4.0	0	2.0

NOTE: Chi-square statistics were used.
[a]GDS long form $M = 7.0$, $SD = 5.9$.
[b]GDS long form $M = 7.3$, $SD = 5.4$.
[c]GDS long form $M = 7.2$, $SD = 5.6$.
*$p < .05$.

The findings of this study must be interpreted with caution. The study was limited by a small sample size and the voluntary nature of participation. Although age was not associated with increased depression in this cross-sectional sample, results may have differed

Table 33-5

Regression Model: Predictors of Depressive Symptoms among Elderly Chinese Immigrants

Predictors	Dependent Measures			
	Unstandardized Coefficient	*SE*	ß	*p*
Age	−.11	.10	−.14	.2690
Gender	.76	.46	.07	.5884
Self-rated health	2.53	.73	.44	.0014
Living alone	4.08	1.36	.36	.0050
Perceived satisfaction with family help	−1.14	.50	−.29	.0269
R^2			.49	
Adjusted R^2			.42	
F			6.95	
df			5, 41	
p			.0001	

had a longitudinal design been used. Future studies should use measures of social support with established reliability and validity for elderly populations and with cultural relevance for this group of ethnic elderly people. Finally, the self-rated measures in the present study may have been affected by the cultural norm of moderation in expressing feelings and emotions. In future studies on this population, the author plans to use a social desirability scale to control for this response tendency. The findings of the present study are most appropriately generalizable to Chinese immigrants who are not mentally impaired and who reside in the community.

Findings of this study did confirm some existing notions about predictors of the mental health status of elderly Chinese immigrants. That self-rated health status, living alone, and satisfaction with family support may be powerful predictors of depression are important empirical findings. These correlates of depression for elderly Chinese immigrants provide new insight into the design of culturally appropriate social work interventions. On the other hand, it is possible that the predictor variables—health status, living alone, and satisfaction with family support—are the result, rather than the cause, of depression.

In any case, the findings suggest that elderly Chinese immigrants, like other elderly groups, are vulnerable to psychological distress in the form of depressive symptoms (Burnette & Mui, 1994, 1996; Mui, 1996a; Mui & Burnette, 1996). This may be due in part to the stresses associated with immigration, language barriers, acculturation, poverty, illnesses, social isolation, perceived satisfaction of family support, splitting of households (children moving out), and adjustment to newborn or new immigrant family members. Indeed, the elderly Chinese immigrants in this study reported changes in their family systems more often than any other stressful life event: More than one-quarter reported having children move out or the immigration or birth of new family members in the previous year. This is important empirical information for social work practitioners working with Chinese families.

The split household may be an indication of intergenerational conflicts and less family support by adult children (Wong & Reker, 1986). This is a difficult emotional issue for elderly Chinese immigrants, who may still have high expectations of filial responsibility and family solidarity. Chinese culture places a strong emphasis on family togetherness and the interdependence of family members. The Chinese community gives high regard to family cohesion in terms of multigenerational family living arrangements. It is almost a norm rather than an exception for adult children to live with their older parents until they get married or even after marriage. It is also culturally desirable for aging parents to live with a married adult child, preferably a married son (Hong & Ham, 1992). Therefore, an adult child's decision to move out is often an extremely stressful transition for aging Chinese parents because it engenders great disappointment and shame. The splitting of the household can cause feelings of failure and embarrassment for all parties involved. Social workers need to be sensitive to the cultural meaning of the changes in the multigenerational family system and be able to help elderly Chinese immigrants accept and adapt to these changes.

Family support is one of the major factors determining the overall quality of life for elderly Chinese immigrants. Perceived dissatisfaction with the quality of help from family members and living alone are associated with higher depression scores. The size of the family network of the Chinese elders did not correlate with the levels of their depressive symptoms, but the perceived satisfaction with family help did. This variable was a quantitative measure and did not provide information concerning the elderly person's subjective evaluation of the quality of family help. This finding is consistent with the literature, which suggests that the effects of support may depend more on its perceived quality than on its quantity (Borden, 1991; Mui, 1992; Wethington & Kessler, 1986). In the present study the perceived satisfaction with family help was a significant variable in explaining depressive symptoms. Chinese elders may have high expectations of family help, but the families of these Chinese elders may not feel the same because of differences in acculturation.

More research is needed both to replicate these findings and to examine the role of traditional norms of family help and care for Chinese elders. This research should be conducted in the context of the Chinese intergenerational family from the perspective of both Chinese elders and their family members. Social work intervention to help elders cope with these life events and evaluation of their unmet needs are important to improve their quality of life.

Furthermore, the integration of new immigrant members into the existing family also affects the whole family system (Hong & Ham, 1992). Under U.S. immigration laws there are different quotas for different categories of family members. Usually, additional family members such as adult children may have to wait years before they can reunite with their family in the United States. Once the new family members immigrate, the reunification affects the family already in the United States because the incorporation of new members into a family system is often a source of unexpected stress for the whole family (Hong & Ham, 1992). The new family members add an additional burden and increase responsibilities for other family members. This may create tremendous conflicts and tensions for the family system, especially for families that are already under pressure and do not have sufficient emotional and financial coping resources. It is therefore important for social workers to be sensitive to the cultural meanings and impact of such changes on Chinese intergenerational families.

In this study health was found to be an important factor in the depression of elderly Chinese immigrants, consistent with other gerontological research (Burnette & Mui, 1994; Mui, 1992, 1993). In general, older Chinese men tended to rate their physical health higher than their female counterparts. The women reported more problems with diabetes and rheumatoid arthritis. For both groups, fatigue was a leading problem. It is unclear whether the reported fatigue was a sign of physical illness, a mental health problem, or a combination of both. Elderly Chinese immigrants might find the expression of physical problems culturally more acceptable. Raskin et al. (1992) found that elderly Chinese immigrants reported fewer positive and negative emotions than white people. It seems that the normative idea in Chinese culture of high tolerance of adversity and moderation in the expression of emotions and feelings still persists. This finding points to the importance of not relying totally on self-reported symptoms, but instead assessing elders in their cultural context. The data suggest that service providers must be sensitive to their clients' unspoken needs and provide information in terms of health education and preventive medicine.

The data also show that living alone was associated with a higher level of depression; this finding is also consistent with previous research (Burnette & Mui, 1994). Living alone may cause social isolation and the loss of interaction with family and friends. Public housing policy and community services should be designed to meet the coresidence needs of Chinese elders. Given that coresidence is preferred by Chinese elders (Chi & Boey, 1993) and that the preponderance of research evidence indicates that coresidence is associated with less depression, social services providers should facilitate shared living arrangements with family members or with others. In families with high levels of intergenerational conflict, family counseling may enable these families to stay together so that the elderly members may benefit from all the advantages of family residence. For Chinese elders who must live alone, supportive counseling may help alleviate some of the stresses and deficiencies that result from living alone. For example, a counselor may help an older person establish new support networks or revive existing family and friendship networks.

CONCLUSION

Recent dramatic increases in the Asian population of the United States and the aging of this population guarantee that in the future social workers will be called on to serve the mental health needs of elderly Asian Americans. Because of the stresses associated with immigration and acculturation, elderly Chinese American immigrants are likely to develop mental health problems. The most prevalent of these problems—depression—can be addressed effectively only with careful attention to the cultural values and expectations of this group. The present study suggests that social workers providing treatment to this group should pay special attention to clients' self-perceived health, their living situation, and their level of satisfaction with help from family members. Consideration of these variables is essential to the design of culturally appropriate mental health interventions for elderly Chinese immigrants.

REFERENCES

Allen, A., & Blazer, D. G. (1991). Mood disorders. In J. Sadavoy, L. W. Lazarus, & L. F. Jarvik (Eds.), *Comprehensive review of geriatric psychiatry* (pp. 337–352). Washington, DC: American Psychiatric Press.

American Psychiatric Association. (1988). *Mental health of the elderly*. Baltimore: Author.

Berry, J. M., Storandt, M., & Coyne, A. (1984). Age and sex differences in somatic complaints associated with depression. *Journal of Gerontology, 39*, 465–467.

Blazer, D., Swartz, M., Woodbury, M., Manton, K. G., Hugges, D., & George, L. (1988). Depressive symptoms and depressive diagnoses in a community population. *Archives of General Psychiatry, 45*, 1078–1084.

Borden, W. (1991). Stress, coping, and adaptation in spouses of older adults with chronic dementia. *Social Work Research & Abstracts, 27*(1), 14–21.

Brink, T. L., Yesavage, J. A., Lum, B., Heersma, P., Adey, M., & Rose, T. A. (1982). Screening tests for geriatric depression. *Clinical Gerontologist, 1*, 37–44.

Brislin, R. W. (1986). The wording and translation of research instruments. In W. J. Lonner & J. W. Berry (Eds.), *Field methods in cross-cultural research* (pp. 137–164). Beverly Hills, CA: Sage Publications.

Burnette, D., & Mui, A. C. (1994). Determinants of self-reported depressive symptoms by frail elderly persons living alone. *Journal of Gerontological Social Work, 22*(1–2), 3–18.

Burnette, D., & Mui, A. C. (1996). Psychological well-being of three cohorts of older American women who live alone. *Journal of Women and Aging, 8*(1), 63–80.

Butler, R. N., Lewis, M. I., & Sunderland, T. (1991). Aging and mental health: Positive psychological and biomedical approaches. New York: Macmillan.

Cantor, M. H. (1979). The informal support system of New York's inner-city elderly: Is ethnicity a factor? In D. E. Gelfand & A. J. Kutzik (Eds.), *Ethnicity and aging: Theory, research, and policy* (pp. 153–174). New York: Springer.

Chi, I., & Boey, K. W. (1993). *A mental health and social support study of the old-old in Hong Kong* (Resource Paper Series No. 22). Hong Kong: University of Hong Kong, Department of Social Work and Social Administration.

Chiu, H.F.K., Lee, H.C.B., Wing, Y. K., Kwong, P. K., Leung, C. M., & Chung, D.W.S. (1993). *Reliability, validity and structure of the Chinese Geriatric Depression Scale in a Hong Kong context: A preliminary report.* Unpublished manuscript, Chinese University of Hong Kong.

Gelfand, D., & Yee, B.W.K. (1991). Influence of immigration, migration, and acculturation on the fabric of aging in America. *Generations, 15*(4), 7–10.

Gibson, R. C. (1989). Minority aging research: Opportunity and challenge. *Journal of Gerontology: Social Sciences, 44*, S2–S3.

Gottlieb, G. L. (1991, November). *Barriers to care for older adults with depression.* Paper presented at the National Institutes of Health Consensus Development Conference on the diagnosis and treatment of depression in late life, Bethesda, MD.

Hong, G. K., & Ham, M.D.C. (1992). Impact of immigration on the family life cycle: Clinical implications for Chinese Americans. *Journal of Family Psychotherapy, 3*(3), 27–39.

Husaini, B. A., Castor, R. S., Linn, G., Moore, S. T., Warren, H. A., & Whitten-Stovall, R. (1990). Social support and depression among the black and white elderly. *Journal of Community Psychology, 18*, 12–18.

Jackson, J. S. (1989). Race, ethnicity, and psychological theory and research. *Journal of Gerontology: Psychological Sciences, 44*, P1–P2.

Kemp, B. J., Staples, F., & Lopez-Aqueres, W. (1987). Epidemiology of depression and dysphoria in an elderly Hispanic population: Prevalence and correlates. *Journal of the American Geriatric Society, 35*, 920–926.

Kessler, R. C., Foster, C., Webster, P. S., & House, J. S. (1992). The relationship between age and depressive symptoms in two national surveys. *Psychology and Aging, 7*(1), 119–126.

Krause, N. (1986). Social support, stress, and well-being among older adults. *Journal of Gerontology, 41*, 512–519.

Kuo, W. H. (1984). Prevalence of depression among Asian Americans. *Journal of Nervous and Mental Disease, 172*, 449–457.

Lapierre, S., Pronovost, J., Dube, M., & Delisle, I. (1992, September). Risk factors associated with suicide in elderly persons living in the community. *Canada Mental Health*, pp. 8–12.

LaVeist, T. A. (1995). Data sources for aging research on racial and ethnic groups. *Gerontologist, 35*, 328–339.

Linn, M. W., Hunter, K. I., & Perry, P. R. (1979). Differences by sex and ethnicity in the psychosocial adjustment of the elderly. *Journal of Health and Social Behavior, 20*, 273–281.

Loo, C., Tong, B., & True, R. (1989). A bitter bean: Mental health status and attitudes in Chinatown. *Journal of Community Psychology, 17*, 283–296.

Mahard, R. E. (1988). The CES-D as a measure of depressive mood in elderly Puerto Rican population. *Journal of Gerontology, 43*, P24–P25.

Markides, K. S., & Mindel, C. (1987). *Aging and ethnicity.* Beverly Hills, CA: Sage Publications.

Mui, A. C. (1992). Caregiver strain among black and white daughter caregivers: A role theory perspective. *Gerontologist, 32*, 203–212.

Mui, A. C. (1993). Self-reported depressive symptoms among black and Hispanic frail elders: A sociocultural perspective. *Journal of Applied Gerontology, 12*, 170–187.

Mui, A. C. (1996a). Correlates of psychological distress among Mexican, Cuban, and Puerto Rican elders living in the U.S. *Journal of Cross-Cultural Gerontology, 11*, 131–147.

Mui, A. C. (1996b). Geriatric Depression Scale as a community screening instrument for elderly Chinese immigrants. *International Psychogeriatric, 8*(3), 1–10.

Mui, A. C., & Burnette, D. (1994a). A comparative profile of frail elderly persons living alone and those living with others. *Journal of Gerontological Social Work, 21*(3–4), 5–26.

Mui, A. C., & Burnette, D. (1994b). Long-term care service use by frail elders: Is ethnicity a factor? *Gerontologist, 34*, 190–198.

Mui, A. C., & Burnette, D. (1996). Coping resources and self-reported depressive symptoms among frail older ethnic women. *Journal of Social Service Research, 21*(3), 19–37.

National Institute of Aging. (1990). *Special Report on Aging, 1990.* Washington, DC: U.S. Department of Health and Human Services, Public Health Service.

New York Center for Policy on Aging of the New York Community Trust. (1993). *Growing older in New York City in the 1990s.* New York: Author.

Olin, J. T., Schneider, L. S., Eaton, E. M., Zemansky, M. F., & Pollock, V. E. (1992). The Geriatric Depression Scale and the Beck Depression Inventory as screening instruments in an older adult outpatient population. *Psychological Assessment, 4,* 190–192.

Ouslander, J. G. (1982). Physical illness and depression in the elderly. *Journal of the American Geriatric Society, 30,* 593–599.

Parmelee, P. A., Lawton, M. P., & Katz, I. (1989). Psychometric properties of the Geriatric Depression Scale among the institutionalized aged. *Psychological Assessment, 1,* 331–338.

Rankin, S. H., Galbraith, M. E., & Johnson, S. (1993). Reliability and validity data for a Chinese translation of the CES-D. *Psychological Reports, 73,* 1291–1298.

Raskin, A., Chien, C. P., & Lin, K. M. (1992). Elderly Chinese and Caucasian Americans compared on measures of psychic distress, somatic complaints and social competence. *International Journal of Geriatric Psychiatry, 7,* 191–198.

Reifler, B. (1991, November). *Depression: Diagnosis and comorbidity.* Paper presented at National Institutes of Health Consensus Development Conference on the diagnosis and treatment of depression in late life, Bethesda, MD.

Ross, C. E., & Huber, J. (1985). Hardship and depression. *Journal of Health and Social Behavior, 26,* 312–327.

Snowden, L. R., & Cheung, F. K. (1990). Use of inpatient mental health services by members of ethnic minority groups. *American Psychologist, 45,* 347–355.

Spitzer, R. L., Endicott, J., & Robins, L. N. (1978). Research diagnostic criteria: Rationale and reliability. *Archives of General Psychiatry, 35,* 773–782.

Thompson, L. W., Futterman, A., & Gallagher, D. (1988). Assessment of late life depression. *Psychopharmacology Bulletin, 24,* 577–586.

U.S. Bureau of the Census. (1991, April). *Census and you* (Press Release No. CB91-100). Washington, DC: U.S. Government Printing Office.

Wethington, E., & Kessler, R. (1986). Perceived support, received support, and adjustment to stressful life events. *Journal of Health and Social Behavior, 27,* 78–89.

Wong, P.T.P., & Reker, G. T. (1986). Stress, coping, and well-being in Anglo and Chinese elderly. *Canadian Journal on Aging, 4*(1), 29–36.

Ying, Y. W. (1988). Depressive symptomatology among Chinese-Americans as measured by the CES-D. *Journal of Clinical Psychology, 44,* 739–746.

Yu, E.S.H. (1986). Health of the Chinese elderly in America. *Research on Aging, 8*(1), 84–109.

This study was supported by the 1994–95 Columbia University School of Social Work Faculty Innovative Research Award.

34

Help-Seeking among Asian and Pacific Americans:
A Multiperspective Analysis

Greg Yamashiro and Jon K. Matsuoka

Asian American and Pacific Islander is an umbrella term that subsumes a number of unique cultural groups into one category. Included in the Asian American population are Chinese, Japanese, Filipino, Korean, Vietnamese, and other groups from Asian and Southeast Asian countries, and included in the Pacific Islander population are Hawaiians, Samoans, Guamanians, and Tongans, to name a few. The utility of the term is more political in nature (it is used for federal funding and the census) because it provides a means by which to organize communities that reside in the Pacific Basin and have political ties to the United States or immigrants or descendants of immigrants from Asia or the Pacific that reside in the United States.

It might be said that Asian Americans and Pacific Islanders are as common as the ocean they share and as diverse as the physiography of their respective homelands. Perhaps the most significant commonality is an ontological orientation that serves as a basis for a worldview. Eastern and Pacific epistemology is molded by natural and spiritual phenomena that define reality as illusory and temporary. Cultural qualities emphasize collective identities and communalism, holism, and fatalism. One example of this common cultural base is the term "local" used to describe those born and raised in Hawaii. The term applies to members of Asian American and Pacific Islander groups who subscribe to particular values, worldviews, behavioral styles, and languages. Local culture in Hawaii represents a social evolutionary process that began with the melding of common cultural elements. Uba and Sue (1991) noted that differences among Asian American and Pacific Islander groups were evident in "differing degrees of acculturation, migration experiences, occupational skills, worldviews and values, patterns of help-seeking from public services, personality syndromes, and basic sociodemographic data including geographic residence, age, place of birth, and poverty levels" (p. 3).

Asian and Pacific Americans may be the fastest growing racial and ethnic group in the United States (Uba & Sue, 1991). Population growth among Asian and Pacific Americans is attributed primarily to rates of immigration rather than to fertility. This growth factor has

This chapter was originally published in the March 1997 issue of *Social Work*, Vol. 42, pp. 176–186.

implications for help-seeking behaviors and perceptions of mental illness. For example, those immigrating to the United States from Asia and Pacific Islands generally possess values and perceptions consistent with the traditional attitudes of their homelands; those born and socialized in the United States generally possess attitudes that are more consistent with the norms and values of American society. One common notion about Asian and Pacific Americans is that as a group they significantly underutilize mental health services (Bui & Takeuchi, 1992; Cheung & Snowden, 1990; Leong, 1994; Snowden & Cheung, 1990; Sue & McKinney, 1975; Sue & Morishima, 1982; Tracey, Glidden, & Leong, 1986). A nationwide study of Asian Americans and Pacific Islanders found that in all states and territories except Colorado, members of this group underutilized formal mental health services (Matsuoka, Breaux, & Ryujin, in press).

This underutilization of or resistance to seeking professional mental health services may have its origin in a number of cultural themes. *Help-seeking* used in this context is the propensity to seek professional mental health services. A study by Tracey et al. (1986) supported the claim that the help-seeking process was different for Asian Americans than for white Americans. Overall, Asian Americans would rarely endorse emotional and interpersonal problems as their central problem. This difference in perception of emotional or psychological stress may influence their help-seeking behaviors.

It is disturbing to note that there is far less empirical research about mental health services utilization among Asian and Pacific Americans than among other ethnic groups (Uehara, Takeuchi, & Smukler, 1994; Vega & Rumbaut, 1991). Compounding matters is the societal view of Asian and Pacific Americans as a "model" ethnic group. This idealized perception may overshadow studies that show Asian and Pacific Americans as having higher than normal levels of disturbance (Sue & McKinney, 1975; Tracey et al., 1986) and higher rates of inpatient service utilization than European Americans (Leong, 1994). A greater understanding is needed of the reasons Asian and Pacific Americans underutilize mental health services and of ways to address the mental health needs of this burgeoning population.

An effective approach to understanding the complex themes related to examining help-seeking behaviors among Asian and Pacific Americans is to break down the "boundary maintenance rhetoric" common among theories and cross-theoretical borders (Pescosolido, 1992). It is important to move beyond theoretical exclusivity by focusing on major conceptual themes and by borrowing from various ideologies related to the problem. Through this process of analysis, a more comprehensive, culturally sensitive perspective may emerge. This chapter examines cultural themes and concepts associated with service utilization to paint a comprehensive picture of Asian and Pacific Americans seeking professional assistance. This approach to understanding provides a multilevel framework based on traditional behavioral and cognitive styles that may explain patterns of help-seeking in a Western context.

HUMAN ECOLOGY

The human ecological perspective is a way to conceptualize exchanges between systems or spheres within which people function (Germain, 1979; Hawley, 1986; Ogbu, 1981; Siporin, 1980). This perspective integrates various theories of human behavior, especially concepts from ecology and general systems theory. The model can be visualized as concentric circles that rotate around the center, which, depending on the culture, is known as the individual or family. Change at the outer macrolevels (for example, natural environment, society, community) has reverberating effects on each system, moving toward the center. Change can be initiated in any of the systems, and the dynamics of effect can move in any direction.

What occurs at the interface between the systems is key to understanding person–environment fit, the source of stressors and problem etiology, and adaptational processes and coping strategies. The self or family is understood in terms of its relational meaning to other systems. The ecological model can be applied to social work's understanding of "goodness-of-fit" and assessments of how social change affects people depending on their worldview or psychological constitution.

A human ecological model also provides a framework for reconceptualization of traditional assumptions about human phenomena and social problems. For example, an ecological analysis offers a radical shift from traditional ideology that defines "functional" in a Western social context. Traditional Asian and Pacific people may view this social context as pathological. The helping professions are charged with working with dysfunctional individuals to enhance their adaptive capabilities through cognitive restructuring and behavior modification. This approach is built on the premise that society is sane and problematic individuals lack requisite behavioral or cognitive capabilities. From an Asian and Pacific perspective, deviance may be understood as a predictable response to inappropriate options or a natural reaction to oppressive conditions.

The human ecological model allows for an analysis of human behavior beyond the traditional focus on individual motivations and psychological determinants. The analysis includes interpersonal dynamics, worldview, sociohistory, and demographics. These factors are central to an analysis of help-seeking related to culture-based behaviors, developmental issues, and cohort mentality.

AN INTERPERSONAL ECOLOGY

An ecological approach is well suited to assessing the interplay of an individual's social and psychological spheres. Because of their group orientation, Asian and Pacific Americans are sensitized to their environment and strive to maintain harmony and equilibrium in their multiple levels of experience. Johnson, Marsella, and Johnson (1974) and Johnson and Marsella (1978) found that Asian and Pacific Americans expressed more concern and sensitivity toward others in social situations than did white Americans. This sensitivity relieves others of the discomfort of making personal requests and is usually contingent on a gesture of future reciprocation. The ultimate goal is to maintain a sense of social and emotional balance through a mutual system of give and take. Establishing a balanced emotional economy with significant others is critical to mental health and the diminishment of neurosis (Reynolds, 1989).

A similar quest for balance occurs between individuals and their external world. A general sense of fatalism derived from Eastern philosophy relates to how Asian and Pacific Americans accept the natural course of life events. *Karma* is a widely held belief that one exists within a framework defined by previous deeds and future destinies. Life is perceived as ultimately beyond the control of the individual and as determined by a series of trials throughout one's lifetime (Walsh, 1989). A predilection for tolerance and mutual concession that stems from this belief system prepares Asian and Pacific Americans for undesirable life events. A general acceptance of life conditions, however, should not be mistaken for passivity or acceptance of negative events. In contrast, the belief holds that people cannot defy their karma; however, they can control how they live within that fate. This system of attribution allows individuals to discriminate between areas of life than can be affected by their efforts and those that cannot and to exercise the resources needed to enhance adaptive capacities and improve environments.

The general belief in fate explains the quiescence in the face of unpleasant life situations among Asian and Pacific Americans. Religious and philosophical beliefs stipulating that life is experienced as a complex series of trials and destinies may diverge from Western psychotherapeutic approaches to helping and coping. In Eastern culture it is believed that the onus is on the individual or family to overcome the problem; therefore, Asian and Pacific peoples are not likely to seek the assistance of others, especially those from another culture.

These aspects of an Asian and Pacific American ecology have implications in terms of barriers to help-seeking in a Western social context. The concern with maintaining social balance and equilibrium poses problems for those who view formal services as a unilateral process in which they are the sole beneficiaries. Although fee-for-service is a means to compensate the provider, the kind of service offered may not fit the traditional notion of what is typically bought or paid for. More appropriate gestures of reciprocity or exchange may come in forms that are not acceptable in the context of formal services (for example, gifts, food or meals, invitations to social activities). In the Western system, the professional who receives invitations to events or gifts from a client is faced with an ethical dilemma.

Worldview

Worldview has been defined as the way people perceive their relationship to nature, institutions, and other people and objects (Kearney,

1984). Worldview constitutes psychological orientation to life and can determine how people think, behave, make decisions, and understand phenomena. Worldviews can provide essential information for assessing mental health status, assisting in diagnosis, and designing treatment programs.

The Asian and Pacific worldview reflects a greater synthesis between the self and the phenomenal world and requires more intuitive and direct cognitive processing. Reasoning and introspection are often viewed as obstructions that interfere with human activity (Reynolds, 1989). A basic assumption underlying psychological thinking relates to a collective orientation related to the self in the context of other systems of human existence. There is much less emphasis on individualism and more on a corporate identity and a more positive interpretation of dependence and interdependencies within the person, the family, and society (Pedersen, 1991).

Religious beliefs have a major influence on worldview. The influences of Buddhism and Confucianism are central to Asian philosophy and lifestyle. Buddhist doctrines are based on four truths: (1) All life is subject to suffering; (2) the desire to live is the cause of repeated existence; (3) the annihilation of desire gives release from suffering; and (4) the way of escape is through the eightfold path of right belief, right thought, right speech, right action, right livelihood, right effort, right mindfulness, and right concentration to escape from desire (Pedersen, 1991). Confucianism emphasizes the notion of face, filial piety, and proper conduct.

Worldviews are manifested in a variety of behavioral forms, one of which relates to how individuals express themselves. In Western culture, much value is placed on self-expression through language. The ability to articulate ideas is often viewed as a measure of one's intellect, and the ability to elicit and express one's feelings is considered an admirable quality. Thoughts or feelings that are difficult to symbolize through language are thought to be either nonexistent or too abstract to be worthy of trying.

In Western psychology, affect is viewed as a consequence of a person's cognitions. How people perceive the world is correlated with their emotional disposition. Affect is often objectified and transformed into semantic content to be manipulated in a way to make the person "feel better." The basic tenet underlying cognitive restructuring is that changing one's perceptions or self-talk leads to a corresponding change in mood.

In Eastern psychology, less emphasis is placed on the compartmentalization of different aspects of the psyche. Phenomena are not broken into usable steps or pieces but are viewed in a more holistic framework. Less emphasis is placed on the dynamic between affect and cognition. Affect is not conceived of as a secondary process mediated by human logic but is considered a primitive and independent system. In support of this viewpoint, Zajonc (1984) suggested that a person's first-level response to the environment is affective and that thoughts enter into an experience only afterward. He surmised that the emotional impact of a situation is largely vague and global but determines future modes of action and anticipatory effects. Modes of operation influence language comprehension and production as well. For example, he surmised that affect is not always transformed into semantic representations but instead is encoded in visceral or muscular symbols. He speculated that information contained in feelings is acquired, organized, categorized, represented, and retrieved differently from information having direct verbal referents.

In Asian and Pacific cultures, language may not accommodate all that individuals think and feel—especially for those who are not socialized to use language as a primary means for expressing feelings. People from these cultures may be prone to relate to symbolic gestures; physical and intuitive sensations; or deeply entrenched, precognitive affect. Attempts to describe feelings verbally are likely to lose something in the translation or may be impossible to present in verbal referents.

Several earlier studies found that differences in maternal styles between Asian and American mothers resulted in a variety of personality outcomes, including verbosity among their children (Caudill & Plath, 1969; Kurokawa, 1969; Lebra, 1976). American mothers tend to be more verbal and consequently have children who have higher levels of vocalization and motor activity. Asian mothers, on the other hand, accommodate their children physically, and their children tend to be less verbal and more physically passive. Cultural ideology shapes child-rearing practices and the development of national or ethnic character. Given that each culture has prescribed verbal norms, one must question the appropriateness and universality of verbal psychotherapies.

Sociohistory and Cohort Mentality

Social learning provides a context for understanding Asian and Pacific American motivation. The learning and socialization experiences can be conceptualized as a twofold process. First, a majority of Asian and Pacific Americans are immigrants or refugees. The social processes related to immigration and acculturation have profound effects on the psychological formation of generational cohorts. Second, Asian and Pacific Americans are socialized by culturally distinct parenting and community dynamics.

A natural tendency among all immigrants to the United States is to resettle in geographic areas near others from their former country. Thus, the formation of ethnic enclaves recreates cultural symbols and institutions and provides a security zone for the perpetuation of traditional lifeways. The element of oppression, especially racism directed toward groups of color, reinforces social separation and the development of subcultural systems ranging from the arts to financial assistance to various forms of self-help. The development of self-reliance is not only a consequence of achievement motivation, but also a result of external social forces intended to restrict the socioeconomic mobility of racial and ethnic groups.

The ideology of self-reliance was, in part, determined by a mistrust generated toward outside institutions and their representatives who took advantage of or misinterpreted situations, thus leading to the victimization of Asian and Pacific Americans. A legacy of mistrust is transmitted across generations. For example, parents convey to their children that skepticism is healthy when dealing with white-controlled institutions. Concurrent with this legacy is the development of "informal" services that fill the void of nonutilization of formal services, including informal services provided by clergy or spiritual leaders, community or clan leaders, and practitioners of traditional healing methods. These informal services are consistent with beliefs associated with psychiatric problems, coping, and service provision.

Nearly all of the studies on utilization of mental health services by Asian and Pacific Americans are based on measures of formal services (for example, Leong, 1994; Matsuoka et al., in press; Snowden & Cheung, 1990). An unknown element are rates of utilization of informal services. This type of data is critical to understanding problem etiologies, types and manifestations of psychiatric problems, treatments of choice, and success rates. It also lends itself to developing hybrid methodologies based on traditional and Western models to accommodate acculturating individuals.

Complicating the issue of help-seeking of formal services is the consideration that Asian and Pacific immigrants may speak little or no English and may reside in areas far away from services. These barriers to service access ultimately reinforce myths explaining why these groups underutilize formal services and may result in reduced outreach efforts or attempts to develop culturally appropriate services. Immigrants who enter the service system are faced with communicating their needs to non–native speakers, dealing with those who are unfamiliar with the nuances of culture-based motives and behaviors, and dealing with logistical problems such as finding transportation to an unfamiliar or a distant place.

Acculturation and Help-Seeking

Acculturation is a likely predictor of service utilization by Asian and Pacific Americans; it is a strong determinant in help-seeking behavior because language and familiarity with service organizations facilitate seeking professional help. Atkinson and Gim (1989) found in their study of Asian American students that attitudes toward professional psychological help were directly related to levels of acculturation. Students who measured higher on acculturation were more likely to recognize a personal need for professional psychological help, to be tolerant of the stigma associated with psychological help, and to be open in discussing their problems with a psychologist. This study suggests that more acculturated individuals are likely to seek professional help and that third- and fourth-generation Asian Americans would seek formal help at the same rate as European Americans.

On the contrary, Narikiyo and Kameoka (1992) found in their study of Japanese American and European American students that acculturation does not necessarily correlate with rates of formal help-seeking. Similar perceptions of mental illness were found across the two groups; however, an analysis of actual utilization of mental health services showed underuse by Japanese Americans. The authors suggested that although the Japanese Americans were seemingly acculturated, cultural values continued to influence beliefs about mental illness and help-seeking.

Studies have shown that sociodemographic factors are also determinants in help-seeking behaviors (Tijhuis & Foets, 1990). Variables such as gender, age, socioprofessional level, education, and income all contribute to how individuals approach help-seeking. There is some evidence to substantiate the importance of demographic factors in help-seeking among Asians and Pacific Islanders. Ying and Miller (1992) found in their study of Chinese Americans that younger adults, women, unmarried people, and those with higher socioeconomic status were more likely to use mental health services. These factors are also likely to correlate with levels of acculturation.

Sociobiology

The basic premise of *sociobiology* is that individuals possessing characteristics that render them more capable of surviving and reproducing will do so and be more successful (Dawkins, 1976; Wilson, 1978). An ancient tradition in Asian and Pacific Islander cultures is arranging marriages to ensure that one's offspring is united with an appropriate partner for the primary purpose of procreation. The assessment of a suitable spouse is based on the health and mental health of the prospective person's family and his or her social status and ranking and genetic purity. All of these factors are believed to contribute to the health and prosperity of successive generations, thus ensuring the survival of familial or genetic lines.

In traditional Eastern cultures, families are conceptualized as superorganic structures existing across past and future generations. Family background checks commonly include a thorough investigation for any signs of mental illness in the blood line. Because mental illness is believed to be genetically inherited, evidence of mental illness in a family's lineage could render their offspring unsuitable for marriage. Families with histories of mental illness have a vested interest in concealing their background (Fugita, Ito, Abe, & Takeuchi, 1991). Seeking outside assistance means risking the family secret being made public.

Studies have indicated that Asian American psychiatric clients entering the mental health system are diagnosed as more severely disturbed and psychotic than white clients (Berk & Hirata, 1973; Palley,

1968). These findings imply that Asian families wait until they have exhausted all other family resource options before entering the system of formal mental health services. By the time they do, the pathology may have reached crisis proportions. Another possible explanation for the severity of diagnosis is cultural insensitivity to differential manifestations of psychiatric symptoms. The findings suggest patterns of avoidance and resistance to services and a strong desire to contain knowledge about mental illness to a small sphere of people. The issue of secrecy has direct implications for confidentiality.

Social Learning

Social learning is a theoretical perspective that integrates behavioral and cognitive elements to explain human behavior. This perspective provides a context for understanding behavior as a function of the person–situation interaction. People are not driven exclusively by inner forces or buffeted by environmental stimuli; rather, behavior is explained in terms of a continuous reciprocal interaction of person and environment (Bandura, 1977).

Deeply entwined in the learning and socialization practices of Asian and Pacific families are methods of social control that rely on the shaming of refractory behaviors. A critical element of shame is a collective identity in which the behavior of one person reflects on the entire group or family system. This approach to behavioral attribution places immense social pressure on all members of the family to act in culturally appropriate ways, to conform to and fulfill role prescriptions, and to pursue honorable careers. The desire to avoid behaviors that bring shame to the family provides a powerful means of self-regulation. By arranging cognitive supports and producing real or anticipated consequences, people are able to exercise some measure of control over their own behavior. Thus, regulating or controlling one's behaviors and emotions is considered a virtue reflecting personal strength and character.

In the traditional family, a member who suffers from mental illness is concealed from the public. Tracey et al. (1986) stated that Asian American concerns about protecting the family name lead many to avoid formal services for fear of being viewed negatively by members of the community. The concept of "saving face" implies that psychological disturbance either is hidden or ignored or is attributed to a source associated with a less severe social stigma. This phenomenon may explain the tendency toward somatization among Asians and Pacific Americans. Physical manifestations of psychological disturbance are more acceptable because they imply a different set of etiological conditions.

Compounding the importance of family reputation is the concept of face perpetuated in the philosophy of Confucianism (Pedersen, 1991). Asian and Pacific Americans may perceive that losing face because of mental illness in the family would subject the individual or family to a religious or spiritual crisis. Further, the concept of karma reflects a blend of the concepts of religion and mental illness. The idea that mental illness is deserved because of some past impropriety may lead an individual to experience even greater shame and negative social consequences (Mokuau, 1990). Thus, through religion and social modeling, members of this population learn that it is far more desirable to hide mental illness than to admit psychological problems by seeking outside help.

Another aspect of social learning related to Asian philosophy is the notion of enduring suffering. The first doctrine of the Buddhist religion suggests that all life is subject to suffering. Implied in this religious paradigm is the understanding that psychological stress is part of human existence. Obstacles or conditions that contribute to stress are the norm, and the ability to work through and transcend such conditions are the key to character development. A person cannot acquire wisdom or achieve a state of equanimity without having endured a life of discomfort or continual suffering. This firmly entrenched belief may be central to explaining a reluctance to seek formal services.

Derivatives of this concept of suffering are reflected in a variety of Japanese beliefs such as *gaman* (to endure) and *shikata ga nai* (whatever has happened cannot be helped). In essence, one must endure and suffer or face *hazu kashii* (ridicule and embarrassment) (Fugita et al., 1991). Other Asian groups have similar expressions and consequences that associate the concept of suffering with normal life expectations (Mokuau, 1990).

IMPLICATIONS FOR SOCIAL WORK PRACTICE

Different cultures produce individuals with different value orientations and worldviews; yet, in American society, people seeking mental health services are likely to be subjected to the same forms of treatment despite their psychocultural orientation. Western treatment approaches may have been successful to some extent in treating Asian and Pacific American clients, but success often depends on the degree to which the client is acculturated to Western norms. The more acculturated the person, the more likely he or she is to respond to Western psychotherapeutic techniques (Mokuau & Matsuoka, 1992).

An analysis of the Asian and Pacific American worldview leads to numerous implications for treatment. For example, in the West, it is presumed that people react emotionally only after considerable cognitive operations have occurred. If in the East it is presumed that people respond emotionally to visceral cues or sense memory, then techniques attempting to manipulate a person's thought patterns are futile. Scientific methods in which clinicians gather data on erroneous thoughts and then systematically challenge their validity would not have much bearing on a client who has not learned to make connections between thoughts and feelings. Perhaps in the case of many Asian and Pacific Americans, relaxation or meditation techniques may be useful because they call on a different cognitive strategy (Reynolds, 1989).

The holistic orientation in the East reflects a system of logic divergent from that in the West. Instead of a one-to-one correspondence of treatment to problem, which is reflected in Western idiographic methods and multimodel approaches, the Eastern orientation reflects a one-to-many correspondence because of more intricate connections between systems. This orientation to treatment may be most effective with Asian and Pacific clients who believe in the practices of traditional healers. For example, the practices of prayer and meditation, ritual, or offerings are means by which individuals can extricate themselves from undesirable life situations.

A prerequisite to working with Asian and Pacific American clients is an understanding of the rudimentary norms and values governing their behaviors. The salient factors that shape personality begin at birth, and attempts to undo these traits imply that one must eradicate years of learning and conditioning that occurred during the most critical period of development. For example, social workers must understand and appreciate clients whose cultural norms encourage such behaviors as brevity and economy of speech (Ishisaka, 1977).

The literature clearly indicates a need for more culturally sensitive marketing strategies for mental health services (Matsuoka et al., in press). Offering appealing options to prospective Asian and Pacific American clients requires removing impediments to services. For example, the issue of shame and losing family face must be addressed in all measures that ensure confidentiality during intake and service. Bilingual and bicultural social workers provide a climate of familiarity and are better prepared to understand the intricacies and nuances of the behaviors and symptoms. The recruitment and retention of Asian and Pacific Americans in the helping professions and in schools of social work are necessary.

Education and training curricula must extend beyond token gestures of cultural sensitivity. A serious exploration is needed of dysfunction from an emic perspective that examines mental disorders as an outgrowth of a unique cultural context and psychosocial indicators of knowledge, skills, attitudes, and values. The social work curriculum needs to be reassessed in terms of its fundamental cultural biases. Mental health and mental illness are often conceptualized in terms of universal developmental and socialization experiences, predisposing factors and etiological conditions, and cognitive–behavioral manifestations. The formulation of culturally appropriate intervention and prevention strategies must begin with an examination of the Eastern worldview and how it is operationalized in terms of child rearing and human development, oppression, trauma and reactions to stress, family pathology, and coping styles.

Another key to marketing is to determine who the prospective clients are and where they reside. Client demographics, especially race and ethnicity, are often contingent on the location of the service agency. For the most part, U.S. society is organized by ethnic or racial enclaves separated by distinct geographic boundaries. Within these boundaries occur economies and services designed according to the cultural proclivities of the client. The same type of marketing strategy found in the economic sector can be applied to human services. Research may play a key role in conducting needs assessments and using new technologies such as the Geographic Information System (GIS) to map out population centers in relation to available human services and the prevalence of social problems. Data derived from this system could provide valuable information for planning and decision making. For example, GIS maps could enable a program planner to decide how and where to conduct outreach efforts.

The provision of culturally sensitive mental health services is perhaps the most important strategy for increasing service utilization by Asian and Pacific Americans. Sue (1977) suggested three program alternatives for mental health services for Asian Americans: (1) training existing personnel to be culturally sensitive, (2) establishing parallel services that provide ethnic-specific services, and (3) providing nonparallel services that have no precedence in the conventional mental health system. The first and second suggestions have long been incorporated into the system of professional training and service delivery. The third suggestion, however, is on the verge of becoming more commonplace as indigenous practitioners, many of whom have been trained in formal Western institutions, are looking for more effective strategies to address chronic social problems in their communities. Prevention and healing strategies in many Asian and Pacific American communities are based on the premise that dysfunction and mental illness are the result of cultural disenfranchisement and separation from entities that provide psychological and spiritual support.

Many community-based programs are designed to restore cultural institutions that are perceived to be at the heart of psychological well-being. For example, the restoration of traditional economies serves as a foundation for cultural practices that buffer individuals from antisocial behavior and mental disorders (Matsuoka & McGregor, 1994). The Opelu Project in Hawaii is designed to resemble a traditional land and economic system that allowed Hawaiians to exist on mountain-cultivated taro and marine resources. Along with being an economic enterprise, the project is designed to resocialize Hawaiian youths and adults with criminal and psychiatric histories through an understanding and appreciation of their cultural history, values, identities, and involvement in work programs. The adage promoted at the Opelu Project is that "work is therapy."

In many Asian and Pacific American communities, there is a desire to destructuralize existing programs and services and adapt or recreate them to fit the cultural dimensions of the community being served. With a high degree of flexibility built into services, supplemental programs could be created to meet a variety of community needs.

Traditional Eastern and Pacific service orientations have gained a bad reputation among strict empiricists, who have denounced them for their nonmeasurable qualities. Thus, the perceptions of the West have often subsumed Asian and Pacific philosophical orientations, and valuable lessons have been lost in the process. However, programmatic innovations point to a new direction in multicultural social work practice. Research measuring program effectiveness is essential to promoting the credibility of these efforts and soliciting funds for refining and expanding services.

CONCLUSION

As the population of Asian and Pacific Americans increases, issues such as the utilization of mental health services and patterns of help-seeking will be of growing concern. Social workers must be sensitive to the service issues surrounding this population. The focus of this chapter is help-seeking behaviors; other aspects of mental health service utilization have not been addressed. Issues such as the high attrition rate and high levels of psychological dysfunction among Asian and Pacific Americans who seek professional help deserve further exploration.

Despite the limitations of the literature, it is clear that Asian and Pacific Americans, compared to white Americans, display different approaches to coping and help-seeking. It is also clear that there are a multitude of issues and variables that must be examined to truly understand service underutilization by Asian and Pacific Americans. A new vision of mental health services needs to be developed to ensure that myths about mental health among racial and ethnic groups are dispelled and that those in need have access to appropriate services. Responsibility lies with scholars and mental health practitioners to devise new approaches for successfully treating various ethnic and cultural groups. Indigenous healing practices and other culturally appropriate treatments provide a broad basis for selection and experimentation. Components and principles of therapeutic models from Asia and the Pacific can be synthesized with existing Western models. A primary objective is to develop a complementary package of therapeutic strategies for treating acculturating and bicultural individuals.

REFERENCES

Atkinson, D. R., & Gim, R. H. (1989). Asian American cultural identity and attitudes toward mental health services. *Journal of Counseling Psychology, 36,* 209–212.

Bandura, A. (1977). *Social learning theory.* Englewood Cliffs, NJ: Prentice Hall.

Berk, B. B., & Hirata, L. C. (1973). Mental illness among the Chinese: Myth or reality? *Journal of Social Issues, 29,* 149–166.

Bui, K.-V. T., & Takeuchi, D. T. (1992). Ethnic minority adolescents and the use of community mental health care services. *American Journal of Community Psychology, 20,* 403–417.

Caudill, W., & Plath, D. (1969). Who sleeps by whom? Parent–child involvement in urban Japanese families. *Psychiatry, 32,* 12–43.

Cheung, F. K., & Snowden, L. R. (1990). Community mental health and ethnic minority populations. *Community Mental Health Journal, 26,* 277–291.

Dawkins, R. (1976). *The selfish gene.* New York: Oxford University Press.

Fugita, S., Ito, K. L., Abe, J., & Takeuchi, D. T. (1991). Japanese Americans. In N. Mokuau (Ed.), *Handbook of social services for Asians and Pacific Islanders* (pp. 61–78). New York: Greenwood Press.

Germain, C. B. (1979). Ecology and social work. In C. B. Germain (Ed.), *Social work practice: People and environments* (pp. 1–22). New York: Columbia University Press.

Hawley, T. (1986). *Human ecology: A theoretical essay.* Chicago: University of Chicago Press.

Ishisaka, A. (1977). *Audio-training tapes focused on the mental health of Indochinese refugees.* Seattle: U.S. Department of Health, Education, and Welfare Region X, and the Asian Counseling and Referral Service.

Johnson, F. A., & Marsella, A. J. (1978). Differential attitudes towards verbal behavior in students of Japanese and European ancestry. *Genetic Psychology Monographs, 97,* 43–56.

Johnson, F. A., Marsella, A. J., & Johnson, C. L. (1974). Social and psychological aspects of verbal behavior in Japanese-Americans. *American Journal of Psychiatry, 131,* 580–583.

Kearney, M. (1984). *World view.* Novato, CA: Chandler & Sharp.

Kurokawa, M. (1969). Acculturation and childhood accidents among Chinese and Japanese Americans. *Genetic Psychology Monographs, 79,* 89–159.

Lebra, W. (1976). *Cultural-bound syndromes, ethnopsychiatry, and alternate therapies.* Honolulu: University of Hawaii Press.

Leong, F. (1994). Asian Americans' differential patterns of utilization of inpatient and outpatient public mental health services in Hawai'i. *Journal of Community Psychology, 22,* 82–96.

Matsuoka, J., Breaux, C., & Ryujin, D. (in press). National utilization of mental health services by Asian Americans and Pacific Islanders. *Journal of Community Psychology.*

Matsuoka, J., & McGregor, D. (1994). Endangered culture: Hawaiians, nature, and economic development. In M. Hoff & J. McNutt (Eds.), *The global environmental crisis: Implications for social welfare and social work* (pp. 100–116). Newcastle, England: Avebury Press.

Mokuau, N. (1990). The impoverishment of native Hawaiians and the social work challenge. *Health & Social Work, 15,* 235–242.

Mokuau, N., & Matsuoka, J. (1992). The appropriateness of personality theories for social work with Asian Americans. In S. Furuto, R. Biswas, D. Chung, K. Murase, & F. Ross-Sheriff (Eds.), *Social work practice with Asian Americans* (pp. 67–84). Newbury Park, CA: Sage Publications.

Narikiyo, T. A., & Kameoka, V. A. (1992). Attributions of mental illness and judgements about help seeking among Japanese-American and white American students. *Journal of Counseling Psychology, 39,* 363–369.

Ogbu, J. U. (1981). Origins of human competence: A cultural–ecological perspective. *Child Development, 52,* 413–429.

Palley, N. (1968). Cultural problems in psychiatric therapy. *Archives of General Psychiatry, 19,* 45–49.

Pedersen, P. (1991). Balance as a criterion for social services for Asian and Pacific Islander Americans. In N. Mokuau (Ed.), *Handbook of social services for Asians and Pacific Islanders* (pp. 37–57). New York: Greenwood Press.

Pescosolido, B. A. (1992). Beyond rational choice: The social dynamics of how people seek help. *American Journal of Sociology, 97,* 1096–1138.

Reynolds, D. K. (1989). *Flowing bridges, quiet waters: Japanese psychotherapies, Morita and Naikan.* Albany: State University of New York Press.

Siporin, M. (1980). Ecological systems theory in social work. *Journal of Sociology and Social Welfare, 7,* 507–532.

Snowden, L. R., & Cheung, F. K. (1990). Use of inpatient mental health services by members of ethnic minority groups. *American Psychologist, 45,* 347–355.

Sue, S. (1977). Community mental health services to minority groups—Some optimism, some pessimism. *American Psychologist, 32,* 616–624.

Sue, S., & McKinney, H. (1975). Asian Americans in the community mental health care system. *American Journal of Orthopsychiatry, 45,* 111–118.

Sue, S., & Morishima, J. K. (1982). *The mental health of Asian Americans.* San Francisco: Jossey-Bass.

Tijhuis, M.A.R., & Foets, M. (1990). An orientation toward help-seeking for emotional problems. *Social Science and Medicine, 31,* 989–995.

Tracey, T. J., Glidden, C., & Leong, F. T. (1986). Help seeking and problem perception among Asian Americans. *Journal of Counseling Psychology, 33,* 331–336.

Uba, L., & Sue, S. (1991). Nature and scope of services for Asian and Pacific Islander Americans. In N. Mokuau (Ed.), *Handbook of social services for Asians and Pacific Islanders* (pp. 3–19). New York: Greenwood Press.

Uehara, E. S., Takeuchi, D. T., & Smukler, M. (1994). Effects of combining disparate groups in the analysis of ethnic differences: Variations among Asian American mental health service consumers in level of community functioning. *American Journal of Community Psychology, 22,* 83–99.

Vega, W., & Rumbaut, R. (1991). Ethnic minorities and mental health. *Annual Review of Sociology, 17,* 351–383.

Walsh, R. (1989). Toward a synthesis of Eastern and Western psychologies. In A. Sheikh & K. Sheikh (Eds.), *Eastern and Western approaches to healing: Ancient wisdom and modern knowledge* (pp. 542–555). New York: John Wiley & Sons.

Wilson, E. O. (1978). *On human nature.* Cambridge, MA: Harvard University Press.

Ying, Y., & Miller, L. S. (1992). Help-seeking behavior and attitude of Chinese Americans regarding psychological problems. *American Journal of Community Psychology, 20,* 549–556.

Zajonc, R. (1984). On the primacy of affect. *American Psychologist, 39,* 117–123.

35 American Indian Perspectives on Addiction and Recovery

Christine T. Lowery

Deloria (1970, p. 13) compared the tribal–nontribal orientation this way: Where the tribal society is "integrated toward a center," the nontribal society is linear; a circle surrounded by tangent lines represents the two orientations. Where the circle and the lines touch, opportunities for the joining of tribal and nontribal perspectives exist "between spirit and science." This makes a case for an emic perspective for American Indian women in recovery—with acknowledgment of the diversity among Native Americans. An emic perspective calls for a cultural-specific framework in which behavior within the culture can be examined and American Indian women can be understood on their own terms. This perspective is certainly not new to social workers trained during the past 20 years. However, the literature on addictions and the American Indian usually ends with recommendations for culturally based or spiritually based interventions.

This narrative report is purposefully organized to reflect the movement between "spirit and science," to reach beyond an intellectual understanding of what constitutes "healing the spirit" for many American Indians addicted to alcohol and drugs. Four broad concepts are presented: (1) balance and wellness; (2) the colonization experience and addiction as a crisis of the spirit; (3) issues of abuse, including sexual abuse; and (4) a time of healing illustrated by a Lakota commemorative event. I have divided these concepts into four circles, noting that all four circles intersect. The first circle speaks to the spiritual and cultural understanding of American Indian wellness and health based on Ottawa, Eastern Cherokee, and Ojibwa medicine wheels and supported by Antonovsky's (1979) salutogenic theory. The second circle frames alcoholism within the context of the colonization experience for Native Americans, integrating the spiritual work of Napoleon (1991) and theoretical framework of Antonovsky. The third circle discusses issues of abuse or "betrayals of the spirit." A qualitative model for Indian women's long-term recovery focused on "reclaiming the spirit" is reviewed, and an intervention for "betrayals of the spirit" is introduced (Lowery, 1994, in press[b]). The

This chapter was originally published in the May 1998 issue of *Health & Social Work*, Vol. 23, pp. 127–135.

fourth circle recounts a story about the Big Foot Memorial Ride, which speaks to Lakota prophecy and the Seventh Generation as a time of healing for Indian peoples.

FIRST CIRCLE: AN AMERICAN INDIAN WELLNESS PERSPECTIVE— SCIENCE OF THE SPIRITUAL

Deloria (1995) told a story of the introduction of a new field of study at the 1992 American Association for the Advancement of Science meeting in Chicago. *Zoopharmacognosy* describes the use of medicinal plants by animals. The potential use for human beings was somehow "a startling departure from ordinary scientific insights" (Deloria, p. 58). Deloria cited Harvard ethnobotanist Shawn Sigstedt, who was quoted in a laudatory report by *Newsweek*, as suggesting that "bears may have taught the Navajos to use a species of the *Ligusticum* plant, just as they had claimed!" (p. 59). Although this idea was a seeming breakthrough for Western peoples, Deloria (1995) questioned, "Why didn't people take Indians seriously when we said that animals and birds give us information on medicinal plants? Why is such knowledge only valid and valuable when white scientists document and articulate it!" (p. 59).

"Science"

The word "science" comes from the Latin *scientia* or knowledge, rooted in "scire," to know (*Webster's New Universal*, 1983). Science is systematized, organized knowledge based on observation, study, and experimentation—a process not unfamiliar to indigenous groups who transmit knowledge orally from generation to generation. From an American Indian cultural perspective, acknowledgment of the world of the spirit provides another knowledge base and another way of knowing and provides power through perception for understanding and healing.

Spiritual Science: The Medicine Wheel

The medicine wheel is an ecological concept and organized knowledge used by many Plains tribes—with tribe-specific details—that demonstrates the wholeness of life and the significance of health and balance; it has been tested through observation and experience over time. Concepts of illness and health are not dichotomous, but are woven into the fabric of life and the environment and through generational time. Indian medicine is used not only for treating illness, but also for providing guidance and protection, betterment of environmental conditions, or improvement of life (Garrett, 1990).

Generally the medicine wheel is a circle divided into four quadrants with different colors associated with each direction. The direction north is located at the top of the wheel, east is to the right, south is at the bottom, and west is to the left. Movement around the wheel flows in a clockwise or counterclockwise direction, depending on the tradition of a particular tribe. The combination of Ottawa, Ojibwa, and Eastern Cherokee Four Directions medicine wheel described by Garrett (1990) moves counterclockwise starting with the east quadrant. The Spirit path (east) recognizes that everything has a spirit and acknowledges the silent, deep respect this engenders; the Wisdom path (north) encompasses the spirit and the mind for listening and learning; the Physical path (west) recognizes the need for introspection or balancing the self; and the Peace path (south) represents the natural way of youth and innocence and "energizes the life forces" (Garrett, 1990, p. 190).

Antonovsky's (1979) salutogenic theory (origins of health) presents a coinciding perspective, a place where the circle and tangent lines meet, where tribal and nontribal orientations intersect (Deloria, 1970). Antonovsky not only examined stresses inherent in the entire life cycle—a developmental perspective—but also considered historical, sociocultural, and contextual perspectives as well. The salutogenic theory is compatible with the minimum requirements of an American Indian theory of addiction and recovery, which would encompass the perspective of two worlds, the world in which we live and the world of the spirit; include a balanced understanding of alcoholism and recovery that focuses on healing the spirit; and center on lifestyle and health ways, including the physical, mental, emotional, and spiritual. Antonovsky's theory considers culture and beliefs as a significant way in which groups of people manage tension; provides a health ease–dis-ease continuum rather than a health–illness dichotomy, and focuses on the origins of health (salutogenesis) rather than the origins of disease (pathogenesis), the traditional perspective on alcohol addiction.

The essence of Antonovsky's (1979) salutogenic theory is the "sense of coherence . . . [a] long-lasting way of seeing the world and one's life in it . . . a crucial element in the basic personality structure of an individual and in the ambiance of a subculture, culture, or historical period" (Antonovsky, p. 124). The key variables in the salutogenic theory are lawfulness, comprehensibility, consistency, predictability, and the ability to accurately judge reality. Social embroilment is historical–universal, contextual, and immediate, and stressors are ubiquitous.

SECOND CIRCLE: "THE WORLD TURNS UPSIDE DOWN"— THE TRAUMA OF A PEOPLE

Significantly, for understanding American Indians within a tribal and historical context, Antonovsky's (1979) theory considers culture as a way a group answers the questions facing it on a daily basis, gives a sense of place in the world, and provides a worldview appropriate to that structure. This theory also accounts for the destruction of a sense of coherence among groups of people and, in general terms, outlines how the sense of coherence can be restored and maintained among people who have experienced historically traumatic events, a context that serves as the background for American Indians and indigenous peoples globally.

The Story of the Yup'ik

In the tradition of story telling, Napoleon (1991) gave us a cultural–historical example of cataclysmic change and its consequences for the Yup'ik (Eskimo) in *Yuuvaraq: The Way of the Human Being*. Napoleon, a Yup'ik man, was paroled in 1993 after serving eight years in prison for the murder, in a drunken state, of his young son (Davidson, 1993). "The way of the human being" was shaped by the tundra, the river, and the Bering Sea for the Yup'ik. The way of the human being described interactions both in this world and the spirit world; in the physical world, the human spirit was the weakest and every physical manifestation had a spiritual cause. The Yup'ik lived in deference to the spirit world, and the shamans were the most important men and women in the village (Napoleon, 1991).

The harshness of the Yup'ik environment supports an ontological perspective, resting authority in the world of the spirit—authority legitimately placed and acting in the interest of the people (Antonovsky, 1979). Therefore, Antonovsky suggested that the sense of coherence of a people would be enhanced by the fact that control is in the hands of the deities—a situation that characterizes the beliefs of many tribal societies. Repeated, reasonable challenges to the sense of coherence followed by successful resolution would likely serve to strengthen the Yup'ik.

However, since the turn of the 20th century, this has not been the Yup'ik history. Contact with white men brought viruses and diseases that the Yup'ik shamans had never encountered and the people could not overcome. The "Yup'ik world turned upside down" in the face of the "Great Death"—an influenza epidemic originating in Nome in 1900 (Napoleon, pp. 10–11). It spread throughout Alaska, killing 60 percent of the Eskimo and Athabascan people. It claimed whole families and whole villages and spawned a generation of orphans, the great-grandparents and grandparents of the people living today. "The world the survivors woke to was without anchor. The *angalkuq* [shamans], their medicines, and their beliefs had all passed away overnight. They woke up in shock, listless, confused, bewildered, heartbroken, and afraid" (Napoleon, 1991, p. 11).

What was left were small groups of people separated by large distances, people who had no explanations for what had happened or resources to deal with their grief. For many, the pain was too great to even speak of. The numbed survivors could not respond to the cultural stressors that followed. They repressed their spirits, forsook their ceremonies, substituted Christianity, and "pretended it didn't happen"—*nallonguaq* became the way to deal with problems in Yup'ik life.

Antonovsky's (1979) concept of "lawfulness" provides a window through which to view the impact of this cataclysmic event and through which to understand the context of alcoholism and suicide among the Yup'ik: When there are no explanations, when there are no reasons, the sense of coherence cannot be maintained (Antonovsky, 1979).

Crisis of the Spirit

By the 1960s and 1970s, the Alaska Natives had benefited from civil rights and antipoverty programs, but violence and alcoholism were rampant.

> Something self-destructive, violent, frustrated, and angry has been set loose from within the Alaska Native people. And it is the young that are dying, going to prison, and maiming themselves. Their families, their friends, their villages say they cannot understand why. Every suicide leaves a stunned family and village. Every violent crime and every alcohol-related death elicits the same reaction. The alcohol-related nightmare has now become an epidemic. No one seems to know why. (Napoleon, 1991, p. 20)

It is the "crisis of the spirit" that precipitates the imbalance of alcoholism. Napoleon (1991) wrote, "The primary cause of alcoholism is not physical but spiritual and the cure must also be of the spirit" (p. 2). This crisis of the spirit entails an all-encompassing feeling of hopelessness. Traditional values of gratitude and reciprocity are absent. No one in his "right mind" wants to beat his wife, leave his children, and ruin his life (Napoleon, 1991). The sense of coherence of an entire people was shattered at the turn of the century. There was no lawfulness, no cultural explanation, no magic, no predictability. The world truly went upside down. Is such a catastrophe permanent? Can the Yup'ik regain their sense of coherence? Movement in either direction on the health ease–dis-ease continuum can occur (Antonovsky, 1979). Unlike the cataclysmic, negative "overnight" change in the story of the Yup'ik, the movement toward health is hard work and involves conscious choice. "Change, then, can take place. But change of this type is always within the context of one's previous level of the sense of coherence, is always slow, and is always part of the web of life experiences that transmit stimuli that are more or less coherent" (Antonovsky, p. 189).

Healing the devastation to the spirit that American Indians addicted to drugs and alcohol suffer must differ from generic substance abuse treatment for the dominant society, in that the history of Native Americans is marked by the grief, anger, and loss of spirit of many peoples. Although resistance and rights claims are still part of Native Americans' existence, the Peoples of the Eagle have survived colonization along with the Peoples of the Condor (indigenous peoples) to the south and the peoples of the far north. They are not alone in this devastation, and they are not alone in the healing.

American Indians are often categorized as powerless populations. Native Americans are not powerless; the powers that they carry are not valued in the dominant society. Their cultural teachings of interdependence—obligation and caretaking, the sharing of power, the recognition of the spirit in all things, the responsibility given by the

Creator to preserve Mother Earth, and acknowledgment of those who have come before them and those who will come after them—are all part of who American Indians are. These teachings provide the strength from which Indian peoples come.

We all need to take this charge seriously. We must acknowledge that all living things are connected and that human beings are only a part of this total ecology. We must acknowledge that alcoholism is a crisis of the spirit. We must acknowledge that this crisis requires a healing of the spirit, of the mind, and of the body within a larger framework of existence—the extended family network nested within community clan, tribe, and nation (Garrett, 1990; Napoleon, 1991).

THIRD CIRCLE: INDIAN WOMEN AND ISSUES OF ABUSE

Among the correlates of addiction, abuse is highly relevant in the treatment processes for women: physical and emotional abuse received as children, sexual abuse, domestic violence, and the neglect and abuse of their own children, by the women themselves or others (Covington, 1982; Gomberg, 1986; Wilsnack, 1984). To understand the full impact of abuse, it must be considered in the context of societal abuses such as racism, discrimination, sexism, and in some cases, homophobia. Physical, verbal, emotional, and sexual abuse, including rape, were consistent in the lives of American Indian women in two qualitative studies of addiction and recovery started in 1993 (Lowery, 1994, in press[b]). Life histories were gathered from 10 women, ages 25 to 53, and addiction and recovery processes were analyzed thematically. These women represent the following American Indian tribes: Nez Perce, Yakama, Blackfoot, Haliwa-Saponi, Ojibwa, Hochunk, and Hopi. Half of the women are of mixed ancestry and two are lesbians.

According to descriptive reports of nine Indian women's treatment programs in seven states, noted in an Indian Health Service (IHS) research report (Center for Reproductive Health Policy Research [CRHPR], 1995), there was no specific evidence of counseling for the gamut of abuse issues, including sexual abuse, and only the program in Nebraska listed counseling for domestic violence. At the same time, the treatment staffs in the nine centers identified physical, sexual, and emotional abuse as the most frequently mentioned childhood life experience and the second most frequent adult life experience for the participants (after being a single parent) (CRHPR, 1995). Chart reviews corroborated this locus, with 81 percent of the charts reviewed showing evidence of some type of child abuse experienced by the participants, including 44 percent who experienced physical abuse and 43 percent who experienced sexual abuse (CRHPR, 1995). As adults, 78 percent had experienced some type of abuse; 80 percent noted physical abuse as the most prevalent (CRHPR, 1995).

The barriers to recovery most frequently mentioned by women in focus groups in the IHS study included negative feelings and emotions, low self-esteem, lack of family support, alcohol and drug use by family and friends, unhealthy relationships with men, and societal problems such as discrimination (CRHPR, 1995).

Indian women in a chemical dependence project in Minnesota (almost half had no treatment history) related that their decision to stop using drugs or to stop drinking came from a spiritual experience: a dream, a vision, a voice telling them it was time to stop (Hawkins, Day, & Suagee, 1993). The treatment staff in the IHS-sponsored study of Indian women in treatment considered spiritual and cultural involvement as the most frequently mentioned milestone to recovery (CRHPR, 1995). The women noted that the major difference between the current treatment program compared to other treatment programs they had been in was the emphasis on culture (CRHPR, 1995). They said that the "presence of other American Indian/Alaska Native women" was the most helpful aspect of alcohol and drug treatment and also mentioned culturally based activities. And most notably for social workers, the women called for more counseling services: "While individual and group counseling services were available at all the treatment centers, many women felt that the frequency of their availability and the level of counseling expertise were inadequate. Participants felt that more individual and group counseling sessions should be provided, specifically for depression awareness and management, sexual abuse and relationship issues, and self-esteem. Some women mentioned that they had been in treatment for as long as three weeks and still had not had an individual counseling session (CRHPR, p. 89).

The Indian Women's Recovery Model

A balanced understanding of alcoholism and recovery would include healing the spirit; there are pathways in and there are pathways out. A balanced understanding of healing the spirit is relational. American Indian women see their children and relatives surrounded by the power of the landscape in the physical environment. They recognize their sense of place and the place of their children in kinship systems (sometimes reconstructed kinship systems in reconstructed urban places) at gatherings, powwows, feasts, and ceremonies. Such experiences enhance their understanding of the spiritual and their knowledge of their relationship with all things. When one can see and feel this, meaning is given to the concepts of health and life. One can see the path to healing and one understands how to bring others along. For healing cannot be done alone or only at the physical level. Healing is communal, and the communal and the relational are the spirit.

A long-term recovery model for Indian women, based on these principles, was developed from a qualitative study of the lives of six Indian women who had stopped drinking for at least two years (Lowery, 1994, in press[b]). The model uses the Eastern Cherokee, Ottawa, and Ojibwa medicine wheels (Coggins, 1990; Garrett, 1990) to organize the four major themes that emerge from the life histories of the six women. Moving clockwise around the wheel, "positive discontinuity" includes the personal elements of breaking the cycle; "expanding the circle" denotes reconnecting relationships; "reclaiming the mother" is a metaphor for acknowledging and understanding the realities of the past, including issues of abuse; and "developing a new continuity" is both present and future oriented and focuses on contributing to Indian peoples and others (Lowery, 1994, in press[a, b]).

The model is developmental and emphasizes the relational nature of the lives of the women from an intergenerational perspective and an ecological perspective. The model acknowledges the cultural understanding that healing the spirit is central to recovery, and "reclaiming the spirit" is at the center of the wheel. Reclaiming the mother is a significant part of the work of reclaiming the spirit.

Betrayals of the Spirit

From the life history data in interviews with four Indian women ages 25 to 30, six childhood–adolescent stances (ages five to 14) that need to be healed were identified: (1) You were not available to me, (2) you did not protect me, (3) you abused me, (4) you rejected me, (5) you shamed me, (6) you abandoned me.

Knowing who one is provides not only a context for change, but also a context for living. Jackie, a 35-year-old Nez Perce woman, reviewed her struggle to confront her addiction to alcohol, marijuana, and cocaine:

> [A treatment program designed for me would] teach me the value of life, how precious it is. Show me what kinds of experiences there are still left to have, like being with people and being part of your culture in one way or another. Now, I'm really involved with my community. [Show me] how that feels, how it feels to have relatives, to have people around you that are strong. Show me what it feels like to be part of a people.
>
> But first I had to know there was a life, that there was something I could do other than drinking and drugging. I had to know what my culture was about. I had to know what my life was about. But no one could say, "You've got to stop." I had to make a choice. I had to see that there was something I had to do. I wanted to be able to see myself. And I think that's what happened when I quit drinking. I could see myself. I really saw this person whom I felt could have so much. Somehow I got from my family that I could be something really special, right? From my grandmother and from my parents and some people around me, that I really had something that was worth keeping, worth saving, you know I never listened to that. (Lowery, in press[b])

An intervention called "Reclaiming the Mother," a series of questions for discussion in dyads or triads, is one step in the healing process that was demonstrated in workshops at the National American Indian Conference on Child Abuse and Neglect in 1996. In the process of shared stories, the caretaker (mother, foster parent, grandparent, father, or other relative) is verbally placed in the context of his or her own sociohistorical time, within the context of his or her own life development and life transitions, and within the context of the resources available to him or her. Finally, the intervention calls for a review of the gifts given in spite of an alcoholic family system or community.

The mother–daughter relationship is significant in understanding emotional pain in the life histories of the women interviewed. This relationship serves as a bridge for acknowledging one's own role as a mother and nurturer and permits the mothering of oneself and one's own children, a process of intergenerational healing described by Jackie. She talked about periods when her mother, in a drunken state, would talk about her family of origin, her pain, and her medicine—all elements that had little meaning for a young Jackie who was struggling with issues of her parents' alcoholism and neglect:

> All of a sudden when [my mother] was talking like this, I was just kind of like half asleep and I was just listening to her because [when she's drunk] she gets on these rags, you know. She just starts going on and on about how she was treated when she was a kid, too. I think that she was really trying to tell me that she understood that I was in pain. And I really was in pain as a kid. I was really in a lot of pain because of the perception I had that [my parents] were dying, and they didn't care about us. (sighs) I was really, I was too thoughtful as a kid I guess, too serious, but she was trying to express to me that she understood the abuse that I felt like I was getting. And that she felt it, too. That she had it in her life, also. And it was violent, really violent for her. But that she did learn something. She really did gain something from [it all], and she'd start talking about different medicine men that she'd worked with or medicine women and then she'd just say something like that she had a gift. I remember laying there and looking up at the ceiling and she had a gift and she goes, "My medicine and my way is to talk to the spirits."
>
> So that would be those types of episodes I would sort of shrug off in my urban way. And now realize that they were really serious things, some things that she was trying to show me. She was trying to show me something that I just let pass. . . . I regret it, I really regret it now. Then later, of course, she would take us to medicine people because she knew who they were. She'd take us there. And they would do medicine over us. And she'd talk to them about us. (Lowery, in press[b])

Jackie began the verbal process of putting her mother in her own historical context. She not only recognized the role incongruence her mother may have experienced, but she also recognized the imprinted Western notions of parenting that she and her siblings had adopted because of their relocation to an urban area—their only consistent environmental reference point while they were growing into adolescence (Lowery, in press[a]).

Jackie traced the traumatic shift from the nomadic lifestyle of the Nez Perce to nonmovement on a reservation for her grandmother and the anguish that gripped her people. Jackie's mother was born into this milieu and was part of a generation that experienced outside contact as young people. Jackie acknowledged her mother's own separation from her people and the expected life she was supposed to live, an obligation to be a mother—whether she wanted to or not: "And I understand more about how she couldn't be the mother that I felt like I had to have. She could only be the mother she was. And I can't have any judgments about that anymore. And that really releases me from a lot of pain. And makes me understand better what she was trying to teach me, what she was trying to show me. And she did make her choices" (Lowery, in press[b]). Jackie concluded that her mother drank her pain away and that she had done the same. Now she was trying to escape that pattern, just as her own daughters were trying to escape her pattern of drinking. Jackie put this all in the context of genocide: "I think that's what we're all doing. I guess it's like we're progressing. It takes this many generations to get over the genocide. My grandmother said, 'It's going to take a long time for us to get over it. The things that we've had to go through as a people.' I mean how can you expect to be conquered like that, to be practically destroyed, having your population go from 40 million to 1.5 [million]. What do you think's going to happen? [People] are going to suffer. [People] are going to hurt. All the generations are going to feel it. So I can see where maybe my grandchildren will have more of a chance to be really truly native people again even though [now] they are so racially mixed" (Lowery, in press[b]).

FOURTH CIRCLE: THE PROPHECY

Indian peoples recognize that they are in the time of the Seventh Generation, a time prophesied by the Lakota to be one of healing. The signs are consistent, and American Indians ascribe cultural and spiritual meaning to these signs: for example, the 1990 commemoration of the Wounded Knee Massacre with the Big Foot Memorial Ride; the 1992 historic meeting of the Peoples of the Eagle and the Peoples of the Condor in opposition to the celebrations around Columbus's "discovery" and the 1994 birth of the White Buffalo calf, a sacred symbol to the Lakotas, in Janesville, Wisconsin.

Beasley (1995), a white journalist, related one story of the Big Foot Memorial Ride in his book *We Are a People in This World*. The six-day ride, which took place from December 23 to December 28, 1990, commemorated the 1890 massacre of 300 Lakota elders, men, women, and children at Wounded Knee. Riders followed the route taken by Big Foot and his people after Sitting Bull was murdered. The first ride in 1986 had 19 riders. By 1990, the ride had taken place three times, and for the fourth ride there were 200 riders. There were people who fasted, there were people who walked, there were people who cooked and drove vans. There were Lakotas and white people and even a group of walkers from Japan. This was a sacrificial ride; the temperatures were below zero and the wind was unmerciful (Beasley, 1995).

On the third day of the ordeal, a French rider dropped out, leaving a horse available, and Bo (Ulbo) de Sitter, a photojournalist from

Amsterdam, was asked if he wanted to make the 26-mile ride from Red Water Creek near Kyle, South Dakota, to Red Owl Springs. At the end of the long day, the riders topped the hill overlooking the camp, where fires glowed and food was being prepared. At the direction of the spiritual leader, the riders fanned out, lined up stirrup to stirrup facing the light of a setting sun. Two hundred riders descended into camp in unison. "Nobody said a word, nobody broke rank, nobody ran ahead" (Beasley, 1995, p. 93). The women saw the riders first and began ululating in high-pitched voices. The men ran from the tipis, drumming and shouting.

"We could have been a returning war party," Bo romanticized. "For a few moments, it was like what it must have been 150 years ago." There was no wind, the fading light was soft. "The silhouettes of the trees against the pale sky were like inky drawings. Many of the riders were crying. I was shaking like a leaf. The solidarity, the togetherness, was overwhelming. It was the most fantastic moment of my life" (Beasley, 1995, p. 94).

I read this section over and over, for Bo de Sitter described the environmental–relational context that is the spirit. Through my own tears and with my own cultural understanding, I could see the spirits of the 300 Lakota elders and warriors, women and children, descending the hill, leading the riders; shouting to one another in old Lakota and calling the names of their descendants in this generation of healing, ensuring the promise of reclaiming our spirits, and completing the circle that joins our world with theirs.

For all my Laguna grandmothers . . .

CONCLUSION

The introduction of the spiritual into the contextual factors for social work has elicited varied responses ranging from the tiresome ("Now we're expected to teach religion!") to the thoughtful. As people of different cultures diversify social work faculties, they bring with them different worldviews, including explanations of their spiritual places in the world. These cultural backgrounds color teaching styles, course content, the way teachers work with students and colleagues, the way people live their lives, and research priorities. As teachers, administrators, supervisors, and practitioners, social workers recognize the responsibility to model openness to the students and colleagues who are privileged to have direct contact with social work clients. Social workers recognize opportunities to incorporate healthy practices from different cultures to strengthen our organizational cultures and social work practice.

Components of healing are spiritual, relational, and intergenerational. It is at this intersection that we must continue to focus attention for social work practice and research on behalf of American Indian women addicted to alcohol and drugs. The demands of alcohol treatment for men and women are overwhelming. A 90-day treatment program (even less under managed care) cannot fully address issues of childhood trauma; sexual abuse; mental illness; the long-lasting effects of racism, discrimination, poverty, and societal stress and complicated legal problems, even after a period of detoxification. However, awareness of the complexity of the issues with which Indian women with substance abuse problems must deal and trained intervention through a referral network that includes helpers who understand how to explore cultural meanings of depression, for example, can have some positive effects over time. Providing consultation for treatment and referral staff for specific topics like sexual abuse and incest can expand how these helpers recognize and assess problems and refer and serve Indian women in treatment.

Research, including qualitative research studies, should examine the intersection of family violence and substance abuse, including sexual abuse and incest; mental health (depression) and substance abuse; Indian women in prisons and the risk-factors for depression, suicide, and substance abuse; treatment issues for Indian women, including lesbian women; and historical trauma.

The profession has much work to do in providing adequate healing in a cultural context for American Indians. In many ways we do succeed. It is within the community that treatment programs have opportunity for programming that will contribute knowledge through community education nights that bring in past residents, outpatients, and their families for discussions or community talking circles, if the talking circle has meaning in a particular community. For example, the Winyan Wasaka (strong women) and the Ikce Wicasa (common man) Projects at the Denver Indian Health and Family Services address feelings related to historical trauma and identify both traditional and modern ways of renewing gender power and constructing new roles (Braveheart & Debruyn, 1995).

However, the social work profession needs to do more. We need to talk about the tandem biopsychosocial–historical development of children (including those affected by fetal alcohol syndrome) and their parents and grandparents and the effects of alcoholism on the body, the mind, and the spirit and the effects over generations. We need to explore the impact of alcoholic behaviors on family systems and understand how this behavior impedes the emotional and spiritual development of peoples, tribes, and nations. We need to pair the historical accounts of regional tribal groups with cultural practices of healing, grieving, and cleansing like the "Releasing of the Spirits, the Wiping of the Tears" conducted in December 1990 to heal the circle 100 years after the Wounded Knee Massacre (Braveheart & Debruyn, 1995).

We need to teach in the language of the tribe when feasible and to discuss the native concepts that convey the values that will help Native Americans live and explore concepts with which to teach their children to live. As a profession, we need to heal our spirits in the discussions of the violence—personal and societal—that American Indians have faced as women and as people of color within the context of colonization. Our work must be developmental within the context of the cultural and the spiritual.

REFERENCES

Antonovsky, A. (1979). *Health, stress, and coping.* San Francisco: Jossey-Bass.

Beasley, C., Jr. (1995). *We are a people in this world: The Lakota Sioux and the massacre at Wounded Knee.* Fayetteville: University of Arkansas Press.

Braveheart, M. J., & Debruyn, L. (1995). So she may walk in balance: Integrating the impact of historical trauma in the treatment of Native American Indian women. In J. Adlemen & G. M. Enguidanos (Eds.), *Racism in the lives of women: Testimony, theory, and guides to antiracist practice* (pp. 345–364). Binghamton, NY: Harrington Park Press.

Center for Reproductive Health Policy Research. (1995, November). *Evaluating the effectiveness of alcohol and substance abuse services for American Indian/Alaska Native women* (DHHS Contract No. 282-92-0048). San Francisco: University of California, Institute for Health Policy Studies.

Coggins, K. (1990). *Alternative pathways to healing.* Deerfield Beach, FL: Health Communications.

Covington, S. S. (1982). *Sexual experience, dysfunction, and abuse: A descriptive study of alcoholic and nonalcoholic women.* Unpublished doctoral dissertation, Union Graduate School.

Davidson, A. (1993). *Endangered peoples.* San Francisco: Sierra Club Books.

Deloria, V., Jr. (1970). *We talk, you listen.* New York: Dell.

Deloria, V., Jr. (1995). *Red earth, white lies: Native Americans and the myth of scientific fact.* New York: Charles Scribner.

Garrett, J. T. (1990). *Indian health: Values, beliefs, and practices in minority aging* (HHS Publication No. HRS, P-DV-90-4, pp. 179–191). Washington, DC: U.S. Department of Health and Human Services.

Gomberg, E.S.L. (1986). Women with alcohol problems. In N. J. Estes & M. E. Heinemann (Eds.), *Alcoholism: Development, consequences, and interventions* (pp. 241–256). St. Louis: C. V. Mosby.

Hawkins, N., Day, S., & Suagee, M. (1993). *American Indian women's chemical health project.* Minneapolis: Minnesota Department of Human Services, Chemical Dependency Division.

Lowery, C. T. (1994). *Life histories: The addiction and recovery of six Native American women.* Unpublished doctoral dissertation, University of Washington, School of Social Work, Seattle.

Lowery, C. T. (in press[a]). From the outside looking in: Rejection and belonging for four urban Indian men in Milwaukee, Wisconsin, 1944–1995 *American Indian Culture and Research Journal* (Special Issue on urban Indians).

Lowery, C. T. (in press[b]). A qualitative model of long-term recovery for American Indian women. *Journal of Human Behavior in the Social Environment.*

Napoleon, H. (1991) *Yuuvaraq: The way of the human being.* Fairbanks, AK: Center for Cross-Cultural Studies.

Webster's new universal unabridged dictionary (2nd ed.). (1983). New York: Dorset & Baber.

Wilsnack, S. C. (1984). Drinking, sexuality and sexual dysfunction in women. In S. C. Wilsnack & L. J. Beckman (Eds.), *Alcohol problems in women: Antecedents, consequences, and interventions* (pp. 189–227). New York: Guilford Press.

Portions of this chapter were presented at the "American Indian/Alaskan Native Alcohol Research: Past, Present and Future" Conference cosponsored by the National Institute on Alcohol Abuse and Alcoholism and the Indian Health Service, October 28–29, 1996, Washington, DC, and at the Musher Seminar Series on Science and Human Behavior, Columbia University School of Social Work, December 2, 1996, New York.

Part VIII

HIV/AIDS

36 Women Living with HIV/AIDS:
The Dual Challenge of Being a Patient and a Caregiver

Kristin L. Hackl, Anton M. Somlai,
Jeffrey A. Kelly, and Seth C. Kalichman

The Centers for Disease Control and Prevention (CDC, 1995) reported that more than 58,000 American women had been diagnosed with AIDS by 1994. The number of women worldwide infected with HIV was at least 4.7 million in 1992 (Mann, Tarantola, & Netter, 1992). The percentage of American women with AIDS has continued to increase; more than 18 percent of all AIDS cases diagnosed in the United States are women (CDC, 1995). AIDS is now the fourth leading cause of death among American women between the ages of 25 and 44 (National Center for Health Statistics, 1994), and the rate of HIV infection is increasing more rapidly in women than in any other population segment (Ickovics & Rodin, 1992). These increases have been especially pronounced among impoverished women of color (McCray, Onorato, & Field Services Branch, 1992; Quinn, Groseclose, Spence, Provost, & Hook, 1992). Although cases of HIV/AIDS in women were reported as early as 1981, it was not until late 1990 that women were routinely included in clinical studies and attention was focused on gender-specific HIV issues (Nakajima & Rubin, 1991).

Women of color living in major urban areas have been particularly affected by the HIV/AIDS epidemic. As of 1994, 76 percent of all reported AIDS cases in women were in women of color; 54 percent were African American, 20 percent were Hispanic, and about 2 percent were Asian or Native American (CDC, 1994). Women with HIV infection are often faced with socioeconomic stressors that exacerbate the negative consequences of HIV for physical and mental well-being (Cochran, 1989; Osmond et al., 1993; Quinn, 1993; Sobo, 1993). The stressors on HIV-infected women with few financial resources are often compounded by the multidimensional responsibilities of being the family's primary caregiver. Women with HIV infection usually live in high-crime areas, can obtain only low-wage jobs with few benefits, are undereducated, and rarely have access to health care facilities except for emergency services (Chu, Buehler, & Berkleman, 1990; Ickovics & Rodin, 1992; Lifshitz, 1990–91; Wofsy, 1987).

This chapter was originally published in the February 1997 issue of *Health & Social Work*, Vol. 22, pp. 53–62.

Recently diagnosed mothers are faced with difficult issues of disclosure, role identity, and parental responsibilities.

ISSUES FACED BY WOMEN WITH HIV/AIDS

Relationship Disruption

Women who share their HIV or AIDS diagnosis with family or friends risk stigmatization (including reactions of fear, shock, and blame), isolation (as a result of others' fears of casual transmission and the possibility of desertion), and potential loss of self-esteem (lack of confidence and self-blame). Keeping the diagnosis of HIV a secret may hinder a woman's ability to develop effective coping strategies and leave her vulnerable to fear, anger, and depression. These problems may worsen as the progression of HIV disease creates significant changes in behavior, attitudes, and physical appearance.

Two studies found stigma and shame to be prominent themes in determining women's HIV disclosure to medical professionals, family, and friends (Chung & Magraw, 1992; Florence, Lutzen, & Alexius, 1994). Women in these studies frequently reported health care professionals to be hostile, fearful, and lacking in knowledge; HIV-related gynecological complications often had to be explained by the patient to the physician. The women reported that in spite of their HIV infection, family members expected them to remain in the role of primary child and family caregiver. In addition, the women often feared a more rapid disease progression, no longer viewed themselves as attractive or desirable, felt that their reproductive rights were socially disapproved, and feared they could lose custody of their children if others became aware of their HIV status.

The need for better understanding of the psychosocial needs of women with HIV infection is widely recognized. Women living with HIV often report a desire for support groups or individual therapy to deal with the depression, hopelessness, and anxiety surrounding the unpredictability of disease progression. Development of effective support services is particularly challenging with impoverished women, for whom HIV infection is but one of many life stressors (Cates, Graham, Boeglin, & Tielker, 1990; Chung & Magraw, 1992; Kelly, 1992; Kelly, Murphy, Sikkema, & Kalichman, 1993; Murphy, Bahr, Kelly, Bernstein, & Morgan, 1992; Reidy, Taggart, & Asselein, 1991; Tiblier, Walker, & Rolland, 1989; Wofsy, 1987; Zuckerman & Gordon, 1988).

Family Caregiving Concerns

Traditional family caregiving responsibilities of HIV-infected women are often complicated by lack of social support and feelings of grief and loss. Chung and Magraw (1992) reported that HIV-positive women have a strong negative reaction to crisis situations and receive less social support at such times. Strong emotional attachment to loved ones and the nurturing demands placed on women by their family members may create significant stress. Although society assigns nurturing responsibilities to women in crisis situations, little value is placed on these services. The care recipient receives the benefit, often to the detriment of the caregiver's physical and mental health.

As women living with AIDS struggle to continue caregiving responsibilities, they must also wrestle with the grief and loss issues that accompany their own terminal illness. Anger and frustration about future goals, mourning of the loss of a long life, and the risk of losing custody of their children as a result of their HIV status were identified as common bereavement issues among HIV-infected women (Sherr et al., 1993). Women living with AIDS also grieve the loss of their family unit.

Effects of Disclosure on Children

The decision to disclose HIV illness places a complex burden on the mother. Parents often have difficulty discussing their HIV status with their children and—in those instances when a child is also infected—discussing the youngster's illness (Nagler, Adnopoz, & Forsyth, 1995). HIV-infected mothers may experience overwhelming guilt regarding their belief that their behaviors have brought harm directly (in vitro infection) or indirectly (leaving orphans through death) to their children.

Young children are often aware of the emerging uncertainty in their lives. Children of HIV-infected mothers seen in therapy and not previously told of their parent's infection frequently report knowing something was wrong but feeling unable to ask about the cause (Nagler et al., 1995). Older, noninfected children told of the parent's diagnosis are often sworn to secrecy and may be the parent's sole confidant. Adolescents' need to deal with anticipatory grief for parents or siblings and with issues regarding their own future, safety, and mortality may go unmet (Johnston, Martin, Martin, & Gumaer, 1992; Nagler et al., 1995). In some cases, the children of AIDS-diagnosed mothers lacking health care access refused to attend school so they could stay by their mother's side for fear she would die while they were gone (Tiblier et al., 1989).

Guardianship Issues

By 2000 the number of children and adolescents in the United States who will have lost their parents to AIDS is expected to reach between 82,000 and 125,000 (Levine, 1995). Making custody arrangements for children is often difficult and painful. Many HIV-infected women lack funds for and access to legal counsel. Mistrust of the legal system in many communities of color may contribute to the belief that disclosure of HIV status will result in immediate loss of custody (Siegel & Gorey, 1994). Many states do not allow for identification of a standby guardian. A mother may have the choice of naming a guardian in her will (which may not be court honored), filing guardianship papers, giving up parental decision-making rights, or even losing custody.

Cultural beliefs may also influence whether a mother makes formal guardianship arrangements. Particularly within ethnic communities of color, women may assume that others within their family systems will step into the parent role after their death. Relatives—even distant cousins—often consider it a duty to care for a sick family member (Groce, 1995). If there are several children, it may be difficult or impossible to place them together. Siblings who develop strong interdependence during their mother's HIV illness may be separated late in the mother's illness or after her death, compounding their feelings of fear, grief, and abandonment (Hudis, 1995; Siegel & Gorey, 1994).

Adolescents, who often assume early caregiving responsibilities for the sick parent, may not want to surrender those responsibilities and return to a dependent role. Hudis (1995) reported that adolescents of mothers with AIDS often exhibit destructive behaviors including criminal activity, drug use, and pregnancy, all of which complicate custody arrangements and also place the adolescent at risk of infection.

METHOD

The present study sought to identify the salient life issues and coping strategies used by HIV-positive women. Intensive semistructured interviews were conducted to explore the women's experiences with the HIV diagnosis and the processes through which they attempted to accept, adapt to, and prioritize aspects of the disease in their daily lives. The interview quotations that follow illuminate the issues faced by women living with HIV as both medical patients and family caretakers and illustrate how these issues influence their coping abilities and mechanisms. Of interest were the women's immediate reactions to the HIV diagnosis, the coping skills they used after learning of their diagnosis, their use of established social networks as a support system, their perception of their coping ability, and anticipation of the future.

Interview Protocol

The interviews consisted of a series of open-ended probe questions designed to elicit a narrative describing primary concerns and coping issues. Each woman was told that the interview purpose was to get a sense of how she was doing with HIV, what she saw as the main challenges confronting her, and how she dealt with these challenges. All interviews were conducted by a clinician experienced in qualitative, open-ended interviewing.

A range of psychosocial and coping issues were probed by the interviewer (Table 36-1). These open-ended questions focused on diagnosis, emotional response, disclosure, intimacy, affect, and future plans, and mirroring statements elicited additional information on inquiry areas. Interviews required about one hour. In addition to the semistructured interview, each woman completed the Beck Depression Inventory (BDI) (Beck & Steer, 1993), a well-standardized measure of clinical depression (Drebing et al., 1994; Volk, Pace, & Parchman,

Table 36-1

Sample Interview Questions

Topic	Questions
Diagnosis	What made you decide to get tested?
	How did you learn of your diagnosis?
	Was there anything that made you feel you might be at risk?
Emotional response	How did you react to hearing that you were HIV positive?
	What was your strongest feeling after learning that you were HIV positive?
	Where did you go and who did you talk with right after learning you were HIV positive?
Disclosure	Have you discussed your diagnosis with anyone?
	Who was the first person you told, and why?
	What has been the response of the people you've told?
	Have you told your children?
Intimacy	How is your relationship going now?
	In what ways does your man give you support?
	How did you feel when he walked out?
	Since you and your partner are both positive, how often do you discuss your status?
	Who in your life gives you the most emotional support?
Affect	Could you describe an average day since you learned of your HIV status?
	How well do you feel you're dealing with the diagnosis now?
	What is the hardest part of having HIV?
	What helps you most in dealing with HIV?
Future concerns and plans	What is your biggest concern?
	What are you most afraid of?
	What do you hope for?
	What do you feel might help you cope more effectively?
	Where does HIV rank in the order of other things you have to deal with in your life?
	What are your expectations now?

1993). Each of the 21 items is rated on a scale from 0 to 3, with a cutoff score of 16 indicative of possible depression (Beck & Steer, 1993). The mean BDI score for the eight participants was 22.9 (SD = 12.9; range, 0 to 37), indicating significant levels of depression.

Participants

Participants were recruited for the study from a hospital-based infectious disease outpatient clinic affiliated with the Medical College of Wisconsin. Women attending the clinic learned of the study through signs in the waiting room and face-to-face contact with staff. All the women lived in the Milwaukee area, and participants received a small incentive payment for their participation.

Eight women completed the semistructured interviews. Five of the women were African American, two were white, and one was

Hispanic. The mean age of the women was 35.6 years (range, 23 to 47), and their mean education level was 12 years (range, 11 to 14). On average, it had been 11 months since HIV diagnosis (range, 1 to 46 months); two of the women already had an AIDS diagnosis, whereas the others were asymptomatic or at earlier stages of disease progression. Clinic records indicated that the women had a mean T cell count of 594 (range, 123 to 1,050) at the time of the interview. Five women reported being involved in an intimate relationship. Seven of the eight women had children, and one mother was pregnant. The children ranged from two to 25 years old, and only four children of the study women (ages 16, 18, 23, and 25) knew of their mothers' diagnosis.

Interview Coding

All interviews were audiorecorded with the written consent of the participant. Audiotapes of the interviews were then transcribed. Transcriptions were coded by a clinical social worker experienced in qualitative analysis to determine the frequency with which participants raised key thematic issues during the interview. Because we did not know in advance which issues would be raised most frequently, thematic categories were compiled during the coding process. Participant statements during the full interview were coded into categories such that each thematic statement would be counted as one thematic occurrence. Although longer responses sometimes elicited additional thematic issues, length of response within a theme area did not increase the count frequency; short and lengthy responses addressing the same thematic issue each were counted as one occurrence of the theme.

FINDINGS

Concerns of Women Diagnosed with HIV Infection

The primary concerns of the women in the study were stigma (46 thematic citations); child concerns and caretaking roles (36 thematic citations); social support needs (33 thematic citations); concerns about death, dying, and despair (33 citations); and HIV/AIDS information needs (26 thematic citations) (Table 36-2).

Stigma. Issues of rejection, shame, and the potential loss of future relationships were the concerns the women raised most frequently. The women feared disclosing their HIV status because of perceived family, peer, and societal rejection. One woman indicated that it would be better to suffer in silence than to face social judgments about her. The potential shame, particularly from extended family, was expressed by one woman who, after disclosing her HIV status to her brother, said she felt that "he looks down on me. I think he feels I've shamed him. He doesn't want me to come around anymore." Difficulties establishing and maintaining intimate relationships were often raised; one woman simply asked, "Who's going to want me now?" Another participant reported, "I had another concern about me being

Table 36-2

Primary Life Concerns Reported by Women Living with HIV

Concern Theme	Number of Times Cited	Specific Concern and Number of Citations
Stigma	46	Disclosure may result in societal rejection (28)
		Extended family is threatened by potential shame (14)
		Diagnosis negatively affects future relationships (4)
Child care concerns and roles	36	Woman failed to protect children from caretaking crisis (14)
		No responsible person has been identified to care for children (13)
		Children will be stigmatized by parent's diagnosis (9)
Social support needs	33	Woman expressed desire for support networks (21)
		Disclosure isolates and prevents reaching out to others (12)
Death, dying, and despair	33	Woman feels sense of hopelessness (19)
		Woman fears the dying process (9)
		Suicide is an alternative to anticipated suffering (5)
HIV/AIDS information needs	26	Woman believes imminent death is medical prognosis (21)
		Availability of psychological resources is unknown (5)

young and single and wanting to be with somebody, and then what am I supposed to do? You know, I say, 'Hi, I'm HIV positive'?"

Child Concerns and Caretaking Roles. Parental caregiving issues were the second most frequently raised concern of these HIV-infected women: "The scariest thing for me right now is I'm pregnant, and we're both worried about whether the baby will pick this up. That's pretty scary." Other concerns frequently involved identification and quality of guardianship: "He [my son] will be here all alone, and I feel like I've failed him." "I don't have anyone in my family responsible enough to take care of my 12-year-old." "My biggest challenge is finding some place for my children." They were also worried about the inability to protect their children from crisis ("My biggest worry right now is how I'm going to tell my daughter.") and about stigma resulting from the parent's diagnosis ("I don't want my children to be looked at funny because of something that I'm going through." "I'm scared because I don't want my kids to be isolated.").

Social Support Needs. The women's responses indicated two significant areas of social support concern: a strong desire for support networks and a fear of reaching out because of the ostracism that can follow HIV status disclosure. Perceived feelings of isolation were consistently present throughout these women's interviews: "I know I'm not the only one, but it feels like I am." "The hardest part is not being able to share, to talk about it." "I don't do too much socializing. I find myself crying, just crying a lot." The primary reason given by the women for wanting social support was to have an environment in which they could openly share their fears and feelings with people who were experiencing the same types of isolation and pressure.

Concerns about Death, Dying, and Despair. Intense feelings of hopelessness, fear of suffering during the dying process, and suicidal thoughts were consistently discussed by these participants. Illustrating these themes, the women said, "We all know that we live, we die, but when it hits you, you know, it's strange." "We're [HIV-positive people are] just sittin' around, you know, and waitin' to die." "Sometimes I feel that I appreciate things more, and then there are other times that I can't really feel as happy as I once did about anything. Like there's a shadow over me."

HIV/AIDS Information Needs. The belief that the HIV diagnosis meant imminent death and the perceived lack of psychosocial resource supports were reported as key information issues. The lack of medical information regarding the prognosis for living with HIV created confusion for many of these women. The women knew they had HIV, but most felt they knew little else about the disease. One woman was told that her pregnancy could cause a false-positive test result. Even after diagnosis, several women did not understand transmission routes, how to get HIV prevention information, or how to find physicians who specialize in HIV/AIDS treatment. Most women interviewed believed that an HIV diagnosis meant that they had AIDS and would die within a year or two. Several had thoughts of suicide immediately after being diagnosed.

When questioned about their interest in support groups, most of the women stated that they had no idea where to begin looking for a group. One woman spoke of halfway-house residents who wanted to start an HIV-positive support group but were unable to find a resource to help them. Several women indicated that they would be happy to attend a gay men's group but felt there were specific female issues (such as gynecological and child care concerns) that would not be covered. The lack of available psychosocial resources was described by one participant who reported, "I went to a support group meeting, stayed there over three hours, and nobody showed up."

Coping Strategies Used by Women with HIV Infection

The interviews were next coded to identify coping strategies being used by the women. The primary coping strategies were denial (48 thematic citations), concealment of their health status from others (32 citations), isolation from others (23 citations), and crying (15 citations) (Table 36-3).

Table 36-3

Primary Coping Strategies Reported by Women Living with HIV

Coping Strategy	Number of Times Cited	Specific Concern and Number of Citations
Denial	48	Use of distractions for avoidance (26)
		Refusal to accept the diagnosis (12)
		Blocking or blunting thoughts of HIV/AIDS (10)
Concealment	32	Fear of societal stigmatization and rejection (23)
		Desire to avoid placing stressors on children (7)
		Fear of abandonment by current or future partners (2)
Isolation	23	Isolation to avoid potential rejection (13)
		Depression-related isolation (for example, self-blame) (10)
Crying	15	Intensity and frequency of crying (8)
		Emotional response to pent-up needs (7)

Denial. The emotion-focused coping strategy of denial was characterized by the use of distractions, blocking or blunting techniques, and nonacceptance of the HIV diagnosis. Typical denial responses included, "I block it out, I try not to deal with it." "I try to block it away and say 'No, this can't be true,' because I guess that it would help me to be a little stronger in a sense, you know, to deal with it." "I'm just not going to believe that I am [dying], and maybe I won't."

Concealment of Health Status. Fears of social rejection and stigma, additional external stressors on their children, and potential abandonment by a partner were reasons given for the use of concealment as a coping strategy. One woman disclosed the following: "I told my pastor, and he told someone else in church. Several people in church know now, so I don't even go back to church. I know people were looking at me real funny." Another participant, who had lived in a halfway house, spoke of personal safety issues: "I didn't share it [my diagnosis] with any other women until I got out of the [halfway] house because I knew it probably would have been fatal." One woman regretted telling her mother. Although two of the women had disclosed to older teenage children, all women we interviewed continued to conceal their HIV status from their younger children: "I don't think she [my daughter] has any idea that I have HIV." "He [my son] knows something, but he doesn't know I'm HIV positive. He knows there is something wrong and it's more than headaches."

Isolation from Others. To avoid rejection by others, some participants used isolation as a coping strategy to protect themselves. This strategy was described by women in the following ways: "I can't tell them I'm HIV, nobody would come around here and help me." "I won't even answer the door if it's them [my family members]. I'll let the phone ring and let the voice mail pick it up."

Crying. As a coping response to emotional distress, participants reported increased intensity and frequency of crying. This coping strategy was used most often when the women were unable to discuss their fears ("When I'm depressed and I can't talk about it, I just cry a lot") and when denial failed ("I try to block it out, but when I can't block it out, I start crying"). Women reported, "I just want to be alone and just cry" and "I just started crying, and she [a friend] asked what's wrong, what's going on, and I told her I'm going to die."

DISCUSSION

These HIV-infected women experienced significant levels of stigma that severely affected their parental caregiving, social support, and health-seeking roles. In addition, the women frequently used ineffective coping strategies such as denial, concealment, and isolation. The findings show that women living with HIV have special needs in the areas of social services, support systems, and stressors related to their dual roles of being patients and family caretakers. These needs can be addressed by health care systems providing services to HIV-infected women.

A theme that emerged in the interviews was the women's ongoing struggle to balance their own health concerns with the demands and needs of their families. Although several women in the study described positive lifestyle changes (such as getting off drugs and eating more nutritious food), most of their attention seemed to be focused on maintaining a happy environment for their children in spite of debilitating illness.

For most of the women we interviewed, silence regarding the HIV diagnosis required hiding medication (or, in the case of one woman, refusing medication) to avoid children's questions about their health. Medical appointments were often scheduled when children were in school or when child care could be arranged. Even women who had cared for dying partners rarely told their children of their own need for hospitalization. Women in our study reported that increased HIV-related fatigue was handled by sleeping during the day when possible. However, this resulted in increased guilt when household chores and meal preparation were not completed when children arrived home.

All of the women described strong feelings of guilt and concern for their children's future. Regardless of transmission route, the women generally expressed guilt about becoming infected. Several women perceived that becoming infected meant they had failed their children. Although two of the women had disclosed their HIV illness to older children, most mothers were reluctant to disclose the illness until it was absolutely necessary. The tenor of these women's interviews indicated their need to maintain a sense of parental status and dignity and to protect their children's well-being.

Social Services Needs of Women with HIV

Support groups and individual therapy services offered on site in health care settings should be routinely made available to women with HIV. Support groups can offer a safe forum to address issues of loss (for example, partner, children, job); to share ideas about healthy life choices; to express anger toward the disease; and to discuss child care, relationship, and body image issues. Individual therapy assists clients with resolution of low self-esteem and negative family dynamics, realistic goal setting, and disease acceptance. Gender-specific treatment models that help disadvantaged women of color address their stress management, support building, self-efficacy, and self-esteem enhancement needs are especially important. Such methods would offer alternatives to the ineffective coping skills that women in this study reported using.

Interventions, while focusing on the women's needs, must also provide supportive services to their family systems as the women define them. Group or individual interventions directed toward those affected (HIV-positive or -negative children, spouses or partners, and extended family members) can augment a woman's support network, facilitating increased HIV/AIDS knowledge, social contact, and a more effective approach to problem solving. Family members should be provided with information on medical treatment as well as mental health and social services (including respite care) resources. Family education can help women consolidate their support resources before they become seriously ill. Perhaps most important, such approaches may help destigmatize HIV within the family unit. Affected individuals, particularly children, may benefit from family-focused therapies in a safe environment where it is acceptable to express fears, anger, and anticipatory grief. It is likely that garnering expanded and diverse systems of support will help HIV-infected women develop coping methods other than denial, concealment, or isolation as primary coping techniques.

Role of Health Care Systems

Current traditional medical models were ineffective in meeting the psychosocial needs of the women living with HIV/AIDS in this study. An integrated health care system directed toward women's overall health may more effectively meet the unique challenges of HIV-positive women. Low-cost clinic transportation and on-site child care would eliminate two major access barriers. Health care professionals must allocate time to fully explain aspects of HIV illness, the importance and possible side effects of medications, and ways to overcome socioeconomic barriers to care regimens. HIV treatment clinics accustomed earlier in the epidemic to providing care to gay men with HIV disease—a group often knowledgeable about AIDS care—may require considerable adaptation of their service programs to meet the different needs of disenfranchised women with few financial resources.

Services to improve the mental and emotional health of HIV-infected women include support groups, individual counseling, instruction in relaxation, stress management and meditation practices, and skills-building training in the development of effective coping strategies. Social services professionals can also assist women in completing complex medical and disability forms and provide information on low-cost housing, child care, food pantries, and other services in the neighborhood. Caregiving support programs can offer women information on subjects ranging from respite care, living wills, and guardianship designation to funeral planning and spiritual development. Agencies should develop systems models to provide access to multiple medical, social, and informational services in a stigma-free environment. Research is required on the cost-effectiveness of care and the impact on the length and quality of life of those being served by comprehensive social health care models.

CONCLUSION

This study has several limitations. As an in-depth qualitative study, the number of women participating in it was small, and they had known of their HIV diagnosis, on average, for less than one year. Because all interviews were conducted by a single interviewer, it will be important to replicate these findings in other interview contexts.

Additional research is needed to determine whether coping issues and needs change over time elapsed since diagnosis, the extent to which these findings generalize to women in other areas and in other care systems, and the influence of newer HIV treatment regimens on coping. Those who carry the heaviest responsibility for the survival of the family are given the least recognition or support. Women living with HIV/AIDS are not invisible, just ignored; not weak, just weary; not defeated, just dying.

REFERENCES

Beck, A. T., & Steer, R. A. (1993). *BDI: Beck Depression Inventory manual.* New York: Psychological Corporation.
Cates, J., Graham, L., Boeglin, D., & Tielker, S. (1990). The effects of AIDS on the family system. *Families in Society, 71,* 195–201.
Centers for Disease Control and Prevention. (1994). *HIV/AIDS Surveillance Report, 6*(2), 12, 31.
Centers for Disease Control and Prevention. (1995). Update: AIDS among women—United States, 1994. *Morbidity and Mortality Weekly Report, 44,* 81–84.
Chu, S., Buehler, J., & Berkleman, R. (1990). Impact of the human immunodeficiency virus epidemic on mortality in women of reproductive age, United States. *JAMA, 264,* 225–229.
Chung, J. Y., & Magraw, M. M. (1992). An approach to psychosocial issues faced by HIV positive women. *Hospital and Community Psychiatry, 43,* 891–894.
Cochran, S. D. (1989). Women and HIV infection: Issues in prevention and behavior change. In W. M. Mays, G. W. Albee, & S. F. Schneider (Eds.), *Primary prevention of AIDS: Psychological approaches* (pp. 309–327). Newbury Park, CA: Sage Publications.

Drebing, C. L., Van Gorp, W. G., Hinkin, D., Miller, E. N., Satz, P., Kim, D. S., Holston, S., & D'Elia, L. F. (1994). Confounding factors in the measurement of depression in HIV. *Journal of Personality Assessment, 62,* 68–83.

Florence, M., Lutzen, K., & Alexius, B. (1994). Adaptation of heterosexual infected HIV-positive women: A Swedish pilot study. *Health Care for Women International, 15,* 265–273.

Groce, N. E. (1995). Children and AIDS in a multicultural perspective. In S. Geballe, J. Gruendel, & W. Andemann (Eds.), *Forgotten children of the AIDS epidemic* (pp. 95–106). New Haven, CT: Yale University.

Hudis, J. (1995). Adolescents living in families with AIDS. In S. Geballe, J. Gruendel, & W. Andemann (Eds.), *Forgotten children of the AIDS epidemic* (pp. 83–94). New Haven, CT: Yale University.

Ickovics, J., & Rodin, J. (1992). Women and AIDS in the United States: Epidemiology, natural history, and mediating mechanisms. *Health Psychology, 11,* 1–16.

Johnston, M., Martin, D., Martin, M., & Gumaer, J. (1992). Long term parental illness and children: Perils and promises. *School Counselor, 39,* 225–231.

Kelly, J. (1992). Psychosocial aspects of AIDS. *Current Opinion in Psychiatry, 5,* 820–824.

Kelly, J., Murphy, D., Sikkema, K., & Kalichman, S. (1993). Psychological interventions to prevent HIV infection are urgently needed: New priorities for behavioral research in the second decade of AIDS. *American Psychologist, 48,* 1023–1034.

Levine, C. (1995). Orphans of the HIV epidemic: Unmet needs in six US cities. *AIDS Care, 7*(Suppl. 1), 557–562.

Lifshitz, A. (1990, December–1991, January). Critical cultural barriers that bar meeting the needs of Latinas. *SIECUS Report,* pp. 16–17.

Mann, J., Tarantola, D. J., & Netter, T. W. (1992). *AIDS in the world: A global report.* Cambridge, MA: Harvard University Press.

McCray, E., Onorato, I. M., & Field Services Branch. (1992, July). Sentinel surveillance of human immunodeficiency virus infection in sexually transmitted disease clinics in the United States. *Sexually Transmitted Diseases, 19*(4), 235–241.

Murphy, D., Bahr, R., Kelly, J., Bernstein, B., & Morgan, M. (1992). A needs assessment survey of HIV-infected patients. *Wisconsin Medical Journal, 91,* 291–295.

Nagler, S., Adnopoz, J., & Forsyth, W. (1995). Uncertainty, stigma, and secrecy: Psychological aspects of AIDS for children and adolescents. In S. Geballe, J. Gruendel, & W. Andemann (Eds.), *Forgotten children of the AIDS epidemic* (pp. 71–82). New Haven, CT: Yale University.

Nakajima, G., & Rubin, H. (1991). Lack of racial, gender, and behavior-risk diversity in psychiatric research on AIDS/HIV in the United States [poster M. B. 2044]. *Proceedings of the Seventh International Conference on AIDS, 1,* 193.

National Center for Health Statistics. (1994). *Annual summary of births, marriages, divorces, and deaths: United States, 1993.* Hyattsville, MD: U.S. Department of Health and Human Services, Public Health Service.

Osmond, M. W., Wambach, K. G., Harrison, D. F., Byers, J., Levine, P., Imershein, A., & Quadagno, D. M. (1993). The multiple jeopardy of race, class, and gender of AIDS risk among women. *Gender & Society, 7,* 99–120.

Quinn, S. (1993). AIDS and the African American woman: The triple burden of race, class, and gender. *Health Education Quarterly, 20,* 305–320.

Quinn, T. C., Groseclose, S. L., Spence, M., Provost, V., & Hook, F. W. (1992). Evolution of the human immunodeficiency virus epidemic among patients attending sexually-transmitted disease clinics: A decade of experience. *Journal of Infectious Diseases, 165,* 558–568.

Reidy, M., Taggart, M. E., & Asselein, L. (1991). Psychosocial needs expressed by the natural caregivers of HIV infected children. *AIDS Care, 3,* 331–343.

Sherr, L., Petrak, J., Melvin, D., Davey, T., Glover, L., & Hedge, B. (1993). Psychological trauma associated with AIDS and HIV infection in women. *Counseling Psychology Quarterly, 6,* 99–108.

Siegel, K., & Gorey, E. (1994). Childhood bereavement due to parental death from acquired immunodeficiency syndrome. *Journal of Developmental and Behavioral Pediatrics, 15,* 581–593.

Sobo, E. J. (1993). Inner-city women and AIDS: The psychosocial benefits of unsafe sex. *Culture, Medicine, and Psychiatry, 17,* 455–485.

Tiblier, K., Walker, G., & Rolland, J. (1989). Therapeutic issues when working with families of persons with AIDS. In E. D. Macklin (Ed.), *AIDS and families: Report of the AIDS Task Force, Groves Conference on Marriage and Family.* New York: Hawthorne.

Volk, R. J., Pace, T. M., & Parchman, M. L. (1993). Screening for depression in primary care patients: Dimensionality of the short form of the Beck Depression Inventory. *Psychological Assessment, 5,* 173–181.

Wofsy, C. (1987). Human immunodeficiency virus infection in women. *JAMA, 257,* 2074–2075.

Zuckerman, C., & Gordon, L. (1988). Meeting the psychosocial and legal needs of women with AIDS and their families. *New York State Journal of Medicine, 88,* 619–620.

This research was supported by center grant #P30-MH52776 from the National Institute of Mental Health. An earlier version of this chapter was presented at the 11th Annual Conference on AIDS, July 1996, Vancouver, BC.

37 Psychological and Spiritual Growth in Women Living with HIV

Heather T. Dunbar, Charles W. Mueller,
Cynthia Medina, and Tamra Wolf

A s of 1996, more than 70,000 women had been diagnosed with AIDS. In 1995 women accounted for 19 percent of new adult and adolescent AIDS cases, the highest yearly percentage ever. Women, and particularly women of color, are the fastest growing group of people with AIDS. From 1992 through 1994 the number of women with AIDS increased 26 percent. In addition, reported adults with HIV (and not AIDS) are even more likely to be women (Centers for Disease Control and Prevention, 1995). HIV and AIDS are particularly affecting young and middle-age women. The median age of women reported with AIDS is 35 years, and women ages 15 to 44 years account for 84 percent of all female cases (Centers for Disease Control and Prevention, 1994). AIDS is the fourth leading cause of death in American women ages 25 to 44 and, in 15 major U.S. cities, the leading cause of death for women in this age group.

Most of the literature on women living with HIV is focused on medical factors or describes the multiple obstacles faced by women living with HIV (for example, Allers & Benjack, 1991; Brown & Rundell, 1993; Campbell, 1990; Hankins, 1990; Hankins & Handley, 1992; Ickovics & Rodin, 1992; Kaplan, 1995; Lea, 1994; Mays & Cochran, 1988; North & Rothenberg, 1993; Seals et al., 1995; Smeltzer, 1992; Zierler et al., 1991). A much smaller theoretical and empirical literature has begun to explore how women living with HIV cope. Using a stress–coping model, studies have examined how factors such as age, medical symptoms, social support, psychological makeup, and cognitive styles influence the stress–coping relationship (for example, Anderson, 1995; Commerford, Gular, Orr, Renznikoff, & O'Dowd, 1994; Florence, Lutzen, & Alexius, 1994; Regan-Kubinski & Sharts-Hopko, 1995; Semple et al., 1993). Implicit in this stress–coping literature is the underlying assumption that these women must adjust to the stress so they can proceed with normal life.

Although the empirical literature has begun to examine important issues related to women with HIV/AIDS, there is a noticeable lack of empirical studies that examine how some women have used the stress of HIV to transform their lives in positive and productive ways.

This chapter was originally published in the March 1998 issue of *Social Work*, Vol. 43, pp. 144–154.

This void is in stark contrast to the "first-person" literature written by women living with HIV. These personal accounts often depict women actively using their HIV diagnosis as a stimulus to healthier and fuller lives (Dunbar & Mueller, 1995). This observation is not meant to suggest that the situations confronting women living with HIV are without pain, suffering, and extreme (and at times, inappropriate) challenges and obstacles. However, the vastly disproportionate focus of the existing literature on negative aspects of HIV, with only a few more recent studies on coping, is unjustified. By failing to recognize the growth some women with HIV have created in themselves, social work professionals can inadvertently minimize the personal strengths and power of their clients. This mindset tends to keep these clients in simple categories (for example, victim) and may impede ethical social work practice, which includes primacy of clients' interests, rights, and prerogatives (National Association of Social Workers, 1996).

In an earlier study, we analyzed published firsthand accounts of women living with HIV and AIDS and developed a tentative model describing their process of growth (Dunbar & Mueller, 1995). We proposed a model of "transcendence" that identified four critical, interrelated components. First, these women's accounts reflected a process of introspection about themselves, their past, and their current ways of coping. Second, many accounts described a process of life affirmation that often served as a strong motivational base for coping. Third, many women described reconceptualizing time, with the recognition of impending death and the intention to live in the present. Fourth, some women described a new or renewed sense of unity with others and the world as a whole. Although this model provided a new way of conceptualizing the experiences of women living with HIV, it was based on post hoc analyses of published accounts. Such analyses are subject to numerous problems, including extremely selective sampling (only women who were able and had the opportunity to publish) and subjective interpretation biases of the authors.

The present study was designed to explore the gap between the positive anecdotal accounts of psychological and spiritual growth and the more problem-focused quantitative studies of women living with HIV. Specifically, the study attempted to answer three questions. First, will "everyday," unpublished women living with HIV describe positive aspects of living with HIV when asked? Second, how well would our model, as described in Dunbar and Mueller (1995), reflect these descriptions? Third, how could our ideas be revised given the accounts provided by these women? The findings reported in this chapter are based on data from a larger qualitative study focused on multiple facets of women's experiences living with HIV.

METHOD

Participants

Thirty-four confirmed HIV-positive women participated in this study (at least six of the participants have died since being interviewed).

Participants were between the ages of 26 and 53, with an average age of 36. Twenty-five (74 percent) participants were mothers (mean number of children = 1.79). About one-third (11) had known of their HIV status for more than five years. Thirteen participants had AIDS diagnoses, 39 percent had entered or completed college, nearly one-third were employed at the time of the interview, and about one-third were in current relationships with an HIV-positive partner (Table 37-1). The ethnic composition of the participants was diverse, with 15 (44 percent) women reflecting the rich mix of heritages in the community studied, including Hawaiian, Filipina, Chinese, Portuguese, Japanese, Hispanic, African American, and white. All women contacted by the research team agreed to participate in the study.

Many of the participants had histories of trauma. Eighty-two percent ($n = 28$) of the participants reported, without direct prompting, having been physically or sexually assaulted. Many described histories of severe substance abuse or earned income via the sex industry, often for nearly all of their adult lives. The lifelong hardships many of these women had faced make the current findings related to healing and growth all the more remarkable, hopeful, and important.

Procedures

Women were recruited on a statewide basis. Participation was voluntary, with referrals made by AIDS service organizations, chemical

Table 37-1

Demographic Characteristics of the Participants

Characteristic	n	%
Current HIV status		
Asymptomatic	14	41
Symptomatic	7	21
AIDS	13	38
Highest educational achievement[a]		
< High school graduate	5	15
High school graduate	15	44
Some college	8	24
≥ College graduate	5	15
Current employment status		
Unemployed	24	71
Employed	10	29
Current partner's HIV status[b]		
Positive	11	32
Negative	8	24
Unknown	7	21
No partner	8	24

[a]Missing value for one participant.
[b]These values do not represent women whose partners had already died from an AIDS-related illness. Some were involved in new relationships, and others were not.

dependency treatment programs, community health and homeless outreach workers, physicians, women's clinics, press releases, public service announcements, and prior participants' word of mouth.

Potential participants (or their surrogates, for example, a case manager) were asked to call a telephone number established for use in this study. A prerecorded message asked them to suggest a way to be reached so that confidentiality and security were maintained. During this return call the procedures and goals of the study were explained and an interview time and location arranged. Interviews were conducted in interviewers' or participants' homes or in other private locations such as a church meeting room or a secluded area of a park. Before the interview, participants reviewed and signed a detailed informed consent form. All interviews were audio recorded. At the completion of the interview, each participant received a $50 cash compensation.

Interviews ranged from 90 to 210 minutes. Twice interviews required two sessions. As expected, many interviews were extremely emotionally laden. Interviewers recognized the need for and worked toward developing an honest alliance with the participants. For many of the participants, this created a unique opportunity to talk openly about their feelings related to their HIV status. At times, interviews were interrupted to give the participant an opportunity to release feelings (for example, cry) and recover. For risk-mitigation purposes, on-call access to a licensed mental health professional outside of the research team was maintained. However, these services were not required and were not called on during the course of this study.

Interviews were semistructured, consisting of open-ended questions followed by prompts to elicit further information or clarification. Eleven general content areas were discussed, roughly in the following order: (1) immediate impressions after diagnosis, (2) history of HIV-related medical events, (3) HIV as a source of stress, (4) coping strategies, (5) impact of prior life experiences on living with HIV, (6) positive outcomes of living with HIV, (7) specific questions about the model of transcendence from our earlier research, (8) experiences with HIV service providers, (9) desire for further formal or informal support, (10) advice or recommendations to other women living with HIV, and (11) demographic information.

Interviewers were careful to fully explore the self-generated descriptions of growth in response to the open-ended questions before they mentioned any words or concepts from the Dunbar and Mueller (1995) model. Specifically, in part 6, women were asked, "Some women speak of responding positively in the face of this very serious illness. In your experience living with HIV/AIDS, have you experienced any unexpected good or positive outcomes?" This question was followed by various prompts (for example, "Anything else?" "Any other positives?" "Could you tell me more about that?"). Participants were then asked about factors they believed made an impact on these positive outcomes. Only then were participants exposed to the Dunbar and Mueller model. We felt that this tunnel technique, from open-ended to specific questions, allowed for spontaneous unbiased descriptions and, later, comments about the earlier model.

All tape recordings were reviewed, and verbatim responses were recorded and organized into a text management program (AskSam for Windows, 1994). Total transcribed material exceeded 500 single-spaced typewritten pages. At the completion of the study, all participants were invited to attend a half-day luncheon and debriefing where initial findings were presented, discussed, and reformulated as indicated.

In this chapter, we report on responses that organized under two categories: positive outcomes of living with HIV and the model of transcendence. Some participants spoke of positive aspects before we asked specifically about this, and these responses were included in our analysis.

FINDINGS

Before or when asked whether they had discovered any unexpected positive outcomes in the face of this very serious illness, 28 of the 34 women (82 percent) answered in the affirmative. These women spoke of rebuilt relationships, newfound values, a new sense of meaning and purpose, profound self-awareness and self-acceptance, and discoveries of connections with nature, God, and higher powers. They reported being able to use the pain and despair of the HIV diagnosis as an opportunity for self-awareness and growth, and some women described a profound healing in their lives that made room for a richer existence. Clearly, the recognition and assimilation of positive, growth-related outcomes is not restricted to a select few women living with HIV, a fact that has important practice implications.

We found mixed evidence about how well our earlier model fit. First, in answer to the open-ended questions, very few women explicitly used terms from the model; the tone of their responses reflected a more worldly and practical and a less philosophical view than inherent in the earlier model, and new or modified themes emerged that we will explore later in this chapter. Second, when shown the model (a listing of the four components and a brief description of each), nearly all the women who had described positive outcomes stated they recognized some truth or suitability to the model. Indeed, some women simply replied that these topics were already covered earlier in the discussion. However, no participant indicated that the model was exactly right.

As we worked through the data, we realized that our tentative model should be modified. Five rather than four themes emerged: reckoning with death, life affirmation, creation of meaning, self-affirmation, and redefining relationships.

Reckoning with Death

On testing positive for HIV, many women described a period of shock and denial, eventually followed by a reckoning with their own impending death.

> The only difference between me and you at this point . . . is that I know I might leave my body sooner than I thought I might. It only puts me closer to knowing that I'm mortal.

* * *

> I think AIDS brought the reality of death right home.

Some participants reported facing the prospect of death soon after testing positive for HIV, but others took years to break through the shock, psychic numbing, and denial. For some, their own or a partner's AIDS symptoms led to a more active confrontation of death. For others it was simply a matter of having time to reflect that allowed them to face the prospect of dying. Regardless, women described the period of reckoning as a painful process associated with feelings of hopelessness, despair, and rage. This began a period of grieving for the imminent loss of life:

> I went through these classes at the [community HIV organization], picturing your own death and who would be there and stuff, and that tore me up. Even to this day too, I still cry for myself when I think of that, and I am not only crying for me but for all the other people out there that are losing and dying. I am crying for the world.

As this woman described it, acceptance of death was not an event, but rather a process wherein she periodically needed to reconsider her relationship with death. Several women described this process of cyclical reconsideration with deepening levels of acceptance.

For several women with long substance abuse histories, this reckoning came with sobriety, and one described her struggle to remain sober in the face of such intense challenges:

> I couldn't medicate, and so I had to feel, and I didn't understand feelings anyway. I'm still trying to understand them. It was really hard for me to understand.

Letting go of the denial was also described by some as a release. Women described finally being able to cry "from the heart, not just the eyes." This reckoning with death led to growth for these women. It has been argued that chaos is an omen of psychological growth (Butz, 1992; Gleik, 1987). For many of these women, the chaos that came with this reckoning led to psychological and spiritual development.

Life Affirmation

Many women who spoke of reckoning with death described a subsequent discovery of the will to live. Affirming life in the face of a fatal illness is profound, for in the face of death, life takes on a different meaning. As Rychlak (1981) aptly asserted, life and death exist in such a way that they mutually imply and define one another. Ironically, it was the participants who decided to live consciously and fully who seemed to experience the greatest grief. One participant described a period of depression in which she tried to numb herself with excessive substance use. She came out of her depression slowly as a result of affirming her will to live:

> The other day I was in the car with my daughter, she was driving. And I was really happy. We'd been up to [a scenic overlook], and I'd had a real nice day. It was a beautiful view that I saw on the top—it was just gorgeous! And in the car afterwards I was feeling, "God! I'm gonna lose all this." I felt good, but at the same time I started crying, 'cause I thought, I don't want to lose all this.

Paradoxically, the "death sentence" of HIV provides the opportunity to commit to life redefined. Many participants reported the need to choose to give up or to live well:

> You finally realize that you have to live with it or else you will die, so you have to accept it and I think face it head on.

And some participants grew to fully embrace the prospect of death:

> The life affirmation is never ending until we actually die . . . and still we affirm life because death is a part of life, something that is to be embraced and not feared.

As these women described it, a prominent aspect of this redefinition of life is a reconsideration of values. Life was recognized as finite, and thus time became more precious to these women. Participants spoke repeatedly of reprioritizing and redefining values with respect to how to spend the time they had:

> I went through a process where I would see beauty in real simple things: flowers, a rainbow, these mountains, a rainstorm, a pond, a river. I never stopped to notice these things before. Yeah, you saw a rainbow, but now a rainbow represents to me the entire life force. I treasure a sunset in my heart. It's a deeper appreciation. . . . I think I have been on a steady course of becoming less materialistic . . . that is just not important anymore.

Creation of Meaning

To live fully in recognition of death, some women spoke of finding new meaning in life. Many of these women described a period of life review as the first step in finding new purpose. For several participants, the affirmation to live consciously required examining and working through unresolved past issues. These women spoke of reviewing past histories of trauma and abuse and reframing the painful incidents such that their survival was a tribute to their strength. "I truly believe that when you survive suffering you have a whole f___ing lot to give. If I was brought up with a silver spoon in my mouth . . . I'd definitely be dead." Other women spoke of becoming more firmly rooted in their spiritual selves and finding meaning this way:

> Well, we're in a body, here on this earth. We have some sort of purpose for being here; it may not be clear to us in this whole life-time what that purpose is, but we have a purpose. And it may not be some huge purpose. It may be only to learn patience, virtue, kindness.

A deeply understood life meaning can translate into a focused purpose for the remainder of life. Like the woman quoted below, several women found this purpose in educating others about HIV and AIDS:

> You know, even if I just reach one person, then this disease didn't come to me in vain, and there was a reason for me having it. And hopefully through my experiences, strength, and hope, it might prevent somebody else from getting it.

Self-Affirmation

As past experiences became better integrated and life became more purposeful, these women spoke of finding a more positive sense of self. Many women saw HIV as an opportunity to care for themselves, whereas in the past their focus had been almost exclusively on care of others. A particularly challenging aspect of self-care for these women was asking for help from others. As HIV affected their physical health, many participants found themselves unable to maintain home, employment, and child care responsibilities. Given that identities were bound with these roles, it was very difficult for these women to confront new physical limitations. One woman described it this way:

> It's devastating when you are a woman and you have a child and you can't do the kinds of things that your child wants you to do.... Having to ask for help has been a difficult task for me, but I finally learned how to do it.

The discovery of HIV became a bridge for women to integrate self-care into the role of caregiver. Many participants used their HIV status as an opportunity to reframe thoughts about selfishness and self-nurturance:

> You know, I think as a mother, as a woman, as a wife, I am always taking care of everybody else.... But I finally realized that ... if I don't start taking care of my own self, then I am not going to be around to take care of anybody else.

Redefining Relationships

With their new outlook on life, many women spoke of resolving and clarifying relationships with family, friends, and acquaintances. Participants spoke repeatedly in these interviews about becoming more honest in their relationships with others. This included ending relationships that did not meet new, more discriminating and honest criteria:

> I was able to get out of a relationship that I was engaged. I was keeping myself in that situation for financial purposes, for security, for all the wrong reasons. . . . I kept trying to have everyone else love me and accept me when I wasn't doing it for myself.

Women also spoke of evaluating the significance of friendships and nonintimate relationships in their lives. Many women felt they no longer had the time or energy to give to relationships that did not meet their needs:

> I am a lot harder on myself and on other people that I see. . . . I don't try to fix people any more. . . . I don't wait around for it to happen. . . . I'm very intolerant with people that I feel are wasting their life away. . . . Who I choose as friends is different.

Several participants also described resolving long-standing problems in intimate relationships. One woman spoke poignantly of asking her father to join her in therapy:

> Having my dad come and do that therapy work was really helpful because it answered questions like "whys" of certain situations and incidences. He was surprised about some of the feelings that I had but, hey, I felt I got it all cleared out. I mean not like eternally, but to where if I were to pass away tomorrow, I would have left a clean slate with my dad.

Facilitative Factors

First indirectly and then directly, we asked participants to identify factors that facilitated or supported the positive experiences they had discussed. Responses were quite variable, and the most valid conclusion we can draw from these data is that each woman's process of growth was uniquely her own. However, three common themes emerged.

First, the availability of accurate knowledge about HIV; accepting nonjudgmental responses from others; and emotional, spiritual, and social support were the most commonly cited facilitative factors external to the participant. The support of others came from friends and family, from other people with HIV or AIDS, and from an accepting community. Being able to share with others the pain of living with the disease enhanced the healing process for many women. Many participants spoke about struggling with whom to inform about their positive status because of the stigma associated with HIV/AIDS. This stigma prevented many women from connecting with others, furthering their isolation and pain. But when women were able to disclose to others, many found their pain lessened. Several women shared statements like the following when asked what helped their healing process:

> The attitude of the media and other people towards HIV, the way people treat you when they find out and then you can move on. They don't run from you, so "OK, cool," and you can move on.

Second, many women pointed to their own self-determination as a factor that enabled their positive experiences:

> You can either cry about it and wallow in it, or you can try to pick
> yourself up and enjoy life for what it is. So for me it was just try-
> ing to get over the emotional hurt, letting go of that and trying to
> be as happy as I can be.

Finally, many women attributed much of their growth to the passage
of time. They pointed out that in the beginning, the growth process
took tremendous amounts of energy, but gradually it became easier.
The growth seemed to provide additional emotional energy for further growth and healing:

> I don't even think about these things anymore. It takes a long time
> to accept death. In the beginning it takes a lot of focus and energy,
> and then it gradually lessens.

* * *

> That [transcendence] is something I am still working on. I just
> don't think that it's something that happens overnight. I think it's
> something that you're constantly doing to a certain extent, be-
> cause you're always seeing a different light on things. It's chang-
> ing, so as things change, you change.

DISCUSSION

Most (82 percent, $n = 28$) participants in this study reported positive
personal responses to their HIV diagnoses. Although not a random
sample of women living with HIV, these participants are more representative than those published in anecdotal accounts. The overwhelming majority had lived troubled and traumatized lives. Many
would likely have received psychiatric diagnoses. Indeed, many of
these women represent a sector of the population that is often
scorned and stigmatized by the larger community. Given these dis-
advantages, these women's descriptions of growth, self-awareness,
and bravery in the face of a positive HIV diagnosis are remarkable.

The present findings provide partial support for the model of
transcendence we explored earlier (Dunbar & Mueller, 1995). After
women described in their own words the positive experiences they
had created through living with HIV, we showed them a depiction of
the transcendence model. Every woman shown the model expressed
recognition and found at least partial truth in it. However, we have
come to see the process differently.

First, the experiences described by these women were less ethereal
than those described by our earlier model. We were struck by the
everyday nature of the participants' frame of reference. Although
spiritual experiences and growth were expressed, these were often
related to the day-to-day experiences of life. For this reason we have
chosen to describe this process as one of "growth" rather than of
"transcendence," and we specifically include spiritual development
within this growth.

Second, we feel that the five themes described in this chapter better
fit the experiences of these women than did our earlier model (Dunbar

& Mueller, 1995). Because we had developed a framework for considering the growth that HIV might elicit in women's lives, we were able to inquire about the process by which such growth took place. This allowed us to compile a more complete picture than published accounts allowed. For instance, the quest for meaning was not alluded to in published accounts (Kurth, 1993; Reider & Rupelt, 1988). Although those essays spoke clearly about life's meaning, we were not able to determine whether those published women's ideas significantly developed or altered after diagnosis. In interviews with women in this study, we asked whether current beliefs and behaviors were developed before or since the discovery of their HIV-positive status. This line of inquiry solicited and found information about postdiagnosis psychological and spiritual growth. This line of inquiry also brought a different understanding of the "reconstruction of time" as it was described in the earlier model of transcendence. With questions as to the underlying process of reordering values and time, we discovered that this concept was really more aptly described as part of a larger reconsideration of the self in relation to a now shortened life.

Third, the mention of relationships and their increased importance in participants' lives was so pervasive among these women that we felt it warranted greater focus. A relationship-oriented focus has been well documented as a common characteristic of women (Gilligan, 1982). Interestingly, relationships presented paradoxes in the lives of these women. Although relationships with children, partners, and friends were often described as reasons for continuing to live and heal, they were also recognized as cause for extraordinary stress.

This finding of a greater relational focus might also relate to the strong representation of women of Asian and Pacific Islander ancestry in this study. For instance, most Asian and Pacific Islander groups have stronger cultural values toward collectivism than do Western cultures (Mokuau, 1991; Triandis, 1995). These values may have contributed to a stronger emphasis on resolution of relationships than would be expected using the prior model.

Exactly how and to what extent personal histories of trauma influenced the later growth of these women remains unclear. Some participants spoke specifically about being able to cope with HIV because they had learned to cope with other traumas earlier in their lives. However, we searched for but did not find reliable differences in responses between those we know and those we do not know were traumatized earlier in their lives. Nevertheless, it remains instructive that we found very little evidence that prior trauma and the necessary personal adjustments required to survive it precluded significant profound psychological and spiritual growth.

PRACTICE IMPLICATIONS

Our findings suggest that many and probably most women living with HIV can describe positive psychological and spiritual growth, consistent with the five themes described in this chapter. These findings have direct implication for social workers, particularly those in clinical practice.

Anticipate, Recognize, and Encourage Growth

A clinician who anticipates actual and potential growth in clients will be able to validate such experiences and feelings and to devise interventions that encourage further development. Although the longitudinal trajectory of growth seems erratic and, at times, unpredictable, the clinician should include growth-related assessment both at the initial interview and periodically throughout the therapeutic relationship. Feedback from our participants indicates that once a therapeutic relationship has begun, open-ended questions about positive aspects of living with HIV, such as those asked in this study, can communicate to clients the clinician's willingness to examine this part of their lives.

Interventions with a growth focus include empowering clients to develop their own agendas for positive growth and helping them develop the skills to enact these plans. Being able and willing to recognize strengths in a client does not translate into denying the pain of living with HIV. In fact, clinicians need to be mindful that jumping too early to this topic could be counterproductive. However, denying the powerful growth potential and experiences of clients diminishes both the client and the therapeutic relationship.

Assist Clients with Death and Dying Issues

Although there are recent positive signs of pharmacological advances in the treatment of HIV, many questions remain about the efficacy, cost, and availability of these treatments. Testing positive for HIV still carries with it strong death themes. Social workers serving women with HIV need to be adequately trained in death and dying practice approaches and must be prepared to pay particular attention to the special issues confronting women with HIV. First, for most people, AIDS leads to an early death. Second, many infected women had difficult lives before infection. They must deal with two types of loss, one related to their anticipated death and one related to adjusting to and surviving their difficult earlier life periods. The majority of women in this study had begun to reckon with death in clear and direct ways. Indeed, some HIV-infected women may surpass their clinicians in the extent to which they have worked through death issues. Clinicians must be ready to learn from and facilitate growth in this area, even when their clients' views exceed their own resolution of such issues.

Identify and Facilitate Life Affirmation

Affirming the will to live is a struggle for many terminally ill clients. Many of the women in our study needed considerable time to do so and often took detours, including substance abuse, denial, and avoidance, on their way. However, once the client has affirmed life and reckoned with death, each day takes on a special meaning. Practitioners should identify the important motivators for clients and help them move toward life affirmation and develop realistic but important goals for both the short- and long-term future. Some clients also need help developing strategies and skills to implement their plans. Interestingly, some terminally ill clients complain that their practitioners are able to discuss death themes adequately, but then have difficulty letting go of this and talking about living life. Clinicians need to be very careful to avoid conceptualizing the client solely as victim and as having little or nothing to live for.

Recognize the Importance of Spiritual Well-being and the Creation of Meaning

The ability to find meaning in life assisted many participants in the process of healing and growth. For many women in this study, the source of their renewed life's meaning was deeply spiritual. Unfortunately, traditional Western psychotherapies tend to ignore spiritual and transcendental issues. By doing so, these approaches surely overlook vital sources of growth. Developing, implementing, and testing alternative models, such as the transegoic model described by Smith (1995), are strongly encouraged. Clinicians who can use methods of therapy that support and encourage spiritual development in an individual or group setting can make a real difference. Clinicians uncomfortable with spiritual issues and practice strategies should make referrals to other colleagues or professionals able to facilitate this dimension of growth in their clients.

Encourage Self-Evaluation, Self-Affirmation, and Self-Care

Many women in this study were able to make a realistic self-evaluation, come to some sort of resolution with themselves, and move to self-affirmation and self-care. Practitioners should be prepared to assess clients' progress on this continuum and facilitate movement at any level. We found a very direct honesty in the women who were growing the most. Of course, a committed, genuine, and supportive therapeutic relationship can create the basis for such honest self-evaluation and lay the groundwork for self-affirmation and care. This process takes time.

Facilitate Relationship Resolution and the Development of New Relationships

We found that honest self-evaluations led to the desire for honest evaluations of relationships. Some relationships can be improved; others can be ended. In particular, women with HIV who have lived difficult lives may need and desire to release themselves from unnecessary relational burdens (for example, an abusive husband). Helping women examine their options, develop other ways to meet their real physical and psychological needs, and develop the skills to change the relationships in their lives can have a lasting effect. In addition, conducting planned family interventions can help the client work toward resolution or disengagement, and arranging opportunities for the development of other social supports can be helpful. Indeed, empowering the client to structure her environment to suit her needs and wishes can be an excellent way to extend the benefits of therapy into the natural ecology of everyday life.

Keep Biases in Check

At all levels of practice, recognizing the real growth and growth potential in HIV-infected women inspires an attitude of respect and admiration. This respect may be clouded by personal issues on the part of the clinician. Clinicians must be aware of their own negative judgments regarding aspects of clients' past or current lifestyles, including drug use, sexuality, abusive relationships, or even spirituality. Such judgments effectively block supportive communication between therapist and client. To facilitate growth and further positive development, it is imperative that clinicians explore and work through any feelings of blame or negative judgments regarding the client.

IMPLICATIONS FOR FURTHER RESEARCH

This study provided a preliminary theory developed from a snapshot of the lives of 34 women living in various stages of HIV disease. A longitudinal study designed to detect important social, psychological, and spiritual changes throughout women's experiences of HIV disease, as well as the factors influencing these changes, would be very valuable to service providers and professionals and ultimately to the growing numbers of women who live with HIV and AIDS. In addition, theory-testing quantitative strategies would help provide a clearer and more reliable and valid understanding of these growth processes.

REFERENCES

Allers, C. T., & Benjack, K. J. (1991). Connections between childhood abuse and HIV infection. *Journal of Counseling and Development, 70*, 309–313.

Anderson, S. (1995). Personality, appraisal, and adaptational outcomes in HIV seropositive men and women. *Research in Nursing and Health, 18*, 303–312.

AskSam for Windows 2.0b. (1994). [Computer software]. Perry, FL: AskSam Systems, Inc.

Brown, G., & Rundell, J. (1993). A prospective study of psychiatric aspects of early HIV disease in women. *General Hospital Psychiatry, 15*, 139–147.

Butz, M. (1992). Chaos: An omen of transcendence in the psychotherapeutic process. *Psychological Reports, 71,* 827–843.

Campbell, C. (1990). Women and AIDS. *Social Science and Medicine, 30,* 407–415.

Centers for Disease Control and Prevention. (1994). Update: AIDS among women—United States 1994. *Morbidity and Mortality Weekly Review, 43,* 81–84.

Centers for Disease Control and Prevention. (1995). *HIV/AIDS surveillance report: U.S. HIV and AIDS cases reported through December 1995: Year-end edition.* Atlanta: Author.

Commerford, M., Gular, E., Orr, D., Renznikoff, M., & O'Dowd, M. (1994). Coping and psychological distress in women with HIV/AIDS. *Journal of Community Psychology, 22,* 224–230.

Dunbar, H., & Mueller, C. (1995). Women and HIV: The process of transcendence. *Arete, 20,* 6–15.

Florence, M., Lutzen, K., & Alexius, B. (1994). Adaptation of heterosexually infected HIV-positive women. *Health Care for Women International, 15,* 265–273.

Gilligan, C. (1982). *In a different voice: Psychological theory and women's development.* Cambridge, MA: Harvard University Press.

Gleik, J. (1987). *Chaos: Making a new science.* New York: Viking.

Hankins, C. (1990). Issues involving women, children and AIDS primarily in the developed world. *Journal of Acquired Immune Deficiency Syndromes, 3,* 443–448.

Hankins, C., & Handley, M. (1992). HIV disease and AIDS in women: Current knowledge and a research agenda. *Journal of Acquired Immune Deficiency Syndromes, 5,* 957–971.

Ickovics, J., & Rodin, J. (1992). Women and AIDS in the United States: Epidemiology, natural history, and mediating mechanisms. *Health Psychology, 11,* 1–16.

Kaplan, M. (1995). Feminization of the AIDS epidemic. *Journal of Sociology and Social Welfare, 22,* 5–21.

Kurth, A. (1993). *Until the cure: Caring for women with HIV.* New Haven, CT: Yale University Press.

Lea, A. (1994). Women with HIV and their burden of caring. *Health Care for Women International, 15,* 489–501.

Mays, V. M., & Cochran, S. D. (1988). Issues in the perception of AIDS risk and risk reduction activities by black and Hispanic/Latina women. *American Psychologist, 43,* 949–957.

Mokuau, N. (1991). *Handbook of social services for Asian and Pacific Islanders.* Westport, CT: Greenwood Press.

National Association of Social Workers. (1996). *NASW code of ethics.* Washington, DC: Author.

North, R. L., & Rothenberg, K. H. (1993). Partner notification and the threat of domestic violence against women with HIV infection. *New England Journal of Medicine, 329,* 1194–1196.

Regan-Kubinski, M., & Sharts-Hopko, N. (1995). Illness cognition of HIV-infected mothers. *Issues in Mental Health Nursing, 16,* 327–344.

Reider, I., & Rupelt, P. (1988). *AIDS: The women.* San Francisco: Cleis Press.

Rychlak, J. (1981). *Introduction to personality and psychotherapy* (2nd ed.). Boston: Houghton-Mifflin.

Seals, B., Sowell, R., Demi, A., Moneyham, L., Cohen, L., & Guillory, J. (1995). Falling through the cracks: Social service concerns of women infected with HIV. *Qualitative Health Research, 5*(1), 496–515.

Semple, S., Patterson, T., Temoshok, L., McCutchan, J., Straits-Troster, K., Chandler, J., & Grant, I. (1993). Identification of psychobiological stressors among HIV-positive women. *Women and Health, 20,* 15–36.

Smeltzer, S. (1992). Women and AIDS: Sociopolitical issues. *Nursing Outlook, 40,* 152–156.

Smith, E. (1995). Addressing the psychospiritual distress of death as reality: A transpersonal approach. *Social Work, 40,* 402–413.

Triandis, H. C. (1995). *Individualism and collectivism*. Boulder, CO: Westview Press.
Zierler, S., Feingold, L., Lanter, D., Velentgas, P., Kantowitz-Gordon, I., & Mayer, K. (1991). Adult survivors of childhood sexual abuse and subsequent risk of HIV infection. *American Journal of Public Health, 81*, 572–578.

This study was supported in part by a grant from The Life Foundation: The AIDS Foundation of Hawaii on Oahu, the Hawaii Community Foundation, and a donor who chooses to remain anonymous. We thank the women who participated in this study, the service providers who made it possible, Dr. Rosemary Adam-Terem for making on-call services available, and three anonymous reviewers.

38

Exploring AIDS–Related Knowledge, Attitudes, and Behaviors of Female Mexican Migrant Workers

Pamela Balls Organista, Kurt C. Organista, and Pearl R. Soloff

During the past 10 years, women have become the fastest grow-ing group likely to contract AIDS, and women of color are the majority of these cases (Nyamathi, Bennett, Leake, Lewis, & Flaskerud, 1993). Although Latinos constitute only 8 percent of the U.S. population, Latino women, or Latinas, represent 21 percent of all adult female AIDS cases (Amaro, 1988). A review of the literature shows that the risk of contracting AIDS is between eight and 11 times greater in Latinas compared with non-Latino white women, primari-ly as a result of unprotected sex with high-risk partners (Marin & Marin, 1992; Singer et al., 1990; Yep, 1995). Compared with white women, Latinas also differ in having higher fertility rates and lower contraceptive use (Amaro, 1988), lower condom use (Marin, Tschann, Gomez, & Kegeles, 1993), and greater reluctance to suggest condom use to their male partners (Marin & Marin, 1992). Hence, both risk of contracting AIDS and barriers to prevention are formidable where Latinas are concerned.

There are approximately 4.1 million migrant workers in the Unit-ed States, predominantly of Mexican background (U.S. Department of Health and Human Services, 1990). Although Mexican migrants have historically been almost exclusively male, the number of fe-males participating in migratory labor has increased. During the past two decades, 50 percent of all Mexican immigrants have been women (Vernez & Ronfeldt, 1991). Thus, Mexican women are a sig-nificant portion of the Mexican immigrant population and migratory labor population.

Although AIDS-related data are slowly beginning to emerge on U.S. Latinas, almost nothing is known about marginalized sub-groups such as Mexican migrant laborers, who are part of a unique population at increasing risk of contracting AIDS. In a recent review of the literature, Organista and Balls Organista (1997) reported that HIV screening at labor camps in South Carolina and Florida revealed

This chapter was originally published in the May 1998 issue of *Health & Social Work*, Vol. 23, pp. 96–103.

infection rates ranging from 3.5 percent to 13 percent in migrant farm workers. With regard to Western stream migrants, less information is known. One study by Lopez and Ruiz (1995) found a 9 percent lifetime history of sexually transmitted diseases (STDs) and two active cases of syphilis in their sample of Mexican farm workers ($N = 176$). In addition, 9.1 percent of women reported sex with someone who injected drugs during the past year. These investigators concluded that although no cases of HIV were identified, high rates of unsafe sex practices reported by respondents warranted prevention efforts with this population.

Many migration-related factors frame a significant risk of health problems, including exposure to HIV. These factors include limited education; cultural, linguistic, and geographic barriers to health care; and poverty-related low wages, hazardous working conditions, chronic underemployment, constant mobility, and substandard housing (National Commission to Prevent Infant Mortality, 1993). At this time, much research is needed to begin to gather data on AIDS-related knowledge, beliefs, and behaviors in migrant laborers to inform prevention policies and programs. Such information should consider both gender-related and cultural factors.

Although AIDS-related information on Mexican migrants is scarce, the few studies that do exist indicate problematic knowledge and very low condom use (Bletzer, 1990; Bronfman & Minella, 1992; Organista, Balls Organista, Garcia de Alba, Castillo-Moran, & Carrillo, 1996). There are indications that female Mexican migrants are far less knowledgeable than their male counterparts. For example, Schoonover Smith (1988) compared knowledge of STDs in black ($n = 60$) and Mexican ($n = 60$) farm workers and found that Mexican workers knew less about transmission, treatment, and prevention and that Mexican women were the least knowledgeable on all subjects.

The cited findings speak strongly to the need for further research on the problem of AIDS in migrant laborers generally, and female migrants in particular, so that health care workers can design cultural- and gender-appropriate prevention programs. This chapter reports findings from a pilot study that assessed AIDS-related knowledge, attitudes, behaviors, and general contraceptive use in a sample of female Mexican migrant workers who travel back and forth across the U.S.–Mexico border to live and work in the United States for extended periods of time.

METHOD

Participants

Participants were 32 Mexican migrant women who have lived and worked in the United States since 1982. These women had a mean age of 34.2 years ($SD = 13.6$), 7.16 ($SD = 3.96$) years of education, and 6.1 ($SD = 5.8$) years spent in the United States (Table 38-1). This sample was part of a larger sample of 87 Mexican migrants (32 females and 55 males) surveyed. Although most female participants were

Table 38-1

Demographic Information on Female Mexican Migrant Workers (*N* = 32)

Characteristic	%	*M*	*SD*
Age		34.2	13.6
Years of education		7.2	3.8
Years spent in the United States		6.1	5.8
Birthplace			
La Cienega/nearby towns	75.0		
Neighboring towns	6.3		
Other places in Mexico	12.5		
United States		6.3	
Current residence			
La Cienega	50.0		
United States	50.0		
Marital status (married/living together)	56.3		
Language (Spanish only or mostly Spanish)	90.6		

originally from the sending community surveyed, 50 percent reported currently living in the United States.

Procedures

In collaboration with faculty at the School of Public Health at the University of Guadalajara, we conducted the survey in December 1992 in a small agricultural sending community 210 kilometers from the city of Guadalajara in Jalisco, Mexico. According to the 11th Mexican census conducted in 1990, this agricultural town is about 200 years old and has a population of about 1,200 inhabitants from 220 families. About 50 percent of the population is under 14 years of age, and it is estimated that an average of two members of each family have lived or are currently living in the United States.

The second author, a team of medical students from the University of Guadalajara, and research assistants from the United States spent three days at the research site interviewing respondents. Eligibility criteria were that participants must have lived and worked in the United States during the past 10 years (that is, during the major years of the AIDS epidemic) and that they must be at least 18 years old. Every household in the community was approached. Participation was voluntary and anonymous, and there were no refusals from eligible participants. Migrants that were currently living in the United States were visiting for the Christmas holiday as well as the town's annual celebration of its patron saint.

Interviewers received six hours of training over a three-day period that included becoming familiar with the questionnaire, group discussions of how to discuss sexuality in a professional manner, having participants interview each other in pairs, and finally an assessment of interviewing skills. Potential interviewers that manifested excessive difficulty with the questionnaire were excluded from the study. Female migrants were interviewed by female interviewers in a private setting, either in the respondent's home or nearby.

Measures

Respondents were administered a modified version of the unpublished Hispanic Condom Questionnaire (HCQ) developed by Marin and associates (1993) at the Center for AIDS Prevention in San Francisco. The HCQ is composed of various single items and subscales that assess AIDS and condom-related knowledge, beliefs, and reported sexual practices, as well as level of acculturation and sociodemographic background information. Items use the term "AIDS virus" rather than "HIV" because respondents might not understand the latter terminology. Most HCQ items are arranged on four- or five-point Likert scales. The HCQ has been used to describe condom use (Marin, Gomez, & Hearst, 1993) and to predict condom use (Marin, Gomez, & Tschann, 1993) in a nine-state sample of U.S. Latinos.

Because the HCQ has only been used with Latinos in the United States, modifications were necessary to make the HCQ appropriate for Mexican migrants. Modifications were based on discussions with Marin and on information gathered from focus groups (one with women and another with men) conducted at the study site six months before the survey. Examples of HCQ modifications included the addition of questions about AIDS transmission from kissing, perspiration, and the AIDS test, because several focus group participants inquired about these areas as possible modes of transmission. Another modification of the HCQ was changing the wording of items to create a gender-neutral version of the instrument. In the original HCQ there are two versions, one for men and another for women, that inquire about sexual relations with the opposite sex. In the current study it seemed more convenient and neutral not to bias inquiry toward heterosexual practices (for example, the term "sex partner" was used in place of the terms "male or female sex partner").

Knowledge of AIDS Transmission and Condom Use. Ten items were used to assess knowledge and misconceptions about the transmission of HIV (for example, getting AIDS from blood and from public toilets). Participants also were asked, "Have you personally known someone that had AIDS or was infected with the AIDS virus?"

Knowledge of proper condom use was assessed by three items: (1) Do you think Vaseline is a good lubricant for condoms? (2) Is it necessary to unroll a condom before putting it on the penis? (3) Is it necessary to grab the condom while withdrawing the penis after ejaculating? Participants were asked if they had ever used a condom in their life, how frequently they had used condoms in the past 12 months with a regular sex partner and with occasional sex partners, and how frequently they carried condoms.

Beliefs about AIDS and Condom Use. Worry about contracting AIDS was assessed by the single item, How often do you worry about contracting AIDS? A five-item subscale was used to assess negative beliefs about condom use: (1) Would you feel less sexual pleasure? (2) Would your partner feel less sexual pleasure? (3) Would you feel guilty? (4) Would you feel embarrassed? (5) Would it interrupt the sex act to put on a condom? (alpha = .62).

Perceived Condom-Related Social Norms. A three-item factor was computed to assess beliefs about condom use with a regular sex partner: If you insisted on using condoms, do you believe your regular sex partner (1) would get angry? (2) would refuse to have sex with you? (3) would become violent? (alpha = .72). A four-item factor was computed to assess beliefs about condom use with an occasional sex partner: (1) If you insisted on using condoms, do you believe your occasional sex partner would get angry? (2) Would your occasional partner refuse to have sex with you? (3) If you used a condom with your occasional sex partner, do you believe you could contract a venereal disease like syphilis or gonorrhea? (4) Do you believe you could contract AIDS? (alpha = .53). Although this factor had below satisfactory internal consistency reliability, the mean score was so similar to the score for beliefs about condom use with a regular partner that we decided to report it.

A single item was used to assess participants' beliefs about whether men or women were responsible for carrying condoms: Who has the responsibility for carrying condoms? A five-item factor was computed to assess negative social reactions to women carrying condoms. Did participants believe (1) that their friends would think badly of them if they were to carry condoms? (2) that a woman carrying condoms was ready to have sex with someone she just met? (3) that men would perceive them as ready to have sex with acquaintances if they were to carry condoms? (4) that a regular partner would respect them for carrying condoms? (5) that occasional sex partners would respect them for carrying condoms? (alpha = .74).

Finally, a three-item factor was used to assess how many friends carried and used condoms with a regular partner and with occasional sex partners (alpha = .83).

Acculturation and Other Background Information. The HCQ contains an acculturation subscale consisting of four language-related items from the Short Acculturation Scale (Marin, Sabogal, Marin, Otero-Sabogal, & Perez-Stable, 1987). Items are arranged on five-point scales ranging from only Spanish = 1 to only English = 5, with both equally = 3 as a midpoint. As expected, this factor had a mean of 1.46 (*SD* = .74), indicating very low acculturation in this migrant sample (alpha = .80). In addition to acculturation, various questions about sociodemographic background were asked, including information about contraceptive use in general.

RESULTS

AIDS and Condom-Related Knowledge

Results were mixed regarding knowledge of AIDS transmission (Table 38-2). Whereas accuracy was high for knowledge of actual

Table 38-2

Knowledge of AIDS Transmission among Female Mexican Migrant Workers (*N* = 32)

Question	% Responding	
	Yes/Probably Yes	No/Probably No
Do you believe it is possible to contract the AIDS virus from		
Mosquito bite?	43.8	56.3
Sitting in public bathrooms?	37.5	62.5
Kissing someone on the mouth?	37.5	62.5
Semen?	93.8	6.3
Vaginal fluids?	81.3	12.5
Blood?	100.0	0
Perspiration?	9.4	90.6
The AIDS test?	21.9	78.2
Do you believe that AIDS is only a problem for homosexuals and drug addicts?	25.0	75.0
Do you believe that it is possible to know by appearance that a person has the AIDS virus?	21.9	78.1

NOTE: All items were arrayed on four-point scales where yes = 1, probably yes = 2, probably no = 3, no = 4.

major modes of HIV transmission (that is, blood, semen, and vaginal fluids), nearly one-half (43.8 percent) of the respondents thought that AIDS could be contracted from a mosquito bite; one-third (37.5 percent) indicated that AIDS could be contracted from public bathrooms or kissing on the mouth; and one-fifth (21.9 percent) thought AIDS could be contracted from the AIDS test. In addition, one-fourth of the respondents indicated that AIDS is a problem only for homosexuals and drug addicts, and one-fifth indicated that it is possible to know by appearance that someone has the AIDS virus.

Knowledge of proper condom use was problematic for this group. Two-thirds of the respondents said either "yes" or "don't know" to the items asking if Vaseline was a good lubricant for condoms and if one should unroll a condom before putting it on the penis. Also, fewer than half of the respondents knew that a condom should be grabbed while withdrawing after ejaculation.

Condom-Related Behaviors

Forty-two percent of the 32 participants reported having used a condom at some time in their life. Thirty-four percent of the women reported having no regular or occasional sex partner within the past year. Of the 21 women who were sexually active during the past year, the percentage who had always used condoms with regular and occasional sex partners during the past year was 28.6 percent and 22.2 percent, respectively, and the percentage who had never used condoms with regular and occasional sex partners was 57.1 percent and 44.4 percent, respectively. Also, 75 percent of respondents reported that they almost never carried condoms currently.

AIDS and Condom-Related Beliefs

Overall, the 32 participants in the current sample indicated that they had some worry about contracting AIDS. Thirty-one percent reported that they worried "frequently to very frequently," 50 percent stated that they worried "a little," and 19 percent stated that they "did not worry at all."

Negative Beliefs about Condom Use. An obtained mean of 2.3 on the scale measuring beliefs about condom use indicated that when respondents were asked if they believed that various negative consequences would occur with condom use (for example, feel less pleasure, interrupt sex act), they answered "probably not."

Perceived Condom Social Norms. Respondents did not believe that a regular sex partner would become angry, would refuse sex, or would become violent if they were to insist on using a condom ($M = 3.2$ on a four-point subscale ranging from yes = 1 to no = 4). With regard to occasional sex partners, respondents similarly indicated that they would not expect negative reactions and would not fear contracting AIDS or another venereal disease if they were to use condoms ($M = 2.9$).

Regarding gender-related responsibility for carrying condoms, respondents generally reported that it was the responsibility of both men and women to carry condoms. However, when asked about negative social reactions to women carrying condoms, they reported uncertainty as indicated by a mean score of 2.6 on this five-item factor in which probably no = 2 and probably yes = 3. A closer examination of factor items revealed that 28 participants (89 percent) answered "probably yes" when asked if men would perceive them as ready to have sex with acquaintances if they were to carry condoms ($M = 2.75$). In contrast, the women answered "probably no" ($M = 2.3$) when asked if participants would perceive the women as promiscuous if they were to carry condoms. Furthermore, respondents answered "probably no" when asked if regular and occasional sex partners would respect them for carrying condoms ($M = 2.9$ and 2.7, respectively) and indicated uncertainty when asked if friends would think badly of them for carrying condoms. Finally, when asked if their friends carried and used condoms with regular and occasional sex partners, respondents reported that fewer than half did so ($M = 2.47$ on a five-point scale where less than half = 2 and half = 3).

General Contraceptive Use. With regard to contraceptive use during the past year, other than condom use, 34.4 percent of the 32 women reported no current use of any type of contraceptive, 43.8 percent reported using birth control pills, 3.1 percent reported using an IUD, and 9.4 percent reported using other methods. (Data are missing for three participants, or 9.4 percent.) The women also reported an average of 2.4 children and no current pregnancies or births within the past three months.

DISCUSSION

Female Mexican migrant workers in the current study were highly knowledgeable about the major actual modes of AIDS transmission, but one-third to one-half also believed that they could contract AIDS from casual sources such as mosquito bites, public bathrooms, kissing on the mouth, and the AIDS test. This pattern of AIDS transmission knowledge was also reported by Marin and Marin (1990) in their study of mostly immigrant Latinos in San Francisco ($N = 460$) and by Foulk, Lafferty, Ryan, and Robertson (1989) in their study of male migrant laborers. Misconceptions about casual modes of transmission could compromise supportive responses to friends or family members infected with HIV within the Mexican migrant population. Also, the fact that more than one-fifth of the respondents believed that they could contract HIV from the AIDS test would suggest high inhibition to obtaining such screening.

Participants also indicated considerable lack of basic, proper knowledge of condom use consistent with Marin and Marin's (1990) conclusion that Latinos low in acculturation have high needs for receiving fundamental AIDS and condom-related education. Health social workers charged with delivery of HIV prevention services to migrants that are culture and gender sensitive must address many basic issues including the provision of services in Spanish (91 percent of the women in the current sample spoke only or mostly Spanish), literature geared to appropriate reading levels (average seven years of education in this sample) as well as non-reading-based (that is, hands on) education, outreach to where migrants live and work (for example, Latino communities, labor camps, sending communities), use of popular Spanish media, and the development of gender-sensitive messages. Given the tendency for traditional Latino men and women not to talk directly about sexual matters, de la Vega (1990) suggested that sex education for Latinos may necessitate placing men and women in separate rooms with same-gender sex educators and then reuniting them afterward to begin a dialogue about preventing AIDS.

Although our review uncovered no interventions that used the specific population of Latina migrants, there are a few studies that have studied impoverished Latinas that lend support to the findings of the current study. Flaskerud and Nyamathi (1990) and their colleagues (Nyamathi, Flaskerud, Bennett, & Leake, 1994) have evaluated culture- and gender-sensitive programs with low-income Latinas. One study included 250 Latinas, predominantly immigrants of Mexican descent (Flaskerud & Nyamathi, 1990). Results showed that a 12-minute slide–tape AIDS education program was successful in producing pretest to posttest gains in AIDS knowledge that were maintained at two to three months' follow-up in the experimental group compared with the control group. Positive changes in attitudes were also found pretest to posttest, but these were not maintained at the two- to three-month follow-up. The authors concluded that experiential learning is needed rather than simply AIDS education alone.

Regarding condom use, participants did not anticipate negative consequences for using condoms, and they did not expect negative reactions from sex partners for insisting on condom use. However, positive attitudes did not translate to frequent condom use (for example, only about 23 percent of sexually active women had used condoms with their partners during the past year).

With regard to negative social reactions to women carrying condoms, the women generally reported that men would perceive them as promiscuous and that regular and occasional sex partners would not respect them for carrying condoms. Respondents were also uncertain about what friends might think of them and also reported that fewer than half of their friends carried and used condoms. With apparent gender-related norms like these, it is not surprising that 75 percent of the women interviewed reported never carrying condoms.

CONCLUSION

Much has been written about the traditional power differential between men and women in Latino culture that makes the task of empowering women to protect themselves with condoms a difficult task (Marin et al., 1993). Our findings regarding Mexican social condom norms biased against women seem consistent with this position. Mikawa et al. (1992) similarly found that condom use was associated with male gender role in their study of recent Mexican immigrants.

Although gender bias against Mexican women carrying condoms may be real, culture- and gender-sensitive strategies for increasing condom use among female migrants and Latinas in general should not be abandoned. For example, the central, culture-based role of being a protective mother could be used to persuade Latinas to begin thinking about precautions to prevent the congenital transmission of AIDS to children. Social workers could also emphasize the Latina's role as a primary caretaker who must take care of her health to support her children and to see them grow up. In the United States 24 percent of pediatric AIDS cases are Latino children (Centers for Disease Control, 1993). This disproportionately high rate of AIDS underscores the urgent need to help Latinas take a more active role in protecting themselves and their children from this complex epidemic. In Amaro's (1988) discussion of AIDS prevention with Hispanic women, she stated that a logical place to begin interventions is to conduct focus groups aimed at empowering the women by discussing what they believe would be good prevention strategies.

Interestingly, the prospect of empowering Mexican migrant women to become active in self-protection against AIDS may be consistent with the gender-role expansion experienced by these women.

For example, Guendelman (1987) found that seasonal migration to the United States expanded the traditional roles of Mexican women to include earning wages, greater purchasing power, more involvement in family decision making, more division of household responsibility with husbands, greater feelings of autonomy, and even lower stress levels than nonworking migrant women. As with the current study, the women in Guendelman's study also were from sending communities in Jalisco, Mexico. Hence, Mexican women in the migrant labor stream may be more ready to assume an active role in AIDS prevention than previously thought.

Although findings from this pilot study are based on a small sample, they are consistent with similar research on Mexican migrants and Latinas in the United States. Therefore, one can conclude that misinformation exists regarding casual modes of HIV transmission and proper condom use and that there is a cultural bias against women carrying condoms. Findings highlight the need for continued AIDS research that includes larger and more representative samples of Mexican migrants and the future development of culture- and gender-sensitive preventive interventions for this group.

REFERENCES

Amaro, H. (1988). Considerations for prevention of HIV infection among Hispanic women. *Psychology of Women Quarterly, 12,* 429–443.

Bletzer, K. V. (1990). Knowledge of AIDS/HIV infection among migrant farmworkers. *AIDS and Public Policy Journal, 5,* 173–177.

Bronfman, M., & Minella, N. (1992). *Habitos sexuales de los migrantes temporales Mexicanos a los Estados Unidos de America, practicas de riesgo para la infección por VIH* [Sexual habits of seasonal Mexican migrants to the United States of America, risk practices for HIV infection]. Mexico, D.F.: El Colegio de Mexico.

Centers for Disease Control. (1993, February). *HIV/AIDS Surveillance* (Year-end edition, December 1992). Atlanta: National Center for Infectious Diseases, Division of HIV/AIDS.

de la Vega, E. (1990). Considerations for reaching the Latino population with sexuality and HIV/AIDS information and education. *SIECUS Report, 18*(3), 1–8.

Flaskerud, J. H., & Nyamathi, A. M. (1990). Effects of an AIDS education program on the knowledge, attitudes and practices of low-income black and Latina women. *Journal of Community Health, 15,* 343–355.

Foulk, D., Lafferty, J., Ryan, R., & Robertson, A. (1989). AIDS knowledge and behavior in a migrant farm-worker population. *Migration World, 17,* 36–42.

Guendelman, S. (1987). The incorporation of Mexican women in seasonal migration: A study of gender differences. *Hispanic Journal of the Behavioral Sciences, 9,* 245–264.

Lopez, R., & Ruiz, J. D. (1995). *Seroprevalence of human immunodeficiency virus type I and syphilis and assessment of risk behaviors among migrant and seasonal farmworkers in Northern California.* (Manuscript prepared for Office of AIDS, California Department of Health Services). Sacramento: California Department of Health Services.

Marin, B. V., Gomez, C., & Hearst, N. (1993). Multiple heterosexual partners and condom use among Hispanics and non-Hispanic whites. *Family Planning Perspectives, 25,* 170–174.

Marin, B. V., Gomez, C., & Tschann, J. M. (1993). Condom use among Hispanic men with multiple female partners: A nine-state study. *Public Health Reports, 25,* 742–750.

Marin, B. V., & Marin, G. (1990). Effects of acculturation on knowledge of AIDS and HIV among Hispanics. *Hispanic Journal of the Behavioral Sciences, 12,* 110–121.

Marin, B. V., & Marin, G. (1992). Predictors of condom accessibility among Hispanics in San Francisco. *Public Health Briefs, 82,* 592–595.

Marin, G., Sabogal, F., Marin, B. V., Otero-Sabogal, R., & Perez-Stable, E. J. (1987). Development of a short acculturation scale for Hispanics. *Hispanic Journal of the Behavioral Sciences, 9,* 183–205.

Marin, B. V., Tschann, J. M., Gomez, C., & Kegeles, S. M. (1993). Acculturation and gender differences in sexual attitudes and behaviors: Hispanic vs. non-Hispanic white unmarried adults. *American Journal of Public Health, 83,* 1759–1761.

Mikawa, J. K., Morones, P. A., Gomez, A., Case, H. L., Olsen, D., & Gonzales-Huss, M. J. (1992). Cultural practices of Hispanics: Implications for the prevention of AIDS. *Hispanic Journal of the Behavioral Sciences, 14,* 421–433.

National Commission to Prevent Infant Mortality. (1993). *HIV/AIDS: A growing crisis among migrant and seasonal farmworker families.* Washington, DC: Author.

Nyamathi, A., Bennett, C., Leake, B., Lewis, C., & Flaskerud, J. (1993). AIDS-related knowledge, perceptions, and behaviors among impoverished minority women. *American Journal of Public Health, 83,* 65–71.

Nyamathi, A., Flaskerud, J., Bennett, C., & Leake, B. (1994). Evaluation of two AIDS education programs for impoverished Latina women. *AIDS Education and Prevention, 6,* 296–309.

Organista, K. C., & Balls Organista, P. (1997). Migrant laborers and AIDS in the United States: A review of the literature. *AIDS Education and Prevention, 9,* 83–93.

Organista, K. C., Balls Organista, P., Garcia de Alba, G.J.E., Castillo-Moran, M. A., & Carrillo, H. (1996). AIDS and condom-related knowledge, beliefs and behaviors in Mexican migrant laborers. *Hispanic Journal of Behavioral Sciences, 18,* 392–406.

Schoonover Smith, L. (1988). Ethnic differences in knowledge of sexually transmitted diseases in North American black and Mexican American farmworkers. *Research in Nursing and Health, 11,* 51–58.

Singer, M., Flores, C., Davison, L., Burke, G., Castillo, Z., Scanlon, K., & Rivera, M. (1990). SIDA: The economic, social, and cultural context of AIDS among Latinos. *Medical Anthropology Quarterly, 4*(1), 72–114.

U.S. Department of Health and Human Services. (1990). *An atlas of state profiles which estimate number of migrant and seasonal farmworkers and members of their families.* Washington, DC: Office of Migrant Health.

Vernez, G., & Ronfeldt, D. (1991). The current situation in Mexican immigration. *Science, 25,* 1189–1193.

Yep, G. A. (1995). Communicating the HIV/AIDS risk to Hispanic populations: A review and integration. In A. M. Padilla (Ed.), *Hispanic psychology: Critical issues in theory and research* (pp. 196–212). Thousand Oaks, CA: Sage Publications.

Preparation of this chapter was supported in part by three grants from the University of California, Berkeley, to Kurt C. Organista: a junior faculty research grant (Committee on Research), a career development grant (Office of the Chancellor), and a faculty minigrant (Chicano/Latino Policy Project). The authors gratefully acknowledge the assistance of Ricardo Organista, Patricia Torres, and 20 medical students from the University of Guadalajara.

39 Methodological Considerations in Surveying Latina AIDS Caregivers: Issues in Sampling and Measurement

Helen Land and Sharon Hudson

The need for knowledge gained through research on people of color, particularly Latinas, has never been more pronounced than in the second decade of the AIDS epidemic. Although descriptive information is available on Latinos in general, studies that highlight the dynamic interaction among cultural values, methodological issues, and the sensitive nature of AIDS research are lacking. Ample evidence suggests that because of cultural and behavioral differences, the Latino population may require the adaptation of traditional research methods (Becerra & Zambrana, 1985). This chapter discusses methodological issues in conducting cross-cultural research that may impede understanding of populations of color, Latinos in general, and Latinas affected by AIDS caregiving in particular. These issues include gender, socioeconomic status, and culture as these factors affect reaching and maintaining a sample, interviewing procedures, and issues in measurement.

Although some of the discussion is drawn from a thorough review of the literature on methodological issues in cross-cultural research on Latino populations, other material is drawn from direct experience in conducting a study of the stress process in Latina family AIDS caregivers. Thus, the discussion in this chapter is based on several sources of information. As we address problematic conditions, where possible, we present suggestions for remediating these difficulties and advancing cross-cultural research.

LATINA AIDS CAREGIVERS

Latina AIDS caregivers bring to their roles histories, cultural values, ties to the surrounding community, and behaviors associated with health risks that are different from those of their white counterparts. Examining these differences is essential in light of the dramatic increase in AIDS among women of Latin origin, many of whom are foreign born (Maldonando, 1991). In fact, Latinas are among the fastest growing group of people infected with AIDS, manifesting a

This chapter was originally published in the December 1997 issue of *Social Work Research*, Vol. 21, pp. 233–246.

171 percent increase of new cases in the past three years (Fernandez, 1995). Often, these women also provide care for AIDS-infected children, husbands, and extended family members. Particularly in Latin cultures, caregiving falls to women because of the strong cultural expectation that they will assume caregiving roles, especially among more recent immigrants (Lockerly, 1991; Mintzer et al., 1992).

A number of factors put Latina caregivers at significant physical risk of health problems and psychological risk of depressive symptoms, regardless of their own HIV status. First, they are often coping with the stress of acculturation, they are isolated because of the stigma associated with AIDS, and they are often not knowledgeable about AIDS services.

Second, the Hispanic cultural value of *sympatia* may delay seeking help. A sympatica person tends to put others before herself (Marin, 1990); therefore, Latinas are often reluctant to seek help or early care for illness for fear of burdening or stigmatizing their families (Salcido, 1996). Hence, the needs of Latina caregivers who have HIV or AIDS are often identified later in the course of the illness. HIV-positive caregivers themselves may present with accelerated disease manifestations as they attend to infected relatives who require more extensive care (Medrano & Cuvilly-Klopner, 1992). In Latina AIDS caregivers, these circumstances evolve as a consequence of substantial misinformation concerning HIV, coupled with a strong tendency to underestimate personal risk (Kalichman, Hunter, & Kelly, 1992; Marin & Marin, 1989). Most are at high risk of contracting HIV because of sociocultural and religious sanctioning against the use of condoms (Rosen & Blank, 1992).

Third, many Latina caregivers coping with AIDS reside in poverty-ridden communities, where health, mental health, and social services are limited for monolingual Spanish-speaking people and where they are underrepresented in health care planning (Munoz et al., 1982). Because many Latina caregivers are undocumented, they often fail to qualify for health and mental health benefits, child care, rent subsidies, or other support services (Dennenberg, 1992; Land, 1994).

Fourth, help-seeking behavior in Hispanics differs dramatically from such behavior in other groups; for example, outside resources such as respite care frequently may be viewed as unnecessary by the family (Cox & Monk, 1993; Hu & Snowden, 1992; Keefe, Padilla, & Carlos, 1979; Martinez, 1978; Starret, Mindel, & Wright, 1983). In the Latino community, female AIDS caregivers constitute the backbone of family attendant care. Many are bereaved from the loss of a spouse or child as they continue to provide care. The multiple demands of AIDS caregiving, coupled with limited resources, often result in stress and role strain that predictably push the boundaries of human physical and emotional capabilities. The negative effects of chronic stress and psychosocial risk factors on the immune system of caregivers have been documented (Kiecolt-Glaser & Glaser, 1995). Moreover, high rates of depression among Latinas have been extensively cited in the literature (Land, 1994; Martinez, 1993). Thus, Latina AIDS caregivers

constitute a growing, vulnerable group at risk of physical manifestations of AIDS and of stress and its psychological sequelae, particularly depressive symptoms.

Programs designed to reach Latin women are recent and may still
operate on a male orientation to the disease. Low rates of participation
in such programs are common and problematic (Weeks, Schensul,
Williams, Singer, & Grier, 1995). Programmatic literature repeatedly
emphasizes the need to attend to women's personal issues within the
broader context of gender, culture, and socioeconomic status rather
than to provide a template approach to AIDS service provision (Weeks
et al., 1995). Questions addressing satisfaction with access to services,
sufficiency of service delivery, understanding of needs and stress
levels of Latinas, and their psychological and physical well-being
remain unanswered. Yet research designed to understand the needs
of Latinas affected by AIDS, particularly regarding the interplay of
culture, gender, and socioeconomic status in their lives, is scant.

STUDY

Because of the many pressing concerns of this population, we undertook a study of Latina AIDS caregivers. Following the stress paradigm of Pearlin (1989) and Pearlin, Mullan, Semple, and Skaff (1990),
the study was designed to examine a number of issues in Latina AIDS
caregivers: the stress and coping process as it relates to physical and
mental well-being of caregivers, the possible buffering effects of service utilization for those who received care, with special attention to
service satisfaction and issues of cultural sensitivity in service provision, and the role of various forms of social support and self-efficacy
in the stress process. In addition, we sought to examine how various
sociodemographic background variables related to respondent stress.
Both quantitative and qualitative methods were used.

Respondents

We interviewed a cross-sectional purposive sample of 155 Latinas
over age 16 who were actively caring for a loved one with AIDS at
the time of the study. Data were collected in the greater Los Angeles
area from February 1995 through August 1996. We recruited 18 AIDS
services organizations to act as referral sources for our study. Respondents were referred from agencies and clinics, as well as
through hospitals, media announcements, and flyers, and by word of
mouth. Of the total, 50 were referred through AIDS services organizations, 100 through direct contact with prospective respondents at
outpatient clinics, and the remainder through media announcements
or from other respondents. Many women were infected themselves
and thus carried a dual status of caregiver and patient. A variety of
caregiving statuses were represented; most women were caring for a
son, daughter, or spouse/partner. The majority were poor and
unemployed. About two-thirds were foreign born and spoke only

Spanish. Of the 193 women referred to the study, only seven refused to participate after initial contact with an interviewer; another 17 were ineligible, and 14 could not be contacted. Others may have been informed but refused referral to the study; we have no knowledge of how many others may have refused or what might have influenced their decision.

Questionnaire

The interviewers administered normed, validated instruments and questionnaires constructed for the purposes of this study. Standardized instruments included the Pearlin et al. (1990) indexes that measure levels of caregiving burden, life stress, coping, social support, and mastery; the Brief Symptoms Inventory (Acosta, Nguyen, & Yamamoto, 1994; Derogatis, 1992; Derogatis & Melisaratos, 1983), which measures general mental well-being; and the Rosenberg (1965) Self-Esteem Scale. Some validated instruments were revised to accommodate Latin cultural variation. Background variables such as age, education, income, ethnicity, place of birth, and household size were also included in the survey instrument. In addition, a number of qualitative, in-depth, and open-ended questions pertaining to service use were asked. Information gathered from pilot interviews, community services providers, and indigenous community caregivers guided construction of open-ended questions.

Respondents were queried about barriers to service use, and specific probes addressed lack of neighborhood-based services, lack of knowledge of services, the availability of Spanish-speaking services, culturally sensitive services provision, and issues of feeling responsible for fulfilling all caregiving obligations. In addition, questions probed for information about preferences for types of services for caregivers and people with AIDS (PWA) and service location (agency-based or in-home).

Obtaining and Maintaining a Sampling Frame

Despite their substantial number, Latinas coping with AIDS have unique problems that often intensify difficulties in reaching a sample, difficulties that slow the research process. Some issues relate to problems of reaching Latino populations in general, and others are specific to people coping with AIDS; for example, generally higher refusal rates among Latinos than white people have been noted in the literature (Howard, Samet, Buechley, Schrag, & Key, 1983; Vernon, Roberts, & Lee, 1984), especially when questions deal with sensitive topics such as sexual behaviors and substance use (Flaskerud & Nyamanthi, 1989; Marin & Marin, 1989). The stigma of AIDS present in the Latin community can increase refusal rates for a number of reasons. First, because AIDS is a life-threatening and stigmatizing illness, a sense of increased vulnerability is often present in the family, resulting in the need to protect the person with AIDS from any possible outside threat. In our experience, many caregivers feared exposure of an

AIDS status to neighbors, friends, and even family members residing in the home who were uninformed about the diagnosis.

Second, because some prospective respondents were undocumented, they were reticent to speak readily with unknown professionals or perceived government bureaucrats. Although this is the case in general with undocumented populations, higher refusal rates can be expected when topics under study may jeopardize the respondent's residency in the United States (Catania, McDermott, & Pollack, 1986). In our experience, the need to maintain privacy for fear of being deported because of an AIDS health problem heightened anxiety about participation in our study.

For many of the same reasons, our experience demonstrated that soliciting involvement through advertising was a far less effective method of obtaining a sample among Latinas than other groups. For example, in a parallel study of white caregivers, approximately half of the sample of 462 were recruited through media advertising or through flyers, whereas only three of 155 were gained through this sampling technique in the Latina study. In fact, no respondents were obtained through newspaper solicitation in the Latina caregiver study. Advertising in newspapers may be the least effective recruitment technique for this group, because many Latinas affected by AIDS do not rely on either Spanish- or English-language newspapers for access to information. We found that solicitation through Spanish-language radio had a slight advantage, but only gained three respondents. Although the literature suggests that public service announcements through Hispanic radio and television stations are excellent methods of recruitment (Humm-Delgado & Delgado, 1983), our experience differed greatly. Although few referrals were gained through this method, those speaking English were the only ones to respond.

Recruitment through radio and television may be slightly more effective than through newspaper advertisements because of the culture's strong oral tradition; however, any advertising method lacks the validation of a personal contact between the prospective respondent and the study representative. In such instances, it is the cultural value of *personalismo* that is operating. *Personalismo* is a strong Latino cultural value emphasizing the importance of open, personal relations in social dealings (Gaw, 1993). We believe that interactions involving *personalismo* lent legitimacy to our study in the eyes of prospective respondents. Furthermore, we believe that this cultural value may be highly useful to incorporate in recruitment efforts in nearly any area of study involving Latinos.

Because of the need for personal contact in recruitment of respondents, AIDS services organizations (ASOs) are a likely source of referrals for research studies. As in many other research endeavors, however, agencies present difficulties as they enact a gatekeeping role. Our experience suggests that in studying AIDS, particular difficulties arise that are worthy of discussion. For example, whereas some agencies may allow a search process whereby clients who fit study criteria can be identified and contacted, no AIDS services agency in our pool would agree to this procedure. And even if this procedure were allowed, again, cold contact is contraindicated in Hispanic populations. Furthermore, well-established older agencies insisted on obtaining signed releases from prospective respondents rather than obtaining verbal consent for them to be referred to the study.

Issues involved with signed releases of information are sensitive ones and require our attention. Perhaps one reason for this procedure lies in the heritage of many ASOs. Many well-established, larger ASOs came into being serving a largely closeted gay male population suffering from a disease with considerable stigma. Agency cultures may be instilled with the necessity of gaining signed releases from clients for any activity outside the agency because reprisal from the greater community (such as employers and insurance companies) was common for their clients. People with AIDS frequently lost their jobs and life or health insurance coverage as their diagnosis became known. The mentality of protecting anonymity regarding HIV-related issues remains a legacy in the second wave of AIDS.

Although signing a release may not be a new experience for majority culture respondents, it is quite new and off-putting for some Latin populations in general, and is a particularly sensitive issue for Latinos coping with AIDS. We found that the necessity of signing a release form before having any contact with the research staff elevated anxiety in some prospective respondents and was viewed with suspicion, especially by those who were undocumented. Signing a release form implied permanence of participation in the study (a misunderstanding) and legal and public documentation of citizenship status (a fear). Few of our respondents had ever participated in a research study and initially were somewhat wary of signing forms until their purpose was carefully explained by trained interviewers. Moreover, such procedures violate Latin values of *personalismo* and *confianza* (confidence, trust, assurance), and in our project, such procedures were viewed as threatening or insulting, subsequently raising refusal rates. Because the topic undertaken for study is highly sensitive and stigmatized, sampling issues that may be problematic when recruiting Latino participants in general take on heightened significance when studying AIDS.

Additional potential difficulties pertaining to populations of color with AIDS concern issues of who is served and where. AIDS is a disease that has affected a changing population over the past decade. Latino clients are underrepresented in centrally located agencies that have historically served predominantly gay males and in agencies located a long distance from Latino neighborhoods. We believe this situation exists because many ASOs have not uniformly adapted to the diversity now represented in the second wave of AIDS. For example, some agencies do not attend to provision of family services. Yet most Latinos define AIDS caregiving as a family issue, not an issue for the individual caregiver or the PWA. Thus, cultural values are interwoven with definitions of responsibility in caregiving and expected service styles. In a study by Cox and Monk (1993), Hispanic

Alzheimer's caregivers turned first to their families for advice and information; only on advice from family did they then seek help from a physician. Values many Latinas hold such as *familismo* (reciprocity, loyalty, and valuing the family and extended family life as a whole), *responsibilidad* (exhibiting responsibility toward one's family), *respeto* (observing proper gender and age respect and consideration), *orgullo* (pride in one's heritage), *personalismo,* and *confianza* are sought by Latinos in the client–worker relationship and in the cultural values exhibited by services agencies. Some agencies may lack knowledge of these particular cultural artifacts and values (Golding & Baezconde-Garbanati, 1990; Land, 1994; Singer, Castillo, Davidson, & Flores, 1990; Singer, Flores, et al., 1990; Weeks et al., 1995). For example, Latino women report interpersonal interactions in such organizations that limit opportunities for the entire family to be fully supported in the AIDS crisis (personal communication with M. Garay, family mental health specialist, AIDS Service Center, Pasadena, CA, March 26, 1996). In addition, many Latinas may find the directness of agency preventive outreach efforts (such as advocating safe sex through pictures, explicit literature, or signs) to be quite offensive and embarrassing. Hence, they are less likely to return for services (personal communication with M. Garay, March 26, 1996).

General research on Hispanics repeatedly emphasizes the need for investigators to gain sponsorship of community agencies and organizations to facilitate synchronicity of attitudes and cultural values among workers, clients, and the organization (Becerra & Zambrana, 1985; Marin & Marin, 1989; Sue, 1988). We found that because their service styles are more concordant with Latin values, smaller neighborhood-based ASOs and clinics and hospitals located in Latino communities, particularly those staffed by women, provided easier access to a Latina sample. Such facilities display less hierarchical bureaucracies and therefore allow personalized communication for referral to research studies and direct access to prospective respondents for sample recruitment. For these reasons, these facilities are valuable sources for sample recruitment. Because of the relatively small client population in such organizations, the researcher may need to contact a greater number of sources to recruit a sufficient number of participants. Nevertheless, we highly recommend this procedure.

Researchers also must consider the circumstances of risk when conducting AIDS research. The mode of HIV infection can influence where HIV-positive people or their caregivers can be approached. Latinas, most of whom are infected by noninjecting sex partners, are best reached in their neighborhoods through clinics, community hospitals, or family-based agencies and through networks of family and friends. Other populations, however, such as those infected primarily through injection drug use, may be best recruited through methods such as street outreach (Weeks et al., 1995).

DATA COLLECTION ISSUES

Interviewing Procedures

As with other research on Latin populations, face-to-face interviews of AIDS caregivers are preferable to other methods of data collection (Zapka, Chasen-Taber, Bigelow, & Hurley, 1994). Response rates on mailed surveys, for example, are lower for Hispanics than for majority culture respondents (Howard et al., 1983). The potential of nonresponse or inaccurate response is ever present; therefore, the use of interviewers to administer questionnaires in person is the best method for reducing this source of bias.

Face-to-face interviewing at a site chosen by the respondent allows both the interviewer and the respondent greater control over the situation. In our study, we found that in-home interviewing was generally preferable to these respondents and had several advantages. First, the women often care for more than one person, and they may be needed in their homes. In addition, the need to arrange for child care for preschoolers and transportation for women and their children to agency or other sites for interviewing is eliminated. Also important, interviewing in the home is often viewed by Latina AIDS caregivers as being sensitive to their responsibility to meet the needs of their family members during this time of heightened stress, thus providing greater comfort for them. However, there are limitations to in-home interviewing; these include interruptions and, at times, lack of privacy. These issues can be minimized when discussed in the preinterview contact.

Protocols for contacting respondents, screening them, and describing the study need to be designed with sensitivity to conducting AIDS research within the Latin community. For example, in our study, to protect privacy interviewers were trained not to mention the word "AIDS" to anyone but the caregiver and not to leave a telephone message about the study. In some cases, even close family and friends of the PWA residing in the caregiver's home were unaware of the AIDS diagnosis. An additional difficulty encountered was that some recently immigrated respondents were hesitant or could not give some information, such as their zip code or two contact sources. In some cases, they did not know the information (for example, contacts' telephone numbers), whereas in others they were reluctant to provide this information, because they did not want to explain to their contacts about their participation in an AIDS study.

In AIDS research, as with other research among Latinos, obtaining at least two contacts is important. This is an effective method of stemming attrition in a population where migration rates are high. Whereas those who are more acculturated seem to be easier to recontact (McGraw, McKinlay, Crawford, Costa, & Cohen, 1992), women who are foreign born, younger, unemployed, and poor tend to be more difficult to recontact (Aneshensel, Becerra, Fielder, & Schyler, 1989; Iverson & Sabroe, 1988). These findings are especially pertinent to Latina AIDS caregivers, as many have these background characteristics. Furthermore, they are likely to be even more difficult to follow than Latinos in general, because their residency may change with changes in caregiving responsibilities.

Gaining Consent, Administering the Interview, and Following Up

Because Latinas come from a sociocultural background that is different from dominant American culture, their expectations about interview questions and protocol may differ from those of the researcher (McGraw et al., 1992). In general, when interviewing Latinos, and in keeping with Latino values of *personalismo, confianza,* and *respeto,* time should be taken to establish a personalized, trusting, and respectful rapport before initiating official interview procedures. Culturally sensitive interviewing with Hispanics must include forming closer ties with respondents than is usual in standard survey methods (Becerra & Zambrana, 1985). Such procedures serve to heighten the authenticity of the interview; in addition, they reduce responses reflecting trait and social desirability and acquiescence, responses particularly noted among Latinos (Ross & Mirowsky, 1984). Researchers should note that these procedures require more interviewer training, more time per interview, and greater cost; hence, more resources should be allocated per interview.

Because language is a strong predictor of acculturation level (Solis, Marks, Garcia, & Shelton, 1990), it may be that Latinas who are monolingual are less acculturated, more invested in traditional Latino values, and less exposed to research interviewing procedures. In our study, interviews conducted with monolingual Spanish-speaking respondents took an average of 40 minutes longer than those conducted in English. In addition to the above-mentioned cultural issues that may increase interview time, other important issues specific to caregivers must be taken into account. Latina AIDS caregivers in particular are often quite isolated, very burdened with multiple family caregiving responsibilities, and at times, bereaved. Their need to ventilate is pressing. Because of this situation and the oral traditions of their culture, respondents may often answer questions in a nonlinear style, through dialogue and storytelling. This process is not inhibiting as long as the respondent, in the end, answers the question at hand. Interviewers should be trained to allow respondents sufficient time to talk and respectfully refocus the respondent. This procedure often yields positive results.

Measurement Issues

When conducting cross-cultural research in general, many issues have been raised about cultural bias or degree of fit in the measurement of psychosocial variables. Difficulties can arise in the measuring process; in the face, content, and construct validity of the instrument; in the translation of the instrument; in the consistency of item functioning; and in the format of the instrument itself. Because measurement issues are tied to the population of interest, our discussion of measurement centers particularly on cross-cultural research and research on Hispanics in general, and we also give some attention to the specifics of conducting research on Latinas and AIDS and suggest guidelines for circumventing difficulties.

Measuring Process

With regard to the measuring process, the literature indicates that cultural values and norms may mediate the extent to which information is revealed or items are endorsed (Kinzie et al., 1982; Rogler, 1993). Respondents may differ on their endorsement of items depending on whether they were interviewed in their primary language (Escobar et al., 1986). Moreover, the context of the interview may predict what content is revealed, including such factors as interviewer characteristics, types of questions asked, and the location of the interview. Differences in display rules for emotion vary across cultures and may influence what is said and to whom, especially on sensitive topics such as AIDS (Manson, 1995). In our study, we were careful to match interviewer and respondent characteristics on ethnicity, gender, and language and to train interviewers about the importance of establishing *confianza* and *personalismo* with respondents. We found that respondents were forthcoming with information on emotionally laden material and openly expressed their emotions about AIDS caregiving.

The literature indicates that in Latin cultures, preference for open-ended and indirect questions about sensitive topics yields greater ease in responding (Becerra & Zambrana, 1985; Salcido, 1990). Thus, a forced choice answer with an item stem "How were you infected with HIV/AIDS" can be rephrased as "Do you have thoughts or an opinion on how you caught the virus?" Especially on sensitive topics, some researchers have found an interaction between ethnicity and interview mode regarding what respondents reveal, with Hispanics revealing more content in face-to-face interviews than through other modes (Aquino & LoScioto, 1990). Some literature indicates that respondents selectively report the elements they believe to be situationally relevant to the interview. What is reported in a physician's office may be different from content reported in the home of the respondent (Kinzie et al., 1982). The researcher must take all of these concerns into account in designing the process of measurement and, where possible, match research content to context.

Issues of Validity

With regard to the content of the instrument, a number of issues arise in measurement of constructs across cultures. Face validity may be lacking, as some cultural content may be underrepresented. For example, the instrument may lack attunement to cultural values such as *familismo* or important relationships such as the *Padrinos* (godparents) or fail to represent adequately content related to gender, ethnicity, or socioeconomic status. For example, health culture is an important construct that is likely to vary among different populations. Health culture is "the information and understanding that people have learned from family, friends and neighbors as to the nature of a health problem, its cause, and its implications" (Rubel & Garro, 1992, p. 627). As the social networks of Hispanics focus primarily on the family, family members are likely to shape the health culture of Hispanic women. The influence of *familismo* on Hispanic health culture suggests that when Hispanic women experience a health problem or symptom that causes uncertainty or stress, they are likely to turn first to family for information. Failure by mental health and health delivery professionals to adequately address the many expectations influenced by the health culture may result in compromised compliance and limited use of services by Hispanic groups (Canino & Canino, 1993; Martinez, 1993). Thus, including content on the effect of *familismo* on the shaping of health culture is important in studies focusing on health issues, particularly AIDS, in Hispanic populations.

A second issue influencing the validity of research with diverse populations is that concepts treated as differentiated may, in fact, be unitarily defined across cultures or vice versa. Such was the case in Manson, Shore, and Bloom's (1985) study of Hopi culture, in which distinctions were found among guilt, shame, and sinfulness; these distinctions were not present in a validated measure of depression. Conversely, that which is differentiated in dominant cultures (such as extended family versus nuclear family) may be unitarily defined in Latino and other cultures. Moreover, culture-bound syndromes such as the Latino *susto* (symptoms of anxiety and depression following a fright and involving possible soul loss) or *ataque de nervios* (a type of anxiety–panic condition) existing in Latino cultures (Gaw, 1993) may be missing from measures of distress, an often-used outcome variable in behavioral research.

Variations exist in the intensity and expression of the language of affect. Cultures may place differential emphasis on emotions and assign unique attributions in the intensity of their experiences. For example, anger, an often-used word in U.S. assessment instruments, may be experienced in a range from moderate irritation to rage episodes, depending on the culture's sanctioning of expression of affect (Westmeyer, 1985). As previously noted, such content may be underrepresented in measuring instruments.

Many standardized scales, particularly those that tap culturally based behavior, such as dimensions of coping or role definitions, are not designed for use with ethnic minority populations or cross-cultural research. In our experience, validated coping inventories do not adequately represent coping mechanisms used in Latino culture and are not useful or valid in their original state. For example, in many Latino cultures, religiosity and spirituality are very much linked to emotional well-being and coping styles (Alarcon, 1995;

Landrine & Klonoff, 1994; Lukoff, Lu, & Turner, 1992), yet content tapping spirituality is lacking from most instruments. This content is crucial in studying manifestations of coping and health behavior in AIDS research.

We found that standardized coping instruments need to be supplemented with coping mechanisms often used by Latinas during crisis points such as in caring for terminally ill relatives. Latino coping mechanisms include the employment of religious sacrificial rituals such as *mandas,* a religious ritual in which a sacrifice to God or a favored saint is made in prayerful hope that intercession will occur in a critical or life-threatening situation. Often, cutting the hair is seen as such a sacrifice (personal communication with M. Garay, March 26, 1996). Other sacrificial rituals include fasting and crawling on one's knees to the altar, saying devotional prayers, and using holy artifacts such as water or soil from holy sites.

Frequently, alternative healing or coping methods include using herbal remedies and visiting an indigenous healer such as a *cuandero* or a Yourbal priestess. In addition, the practice of *Ifa/Santaria* is used by some Latin subcultures and should be included in measures of coping. Derived from the synchronization of Catholic and African spiritual traditions in which Catholic saints represent African deities, *Santaria* encompasses such rituals as owning healing amulets, exorcising evil spirits from the home, and reciting prayers for intercession to favored saints. *Espiritismo* is an especially important ritual for the bereaved and involves efforts to communicate with the spirits of the dead (Canino & Canino, 1993; Martinez, 1993). In our Latina caregiver study, we also found it necessary to add content on cultural sanctioning of certain coping methods. For example, we asked open-ended questions on methods of coping that the respondent wished she could use to relieve stress but felt she could not because of the need to protect an AIDS diagnosis or because of cultural or family sanctions against certain coping strategies.

Definitions of self and loci of emotion also may differ markedly across cultures and influence the validity of an instrument (Aneshensel, Clark, & Freichs, 1983; Sagetta & Johnson, 1980). For example, symptom configurations of disorders such as anxiety or depression may be defined largely as intrapsychic, individually defined experiences in dominant European American culture (for example, I feel blue, I fear things I do not normally fear) (Sampson, 1985; Waterman, 1981). By contrast, Hispanics may be best described as sociocentric in worldview; the self is, in large part, defined through relationships with others. The prevalence and importance of values such as *familismo* in Hispanic cultures speak to the sociocentric worldview. Hence, such symptom configurations are influenced by collaterally defined experiences in Latino culture (for example, I am no longer able to care for my family, I feel that people thought less of my family) (Manson, 1995; Sampson, 1985). Therefore, what constitutes a construct such as depression, an often-used outcome variable in behavioral research, may vary significantly across cultures. This possibility should be addressed in choosing instruments for use with diverse groups. In this regard, indigenous caregivers and health providers are irreplaceable advisers and should be consulted regularly in the review and editing of instruments to increase content and face validity.

Translation

In general, translation of instruments requires more than translation and back-translation by independent parties. Language inequivalence may be evident in colloquialisms, slang, taxonomies, and culture-specific labels and sayings, such as Spanish sayings, or *dichos*, that capture construct definitions or defining experiences for respondents (Zuniga, 1992). For example, unlike Spanish, the English language is replete with compound words such as "caregiver," "weekend," and "babysitter" that do not translate simply. Similarly, expressions such as "being pushed around in life" and operating on an "equal plane" with others do not have concordant counterparts in Spanish.

Word-for-word, literal translations are generally inadequate. Accurate translation involves establishing various types of equivalence including semantic, idiomatic, experiential, and conceptual equivalence (Flaherty et al., 1988). Whereas semantic equivalence addresses equivalence in the meanings of words, idiomatic equivalence addresses establishing equivalence through comparable expressions. For example, in our AIDS caregiver instrument, the phrase "get away from it all" in English was translated in Spanish to *"escaparme de todo,"* meaning "escape from everything."

Experiential equivalence attempts to fit the translation to the target cultural context. For example, in traditional Latino culture, the preferred method of child care may be the use of relatives rather than day care or an employed babysitter. Conceptual equivalence refers to equivalence in the validity of the concept and the events experienced by the people in the target culture. For example, in conducting AIDS research in Hispanic communities, the conceptual equivalence of receiving services through a visiting nurse may translate as receiving the services of an indigenous caregiver whose specialty is injecting and administering medical treatment. Preparation of accurate translations must involve all of these types of equivalence. The researcher cannot simply translate an instrument and disregard nuances mediated through culture (Rogler, 1993).

Several guidelines on translation can be applied to cross-cultural research in general. First, when possible, several translations and back-translations from both professional and culturally indigenous staff should be produced. Ideally, some translators should be blind to the study purpose, and others should be informed. Second, it is helpful to constitute a multidisciplinary committee of professionals and culturally indigenous consultants to review and compare source translations in preparation of the final version of instruments. The team verifies cross-cultural equivalence by rejecting or modifying items or generating new items to be added to the final version.

Third, it is advantageous to use structured methods for decision making, such as decentering techniques that define both source and final versions as being equally important. Fourth, it is essential to check for equivalence in source and final versions through pretesting on target populations. Probes and discussion with respondent–informants should be used for clarification where confusions exist (Guillemin, Bombardier, & Beaton, 1993).

Differential Item Functioning

Today, as researchers grapple with interacting issues of diversity in race, ethnicity, culture, socioeconomic status, and gender, achieving objective measurement is crucial in conducting cross-cultural research. Objectivity requires that the measurement be independent of the object being measured. Thurstone (1928) noted, "A measuring instrument must not be seriously affected in its measuring function by the object of measurement. To the extent that its measuring function is so affected, the validity of the instrument is impaired or limited" (p. 547).

Studies of differential item functioning (DIF) attempt to ascertain whether characteristics such as race and gender, which may appear to be extraneous to respondent status or functioning on a given measure, actually affect measurement (Dancer, Anderson, & Dearlin, 1994). For example, the ruler underlying a questionnaire item may take on one set of properties with Latinos and another set with African Americans. Yet many times researchers assume that experiences are linear and additive in nature, not unlike a ruler, and that the markers on the ruler are invariant across groups. In fact, research indicates that for many constructs, the threshold at which "normal" is demarcated from "abnormal" does vary by gender and cultural group. For example, the persistently higher prevalence of depressive symptoms reported among women than men and among Puerto Ricans than white middle-class Americans may represent culturally patterned variation in the experience of the disorder rather than higher rates of the disorder (Manson, 1995). Hence, normative differences between groups imply the presence of different cutoff points or the need to culturally specify the markers in the measuring instrument.

Research in DIF uses log-linear models to examine item validity, that is, whether or not there is an interaction between the item response and the respondent's background variable on the measure of interest; for example, terms denoting the interactions of ethnicity and gender with item response are included in a log-linear model as a test for the influence of background variables on the item response. If the model containing either interaction term fits the data, it is considered evidence of DIF (Dancer et al., 1994).

Other methods for detecting DIF include the use of the Mantel-Haenszel (M-H) statistic (Holland & Thayer, 1986). This procedure compares the performance of respondents from two groups at each interval score of the test. The score is weighted by the number of respondents at each interval. The statistic yields an odds ratio that is then transformed into the delta scale (where delta is a normal deviate with a standard deviation of 4). The delta difference M-H, representing the difference in difficulty between the groups compared after the total score has been taken into account, permits judging the magnitude of the differential performance in terms of a familiar scale. The results are given in terms of the M-H difference statistic (Scheuneman & Gerritz, 1990).

Attention to how a respondent's background characteristics interact with a measure is particularly important to cross-cultural research in general, because instruments play an evermore prominent role in the diagnosis of dysfunction, placement in treatment programs for people at risk, and acquisition of knowledge of understudied populations. Moreover, recognizing such influences is fundamental to culture-sensitive theory construction as well as to effective service delivery for diverse populations.

Several studies have documented DIF; hence, concern regarding objective measurement appears to be well founded (Becker, 1990; Scheuneman & Gerritz, 1990; Schmitt & Dorans, 1990). In a study of mental health status and suicidal probability, Dancer et al. (1994) found that response rates among psychiatric patient and suicidal respondents of African American and European American heritage were very similar but were nearly the reverse of the response rates for Latinos. Content of some items reflecting DIF for ethnicity centered on themes of social relationships, self-esteem, hostility, and depression. In addition to those themes, some items showing DIF for gender centered on the themes of coping with responsibilities.

These findings make intuitive sense as substantial cultural differences exist between non-Hispanic white people, U.S.-born Hispanics, and Mexican-born Hispanics in the underlying dimensions of measures such as the Center for Epidemiologic Studies Depression Scale (Golding & Aneshensel, 1989). Other European–Latino differences exist in measures of self-esteem (Gil, Vega, & Dimas, 1994), social relationships, and coping styles (Mena, Padilla, & Maldonado, 1987; Moyerman & Forman, 1992) and in measures of aptitude, in which results suggest that differences in prior learning, experience, and interest patterns may be linked with DIF (Scheuneman & Gerritz, 1990).

Results demonstrating DIF for gender are also consistent with other findings. Gender differences exist in how men and women engage in social relationships (Lin & Westcott, 1991), cope with responsibilities (Gore & Colton, 1991), and express symptoms (McGrath, Keita, Strickland, & Russo, 1990; Thoits, 1991); therefore, it is likely that gender has a bearing on response to some items measuring those factors. One possible interpretation of DIF findings for race, ethnicity, and gender is that the performance of the measured group may be different from those for which the test was developed.

Analyzing whether DIF exists within items requires access to comparison samples or information on established scale norms of certain groups. Although the effort to document DIF is quite valuable and necessary for accurate data interpretation, it adds methodological complexity and another step in the research process and often requires greater resources. Cross-cultural research calls for using research designs with comparison groups to permit investigation into DIF in various indexes.

Attention to DIF is particularly relevant to this discussion, given the increasing rates of AIDS infection and other health problems among Hispanics and the consequential increase in the need for services. Of particular concern are potential differences in item functioning within behavioral indexes (as a result of gender, culture, and socioeconomic status) that may influence health risks. For example, if different norms exist for measures of help-seeking behavior, learning styles, coping mechanisms, and appraisal of stress and well-being, many AIDS prevention, outreach, and support services will require programmatic revision. In fact, more accurate measurement of health behavior in general should result in more effective service planning and risk reduction for women of color and others.

Format

The construction of measuring instruments is inherently influenced by cultural assumptions in the people that create the tools; hence, the format of the instrument may be influenced by degrees of cultural familiarity and preference. For example, instruments with negative item stems, multiple choice answers, and mark-sense answer sheets have been noted as being problematic for respondents of various cultural backgrounds (Flaskerud, 1988; Morishima & Mizokawa, 1979). Several methods are helpful in overcoming these problems and are an expected part of conducting cross-cultural research in general. One format difficulty is the widespread use of the Likert-type scale in cross-cultural research. This difficulty arises from the noted inability of varying cultural groups to reliably respond to this format (Baranowski, Tsong, & Broderick, 1990). Investigators have documented variability across ethnic and racial groups in respondent endorsement of markers of intensity on Likert scales. For example, Bachman and O'Malley (1984) reported that African Americans were more likely to use extreme categories on different indexes using the Likert format than were white people or Latinos.

Some studies have manipulated the method of questionnaire administration to control for inaccurate responses, but problems with Likert scales persist. In one study using a paper-and-pencil self-administered instrument for Latinos, 36 percent failed to complete questionnaires correctly (Flaskerud, 1988). Flaskerud noted that failures attributed to nonliteracy were excluded in the analysis. Flaskerud further stated that because the instrument was not back-translated for semantic equivalence, some misinterpretation may have been evident.

In another study, the same translated scale was used, but the method of administration was changed to face-to-face interviewing for nonliterate participants. The change of method did not affect problems with the use of the scale. Despite repeated attempts to clarify instructions and reread the response continuum, the majority of both literate and nonliterate groups experienced difficulty with the Likert format. Respondents preferred a dichotomous "si" or "no" response, experienced complications with the meaning of ordered contrasts, and ignored the range of the scale continuum. Even when items were read aloud and each separate response was inserted into the item stem, respondents experienced confusion. Interviewers continued to report struggles with getting respondents to select one answer and to use and understand the established format. Because respondents resisted the format, irrespective of literacy or method of administration, the problems with the format point to potential cultural barriers in its use (Flaskerud, 1988).

It is possible that the difficulty experienced by respondents in using Likert scales is related to some of the methodological problems discussed earlier, such as an interaction between the format and the content of the measure, cultural sanctions against revealing certain types of information, the degree of respondent comfort with the research experience, or the nature of the response required. Use of the Likert format also may be problematic because of a lack of acculturation of some respondents, education level, or poor translation or lack of semantic equivalence between versions of response continua. Still, difficulty may be related specifically to the format itself. It is possible that the degree of variance the Likert scale attempts to measure is meaningless among some cultural groups (Flaskerud, 1988).

In our study of Latinas, we often found a preference for a dichotomous response. When respondents had difficulty with the Likert format, we found most useful a two-tier method. First we obtained a "yes" or "no" response, and then we solicited the intensity of the response. For example, an item on a social support scale reads, "How much have you lost contact with other people?" The respondent might answer dichotomously saying, "Yes, I have," or "No, I have not." If the respondent answered "yes," she was asked which response came closer: "completely," "quite a bit," or "somewhat." In addition, response cards representing a visual graphic of the intensity continuum often helped with obtaining a graduated response (Figure 39-1).

CONCLUSION

The need for cross-cultural research is evident in the changing demographic picture of the AIDS crisis as well as in other health concerns. The growing awareness of important clinical subgroup differences based on ethnicity, culture, gender, and socioeconomic status indicates that further discussion of methodological concerns and possible solutions in cross-cultural research is needed. Cultural bias is a considerable concern in AIDS and other behavioral research, as it may exist in many forms and ultimately affect client services in a number of ways. Particularly in today's world of managed care and service utilization review, decisions are continually being made about which populations

Figure 39-1
Likert Scale Response Card for Latina Respondents

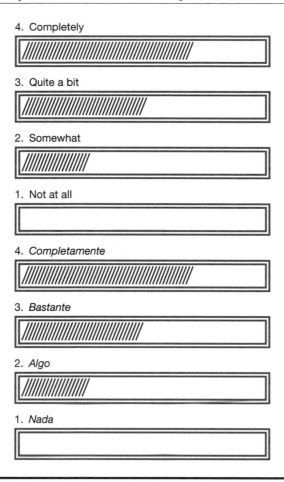

4. Completely

3. Quite a bit

2. Somewhat

1. Not at all

4. *Completamente*

3. *Bastante*

2. *Algo*

1. *Nada*

are eligible to receive limited services, under what circumstances, and for what length of time. The measures by which those decisions are made may reflect cultural, socioeconomic status, and gender bias. Bias may also be present in evaluations of existing ASOs and in pilot study data of service needs, which are often used to initiate new AIDS programs.

A number of methodological and design considerations warrant attention, including how respondents are reached in needs assessments, who is studied, the sensitivity of any measures to cultural variation, the populations that receive the most services, and the conditions that prevail during the study. For example, findings indicate that HIV attitudes held by Latinas remain unchanged even as practices and the knowledge base improve with exposure to educational programs targeted to women (Flaskerud & Nyamanthi, 1990). Findings such as these point to the necessity to explore the mediating role of culture in research design. Both etic and emic traditions are useful in this endeavor, yet both have limitations. The emic tradition examines behavior from within the cultural system and is based on data from only one culture. Conversely, the etic approach studies behavior from outside the cultural system, examines data from many cultures, and extracts common elements across cultures (Berry, 1980; Triandis & Marin, 1983).

The central limitation of segregated cross-cultural research is that it fails to use experimentation and to develop theory. The primary limitation of mainline theories is that they ignore culture and therefore lack universality (Bentancourt & Lopez, 1993). Modifications within the etic and emic approaches are possible. One method useful in overcoming these limitations is to begin with an observation from the study of cultures and move toward its implication for behavioral theory (Triandis, Bontempo, Villareal, Asai, & Lucca, 1988). Another useful method is to begin with an established theory and incorporate and transport cultural elements to broaden its theoretical domain (Bentancourt & Weiner, 1982). Social work, with its ecological framework, is ideally situated to use both methods and to add to the body of knowledge, so that the needs of Hispanic and other diverse groups that constitute social work clientele will be addressed.

REFERENCES

Acosta, F., Nguyen, L., & Yamamoto, J. (1994). Using the Brief Symptom Inventory to profile monolingual Spanish-speaking psychiatric outpatients. *Journal of Clinical Psychology, 50,* 723–726.

Alarcon, R. (1995). Culture and psychiatric diagnosis: Impact on DSM-IV and ICD-10. *Psychiatric Clinics of North America, 18,* 449–465.

Aneshensel, C., Becerra, R., Fielder, E., & Schyler, R. (1989). Participation of Mexican-American female adolescents in a longitudinal panel survey. *Public Opinion Quarterly, 53,* 548–562.

Aneshensel, C., Clark, V., & Freichs, R. (1983). Ethnicity and depression: A confirmatory analysis. *Journal of Personality and Social Psychology, 44,* 385–398.

Aquino, W., & LoScioto, L. (1990). Effects of interview mode on self-reported drug use. *Public Opinion Quarterly, 54,* 362–395.

Bachman, J., & O'Malley, P. (1984). Black–white differences in self-esteem: Are they affected by response styles? *American Journal of Sociology, 90,* 624–639.

Baranowski, T., Tsong, Y., & Broderick, M. (1990). Scaling of response scale adverbs among black American adults. *Perceptual Motor Skills, 71,* 547–559.

Becerra, R., & Zambrana, R. (1985). Methodological approaches to research on Hispanics. *Social Work Research & Abstracts, 21*(2), 42–49.

Becker, B. (1990). Item characteristics and gender differences on the SAT-M for mathematically able youths. *American Educational Research Journal, 27,* 65–72.

Bentancourt, H., & Lopez, S. (1993). The study of culture, ethnicity, and race in American psychology. *American Psychologist, 48,* 629–637.

Bentancourt, H., & Weiner, B. (1982). Attributions for achievement related events, expectancy, and sentiments: A study of success and failure in Chile and the United States. *Journal of Cross-Cultural Psychology, 13,* 363–400.

Berry, J. W. (1980). Introduction to methodology. In H. C. Triandis & J. W. Berry (Eds.), *Handbook of cross-cultural psychology* (Vol. 2). Boston: Allyn & Bacon.

Canino, I. A., & Canino, G. J. (1993). Psychiatric care of Puerto Ricans. In A. Gaw (Ed.), *Culture, ethnicity, and mental illness* (pp. 467–500). Washington, DC: American Psychiatric Press.

Catania, J., McDermott, L., & Pollack, L. (1986). Questionnaire response bias and face-to-face interview sample bias in sexuality research. *Journal of Sex Research, 22*(1), 52–72.

Cox, C., & Monk, A. (1993). Hispanic culture and family care of Alzheimer's patients. *Health & Social Work, 18,* 92–99.

Dancer, L., Anderson, A., & Dearlin, R. (1994). Use of log-linear models for assessing differential item functioning in a measure of psychological functioning. *Journal of Consulting and Clinical Psychology, 62,* 710–717.

Dennenberg, R. (1992).What the numbers mean. In C. Chris & M. Pearl (Eds.), *Women, AIDS and activism* (pp. 1–4). Boston: South End Press.

Derogatis, L. (1992). *BSI: Administration, scoring and procedures manual II.* Baltimore: Clinical Psychometrics Research.

Derogatis, L., & Melisaratos, N. (1983). The Brief Symptom Inventory: An introductory report. *Psychological Medicine, 13,* 595–605.

Escobar, J. I., Burnam, A., Karino, M., Forsythe, A., Landswerk, J., & Golding, M. (1986). Using the Mini Mental State Examination in a community population of mixed ethnicity: Cultural linguistic artifacts. *Journal of Nervous and Mental Disease, 174,* 607–614.

Fernandez, I. (1995). Latinas and AIDS: Challenges to HIV prevention. In A. O'Leary & L. S. Jemott (Eds.), *Women at risk: Issues in primary prevention of AIDS* (pp. 159–174). New York: Plenum.

Flaherty, J. A., Gaviria, F. M., Patnak, D., Michell, T., Wintrob, R., Richman, J. A., & Birz, S. (1988). Developing instruments for cross-cultural psychiatric research. *Journal of Nervous and Mental Disease, 176,* 257–263.

Flaskerud, J. (1988). Is the Likert scale format culturally biased? *Nursing Research, 37,* 185–186.

Flaskerud, J., & Nyamanthi, A. (1989). Black and Latina women's AIDS related knowledge, attitudes and practices. *Research in Nursing and Health, 12,* 339–346.

Flaskerud, J., & Nyamanthi, A. (1990). Effects of an AIDS education program on the knowledge, attitudes, and practices of low income black and Latina women. *Journal of Community Health, 15,* 343–355.

Gaw, A. (Ed.). (1993). *Culture, ethnicity, and mental illness.* Washington, DC: American Psychiatric Press.

Gil, A., Vega, W., & Dimas, J. (1994). Acculturative stress and personal adjustment among Hispanic adolescent boys. *Journal of Community Psychology, 22,* 43–54.

Golding, J., & Aneshensel, C. (1989). Factor structure for the Center of Epidemiologic Studies Depression Scale among Mexican-Americans and non-Hispanic whites. *Journal of Consulting and Clinical Psychology, 1,* 163–168.

Golding, J. M., & Baezconde-Garbanati, L. A. (1990). Ethnicity, culture, and social resources. *American Journal of Community Psychology, 18,* 465–486.

Gore, S., & Colton, M. (1991). Gender, stress, and distress: Social–relational influences. In J. Eckenrode (Ed.), *The social context of coping* (pp. 139–164). New York: Plenum.

Guillemin, F., Bombardier, C., & Beaton, D. (1993). Cross-cultural adaptations of health-related quality of life measures: Literature review and proposed guidelines. *Journal of Clinical Epidemiology, 46,* 1417–1432.

Holland, P., & Thayer, D. (1986). *Differential item performance and the Mantel-Haenszel procedure* (RR-86-31). Princeton, NJ: Educational Testing Service.

Howard, C., Samet, J., Buechley, R., Schrag, S., & Key, C. (1983). Survey research in New Mexico Hispanics: Some methodological issues. *American Journal of Epidemiology, 117,* 27–34.

Hu, T., & Snowden, L. (1992). Cost and use of public mental health services by ethnicity. *Journal of Mental Health Administration, 19,* 278–287.

Humm-Delgado, D., & Delgado, M. (1983). Assessing Hispanic mental health needs: Issues and recommendations. *Journal of Community Psychology, 11,* 363–375.

Iverson, L., & Sabroe, S. (1988). Participation in a follow-up study of health among unemployed and employed people after a company close down: Dropouts and selection bias. *Journal of Epidemiology and Community Health, 42,* 396–401.

Kalichman, S., Hunter, T., & Kelly, J. (1992). Perceptions of AIDS susceptibility among minority and nonminority women at risk for HIV infection. *Journal of Consulting and Clinical Psychology, 60,* 725–732.

Keefe, S. E., Padilla, A. M., & Carlos, M. L. (1979). Mexican-American family as a social support system. *Human Organization, 38*(2), 144–152.

Kiecolt-Glaser, J., & Glaser, R. (1995). Psychoneuroimmunology and health consequences: Data and shared mechanisms. *Psychosomatic Medicine, 57,* 269–274.

Kinzie, J., Manson, S., Vinh, D., Nguen, T. T., Anh, B., & Pho, R. (1982). Development and validation of a Vietnamese depression rating scale. *American Journal of Psychiatry, 139,* 1276–1281.

Land, H. (1994). AIDS and women of color. *Families in Society, 75,* 335–361.

Landrine H., & Klonoff, E. (1994). Cultural diversity in causal attributions for illness: The role of the supernatural. *Journal of Behavioral Medicine, 17,* 181–193.

Lin, N., & Westcott, J. (1991). Marital engagement/disengagement, social networks and mental health. In J. Eckenrode (Ed.), *The social context of coping* (pp. 213–238). New York: Plenum.

Lockerly, S. (1991). Caregiving among racial and ethnic minority elders: Family and social supports. *Generations, 15*(4), 58–62.

Lukoff, S., Lu, F., & Turner, R. (1992). Toward a more culturally sensitive DSM-IV: Psychoreligious and psychospiritual problems. *Journal of Nervous and Mental Disease, 180,* 673–681.

Maldonando, M. (1991). Latinos and HIV/AIDS, implications for the 90's. *SIECUS Report, 19*(2), 11–15.

Manson, S. (1995). Culture and major depression: Current challenges in the diagnosis of mood disorders. *Psychiatric Clinics of North America, 18,* 487–501.

Manson, S. M., Shore, J. H., & Bloom, J. D. (1985). The depressive experience in American Indian communities: A challenge for psychiatric theory and diagnosis. In A. Kleinman & B. Good (Eds.), *Culture and depression: Studies in the anthropology and cross-cultural psychiatry of affect and disorder* (pp. 331–368). Berkeley: University of California Press.

Marin, B. (1990). Hispanic culture: Implications for AIDS prevention. In J. Boswell, R. Hexter, & J. Reinish (Eds.), *Sexuality and disease: Metaphor, perceptions and behavior in the AIDS era* (pp. 1–28). New York: Oxford University Press.

Marin, G., & Marin, B. V. (1989). A comparison of three interview approaches when studying sensitive topics with Hispanics. *Hispanic Journal of Behavioral Sciences, 11,* 330–340.

Martinez, C. (1993). Psychiatric care of Mexican-Americans. In A. Gaw (Ed.), *Culture, ethnicity, and mental illness* (pp. 431–466). Washington, DC: American Psychiatric Press.

Martinez, R. (1978). *Hispanic culture and health care: Fact, fiction, and folklore.* St. Louis: C. V. Mosby.

McGrath, D., Keita, G., Strickland, B., & Russo, N. (1990). *Women and depression: Risk factors and treatment issues.* Washington, DC: American Psychological Association.

McGraw, S., McKinlay, J., Crawford, S., Costa, L., & Cohen, D. (1992). Health survey methods with minority populations: Some lessons from recent experience. *Ethnicity and Disease, 2,* 273–287.

Medrano, L., & Cuvilly-Klopner, M. (1992). AIDS and people of color. In H. Land (Ed.), *AIDS: A complete guide to psychosocial intervention* (pp. 117–140). Milwaukee, WI: Families International.

Mena, F., Padilla, A., & Maldonado, M. (1987). Acculturative stress and specific coping strategies among immigrant and later generation college students. *Hispanic Journal of Behavioral Sciences, 9,* 207–225.

Mintzer, J. E., Rubert, M. P., Lowenstein, D., Gomez, E., Millor, A., Quinteros, R., Flores, L., Miller, M., Rainerman, A., & Gisdorfer, C. (1992). Daughters caregiving for Hispanic and non-Hispanic Alzheimer's patients: Does ethnicity make a difference? *Community Mental Health Journal, 28,* 292–303.

Morishima, J., & Mizokawa, D. (1979). The education for, by, and of Asian/Pacific Americans. *Research Review of Equal Education, 4,* 1–39.

Moyerman, D., & Forman, B. (1992). Acculturation and adjustment: A meta-analytic study. *Hispanic Journal of Behavioral Sciences, 14,* 163–200.

Munoz, R. et al. (1982). On the AHCPR depression in primary care guidelines: Further considerations for practitioners. *American Psychologist, 49,* 42–61.

Pearlin, L. (1989). The sociological study of stress. *Health and Social Behavior, 30,* 241–256.

Pearlin, L., Mullan, J., Semple, S., & Skaff, M. (1990). Caregiving and the stress process: An overview of measures. *Gerontologist, 30,* 583–594.

Rogler, L. (1993). Culturally sensitizing psychiatric diagnosis: A framework for research. *Journal of Nervous and Mental Disease, 181,* 401–408.

Rosen, D., & Blank, W. (1992). Women and AIDS. In H. Land (Ed.), *AIDS: A complete guide to psychosocial intervention* (pp. 141–152). Milwaukee: Families International.

Rosenberg, L. (1965). *Society and the adolescent self-image.* Princeton, NJ: Princeton University Press.

Ross, C., & Mirowsky, J. (1984). Socially desirable response and acquiescence in a cross-cultural survey of mental health. *Journal of Health and Social Behavior, 25,* 189–197.

Rubel, A. J., & Garro, L. C. (1992). Social and cultural factors in the successful control of tuberculosis. *Public Health Reports, 107,* 626–636.

Sagetta, R., & Johnson, D. (1980). *Basic data on depressive symptomatology, United States, 1974–1975* (Vital and Health Statistics, Series 11; DHEW Publication No. 80-1666). Washington, DC: U.S. Government Printing Office.

Salcido, R. (1990). Mexican-Americans: Illness, death and bereavement. In J. Parry (Ed.), *Social work practice with the terminally ill: A transcultural perspective* (pp. 99–112). Springfield, IL: Charles C Thomas.

Salcido, R. (1996, October). *Colloquium on ethnic-sensitive practice.* School of Social Work, University of Southern California, Los Angeles.

Sampson, E. E. (1985). The decentralization of identity: Towards revised concept of person and social order. *American Psychologist, 40,* 1203–1211.

Scheuneman, J., & Gerritz, K. (1990). Using differential item functioning procedures to explore sources of item difficulty and group performance characteristics. *Journal of Educational Measurement, 27,* 109–131.

Schmitt, A., & Dorans, N. (1990). Using differential item functioning procedures to explore sources of item difficulty and group performance characteristics. *Journal of Educational Measurement, 27,* 109–131.

Singer, M., Castillo, M., Davidson, L., & Flores, L. (1990). Owning AIDS: Latino organizations and the AIDS epidemic. *Hispanic Journal of Behavioral Sciences, 12,* 196–211.

Singer, M., Flores, C., Davidson, L., Burke, G., Castillo, Z., Scanlon, K., & Rivera, M. (1990). SIDA: The economic, social, and cultural context of AIDS among Latinos. *Medical Anthropology Quarterly, 4,* 72–114.

Solis, J., Marks, G., Garcia, M., & Shelton, M. (1990). Acculturation, access to care, and use of preventive services by Hispanics: Findings from HHANES 1982–84. *American Journal of Public Health, 80,* 11–19.

Starret, R. A., Mindel, C. H., & Wright, R. (1983). Influence of support systems on use of social services by Hispanic families. *Social Work Research & Abstracts, 19*(4), 35–40.

Sue, S. (1988). Therapeutic services for ethnic minorities. *American Psychologist, 43,* 301–308.

Thoits, P. (1991). Gender differences in coping with emotional distress. In J. Eckenrode (Ed.), *The social context of coping* (pp. 108–138). New York: Plenum.

Thurstone, L. (1928). Attitudes can be measured. *American Journal of Sociology, 33,* 529–554.

Triandis, H., Bontempo, R., Villareal, J., Asai, M., & Lucca, N. (1988). Individualism and collectivism: Cross-cultural perspectives on self-help group relations. *Journal of Personality and Social Psychology, 54,* 323–338.

Triandis, J., & Marin, G. (1983). Etic plus emic versus pseudo-etic: A test of basic assumption of contemporary cross-cultural psychology. *Journal of Cross-Cultural Psychology, 14,* 489–500.

Vernon, S., Roberts, R., & Lee, E. (1984). Ethnic status and participation in longitudinal health surveys. *American Journal of Epidemiology, 119,* 99–113.

Waterman, A. S. (1981). Individualism and interdependence. *American Psychologist, 36,* 762–773.

Weeks, M., Schensul, J., Williams, S., Singer, M., & Grier, M. (1995). AIDS prevention for African-American and Latina women: Building culturally and gender appropriate intervention. *AIDS Education and Prevention, 7,* 251–263.

Westmeyer, J. (1985). Psychiatric diagnosis across culture boundaries. *American Journal of Psychiatry, 142,* 798–805.

Zapka, J., Chasen-Taber, L., Bigelow, C., & Hurley, T. (1994). Methodological issues for health-related surveys of multicultural older women. *Evaluation and the Health Professions, 17,* 485–500.

Zuniga, M. (1992). Using metaphors in therapy: Dichos and Latino clients. *Social Work, 37,* 55–60.

This research was supported by the Universitywide AIDS Research Programs, State of California.

40

HIV/AIDS in a Puerto Rican/ Dominican Community:
A Collaborative Project with a Botanical Shop

Melvin Delgado and Jorge Santiago

T he spread of HIV/AIDS in the Latino community in the United States and Puerto Rico has been extensive, affecting thousands of individuals, families, and communities (Chachkes & Jennings, 1994; Jackson, 1989; Lambert, 1990a, 1990b; Marin, 1996). Innovative approaches are needed to reach Puerto Rican, Dominican, and other Latino communities in the fight against this epidemic. To be effective, these approaches must involve all sectors of the Latino community and must reach out to individuals unwilling or unable to access conventional programs.

This chapter describes a collaborative project undertaken by a university, a community-based organization, and a botanical shop (Projecto Cooperacion) to reach Latinos with HIV/AIDS in a large New England city (Lawrence, Massachusetts). This project was successful in involving a culture-based institution, increasing referrals for HIV testing, and distributing information about HIV/AIDS to a sector of the community that might otherwise not have received it.

OVERVIEW OF THE LITERATURE

The literature has addressed the impact of HIV/AIDS in the Latino community in general and in Puerto Ricans, the largest Latino subgroup in the northeast United States (Knox, 1990; Lambert, 1990a). According to Kilbourne, Gwinn, Castro, and Oxtoby (1994), Latinos, and particularly Puerto Ricans, are the most overrepresented ethnic group among those who contract HIV and AIDS through intravenous drug use: "Data on cumulative AIDS incidence rates by place of birth indicate that Puerto Ricans are the single ethnic group most disproportionately affected by AIDS in the United States when compared with Hispanic AIDS cases amongst those of Latin American descent. Persons of Puerto Rican descent were the only Hispanic subgroup in whom most cases were in heterosexual injection drug users" (p. 105).

Diaz, Buehler, Castro, and Ward (1993) substantiated Kilbourne et al.'s (1994) findings and added that men born in the Dominican

This chapter was originally published in the March 1998 issue of *Social Work*, Vol. 43, pp. 183–186.

Republic had the second highest rate behind Puerto Rican men. The most common means of contracting HIV and AIDS among Latina women in the United States is intravenous drug use (Kilbourne et al., 1994); these findings also are applicable to Puerto Rico (Lambert, 1990b; Menendez, Blum, Singh, & Drucker, 1994).

Kilbourne et al. (1994) summarized the practice needs of Latinos at risk for contracting HIV:

> Programs for preventing HIV infection among Hispanic women and men should focus on drug treatment and prevention of needle-sharing in addition to stressing precautions for heterosexual contact. Existing drug prevention and drug rehabilitation programs should include HIV prevention services, including HIV-antibody testing and counseling, information about early interventions for HIV-positive persons, access to early interventions, and referral for social services and medical management of HIV infection. (p. 115)

Community-based, coordinated efforts are needed to address the tremendous needs of the Puerto Rican, Dominican, and other Latino communities related to the HIV epidemic.

BOTANICAL SHOPS

Botanical shops, like other indigenous culture-based institutions, have not received much attention from social workers and other helping professionals, even though these resources play a critical role in Latino communities (Delgado, 1996). Delgado observed that botanical shops are "community-based ... outlets for important Puerto Rican [and other Latino] cultural traditions pertaining to healing/spirituality and are places where customers can socialize with others who share beliefs" (p. 72).

These shops usually are small storefronts and are found in virtually every Latino community in the United States (Fetherston, 1992; Helfound, 1994; Montana, 1991; Spencer-Molloy, 1994). Fetherston's description of a New York *botanica* provides a vivid picture of the range of products for sale in such establishments: "Santos Variety is a slightly misleading name for the store, since the variety is confined to four groups of products: the greeting cards in Spanish and English on the rack at the center of the sales floor, the music on cassettes in the center case, the cotton crocheted yarn in a rack in the back, and the paraphernalia of Santeria that lines the walls and dominates the scene" (p. 32).

Botanicas carry a variety of herbal medicines, healing paraphernalia, and other assorted products and provide consultation on ailments both physical and emotional. *Botanica* owners are often consulted about problems and ailments that can just as easily be treated in local health centers. In addition, owners can refer customers to local folk healers if the presenting problem is beyond their expertise or capabilities (Borrello & Mathias, 1977). These institutions can thus play a critical role in helping Latinos with HIV/AIDS and must be a part of any community-oriented prevention and early identification initiative (Singer, Gonzalez, Vega, Centeno, & Davison, 1994).

PROJECTO COOPERACION

The city of Lawrence, Massachusetts, is located about 25 miles north of Boston. It has a total population of 72,000, of whom 29,200 are Latino, almost equally divided between Dominicans and Puerto Ricans (Gaston Institute, 1992). Latinos represent 41.6 percent of the total population, making Lawrence the city with the highest percentage of Latinos in the state.

According to a recent Massachusetts Department of Public Health report, HIV/AIDS-related cases accounted for 26 percent of all Latino deaths, making this disease the primary killer among the state's largest community of color (Chacon, 1996; Knox, 1990). In 1995 Lawrence had an AIDS rate of 274.9 per 100,000, the fourth highest rate among the state's cities (Massachusetts Department of Public Health, 1996).

A collaborative project called Projecto Cooperacion was undertaken between the author's urban-based school of social work and Centro Panamericano, a community-based agency. This agency was selected for the project because of its high reputation within the Latino community and its history of providing community-based HIV/AIDS services. In addition, the Centro's executive director and the author, a university-based researcher, had a long-standing working relationship, facilitating collaboration.

The project used a developmental framework for planning and implementing activities (Delgado, 1994). This framework consists of five stages: (1) initial contact and relationship building (the interviewer interviewed a total of five *botanica* owners); (2) assessment of institutional capacity and willingness to participate in a joint project (the author did a follow-up interview to recruit the participation of two owners in the pilot project); (3) training on HIV/AIDS (the two owners underwent training); (4) distribution of educational materials (HIV/AIDS materials in Spanish were made available in the two *botanicas*); and (5) establishment of a referral system (procedures were developed to facilitate referrals for HIV testing).

An assessment of all the botanical shops located within a clearly defined geographic section of Lawrence was completed in 1995 (Delgado & Santiago, in press). Eight shops were located; five owners consented to be interviewed. Two botanical shops were selected for the project; one shop had been in existence 12 years and the other less than one year. One of the goals of the selection process was to assess how length of operation would help or hinder collaboration. Unfortunately, the more recently established botanical shop went out of business shortly after the project began. The owner of this shop successfully completed the training and distributed some materials but did not participate in the other aspects of the project.

Training on HIV/AIDS

The training of the two shop owners consisted of eight hours of instruction provided on a Sunday. This scheduling facilitated participation because the businesses did not have to close for the owners to receive training. Participants were each paid $250 for their time. The all-day training was conducted in Spanish by the HIV/AIDS worker at Centro Panamericano and used didactic, discussion, and role plays as instructional tools. The following topics were covered: (1) cause of HIV/AIDS, (2) methods of spread of the disease, (3) length of time before symptoms appear, (4) common symptoms, and (5) testing procedures. Materials provided by the Massachusetts Department of Public Health were the basis for the information on HIV/AIDS. However, every effort was made to use examples from the Latino community and to use a vocabulary that was sensitive to the cultural background of the participants.

Distribution of Public Education Materials

Owners were provided with posters, brochures, and other printed (Spanish) materials related to HIV/AIDS. In addition, condoms and bleach for cleaning needles were distributed.

Referral System

In the three-month period (June through August 1996) following the initial training, the one participating botanical shop referred for testing nine of the 53 individuals tested by Centro Panamericano. All of those referred were at high risk for HIV because they injected drugs and displayed symptoms commonly associated with AIDS.

Concerns of Botanical Shop Owners

The botanical shop owners raised concerns about the confidentiality of those they referred for HIV testing. The procedures for testing and record keeping were explained, and this satisfied their concerns. The owners were also concerned that Centro Panamericano would discourage those referred from returning to *botanicas* at some future date. Owners were assured that Centro Panamericano was not in competition for clients.

FUTURE PLANS

The initial success of Projecto Cooperacion has encouraged the following results:

- the future involvement of additional botanical shops to be phased in over two years
- the use of botanical shop owners as key informants in asset- and needs-assessment studies to develop a better understanding of trends and community concerns

■ the development of a consultation program to assist botanical shop owners with their questions and concerns about HIV/AIDS. Owners, in turn, will be asked to provide consultation to Centro Panamericano in situations where clients have used or currently use herbs and other healing methods in addressing the symptoms of AIDS.

CONCLUSION

Social work academicians have repeatedly been called on to actively seek collaborative partnerships with practitioners (Hess & Mullen, 1995). Partnerships take on added significance and challenges when they involve indigenous-based institutions (Delgado, 1994). These triadic partnerships increase the likelihood that projects will help their ultimate beneficiary—the community.

This chapter discusses one of an endless number of possible relationships that can be developed in service to the Latino community. These partnerships are not without challenges and considerable expenditure of time and energy. Nevertheless, the rewards make such efforts worthwhile for the profession, the community-based agencies, and the community.

REFERENCES

Borrello, M. A., & Mathias, E. (1977). Botanicas: Puerto Rican folk pharmacies. *Natural History, 86,* 64–73.

Chachkes, E., & Jennings, R. (1994). Latino communities: Coping with death. In B. O. Dane & C. Levine (Eds.), *AIDS and the new orphans: Coping with death* (pp. 77–99). Westport, CT: Auburn House.

Chacon, R. (1996, April 7). Hispanics struggle with high AIDS rate. *Boston Globe,* pp. 29, 34.

Delgado, M. (1994). Hispanic natural support systems and the AODA field: A developmental framework for collaboration. *Journal of Multicultural Social Work, 2,* 11–37.

Delgado, M. (1996). Puerto Rican elders and botanical shops: A community resource or liability? *Social Work in Health Care, 23,* 67–81.

Delgado, M., & Santiago, J. (in press). Botanical shops in a Puerto Rican/Dominican community in New England: Implications for health and human services. *Journal of Health and Social Policy.*

Diaz, T., Buehler, J., Castro, K. G., & Ward, T. W. (1993). AIDS trends among Hispanics in the United States. *American Journal of Public Health, 83,* 504–509.

Fetherston, D. (1992, August 17). Shop where business is a religion. *Newsday,* p. 32.

Gaston Institute. (1992). *Latinos in Lawrence.* Boston: University of Massachusetts.

Helfound, D. (1994, July 28). Faith in folk medicines; many immigrants trust their well-being to spiritual healers. *Los Angeles Times,* p. 6.

Hess, P. M., & Mullen, E. J. (1995). Bridging the gap: Collaborative considerations in practitioner–researcher knowledge-building partnerships. In P. M. Hess & E. J. Mullen (Eds.), *Practitioner–researcher partnerships: Building knowledge from, in, and for practice* (pp. 1–30). Washington, DC: NASW Press.

Jackson, D. Z. (1989, June 18). Why blacks, Latin-Americans are at a higher risk for AIDS. *Boston Globe,* p. 86.

Kilbourne, B. W., Gwinn, M., Castro, K. G., & Oxtoby, M. J. (1994). HIV infection and AIDS among women: Impact on Hispanic women and children residing in the United States. In G. Lamberty & C. Garcia Coll (Eds.), *Puerto Rican women and children: Issues in health, growth, and development* (pp. 103–117). New York: Plenum Press.

Knox, R. A. (1990, June 18). Burden for Puerto Ricans reaches crisis stage. *Boston Globe,* pp. 1, 8–9.

Lambert, B. (1990a, June 15). AIDS travels New York–Puerto Rico "air bridge." *New York Times,* pp. B1, B4.

Lambert, B. (1990b, June 15). The best AIDS programs are too few for too many. *New York Times,* p. B4.

Marin, B. V. (1996). Cultural issues in HIV prevention for Latinos: Should we try to change gender roles? In S. Oskamp & S. C. Thompson (Eds.), *Understanding and preventing HIV risk behavior: Safer sex and drug use* (pp. 157–176). Thousand Oaks, CA: Sage Publications.

Massachusetts Department of Public Health. (1996, September 1). *Massachusetts AIDS surveillance monthly update.* Boston: Author.

Menendez, B., Blum, S., Singh, T. P., & Drucker, E. (1994). Puerto Ricans and AIDS: Research and policy. *Centro de Estudios Puertorriquenos, 6,* 14–21.

Montana, C. (1991, August 25). Unconventional wisdom has it some Hispanics put faith in ancient, unusual rites. *Chicago Tribune,* p. 1.

Singer, M., Gonzalez, W., Vega, E., Centeno, I., & Davison, L. (1994). Implementing a community based AIDS prevention program for ethnic minorities: The Comunidad y Responsibilidad project. In J. P. Van Vugt (Ed.), *AIDS prevention and services: Community based research* (pp. 59–92). Westport, CT: Bergin & Garvey.

Spencer-Molloy, F. (1994, March 2). Doctor negotiates path between folk and traditional medicines. *Hartford Courant,* p. D9.

41 Children with HIV/AIDS and Their Families: A Successful Social Work Intervention Based on the Culturally Specific Health Care Model

AnaMaria Goicoechea-Balbona

R esearch has confirmed the benefits of early diagnosis of HIV/AIDS, such as early sociomedical intervention to lessen the severity of HIV/AIDS and its accompanying social, economic, and related problems (Johnson, Nair, & Alexander, 1987; Ploughman, 1995/1996; Rogers, 1992). Research has also shown that early detection of HIV/AIDS in children can improve their health by modifying conditions that influence their care and management (Goedert & Cote, 1994). Prompt diagnosis can lead to early health care benefits, such as case management, emotional and financial support, and legal aid, as well as awareness of the danger of immunizations on HIV-compromised immune systems (Scofield, 1995). Families can be informed of the availability of prophylactic treatment and antiviral drugs to prevent secondary infections. They also can be told of the required nutrients and feeding techniques when children have difficulty swallowing and eating (Marder & Linsk, 1995; Miller, Turner, & Moses, 1990; Shelov, 1994). Understanding the lifestyles and experiences of the families of affected children is of critical importance for health social workers who tend to be outsiders to the culture (McCoy et al., 1996; Walker, Pomeroy, McNeil, & Franklin, 1996; Williams & Ellison, 1996).

Evidence suggests that ethnically diverse families who are oppressed by race and socioeconomic status are less likely to seek early treatment and tend to die sooner (National Commission on AIDS, 1992). AIDS research suggests that researchers and health care providers should develop "a relationship of trust with those whose lives are the subject of study... to determine the accuracy, sensitivity, and complexity of the data" (Coyle, Boruch & Turner, 1991). Higher rates of HIV/AIDS among African Americans (Dicks, 1994; Flaskerud & Rush, 1989; Fullilove, Fullilove, Haynes, & Gross, 1990; Mays & Cochran, 1987), Latinos (Brett et al., 1996; Jimenez & Jimenez, 1992; Organista, Balls Organista, Garcia de Alba, Castillo-Moran, & Carrillo,

This chapter was originally published in the February 1998 issue of *Health & Social Work,* Vol. 23, pp. 61–69.

1996; Singer et al., 1990), and some Native Americans (DePoy & Bolduc, 1992; Williams & Ellison, 1996) corroborate concerns about the effects of long-standing unmet needs. Data exist suggesting that rural and ethnically diverse communities (Andersen & Civic, 1989; Nieto, 1989; Rounds, 1988a, 1988b) whose revenues come from seasonal and migratory labor (Goicoechea-Balbona, 1994, 1997; Zimmerman, Israel, Colman, & Prevots, 1995) are at a disproportionately higher risk of HIV/AIDS infection because of economic, political, and social inequities (National Public Radio, 1993; White-Means, 1992).

As HIV infection increases in nonmetropolitan areas, comprehensive information on the cultural aspects and needs of rural families with HIV/AIDS and the ways in which rural areas respond to the epidemic become more important (Berry, McKinney, & McClain, 1996; Centers for Disease Control and Prevention [CDC], 1994; Farmer, 1992; Sundwall, 1991; Treichler, 1992). The ethnic diversity of people with AIDS (PWAs), as well as their marginal positions in rural areas, challenges the mission of public health in America (Ell, 1996; Poole & Van Hook, 1997; Rounds, 1988a).

In a previously published article (Goicoechea-Balbona, 1997), I presented the development and application of the Culturally Specific Health Care Model (CSHCM) to ensure awareness of and access to health care services by PWAs. In this chapter, I document a successful research and practice intervention to introduce the CSHCM and to provide process and outcome data on health care utilization by rural families and children with HIV/AIDS. The intervention's goals are to explore the shared beliefs and behaviors that prevent the families from pursuing medical treatment for which they had been scheduled after their children had been diagnosed with HIV or AIDS.

In trying to understand the shared beliefs and behaviors, several questions framed the design. How could I reach the children's families and plan appropriate care and follow-up in a two-week period? Would I have time to gain the families' trust and explore their perceptions of HIV/AIDS? Would I be able to cross cultural lines to understand the families' concerns, language, and emotions?

BACKGROUND

The state of Florida had 4,723 reported AIDS cases in 1988 out of a population of 12,503,800, a rate of 37.8 cases per 100,000 people. These statistics can be compared to 219 reported AIDS cases, or 132 cases per 100,000 people, in the rural Florida town of Belle Glade, which is in West Palm Beach County and has a population of 16,536. Statistically, Belle Glade has a 3.5 times higher rate of reported AIDS cases than does Florida as a whole. A report on West Palm Beach County from the state AIDS surveillance office indicated that among residents of rural towns within an area of 20 miles, Belle Glade reported 172 cases; Pahokee, 25; and South Bay, 22 (AIDS Surveillance Organization, 1988). Seventy-eight percent (171) of AIDS cases were among African Americans, 20 percent were among Haitians, and the remaining 2 percent were among whites and Hispanics, with a growing number of pediatric cases (Department of Health and Rehabilitative Services, 1988; Goicoechea-Balbona, 1988, 1989; LaLota, 1989).

TARGET COMMUNITY

From 1982 to 1987 the CDC and the Florida State Department of Health and Rehabilitative Services delineated AIDS in Belle Glade, in a target community corresponding to three locally defined neighborhoods (LDNs). Castro et al. (1988) directly linked people from these LDNs to at least one other partner or to a person with AIDS-related complex. Risk factors in this target community included sexual contact, sharing needles during intravenous drug abuse, or perinatal exposure (AIDS Programs Surveillance, 1987; Castro et al., 1988; National Public Radio, 1993). Most of the HIV/AIDS-infected children and their families lived in an area in the central part of Belle Glade that had a population of 7,207 (U.S. Bureau of the Census, 1981). As reported, the incidence of congenital HIV transmission is closely related to the spread of HIV infection among women (Ellerbrock et al., 1992). By testing newborns for HIV antibodies, officials from the CDC and from the state AIDS programs attributed Belle Glade's higher rate of pediatric AIDS to heterosexual transmission. Babies from Belle Glade born at Pahokee Memorial Hospital have been "blind tested" since 1988 (LaLota, 1989). During blind testing, the health care providers and families are unaware of the babies' conditions (Coyle et al., 1991). Compared to the rest of Florida, West Palm Beach County, where Belle Glade, Pahokee, and South Bay are located, has a higher proportion of reported positives for HIV than other regions (Castro et al., 1988; Ellerbrock et al., 1992; McCoy et al., 1996; Nwanyanwu et al., 1993; Ploughman, 1995/1996).

METHOD

The events described in this chapter occurred in 1988 while I took a summer practicum as a health educator at the Belle Glade HIV Prevention Center. During the summer practicum, I met a diverse group of professionals who became my cultural guides in a qualitative project that included a social work intervention (Goicoechea-Balbona, 1994, 1997; Goicoechea-Balbona & Greif, 1992). The intervention came to be when newly arrived pediatricians shared their concerns about the inability of the community migrant health center staff to reach the families with babies at high risk of or with AIDS. At my request indigenous health providers from another agency, working with adult case management, collaborated with the social work intervention—a two-week practice experience to identify needs and implement a plan to reach the children's families.

Four elements or themes were recognized to provide an empowerment perspective: (1) a culturally specific description of the target community at high risk of AIDS, (2) a culturally sensitive approach to assessment and intervention, (3) the use of key indigenous providers, and (4) interdisciplinary collaboration among providers. The defined elements linked research and practice forming the CSHCM, which is based on Freire's (1985b) philosophy for education and social change and on Solomon's (1976) recommendation that the approach be culturally sensitive and specific.

Freire's (1985a) empowerment perspective "refers to the process in which men, not as recipients, but as knowing subjects achieve a deepening awareness both of the sociocultural reality that shapes and of their capacity to transform that reality" (p. 93). Solomon (1976) refers "to the on-going efforts [to engage] the client in the problem-solving . . . to ensure that the client's strengths are recognized, held up for mutual consideration, and utilized" (p. 315). To reach the target families, the CSHCM's empowerment relied on key indigenous health care providers, who have cultural knowledge, commitment, and belief in the ability to change their own lives as well as the lives of their targeted at-risk community. Ability is defined by the energy found in those commitments, values, and beliefs that were openly shared and observed during the social work intervention phase. Professionals and activists to whom I was introduced belong to the same cultural and ethnic groups—African American and English-, French-, or Spanish-Caribbean—as the children with HIV/AIDS and their families. Most came from the rural region and have similar historical and economic realities. These similar circumstances provided a sense of ownership critical to the model's success. Ownership also was based on the interdisciplinary collaboration between the identified key providers and other health providers such as physicians and nurses who identify with the community at risk. Subsequently, ownership facilitated reaching the families to understand the existing barriers and providing a plan for action.

As previously stated, I participated in the research and practice intervention as an outsider, with all my biases. I became the research and practice instrument for the "legitimated voices" of key indigenous providers (Stanfield, 1994), adhering to Solomon's advice proposing "nurturance of . . . self-esteem as a prerequisite to sustained empowerment" (Simon, 1994, p. 154). The CSHCM methodology depends for accuracy and legitimacy on this learning and collaborative relationship with key indigenous providers (Coyle et al., 1991). The CSHCM provides what Solomon demands: the understanding of the targeted community's culture and its "shared values, norms, traditions, customs, . . . folklore, and institutions" (Orlandi, 1992, p. vi) and incorporates them into every aspect of the social work process, from the initial observation of the problem during the assessment to the implementation of the intervention.

PARTICIPANTS AND SETTING

A federally subsidized community migrant health center (CMHC) had been built in 1985 on the outskirts of Belle Glade to serve the target rural community in an attempt to ameliorate the AIDS crisis

(Goicoechea-Balbona, 1994). Although staffing the CMHC had been difficult, the rural community was not completely aware of how to use or take advantage of it. There also existed differences among practitioners from diverse ethnic and community groups. These differences were part of the local norms that affected interdisciplinary collaboration between providers and agencies.

Significant changes in attendance were observed on days the clinic was open. On these days the CMHC was full. Families would spend the whole day waiting to get their children immunized or examined. Many senior citizens and children occupied the seats and spaces in the lounge, and waiting times were long. Yet people who had been diagnosed with HIV/AIDS were not present. The staff had contacted them, but to no avail. They did not follow up and use the new services.

Pediatricians staffing the CMHC were concerned that many children who had been diagnosed with HIV or AIDS were not returning for treatment (Goicoechea-Balbona, 1988). The linking process—working as a team and communicating across disciplines—began with the list of nine children from Belle Glade who needed immediate medical attention. Modifying conditions for the nine children was the first step. Reaching the families and identifying their shared beliefs and behaviors would clarify possible causes for low utilization of treatment and services and encourage new approaches by the providers.

THE PROCESS

Home Visits

My task was to identify the beliefs and behaviors that presented barriers to health care utilization. I joined the key indigenous health providers from the Comprehensive AIDS Program (CAP) as they worked on their adult cases with the attending physicians. During those rounds, I visited the children's homes. Before and during those visits, I gathered demographic and psychosocial information and flagged the specific concerns previously mentioned by the families. The interdisciplinary work required a willingness to intervene to solve the sociomedical problems and to become aware of long-standing rural inequities. By working together, community-oriented primary health care was implemented by this diverse group of health care providers.

During the home visits and clinic visits, information was exchanged on how to care for the children and how to protect other family members from infection. Families were encouraged to talk about their grief and pain. Stories from several families follow.

Case 1. Malcolm, at age nine months, was HIV positive. His mother was developmentally delayed and could not provide adequate home care, let alone bring him to the clinic regularly. Both Malcolm and his mother lived with his grandmother in a typical cement block home. Tall grass scorched by the summer's blazing heat surrounded the house. Humidity was high and draining. Ventilation was provided by a door propped open by two lamp poles. The interior, especially the living room, was crammed with furniture. On approaching the entrance, the health providers and I raised our voices to let the family know who we were. Malcolm's mother answered our inquiries with a bit of shyness, as her baby sat smiling on her lap, placidly playing with his hands.

Malcolm's grandmother was willing to bring Malcolm to the clinic but had no transportation. Also, she was not Malcolm's legal custodian. Hence, the grandmother was unable to get Medicaid coverage for his medical expenses.

At first the barriers preventing Malcolm from utilizing health care seemed to be financial and transportation issues. The simple solution was finding transportation and filing custody papers to assure Malcolm of his benefits under Medicaid. However, underlying Malcolm's low utilization of health care were the cultural values of strength and responsibility. Throughout her life, the grandmother had been supportive of her daughter, meeting all her needs. Now as a senior citizen, the grandmother was still working and caring not only for her daughter but also for her grandson. Before these cultural values had been recognized by the indigenous key providers, their effect had not been considered. The key providers started a dialogue that uncovered these values. By recognizing and respecting these values, we were able to convince Malcolm's grandmother to pursue treatment for him.

Case 2. Harry, at 10 months old, had been to the clinic to rule out sepsis meningitis but had tested HIV positive. His family never brought him back to the clinic. Harry and his mother were living with his maternal grandmother, who worked at night and cared for most of her grandchildren during the day.

When we first visited Harry, we found an attractive brick house and a welcoming grandmother. Harry's grandmother was caring for her five small grandchildren. The children played and watched TV while Harry lay in their midst, sharing his bottle and pacifier. The grandmother felt at ease explaining Harry's condition. He could not swallow food, frequently had high temperatures, and had constant diarrhea. He had been given home remedies and what care she knew, but nothing provided relief.

At first the barriers to Harry receiving health care seemed to be the inability to keep his clinic appointments, failure to disinfect his environment with a bleach solution, and improper handling of loose stools. Underlying the situation, however, were the pain and confused feelings of Harry's mother. Pregnant with her third child, she was overwhelmed by the HIV diagnosis. The grandmother mentioned problems such as not having any other physician, being frightened by the HIV diagnosis and its implications, not having the time required to answer questions or having to complete paperwork that revealed personal information to the clinic's providers before even seeing the pediatricians, and having difficulty understanding the disease.

The indigenous key providers encouraged the conversation and answered the grandmother's many questions. Pursuing why Harry's mother would not take him to the clinic, we learned that because of a child-support investigation regarding her Aid to Families with Dependent Children (AFDC) status, Harry's mother "did not want any more hassles with the law." She was working without health insurance or benefits and was afraid that she would lose her job. She could not afford another crisis.

The indigenous key provider was able to overcome the objections by sharing information and explaining the procedures, for which I made all the necessary arrangements. Harry was seen at the clinic the same day and admitted to the hospital. When Harry was discharged, the grandmother met the physician and remained involved with Harry's care. The indigenous key providers assured her of their constant support. Finally, this hard-working grandmother had relief and affirmation. A trusting relationship had been formed.

Case 3. Shaw, age two, was born HIV positive. He lived with his mother, who had AIDS and no job. Two family members, his grandmother and her companion, paid the rent and other household expenses, using their retirement benefits and income from other grandchildren receiving AFDC. The 14 family members all slept in a two-room trailer in which the temperature could reach 130°F. They had received medication for meningitis after testing positive for it. Shaw's mother had been hospitalized three times that winter. She and Shaw had no Medicaid or insurance. Shaw's mother engaged in prostitution on weekends to supply her son with diapers and other items.

Shaw's brother had not been tested for HIV or AIDS. The pediatrician wanted consent to test the brother, who had been living with the grandmother during the mother's absence.

At first the barrier preventing these two children from utilizing health care seemed to be their mother. Her temper was intimidating, and she had a reputation among the health care providers as being difficult. However, whenever we addressed her son's needs, she responded responsibly and amicably. She needed our acceptance and support. By understanding her concerns and emotions and acknowledging her strength in coping with the demands of HIV/AIDS, we were able to work with her.

Case 4. Joey was 17 months old and had been discharged from the hospital after treatment for streptococcal pneumonia, *Staphylococcus aureus*, candidiasis, acute gastroenteritis, and dehydration. He had not returned to see the doctor. Joey lived in a nearby town with his grandmother, who was his caretaker.

At first the barriers to treatment, which were lack of a telephone and transportation, seemed easily overcome. The pediatricians were made aware of the problems. Arrangements to transport Joey and his grandmother to the clinic were made. During subsequent home visits, however, the already taxed grandmother disclosed other barriers that contributed to her mental, emotional, and physical distress.

Joey's mother was a homeless addict with AIDS. Another grandchild, Joey's brother, had died in infancy. The grandmother was caring for her grandchildren alone. She had no respite care and no one to whom she could turn for financial help. The grandmother urgently needed some kind of help.

Case 5. Wanda, who was $2\frac{1}{2}$ years old and HIV positive, had been hospitalized for cellulitis at 24 months and had not returned to see the doctor. Wanda's mother did not understand the need to visit the clinic to bring in her "beautiful" child who was walking and talking. Wanda's mother did not ask questions. She seemed unaware of Wanda's seropositive status and of how HIV is transmitted. Wanda's mother did mention that if her employers learned about her HIV-positive status, she could lose her job. Wanda's mother received us in her parents' trailer. Wanda's father, an elderly Caribbean gentleman from one of the English-speaking islands, assured us he would provide the needed transportation and support to keep clinic appointments. The grandparents would take full responsibility, but the providers could not breach confidentiality and provide information. We could not ask the mother any pertinent questions. We had to wait until another visit to determine her HIV/AIDS knowledge and prevention attitude.

This case presented complicated barriers from the start. Becoming aware of this family's responses, as well as recognizing particular lifestyles and languages, helped clarify the levels of risks.

Other Cases. Cases 6, 7, and 8 were never found. Research verified that one baby had died. The other two had gone underground, and neighbors would not disclose their whereabouts. The barriers to health care utilization in these three cases could not be surmounted. They were cultural barriers of loyalty and confidentiality. These barriers related in some way to existing immigration laws; no one wanted to be deported. Although the barriers to health care utilization were subtly manifested by the six families who were contacted during the intervention, other more blatant examples occurred during the practicum.

For 18 months a young husband from one of the Caribbean islands knew he was infected with AIDS and visited a private practitioner until he ran out of money. Lacking money for treatment because he had lost his managerial job and his health insurance, he refused to go to the health department. Ultimately, he became comatose and died.

The key indigenous providers, who had been unable to convince him to seek help from the public health agency continued to follow his wife and his son, who were also HIV positive. These same providers had been rebuffed when another father dying of AIDS was offered testing and social support for his three small children. He did not want them tested and asked the key providers not to come back.

OUTCOME

The key providers at CAP, the physicians at the CMHC, and the author shared knowledge and, with combined efforts, supported and treated the families. Mobilization of the National Health Service Corps provided comprehensive, community-oriented primary health care and interdisciplinary partnership among professionals from diverse agencies. Consensus about how to get the children the needed medical attention was reached as we listened and conferred with the target families. Underlying our observations was the special strength of self-help. This strength had to be recognized and respected as a powerful resource for the families in their struggles against HIV/ AIDS. At the same time, conversations betrayed the overwhelming despair these families were experiencing regarding their children. Mothers lamented about their children: "God, why my baby?" "I can't understand when the doctor gives me the information." Grandmothers lamented about their daughters: "She's pregnant again and hasn't been to see the doctor." "Her first baby died, too."

Of great importance was the collaborative process with the families carried out by the key indigenous providers, who guided, facilitated, and enabled the interventions to succeed. During the study, the families and the health care providers demonstrated mutual respect. Without the key providers, the crucially needed access to the target families was impossible. The inability to reduce the consequences of HIV/AIDS brought confusion. Manifested as resistance to health care, these feelings were born from paralyzing fear and seemed to reinforce the families' distrust. The key providers encountered pride, self-esteem, and family and ethnic loyalty coupled with utter denial and despair. Deportation policies were driving some of the families to isolate themselves and to go underground. Changes in the 1986 U.S. immigration laws and the "war on drugs" pushed the families at risk of AIDS into an underground way of life (Goicoechea-Balbona, 1994). Denying entrance or revoking work permits to immigrants with HIV/AIDS from particular Caribbean and African nations contributed to my inability to contact the families of the three babies in cases 6, 7, and 8, who were never located. The observed families were paralyzed by the diagnosis of HIV/AIDS. By not hearing the recommendations, the families resisted acknowledging the significance of the message.

CONCLUSION

Intervention in Belle Glade revealed culturally specific and intergroup differences (Oppenheimer, 1992). The inability to identify, treat, and cure AIDS in the early 1980s had created an overwhelming feeling of impotence and incompetence among the rural poor of Belle Glade as it had throughout the rest of the nation (Burkett, 1995; Perrow & Guillen, 1990). Immigration and public health policies seemed also to contribute to the families' fears (Fairchild & Tynan, 1994; Tienda, 1989).

By using the CSHCM the intervention became interdisciplinary and culturally sensitive (Solomon, 1976). It was attuned to the varied beliefs, existential burdens (Krieger, 1988; Walker et al., 1996), and distinct lifestyles (Anderson & Shaw, 1994) of the rural families affected by the epidemic.

Existing cultural knowledge of the key providers produced new knowledge representative of the target community under study. How to preserve self-esteem while finding a way to get the children medical help required tact, discernment, and patience, together with a committed plan for action.

The four elements of the CSHCM were used in the case studies and validated the observations and answered the working questions (Lang, 1994; Solomon, 1976; Stanfield, 1994). The degree of participation was ascertained during the analysis phase of the project (Goicoechea-Balbona, 1997). Lang (1994) stated, "If a dual purpose can be established for practitioners, giving 'knowing' equal importance with 'doing,' and if a pattern for managing both activities concurrently can be established, then the social work practitioner will be able to incorporate a knowledge-developing dimension into the processing of practice data" (p. 271).

The CSHCM can serve as a foundation for organizing the delivery of services (Coyle et al., 1991; Novick, 1994). The model discussed and followed by the intervention in this chapter can be generalized to identify sociocultural behaviors or barriers and to develop treatments and services for specific target communities (Ell, 1996).

In the introduction, I called for a successful intervention through the CSHCM. During my participant observation, social work principles were consistent and were followed. I recognize the limitations of a target and captive community (Castro et al., 1988; Treichler, 1992), of blind nationwide infant testing (Bayer, 1992, 1993), of warning or not warning as dictated by superconfidentiality (Hartog, 1990), and of a public health versus public policy debate (Fairchild & Tynan, 1994; Novick, 1995; Ploughman, 1995/1996) and the complex and ethical issues faced when confidentiality, beliefs, and values compete with protecting life (Bayer, 1993; Loewenberg & Dolgoff, 1996; Novick, 1995). Their effects on health care utilization need to be studied further.

REFERENCES

AIDS Programs Surveillance. (1987, August 15). *AIDS surveillance.* (Department of Health and Rehabilitative Services AIDS Program, Disease Control, State Health Office, Reports No. 36 and No. 34 [June 15, 1987]). Tallahassee: Florida Department of Health and Rehabilitative Services.

AIDS Surveillance Organization of West Palm Beach County. (1988, May 1). *AIDS surveillance.* (Department of Health and Rehabilitative Services AIDS Program, Disease Control, State Health Office, Report No. 45). Tallahassee: Florida Department of Health and Rehabilitative Services.

Andersen, H., & Civic, D. (1989). Psychosocial issues in rural AIDS care. *Human Services in Rural Environment, 13,* 11–16.

Anderson, D. B., & Shaw, S. L. (1994). Starting a support group for families and partners of people with HIV/AIDS in a rural setting. *Social Work, 39,* 135–138.

Bayer, R. (1992). Entering the second decade: The politics of prevention, the politics of neglect. In E. Fee & F. Fox. (Eds.), *AIDS: The making of a chronic disease* (pp. 207–226). Berkeley: University of California Press.

Bayer, R. (1993). The ethics of blinded HIV surveillance testing. *American Journal of Public Health, 83,* 496–497.

Berry, D. E., McKinney, M. M., & McClain, M. (1996). Rural HIV-service networks: Patterns of care and policy issues. *AIDS & Public Policy Journal, 11*(1), 36–46.

Brett, K. M., Yamamura, Y., Kam, W. T., Rios, C. F., Rodriguez, N., & Marconi, K. M. (1996). Movement patterns of persons with HIV receiving treatment in public clinics in the southern region, Puerto Rico. *Hispanic Journal of Behavioral Sciences, 18,* 407–414.

Burkett, E. (1995). *The gravest show on Earth.* Boston: Houghton-Mifflin.

Castro, K. G., Lieb, S., Jaffe, H. W., Narkunas, J. P., Calister, C. H., Bush, T. J., Witte, J. J., & Belle Glade Field Study Group. (1988). Transmission of HIV in Belle Glade, Florida: Lessons for other communities in the United States (Reports). *Science, 239.*

Centers for Disease Control and Prevention. (1994). *HIV/AIDS Surveillance Report, 6*(1), 1–27.

Coyle, S. L., Boruch, R. F., & Turner, C. F. (Eds.). (1991). *Evaluating AIDS prevention programs.* Washington DC: National Academy Press.

DePoy, E., & Bolduc, C. (1992). AIDS prevention in a rural Native American population: An empirical approach to program development. In J. Morales & M. Bok (Eds.), *Multicultural human services for AIDS treatment and prevention: Policy, perspectives, and planning* (pp. 51–69). New York: Harrington Park Press.

Department of Health and Rehabilitative Services. (1988). *Prevention II.* Tallahassee, FL: Belle Glade Project, 5.8–5.9.

Dicks, B. A. (1994). African American women and AIDS: A public health/social work challenge. *Social Work in Health Care, 19*(3/4), 123–143.

Ell, K. (1996). Social work and health care practice and policy: A psychosocial research agenda. *Social Work, 41,* 583–592.

Ellerbrock, T. V., Lieb, S., Harrington, P. E., Bush, T. J., Schoenfisch, S. A., Oxtoby, M. J., Howell, J. T., Rogers, M. F., & Witte, J. J. (1992). Heterosexually transmitted human immunodeficiency virus infection among pregnant women in a rural Florida community. *New England Journal of Medicine, 327,* 1704–1709.

Fairchild, A. L., & Tynan, E. A. (1994). Policies of containment: Immigration in the era of AIDS. *American Journal of Public Health, 84,* 2011–2022.

Farmer, P. (1992). *AIDS and accusation: Haiti and the geography of blame.* Berkeley: University of California Press.

Flaskerud, J. H., & Rush, C. (1989). AIDS and traditional health beliefs and practices of black women. *Nursing Research, 38,* 210–215.

Freire, P. (1985a). *Pedagogy of the oppressed.* New York: Continuum. (Original work published 1969).

Freire, P. (1985b). *The politics of education: Culture, power, and liberation.* Westport, CT: Bergin & Garvey.

Fullilove, M. T., Fullilove, R. E., Haynes, K., & Gross, S. (1990). Black women and AIDS prevention: A view towards understanding the gender rules. *Journal of Sex Research, 27*(1), 47–64.

Goedert, J. J., & Cote, T. R. (1994). Public health interventions to reduce pediatric AIDS [Editorial]. *American Journal of Public Health, 84,* 1065–1066.

Goicoechea-Balbona, A. (1988). Summer internship and practicum, Report to Dr. Joyner Simms et al., Tallahassee AIDS Program, Tallahassee, FL.

Goicoechea-Balbona, A. (1989). Case management—Pediatric AIDS, a community study: Belle Glade, FL. In G. C. St. Denis (Ed.), *Public health social work and primary health care.* Bureau of Maternal Child Health and the University of Pittsburgh Graduate School of Public Health.

Goicoechea-Balbona, A. (1994). Why we are losing the AIDS battle in rural migrant communities. *AIDS & Public Policy Journal, 9,* 36–48.

Goicoechea-Balbona, A. (1997). Culturally Specific Health Care Model for ensuring health care use by rural, ethnically diverse families affected by HIV/AIDS. *Health & Social Work, 22,* 172–180.

Goicoechea-Balbona, A., & Greif, G. L. (1992). AIDS among a rural migrant population. *AIDS & Public Policy Journal, 7,* 247–250.

Hartog, J. P. (1990). *Florida's Omnibus AIDS Act: A brief legal guide for health care providers under contract with the Department of Health and Rehabilitative Services State Health Office AIDS Program, HIV Test Results: Superconfidentiality,* pp. 19–20.

Jimenez, M. A., & Jimenez, D. R. (1992). Latinos and HIV disease: Issues, practice and policy implications. *Social Work in Health Care, 17*(2), 41–51.

Johnson, J. P., Nair, P., & Alexander, S. (1987). Early diagnosis of HIV infection in the neonate. *New England Journal of Medicine, 316,* 273–274.

Krieger, I. (1988). An approach to coping with anxiety about AIDS [Briefly Stated]. *Social Work, 33,* 263–264.

LaLota, M. (1989). *Newborn study HIV seroprevalence, Oct. 1988 to March 1989.* Tallahassee: Florida Department of Health and Rehabilitative Services.

Lang, N. C. (1994). Integrating the data processing of qualitative research and social work practice to advance the practitioner as knowledge builder: Tools for knowing and doing. In E. Sherman & W. J. Reid (Eds.), *Qualitative research in social work* (Part 2, pp. 265–278). New York: Columbia University Press.

Loewenberg, F. M., & Dolgoff, R. (1996). *Ethical decisions for social work practice.* Itasca, IL: F. E. Peacock.

Marder, R., & Linsk, N. L. (1995). Addressing AIDS long-term care issues through education and advocacy. *Health & Social Work, 20,* 75–80.

Mays, V. M., & Cochran, S. D. (1987). Acquired immunodeficiency syndrome and black Americans: Special psychosocial issues. *Public Health Reports, 102*(2).

McCoy, C. B., Metsch, L. R., Inciardi, J. A., Anwyl, R. S., Wingerd, J., & Bletzer, K. (1996). Sex, drugs and the spread of HIV/AIDS in Belle Glade, Florida. *Medical Anthropology Quarterly, 10*(1), 83–93.

Miller, H. G., Turner, C. F., & Moses, L. E. (Eds.). (1990). *AIDS: The second decade.* Washington, DC: National Academy Press.

National Commission on AIDS. (1992). *The challenge of HIV/AIDS in communities of color.* Washington, DC: National Archives and Records Administration.

National Public Radio. (1993, August 23–27). *AIDS in Belle Glade, FL* [Series]. National Public Radio Morning Edition.

Nieto, D. S. (1989). AIDS and the rural family: Some systems considerations and intervention implications for the human services practitioner. *Human Services in the Rural Environment, 13*(1), 34–38.

Novick, A. (1994). Some needed research in the HIV realm. *AIDS & Public Policy Journal, 9.*

Novick, A. (1995). Analyzing proposed new public policies. *AIDS & Public Policies, 10*(2), 63–64.

Nwanyanwu, O. C., Conti, L. A., Ciesielski, C. A., Stehr-Green, J. K., Berkelman, R. L., Lieb, S., & Witte, J. J. (1993). Increasing frequency of heterosexually transmitted AIDS in southern Florida: Artifact or reality? *American Journal of Public Health, 83,* 571–573.

Oppenheimer, G. M. (1992). Causes, cases, and cohorts: The role of epidemiology in the historical construction of AIDS. In E. Fee & D. M. Fox (Eds.), *AIDS: The making of a chronic disease* (Part 1, pp. 49–83). Berkeley: University of California Press.

Organista, K. C., Balls Organista, P., Garcia de Alba, G.J.E., Castillo-Moran, M. A., & Carrillo, H. (1996). AIDS and condom-related knowledge, beliefs, and behaviors in Mexican migrant laborers. *Hispanic Journal of Behavioral Sciences, 18,* 392–406.

Orlandi, M. A. (Ed.). (1992). *Cultural competence for evaluators.* (DHHS Publication No. ADM92-1884). Washington, DC: U.S. Government Printing Office.

Perrow, C., & Guillen, M. F. (1990). *The AIDS disaster.* New Haven, CT: Yale University Press.

Ploughman, P. (1995/1996). Public policy versus private rights: The medical, social, ethical, and legal implications of the testing of newborns for HIV. *AIDS & Public Policy Journal, 10*(4), 182–204.

Poole, D. L., & Van Hook, M. (1997). Retooling for community health partnership in primary care and prevention [Editorial]. *Health & Social Work, 22*, 2–4.

Rogers, D. E. (1992). Report card on our national response to the AIDS epidemic—Some A's, too many D's. *American Journal of Public Health, 82*, 522–524.

Rounds, K. A. (1988a). AIDS in rural areas: Challenges to providing care. *Social Work, 33*, 257–261.

Rounds, K. A. (1988b, June). Responding to AIDS: Rural community strategies. *Social Casework*, 360–364.

Scofield, E. C. (1995). A model of preventive psychosocial care for people with HIV disease. *Health & Social Work, 20*, 102–109.

Shelov, S. P. (1994). Editorial: The children's agenda for the 1990s and beyond. *American Journal of Public Health, 84*, 1066–1067.

Simon, B. L. (1994). *The empowerment tradition in American social work.* New York: Columbia University Press.

Singer, M., Flores, C., Davison, L., Burke, G., Castillo, C., Scanlon, K., Rivera, M., & Hispanic Health Council. (1990). *SIDA: The economic, social and cultural context of AIDS among Latinos. Medical Anthropology Quarterly, 4*(1), 72–114.

Solomon, B. B. (1976). *Black empowerment: Social work in oppressed communities.* New York: Columbia University Press.

Stanfield, J. H. (1994). Ethnic modeling in qualitative research. In N. K. Denzin & Y. S. Lincoln (Eds.), *Handbook of qualitative research* (pp. 175–188). Newbury Park, CA: Sage Publications.

Sundwall, D. N. (1991). *HIV infection in rural areas: Issues in prevention and services.* Report of an Invitational Workshop held July 16–17, 1990, sponsored by Associate Administrator for AIDS & Office of Rural Health Policy.

Tienda, M. (1989). Looking to 1990: Immigration, inequality, and the Mexican Origen People in the United States. In *Immigration of Mexican Origen People.*

Treichler, P. A. (1992). AIDS & HIV infection in the Third World: A First World chronicle. In E. Fee & F. Fox (Eds.), *AIDS: The making of a chronic disease* (Part IV, pp. 377–412). Berkeley: University of California Press.

U.S. Bureau of the Census. (1981). *1980 census of the population: Florida (PC80-ICII).* Washington, DC: U.S. Government Printing Office.

Walker, R. J., Pomeroy, E. C., McNeil, J. S., & Franklin, C. (1996). Anticipatory grief and AIDS: Strategies for intervening with caregivers. *Health & Social Work, 21*, 49–57.

White-Means, S. I. (1992). Health characteristics and utilization of public sector health facilities among migrant agricultural workers in Orange County, New York. *Journal of Health & Social Policy, 4*(1).

Williams, E. E., & Ellison, F. (1996). Culturally informed social work practice with American Indian clients: Guidelines for non-Indian social workers. *Social Work, 41*, 147–151.

Zimmerman, M. A., Israel, B. A., Colman, S. S., & Prevots, D. R. (1995). Delmarva, rural ministries, AIDS prevention for farm workers. In N. Freudenberg & M. A. Zimmerman (Eds.), *AIDS prevention in the community* (pp. 141–145). Washington, DC: American Public Health Association.

42

AIDS Protection and Contraception among African American, Hispanic, and White Women

Alice M. Hines and Karen L. Graves

Women have become the fastest growing subgroup of AIDS cases in the United States and as of 1992 constituted more than 10 percent of all AIDS cases (Centers for Disease Control [CDC], 1992). Most women with AIDS are of reproductive age; approximately 53 percent are African American, and 16 percent are Hispanic (CDC, 1991). In 1993, the number of women who acquired HIV through heterosexual contact increased 139 percent over 1992. Fifty percent of these cases were African American, 24 percent Hispanic, and 25 percent white. Overall, most of the heterosexually acquired AIDS cases were attributed to contact with a partner with HIV infection or AIDS whose risk was unreported or unknown (CDC, 1994).

Prevention efforts to curtail the spread of AIDS have focused primarily on the adaptation of latex condoms used by men during intercourse. In addition to risk of AIDS, negative results of not using condoms can include the contraction and spread of other sexually transmitted diseases (STDs) and unintended pregnancies. To address the overall reproductive needs and risks of women, it is important to examine how condom use is related to the use of other methods to prevent unintended pregnancies (Roper, Peterson, & Curran, 1993). Because AIDS risk-reduction activities are often identical to and linked with contraceptive efforts, especially condom use, it may be useful to look at contraceptive-use behaviors in terms of AIDS protection and effective birth control efforts to uncover sexual practices and factors related to behavior as a means of targeting effective AIDS-related preventive measures (Mays & Cochran, 1988). Sexual behavior is influenced by a variety of racial, cultural, and religious factors in addition to factors related to life stage and socioeconomic status and factors related to the event itself. Knowledge of ways in which these factors relate to safer sexual practices can be used to inform interventions that can then be tailored to the cultural and social realities of a particular group.

This chapter was originally published in the August 1998 issue of *Health & Social Work*, Vol. 23, pp. 186–194.

In addition, recent studies have shown that women, including African American and Hispanic women, are aware of AIDS and ways to prevent the disease but are not changing their behavior (Caetano & Hines, 1995). This finding points to the need to know more about each particular ethnic group. An accurate assessment of women's sexual behavior, including contraceptive-related protection, is critical to the development of effective HIV-prevention programs.

The current study describes the sexual practices of heterosexual women in a population-based sample that oversampled African American and Hispanic women, yielding a sample large enough to look at within-group differences. This study also examines the most recent sexual encounter as a way of obtaining more accurate reports of behavior. The "critical incident" technique involves the study of behaviors linked to a specific event. The purpose of this chapter is to examine characteristics of women in each ethnic group that are related to effective AIDS protection and effective methods of birth control during the 12 months preceding the interview.

METHODS

Sampling

Data were collected in 1991 and 1992 as part of a follow-up survey to a 1984 National Alcohol Survey, the first national household survey to study drinking attitudes, patterns, and problems of African Americans, Hispanics, and the general population. The sample population for the 1984 survey was selected through a multistage probability procedure from among individuals living in households in the 48 coterminous United States. The sampling method of the 1984 survey has been described in detail elsewhere (Santos, 1991).

The sampling design used for the 1991–92 follow up consisted of two samples: a reinterview sample of respondents randomly selected as part of the 1984 national survey and an additional random sample of 18- to 25-year-olds, to replace the 18- to 25-year-olds in the original 1984 sample. Both samples included an oversample of African American and Hispanic respondents. (For a complete description of the 1991–92 sampling design, see Caetano & Kaskutas, 1995.) The survey resulted in 2,247 completed interviews: 737 were conducted with African American respondents, 706 with Hispanic respondents, and 804 with white respondents. Combining the two samples, the overall response rate was 72 percent, ranging from 77 percent for whites to 70 percent for African Americans and 67 percent for Hispanics. The analyses carried out in the current research are based on the responses of African American (N = 275), Hispanic (N = 245) and white (N = 322) women who were sexually active during the past year.

Data Collection. Data were collected by trained interviewers in face-to-face interviews that averaged one hour. The interviews took place in the respondents' homes, and the data-collection instrument was a standardized questionnaire. The interview was conducted in Spanish if desired by the interviewee. To minimize the reluctance or refusal of respondents to answer questions regarding sexual behavior, those questions were contained in a 35-page self-administered questionnaire (SAQ).

Weighting. The sampling design intentionally oversampled African Americans and Hispanics. Percentages represented in this chapter are based on weighting of the sample to attain a representative distribution of African American and Hispanic adults ages 18 years and older and to compensate for unequal probabilities of selection and differential levels of nonresponse across demographic subgroups. Poststratification weights were created on the basis of a comparison of the sample and census data for the African American and Hispanic subsamples. The Ns reported in this chapter are based on the unweighted sample.

DATA COVERAGE

Operational Definitions

With the exception of demographic characteristics, all information for this study was obtained from the self-administered portion of the interview instrument. The following describes only those items relevant to the analysis conducted in the current study:

1. demographics—Measures included age, level of education, marital status, income, employment status, and religious affiliation.
2. ethnicity—Respondents were included in the sample on the basis of the ethnicity of their family of origin.
3. sexual activity—The measures used in this analysis are based on reported heterosexual, voluntary vaginal intercourse in the most recent sexual event during the 12 months preceding the interview.
4. condom use—This measure was based on a series of questions that asked whether the respondent or her partner had done anything to prevent pregnancy or disease during sex. Choices included using a diaphragm; condom (rubber); jelly, foam, cream, or suppository; sponge; pill; IUD; vasectomy or tubal ligation (sterilization); rhythm method; douche; withdrawal (pulling out); other. On the basis of the responses, a categorical variable was created to measure condom use versus other methods. Response categories included no protection, birth control other than condom, condom only, and condom plus other birth control method. For logistic regression analyses, this variable was dichotomized into "condom not used" (no protection, other birth control only) and "condom used" (condom only, condom plus other method).
5. effective birth control—Using the response choices described for the previous measure, a variable was created to assess the effectiveness of the birth control choice. A categorical variable was formed with three levels to measure a range of effectiveness from most to least: (1) pill, tubal ligation, IUD, Norplant; (2) condom,

jelly, foam, sponge, diaphragm; (3) rhythm, withdrawal, douche. For logistic regression analyses, a dichotomous variable was formed: "ineffective birth control" (no birth control used; rhythm, withdrawal, douche) "effective birth control" (pill, tubal ligation, IUD, Norplant; condom, jelly, foam, sponge, diaphragm)

6. concern about AIDS—This measure was based on a series of items that asked respondents to rate the amount of concern they had about contracting AIDS. Three questions asked respondents to report whether they felt afraid, threatened, or worried about contracting AIDS. A scale was created by summing the responses to the three items (alpha = .88), and a categorical variable was formed. A dichotomous variable was created for logistic regression analyses: "no concern" versus "some concern."

7. partner status—Referring to the partner in the most recent sexual encounter, respondents were asked, "Was this the very first time you had sex with that person?" (yes, no).

STATISTICAL ANALYSIS

Statistical analyses were conducted using SPSS (1993) statistical software. The methods consisted of chi-square test procedures and logistic regression techniques.

RESULTS

Sample Characteristics

Analysis indicated that the women in the sample ($N = 842$) differed significantly on all demographic characteristics. Compared with white women, more African American and Hispanic women were in the youngest age range. Hispanic women had fewer years of education than both African American and white women. Income level was lowest for African American women, who were also least likely to be married and more likely to be unemployed. More African American women than Hispanic or white women reported that religion was important or very important.

Condom Use versus Other Methods of Protection. Preliminary analyses indicated that 57.6 percent of African American women, 29.7 percent of Hispanic women, and 54.8 percent of white women in the sample used some form of protection in their most recent sexual encounter. Of those, 31.6 percent of African American women, 13.9 percent of Hispanic women, and 14.9 percent of white women reported using condoms or another contraceptive method plus condoms.

Compared with older African American women, younger African American women were more likely to use some form of protection during the most recent sexual event (Table 42-1). Many young African American women (48.6 percent, $n = 55$) reported using condoms or condoms plus another method of protection. Also, more single African American women used some form of protection than married women. Although the majority of Hispanic women used no protection, a

Table 42-1

Protection Method Used by Age and Marital Status for African American, Hispanic, and White Women (Weighted Percentage, Unweighted Number)

	Age					
	African American		Hispanic		White	
Protection Method	18–29 (n = 114)	30+ (n = 148)	18–29 (n = 95)	30+ (n = 139)	18–29 (n = 105)	30+ (n = 205)
No protection	19.6	63.4	59.6	78.7	26.3	55.1
Birth control method other than condoms	31.9	19.3	22.2	10.8	48.9	34.7
Condom only	23.1	7.5	7.0	10.1	13.0	7.8
Condom plus other method	25.5	9.8	11.2	0.4	11.8	2.4

	Marital Status					
	African American		Hispanic		White	
	Single (n = 165)	Married (n = 99)	Single (n = 83)	Married (n = 151)	Single (n = 93)	Married (n = 217)
No protection	33.6	54.6	57.6	76.3	26.5	52.3
Birth control method other than condoms	25.9	25.4	15.9	16.2	47.6	36.5
Condom only	21.8	4.7	12.5	6.5	11.1	9.0
Condom plus other method	18.7	15.3	13.9	1.0	14.8	2.2

NOTES: For the protection method, $\chi^2(3, N = 262) = 48.7$, $p = .000$ for African American women; $\chi^2(3, N = 234) = 19.0$, $p = .000$ for Hispanic women; $\chi^2(3, N = 310) = 27.5$, $p = .000$ for white women. For the marital status variable, $\chi^2(3, N = 264) = 17.7$, $p = .000$ for African American women; $\chi^2(3, N = 234) = 19.4$, $p = .000$ for Hispanic women; $\chi^2(3, N = 310) = 27.2$, $p = .000$ for white women.

greater percentage of those who did not use protection were young (59.6 percent) and single (57.6 percent). Among white women, about two times as many of those who were young and single reported using some form of protection.

Contraceptive Method by Level of Effectiveness. Comparing across ethnic groups, 48 percent of African American women, 23 percent of Hispanic women, and 51 percent of white women reported using an effective method of birth control during the event (excluding no protection, rhythm, withdrawal, or douche). Use of contraceptive methods of various levels of effectiveness did not differ significantly by age and marital status among African American women (Table 42-2). Among Hispanic women, half of those in the younger age group (51.0 percent, $n = 20$) reported using the most effective types of birth control, whereas the majority of those over 30 years of age (54.6 percent, $n = 23$) said they used birth control at the second level of effectiveness. Differences in marital status and level of contraception effectiveness also appeared among Hispanic women, with the majority of married women (58.4 percent) using the most effective types of birth control. Among single Hispanic women, the highest proportion (36.1 percent) reported using methods at the least effective level, which included rhythm, withdrawal, or douche. There were no significant differences in age and marital status and the level of birth control effectiveness among white women.

Concern about AIDS

Significant differences in whether women were concerned about the possibility of contracting AIDS were found across the three ethnic groups, with African American women reporting the most concern (82.7 percent), followed by Hispanic women (69.8 percent) and white women (65.8 percent) ($\chi^2 (4) = 43.6$, p = .000). For each ethnic group there was an association between the level of concern and condom use versus other methods of protection (Table 42-3). Across all three ethnic groups, a greater percentage of women who reported no concern about contracting AIDS also reported using no protection in their most recent sexual encounter. Across the three ethnic groups, level of effectiveness of birth control method used was not statistically associated with concern about contracting AIDS.

Condom Use and Level of Birth Control Effectiveness According to Partner Status

Among African American women, more of those who were involved with a new partner reported using condoms or condoms plus another method (53.2 percent, $n = 18$) compared with those who had been with the same partner before (28.1 percent, $n = 64$) (Table 42-4). Regarding effectiveness of birth control method used, African American women with a new partner reported using the second highest level of birth control effectiveness (57.9 percent, $n = 10$) compared with those with a previous partner, who reported using the most

Table 42-2

Contraceptive Method: Level of Effectiveness Used, by Age and Marital Status for African American, Hispanic, and White Women (Weighted Percentage, Unweighted Number)

	Age											
	African American				Hispanic				White			
	18–29		30+		18–29		30+		18–29		30+	
Variable	(n = 85)		(n = 48)		(n = 40)		(n = 42)		(n = 76)		(n = 94)	
Pill, IUD, tubal ligation, Norplant	41.8		50.2		51.0		35.7		65.4		60.7	
Condom, jelly, sponge, diaphragm, foam	42.0		29.8		17.5		54.6		27.6		32.9	
Rhythm, withdrawal, douche	16.2		20.0		31.5		9.8		6.9		6.4	

	Marital Status											
	Single		Married		Single		Married		Single		Married	
	(n = 95)		(n = 38)		(n = 34)		(n = 48)		(n = 66)		(n = 104)	
Pill, IUD, tubal ligation, Norplant	40.5		54.7		32.4		58.4		62.2		63.3	
Condom, jelly, sponge, diaphragm, foam	38.2		37.1		31.5		30.7		31.7		29.7	
Rhythm, withdrawal, douche	21.3		8.2		36.1		10.9		6.1		7.0	

NOTES: For all categories except Hispanic women, the variables had no significant effect. For Hispanic women in both age groups, $\chi^2(2, N = 82)$ = 10.2, p = .006; for single and married Hispanic women, $\chi^2(2, N = 82)$ = 6.6, p = .036.

Table 42-3

Condom Use and Contraceptive Method by Level of Concern about AIDS for African American, Hispanic, and White Women (Unweighted Number, Weighted Percentage)

	Condom Use								
	African American		Hispanic				White		
Variable	Not Concerned (n = 49)	Concerned (n = 209)	Not Concerned (n = 70)	Concerned (n = 162)			Not Concerned (n = 98)	Concerned (n = 207)	
No protection	60.5	38.3	80.0	65.3			60.3	37.7	
Birth control method other than condoms	24.2	26.2	15.4	16.5			32.7	43.6	
Condom only	10.6	16.1	4.6	10.4			4.6	11.5	
Condom plus other method	4.7	19.4	—	7.8			2.3	7.2	

	Use of Effective Birth Control								
	(n = 20)	(n = 109)	(n = 17)	(n = 65)			(n = 42)	(n = 125)	
Pill, IUD, Tubal ligation, Norplant	46.9	45.0	59.0	42.1			71.0	61.2	
Condom, jelly, sponge, diaphragm, foam	49.9	35.6	23.7	32.9			19.3	32.9	
Rhythm, withdrawal, douche	3.2	19.5	17.3	25.0			9.7	5.9	

NOTE: For the condom use variable, $\chi^2(3, N = 258) = 9.53$, $p = .022$ for African American women; $\chi^2(3, N = 232) = 8.73$, $p = .033$ for Hispanic women; $\chi^2(3, N = 305) = 15.1$, $p = .001$ for white women. Level of birth control effectiveness was not significant for any group.

Table 42-4

Condom Use and Contraceptive Method in a Relationship with a New Partner versus Previous Partner for African American, Hispanic, and White Women (Unweighted Number, Weighted Percentage)

	Condom Use											
	African American		Hispanic		White	
Variable	NP (n = 34)	PP (n = 226)	NP (n = 42)	PP (n = 189)	NP (n = 19)	PP (n = 291)
No protection	29.1	43.7	58.3	73.3	23.6	46.4
Birth control method other than condoms	17.7	28.1	4.3	19.0	51.0	38.9
Condom only	41.0	9.4	15.1	6.9	10.0	9.6
Condom plus other method	12.2	18.7	22.3	0.8	15.4	5.1

	Level of Birth Control Effectiveness					
	(n = 18)	(n = 133)	(n = 15)	(n = 66)	(n = 15)	(n = 155)
Pill, IUD, tubal ligation, Norplant	30.6	49.4	9.4	62.0	45.7	64.4
Condom, jelly, sponge, diaphragm, foam	57.9	32.1	37.0	29.1	43.3	29.3
Rhythm, withdrawal, douche	11.6	18.5	53.5	8.9	11.1	6.3

NOTES: NP = new partner; PP = previous partner. For the condom use variable, $\chi^2(3, N = 260) = 26.6$, $p = .000$ for African American women; $\chi^2(3, N = 231) = 39.6$, $p = .000$ for Hispanic women; it was not significant for white women. For level of birth control effectiveness, $\chi^2(2, N = 151) = 6.5$, $p = .037$ for African American women; $\chi^2(2, N = 81) = 19.9$, $p = .000$ for Hispanic women; it was not significant for white women.

effective types of birth control (49.4 percent, $n = 66$). More Hispanic women with new partners reported using condoms or condoms plus another method as a form of protection than those with previous partners. Level of effectiveness of birth control method used differed according to partner status for Hispanic women, with more of those with a previous partner using the most effective types (62.0 percent, $n = 41$), compared with those with a new partner (9.4 percent, $n = 1$). In addition, more Hispanic women with a new partner reported using a birth control method of the least effective type (53.5 percent, $n = 8$). Partner status was not associated with condom use or type of effective birth control among white women.

Multivariate Analyses

To control for the simultaneous effects of age, marital status, education, income, employment status, partner status, concern about AIDS, and the importance of religion on condom use and the use of effective birth control, multiple logistic regression analyses were conducted. Because of differences in demographic characteristics among the ethnic groups, separate analyses were conducted for each group and for each of the dependent variables: condom used versus condoms not used and effective birth control used versus not used.

African American women in the 18 to 29 age range and those with incomes lower than $10,000 were more likely to use condoms as a means of protection (Table 42-5). In addition, African American women with new partners were about three times as likely as those with previous partners to use condoms. Among Hispanic women, single women were more likely than those who were married to use condoms, and those involved with a new partner were about eight times more likely than those with a previous partner to use a condom. White women who earned less than $10,000 were more likely to use condoms than those with higher incomes. Also, white women who were concerned about contracting AIDS were three times as likely as those who were not concerned to use condoms. Employment status was also a significant factor for white women; those who were students, retired workers, or homemakers were almost 10 times more likely than those who were unemployed to use condoms.

Different predictors appeared for effective birth control use among the three ethnic groups. Again, younger African American women were more likely to use effective birth control. African American women who were employed were almost $3^1/_2$ times more likely than those who were unemployed to use effective birth control. For Hispanic women, the only predictor of birth control effectiveness level was religiosity; those who felt religion was important were less likely than those who did not to use effective birth control methods. White women who were younger and single were more likely to use effective birth control than those who were older and married. Again, concern about contracting AIDS was a significant factor for white women, with those who were concerned almost twice as likely

Table 42-5
Logistic Regression Results (Unweighted Number, Weighted Percentage)

Condom Use

Variable	African American (n = 246)		Hispanic (n = 222)		White (n = 299)	
	Odds Ratio	CI	Odds Ratio	CI	Odds Ratio	CI
Age (30+)	.21	.10, .43	1.22	.45, 3.28	.67	.30, 1.51
Married	.59	.29, 1.21	.32	.11, .93	.58	.24, 1.36
New partner	2.64	1.13, 6.13	7.89	2.63, 23.6	.88	.19, 4.04
Religion important	1.67	.74, 3.78	1.71	.60, 4.86	.81	.38, 1.71
Education (12+)	.72	.31, 1.70	1.68	.56, 5.01	1.35	.42, 4.33
Income ($10,000+)	.37	.18, .75	.53	.17, 1.67	.26	.10, .67
Concerned about AIDS	1.78	.60, 5.28	2.43	.61, 9.60	2.81	1.08, 7.32
Employment status: Employed	.96	.38, 2.38	.97	.23, 4.12	3.39	.46, 24.7
Student, retired, homemaker (versus unemployed)	.44	.15, 1.26	.77	.16, 3.74	9.46	1.18, 75.5

Level of Birth Control Effectiveness

Variable	African American (n = 246)		Hispanic (n = 219)		White (n = 297)	
	Odds Ratio	CI	Odds Ratio	CI	Odds Ratio	CI
Age (30+)	.20	.10, .38	.61	.30, 1.24	.50	.28, .88
Married	.88	.47, 1.67	.69	.32, 1.47	.50	.26, .95
New partner	1.62	.71, 3.73	1.27	.48, 3.38	1.65	.52, 5.26
Religion important	.87	.42, 1.82	.34	.17, .68	.77	.46, 1.30
Education (12+)	1.38	.63, 3.03	1.55	.69, 3.45	1.91	.79, 4.57
Income ($10,000+)	.60	.31, 1.14	1.63	.65, 4.06	.70	.28, 1.75
Concerned about AIDS	.93	.40, 2.17	1.40	.61, 3.19	1.79	1.03, 3.11
Employment status: Employed	3.37	1.35, 8.37	.44	.16, 1.22	2.54	.83, 7.74
Student, retired, homemaker (versus unemployed)	1.48	.55, 3.95	.48	.15, 1.59	1.98	.60, 6.58

NOTES: CI = Confidence interval. For the condom use variable, $\chi^2(9, N = 246) = 55.2$, $p < .000$ for African American women; $\chi^2(9, N = 222) = 50.7$, $p < .000$ for Hispanic women; $\chi^2(9, N = 299) = 31.1$, $p < .000$ for white women. For level of birth control effectiveness, $\chi^2(9, N = 246) = 48.0$, $p < .000$ for African American women; $\chi^2(9, N = 219) = 21.6$, $p < .010$ for Hispanic women; $\chi^2(9, N = 297) = 37.7$, $p < .000$ for white women.

to use an effective method of birth control than those who were not concerned.

DISCUSSION

Results of this study indicate that a significant proportion of women and their partners in each ethnic group did not use any form of protection during their most recent sexual encounter. Most notably at risk were Hispanic women, 70 percent of whom reported using no protection. This finding supports other research that has suggested that most women at risk of HIV are not using condoms consistently, especially with their main sexual partner (Grinstead, Faigeles, Binson, & Eversley, 1993).

The study also reveals that there are important differences among the three groups of women. More African American women reported using some form of protection and were more likely than the other two groups to use condoms. African American women who used condoms were more likely to be young, have lower incomes, and be involved with a new partner. Using condoms with a new partner perhaps indicates that prevention messages are reaching this group and that most are concerned about protecting themselves against AIDS and other STDs. In addition, nearly one-half of African American women reported using an effective form of birth control. The women who used effective birth control were primarily young and employed, with perhaps a higher degree of independence and ability to afford more expensive types of birth control. In addition, compared with Hispanic and white women, African American women in this sample were the most concerned about contracting AIDS.

Because of their reluctance to use contraceptives, Hispanic women were most at risk both of AIDS and other STDs, as well as unintended pregnancies. Those who used condoms were single and had a new partner. Of the small portion who used protection, only 23 percent used an effective means of birth control. The main predictor of effective contraception was low religiosity. This finding supports other studies that have indicated that using condoms or effective birth control may go against cultural norms that expect Hispanic women to be "modest, faithful, and virginal" and to avoid sexual assertion or expressiveness (Marin & Marin, 1990). It is also possible that given the nature of many prevention programs, most of which are targeted toward women in the general population, Hispanic women may not be able to receive, pursue, or fully understand the information currently available to them regarding the risks and prevention of HIV infection.

The low rate of condom use among Hispanic women also may be tied to the behavior of their partners. Studies suggest that Hispanic women are at risk because they are involved with men who are considered primary partners but who are nonmonogamous and do not use condoms, especially with a primary partner (Hines & Caetano, in press; Marin, Tschann, Gomez, & Kegeles, 1993; Sabogal, Faigeles, &

Catania, 1993). Studies further suggest that in Hispanic culture, condom use may be a male prerogative (Marin, Gomez, & Hearst, 1993).

Findings revealed that white women used contraceptive methods other than condoms, indicating that this group used protection mainly as a means to prevent pregnancy, not for protection against AIDS. Those who used condoms had lower incomes and were concerned about contracting AIDS. Of the women who used effective birth control methods, most were young and single. These results support other research that has indicated that all women, even those who may not perceive themselves at risk for HIV infection and who are not defined as members of "risk groups," should be counseled for HIV risk reduction (Grinstead et al., 1993).

Some limitations of this study need to be considered. Representative population samples generally consist of low-risk people and exclude people with a high frequency of high-risk sexual activity. In addition, those who failed or refused to complete the SAQ represented an older, more economically marginal group than those included in the sample. The information on sexual risk factors was obtained through self-report, which is not entirely reliable and can yield underestimates. Finally, the most recent sexual event might not be representative of respondents' general sexual behavior.

In spite of these limitations, the findings from this study provide information that can help inform prevention efforts in the area of AIDS, STDs, and unintended pregnancies. Results indicate that it may be useful to combine efforts to reduce unintended pregnancies and AIDS protection. All reproductive behavior, including sexual activity, use of contraceptives, and types of protection, is related to the particular beliefs and values held by different cultural and ethnic groups. More accurate knowledge regarding the sexual behavior of women from diverse cultural and ethnic backgrounds can help improve ways in which AIDS-related prevention messages are transmitted and prevention programs are designed.

Information from this study may be of particular use to social work practitioners, many of whom work with women from diverse cultural and ethnic groups in various contexts and settings. Because risk reduction for AIDS and unintended pregnancies relies on altering the intimate behaviors of individuals during sexual activity, ways to do this better are imperative. Behaviors that social workers aim to change in these women are linked to personal identities; psychological issues; social support networks; or social, ethnic, or cultural norms. As culture and ethnicity are associated with HIV and pregnancy-related risk, the design and implementation of education programs that adequately attend to cultural issues related to sexual behavior in a balanced, credible, and realistic manner are necessary. In addition, it may be that AIDS risk-reduction efforts that ignore or misinterpret black and Hispanic women's childbearing decisions will be hindered. It is important to consider ways in which an intervention for one will affect the other.

Social work has developed a significant foundation for the design of community-based interventions that assist individuals in the modification or change of behavior within their own cultural milieu. Social work interventions designed from a systems perspective can take into account the complex ways change in one area can affect behavior in another. Given these theoretical underpinnings, social workers are in a unique position to design and implement effective AIDS and pregnancy prevention programs for women from diverse cultural and ethnic backgrounds.

REFERENCES

Caetano, R., & Hines, A. M. (1995). Alcohol, sexual practices and risk of AIDS among blacks, Hispanics and whites. *Journal of Acquired Immune Deficiency Syndromes and Human Retrovirology, 10,* 554–561.

Caetano, R., & Kaskutas, L. (1995). Changes in drinking patterns among whites, blacks and Hispanics, 1984–1992. *Journal of Studies on Alcohol, 56,* 558–565.

Centers for Disease Control. (1991). HIV/AIDS surveillance. *Morbidity and Mortality Weekly Report, 41,* 1–18.

Centers for Disease Control. (1992). Acquired immunodeficiency syndrome—United States, 1992: Update. *Morbidity and Mortality Weekly Report, 42,* 547–551, 557.

Centers for Disease Control and Prevention. (1994). Heterosexually acquired AIDS—United States, 1993. *Morbidity and Mortality Weekly Report, 43,* 155–160.

Grinstead, O. A., Faigeles, B., Binson, D., & Eversley, R. (1993). Sexual risk for human immunodeficiency virus among women in high-risk cities. *Family Planning Perspectives, 25,* 252–256.

Hines, A. M., & Caetano, R. (in press). Alcohol and AIDS-related sexual behavior among Hispanics: Acculturation and gender differences. *AIDS Education and Prevention.*

Marin, B.V., Gomez, C.A., & Hearst, N. (1993). Multiple heterosexual partners and condom use among Hispanics and non-Hispanic whites. *Family Planning Perspectives, 25,* 170–174.

Marin, B. V., & Marin, G. M. (1990). Effects of acculturation on knowledge of AIDS and HIV among Hispanics. *Hispanic Journal of Behavioral Sciences, 12,* 110–121.

Marin, B. V., Tschann, J. M., Gomez, C. A., & Kegeles, S. M. (1993). Acculturation and gender differences in sexual attitudes and behaviors: Hispanic vs. non-Hispanic white unmarried adults. *American Journal of Public Health, 83,* 1759–1761.

Mays, V. M., & Cochran, S. (1988). Issues in the perception of AIDS risk and risk reduction activities by black and Hispanic/Latina women. *American Psychologist, 43,* 949–957.

Roper, W. L., Peterson, H. B., & Curran, J. W. (1993). Commentary: Condoms and HIV/STD prevention—clarifying the message. *American Journal of Public Health, 83,* 501–503.

Sabogal, F., Faigeles, B., & Catania, J. A. (1993). Multiple sexual partners among Hispanics in high-risk cities. *Family Planning Perspectives, 25,* 257–262.

Santos, R. (1991). One approach to oversampling blacks and Hispanics: The National Alcohol Survey. In W. B. Clark & M. E. Hilton (Eds.), *Alcohol in America: Drinking practices and problems* (pp. 324–344), Albany: State University of New York Press.

SPSS, Inc. (1993). SPSS for Windows (Version 6.0). Chicago: Author.

This research was supported by grant no. AA08564 from the National Institute of Alcohol Abuse and Alcoholism to the Alcohol Research Group.

Part IX

IMMIGRATION

43 Immigrant Policy: Issues for Social Work Practice

Yolanda C. Padilla

mmigrant policy refers to policies aimed at facilitating the social and economic integration of immigrants (Fix & Passel, 1994). Immigrant policy is distinguished from immigration policy, which is concerned with regulating who enters the United States and in what numbers. Immigrant policies are related to social welfare, health, education, and housing and employment programs. Thus, the provision of social services plays a central part in immigrant policy. Because social work is the primary profession involved in social services delivery, social workers must consider the policy context of providing social services to immigrants. Attention to the changing demographic characteristics of immigrants, their primary areas of need, and the opportunities and limitations of current immigrant policies can provide the foundation for appropriate social work intervention.

Although the social work literature has included discussions of practice with immigrants, the underlying concerns have been with their cultural adaptation, namely an understanding of how practice can be sensitive to differences in the worldviews of immigrants given their unique cultural backgrounds. Still, social work has made limited, but important, contributions to the study of immigrant integration at a broader level. Recent analyses by Drachman (1992), Jacob (1994), and Sherraden and Martin (1994) provide a conceptual framework for understanding the relevance of earlier immigrant group experiences to the adjustment of these groups to their countries of destination.

Overall, the social work literature shows that to different degrees, immigrants face a series of stress-producing events that result in the need for assistance and support; such events include separation from family and community, journeys of different durations and levels of danger, and relocation problems associated with finding housing and employment.

Social work's primary concern in the field has been the conceptualization of the psychosocial aspects of immigration and their impact on the successful integration of immigrants. The focus has been on the needs, experiences, and circumstances of immigrants at different

This chapter was originally published in the November 1997 issue of *Social Work*, Vol. 42, pp. 595–606.

phases of the immigration process (premigration, transit, and resettlement) and the need to consider this knowledge in designing responsive service delivery (Drachman, 1992).

In studies of immigration, the emphasis on individual adaptation has given way to the realization that the success of immigrants also depends on the extent to which social and economic conditions and related policies facilitate their integration (Edmonston & Passel, 1994). Therefore, along with an understanding of immigrant experiences, the ability of social workers to provide services to immigrant families is defined by the policy context in which they operate. Although social work practice depends largely on changing policy directives, much less attention has been given to this dimension of social work with immigrants (Le-Doux & Stephens, 1992).

This chapter examines current issues related to immigration in the United States. The increasing numbers of and diversity among immigrants and the pressing needs of these new arrivals present a challenge for social work practitioners. At the same time, federal and state immigrant policies provide the context for the level of resources and services available to help immigrants assimilate economically and socially. It is important to understand immigrant access to government assistance, the extent to which immigrants use social services to meet their needs, and the other strategies they use to survive.

CHANGING DEMOGRAPHIC PROFILE OF IMMIGRANTS

To project the types of services that immigrants need to facilitate their social and economic incorporation, it is necessary first to have a clear knowledge of the changing demographic trends in immigration and some of the major factors shaping those trends. Immigrants make up a significant segment of U.S. society. Moreover, immigration to the United States is characterized by steady growth, dramatic changes in ethnic composition, and declining socioeconomic levels. In 1990 the proportion of immigrants in the total U.S. population was almost 9 percent (Edmonston & Passel, 1994). Over 7 million people immigrated during the past decade, reflecting consistent increases over previous decades (Borjas, 1994), and these increases are expected to continue. By 2040 one in four Americans will be an immigrant (first generation) or the child of immigrants (second generation), and by 2010 children of immigrants will account for 22 percent of the school-age population (Fix & Passel, 1994).

Countries of Origin and Settlement Patterns

The ethnic composition of immigrants is extremely diverse because of shifts in immigration streams in recent history. Before the 1960s the vast majority of immigrants came from Europe or Canada (Bean, Cushing, & Haynes, 1994–95). However, by the 1980s only 12.5 percent of legal immigrants originated in these countries, whereas 84.4 percent were from Asia or Latin America (Bean et al., 1994–95). Asian immigrants came primarily from Korea, the Philippines, Vietnam, and China. Latin American immigrants came primarily from Mexico and El Salvador; other Spanish-speaking immigrants came from the Dominican Republic in the Caribbean (Rolph, 1992). By far the largest group of immigrants in the United States is from Mexico, representing over one-fifth (22 percent) of the foreign-born population (Borjas, 1994). Before the 1960s Mexicans were only 11.9 percent of all immigrants (Borjas, 1994).

The new ethnic communities are not dispersed evenly across the United States but rather tend to be concentrated in particular areas. Fully 74 percent of immigrants locate in only six states: California, Florida, Illinois, New Jersey, New York, and Texas (Rolph, 1992). In addition, immigrants tend overwhelmingly to settle in urban centers, with fewer than 7 percent locating in rural areas in 1987 (Portes & Rumbaut, 1990). Certain metropolitan areas experience disproportionately high rates of immigrant settlement. Immigrants are more than 15 percent of the populations of Chicago, Boston, and Houston; more than 38 percent of Los Angeles; and more than 60 percent of Miami (Fix & Zimmermann, 1994).

Immigration Policy

The changing profile of the immigrant population has been partly shaped by key U.S. immigration policies. The so-called new flow of immigrants from Asia and Latin America began in the late 1960s as a result of the Immigration and Nationality Act of 1965 (P.L. 89-236), which relaxed the restrictions on immigration from countries in those parts of the world (Edmonston & Passel, 1994). Immigration from Asia also greatly increased with the passage of the Refugee Act of 1980 (P.L. 96-212), which gave legal status to refugees and asylees (Rolph, 1992). In addition, the Immigration Reform and Control Act of 1986 (P.L. 99-603) resulted in the legalization of over 2 million long-term undocumented workers. The vast majority of these workers were from Mexico, Central America, and the Caribbean. Immigration from these same parts of Latin America was also expanded with the Immigration Act of 1990 (P.L. 101-649), which granted temporary protective status on an individual basis to people from countries suffering from armed conflict or natural disasters (Rolph, 1992).

Socioeconomic Characteristics

With the vast majority of immigrants originating from Third World countries, the new entrants of the 1980s and 1990s have been considerably less skilled than native-born workers and less skilled than earlier immigrant populations (Bean, Chapa, Berg, & Sowards, 1994). They tend to have significantly lower educational and occupational levels relative to U.S.-born groups. Fully a quarter of immigrants over 25 years of age have fewer than nine years of education, compared with 9 percent of the U.S.-born population (Fix & Passel, 1994).

The lack of English-language proficiency is a major problem. Twenty-five percent of immigrants do not speak English or do not speak it well (Fix & Passel, 1994). Two other factors help explain the lower socioeconomic status of current immigrants. The first factor is the large proportion of recent arrivals: In 1990, 44 percent had come within the preceding 10 years (Fix & Passel, 1994). The second factor is the substantial number of illegal immigrants and refugees, who tend to fare worse than legal immigrants. As of 1990, 87 percent of immigrants had entered the country legally. Of these, 33 percent had become naturalized citizens, 49 percent were legal permanent residents, and 6 percent were refugees and asylees—people admitted into the country for humanitarian reasons. It is estimated that 13 percent of the total immigrant population are undocumented individuals. About 62 percent of illegal entrants are from Mexico, 13 percent from Europe and Canada, and the rest from a large variety of countries in other parts of the world (Fix & Passel, 1994).

In light of the large numbers of recent arrivals and their lower average educational and occupational status, poverty levels are higher among immigrant households than among native households (16.7 percent compared with 12.3 percent), because immigrants are concentrated in low-paying jobs. Regardless of country of origin, recent arrivals fare considerably worse, with an overall poverty rate of 24.8 percent (Fix & Passel, 1994). In 1990 the average poverty rates for foreign-born households from Europe and Canada, Mexico, other Latin American countries, Asia, and Africa were all higher than the poverty rates of U.S.-born citizens. However, this disparity is true only for recent arrivals. Long-term immigrants from each of these regions have lower poverty rates than the U.S.-born population, with the exception of Mexican immigrants (Chiswick & Sullivan, 1995).

Legal status explains important differences in the economic well-being of immigrants. Immigrants from source countries for illegal immigration (primarily Mexico, El Salvador, and Guatemala) earn significantly less than native-born Americans even after having lived in the United States for extended periods. People from refugee countries who are recent entrants earn slightly less but after lengthier stays in the country slightly surpass the U.S.-born populations (Fix & Passel, 1994). However, in a study of Southeast Asian refugees (the largest refugee group in the United States) in California, Potocky (1996) found that refugees were considerably worse off economically than all other ethnic groups when taking into account employment and occupational rates, housing conditions, and other measures of economic well-being, even up to 15 years after arrival.

Direct comparisons of the economic well-being of immigrants relative to U.S.-born individuals of the same ethnic background are more empirically valid than comparisons of immigrants to the general U.S.-born population or to general populations of other U.S. ethnic minority groups, because the processes of economic integration are unique to the history and societal incorporation of each group. Comparisons of immigrants with U.S.-born people of the same ethnic background show dramatic differences by recency of immigration and countries of origin. A detailed analysis (Borjas, 1994) controlled for age and educational levels showed that in 1990 white immigrant groups regardless of period of arrival had higher wages than comparable white U.S.-born groups. The same differential is true for Asian immigrants who have lived in the United States for an extended period, but not for recent arrivals. Finally, relative to U.S.-born Mexican Americans, the income of immigrants of the same age and educational background is significantly lower regardless of length of residence in this country. The reasons for this pattern among Mexican immigrants are not clear, because in the 1960s and 1970s they too were able to gain parity with their U.S.-born counterparts within about 15 years (Chiswick, 1979; Padilla, 1996).

Nevertheless, the socioeconomic advancement of immigrants across generations shows that children of immigrants (the second generation) do considerably better than their parents and indeed surpass the earnings of other native-born people of the same national origin or ethnicity. Research on this topic is less extensive by country of origin because of data limitations. However, detailed multivariate analyses using longitudinal data show that this improvement is true not only for European immigrants, but also for Mexican, Cuban, and other Latino groups (Padilla, 1993). We have yet to see if this pattern will remain true for future generations of contemporary immigrants.

In summary, the socioeconomic status of current immigrants is quite complex and diverse. Immigrants who have entered the country illegally or as refugees or asylees, who have arrived within the past 10 years, and who have come from developing countries are more likely to suffer economic hardship. At present, all of these groups represent significant proportions of the immigrant population resulting from demographic changes in the flows of immigration.

FEDERAL POLICY FACTORS AFFECTING SERVICE PROVISION TO IMMIGRANTS

Unlike immigration policy, which has been a central area of concern, immigrant policy has not been a priority in the United States. The current political context is characterized by a strong anti-immigrant sentiment. Although not substantiated by research, there is a growing concern that immigrants are a drain on the economy because of high welfare use and because they take jobs away from U.S.-born citizens and depress wages. As a result, there has been a push for reducing immigration, particularly illegal immigration (Illegal Immigration Reform and Immigrant Responsibility Act of 1996, P.L. 104-208). The most recent strategy to control immigration includes certain provisions of the 1996 welfare reform legislation that attempt to discourage new immigration by denying a range of social welfare benefits to all foreign-born noncitizens, legal or illegal, currently residing in the country.

U.S. welfare policies toward immigrants have been generally inconsistent and have resulted in a fragmented system of services

(Rosenberg, 1991). The system of assistance involves a combination of services targeted specifically to immigrants and limited access to mainstream social services.

Lack of a Comprehensive National Immigrant Policy

Although the admission of immigrants to the United States has increased, federal support for programs targeted to assist immigrants has declined (Fix & Passel, 1994). Government assistance for immigrants has not responded to changing demographic trends. As the socioeconomic level of immigrant groups has declined over the past 40 years, government assistance has actually decreased. As a result, state and local communities have been forced to take a large role in providing health, education, and social services to immigrants (Fix & Passel, 1994). Furthermore, many of the services are provided through private voluntary agencies rather than public agencies, either through contractual agreements with government entities or through private and religious donations (Le-Doux & Stephens, 1992).

Social welfare policy was first linked to immigration policy with the Migration and Refugee Assistance Act of 1962 (P.L. 87-510) (Tienda & Liang, 1994). This act provided for cash, medical, and educational assistance to refugees. All in all, however, federal immigration policies have not included significant provisions for resettlement assistance. Currently, specific policies for many social welfare provisions are limited to refugees under the 1980 Refugee Resettlement Program and until 1994 to newly legalized people under the Immigration Reform and Control Act (IRCA) of 1986.

Created under the Refugee Act of 1980, the Refugee Resettlement Program guaranteed access to social support, including transportation, relocation allowances, job training, and public assistance programs (such as Aid to Families with Dependent Children, Supplemental Security Income, and Medicaid) (Rolph, 1992). The Refugee Resettlement Program is administered by the Office of Refugee Resettlement, Family Support Administration of the U.S. Department of Health and Human Services. The program provides funding to the states, which then contract with local entities to provide resettlement services. Funding is allocated to provide employment-related services and to help localities that are heavily affected by refugee populations, including grants to states to fund self-help indigenous organizations (Le-Doux & Stephens, 1992).

The second most important immigrant policy is the State Legalization Impact Assistance Grants (SLIAG) provision of IRCA. IRCA created a mechanism to help states and local governments provide public health, public assistance, social services, and education exclusively to previously undocumented immigrants who under this act were granted legal status in the United States (Rolph, 1992). Although the SLIAG provision ended in 1994, it was unprecedented in its inclusion of targeted immigrant services.

Given the limited federal policies, the trend is for states to increasingly take responsibility for assisting immigrants. Not only has federal funding for immigrant programs been curtailed, but the Personal Responsibility and Work Opportunity Reconciliation Act of 1996 (P.L. 104-193), signed into law by President Clinton on August 22, 1996, severely cuts federal services to immigrants. All immigrant groups other than naturalized citizens—primarily undocumented people and refugees, but also legal immigrants—are likely to be affected. Regardless of the course of implementation of this legislation, the move toward block grants will also place the states in the lead. Currently, state programs for immigrants vary widely depending on the state's political characteristics, economy, and immigrant composition (Zimmermann & Fix, 1994). In addition to the programs implemented under current federal policies, states have provided bilingual education for children with limited English (under the Bilingual Education Act, P.L. 89-10) and emergency and prenatal medical services to undocumented immigrants (under the Medicaid public assistance program) (Rosenberg, 1991).

Several state initiatives illustrate the roles state and local governments have played in addition to implementing federally mandated programs. Such initiatives include the development of a campaign to provide basic orientation services to all immigrants in New York (Rosenberg, 1991) and the coordination of services for immigrant children, youths, and families in the areas of mental health, child welfare, public health, and social services in Massachusetts (de Monchy, 1991). In Texas, immigrants have been eligible to receive medical assistance and other primary health care services through local and state indigent health care programs regardless of legal status (Zimmermann & Fix, 1994).

Nevertheless, the lack of federal reimbursement for the provision of services has prompted states with large immigrant populations— such as California, Florida, and Texas—to question the extent of their responsibility for helping immigrants. Although rural areas in southern states often provide special services (for example, migrant school programs, health care, and community-based services) to seasonal migrant farm worker communities who relocate there on a temporary basis, they often lack the resources and infrastructure to assist permanent immigrants.

Eligibility for Mainstream Social Services

In addition to services targeted specifically to immigrants, immigrant policy also includes qualifications for mainstream social programs (Fix & Zimmermann, 1994). On the basis of a complex set of rules, immigrants are eligible to receive services under certain federal programs. Social workers play a pivotal role in the delivery of available government services to immigrants. In providing services to immigrants, there are two key policy-related issues to keep in mind. The first is identifying the person's legal immigration status, and the second is determining what government benefits the person is eligible to receive.

Immigrant legal classification is far more complex than a simple legal–illegal dichotomy. In addition to naturalized U.S. citizens and undocumented individuals, immigrants can be classified as lawful permanent residents, people fleeing persecution, aliens with work authorization, and people allowed to enter the United States with special-purpose visas (also called "nonimmigrants") (National Immigration Law Center, 1994). There are even more specific immigrant statuses within these broad categories (National Immigration Law Center, 1994). For example, people fleeing persecution can be classified as refugees or asylees, depending on whether they sought admission while still in their country of origin or after having entered the United States. Lawful permanent residents include people who were legalized under IRCA and conditional permanent residents (that is, people married to U.S. citizens for less than two years).

A person's immigration classification denotes under what circumstances he or she entered the country (for political or economic reasons), the conditions for remaining in the country (length of time the individual can stay or ability to bring family members into the country), and whether the person is allowed to be employed in the United States. Some immigrant categories are in effect only for restricted periods of time and are based on specific legislation.

More important for human services providers, immigrant status determines what government benefits a client may qualify for. At the federal level the eligibility system for immigrants is quite complicated and exclusionary (Board on Children and Families, 1995; Fix & Passel, 1994; Rolph, 1992). Before passage of the Personal Responsibility and Work Opportunity Reconciliation Act, immigrants across general categories, including some undocumented individuals, were covered by several programs for the poor, including the Special Supplemental Food Program for Women, Infants, and Children (WIC); school lunch and breakfast; emergency Medicaid services; and Head Start. However, eligibility for most federal programs depended on immigrant status, as well as fulfillment of the same program eligibility requirements as U.S. citizens. Furthermore, the level of assistance varied widely. For example, cash assistance to refugees was limited to eight months, and the payment amounts were lower than regular welfare assistance (personal communication with Caitriona Lyons, director of refugee programs, Refugee and Resettlement Services, Austin, Texas, May 21, 1996).

Immigrants eligible for assistance before passage of the Personal Responsibility and Work Opportunity Reconciliation Act could be in the following selected categories:

- lawful permanent residents
- people granted permission to enter the country for humanitarian reasons

- refugees and asylees, including those granted "paroled" refugee status ("parolees") when the number allowed to enter the country has been exceeded
- family members of people granted legal status under IRCA (family unity provision)
- people allowed to remain in the United States under temporary protected status because of unsafe conditions in specific countries of origin
- undocumented immigrants.

For a detailed description of immigrant classification and eligibility for federal social services programs, see National Immigration Law Center, 1994, 1996.

Immigrant Provisions of the Personal Responsibility and Work Opportunity Reconciliation Act of 1996

Some important changes in immigrant eligibility criteria for a number of mainstream social services will take place once the provisions of the Personal Responsibility and Work Opportunity Reconciliation Act begin to take effect in April 1997 (Center for Public Policy Priorities, 1996). Under the new guidelines, most legal ("qualified") immigrants will no longer be eligible to receive food stamps and SSI. States will have the option of maintaining AFDC (changed to Temporary Assistance for Needy Families [TANF] under the new legislation) and Medicaid coverage for current legal immigrants. Otherwise, legal immigrants will remain eligible for other selected federal benefits but will have access to some of the programs only after five years of residence in the United States.

In addition, certain categories of legal residents will, along with undocumented immigrants, be considered "unqualified" for the purposes of eligibility for needs-based assistance: spouses and children of people who sought legal status under IRCA family unity provisions and people in temporary protective status. However, unqualified people will continue to be eligible for emergency Medicaid services and limited grandfathering of current federally subsidized housing. Children of unqualified aliens will continue to receive school breakfast and lunch benefits. States will have the option of providing WIC benefits for these children. Overall, however, state or locally funded programs may provide services to undocumented people only if the state passes a law providing for their eligibility.

SOCIAL WELFARE NEEDS OF IMMIGRANTS

Current knowledge of immigration classification is essential for social workers for several reasons. First, social workers can help clients obtain appropriate lawful immigration status, because this is a first step in becoming eligible for social welfare services. Second, by keeping abreast of changes in program eligibility requirements for immigrants, social workers can provide more accurate information and referral services. Third, social workers need to be aware that the unqualified use of public services by certain categories of immigrants can be a cause for deportation or future denial of lawful permanent resident status under the "public charge" rule. The *public charge rule* refers to the expectation that immigrants will obtain support from family members or other sponsors rather than from government sources during the initial years after arriving in the United States. Consequently, social workers may need to focus on finding alternative nongovernment sources of support for specific immigrant clients in need.

The challenge for both policymakers and social work practitioners is to respond to the needs of immigrants by designing appropriate social services that will contribute to a smooth social and economic transition in an environment of limited government resources. Furthermore, in evaluating the role of social work practice, it is also relevant to understand the alternative immigrant household survival strategies used in the absence of welfare assistance.

Statistical data are available on the demographic characteristics of immigrants, but national data on their needs are much more limited (Board on Children and Families, 1995). Some studies focusing on certain groups of immigrants identify important areas of need among immigrant children and families.

Socioeconomic background and the reasons for immigrating influence the social services needs of immigrants. Some immigrants who have professional backgrounds come to improve their careers or businesses and bring with them access to sources of capital. However, the largest group of immigrants to the United States are labor migrants, who are concentrated in manual, low-paying jobs and often come to escape poverty (Portes & Rumbaut, 1990). Political refugees and asylees who leave their countries because they fear persecution are often also economically disadvantaged. Regardless of socioeconomic status, resettlement always requires support in locating housing; finding work; and connecting to schools, churches, and other institutions in the new society.

Ethnographic studies show that the settlement process involves the development of social, institutional, and economic ties (Massey, 1986). When migrant communities are established, for example, they often provide the social networks necessary to help new immigrants reach their destination, find work, and adapt to the new environment (Massey, 1986; Portes & Rumbaut, 1990). To the extent that immigrants lack access to their own economic resources and networks of social support, they require other sources of assistance.

Resettlement Assistance

Clearly, material resources are a major need among new arrivals, especially among labor migrants; low incomes translate into very poor living conditions for families and children. Over 10 percent of immigrants live in areas of concentrated poverty, a figure that has increased much more rapidly between 1980 and 1990 than that of U.S.-born citizens (Fix & Passel, 1994). Thus, meeting the basic needs of immigrant clients for adequate housing, food, and clothing is a priority for social work. The provision of emergency shelter is often necessary for refugees and asylees, who sometimes flee their countries unexpectedly and unprepared. As a result, they may lack supportive social networks in receiving communities.

The wide range of economic needs among immigrants is related to other areas requiring assistance, including education and language needs. Immigrants with low levels of education and lower occupational status need help obtaining job skills training that will prepare them to work in better-paying jobs. In addition, social workers can be of great assistance in helping clients overcome language barriers. They can advocate for clients by offering bilingual services, serving as translators to other organizations, or providing information and referral services to help secure English instruction.

Although the scarcity of bilingual social workers is a real problem (Harrison, Wodarski, & Thyer, 1992), some communities are developing innovative methods to serve their growing immigrant populations. The state Department of Human Services in Texas, for example, initiated a program—the Volunteer Interpreter Service—that trains bilingual people to serve as volunteer translators for social workers working with clients who have limited English fluency.

Mental Health Services

For refugees and asylees, mental health problems are a critical concern that often goes unaddressed. To different degrees, refugees and asylees suffer trauma associated with having experienced or witnessed violent crimes and deprivation in wars in their countries of origin. Not surprisingly, according to Portes and Rumbaut (1990) and de Monchy (1991), extensive research has shown that refugees have significantly higher rates of need for mental health services than the population in general. Research on the mental health problems of nonrefugee immigrants is much less extensive, but it suggests that mental health is associated with the conditions of settlement—that is, how supportive the new environment is.

Studies among Mexican Americans indicate that mental health problems, such as depression, are indeed greater among immigrants but that they are lower for immigrants who have higher incomes, kin and family support, and strong cultural attachments (Portes & Rumbaut, 1990). Effective mental health intervention by human services providers requires at least four elements: (1) the use of trained bilingual and bicultural staff; (2) training in disorders associated with the immigrant experience, including posttraumatic stress disorder; (3) linkages between social services programs and members of the immigrant community; and (4) integration of traditional methods of healing with other therapeutic approaches (de Monchy, 1991).

Health Care

Because the immigrant population is disproportionately young—29 percent are under age 20 (Rolph, 1992)—child and maternal health care is critical. Yet the data show that immigrant children and their families do not receive adequate health care (Board on Children and Families, 1995; Plascencia & Wong, 1991). Overwhelmingly, the reason for this is the lack of private or public health insurance. Contrary to what the public might think, many immigrants are not eligible for publicly supported health care services, except in emergencies. For example, people seeking asylum, undocumented people, and some categories of legal immigrants are not eligible for Medicaid. In addition, several categories of legal immigrants who are not naturalized citizens risk being denied citizenship for having a record of public service use. Although some believe that immigrants do not seek health services primarily for cultural reasons, there is no empirical evidence to support this belief.

Information on the specific physical health needs of the foreign-born individuals is inconclusive. In some cases, the health of immigrants who have lived in this country longer actually deteriorates (Board on Children and Families, 1995). However, it is not clear what aspects of immigrants' lives result in positive outcomes. Supportive social services can be a key factor in promoting the health of immigrants. Given that the main factor preventing immigrants from obtaining medical care is lack of access to public and private health insurance, social services workers face a tough challenge in the current political environment. Social workers can be a source of information and referral services to connect clients with available programs. For example, many local and state publicly or privately funded medical assistance programs do not restrict immigrant eligibility.

Second, social workers can be supportive of and receptive to immigrant health care practices that produce healthy outcomes. For instance, Hispanic women, particularly immigrant women, tend to have markedly healthier birth outcomes than the general population. At the same time, research shows that they are less likely to smoke during pregnancy and tend to have healthier diets (National Coalition of Hispanic Health and Human Services Organizations, 1995). One way of being supportive of positive health practices is for social workers to collaborate with and serve as a resource to indigenous health promoters, who are found in many immigrant communities.

Patterns of Social Services Use

Given the limited availability of government assistance in adjusting to life in the United States, where do immigrants turn for help? Field studies of selected immigrant communities shed light on some of the coping strategies immigrant families use to meet their needs. According to a study of undocumented Mexican immigrants in a Southern California community, families combine different means (Hondagneu-Sotelo, 1994). First, immigrant families have as many wage earners as possible, including children. Second, they often share their residences with relatives or even with other families. Third, kin networks are an important source of support. Families share and borrow resources and services, such as child care, among kin.

The presence of these types of coping mechanisms was substantiated in ethnographic studies of undocumented Mexicans and Central American immigrants (Chavez, 1990) and Vietnamese and Laotian refugees (Benson, 1990). Some immigrant groups are able to secure work from organized ethnic businesses or enclaves, which serve as a safety net, particularly for those who are unskilled (Light & Bonacich, 1988; Tienda & Liang, 1994).

IMPLICATIONS FOR SOCIAL WORK

Contrary to popular belief, research shows that immigrants, including those who qualify for services, vastly underutilize government programs in comparison with the U.S.-born population (Bean, Van Hook, & Glick, 1994–95; Tienda & Liang, 1994). Thus, there is good reason to believe that many of the needs of immigrant clients have gone unmet, given their generally lower incomes and the need for institutional resources associated with resettlement.

In working directly with clients, social workers need to be cognizant of the pressures on family members associated with their common coping strategies, such as overcrowded living conditions, long work hours, school dropout by older children to work, and gaps in the availability of help. Pryor (1992) suggested that school-based services could be useful in linking families to a wide range of community resources. Community-level services could promote small businesses by securing technical assistance for ethnically diverse entrepreneurs, because they are often a source of employment for immigrants. At the research and policy level, social workers can intervene by highlighting the adverse impact of unmet needs on the long-term social, educational, and economic outcomes of immigrants and the negative effect these difficulties are likely to have on the broader U.S. economy.

Although levels and types of need vary across different socioeconomic classes of immigrants, their overrepresentation among labor migrants and among poor people points to the relevance of social services availability for this population. In assessing the problems of immigrant clients, social workers can build on the strengths that have been shown to sustain the viability of immigrant families, particularly reliance on cultural attachments and values and social support from family, kin, and community. At the same time, such strategies do not begin to fill the holes in the weak government safety net for this segment of the U.S. population.

Social workers need to

- take a national political stance on social welfare legislation that threatens to adversely affect children and other vulnerable immigrant populations through actions such as the recent motion passed by NASW against California's Proposition 187 ("Nation's Social Workers," 1995).

- become involved in the legislative process. With the current move to block grants, states will be redesigning major social programs and under federal legislation will often have the option of providing services to immigrants. Social workers who serve immigrants can provide first-hand testimony on the needs of this population.

- organize for community-based services and form coalitions to respond to the immediate impact of the current welfare reform legislation. Policy analysts project that approximately 500,000 elderly poor and disabled legal immigrants will lose their SSI benefits, that about 900,000 will lose their food stamp benefits, and that many others will lose other forms of assistance necessary to meet their basic needs (Center for Public Policy Priorities, 1996).

CONCLUSION

Immigrants are a significant proportion of the U.S. population, and immigration entails a resettlement process that requires support. Immigrants have been shown to be a revitalizing force in ethnic communities and in the broader society by adding highly motivated workers and small and large business enterprises to the labor market, enriching and maintaining cultural traditions, and strengthening networks of social support (Light & Bonacich, 1988; Moore & Pinderhughes, 1993).

Nevertheless, the adaptation of immigrants presents special challenges related to settling in the new society. The availability of employment and the presence of networks in an existing ethnic community are key factors, but government policies that facilitate resettlement are just as important (Portes & Rumbaut, 1990). Social work plays a crucial role in the social and economic integration of immigrants through the provision of social services and resources. In the context of the limited support currently provided by government to this segment of American society, social workers must respond with creative community-based initiatives that draw directly on the vitality of immigrant families and communities.

REFERENCES

Bean, F. D., Chapa, J., Berg, R., & Sowards, K. A. (1994). Educational and sociodemographic incorporation among Hispanic immigrants to the United States. In B. Edmonston & J. S. Passel (Eds.), *Immigration and ethnicity: The integration of America's newest arrivals* (pp. 73–100). Washington, DC: Urban Institute Press.

Bean, F. D., Cushing, R. G., & Haynes, C. W. (1994–95). *The changing demography of U.S. immigration flows: Patterns, projections, and contexts* (Paper No. 94-95-16). Austin: University of Texas at Austin, Population Research Center.

Bean, F. D., Van Hook, J.V.W., & Glick, J. (1994–95). *Mode-of-entry, type of public assistance and patterns of welfare recipiency among U.S. immigrants and natives* (Paper No. 94-95-17). Austin: University of Texas at Austin, Population Research Center.

Benson, J. E. (1990). Households, migration, and community context. *Urban Anthropology, 19*, 9–29.

Bilingual Education Act, P.L. 89-10, 102 Stat. 274 to 293.

Board on Children and Families. (1995). Immigrant children and their families: Issues for research and policy. *The Future of Children, 5*, 72–89.

Borjas, G. J. (1994). The economics of immigration. *Journal of Economic Literature, 32*, 1667–1717.

Center for Public Policy Priorities. (1996, October 1). *Analysis of federal welfare reform* (Special issue). Policy Page. Austin, TX: Author.

Chavez, L. R. (1990). Coresidence and resistance: Strategies for survival among undocumented Mexicans and Central Americans in the United States. *Urban Anthropology, 19*, 31–61.

Chiswick, B. R. (1979). The economic progress of immigrants. In W. Fellner (Ed.), *Contemporary economic problems* (pp. 357–399). Washington, DC: American Enterprise Institute.

Chiswick, B. R., & Sullivan, T. A. (1995). The new immigrants. In R. Farley (Ed.), *State of the union: America in the 1990s* (pp. 211–270). New York: Russell Sage Foundation.

de Monchy, M. L. (1991). Recovery and rebuilding: The challenge for refugee children and service providers. In F. L. Ahearn, Jr., & L. L. Athey (Eds.), *Refugee children: Theory, research, and services* (pp. 163–180). Baltimore: Johns Hopkins University Press.

Drachman, D. (1992). A stage-of-migration framework for service to immigrant populations. *Social Work, 37*, 68–72.

Edmonston, B., & Passel, J. S. (1994). Ethnic demography: U.S. immigration and ethnic variation. In B. Edmonston & J. S. Passel (Eds.), *Immigration and ethnicity* (pp. 1–30). Washington, DC: Urban Institute Press.

Fix, M., & Passel, J. S. (1994). *Immigration and immigrants: Setting the record straight.* Washington, DC: Urban Institute.

Fix, M., & Zimmermann, W. (1994). After arrival: An overview of federal immigrant policy in the United States. In B. Edmonston & J. S. Passel (Eds.), *Immigration and ethnicity* (pp. 251–281). Washington, DC: Urban Institute Press.

Harrison, D. F., Wodarski, J. S., & Thyer, B. A. (1992). *Cultural diversity and social work practice.* Springfield, IL: Charles C Thomas.

Hondagneu-Sotelo, P. (1994). *Gendered transitions: Mexican experiences of immigration.* Berkeley: University of California Press.

Illegal Immigration Reform and Immigrant Responsibility Act of 1996, P.L. 104-208, 110 Stat. 3009.

Immigration Act of 1990, P.L. 101-649, 104 Stat. 4978.

Immigration and Nationality Act of 1965, P.L. 89-236, 79 Stat. 911 to 920, 922.

Immigration Reform and Control Act of 1986, P.L. 99-603, 100 Stat. 2099.

Jacob, A. G. (1994). Social integration of Salvadoran refugees. *Social Work, 39*, 307–312.

Le-Doux, C., & Stephens, K. S. (1992). Refugee and immigrant social service delivery: Critical management issues. In A. S. Ryan (Ed.), *Social work with immigrants and refugees* (pp. 31–45). New York: Haworth.

Light, I., & Bonacich, E. (1988). *Immigrant entrepreneurs: Koreans in Los Angeles 1965–1982.* Berkeley: University of California Press.

Massey, D. (1986). The settlement process among Mexican migrants to the United States. *American Sociological Review, 51*, 670–684.

Migration and Refugee Assistance Act of 1962, P.L. 87-510, 76 Stat. 121.

Moore, J., & Pinderhughes, R. (1993). *In the barrios: Latinos and the underclass debate.* New York: Russell Sage Foundation.

National Coalition of Hispanic Health and Human Services Organizations. (1995). Meeting the health promotion needs of Hispanic communities. *American Journal of Health Promotion, 9*, 300–311.

National Immigration Law Center. (1994). *Guide to alien eligibility for federal programs.* Los Angeles: Author.

National Immigration Law Center. (1996). *Immigrants and the '96 welfare law: A resource manual.* Los Angeles: Author.

Nation's social workers oppose Prop. 187: Ethics may force social workers to break law. (1995, January). *NASW Network,* p. 7.

Padilla, Y. C. (1993). The effect of geographic mobility on the socioeconomic achievement of young Hispanic men. *Dissertation Abstracts International, 54-03,* 1113. (University Microfilms No. 93-19, 602)

Padilla, Y. C. (1996, August). *The effect of social background on the long-term economic integration of Mexican immigrants.* Paper presented at the meeting of the Society for the Study of Social Problems, New York.

Personal Responsibility and Work Opportunity Reconciliation Act of 1996, P.L. 104-193, 40 U.S.C. §1305 (Note).

Plascencia, F., & Wong, P. (1991). *Survey of newly legalized persons in Texas: Executive summary.* Austin: University of Texas at Austin, LBJ School of Public Affairs, Center for the Study of Human Resources.

Portes, A., & Rumbaut, R. G. (1990). *Immigrant America: A portrait.* Berkeley: University of California Press.

Potocky, M. (1996). Toward a new definition of refugee economic integration. *International Social Work, 39,* 245–256.

Pryor, C. (1992). Integrating immigrants into American schools. *Social Work in Education, 14,* 153–159.

Refugee Act of 1980, P.L. 96-212, 94 Stat. 102.

Rolph, E. (1992). *Immigration policies: Legacy from the 1980s and issues for the 1990s.* Santa Monica, CA: Rand Corporation.

Rosenberg, D. E. (1991). Serving America's newcomers: States and localities are taking the lead in the absence of a comprehensive national policy. *Public Welfare, 49,* 28–37.

Sherraden, M. D., & Martin, J. J. (1994). Social work with immigrants: International issues in service delivery. *International Social Work, 37,* 369–384.

Tienda, M., & Liang, Z. (1994). Poverty and immigration in policy perspective. In S. H. Danziger, G. D. Sandefur, & D. H. Weinberg (Eds.), *Confronting poverty: Prescriptions for change* (pp. 330–364). New York: Russell Sage Foundation.

Zimmermann, W., & Fix, M. (1994). Immigrant policy in the states: A wavering welcome. In B. Edmonston & J. S. Passel (Eds.), *Immigration and ethnicity* (pp. 287–315). Washington, DC: Urban Institute Press.

Research for this chapter was funded by a grant from the Committee for Public Policy on Contemporary Hispanic Issues of the Inter-University Program on Latino Research, Social Science Research Council.

African Immigrants in the United States: The Challenge for Research and Practice

Hugo A. Kamya

Although considerable resources have been devoted to the study of immigrants, historically there has been a lack of attention to African immigrant groups in the United States. Previous research has examined the adjustment of refugees or immigrants in terms of education; language; and economic, social, and psychological well-being (Haines, 1989). Immigrants face a number of problems, including stress related to acculturation, change, loss, and trauma. Immigrants may not be welcomed by the host society. The tenor of this sentiment is echoed by recent legislative initiatives in some states that propose to deny some immigrants access to social services.

An article in *Social Work* underlines the fact that "little thought has been given to specific practice to help refugees" (Jacob, 1994). The immigration status of these newcomers continues to influence provision of, access to, and use of services (Drachman, 1995). Although several authors have written about the need for cross-cultural understanding, acceptance, and support among helping professionals who work with clients from different cultures (Augsburger, 1986; McGoldrick, Pearce, & Giordano, 1985; Padilla, Wagatsuma, & Lindholm, 1985; Pedersen, 1985; Sue, 1990), there is no research that examines stress and coping among African immigrants or takes into account the care and well-being of African immigrants.

This chapter describes the results of a study on a sample of African immigrants in the United States. The research had two purposes: (1) to explore African immigrants' integration into the social environment of the host country in light of several interactive processes involving stress, self-esteem, spiritual well-being, and coping resources and (2) to examine the interplay of immigrants' decisions to emigrate; the role of religion in their lives; length of stay in the host country; and experiences of stress, self-esteem, spiritual well-being, and coping resources. The chapter then discusses implications for future research and practice with African immigrants.

This chapter was originally published in the March 1997 issue of *Social Work*, Vol. 42, pp. 154–165.

BACKGROUND

During the past two decades, the United States has experienced an influx of new immigrants. These immigrants have come mainly from Mexico, the Caribbean, South America, Europe, Asia, and Africa. The cited numbers of these immigrants, however, do not take into account undocumented individuals (Bean, Edmonston, & Passel, 1990).

The immigration status of these newcomers varies. Ahearn (1995) made important distinctions among these new arrivals to the United States—refugees, immigrants, migrants, and illegal aliens. *Refugees* are people who cross national boundaries in search of safety because they fear persecution. *Immigrants* are people who have been granted legal permanent residence by their host countries. *Migrants* are individuals who have been granted temporary residence but intend to return to their countries of origin. *Illegal aliens* are people who enter another country illegally. A preferred term for illegal aliens is "undocumented people." The *1992 Statistical Yearbook of the Immigration and Naturalization Service* (U.S. Department of Justice, 1993) reported that there were 19 million migrants to the United States in 1991. That year, more than 1.8 million immigrants were granted permanent residence. Between 1965 and 1992 over 2.25 million people emigrated from Africa to the United States, about 3 percent of the total number of immigrants to the United States. Data from 1983 to 1992 indicate that African immigrants were between 2 percent and 3 percent of the immigrant population (U.S. Department of Justice, 1993).

Although several things account for this wave of migration, two factors deserve mention. The first is kinship, which has played a major role in the history of immigration. In 1965 the Immigration and Nationality Act (P.L. 89-236) made kinship ties the primary rationing device for admitting new immigrants to the United States. The link to kinship resulted in an increased number of women, children, and older people becoming new immigrants.

A second factor responsible for displacement patterns are the changes in the social, economic, and political landscape around the world. These changes have resulted in a mass exodus of affected peoples into new lands.

Issues Confronting Immigrants

Immigration involves a process of acculturation. At a cultural level, acculturation involves adjusting to a new culture and environment. At an interpersonal level, immigrants must reorganize interpersonal relationships. At an intrapsychic level, immigrants must learn to cope cognitively, attitudinally, and behaviorally in a new cultural system (Kim, 1978; Padilla, 1980).

Immigrants experience greater stress than nonimmigrants during the process of relocation (Dyal & Dyal, 1981). In dealing with and resolving their emotional and cultural conflicts in their new, reconfigured society, immigrants undergo acculturative stress (Born, 1970; Dyal & Dyal, 1981). Whether these stress-related problems are interpersonal conflicts (Caudill & DeVos, 1956), role conflicts (Naditch & Morrissey, 1976), intrafamilial role conflicts in self and family role perception (Kurtines & Miranda, 1980), poor self-esteem (Chan, 1977; Padilla et al., 1985), or loss of control (Naditch & Morrissey, 1976), the subsequent changes resulting from relocation have psychological, spiritual, affective, and cognitive consequences.

There are a number of identifiable experiences of immigrant populations. Kuo (1976) outlined social isolation, cultural shock, cultural change, and goal-striving stress as four significant experiences all immigrants experience. Sluzki (1979) and Richardson (1967) pointed out that migration is a developmental process with various tasks and demands.

Past studies of immigration have focused on identifying situation-specific coping mechanisms used by immigrants to confront these problems (Mena, Padilla, & Maldonado, 1987). The migration process, however, is a multivariable interaction among individuals' internal resources, the support available to them, and the types of stressors they experience (Cervantes & Castro, 1985). Although the interactive process of stress, self-esteem, and coping resources has received attention, the role of spiritual well-being has not.

Research has examined the relationship between stress and coping among various immigrant populations (Dyal & Dyal, 1981). One study showed that self-esteem is predictive of stress perceptions among Japanese people and Japanese Americans (Padilla et al., 1985). The authors of these studies have argued that practitioners need to address certain aspects pertaining to the culture-specific situations of these immigrant populations. The question of well-being must address stress, self-esteem, spiritual well-being, and coping.

African Value System

Limited attention has been given to African immigrants, although they are a particularly vulnerable population. A review of the literature on immigration and emigration between 1990 and 1995 reveals that most studies have focused on Hispanic, Asian, Jewish, and Russian immigrants.

The philosophy or value system of Africans provides some background to understanding their immigration experience. Most Africans believe in a Supreme Being who controls the natural order of things. Some Africans also believe in spirits or spiritual beings who work in concert with the Supreme Being. The African's philosophy is life centered and is expressed in prayers, invocations, and praises. The life motif can be seen in prayers for obtaining life, restoring life, and preserving life from impending dangers; in prayers for recovery from illness; and in prayers for making life more abundant. The life motif also is the basis of the African immigrant's well-being. Although many Africans have embraced major Western and Eastern religious traditions, strong African cultural and religious beliefs, rituals, and values permeate their self-understanding and celebration of life.

Stress, which has been defined as a nonspecific response of the body to any demand, can be studied across a range of dimensions from the cellular level to different cultural levels (Selye, 1976). For Africans, the social dimension of stress as observed in attitudinal, familial, and environmental contexts is very important. *Self-esteem* is defined as one's self-perceptions and self-valuations in personal and social contexts. For Africans, these valuations include the community, the spiritual, and nature. *Spiritual well-being* is defined as satisfaction with one's religious well-being reflected in one's relationship with a Supreme Being, one's existential well-being, and one's sense of meaning and purpose in life. For Africans, the spiritual has a personal and a communal aspect. It also implies the community's preparedness and acknowledgment of something outside itself and the community's experience and involvement of this "other-ness."

Self-esteem and spiritual well-being are intimately tied into the individual's *coping resources,* defined as characteristics or ongoing behaviors that enable individuals and communities to handle stressors more effectively, to experience fewer symptoms on exposure to stressors, or to recover faster from exposure (Zeidner & Hammer, 1990). For Africans, therefore, coping, be it cognitive or social, emotional or physical, is derived from the personal and collective understanding of the spiritual in people's lives.

METHODS

Sample and Procedure

The sample was drawn from a pool of 125 African immigrants who were randomly selected from a list of 300 immigrants that the author obtained from membership lists of churches and common-interest organizations in spring 1993. The subjects of this study identified themselves as African immigrants who had been born and lived in Africa for at least 10 years. They had to be at least 18 years old, to have lived in the United States at least three months, and to consider the United States their current domicile. A survey questionnaire that included a set of demographic questions; several measures of coping, self-esteem, hardiness, and spiritual well-being; and an informed consent form that explained the study's intention and participant requirements were mailed to 125 individuals. This mailing yielded 57 responses (46 percent), of which 52 (42 percent) were usable for analysis.

The respondents included more men (58 percent) than women (42 percent) (Table 44-1). The ages ranged from 17 to 50 years. Most of the respondents were 40 years old or younger (85 percent). Nearly two-thirds (60 percent) of the respondents were single, and 33 percent were married.

Respondents were from nine African nations, with the majority coming from the East African countries of Uganda (44 percent) and Kenya (25 percent). Nearly three-quarters (72 percent) of the respondents had

Table 44-1
Demographic Characteristics of African Immigrant Sample (*N* = 52)

Characteristic	*n*	%
Gender		
Male	30	58
Female	22	42
Age (years)		
Under 21	4	8
21–30	13	25
31–40	27	52
41–50	8	15
Marital status		
Single, never married	31	60
Married	17	33
Single, cohabiting	1	2
Separated	1	2
Divorced	1	2
Country of origin		
Uganda	23	44
Kenya	13	25
Zimbabwe	4	8
Liberia	2	4
South Africa	3	6
Nigeria	1	2
Ivory Coast	1	2
Ethiopia	1	2
Ghana	3	6
Years in the United States		
Under 5	19	37
5–10	18	35
11–15	7	13
16–20	8	15
Reason for emigrating		
Family	3	6
Political	4	8
Education	44	85
Other	1	2

been in the United States less than 10 years. The majority of the respondents (85 percent) chose to immigrate for educational reasons. It is hard to say the extent to which this sample is representative. It is possible that there were more respondents from Uganda and Kenya because these respondents identified the author's country of origin (Uganda) from his name and may have felt more comfortable in responding.

Other sample characteristics included religion of upbringing; 48 percent had been raised as Roman Catholics and 46 percent as

Protestants. Most respondents (81 percent) considered religion a major and positive force in their upbringing, whereas only 65 percent considered it a major and positive force in their current life. Nearly two-thirds (60 percent) had no family members living with them.

There are two limitations worth noting here. First, the sample was drawn mostly from religious organizations. The findings of this study might have been different if the respondents had been drawn from nonreligious organizations, where the level of social support might differ greatly from that of religious organizations, especially in members' willingness to report their situations. Such a sample eliminates the equally important experiences of other people. Second, because the majority of the respondents chose to immigrate for educational reasons, the nature of their responses may reflect an educational status unrepresentative of the African immigrant population as a whole. Thus, the participants may have underreported stress and overreported self-esteem, spiritual well-being, and coping resources, which may limit the validity and reliability of the results.

Measures and Variables

The variables measured were stress, hardiness, self-esteem, coping resources, and spiritual well-being. These variables were measured with the following standardized instruments: the SAFE scale (Mena et al., 1987), the Family Hardiness Index (McCubbin & Thompson, 1991), the Spiritual Well-Being Scale (Paloutzian & Ellison, 1982), the Coopersmith Self-Esteem Inventory (Coopersmith, 1967), and the Coping Resources Inventory (Hammer & Marting, 1987).

The SAFE scale assesses stress in the social, attitudinal, familial, and environmental domains and was constructed specifically for immigrant and acculturating populations. This 24-item Likert-type instrument, with response options ranging from 1= not stressful to 5 = extremely stressful, asks subjects to indicate the extent to which various statements apply to them. A high overall score indicates high stress. This scale had a Cronbach's alpha of .89 for the respondents in this study.

The Family Hardiness Index, a 20-item Likert-type scale, measures hardiness, or the ability to resist stress and to adapt to and effectively deal with new situations. The scale has four subscales: co-oriented commitment, confidence, challenge, and control. Higher sum scores indicate greater hardiness. The scale had a Cronbach's alpha of .82 for the respondents.

The Spiritual Well-Being Scale, a 20-item Likert-type scale, measures overall spiritual well-being and religious and existential well-being. The scale calls for the respondents to assess the degree to which they "strongly agree" or "strongly disagree" with a given statement. Higher scores indicate greater spiritual well-being. Cronbach's alpha coefficients for respondents were .59 and .90 for existential well-being and religious well-being, respectively.

The Coping Resources Inventory, a 60-item scale, assesses personal resources for coping with stress in five domains: cognitive, social, emotional, spiritual or philosophical, and physical. Respondents indicated how often they engaged in various behaviors. Higher scores indicated more coping resources. This scale had a Cronbach's alpha of .89 for this group of participants.

The Coopersmith Self-Esteem Inventory, a 25-item scale, assesses self-esteem as indicated by attitudes toward self in social, academic, family, and personal contexts. Higher scores indicate greater self-esteem. For respondents, the scale had a Cronbach's alpha of .87.

The respondents were also asked questions about their decision to emigrate and the role of religion in their lives. A single question asked the respondents to indicate their perceived say in the decision to come to the United States on a four-point scale. Respondents also indicated the perceived role of religion in their current life. Finally, respondents indicated how long they had been in the United States.

RESULTS

Correlations were done to determine whether, and to what extent, relationships exist among spiritual well-being, hardiness, and coping resources. Results indicate that there was a positive correlation between spiritual well-being and hardiness for African immigrants in the United States ($r = .22$, $p < .05$). Spiritual well-being was significantly correlated with overall coping resources ($r = .32$, $p < .01$), with the spiritual coping resources subscale showing the strongest correlation ($r = .48$, $p < .001$). A strong positive relationship between spiritual well-being and self-esteem ($r = .37$, $p < .001$) and between hardiness and coping resources ($r = .46$, $p < .001$) was found.

The relationships among self-esteem, stress, and coping resources also were investigated. Not surprisingly, there was a negative and strong relationship between stress and self-esteem ($r = .43$, $p < .001$). There were strong positive relationships between self-esteem and coping resources ($r = .46$, $p < .001$).

Decision to Emigrate

The extent to which an immigrant perceived a say in the decision to emigrate to the United States appeared to relate to the immigrant's confidence in his or her personal ability to endure stressors. Previously reported conclusions indicated a close association between having a say in the decision to emigrate and the ability to endure stressors (Berry, Uichol, Minde, & Mok, 1987; Tyhurst, 1951). Furthermore, having a say in the decision to emigrate often highlights a person's sense of control. This study confirmed that people who were able to determine when and where they should move tend to feel more confident and show a greater sense of control over their circumstances. They also tend to feel better about themselves.

Role of Religion

The t-test was done to determine if there were any differences between African immigrants who saw religion as a major influence and
those who saw religion as a minor influence. The degree to which religion was seen as an influence in the immigrants' lives appeared to
affect their spiritual well-being and coping resources. Immigrants for
whom religion was a major influence reported higher scores on the
spiritual well-being scale ($t = -3.42$) and the spiritual coping resources scale ($t = -2.76$) (Table 44-2).

This finding supports the literature that suggests that religion is a
major coping resource for immigrants. Any threat, therefore, to a
person's cultural or religious beliefs poses a threat to the person's
ability to cope (Lazarus & Folkman, 1984; Mbiti, 1970; Paloutzian &
Ellison, 1982). Also, Padilla (1980) suggested that ethnic loyalty, individual pride, and affiliation with one's culture of origin were important factors for an immigrant. Spiritual well-being and the role of religion in immigrants' lives may enhance loyalty and attachment to
their culture of origin. This view of religion as a major influence in
the life of African immigrants finds support in the African philosophy of life, where the sacred and the secular are seen as one reality.

Table 44-2

Mean Scores for Influence of Religion in Relation to Hardiness, Stress, Self-Esteem, Spiritual Well-being, and Coping Resources

Scale	Religion Is		
	Minor Influence ($n = 15$)	Major Influence ($n = 37$)	t
Hardiness			
Overall	45.2	45.4	−0.08
Commitment	2.4	2.5	−1.08
Confidence	2.5	2.4	0.87
Challenge	2.3	2.2	0.73
Control	2.0	1.9	0.37
Stress	37.2	41.7	−0.71
Self-esteem	66.8	76.1	−1.61
Spiritual well-being			
Overall	88.8	101.8	−3.42***
Religious well-being	44.5	52.7	−3.55***
Existential well-being	44.3	49.0	−2.17*
Coping resources			
Total	50.8	54.9	−1.42
Cognitive	53.5	55.9	−0.93
Social	48.0	53.3	−1.67*
Emotional	50.2	49.7	0.17
Spiritual	48.5	55.2	−2.76**
Physical	52.3	54.2	−0.78

*$p < .05$. **$p < .01$. ***$p < .001$.

Religion, therefore, may offer grounding and hope in a foreign land and culture.

Length of Stay

An analysis of variance (ANOVA) was conducted to determine the relative significance of length of stay in the United States. Results of this analysis indicate that hardiness, or the ability to endure stressors, was a significant contributor to length of stay (Table 44-3).

For overall hardiness, the means formed a significant upward trend [$F(2, 49) = 6.20, p < .05$]. Immigrants who reported that they had lived in the United States more than 10 years scored the highest on both the overall hardiness scale and the confidence subscale, suggesting that immigrants who have lived longer in the United States tend to have greater internal strengths for enduring stressors. This finding confirms earlier research that suggested that exposing oneself to new situations is related to resilience (Furnhan & Bochner, 1986; Lasry & Signal, 1975; Mena et al., 1987; Oberg, 1960).

Although not statistically significant, a downward trend was observed between length of stay and spiritual well-being. One possibility is that there was a decline in immigrants' spiritual well-being as

Table 44-3

Mean Scores of Hardiness, Stress, Self-Esteem, Spiritual Well-being, and Coping Resources Scales as a Function of Length of Stay

Scale	Years in the United States			
	0–4	5–10	11–20	F^a
Hardiness				
Overall	41.7	47.3	47.5	6.20*
Commitment	2.4	2.6	2.5	1.41
Confidence	2.2	2.6	2.4	0.93
Challenge	2.1	2.3	2.5	5.97*
Control	1.8	1.9	2.1	0.93
Stress	45.5	35.5	41.4	0.32
Self-esteem	71.7	77.3	70.5	0.03
Spiritual well-being				
Overall	99.8	98.0	98.0	0.74
Religious well-being	51.0	50.9	48.9	0.53
Existential well-being	48.8	47.1	46.9	0.58
Coping resources				
Total	52.7	54.4	54.1	0.17
Cognitive	52.6	57.1	56.2	1.48
Social	51.0	51.6	53.1	0.32
Emotional	50.2	49.1	50.3	0.00
Spiritual	53.4	53.6	52.7	0.05
Physical	53.5	54.2	53.3	0.01

[a]$df = 2, 49$.
*$p < .05$.

they continued to live away from their countries of origin. Indeed, the literature suggests that as immigrants learn to integrate both old and new rules, models, and values into their new realities, they let go of some aspects of their past lives (Shuval, 1993; Sluzki, 1979). If there is a decline in an individual's spiritual well-being, it may very well be the by-product of this integration.

DISCUSSION

Overall, on the major variables investigated in this study, higher scores on the self-esteem, hardiness, and coping resources scales were associated with higher scores on the spiritual well-being scale and with lower scores on the stress scale. The present findings are generally consistent with the literature and earlier studies done with different populations (Ellison, 1983). Some of these studies have focused on the relationships between spiritual well-being and physical well-being and between psychological well-being and relational well-being (Fehring, Brennan, & Keller, 1987; Paloutzian & Ellison, 1982). The findings in this study support the argument that both self-esteem and hardiness are related to spiritual well-being among African immigrants.

The significant relationship between spiritual well-being and coping resources is an important finding, because it sheds light on what coping is and suggests the need for immigrants to develop new social ties and form social networks and roles in their new environments (Kuo, 1976; Padilla et al., 1985; Sluzki, 1979). Also, the strong positive correlation between the Spiritual Well-Being Scale and the Spiritual Coping Resources Inventory subscale suggests the evidence of construct validity for the Spiritual Well-Being Scale.

The findings on stress, self-esteem, and coping are consistent with the literature on self-esteem and stress perceptions (Dyal & Dyal, 1981; Padilla et al., 1985). Other authors have repeatedly argued that self-esteem is a personality dimension closely associated with a person's capacity to cope (Chan, 1977; Mena et al., 1987; Padilla, Alvarez, & Lindholm, 1986). Similarly, the positive relationship between hardiness and coping suggests that immigrants who had greater internal strengths to endure stressors also had greater coping resources. This finding concurs with earlier studies on Asian and Hispanic immigrants (Padilla et al., 1985, 1986), on Cuban immigrants (Naditch & Morrissey, 1976), on cancer patients (Bonner, 1988), and on lawyers (Kobasa, 1979).

IMPLICATIONS FOR RESEARCH

This study used instruments that had been previously used with other populations (Ellison, 1983; Padilla et al., 1985, 1986). The results presented in this chapter suggest that this African immigrant population falls within the normal range when compared with other populations.

An important outcome of this study was the information on the cross-cultural validity of the instruments used. Yet the study also challenges researchers to pursue the development of instruments that are more culturally sensitive and culturally competent. Also, that there is very little empirical data on the relationships between spirituality and psychological constructs underscores the need for further research to examine the relationships between spiritual well-being and other aspects of psychological well-being. One such study could investigate the relationship between spiritual well-being and anxiety among immigrants.

Another future challenge for researchers is examination of the level of acculturation and coping in relation to family upbringing and sex-role socialization among African immigrants. Also, a follow-up study would be helpful in identifying any changes in the immigrants' expressed responses during their cross-cultural transitions, and longitudinal research would help to delineate changes in self-esteem across time more adequately.

Future research should investigate how stereotypes about black Americans and racism may affect the experience of African immigrants. Although several authors have identified certain issues related to beliefs affecting certain immigrant groups, no issues have been extensively studied for recent immigrants from Africa. Such issues include the tension between African Americans and recent immigrants from Africa, often exacerbated by myths about immigrants (Muller, 1993). The tension, generated by the masked preferential treatment given to Africans over African Americans, often contributes to the exploitation of both groups as well as mutual suspicion among members of both groups. Bryce-LaPorte (1972) also spoke of the "double invisibility" African immigrants experience because of their race and their origin.

Although African immigrants share a number of similarities with African Americans, the question of ethnic identity formation may vary. African immigrants in the United States may see themselves as black people, immigrants, or distinct ethnic groups. These levels are compounded by African immigrants' own self-perception, the immediate host community's (African Americans') perception, and the general ordering of forces within the larger host community (the United States). The interactive processes of these levels will determine the unfolding of African immigrants' ethnic identity (Mittleberg & Waters, 1992). Ultimately, some attention must be paid to the ambivalence about identity that many African immigrants experience in this country.

IMPLICATIONS FOR PRACTICE

The degree to which the results of this study showed strong relationships between and among the variables suggests that practitioners ought to be cognizant of these interactive processes when working with the African immigrant population. Although none of the participants in this study indicated they were receiving counseling, most of them preferred helping professionals who showed some interest in their spiritual well-being. Practitioners therefore need to be sensitive to those conditions that enhance individual spiritual well-being. Ellison (1983) suggested that within the course of a therapeutic relationship, spiritual well-being is amenable to change. Seaward (1989), on the other hand, asserted that interventions to improve spiritual well-being are as essential as interventions directed to improving physical and emotional health.

The findings of this study suggest that it is clinically compelling to attend to spiritual concerns. Practitioners ought to be curious, respectful, and open to those instances when immigrants present issues involving their spiritual well-being. Creating space that allows possible exploration of such issues is an important task for practitioners.

Attending to the concerns of people is an interactive process in which both practitioner and individual cocreate meaning systems. Both explore how various factors help to give meaning and organization to one's life. These concerns also become systems or lenses that inform practice. A better understanding of the effect of these factors on the population studied and their interrelationship becomes part of a shared worldview between the practitioner and the client. A practitioner can also explore the feelings aroused by the presence or absence of stress, self-esteem, spiritual well-being, or coping resources.

This study identified social and spiritual coping resources as central to the life of immigrants, underscoring the need for the development of a strong social network for immigrants. Padilla et al. (1985) demonstrated that the most stressful phase of acculturation for immigrants is the re-evaluation of their proper role within the host society and their feelings of not belonging. A lack of awareness of the stressful aspects of a client's social environment may lead to errors in therapeutic interventions, especially for immigrants who seek mental health services. Practitioners may need to pay greater attention to the selection of practice approaches as they work with immigrants. A systems perspective may better address the issues of hardiness, stress, self-esteem, spiritual well-being, and coping.

Obviously, there is a need to respect the worldview of African immigrants as it evolves in a new host culture. Mbiti (1970) noted that an African's identity is found in the community's identity. Individuals are viewed as a part of or extension of the environment because of the belief that everything is functionally connected. Self is viewed as interdependence and relationship (Gergen, 1991). There is an integrated sacred and secular reality that is fused into a harmonious, cooperative, and communal orientation. This Africentric worldview can be understood as a mediator of stress for African immigrants. Differentiation, for example, may be a less important issue from an African point of view than it is for a North American practitioner, for whom individuation may be an important clinical or practice goal. In this context, practitioners need to become sensitive to and listen to the multiple voices that characterize the lives of African immigrants.

Africans bring with them a unique cultural perspective. In addition, they have the same heritage that many African Americans do, and many of those have sought to rediscover this ancestry. Practitioners therefore need to learn more about the culture, philosophy, and religion of Africans so they can provide more culturally competent services. Cultural competence compels providers to encourage help seekers to learn to function in a larger culture and, at the same time, to appreciate their own sociocultural context. Service providers need to ask what constitutes the spiritual for Africans, why certain beliefs carry important meanings for some people, and what variations exist across cultures between and among Africans. How does the experience of the "holy" or "spiritual" relate to the doing or praxis in an African's life? Clinicians ought to explore with Africans the "holy" and the "sacred" in their lives and to examine the language they use to capture these moments. In some cultural groups, silence is described as a "spiritual touch" (Mbiti, 1970).

Practitioners also need to be creative in empowering clients to enhance their worldview. Entering a new culture always threatens one's worldview. This worldview is a valuable resource by which a person evaluates himself or herself and his or her experiences and relationship to the world (Akbar, 1984). By enhancing African immigrants' worldviews, practitioners participate in enhancing the African immigrants' self-esteem, hardiness, and spiritual well-being. Practitioners must explore with immigrants the changing and evolving aspects of their spiritual well-being. Supporting the integration of creative spirituality involves not only holding and nurturing, but also challenging and understanding these perspectives. Such efforts may contribute to a better understanding of immigrants and, ultimately, toward the enactment and implementation of appropriate programs and policies for these populations.

Any attention to issues affecting African immigrants should be placed in context. Hopps and Collins (1995) have documented social work's response to the ever-shifting context of the field. The changes include government and social welfare, structural issues in the economy contributing to poverty and social ills, demographic changes as a result of the settlement of displaced peoples, violence, and changes in the family. Isaacs and Benjamin (1991) suggested that the 1990s are the years of the cultural imperative in the United States. This cultural imperative invites social workers to attend to the social ills of U.S. society, many of which disproportionately affect immigrants.

The ambivalence of U.S. society toward social work (Hopps & Collins, 1995) extends to the ambivalence society has toward immigration. Although immigrant energy and labor fuel the economy, each wave of arrivals is greeted with skepticism. The benefits of immigration are recognized only in retrospect. For African immigrants, this ambivalence has been compounded by the legacy of racism and oppression. Providers need not only to dispel the myths but also to state the facts about immigrants.

The role of social work in empowering clients has been underscored (Allen, Barr, Cochran, Greene, & Dean, 1989; Pinderhughes, 1989; Ross-Sheriff, 1995). The increasing number of immigrants in the United States is a "crisis" that offers this country yet another opportunity to address the potential danger inherent in ignoring its political, economic, and cultural ramifications. Service providers need to support the contributions of African immigrants and explore with them those aspects of their lives that enhance their well-being in all its complexity. Social workers may have to explore well-being as it applies to kin or extended family, spirituality or religion, and the ability to obtain information or needed services (Allen, 1995).

Attending to these concerns demands that social workers be self-aware, appreciate skills as time bound and culture bound, and receive supervision and training when working with African immigrants. Finally, as new issues emerge, there is an urgent need for social workers to develop interest in empirically based practice with this population. Such a commitment holds service providers, theories, and interventions accountable (Bloom & Fischer, 1982; Blythe, Tripodi, & Briar, 1994; Collins, Kayser, & Platt, 1994; Collins, Kayser, & Tourse, 1994; Hopps & Collins, 1995; Sze & Hopps, 1978). Ultimately, service delivery will map its influence on policies that affect African immigrants (Ross-Sheriff, 1995) as African immigrants themselves map their own influence on those policies. As the nature and needs of the populations that are social work's clientele change, so must the focus of the profession's efforts to deliver services. The delivery of services is intricately intertwined with policy and practice implications. Future research must continually examine this relationship.

CONCLUSION

This study found spiritual well-being to be an important variable that interacts with other variables to enhance the well-being of African immigrants. The results of the study underscore the need for increased understanding of the complexity of the cross-cultural transition and acculturation for African immigrants in the provision of social support services.

Because this study did not include respondents from all African countries, future research should include respondents from other African countries. Such direction could further the findings of this study by exploring the cultural diversity among African immigrants as well as the relationships between and among various groups. Follow-up studies that examine these variables qualitatively are needed to provide further depth, richness, and complexity to these findings. One approach may be to conduct individual interviews or use focus groups with a subsample of participants.

Further exploration of the relationships between race and racism and these variables also would be appropriate. Another area of investigation would be to further explore the aspects of racism that keep many immigrants invisible, such as the stereotypes about black people or immigrants, escapees, refugees, or socially marginalized people. These approaches can increase the practitioner's understanding of and ability to advocate for the African immigrant population.

REFERENCES

Ahearn, F. L. (1995). Displaced people. In R. L. Edwards (Ed.-in-Chief), *Encyclopedia of social work* (19th ed., Vol. 1, pp. 771–780). Washington, DC: NASW Press.

Akbar, N. (1984). Africentric social sciences for human liberation. *Journal of Black Studies, 14,* 395–414.

Allen, J. (1995). African Americans: Caribbean. In R. L. Edwards (Ed.-in-Chief), *Encyclopedia of social work* (19th ed., Vol. 1, pp. 121–129). Washington, DC: NASW Press.

Allen, J., Barr, D., Cochran, M., Greene, J., & Dean, C. (1989, October). *Networking bulletin: Empowerment and family support* (Vol. 1, Issue 1). Ithaca, NY: Cornell Empowerment Group.

Augsburger, D. W. (1986). *Pastoral counseling across cultures.* Philadelphia: Westminster.

Bean, F. D., Edmonston, B., & Passel, J. (Eds.). (1990). *Undocumented migrants in the United States.* Santa Monica, CA: Rand Corporation.

Berry, J. W., Uichol, K., Minde, T., & Mok, D. (1987). Comparative studies of acculturative stress. *International Migration Review, 21,* 491–511.

Bloom, M., & Fischer, J. (1982). *Evaluating practice: Guidelines for the accountable professional.* Englewood Cliffs, NJ: Prentice Hall.

Blythe, B., Tripodi, T., & Briar, S. (1994). *Direct practice research in human service agencies.* New York: Columbia University Press.

Bonner, C. M. (1988). *Utilization of spiritual resources by patients experiencing a recent cancer diagnosis.* Unpublished master's thesis, University of Pittsburgh.

Born, D. (1970). Psychological adaptation and development under acculturative stress: Toward a general model. *Social Science and Medicine, 3,* 529–547.

Bryce-LaPorte, R. S. (1972). Black immigrants: The experience of invisibility and inequality. *Journal of Black Studies, 3*(1), 29–56.

Caudill, W., & DeVos, G. (1956). Achievement, culture, and personality: The case of the Japanese. *American Anthropology, 58,* 1102–1126.

Cervantes, R. C., & Castro, F. G. (1985). Stress, coping, and Mexican American mental health: A systemic review. *Hispanic Journal of Behavioral Science, 7,* 1–73.

Chan, K. B. (1977). Individual differences in reactions to stress and their personality and situational determinants: Some implications for community mental health. *Social Science and Medicine, 11,* 89–103.

Collins, P. M., Kayser, K., & Platt, S. (1994). Conjoint marital therapy: A practitioner's approach to single-system evaluation. *Families in Society, 75,* 131–141.

Collins, P. M., Kayser, K., & Tourse, R. (1994). Bridging the gaps: An interdependent model for educating accountable practitioners. *Journal of Social Work Education, 30,* 241–251.

Coopersmith, S. (1967). *The antecedents of self-esteem.* Palo Alto, CA: Consulting Psychologist Press.

Drachman, D. (1995). Immigration statuses and their influence on service provision, access, and use. *Social Work, 40,* 188–197.

Dyal, J. A., & Dyal, R. Y. (1981). Acculturation, stress and coping. *International Journal of Intercultural Relations, 5,* 301–328.

Ellison, C. W. (1983). Spiritual well-being: Conceptualization and measurement. *Journal of Psychology and Theology, 11,* 330–340.

Fehring, R. J., Brennan, P. F., & Keller, M. L. (1987). Psychological and spiritual well-being in college students. *Research in Nursing and Health, 10,* 391–398.

Furnhan, A., & Bochner, S. (1986). *Cultural shock: Psychological reactions to unfamiliar environments.* New York: Methuen.

Gergen, K. (1991). *The saturated self.* New York: Basic Books.

Haines, D. W. (1989). Introduction. In D. W. Haines (Ed.), *Refugees as immigrants* (pp. 1–23). Totowa, NJ: Rowman & Littlefield.

Hammer, A. L., & Marting, S. (1987). *Coping Resources Inventory.* Palo Alto, CA: Consulting Psychologist Press.

Hopps, J., & Collins, P. (1995). Social work profession overview. In R. L. Edwards (Ed.-in-Chief), *Encyclopedia of social work* (19th ed., Vol. 2, pp. 2266–2282). Washington, DC: NASW Press.

Immigration and Nationality Act, P.L. 89-236, 79 Stat. 911–920 (1965).

Isaacs, M., & Benjamin, M. (1991). *Towards a culturally competent system of care: Volume II. Programs which utilize culturally competent principles.* Washington, DC: Georgetown University, Child Development Center, CASSP Technical Assistance Center.

Jacob, A. G. (1994). Social integration of Salvadoran refugees. *Social Work, 39,* 307–312.

Kim, Y. Y. (1978). A communication approach to the acculturation process: A study of Korean immigrants in Chicago. *International Journal of Intercultural Relations, 2,* 197–223.

Kobasa, S. (1979). Stressful life events, personality, and health: An inquiry into hardiness. *Journal of Personality and Social Psychology, 37*(1), 1–11.

Kuo, W. (1976). Theories of migration and mental health: An empirical testing on Chinese-Americans. *Social Science and Medicine, 10,* 297–306.

Kurtines, W. M., & Miranda, L. (1980). Differences in self and family role perception among acculturating Cuban American college students. *Intercultural Relations, 4,* 167–184.

Lasry, J. M., & Signal, J. (1975). Length of time in new country and mental health of immigrants. *Canadian Journal of Behavioral Science, 41,* 244–268.

Lazarus, R. S., & Folkman, S. (1984). *Stress, appraisal, and coping.* New York: Springer.

Mbiti, J. S. (1970). *African religions and philosophy.* New York: Doubleday.

McCubbin, H. I., & Thompson, A. I. (1991). *Family assessment inventories for research and practice.* Madison, WI: Family Stress Coping and Health Project.

McGoldrick, M., Pearce, J., & Giordano, J. (Eds.). (1985). *Ethnicity and family therapy.* New York: Guilford Press.

Mena, F. J., Padilla, A. M., & Maldonado, M. (1987). Acculturative stress and specific coping strategies among immigrant and later generation college students. *Hispanic Journal of Behavioral Sciences, 9,* 207–225.

Mittleberg, D., & Waters, M. (1992). The process of ethnogenesis among Haitian and Israeli immigrants in the United States. *Ethnic and Racial Studies, 15,* 413–435.

Muller, T. (1993). *Immigrants and the American city.* New York: New York University Press.

Naditch, M. P., & Morrissey, R. F. (1976). Role stress, personality, and psychopathology in a group of immigrant adolescents. *Journal of American Psychology, 85,* 113–118.

Oberg, K. (1960). Cultural shock: Adjustment to new cultural environments. *Practical Anthropology, 7,* 177–182.

Padilla, A. M. (Ed.). (1980). *Acculturation: Theory, models, and some new findings.* Boulder, CO: Westview Press.

Padilla, A. M., Alvarez, M., & Lindholm, K. (1986). Generational status and personality factors as predictors of stress in students. *Hispanic Journal of Behavioral Sciences, 8,* 275–288.

Padilla, A. M., Wagatsuma, Y., & Lindholm, K. (1985). Acculturation and personality as predictors of stress in Japanese and Japanese-Americans. *Journal of Social Psychology, 125,* 295–305.

Paloutzian, R. F., & Ellison, C. W. (1982). Loneliness, spiritual well-being and the quality of life. In L. A. Peplau & D. Perlman (Eds.), *Loneliness: A sourcebook of current theory, research and therapy* (pp. 224–237). New York: John Wiley & Sons.

Pedersen, P. (1985). *Handbook of cross-cultural counseling and therapy.* Westport, CT: Greenwood Press.

Pinderhughes, E. (1989). *Understanding race, ethnicity and power: The key to efficacy in clinical practice.* New York: Free Press.

Richardson, A. A. (1967). Theory and method for the psychological study of assimilation. *International Migration Review, 2,* 3–30.

Ross-Sheriff, F. (1995). African Americans: Immigrants. In R. L. Edwards (Ed.-in-Chief), *Encyclopedia of social work* (19th ed., Vol. 1, pp. 130–136). Washington, DC: NASW Press.

Seaward, B. L. (1989). Giving wellness a spiritual workout. *Health Progress, 70*(4), 50–52.

Selye, H. (1976). *The stress of life.* New York: McGraw-Hill.

Shuval, J. T. (1993). Migration and stress. In L. Goldberger & S. Breznitz (Eds.), *Handbook of stress: Theoretical and clinical aspects* (pp. 641–657). New York: Free Press.

Sluzki, C. E. (1979). Migration and family conflict. *Family Process, 18,* 379–390.

Sue, D. W. (1990). *Counseling the culturally different: Theory and practice.* New York: John Wiley & Sons.

Sze, W., & Hopps, J. (1978). *Evaluation and accountability in human services programs* (2nd ed.). Cambridge, MA: Schenkman.

Tyhurst, L. (1951). Displacement and migration. *American Journal of Psychiatry, 107,* 561–568.

U.S. Department of Justice. (1993). *1992 statistical yearbook of the Immigration and Naturalization Service.* Washington, DC: Author.

Zeidner, M., & Hammer, L. (1990). Life events and coping resources as predictors of stress symptoms in adolescents. *Personal Individual Differences, 11,* 693–703.

45 Refugee Children: How Are They Faring Economically as Adults?

Miriam Potocky-Tripodi

Within the field of child welfare, one special group of children has received relatively little scholarly attention: refugee children. These are children who have made international migrations because of political oppression in their home countries. Approximately 100,000 refugees are admitted into the United States each year, and almost 1.3 million have been admitted since 1982 (U.S. Committee for Refugees, 1995c). The primary countries of origin of these refugees have been Southeast Asia (Vietnam, Laos, and Cambodia), the former Soviet Union, Eastern Europe (Hungary, Poland, Romania, and the former Czechoslovakia), Cuba, and Haiti (U.S. Committee for Refugees, 1995c). Each of these groups began arriving in the United States following political upheavals in their respective countries: Southeast Asians in 1975, following the end of the Vietnam War and the consequent Communist domination of the area; Soviets and East Europeans in the late 1940s following Communist coups; Cubans in the early 1960s following the Castro coup; and Haitians in the late 1960s and the 1970s during the oppressive Duvalier regimes.

A substantial proportion of these arriving refugees (26 percent in 1992) are children (Office of Refugee Resettlement, 1993). Refugee children arrive with immediate or extended family members or as unaccompanied minors who are placed with relatives who arrived earlier or, in the absence of relatives, are placed in foster care (Office of Refugee Resettlement, 1993).

On resettlement, refugee children face numerous challenges. In addition to language barriers, a variety of unique stressors are experienced. First, for children who are with their families, there are often intergenerational problems. Frequently, children adopt the customs of the new country much more quickly than their parents, resulting in a role reversal whereby the children become translators of language and cultural norms for their parents (Carlin, 1990; Drachman, 1992; Stepick & Dutton Stepick, 1994). This frequently leads to a lack of respect for elders, which is an extremely important value in many of the original cultures (Carlin, 1990; Drachman, 1992; Matsuoka, 1990; Stepick & Dutton Stepick, 1994). Problems also develop with

This chapter was originally published in the July 1996 issue of *Social Work*, Vol. 41, pp. 364–373.

child discipline; some types of discipline used in the original culture may be considered child abuse in the United States, a fact that the children may use to their advantage by threatening to report their parents to child welfare authorities (Stepick & Dutton Stepick, 1994).

A further source of intergenerational stress is strong expectations for achievement that are often placed on refugee children by their parents. Many older refugees arrive in this country having given up hope on their own advancement; however, they view their children's opportunity to live a better life as giving meaning to or redeeming their own suffering (Carlin, 1990).

Another common problem is posttraumatic stress disorder. A significant number of refugee children have witnessed death, torture, rape, or imprisonment of family members. Disease and starvation are also common. Many refugees leave on boats and may be at sea for lengthy periods without adequate food, shelter, or sanitation. Frequently, refugees undergo a long stay in refugee camps that have poor housing and shortages of clothing and water. All of these factors contribute to posttraumatic stress (Drachman, 1992; Uba & Chung, 1991).

In addition to intergenerational conflicts and posttraumatic stress, refugee children experience difficulties with acculturation and cultural identity. In their homes they are expected to behave in accordance with the native culture, whereas at school they are expected to be Americanized. Thus, they must live a dual life for which they have no role models (Carlin, 1990). A final issue of concern regarding these children is their increasing involvement in criminal activities. Numerous violent crimes have been reported, and the formation of refugee youth gangs is particularly troublesome (Carlin, 1990; Stepick & Dutton Stepick, 1994).

In recognition of some of the unique difficulties faced by refugee children, legislative policies have been developed and implemented to provide services to this population. From the post–World War II period to 1980, refugee assistance was provided on an ad hoc basis in response to crises in different parts of the world (Gallagher, Forbes, & Fagen, 1985). In the late 1970s policymakers recognized that refugee issues were recurrent and persistent over time, necessitating a better-planned response (Gallagher et al., 1985). Therefore, Congress passed the Refugee Act of 1980 (P.L. 96-212) and the Refugee Education Assistance Act of 1980 (P.L. 96-422), which established for the first time a set of comprehensive, permanent, and systematic policies for refugee assistance. These policies guide the provision of cash assistance, medical assistance, and social services to refugees. Services specifically for refugee children include special education, English language training, child welfare (including foster care for unaccompanied minors), and health care.

Although the services provided by this legislation address some of the previously identified problems experienced by refugee children, the overarching goals of these policies for all refugees are to increase economic self-sufficiency and decrease welfare dependence. Because of this fundamental policy focus on economic integration, a number of studies have been undertaken to examine the economic status of refugees (Gozdziak, 1989; Portes & Stepick, 1985; Tran, 1991; Westermeyer, Callies, & Neider, 1990). However, all of these studies have focused on refugees who arrived as adults; no studies have been conducted specifically to examine the long-term economic adjustment of refugees who arrived in the United States as children. Such an examination is important because "the adaptation of [refugee children] will be decisive in establishing the long-term outlook for contemporary immigration" (Portes, 1994, p. 632). Therefore, the present study was conducted to address this gap in knowledge. Specifically, this study examined the economic status of adults who arrived in the United States as refugee children as compared with two reference groups—refugees who arrived as adults and U.S.-born citizens of the same age range as the childhood refugee arrivals.

METHOD

Research Design and Target Populations

This study used the statistical indicators method of community assessment, in which sociodemographic characteristics of individuals in a geographic area are examined to estimate the social well-being of the members of that community (Chambers, Wedel, & Rodwell, 1992). The data for this study were obtained from the 1990 Census of Population and Housing, Public Use Microdata Sample (U.S. Bureau of the Census, 1992), a cross-sectional survey of a 1 percent stratified random sample of the nation's residents. (Full details of the survey and sampling procedure are described in U.S. Bureau of the Census, 1992.)

For this study, two geographic areas were examined—California and Florida, which are among the top four refugee resettlement states in the country (the others are New York and Texas) (Office of Refugee Resettlement, 1993). The study consisted of two phases. Phase 1 focused on California. The largest proportion of refugees in this state are Southeast Asians. They are concentrated in the Los Angeles County, Orange County, and San Francisco Bay areas, although they are also dispersed throughout the rest of the state (Office of Refugee Resettlement, 1993). Therefore, phase 1 examined data for the entire state of California.

Phase 2 focused on Florida and was a replication study conducted to determine whether the economic status patterns observed in California were similar in another state with different refugee populations. The primary refugee groups in Florida are Cubans, Haitians, Soviets/East Europeans, and Nicaraguans. (Although Nicaraguans are not legally considered refugees by the U.S. government, they were included in this study because they meet the United Nations [1951, 1967] definition of refugees as people fleeing political oppression; they began arriving in the United States in the late 1970s and early 1980s during the Somoza and Sandinista regimes.) Unlike California, refugees in Florida are geographically clustered in one part of the state, Dade County (the Miami metropolitan area), with relatively few refugees residing in other parts of the state (Office of Refugee Resettlement, 1993). Therefore, phase 2 of the study focused on Dade County only. The methods and procedures for both phases were identical.

Sample Selection

Respondents were selected for inclusion in the study if they resided in one of the target communities (California and Dade County, Florida), were born in one of the target refugee countries, had arrived in the United States before age 18, and were at least 18 at the time of the census survey in 1990. For each phase of the study, two comparison samples were also selected. The first comparison sample consisted of all adult residents of the target communities who were born in the target countries. This sample allowed for a comparison between the childhood refugee arrivals and the overall adult population of refugees from those same countries (consisting primarily of those who arrived in the United States when they were already adults). The second comparison sample consisted of all U.S.-born residents of the target communities who were in the same age range as the childhood refugee arrivals. This sample allowed for a comparison between the childhood refugee arrivals and their native-born peers of the same age range. Table 45-1 shows the weighted sample sizes (total population estimates), maximum lengths of U.S. residence, and maximum ages for each of the groups. (It should be noted that because of the different periods of initial arrival, the maximum ages of the childhood refugee arrivals differ.)

Data Collection and Variable Selection

All respondents to the census survey completed a questionnaire about items such as income and occupation in addition to basic demographic information. Instruction guides for completing the questionnaire were available in 33 languages (U.S. Bureau of the Census, 1992). The data consisted of over 125 variables. For the present study, seven key economic status indicators (employment status, earnings, public assistance use, employment history [proportion of people who have never worked], poverty, education, and school enrollment) were selected for analysis based on prior empirical literature (Gozdziak, 1989; Portes & Stepick, 1985; Tran, 1991; Westermeyer et al., 1990).

Data Analysis

For purposes of analysis, the Vietnamese, Laotians, and Cambodians were combined into one group (Southeast Asians). Similarly, the Soviets and East Europeans were combined into one group. These combinations were based on the geographic proximity of these countries to each other and their common historical backgrounds in respect to the political oppression that generated the refugee exodus.

Table 45-1

Characteristics of the Populations (1990)

Area, Population, and Characteristic	Weighted Sample Size	Maximum Length of U.S. Residence (years)	Maximum Age of Childhood Arrivals and Peers (years)
California			
Southeast Asians		15	28
Childhood refugee arrivals	87,321		
Total adult refugees	388,310		
U.S.-born age-matched peers	3,534,206		
Dade County, Florida			
Cubans		30	43
Childhood refugee arrivals	89,410		
Total adult refugees	390,440		
U.S.-born age-matched peers	333,180		
Soviets/East Europeans		40	48
Childhood refugee arrivals	940		
Total adult refugees	6,545		
U.S.-born age-matched peers	301,240		
Nicaraguans		15	28
Childhood refugee arrivals	6,835		
Total adult refugees	68,600		
U.S.-born age-matched peers	143,780		
Haitians		20	33
Childhood refugee arrivals	3,215		
Total adult refugees	45,660		
U.S.-born age-matched peers	214,425		

The data were extracted from magnetic tape and CD-ROM and analyzed by computing means or frequency distributions of each economic indicator for each refugee group and its two comparison groups. The analyses were based on total population estimates.

RESULTS

Phase 1

The results for California are summarized in Table 45-2. For most of the indicators, the economic status of the Southeast Asian childhood refugee arrivals was higher than that of the total adult population of Southeast Asian refugees. For example, a higher percentage were employed and a much lower percentage were receiving public assistance. However, the childhood refugee arrivals' status on most of the indicators was lower than that of their U.S.-born age-matched peers. For example, the percentage of childhood refugee arrivals living in poverty was higher than that of their native-born peers. Thus, childhood refugee arrivals had higher economic status than refugees who arrived in the United States as adults but lower economic status than their U.S.-born peers.

Table 45-2

Economic Characteristics of Selected California Southeast Asian Refugees and U.S.-Born Residents (1990)

Characteristic	Childhood Refugee Arrivals	Total Adult Refugees	U.S.-Born Peers
Percentage employed	55.1	44.5	72.7
Yearly earnings ($)	12,109	16,632	14,752
Percentage receiving public assistance	8.2	24.3	4.4
Percentage who have never worked	23.1	31.9	5.7
Percentage living in poverty	28.6	34.1	12.9
Years of education	11.8	11.4	12.8
Percentage enrolled in school	52.3	26.4	32.9

Phase 2

The results for Florida are shown in Tables 45-3 through 45-6. The economic patterns for these refugee groups differ from those observed for Southeast Asian refugees in California. In general, Cuban, Soviet/ East European, and Nicaraguan childhood refugee arrivals had higher economic status than both of their respective comparison samples. Specifically, Cuban childhood refugee arrivals (Table 45-3) had equal or higher economic status than both of their comparison samples on all the indicators. For example, their yearly earnings were greater than those of the total adult Cuban refugee population and the native-born peers. Similarly, Soviet/East European childhood arrivals (Table 45-4) had higher economic status than both of their comparison groups on all but two of the indicators (percentage employed and yearly earnings). Again, Nicaraguan childhood arrivals (Table 45-5) had higher economic status than both of their comparison groups on all but two of the indicators (yearly earnings and years of education). In contrast, the Haitian childhood arrivals (Table 45-6) had a mixed pattern. On four indicators (percentage

Table 45-3

Economic Characteristics of Selected Dade County, Florida, Cuban Refugees and U.S.-Born Residents (1990)

Characteristic	Childhood Refugee Arrivals	Total Adult Refugees	U.S.-Born Peers
Percentage employed	80.3	72.9	76.0
Yearly earnings ($)	23,884	19,674	20,539
Percentage receiving public assistance	2.2	9.6	2.8
Percentage who have never worked	4.4	12.6	5.3
Percentage living in poverty	8.5	16.6	12.9
Years of education	12.9	11.6	13.0
Percentage enrolled in school	20.7	7.2	20.1

employed, yearly earnings, percentage who have never worked, and percentage living in poverty) their economic status was lower than that of both of their comparison groups. However, on two indicators

Table 45-4

Economic Characteristics of Selected Dade County, Florida, Soviet/East European Refugees and U.S.-Born Residents (1990)

Characteristic	Childhood Refugee Arrivals	Total Adult Refugees	U.S.-Born Peers
Percentage employed	55.9	66.4	79.1
Yearly earnings ($)	22,266	33,410	22,388
Percentage receiving public assistance	0	0	3.1
Percentage who have never worked	0	5.1	3.2
Percentage living in poverty	0	7.0	12.0
Years of education	15.4	13.1	13.2
Percentage enrolled in school	27.1	3.9	14.4

Table 45-5

Economic Characteristics of Selected Dade County, Florida, Nicaraguan Refugees and U.S.-Born Residents (1990)

Characteristic	Childhood Refugee Arrivals	Total Adult Refugees	U.S.-Born Peers
Percentage employed	70.8	68.8	67.2
Yearly earnings ($)	10,656	11,409	11,753
Percentage receiving public assistance	0	0.9	2.4
Percentage who have never worked	6.1	17.1	9.9
Percentage living in poverty	14.3	36.0	16.5
Years of education	11.2	11.3	12.5
Percentage enrolled in school	54.1	19.9	33.2

Table 45-6

Economic Characteristics of Selected Dade County, Florida, Haitian Refugees and U.S.-Born Residents (1990)

Characteristic	Childhood Refugee Arrivals	Total Adult Refugees	U.S.-Born Peers
Percentage employed	62.5	70.3	72.1
Yearly earnings ($)	10,091	11,296	15,605
Percentage receiving public assistance	0	4.3	2.9
Percentage who have never worked	21.8	9.1	7.2
Percentage living in poverty	31.4	29.6	14.5
Years of education	12.1	10.7	12.6
Percentage enrolled in school	67.3	23.6	26.0

(public assistance and school enrollment), their status was higher than that of both of their comparison groups. On the remaining indicator (years of education), their status was higher than that of the total adult Haitian refugees but lower than that of the native-born peers. Thus, none of the Florida childhood refugee arrival groups showed the pattern that was observed for the Southeast Asians in California (higher status than the adult refugees but lower status than the native-born peers).

Finally, in terms of comparisons across the Florida childhood refugee arrivals from the different countries, the Cubans and Soviets/ East Europeans were similar to each other, and both had higher economic status than either the Haitians or the Nicaraguans. In turn, the Haitians and Nicaraguans were similar to each other, although Haitians had a much higher poverty rate than the Nicaraguans.

DISCUSSION

The results of this study indicate that the economic status of childhood refugee arrivals differs by refugee group. Cuban and Soviet/East European childhood refugee arrivals in Dade County, Florida, were faring very well economically, having surpassed both refugees who arrived as adults and their U.S.-born peers on most indicators. Southeast Asian childhood refugee arrivals in California were in a transitional stage, having surpassed the adult arrivals but not yet faring as well as their U.S.-born peers. In contrast, Nicaraguan and Haitian childhood refugee arrivals in Dade County, Florida, were not faring well economically. Although the Nicaraguan childhood refugee arrivals had higher economic status than both of their comparison groups on most indicators, they had lower earnings and lower educational attainment, and a higher percentage of them lived in poverty than either the Cuban or Soviet/East European childhood refugee arrivals. Finally, the Haitian childhood refugee arrivals had lower economic status than both of their comparison groups on most indicators and also had lower status than either the Cuban or Soviet/ East European childhood refugee arrivals.

Contributing Factors

There are several likely explanations for these observed differences in economic status across the different childhood refugee groups. First, length of residence in the United States appears to be an underlying factor, with increased length of residence being associated with increased economic status (Soviets/East Europeans have been in the United States the longest, followed by Cubans, Southeast Asians, Haitians, and Nicaraguans). This finding is consistent with prior research and theory (Kuhlman, 1991; Poston, 1994); however, these data illustrate that improvement in economic status is a very lengthy process, extending over decades.

A second factor likely to contribute to the observed economic status patterns are cultural and racial differences across the various refugee groups. The Soviets/East Europeans and Cubans came from relatively more westernized, developed countries and are predominantly white; in contrast, the Southeast Asians and Haitians came from developing countries and are predominantly people of color. Nicaraguans are also from a developing country, and a substantial proportion are also people of color. Therefore, Soviets/East Europeans and Cubans were somewhat better prepared to adjust to U.S. culture and did not face the extent of racism and discrimination experienced by the other groups. These factors are likely to have hindered the economic adjustment of the Southeast Asian, Haitian, and Nicaraguan children.

Third, the differential economic status of the various refugee groups may be related to differential policy implementation. Although all of these groups qualify as refugees under the United Nations Convention and Protocol Relating to the Status of Refugees (United Nations, 1951, 1967), to which the United States is a signatory, in practice the United States gives preferential treatment in asylum applications to certain refugee groups, specifically those from Communist countries (Gallagher et al., 1985). Thus, Soviets, East Europeans, Cubans, and Southeast Asians have generally been given blanket asylum, whereas Haitians and Nicaraguans have been required to prove on a case-by-case basis that they have experienced persecution or have a well-founded fear of persecution in their home countries (Portes & Stepick, 1993; Yarnold, 1990). This has been true even though a portion of the Refugee Education Assistance Act of 1980 (Title 5) was enacted specifically to provide for equitable treatment of Cuban and Haitian entrants. The case of the Nicaraguans represents another policy departure because even though Nicaraguans fled a communist regime during the 1980s, the United States did not issue blanket asylum in an effort to avoid a massive influx of refugees such as occurred in the 1980 Mariel boatlift of Cubans (Portes & Stepick, 1993).

The vast majority of the asylum cases of Haitians and Nicaraguans are denied (U.S. Committee for Refugees, 1995a), and therefore many of these people residing in the United States are considered illegal aliens. As such, they are not entitled to the benefits provided by the Refugee Act of 1980 and the Refugee Education Assistance Act of 1980 (Portes & Stepick, 1993). It is likely that this disentitlement plays a role in these groups' low economic status compared with those of the entitled groups. This conclusion is supported by other researchers, who have noted that "a welcoming reception in areas of destination—including government initiatives to facilitate immigrant adaptation—can have long-term benefits. The opposite is also true" (Fernandez-Kelly & Schauffler, 1994, p. 686).

In addition, two findings emerged in this study that were deviations from the general observed trends and therefore warrant additional attention. First, the yearly earnings of the Southeast Asian childhood arrivals were lower than those of both the adult arrivals and the peer group; this is in contrast to the general trend for this group, wherein the childhood arrivals had surpassed the adult arrivals but were not faring as well as their peers on the other indicators. The likely explanation for this finding is the adult arrivals' longer tenure in the workforce; earnings increase with length of work experience, and over time these young adults' earnings can also be expected to increase and eventually surpass those of the older workers and thus conform to the observed pattern.

Second, it was found that the Cuban and Soviet/East European childhood arrivals economically surpassed even their U.S.-born peers, which is in contrast to the other three groups of refugee childhood arrivals, who were not faring as well as their peer groups. A potential explanation for this finding lies in a possible interaction between parental expectations for achievement and parental resources to foster such achievement. As noted earlier, refugee parents of all groups tend to place high expectations on their children, probably to a greater extent than do U.S.-born parents (Gibson & Ogbu, 1991). Given this, all refugee children might be expected to surpass their U.S.-born peers. However, not all of the refugee groups have equal resources to help their children attain the desired success. Educational research indicates that parents' "cultural capital" (their knowledge, skills, provision of a home environment conducive to learning, and engagement with their child's educational process) plays a significant role in the child's educational achievement (Bordieu, 1983; Vacha & McLaughlin, 1992). Because of Soviet/East Europeans' and Cubans' advantageous backgrounds relative to the other groups, these parents possessed greater cultural capital that combined with their high expectations to propel their children to surpass their U.S.-born peers.

Policy and Program Implications

The findings of this study have clear implications for policy and program development. First, asylum decision-making processes should conform to existing policy, which, as written, provides for equitable treatment across all refugee groups. (In an interesting development on this issue, in May 1995 the Clinton administration reversed the de facto policy that granted virtual blanket asylum to all Cubans. At this time, all Cubans intercepted at sea are being returned to Cuba for in-country processing of asylum claims on a case-by-case basis, making their treatment equitable with that of Haitians [Epstein, Lantigua, & Cavanaugh, 1995].) The argument for equitable asylum treatment has been made for some time by refugee advocates (although in the case of Cubans and Haitians, advocates have argued for Haitian claims to be treated in the same manner as Cuban claims, rather than vice versa) (U.S. Committee for Refugees, 1995b). The results of this study lend further support to this advocacy argument by providing empirical evidence of the sequelae of discriminatory de facto policy. Namely, children who are considered refugees by international convention but are denied asylum in the United States and remain in the country

illegally are likely to suffer economically into their adult years. Therefore, social workers who work with refugees must continue to advocate for more humanitarian treatment of refugee children.

A second policy implication of this study is that refugee policies
should adopt a long-term outlook in recognition of the fact that
refugee economic adaptation is a very lengthy process. Therefore, supportive services for refugee children should be aimed at promoting
long-term adaptation as opposed to short-term "crisis stabilization."
At the programmatic level, a logical point of delivery of such services
is the school system. There is a well-established empirical link between academic achievement in childhood and subsequent economic
adaptation in adulthood (Rumberger, 1987). At the same time, there is
well-established evidence of the negative impact of childhood psychosocial stressors on academic achievement (Rumberger, 1987).
Therefore, school-based programs for refugee children must address
the multiple stressors experienced by these populations.

Specifically, the problems of acculturation, intergenerational conflict, and posttraumatic stress need to be addressed. One means for
doing this is through support groups that encourage the children to
share their feelings and experiences and devise healthy coping
strategies. Additionally, because of the increasing involvement of
refugee children in crime, diversion programs such as culturally focused after-school recreational and sports activities need to be developed. These types of initiatives extend beyond the English-language
training and special education programs that are currently in place
for refugee children. School social workers are the logical agents to
implement these extended programs. Although a detailed proposal
for the implementation of these initiatives is beyond the scope of this
chapter, the hypothesis is advanced that addressing these underlying
issues, which are unique to refugee children, will lead to increased
academic achievement, which will in turn lead to increased long-
term economic adjustment in adulthood.

A final implication is that programs need to be tailored to each
specific refugee group because of their cultural and racial differences. Clearly, Haitian and Soviet children, for example, have had
vastly different experiences, which are subsequently reflected in
their differential economic status. Thus, the same approach will
probably not have the same outcome for the two groups. Therefore,
programs and interventions need to be culture specific to address the
unique experiences of each group.

Suggestions for Future Research

A shortcoming of this study is that the limitations of the census data
did not permit an analysis of how participation or nonparticipation
in existing refugee programs specifically affected individuals. The
conclusions of this study were based on aggregate-level data. Therefore, future program evaluation research is needed that explicitly

examines the links between program participation in childhood and economic outcome in adulthood.

Another relevant area for future research is more in-depth examination of the academic achievement of refugee children. Recent immigration theory suggests a model of "segmented assimilation" whereby some refugee children assimilate into a group of U.S.-born peers who are high academic achievers, whereas other refugee children from the same country assimilate into low-achieving U.S.-born peer groups (Portes & Zhou, 1993). Further research is needed on the factors that lead to this segmentation.

Finally, the issues examined in this study should be explored in regard to refugee children in other parts of the United States. Because this study focused on California and Dade County, Florida, it is not known whether these findings are generalizable to other states and other refugee groups.

CONCLUSION

With respect to some of the refugee groups examined (Soviets, East Europeans, Nicaraguans, and Haitians), arrivals may be expected to decline in the future as democracy is restored in those countries (although oppression in those countries continues to exist, albeit at reduced levels). Nonetheless, refugee populations will undoubtedly emerge in other parts of the world and seek asylum in the United States. Therefore, the findings and implications of this study will continue to be relevant.

Like all children, refugee children represent an investment in the nation's future. Equitable and effective policies and programs that enhance these children's chances for success in adulthood will enhance the well-being of the nation as a whole.

REFERENCES

Bordieu, P. (1983). Forms of capital. In J. Richardson (Ed.), *Handbook of theory and research for the sociology of education* (pp. 241–258). New York: Greenwood Press.

Carlin, J. E. (1990). Refugee and immigrant populations at special risk: Women, children, and the elderly. In W. H. Holtzman & T. H. Bornemann (Eds.), *Mental health of immigrants and refugees* (pp. 224–233). Austin, TX: Hogg Foundation for Mental Health.

Chambers, D. E., Wedel, K. E., & Rodwell, M. K. (1992). *Evaluating social programs.* Boston: Allyn & Bacon.

Drachman, D. (1992). A stage-of-migration framework for social service to immigrant populations. *Social Work, 37,* 68–72.

Epstein, G., Lantigua, J., & Cavanaugh, J. (1995, May 7). U.S. ship taking rafters to Cuba. *Miami Herald,* p. 1A.

Fernandez-Kelly, M. P., & Schauffler, R. (1994). Divided fates: Immigrant children in a restructured U.S. economy. *International Migration Review, 28,* 662–689.

Gallagher, D., Forbes, S., & Fagen, P. W. (1985). *Of special humanitarian concern: U.S. refugee admissions since passage of the Refugee Act.* Washington, DC: Refugee Policy Group.

Gibson, M. A., & Ogbu, J. U. (Eds.). (1991). *Minority status and schooling: A comparative study of immigrant and involuntary minorities.* New York: Garland.

Gozdziak, E. (1989). *New Americans: The economic adaptation of Eastern European, Afghan, and Ethiopian refugees.* Washington, DC: Refugee Policy Group.

Kuhlman, T. (1991). The economic integration of refugees in developing countries: A research model. *Journal of Refugee Studies, 4,* 1–20.

Matsuoka, J. K. (1990). Differential acculturation among Vietnamese refugees. *Social Work, 35,* 341–345.

Office of Refugee Resettlement. (1993). *Refugee resettlement program: Annual report to Congress, FY 1992.* Washington, DC: U.S. Government Printing Office.

Portes, A. (1994). Introduction: Immigration and its aftermath. *International Migration Review, 28,* 632–639.

Portes, A., & Stepick, A. (1985). Unwelcome immigrants: The labor market experiences of 1980 (Mariel) Cuban and Haitian refugees in South Florida. *American Sociological Review, 50,* 493–514.

Portes, A., & Stepick, A. (1993). *City on the edge: The transformation of Miami.* Berkeley: University of California Press.

Portes, A., & Zhou, M. (1993). The new second generation: Segmented assimilation and its variants. *Annals of the American Academy of Political and Social Science, 530,* 74–96.

Poston, D. L. (1994). Patterns of economic attainment of foreign-born male workers in the United States. *International Migration Review, 28,* 478–500.

Refugee Act of 1980, P.L. 96-212, 94 Stat. 102.

Refugee Education Assistance Act of 1980, P.L. 96-422, 94 Stat. 1799.

Rumberger, R. W. (1987). High school dropouts: A review of issues and evidence. *Review of Educational Research, 57,* 101–121.

Stepick, A., & Dutton Stepick, C. (1994). *Preliminary Haitian needs assessment: Report to the city of Miami.* Miami: Florida International University, Immigration and Ethnicity Institute.

Tran, T. V. (1991). Sponsorship and employment status among Indochinese refugees in the United States. *International Migration Review, 25,* 536–550.

Uba, L., & Chung, R. C. (1991). The relationship between trauma and financial and physical well-being among Cambodians in the United States. *Journal of General Psychology, 118,* 215–225.

United Nations. (1951). *Geneva Convention relating to the status of refugees.* Geneva: Author.

United Nations. (1967). *Protocol relating to the status of refugees.* Geneva: Author.

U.S. Bureau of the Census. (1992). *Census of population and housing, 1990: Public use microdata samples, technical documentation.* Washington, DC: Author, Data User Service Division.

U.S. Committee for Refugees. (1995a). Asylum cases filed with INS, April 1991–September 1995. *Refugee Reports, 16*(12), 12.

U.S. Committee for Refugees. (1995b). Oakley looks to future of U.S. refugee resettlement program, present treatment of Cubans and Haitians. *Refugee Reports, 16*(1), 1–5.

U.S. Committee for Refugees. (1995c). Refugees admitted to the United States by nationality, FY 1982–1995. *Refugee Reports, 16*(12), 10–11.

Vacha, E. F., & McLaughlin, T. F. (1992). The social, structural, family, school, and personal characteristics of at-risk students: Policy recommendations for school personnel. *Journal of Education, 174,* 9–24.

Westermeyer, J., Callies, A., & Neider, J. (1990). Welfare status and psychosocial adjustment among 100 Hmong refugees. *Journal of Nervous and Mental Disease, 178,* 300–306.

Yarnold, B. M. (1990). *Refugees without refuge: Formation and failed implementation of U.S. political asylum policy in the 1980s.* Lanham, MD: University Press of America.

Phase 1 of this study is based on the author's doctoral dissertation at the University of Kansas School of Social Welfare. Phase 2 of this study was funded by a grant from the Florida International University Foundation. The author is grateful to Antoinette Rodgers, Fred Newman, and Suman Kakar for their helpful comments.

46

The Influence of Pre-emigration and Postemigration Stressors on Mental Health: A Study of Southeast Asian Refugees

Barbara L. Nicholson

Since 1975, almost 1 million Southeast Asian refugees have emigrated to the United States. Most of these refugees were forced to flee their homelands for political reasons, usually against their will, often suddenly, and under extremely dangerous conditions. Both before and during emigration, all refugees experienced stressful conditions and events that were devastating for many and extremely difficult for most. Many either witnessed or were victims of politically provoked torture and trauma (Carlson & Rosser-Hogan, 1994; Kinzie et al., 1990; Kinzie, Fredrickson, Ben, Fleck, & Karls, 1984; Kleinman, 1990; Lee & Lu, 1989).

In addition, the environment after emigration was fraught with extreme stressors. Refugees were forced to adapt to a new country that was quite different from their own while simultaneously grieving the multiple losses intrinsic to the upheavals in Southeast Asia (Bernier, 1992; Bromley, 1987; Eisenbruch, 1991; Gorst, 1992). Clinical and empirical studies have reported that cultural, language, and value differences added further stress and hindered the process of adaptation (Gong-Guy, Cravens, & Patterson, 1991; Le-Doux & Stephens, 1992; Mayadas & Elliott, 1992).

Although some studies have established a relationship between the traumatic events experienced before and during emigration and mental health difficulties (Carlson & Rosser-Hogan, 1993, 1994; Chung & Kagawa-Singer, 1993; Kinzie et al., 1984, 1990; Mollica, Wyshak, & Lavelle, 1987), other studies have linked acculturation problems with psychological difficulties (Beiser, 1988; Bernier, 1992; Johnson, 1989; Nicassio, 1985; Uba & Chung, 1991). Thus, although numerous studies have linked factors either before or after emigration to mental health outcome, few studies have evaluated the relative importance of two or more of these factors at once.

REVIEW OF THE LITERATURE

Because of the severity and duration of stressors both before and after emigration, many refugees develop serious mental health difficulties. However, most of the evidence citing such problems comes from

This chapter was originally published in the March 1997 issue of *Social Work Research*, Vol. 21, pp. 19–31.

research studies of clinical populations. These studies have reported high prevalence rates of posttraumatic stress disorder (PTSD), depression, and anxiety, as well as problems with somatization (Kinzie et al., 1984, 1990; Kroll et al., 1989; Mollica, Wyshak, & Lavelle, 1987). For instance, Kinzie et al. (1990) found that 71 percent of clinic patients were diagnosed with PTSD, and 81 percent were diagnosed with depression. Mollica, Wyshak, and Lavelle (1987) reported a 50 percent prevalence rate of PTSD and a 71 percent prevalence rate of mixed anxiety and depression. Kroll et al. (1989) diagnosed only 14 percent of the patients as having PTSD but found a prevalence rate of 73.3 percent for depression among the refugees.

Even fewer studies have assessed the prevalence of psychiatric difficulties in a nonclinical sample of Southeast Asian people (Carlson & Rosser-Hogan, 1993, 1994; Gong-Guy, 1986). Gong-Guy reported prevalence rates of 36 percent for depression, 96 percent for anxiety, and 16.3 percent for PTSD in a nonclinical sample of the same four ethnic groups included in the present study. However, Carlson and Rosser-Hogan (1993, 1994) reported much higher rates in their Cambodian sample; 80 percent met criteria for depression, 88 percent for anxiety, and 86 percent for PTSD. The discrepancy between these two reports is considerable.

The nonclinical studies cited were undertaken in earlier stages of refugee adaptation, whereas this study investigated acculturation and mental health issues in a nonclinical sample in which 46 percent of participants had lived in the United States for more than 10 years. In addition, because prior traumatic experiences are often indicated as primary reasons for mental health problems, this study assessed the trauma histories of the four ethnic groups included here. I found only one other study (Carlson & Rosser-Hogan, 1993, 1994) that enumerated traumatic experiences; however, that sample included only Cambodians. No empirical studies report an aggregate score of current stress experienced by this at-risk population. Although the measure designed for this project will need further validation, it holds promise for advancing the knowledge base for future empirical studies.

PURPOSE OF THE STUDY

The path analysis study reported in this chapter assessed the mental health status of a nonclinical sample of Southeast Asian refugees to address several deficits in researchers' current knowledge and understanding of this population. The study examined a causal model that included variables from both before and after emigration that were believed to have either direct or mediating effects on mental health among the refugee population. These factors were analyzed simultaneously to evaluate the relative importance of such variables in predicting outcomes. Prior research has not been sufficiently complex to explore a model that would predict mental health status among these refugees.

Pre-emigration factors include traumatic events either experienced or witnessed before and during emigration, as well as relevant individual background characteristics such as age, education, ethnicity, gender, environment before emigration (rural versus urban), and marital status. Postemigration factors include an index of current stress, self-perceived health status, and income levels.

Using path analysis, I attempted to determine which factors are predictive of mental health status after emigration. Findings from this research should enhance researchers' ability to predict impediments to successful adaptation. Increased knowledge of the specific needs of this at-risk population can help clinicians make more relevant decisions about mental health treatment and prevention for this group.

Pre-emigration Stressors

The trauma the refugees experienced in leaving their homelands provides a basis for the current study. Most Southeast Asian refugees endured tremendous hardship before, during, and after emigration. For example, refugees frequently suffered human rights abuses of any or all of the following types: incarceration, combat, torture, physical abuse, sexual abuse, forced isolation, and the murder of family and friends (Lee & Lu, 1989; Mollica et al., 1993). Many refugees experienced starvation and severe illness, either of themselves or of family members, without access to adequate medical care. Others watched family members and friends die and could not prevent or control these events (Bromley, 1987; Chung & Kagawa-Singer, 1993; Kinzie et al., 1984). According to the *Diagnostic and Statistical Manual of Mental Disorders—Fourth Edition* (DSM-IV) (American Psychiatric Association, 1994), life stressors are considered traumatic if they are catastrophic, outwardly induced, and outside the realm of ordinary human experience. The experiences of these refugees meet these criteria for psychological trauma.

The foregoing description is only a hint of what these refugees endured. Difficult conditions continued after they arrived at refugee camps. Several empirical studies have suggested that prolonged stays in these camps, where conditions were unsafe, unsanitary, and basically intolerable, exacerbated the trauma for most refugees (Chung & Kagawa-Singer, 1993; Mollica et al., 1993). In a study of 1,348 adult refugees from Southeast Asia, Beiser, Turner, and Ganesan (1989) found that stressful camp conditions exerted a significant effect on adjustment after emigration and were a primary cause of subsequent depression.

In addition, characteristics such as age, education, ethnicity, gender, rural or urban locality of origin, and marital status have all been cited as possible correlates of adjustment after emigration. As pre-emigration factors, they have been incorporated into my theoretical model.

Postemigration Stressors

The research findings of Beiser et al. (1989) also emphasized that the grimness of camp conditions was only one of the multiple stressors that influenced adjustment after emigration. Although memories of the camps may diminish over time, bereavement from multiple losses is more powerful and less retractable. Beiser and colleagues viewed this as a significant factor that undermined individuals' capacities to adjust successfully to a new environment after emigration. Other researchers have concurred that grief over the loss of family members and social supports influenced adaptation after emigration and was significantly correlated with negative mental health outcomes (Boehnlein, 1987; Eisenbruch, 1984, 1991). Refugees also suffered loss of homeland, culture, role, status, and material possessions. These losses rendered the process of acculturation even more difficult (Bernier, 1992; Gorst, 1992).

Other stressors had a negative impact on mental health after emigration. On arrival in the United States, the refugees in the study experienced additional stressors inherent in the resettlement process. They faced the challenge of adapting to a new country with cultural norms and values significantly different from those of their homeland without the support of their prior indigenous social networks (Canda & Phaobtong, 1992; Matsuoka, 1993; Mayadas & Elliott, 1992). The myriad tasks involved in acculturation include learning a new language, redefining gender and work roles, rebuilding social networks, and integrating the values and norms of the host society.

Perceived poor health status is a major psychological stressor in the refugee community. Many refugees have legitimate concerns because they have been injured by violent traumatic experiences that include war-related trauma and torture. However, because of traditional values, refugees often experience and express stress in somatic symptoms. Somatization is a culturally acceptable way to contain or experience affective states to avoid expressing emotion (Chung & Kagawa-Singer, 1993; Gong-Guy et al., 1991; Lin, Carter, & Kleinman, 1985; Westermeyer, 1986). Beiser and Fleming (1986) suggested an alternate explanation for this high degree of somatization: Rather than masking depression, somatic conditions may be an alternate way of expressing distress. This study found only a mild negative correlation ($r = -.28$) between perceived health and depression. Consequently, self-perceived health remains separate from depression in my theoretical model. Difficulty involved in all of the areas enumerated may result in a significant loss of income (Johnson, 1989; Uba & Chung, 1991). Therefore, self-perceived health and income levels are included in the postemigration factors that are believed to be potential predictors of mental health outcomes.

METHOD

Participants

The sample for this cross-sectional survey consisted of 447 Southeast Asian refugees. Participants were divided evenly between men and women, working and nonworking, and individuals coming from rural or urban backgrounds. Participants also were evenly distributed among the four primary Southeast Asian ethnic groups represented in the Northeast United States: Vietnamese, Cambodian, Laotian, and Hmong.

In addition, the sampling design controlled for age and length of residence in the United States. Subjects had to have lived in the United States for at least four years so that they would have time to acculturate, to seek employment, and to become comfortable with American culture and mores. In addition, participants had to be at least 35 years of age to control for the effects of developmental life stage at the time of relocation.

I recruited potential participants by contacting and meeting with community and religious leaders and human services workers for help in locating participants. Also, information about the study and requests for participants were placed in strategic areas in each ethnic community. Many participants volunteered after being told about the project by other members of their communities. From these efforts, a stratified convenience sample of about 110 people from each ethnic group was selected from a wider pool of volunteers.

The average age of participants was 45 years (SD = 9.15), and the mean length of stay in the United States was 9.2 years (SD = 3.30). Forty-six percent had lived in the United States for more than 10 years. Approximately 77 percent of the subjects were married. Slightly less than half (45.6 percent) were Buddhist, 29 percent were Christian, 15 percent represented a variety of Eastern religions, and the remaining 10 percent were not affiliated with any religion. A majority of the participants (59 percent) completed grade school or less, 29 percent had completed high school or trade school, and only 12 percent had completed college.

Procedures

The interviewers were selected because of their experience and knowledge of mental health and adaptation, and they were thoroughly trained to administer the two-hour personal interview. Before data collection began, I conducted pilot tests to assess the general ease of administering the interview, the clarity and conciseness of the questions, and the appropriateness of the difficulty level of the instruments. Measures were modified as needed before formal data collection began. In addition, I provided continual supervision, emotional support, and peer group meetings throughout the data-collection phase of the project to ensure that neither the interviewers nor the interviewees experienced any emotional difficulty.

Before each interview began, the interviewers thoroughly described the interview, emphasized each individual's right to withdraw from the study at any time, and obtained informed consent. If participants were literate in their own language, they completed the demographic data on their own. If they were not literate, the bilingual interviewer administered the entire interview protocol. In all cases, the interviewers administered the Harvard Trauma Questionnaire (HTQ) (Mollica et al., 1992), the Hopkins Symptom Checklist-25 (HSCL-25) (Mollica, Wyshak, deMarneffe, Khuon, & Lavelle, 1987), and the Current Stressors Scale (CSS) to ensure that if respondents were negatively affected by the interview, appropriate clinical intervention would be provided. In addition, the interviewers contacted participants one week after the interview to confirm that they did not experience any negative aftereffects as a result of their participation in this study. Fortunately, there were no reports of emotional difficulty either during or after the interview.

Instruments

Criterion Variables. The three mental health criterion variables were measured using the standardized measures listed above, all of which have been used previously with a Southeast Asian refugee population, have been translated into the separate Southeast Asian languages, and have been tested for psychometric properties. The HSCL-25, a widely used standardized instrument for both clinical and nonclinical populations, is a 25-item checklist that measures anxiety and depression in a variety of settings (Mollica, Wyshak, deMarneffe, et al., 1987). This instrument is composed of 10 items measuring anxiety and 15 items measuring depression. Examples of specific items can be found in Mollica, Wyshak, deMarneffe, et al. (1987).

The HSCL-25 has been tested for reliability and validity for use with Southeast Asian refugees (Mollica, Wyshak, deMarneffe, et al., 1987). Specificity and semantic equivalence have been demonstrated. Cronbach's alphas of .89 for anxiety and .89 for depression were obtained for the current sample.

Part 2 of the HTQ (Mollica et al., 1992) measures the criterion variable of PTSD (part 1 of this questionnaire measures the predictor variables of experienced and witnessed traumatic events described below). Part 2 of the HTQ measures PTSD symptoms in Southeast Asian refugees. The PTSD symptom measurement consists of 16 items drawn from *Diagnostic and Statistical Manual of Mental Disorders, Third Edition–Revised* (DSM-III-R)(American Psychiatric Association, [APA] 1987) criteria and 14 items that capture the specific culture-bound experiences of Southeast Asian refugees. The latter include such questions as "feeling that people do not understand what happened to you," "blaming yourself for things that have happened," "feeling guilty for having survived," "feeling ashamed of the hurtful or traumatic event that has happened to you," "feeling that someone you trusted betrayed you," and "feeling that others are hostile toward you." Instructions for the HTQ, as well as its psychometric properties, can be found in Mollica et al. (1992).

Predictor Variables. Part 1 of the HTQ measures pre-emigration predictor variables of several experienced and witnessed traumatic events. The remaining pre-emigration variables, rural versus urban living in home country, gender, and marital status, are self-reports. Part 1 of the HTQ is a checklist developed specifically for use with Southeast Asian refugees. This section measures the number of traumatic events that were experienced, witnessed, or heard about by Southeast Asians before and during emigration, such as death of a family member, starvation, torture, rape, forced labor, severe illness, forced isolation, serious injury, combat, brainwashing, imprisonment, and lack of food or shelter. The HTQ was tested for reliability and validity; Mollica et al. (1992) discussed psychometric properties. An alpha coefficient of .95 was obtained for this study.

Of the three postemigration variables, current stress was measured by the CSS, whereas perceived health status and income levels are single measures rather than scales. The CSS was devised for this project. The scale consists of 24 items devised from clinical experiences with the population being studied. The items of the CSS were factor-analyzed using a principal factors initial solution followed by an Oblimin oblique rotation. A Cattell scree test indicated that a two-factor solution was adequate (Norusis, 1988). The first eigenvector accounted for 28 percent and the second for 12 percent of the variance for a total of 40 percent in the two factors. Cronbach's alpha for the entire scale was .88. However, in analyzing the individual factors, the 17 items in factor 1 resulted in a scale coefficient of .88, whereas the seven items in factor 2 resulted in a scale coefficient of .80. In addition, the scale scores for factor 1 and factor 2 correlated together at only .38, indicating relative independence of the two factors.

The first factor contained more "normal" stressors, whereas the second factor contained more serious and less common stressors. Specifically, examples of the factor 1 items included commonly cited problems for refugees and immigrants such as housing, finances, employment, language, and education, as well as personal or family members' illness or death and loss of kinship networks. Examples of items on factor 2 included, for example, being mugged or burglarized, being raped, losing financial entitlements such as Medicaid and welfare, having legal problems, and providing day care for elderly family members.

The self-perceived health status of the study participants was measured using a four-point Likert-type scale. Response categories were 1 = poor, 2 = fair, 3 = good, and 4 = excellent. Individual scores for this measure consisted of the numerical value associated with the category endorsed. Income levels were measured by self-report on a ratio scale depicting exact salary rates.

RESULTS

Description

Southeast Asian community residents exhibited relatively high levels of psychiatric symptomatology as attested by their scores on the symptom measures of PTSD, depression, and anxiety. On the HTQ, individuals with total scores greater than 2.5 are considered symptomatic for PTSD (Mollica et al., 1992). Although the mean score for symptoms of PTSD in this sample was 1.64 (SD = 0.53), approximately 14 percent scored above the 2.5 range, meeting criteria for a PTSD diagnosis.

On the HSCL-25, individuals with scores of less than 1.75 on the anxiety and depression subscales are considered symptomatic (Mollica, Wyshak, deMarneffe, et al., 1987). In the present study, mean scores for anxiety and depression were 1.67 and 1.74, respectively (SD = 0.60 and 0.55), indicating relatively high levels of these symptoms among study participants. More important, approximately 35 percent scored above 1.75 for anxiety, and 40 percent exceeded the same cutoff point for depression, meeting criteria for major anxiety and depressive disorders.

Study participants had a mean score of 2.47 for the amount of stress caused by life events and psychosocial problems experienced during the past year. In addition to these perceived life stressors, almost 50 percent of the subjects rated their health as only fair or poor. The mean annual income level of participants was between $7,000 and $9,999, although annual incomes ranged from more than $60,000 to no income whatsoever.

In addition, from a list of 17 traumatic events, subjects experienced a mean of 5.04 events. Sixteen percent reported experiences of 10 events or more, and approximately 22 percent noted that they experienced no traumatic events before or during emigration. From the same list of possible events, 27 percent of participants either witnessed or heard about more than 10 events, whereas only 8 percent had neither witnessed nor heard about any traumatic events. The mean number of witnessed events was 6.68.

Path Analysis

Table 46-1 lists the Pearson correlation coefficients between each of the eight predictor and three criterion variables and reports the means, standard deviations, and ranges for each variable. The relatively low correlations among the predictor variables indicate that test results are not contaminated by problems of multicollinearity. In addition, regression diagnostic tests were performed to calculate the tolerance values for each of the independent variables included in the three separate equations predicting mental health outcomes. For the variables directly affecting PTSD, the highest tolerance value was .955 (health) and the lowest was .827 (experienced events). For anxiety, the highest tolerance value was .991 (gender) and the lowest was

Table 46-1

Zero Order Correlations, Means, Standard Deviations, and Ranges for Causal Model

Stressor	1	2	3	4	5	6	7	8	9	10	11	M	SD	Range
1. PTSD	—											1.64	0.53	0–4
2. Anxiety	.54											1.67	0.60	0–4
3. Depression	.63	.61										1.74	0.55	0–4
4. Experienced events	.21	.28	.26									5.04	4.78	0–17
5. Witnessed events	.04	.02	.03	.29								6.68	4.38	0–17
6. Rural/urban	.07	.13	.08	.15	.13							0.45	0.50	
7. Gender	.07	.12	.09	-.03	-.03	-.05						0.50	0.50	
8. Marital status	.09	.07	.13	.11	.01	.05	.12					0.46	0.91	
9. Current stress	.41	.40	.48	.28	.11	.14	.07	.05				2.47	0.67	0–4
10. Perceived health	-.17	-.40	-.28	-.11	-.03	-.14	-.04	-.05	-.19			2.44	0.94	0–4
11. Income	-.22	-.26	-.29	-.15	-.05	-.21	-.16	-.05	-.33	-.38	—	4.77	2.10	0–12

NOTE: PTSD = posttraumatic stress disorder.

.889 (current stress). For depression, the highest tolerance value was .997 (marital status) and the lowest was .888 (income). Because a score of 1 indicates complete independence among variables, such high tolerance values for each model signify almost no collinearity. The variance inflation factor for all three equations was very small, averaging 1.02 and further strengthening the appropriateness of the data for regression analysis.

The distributional characteristics for all predictor variables were analyzed to ensure that the data met the normality requirements for regression analyses. Specifically, the skew for most variables centered around 0 (signifying symmetric distributions) for all predictors with the exception of experienced events at .779. All others were positively skewed below .135 with the exception of health, which was negatively skewed at –.069. These results confirm that the data are symmetrical. Also, kurtosis, the extent to which the predictor variables clustered around a central point given a standard deviation, was normal, centering around zero for all variables except witnessed events at –1.036. All other variables met this distributional standard at below 0.325.

Therefore, I tested the proposed model using multiple regression techniques. (The results of the path analysis generated from the hypothesized causal model are presented in Figure 46-1.) For each criterion variable (PTSD, depression, and anxiety), a separate, stepwise, multiple regression was performed with each of the pre-emigration variables and each of the postemigration stressors as predictor variables. In addition, separate multiple regressions were performed with pre-emigration variables as predictors and postemigration stressors as criterion variables. When a particular regression coefficient failed to achieve significance, the line or path was excluded from the final model. Age, educational level, and ethnicity did not add significantly to the proportion of explained variance and were dropped from the model.

The predicted model accounted for a substantial amount of the variance in mental health status among study participants. Specifically, the multiple regression R^2 adjusted indicated that the combined variables representing factors before emigration and conditions after emigration accounted for 35 percent of the variation in PTSD, 39 percent of the variation in anxiety, and 38 percent of the variation in depression. However, when the postemigration variables were analyzed as criteria, pre-emigration variables predicted only 9 percent of the variation in current stressors, 3 percent of the variation in self-perceived health status, and 7 percent of the variation in income. Consequently, the data indicate that the pre-emigration factors analyzed are only mildly predictive of current stress. Only one pre-emigration variable, experienced trauma, directly affected all psychiatric outcomes, particularly PTSD (ß = .31). However, two postemigration factors, current stress and self-perceived health status, directly affected all psychiatric outcomes. Therefore, postemigration factors are more

Figure 46-1

Causal Analysis of Pre-emigration and Postemigration Factors Affecting Mental Health among Southeast Asian Refugees

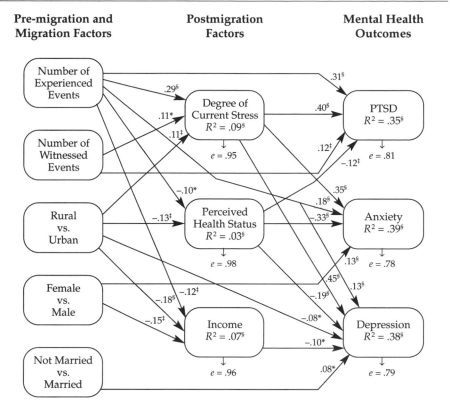

| Pre-migration and Migration Factors | Postmigration Factors | Mental Health Outcomes |

NOTES: PTSD = posttraumatic stress disorder. $N = 444$.
$*p \leq .05.$ $\ddagger p \leq .01.$ $\S p \leq .001.$

powerful in predicting all psychiatric outcomes than are factors from before emigration.

Postemigration Factors. The current stress index was the strongest overall predictor of the three mental health outcomes. Degree of current stress had direct paths to PTSD, depression, and anxiety with coefficients of .40, .45, and .35, respectively. Participants with higher stress levels also had higher levels of psychiatric symptoms. In addition, self-perceived health status also had direct paths to the three outcome measures: PTSD (–.12), depression (–.19), and anxiety (–.33). Thus, refugees who perceived their health as poor were likely to experience higher symptom levels of PTSD, anxiety, and depression than refugees who perceived their health as good. Income had a direct negative effect on depression (–.10), indicating that refugees with lower incomes were more likely to be depressed than were more highly paid refugees. However, income had no direct effect on either anxiety or PTSD.

Pre-emigration Factors. Although current stress was the most powerful predictor of psychiatric outcome, experienced events directly affected PTSD (.31), anxiety (.18), and depression (.13). Individuals who experienced the greatest number of traumatic events had the most severe levels of psychiatric symptoms. Experienced events predicted PTSD more powerfully than either anxiety or depression, and this factor had indirect effects on mental health mediated through its effects on current stress (.29), self-perceived health status (–.10), and income (–.12). Refugees who experienced the most traumatic events had higher levels of stress, perceived their health as poorer, and had lower incomes than their counterparts who experienced fewer traumatic events.

In contrast, there is only one direct path between witnessed events and mental health outcomes—PTSD (.12). Gender directly affected anxiety (.13), and marital status directly affected depression (.08). Women had higher levels of anxiety than men, and unmarried participants were more likely to be depressed than were married participants. The remaining pre-emigration factors had indirect effects on mental health outcomes. Both the number of events witnessed and whether a refugee came from an urban or rural background had indirect effects on all mental health measures mediated through their effects on current stress (.11 and .11, respectively). Refugees who witnessed more traumatic events and who came from rural backgrounds were more likely to experience higher stress levels, which contributed to higher levels of PTSD, anxiety, and depression. Gender had an indirect effect on mental health mediated through income (–.15). Women had lower incomes than men and were more prone to depression.

Study Limitations

This study was limited by several factors. First, single measures for complex problems may trivialize the significance and complexity of specific problem areas. Self-reports are not completely reliable because of the bias inherent in individuals talking about themselves. This unreliability might be particularly true in the Southeast Asian community because discussing problems with people other than family members may involve a "loss of face." In addition, the cross-sectional nature of the design merits discussion as a limitation. Interviewing individuals at one point in time may capture how they are feeling only at that particular time, and the telling of sensitive information may reflect the subject's current mood or feelings about the interviewer. Also, past events, particularly traumatic ones, are often difficult to recall given the human propensity to deny or repress the exact nature of such experiences. Current problems are usually more pressing than past ones. This fact might contribute to the findings that current stressors are more predictive of mental health than past events.

DISCUSSION

The results of this study confirm that nearly 20 years after leaving their home countries, many Southeast Asian refugees exhibited serious psychiatric problems stemming from stressors that occurred both before and after emigration. Specifically, one pre-emigration factor, traumatic events experienced, and two postemigration factors, current stressors and perceived health status, directly affected all three mental health outcomes. In addition, 40 percent of this nonclinical sample had clinical depression, 35 percent had clinical anxiety, and 14 percent had PTSD. Given the results of prior research, the number of traumatic events reported by study participants was lower than anticipated, whereas the degree of current stress created by specific life events and difficulties with tasks of daily living was higher than anticipated.

Of a possible 17 events, the mean number of traumatic events experienced or witnessed was 5.04 and 6.68, respectively. One possible explanation for this low report is that the sample was stratified to include equal numbers of Cambodian, Vietnamese, Laotian, and Hmong participants. However, prior research has documented that Cambodian refugees were subjected to greater trauma than other Southeast Asian groups (Chung & Kagawa-Singer, 1993; Lee & Lu, 1989; Mollica et al., 1993). Therefore, including the groups who may not have experienced equal levels of trauma would decrease the mean number of events reported. Also, to be eligible for this study, participants had to be at least 35 years old and to have lived in the United States for four years. The mean number of years respondents lived in this country was 9.2 years. Therefore, because their emigration experiences were so long ago, they may have underreported traumatic events in an effort to repress past trauma while attempting to adapt to their new environment.

The participants in this study reported high levels of clinical depression and anxiety as well as PTSD. The rates found in this study were less than half those reported in clinical samples (Kinzie et al., 1990; Kroll et al., 1989; Mollica, Wyshak, & Lavelle, 1987). Carlson and Rosser-Hogan (1993) reported 80 percent depression, 88 percent anxiety, and 86 percent PTSD in a small nonclinical sample who were entirely Cambodian and had been in the United States an average of four years less than participants in this study.

However, Gong-Guy (1986), in his nonclinical sample, reported rates similar to those in the current sample for depression (36 percent) and PTSD (16 percent) but a much higher rate for anxiety (96 percent). The similarities in the PTSD and depression scores are most likely explained by the similarities in the sample composition. These results suggest that examining four different ethnic groups of Southeast Asians will produce different results from studies of a single group. A possible explanation for the difference in the anxiety scores reported in the Gong-Guy study is that the data were collected almost 10 years earlier than the current data, suggesting that many in the sample were new arrivals to the United States. Rates of anxiety were probably elevated both by their current emigration experiences and by the frightening acculturative tasks confronting them. After 10 years in a new country, one could assume that anxiety would be lower because many unknowns had been dealt with but that depression in response to multiple losses and chronic or delayed symptoms of PTSD would continue or even be heightened (Beiser et al., 1989; Gorst, 1992).

The PTSD rate in this study was comparable to that in studies by Kroll et al. (1989) and Gong-Guy (1986), both of whom had samples consisting of mixed groups of Southeast Asians. Still, these rates were low compared with the rates found by Carlson and Rosser-Hogan (1993, 1994), Kinzie et al. (1990), and Mollica, Wyshak, and Lavelle (1987). These higher PTSD rates might be explained by the high number of Cambodians participating in all three studies. Carlson and Rosser-Hogan's sample was completely Cambodian, whereas the latter studies not only had high rates of Cambodians, but also were drawn from a clinical population.

The mean score of 2.47 on a four-point scale for current stress is considered high. This finding was congruent with other research that states that difficulties with acculturation can persist for many years after initial resettlement. One of the major tasks of acculturation that creates current stress is grieving losses from the past, as participants reported. Extended bereavement over multiple losses with this refugee population has been observed elsewhere (Beiser et al., 1989; Eisenbruch, 1991; Gorst, 1992; Kleinman, 1990). Common and persistent problems with acculturative tasks reported by participants in this study such as language, employment, educational, and financial difficulties were consistent with those documented in other studies (Johnson, 1989; Matsuoka, 1993; Uba & Chung, 1991).

Almost 50 percent of subjects rated their health as only fair or poor. Many refugees were tortured, starved, ill, or otherwise physically injured during their escapes, and those injuries created deteriorated health for some refugees (Kleinman, 1990; Westermeyer, 1986). In addition, the perceived poor health reported by these participants was consistent with reports from other practitioners and researchers, who have suggested that somatic complaints are frequently the presenting problem for refugees (Chung & Kagawa-Singer, 1993; Gong-Guy et al., 1991; Lin et al., 1985). Somatization is a culturally appropriate way to manage psychological problems and the accompanying intensity of affect. Cultural traditions discourage the overt expression of feelings because such expression would result in a loss of face. Therefore, intense feeling states are often indirectly experienced through somatic symptoms, further hindering the process of acculturation (Lin et al., 1985).

There is a continuing debate in the literature on Southeast Asian refugees about whether pre-emigration or postemigration experiences account for the high rates of mental health disorders experienced by these refugees. Most empirical reports have examined and found correlations between both pre-emigration and postemigration factors and mental health outcomes and have suggested, but not empirically tested, other factors that are important in the overall functioning of this population (Kinzie et al., 1990; Kroll et al., 1989; Matsuoka, 1993; Uba & Chung, 1991). The present investigation, therefore, is the first attempt to apply a causal model to determine whether pre-emigration or postemigration factors predict mental health difficulties. These results support the proposed model by indicating that both sets of factors directly affect levels of psychiatric symptomatology. Although one pre-emigration factor, experienced events, directly affected all three mental health outcomes, two postemigration variables, the degree of current stress and perceived health status, had direct effects on all outcome measures. Overall, the degree of current stress was the strongest, most powerful predictor of mental health status.

Experienced events predicted PTSD more strongly than either anxiety or depression. In addition, experienced events directly affected all postemigration factors. Witnessed events also predicted PTSD but had no direct effects on either anxiety or depression. However, the indirect effect of witnessed events on mental health through their direct effect on current stress is notable. These findings are consistent with studies that directly link traumatic experiences with PTSD among refugees (Carlson & Rosser-Hogan, 1993, 1994; Kinzie et al., 1984, 1990; Mollica, Wyshak, & Lavelle, 1987) but are inconsistent with studies that suggest that past catastrophic experiences fade over time as new acculturative tasks take precedence (Beiser, 1988; Rumbaut, 1990). Although current stressors more strongly predict mental health outcome, past traumatic experiences are primary determinants of how individuals deal with these current stressors and, therefore, how this affects mental health status. Thus, a continuum exists from pre-emigration through postemigration that is linked to mental health. Such a finding lends credence to the suggestion of Kroll et al. (1989) that "an expanded concept of PTSD takes into account the observations that severe, prolonged, and/or massive psychological and physical traumata produce a single syndrome (along a severity continuum) that encompasses major depressive and somatization features as well as the currently listed PTSD categories" (p. 1596).

All refugees experience multiple losses and major upheavals in their life situations before and during emigration. However, after arrival in their host country, they face acculturative tasks that are extremely difficult. Lee and Lu (1989) stated that refugees are challenged by the need to resolve both "loss" and "load" (p. 100). Whereas "loss" involves coming to terms with the multiple sources of loss, "load" involves coming to terms with beginning a new life in a strange and foreign environment. One task cannot be separated from the other, because grief and loss continue while acculturation tasks begin and proceed. The notion of "cultural bereavement" (Eisenbruch, 1991) offers a culturally sensitive theoretical underpinning that makes the movement from before to after emigration through mental health status more understandable. The multiple losses inherent in the refugee experience create a state of cultural bereavement that becomes part of the posttraumatic "recovery" environment, which is not benign—it is full of challenges that make recovery and successful acculturation more difficult.

The measurement of current stress, which takes into account both loss and load, directly affected depression most strongly, followed by anxiety and PTSD. Whereas experienced events predicted the specific symptom cluster of PTSD, current stress, influenced by cultural bereavement and the stressful tasks of acculturation, predicted depression and anxiety. Refugees living in rural areas before emigration experienced more current stress, perceived their health as poorer, and had lower incomes than did their urban counterparts, and thus experienced more mental health problems. These findings are congruent with other studies that have recognized the difficulties inherent in moving from an agrarian culture to a highly industrialized one (Gong-Guy et al., 1991; Johnson, 1989; Matsuoka, 1993). The tasks of acculturation may thus be more difficult for those in rural environments, predisposing them to greater mental health difficulties. Findings that unmarried participants were more depressed than married participants and that women were more anxious than men are confirmed in the literature.

Finally, perceived health status directly affected all mental health difficulties but less strongly than did degree of current stress. Given the emphasis on somatization as a culturally appropriate and alternate way of experiencing difficult affect, this finding was congruent with other research findings (Gong-Guy, 1986; Kroll et al., 1989; Lin et al., 1985).

CONCLUSION

This research has important implications for social work practice, policy, and prevention. The results of this study stipulate that current stress, a factor after emigration, is the strongest predictor of mental health outcomes. Therefore, both practitioners and policymakers should target initial interventions toward assessing and ameliorating factors creating such stress. Policies and programs developed to solve specific acculturative problems, such as lack of language skills, employment, and education, will enhance adaptation and reduce mental health difficulties. In addition, programs that enhance social supports, build natural helping networks, and create mutual assistance programs will help lessen cultural bereavement and will strengthen appropriate cultural ties in the newcomer communities.

Programs should address health-related issues because of both their real and symbolic meanings for these refugees (Bernier, 1992; Lin et al., 1985; Westermeyer, 1986, 1988). After current stresses and health concerns are addressed and appropriate supports and programs are in place, refugees may be better prepared to deal with prior traumatic events. These experiences can then be psychologically processed, increasing adaptive functioning and decreasing mental health problems.

Care should be taken in generalizing the results of this investigation to the Southeast Asian population in general. The stratified sampling design, although representative of different strata of the Southeast Asian population, was limited by its lack of randomization. Replicating this study with a random sample of Southeast Asians would considerably strengthen current findings and increase their generalization to other Southeast Asian groups as well as to other groups of traumatized refugees.

The exact nature and number of daily pressures and their correlates in Southeast Asians have yet to be empirically examined. Also, somatization is an important construct in understanding health and mental health in this population. The results of this study, as well as those of other researchers, continually point out the importance of understanding the culture-specific meaning of somatic symptoms in other than "Westernized" ways. As suggested earlier, somatization may be a criterion variable equal to depression, anxiety, and PTSD, rather than a mediator for these affective disorders. The development of a more culturally sensitive measure for this construct is imperative in ongoing research of the mental health needs of Southeast Asian refugees. An instrument such as the Derogatis Symptom Checklist (Derogatis, Rickles, & Rock, 1976), which includes measures of somatic symptoms, could be translated and used as a fuller measure of somatization than the self-report used in this study.

Cultural bereavement appears to be a significant concept that creates difficulties both before and after emigration. Researchers should design culturally sensitive measures that would separate this condition from other, more Westernized diagnostic categories (for example, depression), which, in turn, would advance knowledge about appropriate treatment techniques. Also, although the present model was of significant value in locating factors that predict mental health outcomes, the addition of other factors would strengthen future efforts for both practice and policy. Given the escalating crisis of refugees worldwide, including in the United States, it is imperative that the social work community have the knowledge and skill to help this population. The information gained from this study takes us one step closer to achieving this goal.

REFERENCES

American Psychiatric Association. (1987). *Diagnostic and statistical manual of mental disorders* (3rd ed., rev.). Washington, DC: Author.

American Psychiatric Association. (1994). *Diagnostic and statistical manual of mental disorders* (4th ed.). Washington, DC: Author.

Beiser, M. (1988). Influences of time, ethnicity, and attachment on depression in Southeast Asian refugees. *American Journal of Psychiatry, 145,* 46–51.

Beiser M., & Fleming, J. A. (1986). Measuring psychiatric disorder among Southeast Asian refugees. *Psychological Medicine, 16,* 627–629.

Beiser, M., Turner, R. J., & Ganesan, S. (1989). Catastrophic stress and factors affecting its consequences among Southeast Asian refugees. *Social Science Medicine, 26,* 183–195.

Bernier, D. (1992). The Indochinese refugees: A perspective from various stress theories. *Journal of Multicultural Social Work, 2,* 15–30.

Boehnlein, J. K. (1987). Clinical relevance of grief and mourning among Cambodian refugees. *Social Science and Medicine, 25,* 765–772.

Bromley, M. A. (1987). New beginnings for Cambodian refugees: Or further disruptions? *Social Work, 32,* 236–239.

Canda, E., & Phaobtong, T. (1992). Buddhism as a support system for Southeast Asian refugees. *Social Work, 37,* 61–67.

Carlson, E., & Rosser-Hogan, E. (1993). Mental health status of Cambodian refugees ten years after leaving their homes. *American Journal of Orthopsychiatry, 63,* 223–231.

Carlson, E., & Rosser-Hogan, E. (1994). Cross-cultural response to trauma: A study of traumatic experiences and posttraumatic symptoms in Cambodian refugees. *Journal of Traumatic Stress, 7*(1), 43–58.

Chung, R. C., & Kagawa-Singer, M. (1993). Predictors of psychological distress among Southeast Asian refugees. *Social Science Medicine, 36,* 631–639.

Derogatis, L., Rickles, K., & Rock, A. (1976). The SCL-90 and the MMPI: A step in the validation of a new self-report scale. *British Journal of Psychiatry, 128,* 280–289.

Eisenbruch, M. (1984). Cross-cultural aspects of bereavement: Ethnic and cultural variations in the development of bereavement practices. *Culture, Medicine and Psychiatry, 8,* 315–347.

Eisenbruch, M. (1991). From post-traumatic stress disorder to cultural bereavement: Diagnosis of Southeast Asian refugees. *Social Science and Medicine, 33,* 673–680.

Gong-Guy, E. (1986). *The California Southeast Asian Needs Assessment.* Oakland, CA: Asian Community Mental Health Services.

Gong-Guy, E., Cravens, R. B., & Patterson, T. E. (1991). Clinical issues in mental health service delivery to refugees. *American Psychologist, 46,* 642–648.

Gorst, U. C. (1992). Adaptation after torture: Some thoughts on the long term effects of surviving a repressive regime. *Medicine and War, 8*(3), 164–168.

Johnson, P. (1989). Resources for coping with economic distress: The situation of unemployed Southeast Asian refugees. *Lifestyles: Family and Economic Issues, 10*(1), 18–43.

Kinzie, J. D., Boehnlein, J. K., Leung, P. K., Moore, L. J., Riley, C., & Smith, D. (1990). The prevalence of posttraumatic stress disorder and its clinical significance among Southeast Asian refugees. *American Journal of Psychiatry, 147,* 913–917.

Kinzie, J. D., Fredrickson, R. H., Ben, R., Fleck, J., & Karls, W. (1984). Posttraumatic stress disorder among survivors of Cambodian concentration camps. *American Journal of Psychiatry, 141,* 645–650.

Kleinman, S. B. (1990). Terror at sea: Vietnamese victims of piracy. *American Journal of Psychoanalysis, 50,* 351–362.

Kroll, J., Habenicht, M., Mackenzie, T., Yang, M., Chan, S., Vang, Y., Souvannasoth, L., & Cabugao, R. (1989). Depression and posttraumatic stress disorder in Southeast Asian refugees. *American Journal of Psychiatry, 146,* 1592–1597.

Le-Doux, C., & Stephens, K. S. (1992). Refugee and immigrant social service delivery: Critical management issues. *Journal of Multicultural Social Work, 2,* 31–45.

Lee, E., & Lu, F. (1989). Assessment and treatment of Asian-American survivors of mass violence. *Journal of Traumatic Stress, 2,* 93–120.

Lin, E. H., Carter, W. B., & Kleinman, A. M. (1985). An exploration of somatization among Asian refugees and immigrants in primary care. *American Journal of Public Health, 75,* 1080–1084.

Matsuoka, J. (1993). Demographic characteristics as determinants in qualitative differences in the adjustment of Vietnamese refugees. *Journal of Social Service Research, 17*(3/4), 1–21.

Mayadas, N. S., & Elliott, D. (1992). Integration and xenophobia: An inherent conflict in international migration. *Journal of Multicultural Social Work, 2,* 47–62.

Mollica, R. F., Caspi-Yavin, Y., Bollini, P., Truong, T., Tor, S., & Lavelle, J. (1992). The Harvard Ttrauma Questionnaire: Validating a cross-cultural instrument for measuring torture, trauma, and posttraumatic stress disorder in Indochinese refugees. *Journal of Nervous and Mental Disease, 180,* 111–116.

Mollica, R. F., Donelan, K., Tor, S., Lavelle, J., Elias, C., Frankel, M., & Blendon, R. J. (1993). The effect of trauma and confinement on functional health and mental health status of Cambodians living in Thailand–Cambodia border camps. *JAMA, 270,* 581–586.

Mollica, R. F., Wyshak, G., deMarneffe, D., Khuon, F., & Lavelle, J. (1987). Indochinese versions of the Hopkins Symptom Checklist-25: A screening instrument for the psychiatric care of refugees. *American Journal of Psychiatry, 144,* 497–500.

Mollica, R. F., Wyshak, G., & Lavelle, J. (1987). The psychiatric impact of war trauma and torture on Southeast Asian refugees. *American Journal of Psychiatry, 144,* 1567–1572.

Nicassio, P. M. (1985). The psychosocial adjustment of the Southeast Asian refugee: An overview of empirical findings and theoretical models. *Journal of Cross-Cultural Psychology, 16,* 153–173.

Norusis, M. J. (1988). *SPSSX advanced statistics guide* (2nd ed.). Chicago: SPSS.

Rumbaut, R. G. (1990). The agony of exile: A study of the migration and adaptation of Indochinese adults and children. In F. Ahearn & J. Garrison (Eds.), *Refugee children: Theory, research and practice.* Baltimore: Johns Hopkins University Press.

Uba, L., & Chung, R. C. (1991). The relationship between trauma and financial and physical well-being among Cambodians in the United States. *Journal of General Psychology, 118*(3), 215–225.

Westermeyer, J. (1986). Migration and psychopathology. In C. Williams & J. Westermeyer (Eds.), *Refugee mental health in resettlement countries* (pp. 113–130). Washington, DC: Hemisphere.

Westermeyer, J. (1988). DSM-III psychiatric disorders among Hmong refugees in the United States: A point prevalence study. *American Journal of Psychiatry, 145,* 197–202.

This research was conducted under the auspices of National Institute of Mental Health grant no. ITO-1MH19164, the Indochinese Psychiatry Clinic, and the Boston College Graduate School of Social Work.

47

Income, Language, and Citizenship Status: Factors Affecting the Health Care Access and Utilization of Chinese Americans

Michael H. Jang, Evelyn Lee, and Kent Woo

T wo decades of empirical research have demonstrated that numerous demographic and socioeconomic factors are related to health care access and use. Having health insurance is one of the more striking correlates to health-related behaviors and services (Feinstein, 1993; Hayward, Bernard, Freeman, & Corey, 1991; House, Kessler, & Herzog, 1990; Lambrew, DeFriese, Carey, Ricketts, & Biddle, 1996; Mandelblatt, Andrews, Kerner, Zauber, & Burnett, 1991; Stein, Fox, & Murata, 1991). The Office of Technology Assessment (U.S. Congress, 1992) conducted a thorough literature review regarding how the health insurance coverage affects utilization and health status. That review showed that, controlling for other factors, people without health insurance generally receive poorer health care services. More specialized studies have shown how health insurance affects physician recommendations (Mort, Edwards, Emmons, Convery, & Blumenthal, 1996), personal health status (Hahn & Flood, 1995), physician rather than hospital utilization (Hafner-Eaton, 1994), follow-up medical care (Kerr & Sui, 1993), and differential health care access by specified ethnic groups (Trevino, Trevino, Medina, Ramirez, & Ramirez, 1996).

Most studies examining access to health care by race or ethnicity concentrate on four general categories: white, African American (black), Hispanic, and "other" (Frazier, Jiles, & Mayberry, 1996; Manton, Patrick, & Johnson, 1987; Polednak, 1986; Trevino et al., 1996). Relatively little research has been conducted concerning health care access and health insurance in the Asian community, particularly for Chinese people living in the United States. Limited research has shown that socioeconomic factors such as lack of health insurance, inadequate formal education, and limited English language fluency have a strong effect on the Chinese population's use of health care services (Mayeno & Hirota, 1994). One study indicated that 23 percent of nonelderly Asian and Pacific Islanders and "others" living in California were not insured (Brown, Valdez, Morgenstern, Wang, & Mann, 1991). The 1989 Behavioral Risk Factor Survey of Chinese in

This chapter was originally published in the May 1998 issue of *Health & Social Work*, Vol. 23, pp. 136–145.

California (Centers for Disease Control [CDC], 1992) revealed that over half of the respondents' annual household incomes were below $10,000 and that 35 percent of Chinese people in Oakland, California, were without health insurance coverage. Education and English-language fluency can also strongly affect health care access in the Asian and Pacific Islander population. The CDC survey of Chinese in California indicated that 58 percent of Chinese people living in Oakland had an eighth-grade education or less. According to a survey in Chicago's Chinatown, 23 percent of respondents could read "a little" or "none" even in their native language (Yu, Huber, Wong, Tseng, & Liu, 1990). And the National Comparative Study of Minority Health Care (Commonwealth Fund, 1995) found that 22 percent of Asian Americans needed an interpreter when seeking health care services.

Most studies that examine "Asian" health care access aggregate all Asian and Pacific Islander subgroups together and do not specifically analyze the Chinese community. Asians as a group have typically not been disaggregated in previous studies. Using data that fail to make adequate distinctions among sociodemographic factors, particularly ethnic and cultural variables, greatly limits both public health research and service provision. As stated in the Behavioral Risk Factor Survey of Chinese (CDC, 1992), "differences reported in that survey underscored the need for tailored data collection approaches—such as characterizing ethnicity, nativity, income, insurance status, and language fluency—to accurately determine the health status of Asians and Pacific Islanders and other racial or ethnic groups" (p. 267). It is because of the need for more specific health-related data on San Francisco's Chinese community that this health study was undertaken. NICOS Chinese Health Coalition, a consortium of 25 health and social services agencies that serve Chinese people in San Francisco, commissioned the study to learn more about critical health care issues, barriers to services, and gaps in services to plan for the future. (The charter members of the group are Northeast Medical Services, Independent Physician Association, the Chinese Hospital, and Self-Help for the Elderly.)

This study examined several issues, including which segments of the Chinese population in San Francisco had a usual source of health care the types of health care respondents used, health care coverage, the factors associated with being uninsured, and the effects of being uninsured on health care access and utilization. This chapter addresses the policy implications of the findings for poor and uninsured individuals, particularly people of immigrant status, and concludes with suggestions for local health planners and advocates.

METHOD

The methods for this study consisted of three basic approaches: (1) focus groups with Chinese residents, (2) interviews with key informants, and (3) a comprehensive community telephone survey of a random sample of Chinese people living in San Francisco.

Focus Group

Research personnel conducted four focus groups with Chinese residents in San Francisco. The focus groups were designed to accomplish three objectives: (1) to interview those groups underrepresented in the community telephone survey, (2) to obtain ethnographic information that could help explain the telephone survey results, and (3) to learn more about health insurance and immigration issues than was possible in the telephone survey alone.

The number of participants per focus group ranged from three to six; the focus groups were conducted in Cantonese and English. The focus group format was semistructured; that is, a list of topic areas was used to guide the direction of the discussion. The content of the discussion, however, was not restricted to the special issues; all relevant concerns were entertained. Issues covered in the focus groups included participants' health insurance and immigration status, health utilization patterns, and experiences with the health care system in San Francisco. Participants were asked about their perceptions of health care for the Chinese community and the barriers that they had personally encountered. In addition, respondents were asked about their health-related behaviors as well as sociodemographic characteristics, such as county of origin.

Interviews with Key Informants

Research staff interviewed 25 key informants associated with San Francisco's health care system, particularly that segment of the system serving the Chinese community. An interview protocol was developed that focused on two primary areas: respondent information (training, roles, responsibilities, duration in present job, and time working with the target population) and health care service information (health insurance, estimated demand for specified services, gaps in services, barriers to service utilization, and most pressing health care issues). The protocols had approximately 35 semistructured questions and provided a way to collect consistent data across interviews and respondents while allowing flexibility. Interviewees included physicians, administrators, and other professionals from San Francisco's Chinese Hospital, North East Medical Services (a nonprofit clinic), elderly day care, long-term care agencies, public health centers, and private medical offices.

Community Telephone Survey

Because this research project sought to obtain generalizable data, we conducted a community household telephone survey. The study used a probability sample drawn from San Francisco residents over the age of 18 (except for people in institutions). The sampling procedure involved generating a set of telephone numbers specifically from the Chinese community. The telephone numbers were randomly selected from listings on PRO-PHONE, a database that contains all telephone numbers in the United States on CD-ROM. The survey used a sampling universe of approximately 50,000 telephone numbers matching 1,200 different Chinese surnames based on the 1990 census. A total of 1,808 residents of the Chinese community were eventually surveyed. The interviews were completed over a seven-week period from September 5 through October 20, 1996.

Paid interviewers administered the survey in English, Cantonese, and Mandarin. The survey instrument consisted of 65 questions and focused on a variety of health-related areas: health insurance, medical history, health-seeking behaviors, prenatal care, mental health, dental care, and knowledge of and opinions about specified community health services. In addition, the instrument secured sociodemographic data about the respondents. Many demographic variables, such as place of birth, years in the United States, level of acculturation, and immigration status, are often missing from national, state, and local data sets. These variables are important in analyzing the distribution of respondents across health-related behaviors and health care access. Most of the survey items were closed-ended to allow for precoded, direct entry. The formats used included simple yes–no responses, Likert-scaled responses, and other types of scales that foster the quantification of responses. To the extent feasible, standardized coding categories were established for open-ended questions.

Acculturation Index

The health care literature suggests that acculturation may be related to health care access. The research team therefore created an acculturation index, which totals the responses to seven questions about citizenship, language fluency, and respondents' attitudes about the United States and their native country. The index ranges from 0 = most acculturated to 7 = least acculturated.

Data Analysis

A database was created from the telephone interviews, and data verifications were performed. A statistical package, SPSS for Windows (Version 6.1), was used to generate frequency distributions, cross-tabulations, and other statistical analyses. To detect statistically significant differences among demographic characteristics, chi-square tests were performed on data, with unknown and refused categories excluded. A more sophisticated analytical technique, logistical regression, was also used to determine the odds ratios of various independent variables for respondents having no health insurance.

RESULTS

Demographic Profile of Respondents

A demographic profile of the 1,808 respondents is presented in Table 47-1. Several points stand out. First, only 18.3 percent of the respondents in the study were born in the United States. (However, if

Table 47-1

Demographic Characteristics of Chinese American Respondents (N = 1,808)

Characteristic	N	%	Characteristic	N	%
Gender			Education (*n* = 1,322)		
Male	843	46.6	8th grade or less	488	27.2
Female	965	53.4	Some high school	168	9.4
Age (years) (*n* = 1,760)			High school		
18–29	323	18.4	graduate/GED	414	23.1
30–39	337	19.1	Some college	256	14.3
40–49	345	19.6	College graduate	368	20.5
50–64	318	18.1	Graduate degree	99	5.5
65 and over	437	24.8	Household income ($)		
Marital status			(*n* = 1,322)		
Married	1,126	62.3	< 15,000	471	35.6
Widowed	167	9.2	15,000–29,999	362	27.4
Divorced	44	2.4	30,000–44,999	220	16.7
Separated	13	0.7	45,000–59,999	129	9.8
Single	457	25.4	60,000–75,000	60	4.5
Number 65 and over			> 75,000	80	6.1
in household			Year of entry into		
None	1,179	65.2	United States		
One	324	17.9	U.S. born	330	18.3
Two or more	305	16.9	Before 1950	41	2.3
Number under 18 in			1950–64	76	4.2
household			1965–69	78	4.3
None	1,104	61.1	1970–74	96	5.3
One or more	704	38.9	1975–79	196	10.8
Ownership or rental			1980–84	285	15.8
of dwelling			1985–90	478	26.4
Own	867	48.0	1991–96	228	12.6
Rent	897	49.6			
Other	44	2.4			
Citizenship status					
U.S. born	330	18.3			
Naturalized citizen	992	54.9			
Not a citizen	486	26.9			

NOTE: GED = general equivalency degree.

children under age 18 had been included in the sample, the percentage of U.S.-born respondents would have been substantially higher.) Second, almost one-fourth (24.8 percent) of the respondents were over 65 years old. And third, more than one-third (35.6 percent) of the respondents had an annual income of less than $15,000 per year.

Some relevant sociodemographic information secured in the survey is not presented in Table 47-1. For example, respondent data indicated that English-language fluency was limited for a large segment of San Francisco's Chinese community. Specifically, 71.8 percent (n = 349) of the noncitizen respondents stated that they spoke only Chinese at home; 55.8 percent (n = 554) of the naturalized citizens spoke only Chinese at home, and only 5.5 percent (n = 18) of the U.S.-born respondents spoke only Chinese at home.

Usual Source of Health Care

Overall, nearly four-fifths (79.5 percent, n = 1,453) of the respondents stated in the telephone survey that they had a usual source of health care. Having a regular source of health care was statistically related to immigration status. Almost nine of 10 (87.3 percent, n = 288) U.S.-born residents had a regular source of health care compared to 65.0 percent (n = 316) of noncitizens. Moreover, the more acculturated a person was, the greater the chance that he or she would have a usual health care source. However, the least acculturated respondents (6 and 7 on the Acculturation Index) did not conform to this pattern and had a relatively high probability of having a usual source of health care. This finding may result from the fact that respondents in this segment of the sample were older (mean age of 55) and poorer (median income less than $15,000) and thus were more likely to be covered by Medicare or Medi-Cal.

Respondents were asked why they did not have a regular health care source. Of the 307 respondents who reported not having a regular source of health care, 55.9 percent said that they simply had not needed a doctor, 48.9 percent reported that they had no health insurance, 45.1 percent said that they went to different places depending on the ailment, and 39.2 percent said that they did not have enough money. Other reasons included being new to the area, language difficulties, unavailability of a nearby clinic, and skeptical attitudes toward Western doctors. These other reasons grouped together applied to fewer than 10 percent of the respondents.

Respondents having a usual place to secure health care (n = 1,438) were asked to classify the source. The response choices included personal doctor, health clinic or health center, health maintenance organization (HMO), hospital other than HMO, and some "other" source. Overall, the largest group of people (43.2 percent) having a usual source of health care went to their personal doctor (Table 47-2). Almost one-fourth (23.2 percent) used an HMO, 17.9 percent went to hospitals other than an HMO, and 14.1 percent visited community clinics or health centers.

The upper-income, educated, and more acculturated respondents tended to seek health care from personal physicians or an HMO, whereas the lower-income and less acculturated respondents used community clinics and health centers. This same pattern applied to citizenship status. Noncitizens were over five times more likely to visit community clinics than were U.S.-born respondents; on the other hand, those born in the United States were more than three times as likely to receive health care from an HMO.

Table 47-2

Usual Source of Care for Chinese Americans, Percentage by Demographic Characteristic

Demographic Characteristic	Clinic or Health Center	HMO	Other Hospital	Personal Physician	Other
Total (*N* = 1,438)	14.1	23.2	17.9	43.2	1.5
Age (years)					
18–29	8.8	36.6	9.3	41.0	4.4
30–41	17.5	21.4	19.2	40.0	2.0
42–53	8.9	30.0	20.7	40.5	0
54–65	15.5	23.3	23.7	37.0	0.9
Over 65	17.5	12.1	15.2	54.4	0.8
Education					
8th grade or less	21.2	11.7	18.3	47.7	1.1
Some high school	17.6	29.6	15.2	37.6	0
High school graduate/GED	12.8	25.8	20.5	39.8	1.2
Some college	14.2	31.7	13.1	38.8	2.2
College graduate	7.5	27.5	16.0	46.1	3.0
Graduate degree	7.8	23.3	24.4	43.3	1.1
Household income ($)					
< 15,000	23.7	11.1	17.2	47.0	1.1
15,000–29,999	18.2	25.5	16.8	38.3	1.1
30,000–44,999	2.9	41.7	20.6	32.6	2.3
45,000–59,999	3.5	31.6	17.5	47.4	0
60,000–75,000	9.1	6.8	18.2	65.9	0
> 75,000	1.4	15.3	19.4	58.3	5.6
Citizenship status					
U.S. born	5.3	33.0	20.2	38.3	3.2
Naturalized citizen	12.4	24.9	17.1	45.0	0.7
Not a citizen	26.7	10.2	18.1	42.9	2.2
Acculturation index (mean)	4.67	4.06	4.11	4.18	3.45

NOTE: GED = general equivalency degree.

Health Insurance

Health insurance is clearly a central component of any analysis of health care. The telephone survey included the question, "Do you or anyone else in your family have any kind of insurance or medical coverage that pays for visits to the doctor (for your exams)?" Overall, 78.1 percent (*n* = 1,412) of the respondents indicated that they had some form of health insurance including 51.0 percent (*n* = 919) with private insurance and 25.6 percent (*n* = 450) with Medicare or Medi-Cal coverage (Table 47-3). Respondents over 65 were more likely to be insured (93.0 percent) than any other age group. Elderly people in California are most insured primarily because they benefit from Medicare and Medi-Cal programs. Generally, people with higher

Table 47-3

Number and Percentage of Chinese American Respondents with Health Insurance Coverage by Demographic Characteristic (N = 1,808)

Characteristic	N	Any Health Insurance		Medicare and/or Medi-Cal		Private Insurance	
		n	%	n	%	n	%
Total		1,412	78.1	450	24.9	919	50.8
Age (years)							
18–29	323	238	73.7	23	7.1	200	61.9
30–41	337	352	74.7	46	9.8	391	83.0
42–53	345	227	74.9	22	7.3	199	65.7
54–65	318	193	69.9	59	2.1	134	48.6
Over 65	437	360	93.0	300	77.5	61	15.8
Education (n = 1,793)							
8th grade or less	488	345	70.7	242	49.6	103	21.1
Some high school	168	111	66.1	35	20.8	74	44.0
High school graduate/GED	414	329	79.5	89	21.5	232	56.0
Some college	256	199	77.7	33	12.9	154	60.2
College graduate	368	326	88.6	39	10.6	275	74.7
Graduate degree	99	92	92.9	13	13.1	76	76.8
Household income ($) (n = 1,322)							
<15,000	471	349	74.1	273	58.0	74	15.7
15,000–29,999	362	237	65.5	66	18.2	165	45.6
30,000–44,999	220	181	82.3	16	7.3	163	74.1
45,000–59,999	129	123	95.3	5	3.9	113	87.6
60,000–75,000	60	56	93.3	3	5.0	47	78.3
>75,000	80	77	96.3	7	8.8	69	96.3
Citizenship status							
U.S.-born	330	306	92.7	39	11.8	258	78.2
Naturalized citizen	992	815	82.2	281	28.3	516	52.0
Not a citizen	486	291	59.9	137	28.2	489	29.8
Acculturation index (n = 1,803)[a]							
0 or 1	76	71	93.4	8	10.5	62	81.6
2 or 3	470	391	83.2	104	22.1	274	58.3
4 or 5	859	664	77.3	193	22.5	457	53.1
6 or 7	398	285	71.6	152	38.2	126	31.7

NOTE: GED = general equivalency degree.
[a] The index ranges from 0 = most acculturated to 7 = least acculturated

levels of education were more likely to have health insurance. Slightly more than nine of 10 (92.9 percent) graduate degree holders had some form of health insurance, followed by 88.6 percent of college graduates and 79.5 percent of high school graduates.

Barring people earning less than $15,000, increasing levels of income were associated with higher rates of insurance coverage. The over-$75,000 income earners led all other subgroups with an insurance coverage rate of 96.3 percent, whereas those in the $15,000-to-$30,000 bracket were the least insured (65.5 percent). A possible explanation for the under-$15,000 group having a higher rate of insurance (74.1 percent) than the $15,000-to-$30,000 group is that Medicare and Medi-Cal target the lower-income bracket. Indeed, 58.0 percent of the people in the lowest income bracket had Medicare or Medi-Cal coverage compared with only 18.2 percent of the $15,000-to-$30,000 group (Table 47-3).

U.S.-born respondents were most likely to have health insurance (92.7 percent), followed by naturalized citizens (82.2 percent) and noncitizens (59.9 percent). This difference may be the result of the greater acculturation of U.S. citizens, their greater incomes, and their better access to and knowledge of the health care system. A clear negative trend exists between the acculturation index and the rate of health insurance; people who were less acculturated were much less likely to have insurance. Slightly fewer than three-fourths (71.6 percent) of those with an acculturation index score of 6 or 7 had insurance compared with 93.4 percent of those with a score of 0 or 1.

Most of the 450 recipients of Medicare or Medi-Cal or both were over 65 (77.5 percent), had an 8th grade education or less (49.6 percent), and belonged to households earning less than $15,000 per year (58.0 percent). U.S.-born respondents were least likely to collect Medicare or Medi-Cal (11.8 percent of U.S.-born respondents compared to 28.2 percent of noncitizens), and those least acculturated were most likely to receive these entitlements (38.2 percent).

Private insurance covered about half (50.8 percent) of respondents. The age group with the highest rate of private insurance was the 30-to-41-year-old group (83.0 percent). The fact that private insurance coverage often is work related may explain why certain age groups are more likely to have this form of insurance. As age increased, the rate of private insurance dropped and bottomed out at 15.8 percent of the respondents over 65.

Private insurance is strongly tied to education. Graduate degree holders had the highest private insurance rates at 76.8 percent, whereas those with the least education had the lowest insurance rates (21.1 percent) (Table 47-3). Income was similarly correlated with private insurance. Moreover, the more acculturated the respondent, the more likely he or she was to have private insurance. And citizenship was related to having health insurance. More than three-fourths (78.2 percent) of the U.S.-born respondents had private health insurance, compared with 29.8 percent of the noncitizen respondents.

Uninsured Respondents

People without health insurance are potentially in situations that threaten their health. It is therefore important to examine how and where these people obtain their health care. The insured respondents were more than twice as likely as the uninsured respondents to have a usual source of health care (Table 47-4). Examining types of care, respondents with insurance depended on the following places for regular care (in order of use): personal doctors (44.6 percent), HMOs (26.0 percent), other hospitals (18.5 percent), and community clinic or health centers (9.9 percent). On the other hand, uninsured respondents used community clinics or health centers first (44.1 percent), followed by personal doctors (33.3 percent), and other hospitals (14.1 percent). These data only include people who had usual places for health care. Interviews with users and providers suggested that uninsured respondents who did not have usual places for care were likely to visit community clinics or health centers, including the emergency room at the county hospital.

Although most uninsured respondents relied on Western doctors first, a larger percentage (compared to those insured) used herbalists

Table 47-4

Health Care Practices of Insured and Uninsured Chinese American Respondents ($N = 1,808$)

Variable	Insured (%)	Uninsured (%)
Has usual place to go when sick	89.5	43.9
Place for usual care		
Clinic or health center	9.9	44.1
HMO	26.0	4.0
Other hospital	18.5	14.1
Personal physician	44.6	33.3
Other	1.2	4.5
Where respondent goes first when sick		
Western trained doctor	82.8	56.6
Herbalist	2.7	8.3
Chinese medicine doctor	5.0	16.4
Nowhere	3.9	12.1
Other	5.6	6.6
Check-up with Western trained doctor in past year	76.4	42.2
Visit to dentist in past year	66.2	29.8
Prostate examination in past two years (men)	26.3	6.5
Breast examination in past two years (women)	59.8	36.3
Pap smear in past two years (women)	62.0	37.2
Health care satisfaction		
Very satisfied	18.8	5.9
Satisfied	58.5	41.9
Somewhat satisfied	19.9	36.6
Not at all satisfied	2.8	15.5

and Chinese medicine doctors. Almost one-fourth (24.7 percent) of uninsured respondents depended on herbalists or Chinese medicine doctors or both when first sick, whereas only 7.7 percent of insured respondents did. Moreover, the respondents generally used a mixture of Chinese and Western health practices to take care of their health needs. For example, 54 percent of the respondents reported that they took soup with Chinese herbal medicine in it at least once a week. Thirty-five percent of the respondents said that they took a Chinese herb or tonic at least once a week. Finally, 43 percent of the respondents reported that home remedies were as good as Western medicine for minor health problems.

Proportionately, insured respondents typically received two or three times more regular check-ups, dental exams, and early detection tests (clinical breast examinations, Pap smears, and prostate examinations) than the uninsured respondents. These facts are of great concern because the costs (to the individual and society) of preventive, routine treatment are usually much less than the costs of the future ailments that could have been prevented or mitigated. Finally, the insured respondents were more likely than the uninsured to be satisfied with the health care they had received.

Factors Associated with Being Uninsured

To get a clearer understanding of what factors are associated with being uninsured, the study used logistical regression analysis (Table 47-5). The dependent variable was whether respondents were

Table 47-5

Logistical Regression Results for Having No Insurance (N = 1,288)

Independent Variable	Odds Ratio	95% CI
Household income ($)		
< 15,000	4.61**	2.22, 6.99
15,000–29,999	4.71**	2.39, 7.03
30,000–44,999	2.41*	0.01, 4.80
45,000–60,000	0.85	–2.28, 3.97
Education		
8th grade or less	1.45	–0.24, 3.13
Some high school	1.30	–0.50, 3.10
High school graduate/GED	1.07	–0.59, 2.74
Some college	1.10	–0.65, 2.85
Not a U.S. citizen	1.45**	0.06, 2.85
Time living in United States	0.96**	–0.06, 1.98
Speaks Chinese only	2.00**	0.50, 3.50
Age	0.97**	–0.04, 1.98
Concordant % (correctly predicted outcomes)	79	

NOTE: CI = confidence interval, GED = general equivalency degree.
$*p < .05. **p < .01.$

uninsured, and the independent variables were income, education, noncitizenship, time spent in the United States, English language skill (speaking only Chinese at home), and age. The income and education baseline category groups were incomes over $60,000 and college graduation.

Everything else being equal, the people with lower incomes were much more likely to lack health insurance. Relative to the over-$60,000 income bracket, those earning $30,000 to $45,000 were 2.4 times more likely to be uninsured; people in households with incomes under $30,000 were 4.7 times more likely to not have insurance (compared to the over-$60,000 group) (Table 47-5). Younger people had greater odds of being uninsured. Education failed to have a significant effect.

Lack of acculturation appeared to be strongly related to not having health insurance; noncitizens had a 45 percent greater chance of being uninsured than did citizens. People who only spoke Chinese had twice the odds of having no insurance. And for each additional year the respondent lived in the United States, the likelihood of having insurance increased by 4 percent.

Perception of Social Problems

To develop a sense of the quality of life experienced by the target population, respondents were asked whether they thought any of the following eight social issues were a problem in the San Francisco Chinese community: drinking, gambling, illegal drugs, mental health problems, domestic violence, elder abuse, child abuse, and gangs.

Each of the eight social issues was felt to be a problem in San Francisco's Chinese community by over one-third of the survey respondents (Table 47-6). Gambling, gangs, and illegal drugs were perceived as the three biggest problems. More than two-thirds of the respondents (69.6 percent) felt that gambling was a problem; just under two-thirds (65.8 percent) felt that gangs were a problem, and slightly fewer than half (46.3 percent) believed that illegal drugs were a problem. The three social issues least perceived as problems by the survey

Table 47-6

Chinese American Respondents' Ranking of Social Problems in the San Francisco Chinese Community (N = 1,808)

Social Problem	n	%
Gambling	1,258	69.6
Gangs	1,190	65.8
Illegal drugs	837	46.3
Domestic violence	803	44.4
Drinking	758	41.9
Elderly abuse	711	39.3
Mental health problems	678	37.5
Child abuse	650	36.0

respondents were elder abuse (39.3 percent), mental health problems (37.5 percent), and child abuse (36.0 percent).

CONCLUSION

Health care and social services providers face numerous challenges in meeting the health and wellness needs of Chinese Americans. In designing a strategy of care for this population, providers must understand that poverty, limited English skills, and noncitizenship status all serve as significant barriers to access and use. Providers must also consider the population's unique cultural beliefs and practices as well as address its most pressing social concerns.

A strategy to increase accessibility and use of health care services among Chinese Americans may well begin by creating health plans that are affordable; linguistically and culturally appropriate; and, in the case of a public plan, nondiscriminatory based on citizenship status. A large proportion of the population are working poor people (63 percent of survey respondents lived in households earning $30,000 or less annually), who are often locked out of the health care system because the industries in which they are employed do not offer insurance. A truly effective strategy would reach out to this sizable group, which is neither wealthy enough to purchase insurance individually nor poor enough to qualify for public benefits.

Linguistically and culturally appropriate outreach and services are essential as well. Much of the population is foreign-born (81 percent of survey respondents were immigrants), and many among them speak only Chinese. Thus, educational workshops—on understanding managed care or practicing basic preventive care—should be available in Chinese. The use of bilingual and bicultural care providers and interpreters in health care settings is also important. Moreover, a health plan honoring the population's cultural practices should be investigated (the majority of respondents reported taking Chinese herbal medicine at least weekly). A plan that allows a client to seek the services of a Chinese herbalist in addition to the services of a Western-trained doctor warrants exploration.

The question of who will care for the many noncitizens within the Chinese American population looms large. Already, 40 percent of noncitizen survey respondents reported having no insurance. This percentage will likely increase as welfare reform is implemented, stripping many noncitizens of state and federal medical benefits and preventing newly arrived immigrants from gaining access to them. Citizenship classes offer a partial solution. Perhaps greater advocacy work should be done to reverse this policy altogether.

Finally, researchers and providers should begin gathering data on and developing treatment strategies for gambling as an addiction among this population. Nearly 70 percent of survey respondents identified gambling as a problem in the Chinese community. For years, through anecdotal information, social workers have linked gambling to the destruction of many of the community's families and individuals. Despite its notoriety, little research has been done to examine the problem, and a culturally relevant remedy has yet to be created.

REFERENCES

Brown, E. R., Valdez, R. B., Morgenstern, H., Wang, C., & Mann, J. (1991). *Health insurance coverage of California in 1989*. Paper presented at California Policy Seminar, University of California, Berkeley.

Centers for Disease Control. (1992). Behavioral Risk Factor Survey of Chinese in California 1989. *Morbidity and Mortality Weekly Report, 41*, 266–270.

Commonwealth Fund National. (1995). *Comparative survey of minority health care.* New York: Author.

Feinstein, J. S. (1993). The relationship between socioeconomic status and health: A review of the literature. *Milbank Quarterly, 71*, 279–322.

Frazier, E. L., Jiles, R. B., & Mayberry, R. (1996). Use of screening mammography and clinical breast examinations in Black, Hispanic, and White women. *Preventive Medicine, 25*, 118–125.

Hafner-Eaton, C. (1994). Patterns of hospitalization and physician utilization among the uninsured. *Journal of Health Care for the Poor and Underserved, 5*, 291–310.

Hahn, B., & Flood, A. B. (1995). No insurance, public insurance, and private insurance: Do these options contribute to differences in general health? *Journal of Health Care for the Poor and Underserved, 6*, 41–59.

Hayward, R. A., Bernard, A. M., Freeman, H. E., & Corey, C. R. (1991). Regular source of ambulatory care and access to health services. *American Journal of Public Health, 81*, 434–438.

House, J. S., Kessler, R. C., & Herzog, A. R. (1990). Age, socioeconomic status, and health. *Milbank Quarterly, 68*, 383–411.

Kerr, E. A., & Sui, A. L. (1993). Follow-up after hospital discharge: Does insurance make a difference? *Journal of Health Care for the Poor and Underserved, 4*, 133–142.

Lambrew, J. M., DeFriese, G. H., Carey, T. S., Ricketts, T. C., & Biddle, A. K. (1996). The effects of having a regular doctor on access to primary care. *Medical Care, 34*, 138–151.

Mandelblatt, J., Andrews, H., Kerner, J., Zauber, A., & Burnett, W. (1991). Determinants of late stage diagnosis of breast and cervical cancer: The impact of age, race, social class, and hospital type. *American Journal of Public Health, 81*, 646–649.

Manton, K. G., Patrick, C. H., & Johnson, K. W. (1987). Health differentials between blacks and whites: Recent trends in mortality and morbidity. *Milbank Quarterly, 65*(Suppl. 1), 129–199.

Mayeno, L., & Hirota, S. M. (1994). Access to health care. In N.W.S. Zane, D. T. Takeuchi, & K.N.J. Young (Eds.), *Confronting critical health issues of Asian and Pacific Islander Americans* (pp. 347–375). Thousand Oaks, CA: Sage Publications.

Mort, E. A., Edwards, J. N., Emmons, D. W., Convery, K., & Blumenthal, D. (1996). Physician response to patient insurance status in ambulatory care clinical decision making. *Medical Care, 34*, 783–797.

Polednak, A. B. (1986). Breast cancer in black and white women in New York State: Case distribution and incidence rates by clinical stage at diagnosis. *Cancer, 58*, 807–815.

Stein, J. A., Fox, S. A., & Murata, P. J. (1991). The influence of ethnicity, socioeconomic status, and psychological barriers on use of mammography. *Journal of Health and Social Behavior, 32*, 101–113.

Trevino, R. P., Trevino, E. M., Medina, R., Ramirez, G., & Ramirez, R. R. (1996). Health care access among Mexican Americans with different health insurance coverage. *Journal of Health Care for the Poor and Underserved, 7*, 112–121.

U.S. Congress, Office of Technology Assessment. (1992). *Does health insurance make a difference?* (Background paper OTA-BP-H-99). Washington, DC: U.S. Government Printing Office.

Yu, E., Huber, W., Wong, S., Tseng, G., & Liu, W. (1990). *Survey of health coverage needs in Chicago's Chinatown: A final report.* San Diego, CA: Pacific/Asian Mental Health Research Center.

48 Resettlement: A Cultural and Psychological Crisis

Phyllis Hulewat

Resettlement is a life crisis. Leaving behind all that is familiar and starting a new life in a new country with a different language and culture produces an immediate family crisis that can have long-term effects. This is true whether a family is coming from Europe, the Far East, or Central America.

When trying to help families cope with the stresses of resettlement, three central concepts need to be addressed. The first concept is the stages of resettlement. Five stages of resettlement have been identified, with different emotional and concrete tasks necessary for the completion of each stage. The second concept is the cultural styles and psychological dynamics of the population being resettled. The degree to which those dynamics create internal dissonance or consonance in the immigrant as he or she attempts to adjust to life in the United States is significant in determining how the resettlement process will proceed. The third concept is the individual dynamics of the family. Each family brings its own cultural understanding as it has been processed through the unique life experiences of its members. These individual dynamics affect the family's ability to tolerate cultural dissonance and to manage the tasks necessary to proceed through the stages of resettlement.

These elements can be seen clearly in all resettlement populations. In this chapter, the Soviet Jewish resettlement experience is used to demonstrate how understanding and identifying these elements as they operate in a particular population affect how services can be designed that help clients deal with personal crises as they adjust to their new lives. Although the Soviet Union no longer exists, for the purposes of this chapter, the families are referred to as Soviet Jews because many of them immigrated before the fall of the Soviet Union, and all were acculturated under the Soviet system.

The understanding of the Soviet culture and the immigration experiences described in this chapter are based on the experiences of the Cleveland Jewish Family Service Association's resettlement of approximately 1,000 Soviet Jews each year between 1979 and 1981 and between 1989 and 1993. The families that resettled between 1979 and 1981 were largely from Russia and Ukraine. The families that resettled

This chapter was originally published in the March 1996 issue of *Social Work*, Vol. 41, pp. 129–135.

between 1989 and 1993 were largely from Russia, Ukraine, and Uzbekistan. During these two periods the Cleveland Jewish Family Service Association was involved with the case management tasks of helping families find housing, connecting them to services, providing acculturation services, and helping them navigate the bureaucracies of their new country. In addition, clinical services were provided to help families deal with the transitional stresses of immigration as well as a whole range of emotional and relationship issues. The most prevalent problems identified were marital conflict, depression, and either anxious and withdrawn or acting out children and adolescents.

The psychological and cultural dynamics characteristic of many Soviet Jews, combined with the crisis of the immigration experience, create dilemmas for the Soviet family that can make the resettlement experience difficult and painful. The dilemma for the worker is how to address the practical and the emotional issues quickly and effectively. If both issues are addressed, the worker can establish a trusting relationship with an untrusting client. Such a trusting relationship can be sustained through the inevitable anger and disappointment that occurs in the resettlement process.

STAGES OF RESETTLEMENT

Sluzki (1979) identified a clear progression of stages for resettlement. The first stage is the preimmigration or preparatory stage, when the decision to leave is struggled with and made. *Splitting*, an adaptive tool often used at this stage, is a defensive maneuver used to protect against intolerable feelings. A toddler first uses splitting to stay connected to his or her mother when he or she is frustrated. The toddler has not yet developed the ability to see both good and bad in one love object, so the angry feelings are split off, and the mother is seen as either all good or all bad. In later life, maladaptive splitting can be seen in adults who can sustain only attachments that they view as perfect. As soon as the inevitable disappointment occurs, the love object becomes an object of hate. There is no middle ground; these adults have never learned to tolerate ambivalence.

At times of stress, splitting can be used as an adaptive mechanism. Idealizing the future and denigrating the past make leaving easier. Understanding how a particular family made the decision to leave can be important in understanding how they will adjust to resettlement.

It is important to stress that although splitting has pathological connotations, especially in relation to its use by individuals with borderline personality disorders, in the context of resettlement splitting can be a healthy defensive maneuver in the face of the traumatic event of immigration. The use of splitting by immigrants does not indicate a characterological problem. This is a slightly different way of thinking about splitting; rather than being an ever-present defense against the intolerable feelings of the disintegration of self as in the person with borderline personality disorder, splitting is a temporary defense against a transitory crisis.

The second stage of resettlement is the actual migration. This experience can be very different for different populations. Soviets who now come directly from Moscow have no transition time to adjust. As difficult as refugee camps can be, the one thing they do offer is transition time.

The third stage of resettlement is the arrival in a new home. This is an exhilarating and exhausting experience, and during this stage people are often unaware of the cumulative effects of the stress they have been under. The tasks associated with this stage are straightforward, and at this point efficiency is valued more than sensitivity. The dominant mood is anxiety and optimism, although an anxious depression may occur as a result of looking for a job and learning a language. Splitting is still very much in evidence at this stage and is the primary defense. As a consequence, the world and the resettlement workers are seen in black-and-white terms. Splitting can still be functional at this time, although it can quickly become dysfunctional if rigidified. This third stage is the stage of resettlement in which resettlement workers are usually the most active.

The fourth stage of resettlement is decompensation. During this period, the family will begin to realize and experience the loss it has suffered. This is a time to make peace, and the ability to balance the past and the present is crucial. At this stage each individual needs to let go of splitting as a defense and reacquire his or her ambivalence. This process may take up to three years or longer.

The fifth and final stage of resettlement is the transgenerational stage, in which unresolved conflicts from the immigration experience are passed on to succeeding generations. According to Golan (1981), "Sometimes the conflict raised by the migration transition can become attenuated or subsided for years only to emerge when the second generation, raised in the country of adoption, picks up what the first generation has heretofore avoided and makes it the theme of a clash between generations" (p. 112).

PSYCHOLOGICAL AND CULTURAL ISSUES

Every immigrant population brings with it unique cultural and psychological dynamics that affect how smoothly the immigrants will resettle. As an example, an analysis of the Soviet Jewish family and culture shows how these dynamics affect resettlement: "Several related themes which can be seen as general characteristics of Soviet family life and dynamics are family enmeshment and lack of autonomous functioning accompanied by incomplete object constancy and difficulty in managing ambivalent feelings" (Hulewat, 1981, p. 53).

Although these characteristics are, of course, broad generalizations and families fall along a wide continuum, the child-rearing practices of Soviet Jews tend to foster enmeshment. It has been the author's experience that Soviet mothers tend to support the dependent side of a child's ambivalence about separation and individuation. This support increases the feelings of omnipotence that the child may experience. The result for some of these children is that they believe they must and can control their mothers because that is the only way to get their needs met. Independent functioning can possibly lead to rejection. "The result is a tendency toward depression and despair, a continued struggle to assert one's feelings of omnipotence and entitlement and prolonged use of the defense of splitting" (Hulewat, 1981, p. 54).

The child-rearing practices that led to this enmeshment were supported by a culture and political system that encouraged splitting and discouraged autonomous functioning. Authoritarian governments do not support the development of internal controls but rather enforce external controls. For Soviet families, financial and emotional dependence on one another was a matter of survival. The world was divided into those who can be trusted and those who cannot be trusted. Thus, splitting and enmeshment were adaptive and enhanced functioning in the former Soviet Union. Also, because there are limited opportunities for Soviet Jews and being a Jew is seen as negative, the Soviet Jew's sense of self becomes invested in his or her career, and status becomes attached to achievements. This view adds additional barriers to the development of self-esteem.

The Soviet Jew's experience in Soviet society and in the Soviet Jewish family work together to encourage those personality characteristics. In resettlement services these characteristics can be seen in clients ranging from those with severely dysfunctional borderline personalities to those in a regressed dependent and anxious state to those who function effectively but may have some tendency toward low self-esteem and the need to maintain compensatory mechanisms.

BEGINNING OF RESETTLEMENT WORK

"Crisis is the turning point at which things will either get better or get worse. . . . In Chinese, the word 'crisis' is made-up of characters for 'danger' and 'opportunity.' Certainly crisis is a dangerous opportunity" (Pittman, 1987, p. 3). Resettlement is an experience that throws a family into a state of crisis that offers them a wide range of opportunities and exposes them to many risks. Viewing resettlement as a crisis, to be managed as any crisis, gives the worker a framework within which to plan how to be helpful. According to Pittman, "To treat families in crisis one must have an air of calm urgency, a clear sense of the nature of the world and how things work, impatient tolerance for people who prefer chaos to change and optimism that life is an exciting series of adventurous obstacles" (p. 27).

When an immigrant family first comes to see their resettlement worker, they are filled with great anxiety and excitement. They are grateful to be in the United States and are anxious to please their worker. They are confused and frightened but usually optimistic and eager to begin their new lives.

The beginning focus for the worker is to welcome the family and get to know them. Most families come with many questions but cannot fully comprehend the answers. At this point, it is imperative that the worker present himself or herself as calm, confident, knowledgeable, and caring. Presenting too much information can overwhelm the family. It is more useful to give clients as much information as possible in writing to be reviewed at later appointments and to spend the first appointment discussing practical realities. Although several things need to be accomplished in the first interview, the primary task is to establish a relationship. In getting to know the client, the focus of the conversation initially will be on how and why the decision to emigrate was made and what losses resulted from making that decision. This discussion also needs to involve the clients' expectations of their new life in America. Other tasks for this first interview include providing information and anticipating with the client what is to come. All these tasks are dealt with in a way that sets the tone for future contact.

Several themes permeate the entire resettlement experience for all Soviet immigrants. From the cultural perspective, it is important for the worker to recognize that he or she may be perceived as an authoritarian figure to be mistrusted and manipulated. From the psychological perspective, the worker may be viewed as omnipotent and as having the power to make the resettlement process a smooth or rough experience, and clients may feel that how they deal with the worker may determine whether the process is smooth or rough. Understanding that the clients are in the third stage of the immigration process alerts the worker to the likelihood that they are using splitting as a defense mechanism and are very task oriented. In addition to understanding all of these perspectives, the worker should anticipate that the client is in a state of crisis and therefore may be regressed.

For example, Mr. and Mrs. V came in to demand that they be given a separate apartment for Mr. V's mother, with whom they had been resettled. Mr. and Mrs. V were both working part-time, but with Mr. V's mother's Supplemental Security Income check they could be financially independent from the Jewish community. The worker discussed the availability of subsidized housing for Mr. V's mother but said that the family could separate only when they could afford it on their own. They were outraged, feeling that they had suffered in the Soviet Union and that the worker and the community owed them a better life. The worker maintained the community's position, which supports the clients' ability to master their environment and be in charge of their own lives. However, the worker also empathized with the clients' wish to live separately and to be cared for and focused on the stress of living together. Once the family accepted the clearly restated community stance, with clear expectations from the worker, who supported their competency and assisted them in mourning the losses of resettlement, Mr. V got a full-time job and the family was able to separate.

It is important to communicate to the family that although the worker is there to help the family in their adjustment and the worker understands their anxiety, there will be times when they may feel that the worker does not seem to understand. Because most clients at this stage of resettlement are using splitting as a defense mechanism, the tendency is to see the worker as good when he or she is doing as the client asks and bad when he or she is not. It is essential that the worker begin discussing from the very beginning how he or she may disappoint the client and how it is important that the relationship sustain that disappointment. Tolerating ambivalence is a key task of the resettlement process as well as a central issue for Soviet clients. It also needs to be a central focus of resettlement work, and it begins with the client–worker relationship.

This discussion of the worker–client relationship parallels the discussion of the losses that accompany immigration. Disappointment in the worker represents the clients' recognition that the United States may not be all they expected. As long as they can blame their worker for their difficulties, they can maintain splitting, keep their ideal view of the United States, and denigrate their country of origin to deny their losses.

Discussing the losses within the worker–client relationship begins the process of helping clients tolerate their ambivalence. G was an elderly woman who immigrated with her daughter and her daughter's family. She developed a warm relationship with her worker, who helped her find an apartment in a subsidized building for elderly people. The worker received a call from the building management shortly after G moved in to report that G had paid only half of her rent. The worker called G, who became very angry, insisted she had paid the rent in full, and accused the worker of extorting money from her. The worker was stunned and hurt but responded by reminding G of their good relationship and addressing G's worries about how she would manage to live independently.

G's initial anxiety about needing more rent money resulted in splitting. The worker was the bearer of bad news and therefore was seen as "bad," even though she had been "good" when she had found G the apartment. It was essential to discuss how G's worry that she could lose her apartment related to losses as a result of resettlement and to restate that the nature of the worker–client relationship included implementing policies as well as appreciating G's feelings about those policies. Then G was able to apologize to the worker and reacquire her tolerance of ambivalence.

THREE KINDS OF ADJUSTMENT

As the weeks passed after arrival, certain groups of immigrants tended to emerge along a continuum of how well they managed to deal with the issues of loss and dependence. The first and largest group, identified as the "help me get started" group, were those who were truly eager to gain control of their lives and move ahead to become independent. The second largest group, identified as the "take care of me" group, were those who were regressed to a dependent state in a way that created a control struggle. The focus of their energy was to get their worker to take care of them. They presented as entitled and grandiose. After a period of struggle, with sound case management, this group would reconstitute their defenses and successfully resettle. The smallest group, identified as the "you must do it my way" group, were those who could not give up the control battle and who remained rigidly committed to having the community meet all of their needs. Their need to control the worker and manipulate the system to get all their needs met took precedence over getting on with their lives. They were often borderline individuals who could not tolerate loss and who needed to continually assert the fantasy of their omnipotence. A fourth group—clients with problems such as illness, marital stress, family dysfunction, or depression in addition to resettlement issues—is not addressed in this chapter.

"Help Me Get Started"

As the first few months pass, the realities of the immigrants' new life begin to sink in. For the largest group of clients, this will stir up a great deal of conflict as splitting becomes less effective and they vacillate between anger and depression. They may be coming to terms with their inability to find employment in their fields, the difficulty of learning English, their financial hardship, or their sadness about who and what they left behind. This is a crucial point in the worker–client relationship. At the same time a client is dealing with his or her sadness and anger because an entry-level job or factory job is all that is available, the worker needs to affirm the need for the client to find work as soon as possible. This can only be done if a trusting relationship has been established.

The task of the resettlement worker is to be a caring, supportive authority figure who supports and encourages independence. This has not been the experience of many immigrants who come to the United States. Taking a stance toward independence can create confusion and even anxiety, but for most clients who function very well when not in a crisis, this stance promotes growth. Prolonged dependence on either community support or welfare retards the resettlement process. Furthermore, it inhibits people in getting on with their lives. The need for early employment, when discussed in the context of the client gaining control of his or her life, becoming independent, learning English quickly, becoming familiar with American culture, and getting American job experience, is often viewed as helpful. When the issue of independence is communicated with caring and patience, the client is better able to deal with it, and dealing with this issue enhances the client's ability to tolerate ambivalence.

"Take Care of Me"

In the second group of clients, tolerating ambivalence is much more difficult. This group of clients is clearly regressed. They are likely to insist that they will not take a job outside their field, that they must study, that they will not live with their in-laws or parents, or that they need more financial assistance. They feel entitled and can be either very ingratiating or provocative. Soviet clients are also likely to push the system, insisting on meeting with supervisors and administrators. They are committed to the dependent side of their ambivalence. The task for the worker is to stress the importance of independence and self-sufficiency in the face of the clients' anger or pleading. The worker must not be manipulated or provoked but must patiently and repeatedly affirm the clients' strengths and appeal to the side of their ambivalence with which they have lost touch: the need to be competent and to master their environment. Giving in to their wish for dependence can encourage the continuation of splitting and therefore delay resolution of the resettlement crisis. Workers who represent the other side of these clients' ambivalence while acknowledging and empathizing with their wish to be taken care of will usually help them reconstitute their defenses and move on to a successful resettlement. Their demands are often an effort to deal with loss by seeking restitution in a narcissistic, entitled way. It is very important that the worker be capable of carefully and realistically assessing the appropriateness or inappropriateness of the clients' demands.

For example, D was a 48-year-old mother with a 23-year-old daughter. D was what is referred to as a "free case," or one in which an arriving family has no relatives in the United States and the community accepts responsibility for their support. D was still married, but she left her husband in the Soviet Union. Because of the kind of work her husband did, he could not receive permission to leave, and the couple decided that to give their daughter a better life, D and her daughter should immigrate without D's husband. They hoped that some day he would be able to follow. D was an accountant in the Soviet Union, and her daughter was a student. Neither spoke English.

D presented in a highly anxious state, expressing her belief that as a single mother she was entitled to extra help. During her first visit with the resettlement worker, she presented only with anxiety in the form of complaints. Her apartment was too far away and too small. She did not have enough furniture. She was afraid to take the bus. Her endless questions were about how to get the worker and the community to take care of her. The worker told D that experience shows that when competent people such as herself remain dependent, their anxiety is prolonged rather than relieved. D and her daughter had to hear this message many times, from the supervisor as well as the worker. Five months after her arrival, D was beginning to make friends in the community. She no longer presented as needy and was taking pride in her ability to get around independently.

"You Must Do It My Way"

The third and smallest category of resettlement clients often consumes most of the worker's time. These clients are committed to establishing control over the worker and the community to have their needs met. The battle takes precedence over the outcome. For these clients, when the worker disagrees with what they want, it is a call to arms, because the need to control is the issue. For the client in the "take care of me" group, the struggle to control is only a means to an end. For this group, it is the end. These are people who deal with fear and anxiety by trying to control and be omnipotent. They were probably troubled all their lives, but the resettlement experience triggered a severe regression. These clients may begin as ingratiating but soon become belligerent. It is very important for the worker not to engage in battle with these clients but rather to accept their resistance. That is, community policy must be stated and adhered to, and the worker must continually acknowledge to the client that he or she is providing this information to the client and that the client may choose to do what he or she wishes with that information—that only he or she is in control of what will happen. Clients in this category spend a great deal of time finding people in the community who will support their cause, often school officials, doctors, or neighbors. Often these families need to move to another community with their splitting still intact so that their first community of resettlement becomes the bad community. Only in a new community can they begin to settle down.

M was a single mother, age 54, with three children in their twenties. When met at the airport, M presented as helpless and very anxious. The worker's immediate response was to try to ease the family's anxiety and let them know that everything would be alright. They came from a small town in an Asian Republic and were quite lost in the big city.

During the first interview M presented as quite helpless but eager to cooperate. She claimed that she and her children were all willing to work. Very shortly afterward, however, it became evident that M did not want to go to work and did not want her children to go to work. All of them turned down job offers. When confronted, M claimed to be a poor, frightened, single mother with three children whom the community should care for. After continued refusal to cooperate in finding work, M was taken off community assistance, and the Department of Human Services was notified that the family was ineligible for welfare because they refused to go to work. This was presented to the family as a community decision that would be reversed if at least one of them would accept employment. M accused the worker of persecuting her and leaving her and her family to starve. The worker presented the community position calmly and let M know that she could choose how she wanted to live.

The agency began receiving calls almost daily from M and from angry people in the community calling on her behalf. Much of the worker's time was spent clarifying agency policy to the callers from the community. Eventually, M and her family left the city. She had become so entrenched in the battle that she could not let go of the fight. The community to which M and her family moved was notified of their behavior so that they could prepare to work with her.

CONCLUSION

Resettlement can present opportunity in the form of economic and emotional freedom as well as risk in the form of regression and rigid resistance to growth and change. Although this chapter focuses on the experiences of Soviet Jews in particular, the issues are international in scope. Each cultural group faces crises and manages losses differently, and workers dealing with immigrants need to understand how their particular clients are managing their losses and their ambivalence.

REFERENCES

Golan, N. (1981). *Passing through transitions: A guide for practitioners.* New York: Free Press.

Hulewat, P. (1981). Dynamics of the Soviet Jewish family: Its impact on clinical practice for the Jewish Family Agency. *Journal for Jewish Communal Service, 58,* 5–60.

Pittman, F. S. III. (1987). *Turning points: Treating families in transition and crisis.* Toronto: Penguin Books.

Sluzki, C. E. (1979). Migration and family conflict. *Family Process, 18,* 379–390.

A previous version of this chapter was presented at the Annual Meeting of the Conference of Jewish Communal Workers, June 3, 1991, Montreal.

Index

About the Editors

Patricia L. Ewalt, PhD, *is dean and professor, School of Social Work, University of Hawaii, Honolulu. She has an MSW from Simmons College School of Social Work and a PhD in health care policy, research, and administration from the Florence Heller School for Advanced Studies in Social Welfare, Brandeis University, Waltham, Massachusetts. She was the editor of* Social Work *from 1993 to 1997.*

Edith M. Freeman, PhD, *is professor, University of Kansas School of Social Welfare, Lawrence. She has an MSW from the University of Kansas School of Social Welfare and a PhD from the Departments of Psychology and Human Development and Family Life. She was the editor of* Social Work in Education *from 1994 to 1998.*

Anne E. Fortune, PhD, *is professor, School of Social Work, University at Albany, State University of New York. She has a PhD from the University of Chicago School of Social Service Administration. She is the current editor of* Social Work Research.

Dennis L. Poole, PhD, *is professor, University of Central Florida, Orlando. He has an MSW from West Virginia University and a PhD from the Florence Heller School for Advanced Studies in Social Welfare, Brandeis University, Waltham, Massachusetts. He was the editor of* Health & Social Work *from 1995 to 1998.*

Stanley L. Witkin, PhD, *is professor, Department of Social Work, University of Vermont. He has an MSW and a PhD from the University of Wisconsin–Madison. He is the current editor of* Social Work.

About the Contributors

Marian A. Aguilar, PhD, LMSW-ACP, is associate professor, School of Social Work, University of Texas at Austin.

Mary Altpeter, MSW, MPA, ACSW, is associate director of operations, Institute on Aging, University of North Carolina at Chapel Hill.

Wendy F. Auslander, PhD, LCSW, is associate professor, George Warren Brown School of Social Work, Washington University, St. Louis.

Sharon E. Barrett, MS, is director, Health Resources and Services Administration, Bureau of Primary Health Care, Office of Minority and Women's Health, Bethesda, Maryland.

Keva Barton, MSW, is program coordinator, Quincy-Geneva Housing Development Corporation, Dorchester, Massachusetts.

Raymond L. Bending, PhD, is senior lecturer, School of Social Work, University of Washington, Seattle.

Kathryn L. Braun, DrPH, is associate professor and director, Center on Aging, School of Public Health, University of Hawaii, Honolulu.

Karin A. Elliott Brown, PhD, is associate professor, School of Health and Human Services, Department of Social Work, California State University, Los Angeles.

Letha A. Chadiha, PhD, is associate professor, Center for Mental Health Services Research, George Warren Brown School of Social Work, Washington University, St. Louis.

Li Chin Cheng, PhD, is assistant professor, Department of Social Work, Soochow University, Taipei, Taiwan.

Valire Carr Copeland, PhD, MPH, is assistant professor, School of Social Work, University of Pittsburgh.

Larry E. Davis, PhD, is professor of social work and psychology, George Warren Brown School of Social Work, Washington University, St. Louis.

Melvin Delgado, PhD, is professor of social work and chair of macro practice, School of Social Work, Boston University.

Debra D. Desselle, PhD, BCD, ACSW, is assistant professor, Department of Sociology and Anthropology, University of North Carolina at Wilmington.

Peter M. Doré, MS, is database administrator, Center for Mental Health Services Research, George Warren Brown School of Social Work, Washington University, St. Louis.

Daniele Dreitzer, MSW, is program manager, American Cancer Society, Las Vegas, Nevada.

Heather T. Dunbar, MSW, is social worker, Casey Family Program, Honolulu.

Kathleen A. Earle, PhD, LMSW, is assistant professor of social work, University of Southern Maine, Portland.

Jo Anne L. Earp, ScD, is professor and chair, Department of Health Behavior and Health Education, School of Public Health, University of North Carolina at Chapel Hill.

Florence Ellison, MSW, is former director of social services in an American Indian community, Petoskey, Michigan.

Leonard G. Epstein, MSW, is senior adviser on cultural competency programs, Health Resources and Services Administration, Bureau of Primary Health Care, Office of Minority and Women's Health, Bethesda, Maryland.

Marilyn H. Gaston, MD, is associate administrator for primary health care, Health Resources and Services Administration, Bureau of Primary Health Care, and Assistant Surgeon General of the United States.

AnaMaria Goicoechea-Balbona, PhD, ACSW, LCSW, is assistant professor, School of Social Work, University of Maryland, Baltimore.

Gloria Gonzales, LMSW, is school social worker, Gadsden Independent School District, Anthony, New Mexico.

Karen L. Graves, PhD, is a scientist, Alcohol Research Group, Western Consortium for Public Health, Berkeley, California.

Gilbert J. Greene, PhD, ACSW, LISW, is associate professor, College of Social Work, Ohio State University, Columbus.

Kristin L. Hackl, MSW, is project coordinator, Center for AIDS Intervention Research, Department of Psychiatry and Behavioral Medicine, Medical College of Wisconsin, Milwaukee.

Wendy L. Haight, PhD, is assistant professor, School of Social Work, University of Illinois at Urbana–Champaign.

Alice M. Hines, PhD, is assistant professor, College of Social Work, San Jose State University, California.

Leslie Doty Hollingsworth, PhD, ACSW, is assistant professor, School of Social Work, University of Michigan, Ann Arbor.

Maggie Hourd-Bryant, MA, is doctoral student, Center for Mental Health Services Research, George Warren Brown School of Social Work, Washington University, St. Louis.

Sharon Hudson, MA, is doctoral candidate, Institute for Prevention Research, University of Southern California, Los Angeles.

Margaret Hughes, PhD, is assistant professor, School of Social Work, San Diego State University, California.

Phyllis Hulewat, MSSA, ACSW, LISW, BCD, is director of counseling, Jewish Family Service Association of Cleveland, Beachwood, Ohio.

Michael H. Jang, MA, is president, Four Winds Research Corporation, San Francisco.

Frances E. Jemmott is senior program officer, California Wellness Foundation, Woodland Hills.

Carla Jensen, PhD, ACSW, LSW, is assistant professor, School of Social Welfare, University of Wisconsin–Milwaukee.

Tamara Lewis Johnson, MBA, MPH, is senior public health adviser, Health Resources and Services Administration, Bureau of Primary Health Care, Office of Minority and Women's Health, Bethesda, Maryland.

Dorothy Harper Jones, PhD, ACSW, CSW, is assistant professor, School of Social Work Michigan State University, East Lansing.

Seth C. Kalichman, PhD, is associate professor, Center for AIDS Intervention Research, Department of Psychiatry and Behavioral Medicine, Medical College of Wisconsin, Milwaukee.

Hugo A. Kamya, PhD, CGP, LICSW, is assistant professor and chair of clinical concentration, Graduate School of Social Work, Boston College, Chestnut Hill.

Valli Kanuha, PhD, is assistant professor, School of Social Work, University of Hawaii, Honolulu.

Lynn Keenan, PhD, is lecturer, School of Social Work, University of Washington, Seattle.

Jeffrey A. Kelly, PhD, is professor and director, Center for AIDS Intervention Research, Department of Psychiatry and Behavioral Medicine, Medical College of Wisconsin, Milwaukee.

Helen Land, PhD, is associate professor, School of Social Work, University of Southern California, Los Angeles.

Evelyn Lee, PhD, LCSW, is associate clinical professor, Department of Psychiatry, University of California, San Francisco.

Belinda R. Lopez, MSW, is school social worker, Las Cruces Public Schools, Las Cruces, New Mexico.

Christine T. Lowery, PhD, is assistant professor, School of Social Welfare, University of Wisconsin–Milwaukee.

Richard A. Mackey, DSW, LICSW, is professor, Graduate School of Social Work, Boston College, Chestnut Hill.

Jon K. Matsuoka, PhD, is professor, School of Social Work, University of Hawaii, Honolulu.

Linda A. McLaughlin, MSW, is medical social worker and doctoral candidate, School of Social Work, University of Hawaii, Honolulu.

Cynthia Medina, MSW, is doctoral student, School of Social Work, University of Hawaii, Honolulu.

Susan O. Mercer, DSW, ACSW, is professor, School of Social Work, University of Arkansas at Little Rock.

Holly J. Mitchell is executive director, California Black Women's Health Project, Los Angeles.

Paula T. Tanemura Morelli, PhD, ACSW, is assistant professor, School of Social Work, University of Hawaii, Honolulu.

Nancy Morrow-Howell, PhD, ACSW, *is associate professor, Center for Mental Health Services Research, George Warren Brown School of Social Work, Washington University, St. Louis.*

Charles W. Mueller, PhD, *is associate professor, School of Social Work, University of Hawaii, Honolulu.*

Ada C. Mui, PhD, ACSW, *is associate professor, Columbia University School of Social Work, New York.*

Barbara L. Nicholson, PhD, LICSW, BCD, *is professor, Salem State School of Social Work, Salem, Massachusetts.*

Bernard A. O'Brien, PhD, *is associate professor and licensed psychologist, Department of Counseling, Developmental Psychology and Research Methods, Boston College, Chestnut Hill.*

John L. O'Neal, MSW, *is doctoral student, George Warren Brown School of Social Work, Washington University, St. Louis.*

Pamela Balls Organista, PhD, *is associate professor and licensed psychologist, Department of Psychology, University of San Francisco.*

Kurt C. Organista, PhD, *is associate professor and licensed psychologist, School of Social Welfare, University of California, Berkeley.*

Debora M. Ortega, MSW, LCSW, *is doctoral candidate and assistant professor, School of Social Welfare, University of Kansas, Lawrence.*

Yolanda C. Padilla, PhD, LMSW-AP, *is assistant professor, School of Social Work, University of Texas at Austin.*

Lynn Pearlmutter, DSW, BCD, ACSW, *is associate professor, School of Social Work, Tulane University, New Orleans.*

Dennis L. Poole, PhD, *is professor, School of Social Work, University of Central Florida, Orlando.*

Miriam Potocky-Tripodi, PhD, *is associate professor, School of Social Work, Florida International University, North Miami.*

Enola K. Proctor, PhD, LCSW, *is Frank J. Bruno Professor of Social Work Research; director, Center for Mental Health Services Research, George Warren Brown School of Social Work, Washington University, St. Louis.*

Cheryl A. Richey, PhD, *is professor, School of Social Work, University of Washington, Seattle.*

John Ronnau, PhD, ACSW, *is dean for curriculum and student affairs, Graduate School of Social Work, University of Utah, Salt Lake City.*

Jorge Santiago, PhD, *is director, Office of Urban Program Development, Northern Essex Community College, Lawrence, Massachusetts.*

Julio V. Santiago, MD, *is professor of pediatrics, School of Medicine, Washington University, St. Louis.*

Jerome H. Schiele, DSW, *is associate professor and chair of PhD program, School of Social Work, Clark Atlanta University.*

Janice H. Schopler, PhD, *was professor and associate dean, School of Social Work, University of North Carolina at Chapel Hill.*

Sherri Seyfried, PhD, ACSW, *is assistant professor, School of Social Work, University of Washington, Seattle.*

Sung Sil Lee Sohng, PhD, *is associate professor, School of Social Work, University of Washington, Seattle.*

Pearl R. Soloff, MSW, CSW, *is research assistant and doctoral candidate, School of Social Welfare, University of California, Berkeley.*

Anton M. Somlai, EdD, *is assistant professor, Center for AIDS Intervention Research, Department of Psychiatry and Behavioral Medicine, Medical College of Wisconsin, Milwaukee.*

Michael S. Spencer, PhD, MSSW, *is assistant professor, Center for Poverty, Risk, and Mental Health, School of Social Work, University of Michigan, Ann Arbor.*

Arlene Rubin Stiffman, PhD, *is professor, George Warren Brown School of Social Work, Washington University, St. Louis.*

Michael J. Strube, PhD, *is professor of psychology, Washington University, St. Louis.*

Mary E. Swigonski, PhD, ACSW, LCSW, *is assistant professor, Department of Social Work, Monmouth University, West Long Beach, New Jersey.*

Sharon Tennstedt, PhD, *is vice president and director, Institute for Studies on Aging, New England Research Institutes, Watertown, Massachusetts.*

Sanna J. Thompson, PhD, *is assistant professor, State University of New York at Buffalo.*

Edwina S. Uehara, PhD, *is associate professor and associate dean for educational initiatives, School of Social Work, University of Washington, Seattle.*

Gerald W. Vest, ACSW, LISW, *is professor emeritus, Department of Social Work, New Mexico State University, Las Cruces.*

Mary L. Walton, MSW, *is principal, MLW Consultancy, Long Beach, California.*

Hilary N. Weaver, DSW, *is assistant professor, School of Social Work, State University of New York at Buffalo.*

Maria Wilhelmus, MSW, JD, *is licensed attorney, Bloomington, Indiana, and doctoral student, School of Social Work, Ohio State University, Columbus.*

Edith Ellison Williams, PhD, *is director of social work, Chicago Read Mental Health Center.*

James Herbert Williams, PhD, ACSW, *is assistant professor, George Warren Brown School of Social Work, Washington University, St. Louis.*

Tamra Wolf, MSW, *is social worker, Giarretto Institute, San Jose, California.*

Kent Woo, BS, *is MSW candidate and executive director, NICOS Chinese Health Coalition, San Francisco, California.*

Greg Yamashiro, MSW, *is doctoral candidate, School of Social Work, University of Washington, Seattle.*

**Multicultural Issues in Social Work:
Practice and Research**

Cover design by The Watermark Design Office

Interior design by Bill Cathey

Typeset in Lucida Sans and Palatino by
Christine Cotting, UpperCase Publication Services, Ltd.

Printed by Boyd Printing Company

ORDER THESE IMPORTANT HANDBOOKS ON DIVERSITY FROM THE NASW PRESS

Multicultural Issues in Social Work: *Practice and Research, Patricia L. Ewalt, Edith M. Freeman, Anne E. Fortune, Dennis L. Poole, and Stanley L. Witkin, Editors.* This new and expanded second volume will delve into issues like promoting same-race adoption for children of color, methodological considerations in surveying Latina AIDS caregivers, and alternative health practices in ethnically diverse rural areas. This book will help researchers, policymakers, and practitioners in their work with diverse populations.

ISBN: 0-87101-302-9. Item #3029. NASW Member $33.55, Nonmember $41.95.

Multicultural Issues in Social Work, *Patricia L. Ewalt, Edith M. Freeman, Stuart A. Kirk, and Dennis L. Poole, Editors.* A collection of 38 articles from 1994 and 1995 issues of the four NASW Press journals. Examines the differences and similarities in the experiences, needs, and beliefs of people in different population groups.

ISBN: 0-87101-266-9. Item #2669. NASW Member $30.35, Nonmember $37.95.

Workplace Diversity: *Issues & Perspectives, Alfrieda Daly, Editor.* This insightful book examines the complex issues involved in workplace diversity and teaches a practical method for applying an organizational change process that is truly inclusive of diverse groups.

ISBN: 0-87101-281-2. Item #2812. NASW Member $22.35, Nonmember $27.95.

Social Work and the Black Experience, *by Elmer P. Martin and Joanne Mitchell Martin.* Written in the African tradition of collaboration, this is the first book to incorporate the rich black spiritual and blues traditions for use in work with black individuals and families. Students, faculty, and practitioners will find this an extraordinarily moving and useful reference.

ISBN: 0-87101-257-X. Item #257x. NASW Member $26.35, Nonmember $32.95.

Lesbians and Gays in Couples and Families: *A Handbook for Therapists, Joan Laird and Robert-Jay Green, Editors.* Laird and Green address the experiences of lesbians and gay men as couples, as parents, and in relationship to their own families of origin. The book contains a wealth of research, as well as recommendations and suggestions for working with gay couples and families in a clinical setting.

ISBN: 0-7879-0222-5. Item #2225. NASW Member $31.15, Nonmember $38.95.
Available from NASW Press by special arrangement with the publisher Jossey-Bass.

Cultural Competence in Substance Abuse Prevention, *Joanne Philleo, Frances Larry Brisbane, and Leonard G. Epstein, Editors.* This educational tool demonstrates how to integrate cultural competence and an AOD curriculum and how to develop highly effective prevention messages and treatment modalities within a cultural context.

ISBN: 0-87101-278-2. Item #2782. NASW Member $23.95, Nonmember $29.95.

(Order form on reverse side)

ORDER FORM

Title	Item #	NASW Member Price	Non-member Price	Total
__ Multicultural Issues in Social Work: *Practice and Research*	3029	$33.55	$41.95	_____
__ Multicultural Issues in Social Work	2669	$30.35	$37.95	_____
__ Workplace Diversity	2812	$22.35	$27.95	_____
__ Social Work and the Black Experience	257x	$26.35	$32.95	_____
__ Lesbians and Gays in Couples and Families	2225	$31.15	$38.95	_____
__ Cultural Competence in Substance Abuse Prevention	2782	$23.95	$29.95	_____
			Subtotal	_____
		+ 10% postage and handling		_____
			Total	_____

❏   I've enclosed my check or money order for $ _____.

❏   Please charge my   ❏ NASW Visa*   ❏ Other Visa   ❏ MasterCard

_____   _____

Credit Card Number   Expiration Date

Signature _____

          Use of this card generates funds in support of the social work profession.

Name _____

Address _____

City _____ State/Province _____

Country _____ Zip _____

Phone _____ E-mail _____

NASW Member # (if applicable) _____

     (Please make checks payable to NASW Press. Prices are subject to change.)

NASW PRESS
P. O. Box 431
Annapolis JCT, MD 20701
USA

Credit card orders call
1-800-227-3590
(In the Metro Wash., DC, area, call 301-317-8688)
Or fax your order to 301-206-7989
Or order online at http://www.naswpress.org

MIBI99